THE
VIRGINIA
HANDBOOK

Blair Howard, Mary Burnham
& Bill Burnham

HUNTER

Hunter Publishing, Inc.
130 Campus Drive
Edison, NJ 08818-7816
☎ 732-225-1900 / 800-255-0343 / Fax 732-417-1744
Web site: www.hunterpublishing.com
E-mail: hunterp@bellsouth.net

IN CANADA:
Ulysses Travel Publications
4176 Saint-Denis, Montréal, Québec
Canada H2W 2M5
☎ 514-843-9882, Ext. 2232 / Fax 514-843-9448

IN THE UNITED KINGDOM:
Windsor Books International
The Boundary, Wheatley Road, Garsington
Oxford, OX44 9EJ England
☎ 01865-361122 / Fax 01865-361133

ISBN 1-58843-512-1
© 2006 Blair Howard, William Burnham, and Mary Burnham
Manufactured in the United States of America

Cover: *Cardinal* (Virginia's State Bird) by Rob & Ann Simpson
Maps by Kim André, Lissa K. Dailey, & Toni Wheeler
© 2005 Hunter Publishing, Inc.

4   3   2   1

Contents

Maps

Introduction

Virginia is a spectacular state; ask any Virginian. And anyone who's ever visited the Old Dominion will tell you it's true. From the majesty of the Blue Ridge Mountains in the west to the mighty river deltas in the east, Virginia is a great green blanket cast down upon the landscape to delight us all. The Commonwealth is the grandfather of these United States. It saw the beginnings of this great country as it was hewn from the virgin timber. It saw the birth of a new nation when the English surrendered at Yorktown. And it saw the nation's rebirth when General Lee surrendered the Army of Northern Virginia at Appomattox, thus bringing the great Civil War to an end.

Visitors to the Commonwealth can step back into a bygone age when those pitifully few pioneers founded Jamestown, the first English settlement in the New World. They can visit numerous Revolutionary War battlefields, and follow in the footsteps of men like Robert E. Lee and Stonewall Jackson from Manassas to Fredericksburg, from Petersburg to Appomattox.

Virginia at a Glance

- ❖ **Nickname:** The Old Dominion
- ❖ **Motto:** *Sic semper tyrannis* (Thus always to tyrants)
- ❖ **Population:** 6.7 million
- ❖ **Major Cities:** Arlington, Hampton-Newport News, Norfolk-Virginia Beach, Richmond, Roanoke
- ❖ **Major Rivers:** James, Rappahannock, York, Potomac and Shenandoah
- ❖ **Capital:** Richmond
- ❖ **State Bird:** Cardinal
- ❖ **State Flower:** Dogwood
- ❖ **State Tree:** Dogwood
- ❖ **Shell:** Oyster

Nature lovers can hike the Appalachian Trail, explore the vast wooded expanses of the George Washington and Jefferson National Forests, and drive the Blue Ridge Parkway and hundreds of miles of scenic highways. They can descend to the center of the earth in the great limestone caverns

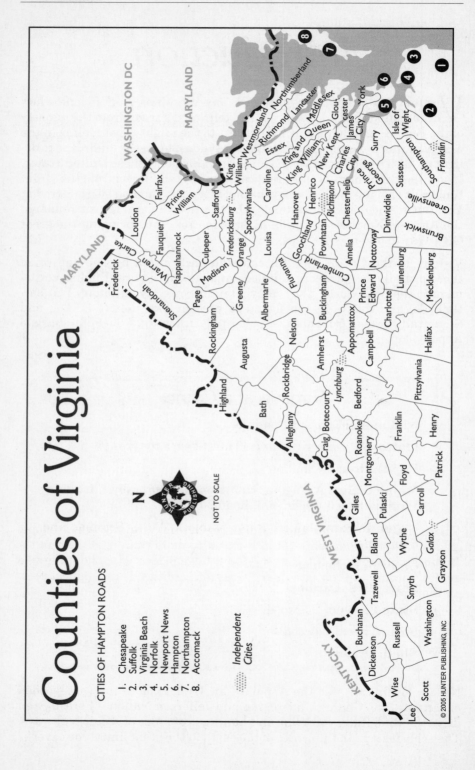

Counties of Virginia

CITIES OF HAMPTON ROADS

1. Chesapeake
2. Suffolk
3. Virginia Beach
4. Norfolk
5. Newport News
6. Hampton
7. Northampton
8. Accomack

N

NOT TO SCALE

Independent Cities

© 2005 HUNTER PUBLISHING, INC

of the Shenandoah Valley and wander the wetlands of the Great Dismal Swamp National Wildlife Refuge.

There's swimming, fishing, biking, golf, and skiing at Virginia's four-season resorts. You can explore more than 50 national and state parks, hundreds of freshwater lakes, and over 3,000 miles of rivers and streams.

For water lovers, there are magnificent beaches and barrier islands to explore. The Eastern Shore on the Delmarva Peninsula offers some of the finest boating and fishing anywhere in the United States.

Geography

Virginia is shaped roughly like a triangle, with its southern boundary as the base and its borders following the topography. To the northeast, Virginia is separated from Maryland and the District of Columbia by the west bank of the Potomac River. To the west and northwest it is bounded by the states of West Virginia and Kentucky, and to the south by Tennessee and North Carolina. To the east, Virginia is bordered by the Atlantic Ocean. America's largest estuary, the Chesapeake Bay, separates the low-lying coastal plains of eastern Virginia and the two eastern counties, Northampton and Accomack, located on the Delmarva Peninsula.

❖ *The name **Delmarva** comes from the names of the three states – Delaware, Maryland, and Virginia – that occupy the area. Virginia's portion occupies the southernmost tip.*

Virginia's southern border is 440 miles long, and the greatest distance, from north to south, is 196 miles. Its total area is 40,817 square miles, which includes more than 1,000 square miles of inland water surface.

The Five Regions

There are five distinct and natural regions in Virginia, which slopes gently upward from sea level in the east to more than 5,000 feet in the mountainous regions of the west. Mount Rogers, located to the southwest on the border between Smyth and Grayson counties, is the highest point in the state at 5,729 feet.

Northern Virginia encompasses the section of the state southwest of the Maryland border from Arlington to Leesburg, to a line running roughly along the southern borders of Greene, Orange, Spotsylvania, and Caroline counties.

The history of Northern Virginia spans more than three centuries. While still very much representative of The Old South with its plantations, Colonial homes, cobblestone streets and old-world charm, this region is also Virginia's most urbanized and dynamic. Burgeoning suburban communities are interspersed with modern skyscrapers, highways, shopping centers and malls.

Visitors to this region can visit the Eternal Flame at the Kennedy Gravesite in the Arlington National Cemetery; gaze in wonder at the world's largest cast bronze statue, the great Iwo Jima Memorial; and tour the Pentagon, the world's largest office building. They can also visit Mount Vernon, George Washington's home, or George Mason's Gunston Hall.

The **Coastal Plain** includes the increasingly metropolitan area of Hampton Roads, the two counties on the Delmarva Peninsula known as the Eastern Shore, and the rural counties that make up the Chesapeake Bay region. The coastal plain extends inland for about 100 miles to a line that runs north and south from Arlington through Richmond, and down to Emporia in Brunswick county on the North Carolina border. The elevation of the Coastal Plain ranges from 0 to 300 feet above sea level. In places, the great plain, slashed from east to west into three peninsulas by the Potomac, the Rappahannock, the York, and the James rivers, remains swampy, undeveloped wetlands. Typical of this is the 750-square-mile Great Dismal Swamp National Wildlife Area south of Suffolk and Chesapeake in the extreme southeastern corner of the state, and extending into North Carolina.

❖   *"Roads" is an Old English term for waterway.*

In the Hampton Roads region, water impacts every aspect of life. Here, freshwater carried by the James and York rivers mingles with ocean water in fertile tidal deltas. Crabbers, oystermen and fishermen plied a living here for generations. Perched strategically at the mouth of the Chesapeake Bay, Hampton Roads is thick with military installations. The white sand beaches of Virginia Beach have elevated the region to a major vacation destination.

Central Virginia consists primarily of the Piedmont Plateau west of the Coastal Plain. It is a region of low rolling hills about 40 miles wide to the north and some 150 miles wide along its southern border. It's an area where the old and the new come together, where quaint old country towns and villages lie side-by-side in perfect harmony with Virginia's modern cities. Here, the foothills of the Blue Ridge give way to the valleys of the great tidal rivers. This is where many great patriots – men like Patrick Henry, Thomas Jefferson, James Monroe, and James Madison – dreamed the dreams that gave birth to a nation.

The **Shenandoah Valley** region, renowned for its majestic mountains, its breathtaking scenery and glorious valley, covers most of western Virginia. It's a section of the Great Valley that extends from New Jersey to Tennessee. In Virginia, it funnels between the Allegheny and Blue Ridge mountains. The Shenandoah Valley, "daughter of the stars," with its rich limestone soil, is one of the most fertile regions in the state – an area that once was the breadbasket of the Confederacy. It is also a region that abounds with natural wonders and opportunities for outdoor activities ranging from hiking to horseback riding, and from tennis to snow skiing.

The Shenandoah's largest city, Roanoke, is a bustling community with a population of more than 95,000 people and a culture all its own. Steeped in the arts and history, Roanoke lies at the heart of an area where year-round festivals offer a myriad of regional foods and crafts.

Southwest Virginia is dominated by the Blue Ridge Mountains and Southwest Highlands, which extend for about 300 miles across the whole state in a southwest-northeast direction. The Blue Ridge are at their widest near the North Carolina border. To the southwest rise the headwaters of Virginia's great Tidewater rivers – the Rappahannock, the York, and the James. To the north, the Potomac and Shenandoah rivers join together at Harpers Ferry in West Virginia to carve a deep gash through the Blue Ridge Mountains. To the south, the Roanoke River rises and crosses over into North Carolina. Farther still lie the highlands of southwestern Virginia, the homeplace of bluegrass music and the source of Virginia's tremendous mineral wealth. It was in this far-off region that Daniel Boone carved out his Wilderness Trail through the Cumberland Gap and so began the push to drive back the frontiers of the new nation.

The pioneering spirit of so long ago still remains among the hills and valleys of the Blue Ridge, the Cumberland Mountains, and the Alleghenies, where, so its people claim, the Great Outdoors begins and ends.

The Land

The entire state is a treasure chest of natural resources: hundreds of square miles of rich grazing land, abundant waterpower, teeming fisheries, thousands of acres of hardwood and softwood forests, and an abundance of solid fuels and minerals.

In Colonial times, Virginia's soils, especially those of the Tidewater and Piedmont regions, were left barren; worn out by the poor land management techniques of the early settlers, and by over-intensive tobacco growing. Today, the land has been reclaimed and revitalized by an intensive and long-term program of crop rotation and other conservation practices. Once again, it supports such crops as tobacco, grain and fruit.

Virginia's ongoing program of land management and conservation led to the building of its two largest flood-control and hydroelectric projects: the Philpott Dam on the Smith River and the John H. Kerr Dam on the Roanoke River. Both projects were completed during the 1950s.

Many state and national agencies have been part of Virginia's efforts at reclamation and its many conservation programs. Much of the credit for the success of these programs must go to the agencies that have directed them. These include the Virginia State Department of Conservation and

Historic Resources, the Marine Resources Commission, and the Commission of Game and Inland Fisheries.

Virginia's commercial resources include the ports of Hampton Roads, navigable rivers, and the scenic and historic attractions for tourists.

Flowers & Trees

The **flowering dogwood** is Virginia's state tree. When the breath of spring blows, it is the dogwoods that awaken first, bursting forth in white and pink flowers. When fall comes, the brilliant red foliage provides colorful country and city walks. Its scarlet berries remain throughout most of the winter.

The **redbud** is another medium-size flowering tree found throughout Virginia. The leaves appear in the early spring, followed by a profusion of small rose-pink flowers. The redbud blossoms at about the same time of year as the dogwood.

The **crape myrtle**, also found throughout the state, is perhaps the South's most beautiful flowering tree. It grows to a height of more than 10 feet and blooms from July until early frost with red, pink, purple and white flowers.

The famous **Southern magnolia**, with its large, fragrant, white flowers, blooms in the summer and can be seen in Virginia's parks and gardens and along many city walks.

Azalea and **rhododendron** are also popular Southern evergreen shrubs. They are found in many of Virginia's gardens and parks, blooming in the spring with varying shades of red, pink and purple blossoms.

The chief commercial trees are **pine** in the Coastal Plain, **hardwoods** in the mountains, and mixed pine and hardwoods on the Piedmont Plateau.

The People

At the time of the founding of Jamestown in 1607, the largest group of Native Americans in the area was the **Powhatan Confederacy**, an association of tribes that covered southeastern Virginia. These were woodland Indians led by Chief Powhatan. It was from Chief Powhatan that the European colonists learned about tobacco cultivation. After several years of warfare between the Indians and the settlers, the marriage of Chief Powhatan's daughter, Pocahontas, to John Rolfe in 1614 brought peace to the area, at least for a time. When the Powhatans attacked the Colonial settlements in 1622 and in 1644, however, the colonists retaliated. The Indians were slaughtered almost to the point of extinction.

Most of the white population of Virginia stems from two immigrant groups. In the Hampton Roads section nearly all of the early settlers were

English. The other group consisted of German and Scotch-Irish immigrants who had pushed down into the Shenandoah Valley from Pennsylvania sometime around 1730. African-Americans, who made up 40% of the population in the 1700s, now total about 20%.

> ❖ *Virginia has the distinction of producing not only the author of the Declaration of Independence and other Revolutionary stalwarts, but 12 American Presidents as well. It is no wonder then that one nickname for the Old Dominion is "Mother of States and Statesman."*

Notable Virginians

Plenty of celebrities and political heavyweights got their start in Virginia.

❖ **L. Douglas Wilder** was born on January 17, 1931, in Richmond. In 1969, Wilder became the first black elected to the Virginia State Senate since Reconstruction. He was Lieutenant Governor of Virginia in 1985, and four years later became the first black Governor in the United States.

❖ **Carter Godwin Woodson**, a noted historian, educator, and editor, was born on December 19, 1875, in New Canton. Woodson graduated from Harvard University in 1912 and three years later, in 1915, founded the Association for the Study of Negro Life and History. He died in 1950.

❖ Actor **Warren Beatty** was born Henry Warren Beatty on March 30, 1937 in Richmond. He landed his first movie role, *Splendor in the Grass*, in 1961 and later began producing his own films, including *Bonnie and Clyde* in 1967 and *Shampoo* in 1975. Other films to his credit include *Heaven Can Wait*, the Academy Award-winning *Reds*, as well as *Dick Tracy* and the political satire *Bullworth*.

❖ **Jerry Falwell**, the noted evangelist and political lobbyist, was born on August 11, 1933 in Lynchburg. Falwell established the Lynchburg Baptist College, now Liberty University, in 1971, and founded the Moral Majority in 1979 to involve the Christian evangelical movement in politics through lobbying and the endorsement of candidates. Falwell resigned as president of the Moral Majority in 1987 and disbanded the group in 1989.

❖ Virginia writers include **William Byrd II** (1674-1744), Pulitzer Prize winning novelists **Willa Cather** (1873-1947), **Ellen Glasgow** (1873-1945) and **William Styron** (1925-), **Earl Hamner Jr.**, creator of *The Waltons* television series, and

Tom Wolfe, author of *The Right Stuff*. Many famous writers made Virginia their adopted home, from 19th-century master of the macabre, **Edgar Allan Poe**, to **Rita Mae Brown**, who writes cat mysteries from Crozet.

❖ Famous Virginia athletes include football Hall of Famer **Fran Tarkenton** (Richmond), basketball stars **Alonzo Mourning** (Chesapeake) and **Allen Iverson** (Hampton), and golf legends **Sam Snead** (Hot Springs) and **Curtis Strange** (Norfolk). A statue of Wimbledon champion **Arthur Ashe** (1943-1993) stands on Monument Avenue in his hometown of Richmond. In the racing world, **Ward** and **Jeff Burton** hail from South Boston, and **Ricky Rudd** from Chesapeake.

❖ Other notable Virginians include explorer and aviator **Adm. Richard E. Byrd**, country music singer **Patsy Cline**, Confederate Generals **Thomas "Stonewall" Jackson**, **Robert E. Lee** and **Joseph Eggleston Johnston**, Supreme Court Justice **John Marshall**, US Army doctor **Walter Reed**, former slave and abolitionist **Booker T. Washington**, the exploring duo of **Meriwether Lewis and William Clark**, psychic **Edgar Cace** and Indian princess **Pocahontas**.

❖ In addition to **George Washington**, other Presidents born in Virginia were **Thomas Jefferson, James Madison, James Monroe, William H. Harrison, John Tyler, Zachary Taylor**, and **Woodrow Wilson**.

❖ Virginia-born performers include singers **Pearl Bailey** and **Ella Fitzgerald** (Newport News), rapper **Missy Elliot** (Portsmouth) and actors **Tim Reid** (Norfolk) and **Blair Underwood** (Alexandria).

Major Cities

Norfolk, Virginia's chief port city, is located in the Hampton Roads area where the James River enters the Chesapeake Bay. It has played a key part in the defense of the United States since Colonial days and is the home port of the United States Atlantic Fleet.

Virginia Beach, the state's most populous city, and Norfolk anchor the Hampton Roads region, a geographic area comprised of seven cities, plus surrounding counties, in southeast Virginia. Other Hampton Roads cities include Newport News, Hampton, Portsmouth, Suffolk and Chesapeake. Military-rich and diverse in population, this is Virginia's fastest growing region, with 1.5 million people.

Richmond, the state capital, is one of the leading industrial cities of the South, and the third largest city in Virginia. It is home to RJ Reynolds, the cigarette manufacturer, and a growing number of high-tech companies.

Alexandria, on the west bank of the Potomac, is a residential city and something of a bedroom community for the nation's capital, Washington DC, located just to the east across the Potomac River.

Roanoke, at the southern end of the Shenandoah Valley, is the largest city in western Virginia, as well as the business and cultural center for the region.

Petersburg, just to the south of Richmond, **Lynchburg** on the upper James River, and **Danville**, close to the southern border, represent Virginia's major tobacco markets.

History

It was during the reign of King James I of England that men of the **Virginia Company of London** arrived in three ships off the shore of a marshy peninsula, some 30 miles inland from the entrance to the Chesapeake Bay. They went ashore there on the 13th of March, 1607, and founded **Jamestown**, the first permanent English settlement in America. The mission of these first settlers was commercial, a fact that set Jamestown apart from the other English foothold in America, the religious settlement of Plymouth in New England.

For three years, the tiny Jamestown colony struggled for survival under the direction of **Captain John Smith**. Only the arrival in 1610 of the new governor, Sir Thomas West, Lord de la Warr, with supplies from England, saved the community from extinction. During the years that followed, life in the new colony took a turn for the better. In 1612, John Rolfe, husband of the Indian princess Pocahontas, introduced tobacco growing, and Jamestown began to prosper.

In 1616 a new charter granted each free colonist 50 acres of land. It is believed that around this same time, the first black indentured servants landed in the New World, and the House of Burgesses, the first representative assembly formed in America, was established to provide a government of the Virginia planters.

In 1624 the tiny settlement became a royal colony and a royal governor was appointed. **Nathaniel Bacon**, a young English lawyer who had emigrated from London to become a planter, was outraged at the way the new colony was being misgoverned by Sir William Berkeley. When Berkeley refused to take measures to stop Indian attacks, Bacon organized the colonists and did it himself. Bacon's movement broadened as dissatisfaction with Berkeley grew. Eventually, it became a full rebellion against the aristocracy in general and Berkeley in particular. The rebellion ended when Bacon died suddenly soon after his followers had burned Jamestown and driven Berkeley and his followers into refuge on board an English man-of-war.

The years that followed Bacon's Rebellion were prosperous ones for the colonists. The tobacco plantations thrived on the cheap labor of black slaves; their owners grew wealthy.

Virginia's prosperity, however, brought heavy taxation. More new taxes were added until finally, in 1765, Patrick Henry's rousing speech against the Stamp Act brought the colonies to the brink of revolution.

Patriots in Virginia rallied opposition against the government in England and, in May 1776, they asked the Continental Congress to make a formal declaration of independence. The resolution, written mostly by Virginian Thomas Jefferson, was introduced to the Congress by Virginia delegate Richard Henry Lee, and was adopted on July 2, 1776.

As the tumultuous events taking place at the Continental Congress were heading rapidly toward a climax, Virginia adopted a state constitution that included a bill of rights. This was followed by the passing of Thomas Jefferson's acts for religious freedom and the outlawing of the laws that restricted the inheritance of land and other wealth to one line of descendants.

And so the **War of the Revolution** began. During the years that followed, many patriotic Virginians, including George Rogers Clark, "Light-Horse Harry" Lee, and Daniel Morgan, fought alongside George Washington. The fighting eventually ended when General George Cornwallis surrendered to Washington at Yorktown on October 18th, 1781.

In 1859, when John Brown made his famous raid on Harpers Ferry, the area we know today as West Virginia was still a part of Virginia. There's no doubt that Brown's raid was instrumental in bringing the nation, already deep in conflict over state's rights, to the brink of civil war.

On December 20th, 1860, the government of South Carolina seceded from the Union. Thereafter, things began to move quickly. A month later, on January 21, the State of Mississippi followed suit and was quickly joined by Florida, Alabama, Georgia, Louisiana, and Texas. On February 20th, 1861, in Montgomery, Alabama, Jefferson Davis took the oath as the first President of the Confederate States of America. In April 1861, Confederate forces fired upon the Federal Garrison at Fort Sumter in South Carolina. On April 15th, President Abraham Lincoln issued a proclamation that called into service 75,000 militia, and Virginia joined her Southern sister states in secession. The Confederate capital was moved from Montgomery, Alabama to Richmond during May and June of 1861. Richmond remained the capital of the Confederate States until it fell to General Ulysses S. Grant's army in April, 1865.

For four years the Civil War raged back and forth across Virginia. Great battles were fought at such places as Manassas, Fredericksburg, Chan-

Summary of Virginia's Notable Historic Events

1606. King James I chartered two companies to colonize Virginia.

1607. Jamestown, the first permanent English settlement in North America, was founded. John Smith became the leader of the colony.

1610. Lord De la Warr arrived with supplies and prevented the desertion of Jamestown.

1612. John Rolfe cultivated tobacco.

1619. House of Burgesses was created. The first representative assembly in America met at Jamestown. The first black indentured servants arrive in America.

1622. Indians massacred many of the colonists.

1624. The king revoked the Virginia Company's charter.

1676. Nathaniel Bacon led the revolt against the Governor.

1693. The College of William and Mary was chartered at Williamsburg.

1699. Virginia's capital was moved from Jamestown to Williamsburg.

1716. The first theater in America was built at Williamsburg.

1775. Patrick Henry delivered his "liberty or death" oration.

1776. Virginia declared its independence.

1778. State authorized the Northwest expedition by George Rogers Clark, born in 1752 near Charlottesville.

1779. Richmond became Virginia's state capital.

1781. Lord Cornwallis surrendered at Yorktown.

1784. Virginia ceded its northwestern lands to the US.

1787. The Constitutional Convention adopted the Virginia Plan.

1788. Virginia was the 10th state to ratify the US Constitution on June 26.

1789. George Washington, born 1732 near Oak Grove, became the first President of the US.

1792. The State Capitol was completed.

1801. John Marshall, born in 1755 in Fauquier County, was appointed Chief Justice of the US.

1819. The State University was founded in Charlottesville.

1831. Nat Turner led the slave rebellion in Southampton County. Cyrus McCormick invented the first successful reaper near Steeles Tavern.

1846. Two Virginians, Zachary Taylor and Winfield Scott, commanded American armies during the Mexican War.

1859. John Brown seized the arsenal at Harpers Ferry.

1861. Virginia seceded from Union. General Robert E. Lee took command of Virginia's forces. Richmond became the Confederate capital. The first major land battle of the Civil War was fought at Bull Run.

1862. The USS *Monitor* and the CSS *Merrimack* engage in a historic sea battle in Hampton Roads. General Stonewall Jackson defeated Union forces in the Shenandoah Valley. Lee was recalled to Richmond.

1863. Virginia lost some of its territory by the admission of West Virginia to the Union.

1865. Lee surrendered the Army of Northern Virginia to Gen. Ulysses S. Grant near Appomattox, ending American Civil War.

1870. Virginia was readmitted to the Union.

1908. Staunton became the first city in the US with a city manager.

Introduction

1915. The Virginia-West Virginia debt dispute was settled.

1926. John D. Rockefeller, Jr. restored Williamsburg.

1951. The SS *United States*, the largest ocean liner ever constructed in the US, was launched at Newport News.

1952. The John H. Kerr Dam on Roanoke River was completed.

1964. The Chesapeake Bay Bridge-Tunnel was completed.

1966. The Supreme Court ruled that Virginia's poll tax was unconstitutional, thus outlawing that type of tax in all states.

1970. Virginia's present state constitution was adopted.

1972. Tropical storm Agnes produced the worst floods in recorded history.

1985. Devastating floods followed Hurricane Juan.

1990. L. Douglas Wilder was sworn in as Governor of Virginia, the first elected black governor in the US.

1993. Republican George Allen inaugurated as governor.

1999. Republicans gain a majority in the state legislature for the first time since Reconstruction.

2001. Terrorists use hijacked passenger planes to destroy New York's World Trade Center and damage the Pentagon in Arlington, VA.

2002. Democrat Mark Warner inaugurated as governor.

2003. Hurricane Isabel causes extensive damage in the Hampton Roads area.

---

cellorsville, in The Wilderness, on the Peninsula, at Petersburg, Mechanicsville, Cold Harbor, Malvern Hill, Five Forks, and Sayler's Creek. Greatest generals like Robert E. Lee, Thomas "Stonewall" Jackson, Jeb Stuart, Jubal Early, Joseph E. Johnston and George Pickett fought side-by-side through the years of war that ravaged the state.

After the fighting ended, Virginians had to rebuild. The once-great cities had been laid waste by four years of death and destruction. It was many years before the war-torn land recovered.

Virginia's original Colonial charter encompassed so much territory that it was virtually unmanageable. At one point, Augusta County west of the Blue Ridge extended all the way to the Mississippi River, and north into Illinois. Piece-by-piece, western sections were cut away to form the present states of Kentucky, Ohio, Illinois, Indiana, Wisconsin and a large part of Minnesota. The bitter conflict within Virginia over secession from the Union in 1861 reduced it even further when, in 1863, the 50 counties in far northwest Virginia broke away to form the new state of West Virginia.

Since the end of the Civil War, despite the massive loss of territory, Virginia's population has steadily increased to the point where, today, it ranks 14th among the states with a population of more than seven million people.

The Rise & Fall of Slavery in Virginia

Indentured servitude was a form of contract labor used in the English colonies of North America. The first indentured servants were believed to have been introduced in 1616. For the next 25 years, large numbers of German, English and Scottish colonists arrived in the New World as indentured servants. Some were convicted criminals, while others were too poor to pay their way to the colonies by any other means. Often the contracts were made with ship captains who, upon arrival in the colonies, sold them to someone else. A contract usually ran from five to seven years, after which the servant became free.

By 1650, many of the first indentured servants had earned their freedom. This caused something of a problem, mainly because replacements were costly and often in short supply. The plantation owners in Virginia began to consider the advantages of slavery, a policy already being exercised by landowners in the Caribbean. And so it was that Virginia legalized slavery in the colony in 1661. By 1672, the English Royal African Company was bringing black slaves into America by the shipload. By the end of the American Revolution the system of indentured labor had died out altogether, and slavery had become the only system of forced labor in the United States.

By the early 1800s, the state's plantation economy relied heavily on slaves, and any threat to this system met with harsh consequences. Such was the fate of a slave named Nat Turner, who in 1831 led a rebellion in Southampton, in southeast Virginia. After terrorizing the countryside for several weeks, Turner and others were finally captured and hanged.

And so, for more than 300 years, a pattern of fear, punishment, and segregation developed, one that persisted well into the 20th century. Things began to change in 1926, when Virginia became the first Southern state to adopt an anti-lynching law.

Politically, however, Virginia remained strongly segregationist. So much so that, for more than five years in the 1960s, the schools in Prince Edward County were closed down as part of a local strategy to avoid racial integration. Other cities and counties joined in the "massive resistance" toward mixing black and white students. By 1990, however, the political climate in Virginia had changed so completely that L. Douglas Wilder, the grandson of Richmond-area slaves, became the first elected black Governor in the United States.

Climate

Although Virginia's climate is generally mild and pleasant, there is a wide variation in temperatures between the eastern and western parts of the state.

❖ *As a rule, for every 1,000 feet of elevation gain, the temperature drops 6°F. Therefore, a late October day can produce 75° temperatures in Hampton Roads, while ice and snow signal the approaching winter in far Southwest Virginia.*

Hampton Roads is tempered by the ocean breezes and the climate stays fairly moderate throughout most of the year. To the west, especially in the Appalachian Highlands, cold winters and cool summers are the norm. Burkes Garden in Tazewell County, a unique bowl-shaped valley in Southwest Virginia, has the latest spring frosts on record for the state. Monthly average temperatures range from 26°F to 88°F.

Average mean temperatures vary across the state from 54°F in the south-western mountains to about 59° along the coast. The average annual pre-cipitation varies from about 50 inches in the extreme southeastern region to around 35 inches in the northwestern part of the state. The area with the longest growing season – about 260 days – extends southward along the western shore of the Chesapeake Bay from Northumberland County to Virginia Beach. At the other extreme is the southwestern region of Vir-ginia, especially in the higher elevations around the Jefferson National Forest, with only some 150 frost-free days a year.

Scenic & Historic Attractions

In 1969, the state coined a slogan that has since become an industry stan-dard: "Virginia is for Lovers." Three and a half decades later, the impor-tance of tourism as a piece of Virginia's economy has grown by leaps and bounds. **Virginia Beach** is the "resort city," its miles of white sand beach lined with high-rise hotels, its neon-encased strip teeming with tourists and businesses hawking T-shirts, beachwear and souvenirs. To the west, the magnificent scenic routes of the **Blue Ridge Parkway** and **Skyline Drive** that run along the top of the western mountains attract visitors throughout the year. Iron markers at strategic locations along almost all of Virginia's highways pinpoint and interpret the state's many **historic spots**. These include the famous battlefields of the Revolutionary and Civil Wars; scenic mountain routes; national parks, like Shenandoah Na-tional Park and Assateague Island National Seashore, home of the Chincoteague ponies; and the homes of such national figures as George Washington, Thomas Jefferson, James Monroe, Woodrow Wilson, Robert E. Lee, and John Marshall.

Virginia is rich in historical sites that trace our nation's beginnings at **Jamestown**, nearly 400 years ago, through pioneer days at **Cumber-land Gap National Historical Park**, to the space age at the new Smithsonian Air and Space Museum's **Udvar-Hazy Center** in northern Virginia.

Government

The chief executive officer of the state is the **Governor**, who heads the **Executive Branch** and is limited to one four-year term. Other members of the Executive Branch are a Lieutenant Governor and an Attorney General, both of whom are elected and serve four-year terms.

Lawmaking is the domain of the **General Assembly**, which consists of the State Senate and the House of Delegates. Virginia's judicial branch of the government is headed by the **Supreme Court**, which has seven justices serving a term of 12 years. The **State Judiciary** is composed of the Supreme Court; a Court of Appeals, where 10 judges serve eight-year terms; and the Virginia Circuit courts, where 122 judges serve for eight years. The **State Legislature** is composed of 40 senators serving four-year terms, and 100 delegates each serving two-year terms. Virginia is represented in the **US Congress** by two members of the Senate and 11 members of the House of Representatives. The state controls 13 electoral votes.

Virginia, traditionally Democratic in state and local politics since the days of Reconstruction, saw a resurgence of Republican-dominated politics in the 1990s. Although voters in Virginia supported the Democratic presidential candidate in all elections until 1968, except those held in 1928, 1952, 1956 and 1960, the state has more recently been considered a lock to support Republican presidential candidates.

Emblematic of that change was the election in 1993 of Republican George Allen, son of the great football coach, as Governor. Four years later his protégé, Republican James Gilmore, took the state's highest office. And in 1999, Virginia voters sent a majority of Republicans to the General Assembly for the first time since Reconstruction. In 2002, however, the governor's seat returned to the Democrats with the election of Mark Warner.

Since 1779, the state capital has been **Richmond**. Virginia became the 10th state in the Union on June 26, 1788. A state constitution was adopted in 1970. An amendment to the state constitution may be passed only by a majority vote of the General Assembly at two consecutive sessions, and must be ratified by a majority vote in an election.

There are **95 counties** in the State of Virginia, most of which are governed by boards of supervisors and county administrators; **40 independent cities**, governed by city councils and city managers; and **189 incorporated towns**.

Education & Culture

Colleges & Universities

The first free school in Colonial Virginia was founded in Hampton in 1634. Virginia's first college, **William and Mary**, was chartered in Williamsburg in 1693 and was the second college to be founded in the colonies. Only Harvard, founded in 1636, is older.

Thomas Jefferson was the first to advocate a free public educational system in America, but it wasn't until 1870 that the present public school system was established.

The **University of Virginia** was founded in Charlottesville by Thomas Jefferson in 1819. Since then the state system of higher education has grown and expanded, until today it rivals any in the nation for its diversity and quality of education. Other state-supported schools include the **Wise Campus** branch of the University of Virginia; the **Virginia Polytechnic Institute and State University** in Blacksburg; **Virginia Commonwealth University** in Richmond; **Old Dominion University** in Norfolk; the **College of William and Mary** in Williamsburg; **Christopher Newport College** in Newport News; **Virginia State University** in Petersburg; **Norfolk State University** in Norfolk; **Radford University** in Radford; **James Madison University** in Harrisonburg; **Virginia Military Institute** in Lexington; **Longwood College** in Farmville; **George Mason University** in Fairfax; and **Mary Washington College**, formerly the women's division of the University in Fredericksburg, now an independent coeducational school.

Virginia is also home to **Washington and Lee University** in Lexington; the **University of Richmond** and **Virginia Union University** in Richmond; **Hampton University**; **Lynchburg College**; **Randolph-Macon College** in Ashland; **Randolph-Macon Woman's College** in Lynchburg; **Sweet Briar College**; and **Hampden-Sydney College**.

Libraries

The state's most important libraries include **Fairfax County Public Library**; **Old Dominion University Library** at Norfolk; **Richmond Public Library**; the **University of Virginia Library** in Charlottesville; the **Virginia Beach Public Libraries**; the **Virginia Polytechnic Institute and State University Library** at Blacksburg; and the **Virginia State Library** in Richmond.

❖ *Most libraries in major cities feature a Virginiana Room, repositories for important documents relating to the state, as well as genealogical information.*

Museums

Among Virginia's notable museums are the **Chrysler Museum of Art** in Norfolk; **Colonial Williamsburg**; **Manassas National Battlefield Park**; the **Mariners' Museum** at Newport News; the **Virginia Air and Space Museum** in Hampton; the **Museum of the Confederacy** in Richmond; **New Market Battlefield Park**; **Roanoke Museum of Fine Arts**; the **Valentine Museum** and the **Virginia Museum of Fine Arts** in Richmond; the **Virginia Military Institute Museum** in Lexington; and the **Woodrow Wilson Birthplace Foundation** in Staunton.

Manufacturing & Employment

During the 1900s Virginia slowly but surely turned away from the old agrarian economy and moved toward an industrial one. Today, while farming is still an important part of the state's gross product, Virginia's economy is more balanced between manufacturing, government, services and high tech. Manufacturing provides almost 60% of Virginia's total income, six times that derived from the farms, mines, forests, and fisheries. Government accounts for 20% of the state's total income, while services contribute 18%.

Virginia ranks as one of the top industrial states in the South, with more than $100 billion in annual manufacturing shipments. The state's manufacturing sector is also one of the most diversified in the nation. About 20% of Virginia's total work force is employed in its industrial plants.

Public administration is also a major source of employment in the state and accounts for about 20% of the state's work force. This includes not only the people employed at the local and state levels, but also those employed by the federal government in civilian and military jobs. Most of the federal employees work in Washington DC, or at the military bases in Hampton Roads.

Virginia's largest industry is the manufacture of transportation equipment, of which shipbuilding and ship repair constitute the largest single sector. Newport News Shipbuilding is the nation's largest private shipbuilder, producing aircraft carriers and nuclear submarines for the US military. The state's vast forest resources provide the foundation for an extensive pulp and paper industry. Virginia's lumber industry produces almost a billion board feet each year, which ranks it among the top 10 states in the nation.

Major Products

Agricultural products range from cattle and dairy products, pigs, chickens and turkeys to soybeans, corn, peanuts, potatoes, tomatoes, apples, and peaches. Smithfield Foods in southeast Virginia is the world's largest producer of pork products.

Virginia's **manufactured products** include transportation equipment, textiles, food products, electric and electronic equipment, printing and publishing, and chemicals. Mined products include coal, stone, sand and gravel, calcinated lime, feldspar, gypsum and dolomite.

There are some 50,000 **farms** throughout Virginia, with an average size of about 190 acres. They produce a diverse variety of crops, including tobacco, still one of the state's most valuable products. The state ranks high in tobacco production, along with the two Carolinas and Kentucky. Today, tobacco is grown mostly in the southern Piedmont region of Virginia.

Other valuable agricultural products include beef, pork, poultry, eggs, and milk.

Mining, too, is a major industry in Virginia. Millions of tons of bituminous coal are dug each year from the Pocahontas coal fields in the southwestern region of the state. Virginia's other chief minerals include stone, sand and gravel, and calicinated lime.

Commercial fishing is also an important industry in Virginia, with almost 20% of the nation's total catch arriving through its port cities. The leading ocean catches are menhaden, flounder, croaker, scup and sea trout.

Transportation

Virginia's first transportation system was born on the waters of the Chesapeake Bay and its river tributaries. During the early 1800s a network of canals was dug along the Potomac and James rivers that stretched inland as far as the mountains. The advent of railroads and modern highways deprived these great inland waterways of much of their traffic.

From the earliest times, commerce moved chiefly along a north and south axis until, in the late 1700s, the emphasis changed to east and west. The leading routes east and west, the **Wilderness Road** and the **Little River Turnpike**, were pioneered by men such as Daniel Boone. Today, Virginia's Department of Transportation maintains about 60,000 miles of primary and secondary state roads. In addition, the state is served by a system of federal and interstate highways, of which **Interstate highways** I-95, I-81, and I-77 are the major arteries running north-south; I-64 and I-66 keep traffic moving east-west.

Virginia's first railroad was a horse-drawn line that hauled coal from Chesterfield County to Richmond beginning in 1831. The first steam-powered railroad connected Petersburg with Weldon, NC. During the Civil War Virginia's railroads suffered great damage. Later, many of the smaller lines were absorbed by the major railroads that serve the state today.

Dulles International Airport and **Ronald Reagan Washington National Airport** – both in northern Virginia, just outside of Washington DC – serve the city and the surrounding metropolitan area. Other major airports serving Virginia are in Richmond, Roanoke, and Norfolk. Also convenient are Tri-Cities Airport in northeast Tennessee and Baltimore/Washington International airport in Baltimore. For complete airport and airline information, www.metawashairports.com, or call ☎ 703-572-2700 (Dulles) or 703-417-8000 (National).

Fishing & Hunting

Outstanding opportunities for fishing and hunting abound throughout the state.

Saltwater fishing on the ocean, the bay, and the river estuaries and creeks is a major sport in Virginia. The state is blessed with more than 120 miles of shoreline on the Atlantic Ocean and more than 300 miles on the Chesapeake Bay. There are also over 1,300 miles of saltwater shoreline on the major river estuaries and their tributaries. There is no closed season for saltwater fishing in Virginia, but there are bag and size limits on some species of fish, unless you are fishing from private property, and a saltwater fishing license is required. For more information on licensing and bag limits, contact the Virginia Marine Resources Commission, 2600 Washington Avenue, 3rd Floor, Newport News, VA 23607, ☎ 757-247-2200, www.mrc.state.va.us. To purchase a license, call 800-986-2628; there is a $3.95 processing fee.

Freshwater fishing and **hunting** are regulated by the Department of Game & Inland Fisheries. The state's many large reservoirs, lakes, rivers and creeks abound with largemouth and smallmouth bass, striped bass, muskie, northern pike, perch, trout, crappie, bluegill and many more species of pan fish. Some of the best freshwater fishing locations include Lake Anna, Smith Mountain Lake, Lake Gaston, Lake Philpott, Lake Moomaw and Buggs Island Lake; all are nationally known for their excellent bass fishing. A non-resident license to fish costs $30. An additional $30 is required for trout fishing in designated stocked waters. A five-day fishing license can be obtained for $6, and a $3 stamp is added to the state license for fishing in Virginia's national parks. Virginia resident licenses are $12 annually, or $5 for five days.

Hunting for upland game and migratory water fowl is allowed in season. A non-resident hunting license costs $60; a three-day license costs $30. For further hunting and fishing information, and for information regarding special licenses, muzzle-loader and archery, contact the **Virginia Department of Game and Inland Fisheries**, Box 11104, Richmond, VA 23230, ☎ 804-367-1000, www.dgif.state.va.us. To purchase a license by phone, call 800-986-2628 ($3.95 procesing fee is paid to Bass Pro Shops).

Outdoor Recreation

Tent and trailer camping and a variety of outdoor sports, water-related activities, hiking, picnicking, horseback riding, golf, etc., are available at 22 of Virginia's state parks, national parks and forests, and at a number of privately operated resorts and outdoor facilities. These are described in some detail in the listings for each town throughout this book.

Shenandoah National Park, as well as the George Washington and Jefferson National Forests, have thousands of acres for outdoor recreation.

You can stay in a posh resort along Skyline Drive or explore remote backcountry in the national forests.

❖ *Virginia also contains a quarter of the total mileage of the Appalachian Trail. The Maine-to-Georgia trail enters the state at Damascus and crosses some of the state's most stirring geography, from the Grayson Highlands of southwest Virginia to the sharp ridge-and-valley systems of western Virginia, en route to its exit at Harpers Ferry.*

Camping reservations may be made up to 180 days in advance by contacting the Reservation Center at **Virginia State Parks**, ☎ 800-933-7275 or 804-225-3867, www.dcr.state.va.us/parks. You can also request a campground directory.

Information & Services

Road & Weather Information

For current road conditions, call the **Virginia Department of Transportation's Highway Help Line** at ☎ 800-367-ROAD.

Road Systems

Virginia is well served by an interstate road system.

❖ **Interstate 64** runs east-west, linking West Virginia to Richmond and Hampton Roads.

❖ **Interstate 66** links Alexandria, Arlington County, Fairfax, Falls Church, Front Royal, Manassas and McLean to the nation's capital from the west.

❖ **Interstate 81** runs north-south almost the entire length of the Blue Ridge and Shenandoah Valley, linking Abingdon, Blacksburg, Bristol, Front Royal, Harrisonburg, Lexington, Marion, Natural Bridge, New Market, Radford, Roanoke, Salem, Staunton, Strasburg, Winchester, Woodbridge and Wytheville. It connects with Interstate 77 at Wytheville, Interstate 64 at Staunton and Interstate 66 near Strasburg.

❖ **Interstate 85** runs south from Petersburg, connecting that city with South Hill and North Carolina.

❖ **Interstate 95** runs north-south and connects Alexandria, Arlington, Ashland, Emporia, Fairfax, Falls Church, Fredericksburg, Hopewell, McLean, Mount Vernon, Petersburg, Richmond, Springfield and Triangle with Washington DC.

❖ **Interstate 77** connects Interstate 81 at Wytheville with North Carolina to the south and with Kentucky to the north.

Information Centers

Ten Virginia **welcome and information centers** are staffed daily from 8:30 a.m. to 5 p.m. at the following locations: at the **northern** end of the state on I-81 in Clear Brook, and on I-66 in Manassas; to the **northeast** on I-95 at Fredericksburg; to the **east** on US 13 in New Church; to the **south** on I-95 at Skippers, and on I-85 at Bracy; to the **southwest** in Bristol on I-81, and in Lambsburg on I-77; to the **west** on I-64 at Covington, and on I-77 in Rocky Gap.

The **Virginia Hospitality & Travel Association** can be reached at 2101 Libbie Avenue, Richmond, VA 23230, ☎ 800-552-2225, www.vhta.org. The **Virginia Tourism Corporation** is located at 901 Byrd Street, Richmond, VA 23219, ☎ 800 VISIT VA (800-847-4882), www.virginia.org. Official state maps are available from the **Department of Transportation** at 1221 E. Broad Street, Richmond, VA 23219, ☎ 804-786-2801, www.virginiadot.org.

Online information about Virginia begins at the Virginia Division of Tourism's Web site, **www.virginia.org**, which has links to tourism and government offices, lodging, history and travel information.

Tourist Information Centers – Major Cities

Alexandria	☎ 703-838-4200
Arlington	☎ 703-228-3988
Fredericksburg	☎ 540-373-1776
Hampton	☎ 757-722-1222
Lexington	☎ 540-463-3777
Newport News	☎ 888-493-7368
Norfolk	☎ 757-441-1852
Petersburg	☎ 804-733-2402
Richmond	☎ 804-782-2777
Roanoke	☎ 540-342-6025
Shenandoah Valley	☎ 540-740-3132
Virginia Beach	☎ 757-437-4700
Williamsburg	☎ 757-253-0192

Introduction

Accommodations Key

Each accommodation listed in this guide is followed by a cost rating. This is based on a double-occupancy, in-season rate for one night's stay in a standard room.

$	Under $100
$$	$100-$150
$$$	$150-$200
$$$$	Over $200

 The DOGGY symbol in the margin of a listing indicates that pets are welcome.

Northern Virginia

Alexandria

History

Alexandria is on the west bank of the Potomac River, six miles below Washington DC, and nine miles from Mount Vernon. The city was established by the Virginia Assembly in 1749 and, in July of that year, building lots were auctioned off from the town square. The town was named for Scotsman John Alexander who, in 1669, purchased the land that included the future Alexandria for "six thousand pounds of tobacco and cask."

English General Braddock made his headquarters in Alexandria and occupied the Carlyle House while planning his campaign against the French in 1755.

At the time of the Revolution, Alexandria was one of the principal Colonial trading centers and ports. Its political, social and commercial interests were of great importance to the many local residents, especially to its nearby resident, George Washington, in Mount Vernon.

Washington maintained a townhouse in Alexandria, and served as a trustee of the town. He also purchased a pew in Christ Church, and was a Worshipful Master of the Alexandria Masonic Lodge number 22. Records reveal that Washington had numerous social and business connections to the town.

General Henry "Light Horse Harry" Lee, a Revolutionary War general and the father of Robert E. Lee, brought his family to Alexandria in 1810. Robert lived there until his departure for West Point in June, 1825.

At the turn of the 19th century, Alexandria was a part of the District of Columbia and, during the years prior to the Civil War, industry grew and flourished and shipping through the Alexandria Canal prospered.

During the Civil War, Alexandria was captured and occupied by Union troops and was a base for operations in Northern Virginia. Troops and supplies were transported to the city via railroad and the port and then dispersed where needed at the front. Wounded soldiers, brought back from the front on trains, crowded the available hospitals and temporary medical facilities in and around the town.

Although Alexandria was a slave trading location prior to the Civil War, it also had several free Black communities. African-American life in the city flourished with the establishment of churches, social and fraternal organizations and businesses. Many of early Alexandria's African-Americans were skilled artisans.

The Torpedo Factory on the waterfront was built during World War I and was used again during the Second World War as a munitions factory. Before its renovation in the late 1970s and early 1980s, its 10 heavy industrial buildings dominated Alexandria's waterfront. Today, it's an award-winning example of adaptive reuse and the centerpiece of a lively waterfront community with a marina, shops, public parks and walkways, restaurants, residences and offices.

Alexandria began its historic preservation and urban renewal projects in the 1960s, and all was achieved through the cooperation of citizen activists and local government. The Civil War centennial restoration of the northwest bastion of Fort Ward was the beginning of Alexandria's official protection of its historic sites and landmarks.

Today, the Old Town historic district is known for its many museums, its architecture, special events, fine restaurants and hotels, and other attractions, which draw more than 1.5 million international and domestic visitors to it each year.

Sights

Adams Center for the History of Otolaryngology, One Prince Street, ☎ 703-836-4444, www.entnet.org/museum, is an unusual museum on the history of treating the ear, nose and throat. Open Monday-Friday.

Alexandria Black History Museum, 902 Wythe Street, ☎ 703-838-4356, http://oha.ci.alexandria.va.us/bhrc/, documents local and national culture and contributions of Black America. Open Tuesday-Saturday.

Woodlawn, 9000 Richmond Highway, ☎ 703-780-4000, www.woodlawn1805.org, is the estate George Washington gave to his adopted granddaughter and his nephew as a wedding gift. Open daily, 10 a.m. to 5 p.m., March through December; combined admission with Pope-Leighy House available.

Frank Lloyd Wright's **Pope-Leighey House** is on the Woodlawn estate; built in 1940 of cypress, brick and glass, the house contains examples of many of Wright's contributions to architecture. Open same hours as Woodlawn; combined admission available. ☎ 703-780-4000, www.popeleighey1940.org.

The **United States Patent and Trademark Office Museum** has a new home at 600 Dulany Street. It features displays on fascinating inventions. Open Monday-Friday. Admission is free.

Ramsay House, the town's Visitor Center at 221 King Street in Old Town, is the oldest house in Alexandria, built in 1724, and has done ser-

Old Town Alexandria

METRO Subway Station
● Parking

Nat'l Airport – 2 miles
Washington DC – 5 miles

Potomac River

Powhatan St

First St

Canal Center Plaza

Montgomery St

Braddock Rd

Madison St

N

Wythe St

Oronoco Park

Pendleton St

Oronoco St

Princess St

N West St
N Payne St
N Fayette St
N Henry St
N Patrick St
N Alfred St
N Columbus St
N Washington St
N St. Asaph St
N Pitt St
N Royal St
N Fairfax St
N Lee St
N Unions St

Queen St

Cameron St

Founders Park

King St

Peyton St
Commerce St

S Fayette St
S Henry St
S Patrick St
S Alfred St
S Columbus St
S Washington St
S St. Asaph St
S Pitt St

Prince St

Waterfront Park

AMTRAK

S West St
S Payne St

Duke St

Wolfe St

S Royal St
S Fairfax St
S Lee St
S Unions St

Wilkes St

Gibbon St

Franklin St

Mount Vernon
10 miles

1. Ramsay House / Visitor Center, Gadsby's Tavern Museum
2. Carlyle House
3. Torpedo Factory Art Center
4. Christ Church
5. Appomattox Statue
6. Friendship Firehouse
7. Robert E. Lee Boyhood Home
8. Black History Resource Center
9. George Washington Masonic National Memorial
10. Stabler Leadbeater Apothecary Shop

© 2005 HUNTER PUBLISHING, INC

Alexandria

vice as a tavern, grocery store and cigar factory. Here visitors can obtain an assortment of informational material, including free parking permits, maps, complete listings of restaurants, hotels and tours. They can also purchase "block tickets" good for reduced admission to three of the city's historic properties.

Guided walking tours depart from the Visitor Center during the spring, summer and fall, weather permitting. The center is open daily except

Thanksgiving, Christmas, and New Year's Day. ☎ 800-388-9119 or visit www.FunSide.com.

Alexandria African American Heritage Park, Holland Avenue, ☎ 703-838-4356, features bronze trees and other sculptures honoring African-Americans of Alexandria, past and present.

Alexandria Archaeology Museum, 105 N. Union Street, inside the Torpedo Factory Art Center, is where archaeologists piece together the city's history. Open daily except Mondays. ☎ 703-838-4399, www.alexandriaarchaeology.org.

Alexandria National Cemetery, Wilkes and Payne streets, was established in 1862 and contains the graves of 3,500 Civil War soldiers.

The **Alexandria Seaport Foundation's Seaport Center** is at the Potomac River waterfront, just south of Founders Park. This floating museum opened in 1999. There is a boat-building program, a marine science lab, a small museum and library, and rental boats. Open daily. ☎ 703-549-7078, www.alexandriaseaport.org.

The Carlyle House, 121 N. Fairfax Street in Old Town Alexandria, is a stately stone mansion built in the Palladian style in 1753. It was the site of a 1755 meeting between General Edward Braddock and five English Colonial governors to plan the early campaigns of the French and Indian War. The house is open daily except Mondays. ☎ 703-549-2997, carlylehouse.org.

Christ Church, at Cameron and N. Washington streets, is well known for its fine Palladian widow, its interior balcony, and its wrought-brass and crystal chandelier, which was brought over from England. The old structure is little changed from the day when it was built in 1773. Both George Washington and General Robert E. Lee were pew holders here. A gift shop and several interpretive exhibits are located at the Columbus Street entrance. The church is open daily except Thanksgiving and New Year's Day. Donations are welcome. For more information, ☎ 703-549-1450, www.historicchristchurch.org.

Friendship Fire House, 107 S. Alfred Street, was built in 1871 and now houses historic firefighting exhibits ☎ 703-838-3891, www.friendshipfirehouse.org.

Fort Ward Museum & Historic Site, 4301 W. Braddock Road, is an authentically restored Union fort of the Civil War era. The museum presents a number of interesting exhibits including many fine pieces of Civil War memorabilia and artifacts. On a fine day visitors to the fort can also enjoy a picnic in the park. Fort Ward is open daily except Mondays, Thanksgiving, Christmas, and New Year's Day. ☎ 703-838-4848, www.fortward.org.

Gadsby's Tavern Museum, 136 N. Royal Street, is a famous old tavern much frequented by George Washington and other patriots. The museum is a combination of two 18th-century buildings and features some interesting Colonial architecture. Be sure to try the food at Gadsby's Tavern Restaurant. Call or see the Web site for hours, ☎ 703-838-4242, www.gadsbystavern.org.

George Washington Masonic National Memorial is at King Street and Callahan Drive. George Washington was perhaps the most prominent American Freemason. The 333-foot-high structure houses a large collection of Washington's belongings, gathered together over many years by members of the Washington family and the Masonic lodge of which he was the first master. Visitors may take a guided tour of a replica of the Alexandria-Washington Lodge's first assembly hall, the museum, and climb to the observation deck high on the top floor for magnificent views of Alexandria and the Potomac River. The memorial is open daily except Thanksgiving, Christmas, and New Year's Day. ☎ 703-683-2007, www.gwmemorial.org.

The Lee-Fendall House, 614 Oronoco Street, was built by Philip Richard Fendall and lived in by the Lee family for 120 years. George Washington and Henry "Light Horse Harry" Lee were both frequent visitors. The house was remodeled in 1850 and is furnished with many of the Lee family belongings. The house is open daily except Mondays, major holidays, Thanksgiving, Christmas, and New Year's Day. ☎ 703-548-1789, www.leefendallhouse.org.

The Lyceum, Alexandria's History Museum, 201 N. Washington Street, was first established as a cultural and scientific center in 1839. Today, the Greek revival building is a museum and information center for Historic Alexandria. The museum is open daily. ☎ 703-838-4994, www.alexandriahistory.org.

The **Old Presbyterian Meeting House**, 321 S. Fairfax Street, ☎ 703-549-6670, was the site of memorial services for George Washington. Open Monday through Friday, www.opmh.org.

The Stabler-Leadbetter Apothecary Shop, 105-107 S. Fairfax Street, was built in 1792 and houses the country's largest collection of apothecary glassware in an original setting. The original building, now a museum of early pharmacy, offers visitors a unique glimpse into the nation's medical past through a fine collection of old prescriptions, patent medicines, scales and other interesting medical memorabilia. The old shop has served many famous customers, including George Washington, Robert E. Lee, and John Calhoun. It is open daily. ☎ 703-836-3713, www.apothecarymuseum.org.

Torpedo Factory Art Center, 105 N. Union Street, is a renovated munitions factory which today houses more than 150 professional artists. There are studios, galleries, a museum, a school, and the Alexandria Archaeological offices located inside the building. The center is open daily

Alexandria

except major holidays, Thanksgiving, Christmas, and New Year's Day. ☎ 703-838-4565, www.torpedofactory.org.

Dressing for the Weather

Springtime in Alexandria is a delightful time of year, with the dogwoods, azaleas and colorful flowering bulbs all in bloom. But the weather can be a little on the chilly side, especially in the evenings. A sweater or jacket is recommended. May and June are usually warm, with temperatures in the 70s and 80s. Wear something cool and comfortable for the hot and humid weather of July and August.

Often a long Indian summer gives way to a cool, crisp autumn, perfect for light woolens. Winters in Alexandria are usually moderate, with only light snowfalls of around one to two inches, although an occasional major storm may occur. January is usually the coldest month, followed by the spring thaw in February.

Annual Events

The **Lee Birthday Celebrations** in January honor "Light Horse Harry" Lee and his son, Robert E. Lee, at the Lee Boyhood Home, 607 Oronoco Street, and the Lee-Fendall House, 614 Oronoco Street. ☎ 703-548-8454 or 548-1789.

The **George Washington's Birthday Celebrations**, held in February, include a race, Civil War re-enactments, and are climaxed by the birthday parade on the national holiday. ☎ 703-991-4474, www.washingtonbirthday.net.

Many fine Colonial and federal-style homes are opened for public viewing during **Historic Garden Week** in April. For more information and tickets, call the Alexandria Visitors Bureau at ☎ 703-549-2289, www.vagardenwalk.org.

Old Town Arts & Crafts Fair in early May brings artisans and live music to Market Square, 301 King Street, ☎ 703-836-2176, www.alexandriavolunteers.com.

Mount Vernon's **Wine Festival & Sunset Tour** in mid-May is an elegant evening and a rare opportunity to see the cellar vaults at George Washington's estate. Advance tickets required; available April 1 at www.Ticketmaster.com or at the estate, ☎ 703-780-2000, www.mountvernon.org.

Alexandria Red Cross Waterfront Festival, held during held in early June, commemorates Alexandria's maritime heritage, and features the

"Tall Ships," Blessing the Fleet, river cruises, races, arts and crafts, many exhibits, good food, a fireworks display, and lots of good music. ☎ 703-549-8300, www.waterfrontestival.org.

The **Virginia Scottish Games**, held the fourth weekend in July, is an athletic competition featuring all the old-time traditional Highland Games events, including Highland dance and music, and a display of antique cars. For more information, call the Alexandria Visitors Bureau at ☎ 703-912-1943, www.vascottishgames.org.

Historic Alexandria Antiques Show & Sale in mid-November brings dealers from all over the country to Holiday Inn & Suites, 625 First Street ☎ 703-549-5811, www.funside.com.

The **Holiday Parade of Boats** in early December lights up the harbor. Activities are centered at the Alexandria Marina at the foot of Cameron Street. ☎ 703-838-5005, www.funside.com.

There are holiday **Candlelight Tours** in Old Town Alexandria and Gunston Hall, www.funside.com.

The **Scottish Christmas Walk**, held the first weekend in December, features a parade, a tour of historic homes, concerts, greens and heather sales, and a dinner dance, all emphasizing Alexandria's Scottish origins. ☎ 703-549-0111, www.campagnacenter.org.

Entertainment

Although Alexandria is only a little more than a stone's throw away from the glittering nightlife offered by the nation's capital, it is well served with a cultural and arts community all its own, including the following.

Rachel M. Schlesinger Concert Hall and Arts Center hosts performances on the Northern Virginia Community College campus at 3001 N. Beauregard Street, ☎ 703-845-6156, www.schlesingercenter.com.

The Birchmere features big-name country and folk acts, 3701 Mt. Vernon Avenue, ☎ 703-549-7500, www.birchmere.com.

Old Town Theater is an historic theater featuring live entertainment and movies, 815½ King Street, ☎ 703-683-8888, www.oldtowntheater.com.

The Alexandria Ballet performs at the historic Athenaeum, 201 Prince Street, Alexandria VA 22314, ☎ 703-548-0035, www.alexandria-athenaeum.org (click the link for Alexandria Ballet Company & School).

The Alexandria Symphony Orchestra offers a full program of music and entertainment. For more information and schedules, contact the symphony at PO Box 1035, Alexandria, VA 22313, ☎ 703-845-8005, www.alexsym.org.

Alexandria

The Little Theatre of Alexandria is at 600 Wolfe Street, ☎ 703-683-0496, www.thelittletheatre.com.

MetroStage, located at 1201 N. Royal Street, offers a season of productions, staged readings and a children's theater series. ☎ 703-548-9044, www.metrostage.org.

The West End Dinner Theatre, 4615 Duke Street, offers fine dining and Broadway musicals, comedies and mysteries. ☎ 703-370-2500.

***The Dandy* Restaurant Cruise Ship**. *The Dandy*, operated by Potomac Party Cruises, is docked at Zero Prince Street. The ship offers gourmet dining, dancing and an unparalleled view of Washington Monument and the nation's capital. ☎ 703-683-6076, www.dandydinnerboat.com.

Headliners & Comedy Club, ☎ 703-397-HAHA, is located in the Holiday Inn Eisenhower Avenue.

Las Tapas, 710 King Street, ☎ 703-836-4000, features Flamenco dancers on certain nights.

The Laughing Lizard, 1322 King Street, offers fine dining, comedy shows and bands. ☎ 703-548-2582.

Shopping

Alexandria offers the discerning visitor a world of shopping opportunities and something for just about everyone from simply browsing the tiny shops and stores to some very serious shopping at the mall.

Literally hundreds of fine shops and stores are situated at various strategic locations in and around the city. These include antique stores and art galleries, more than a dozen book stores catering to both adults and children, a half-dozen gourmet food shops. In addition, are specialty stores catering to all sorts of needs from diving equipment to fine tobacco.

A brochure entitled *A Guide to the Arts and Antiques in Alexandria* is available at the Ramsay House Visitors Center.

Dining

There are more than 200 restaurants in Alexandria, offering innovative menus with international and regional tastes. In most cases, reservations are accepted and are required on Fridays and Saturdays. For a complete listing, visit www.funside.com, where you can also search by cuisine. Unless otherwise noted, all restaurants serve lunch and dinner.

219 Restaurant, 219 King Street in Old Town Alexandria, ☎ 703-549-1141, www.219restaurant.com, features a Creole menu with emphasis on seafood. Jazz is played Tuesday through Saturday. The restaurant is located in a converted private residence, circa 1890, with period millwork, antiques, Victorian paintings and marble fireplaces.

Bilbo Baggins Restaurant, 208 Queen Street in Old Town Alexandria, ☎ 703-683-0300, www.bilbobaggins.net, offers a continental menu, many varieties of wines and micro-brews. This is an upstairs restaurant in a pre-turn-of-the-century building.

Bistrot Lafayette, 1118 King Street, ☎ 703-548-2525, www.bistrotla-fayette.com, serves hearty French Provincial cuisine featuring entrées of lamb, game and seafood. Open Monday-Saturday for lunch and dinner.

Shellfish is the specialty at **Blue Point Grill**, 600 Franklin Street, ☎ 703-739-0404, a lively restaurant with a raw bar and outdoor dining. Open daily for lunch and dinner.

Elysium has no menu – instead the chef tells patrons the nightly dishes, which usually include game and seafood. It's formal and expensive, with impeccable service. Open for dinner Tuesday-Saturday. 116 S. Alfred Street, ☎ 703-838-8000.

Evening Star Café is moderately-priced and casual with a diner-like décor, and surprisingly daring menu and homemade desserts. Open daily for dinner; lunch Tuesday-Saturday. 2000 Mount Vernon Avenue, ☎ 703-549-5051.

The Fish Market, 105 King Street at Union Street in Old Town Alexandria, ☎ 703-836-5676, is in a restored 18th-century warehouse. Specialties include seafood, pasta, crab cakes and clam chowder. The restaurant also has a bar. Reservations are accepted.

Gadsby's Tavern Restaurant, 138 N. Royal Street, across from the Old Town Hall, ☎ 703-548-1288, www.gadsbystavernrestaurant.com. The Colonial menu offers Sally Lunn bread; George Washington's favorite, duck; and English trifle. The tavern features Georgian architecture, Colonial décor and strolling minstrels.

Geranio Ristorante, 722 King Street in Old Town Alexandria, ☎ 703-548-0088, features rustic Mediterranean décor, a fireplace and ceramic lights. The Northern Italian menu includes seafood, veal, and pasta dishes.

Green Olive Buffet & Grill has a great Asian-American buffet featuring seafood and prime rib. It's "heaven" for the Chinese food-lover. 7405 Richmond Highway, Alexandria, ☎ 703-765-5899.

Il Porto Ristorante, 121 King Street in Old Town Alexandria, ☎ 703-836-8833, www.ilportoristorante.com, serves Northern Italian cuisine, featuring pasta, chicken, and seafood dishes. Il Porto is in a fine old 18th-century building with a long history.

Alexandria

La Bergerie, 218 N. Lee on the second floor of Crilley Warehouse in Old Town Alexandria, ☎ 703-683-1007, www.labergerie.com, serves Basque cuisine in a restored 1890s warehouse.

Le Gaulois, 1106 King Street in Old Town Alexandria, ☎ 703-739-9494 has a French Country menu that includes rack of lamb, veal, and rabbit. The restaurant features French provincial décor and a fireplace.

Majestic Café, which opened in 2001, is a reincarnation of the 50-year-old art deco original. 911 King Street, ☎ 703-837-9117, www.majesticcafe.com.

Pat Troy's Ireland's Own, 111 North Pitt Street, ☎ 703-549-4535, www.pattroysirishpub.com, has an Irish-American menu, serving specialties such as lamb and beef stew and corned beef and cabbage. There is entertainment in an Irish pub atmosphere.

RT's Restaurant serves very good New Orleans cooking. 3804 Mount Vernon Avenue, ☎ 703-684-6010.

Taverna Cretekou, 818 King Street in Old Town Alexandria, ☎ 703-548-8688, offers a Greek menu with specialties of seafood and lamb. The restaurant features Mediterranean décor and a brick patio.

Union Street Public House, 121 S. Union Street in Old Town Alexandria, ☎ 703-548-1785, www.usphalexandria.com, serves up specialties of apple-smoked barbecue pork ribs and linguini with lobster and smoked scallops. The restaurant is located in an old sea captain's house and warehouse, circa 1870.

Villa D'Este, 818 North St. Asaph Street, ☎ 703-549-9477, www.villadesteristorante.com, features Northern Italian cuisine.

Accommodations

Hotels & Motels

Alexandria Lodge Old Town, 700 N. Washington Street, ☎ 703-836-5100. The hotel has 39 rooms, and pets are allowed in rooms. A café is nearby. $$

Best Western Old Colony Inn, 1101 N. Washington Street, Old Town Alexandria, ☎ 703-739-2222, www.bestwestern.com, has 49 rooms. Features include coffee in the lobby, bar, high-speed Internet access and an exercise room. $$

Comfort Inn-Alexandria, 5716 S. Van Dorn Street, ☎ 703-922-9200, www.comfortinn-alexandria.com, has 169 rooms. Guests enjoy the new Noble Roman's restaurant, in-room coffee, free continental breakfast, complimentary shuttle to the Metro, outdoor swimming pool, and fitness room. $

Comfort Inn-Landmark, 6254 Duke Street, Alexandria, ☎ 703-642-3422, www.comfortinnalexandria.com, has 150 rooms. Coffee is available in the lobby, and there is a free continental breakfast. Amenities include a bar, swimming pool, exercise room, meeting rooms, valet service, and café. $$

Courtyard by Marriott, 2700 Eisenhower Avenue, Alexandria, ☎ 703-329-2323, has 176 rooms. Features include coffee in the lobby, bar, swimming pool, an exercise room, meeting rooms, valet service, café. $$

Hampton Inn Alexandria, 5821 Richmond Highway, ☎ 703-329-1400, www.hamptoninnalexandria.com. The hotel has 156 rooms. Features include coffee in the lobby, free continental breakfast, swimming pool, meeting rooms, valet service, café. $$

Hampton Inn Old Town, 1616 King Street, ☎ 703-299-9900 www.hamptoninn.com, has 80 rooms and is convenient to the King Street Metro Station. $$

Hawthorn Suites, 420 N. Van Dorn Street, ☎ 703-370-1000, www.hawthorn.com, is newly renovated with 185 large suites and fully-equipped kitchens. Free continental breakfast, hospitality tour, shuttle to the Metro, outdoor pool. $$

Hilton Alexandria at Mark Center, 5000 Seminary Road, ☎ 703-845-1010. The hotel has 495 rooms, and offers coffee in the lobby, a bar, swimming pool, exercise facilities, free supervised children's activities, tennis courts, golf privileges, luxury level accommodations, meeting rooms, valet service, café, gift shop, free local and airport transportation. $$$

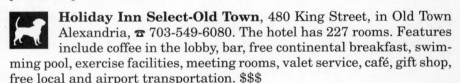

Holiday Inn Select-Old Town, 480 King Street, in Old Town Alexandria, ☎ 703-549-6080. The hotel has 227 rooms. Features include coffee in the lobby, bar, free continental breakfast, swimming pool, exercise facilities, meeting rooms, valet service, café, gift shop, free local and airport transportation. $$$

Radisson Hotel Old Town, 901 N. Fairfax Street, ☎ 703-683-6000, with 258 rooms on the Potomac River. Coffee is available in the lobby, and there is a bar, swimming pool, exercise room, meeting rooms, valet service, café, gift shop, and free local and airport transportation. $$

Red Roof Inn, 5975 Richmond Highway, ☎ 703-960-5200, has 115 rooms. Amenities include coffee in the lobby, free continental breakfast, an exercise room, meeting rooms, valet service, café nearby. $

Sheraton Suites Old Town, 801 North St. Asaph Street, ☎ 703-836-4700 or 800-325-3535, has 247 rooms, including two-room suites, an indoor pool, fitness center, restaurant, and free shuttle to Old Town and airport. $$$

Alexandria

Washington Suites Alexandria, 100 S. Reynolds Street, ☎ 703-370-9600, www.washingtonsuiteshotel.com, has 225 spacious suites with full kitchens and a pool. $$$

Bed & Breakfasts / Inns

The Morrison House, 116 S. Alfred Street, in Old Town Alexandria, ☎ 703-838-8000, 866-834-6628, www.morrisonhouse.com. The inn has 45 rooms. Amenities include afternoon English tea, meeting rooms, bathroom telephones, covered parking, entertainment, bar, health club privileges. The hotel is located in a building from the Federal period, now a European-style inn with individually decorated rooms, a paneled library and a parlor with a fireplace. $$$

Transportation & Information

Alexandria is served by **Ronald Reagan Washington National Airport** (☎ 703-417-8000), about 10 minutes from Old Town; **Washington Dulles International Airport** (☎ 703-572-2700), about 40 minutes away; and **Baltimore/Washington International Airport** (www.bwi.com, ☎ 410-859-7111), about one hour away. All major domestic and international carriers service these airports.

Alexandria has its own **Amtrak** station, and is also served by **Metrorail**, **Virginia Rail Express** (www.vre.org) and its own **DASH** buses.

The **Metro** has four convenient locations: Braddock Road is on the Yellow Line, Eisenhower Avenue is also on the Yellow Line, and King and Van Dorne Streets are both on the Blue Line. Metro Subway hours of operation are from 5:30 a.m. until midnight, Monday through Friday, and from 8:00 a.m. until midnight on Saturday and Sunday. The rush hours are from 5:30 a.m. until 9:30 a.m., and from 3:00 p.m. until 7:00 p.m.

Transportation Contact Numbers

- ❖ **Metro** (subway), ☎ 202-637-7000, www.wmata.com
- ❖ **Metrobus**, ☎ 202-637-7000 (also available for charter)
- ❖ **DASH**, ☎ 703-370-DASH (also available for charter)
- ❖ **Amtrak**, ☎ 800-USA-RAIL (800-872-7245)
- ❖ **Greyhound**, ☎ 800-231-2222

The **Ramsay House** at 221 King Street, ☎ 800-388-9119, is Alexandria's official visitors center, and is located in the heart of the historic Old Town. The center is open daily from 9 a.m. until 5 p.m., except Thanksgiving,

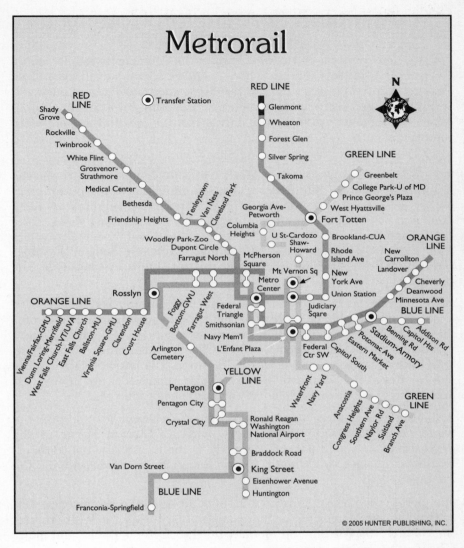

Metrorail

Christmas Day and New Year's Day. Brochures on Alexandria's historic attractions, special events, walking guides, restaurants, hotels, antique stores, art galleries, and museums are provided by experienced and knowledgeable travel councilors.

Free parking passes for out-of-city visitors are available for metered on-street spaces. For more information, contact the **Alexandria Convention and Visitors Association**, 221 King Street, Alexandria, VA 22314-3209, ☎ 703-838-4200, 800-388-9119 or www.FunSide.com.

Arlington & Arlington County

Arlington County is on the west bank of the Potomac River, just across from the nation's capital, where it enjoys all the advantages of its close proximity to the center of government and international business. Arlington is an international community; a melting pot where a hundred different languages are spoken, and the streets blaze with the colors of international garb.

Today's Arlington is fired by a powerful economy. Its highly educated workforce is whisked to work on Metro trains. Its businesses thrive in the hospitality, defense, information, telecommunications, computer, technology, and aerospace industries. The world's decision-makers shop, dine, and live in apartments and homes with breathtaking views of the capital and the Potomac. Airplanes bring visitors and business travelers from all points of the compass into Arlington's Ronald Reagan Washington National Airport and nearby Washington Dulles International Airport.

Arlington is home to more than two dozen international companies, with about 10 of them being worldwide corporate headquarters. The Center for European Community Studies offers the resources of the East Coast's official documentation center for the European Community. The US Patent Office eases access to the world's markets. The nation's defenses are looked after at the Pentagon. All of the world's embassies are located just across the Potomac in the heart of the District of Columbia.

Arlington's many attractions draw millions of visitors from all over the world. Arlington National Cemetery, with its Eternal Flame at the gravesite of President John F. Kennedy, is the most visited of these attractions, followed by Arlington House Robert E. Lee Memorial and the Pentagon.

Just across the river in Washington, in addition to the Kennedy Center, are the Lincoln Memorial, the Smithsonian Institution, the White House, the Capitol, the Washington Monument, the Supreme Court, and many other famous points of interest.

A short walk across the Roosevelt Bridge to the Kennedy Center for the Performing Arts offers visitors an international showcase of music, theater, opera, and dance. Arlington lists some 20 groups that contribute to the area's cultural offerings. These include ballet and contemporary dance companies, opera and choral groups, four theater companies, and a puppet theater. Last, but not least, the Arlington Symphony caps this glittering community of international artists.

History

Arlington's history dates back about 9,000 years. For centuries the Iroquois fished the waters of the Potomac and hunted the immense forests of Virginia's Piedmont region, unaware of the existence of a world beyond the great waters. Then, in 1607, **Captain John Smith**, an English explorer, sailed up the Potomac as far as Little Falls above Arlington. And so it began.

Over the years that followed Smith's epic voyage into what was to become Arlington County, the land along the Potomac was cleared and settled. At first the farms and holdings were small and far between. Then, as wealthy members of the English aristocracy began to see the great potential offered by the New World, great homes and plantations were established. One of the largest landowners in the area in those early times was the Custis family. Its most famous member was Martha Dandridge Custis, who married George Washington in 1759. It was Custis land that, in the late 1790s, became the site of **Arlington House**.

In 1791 much of what is now Arlington was included in Congress's description of the land that would become the nation's capital. The boundaries then included an area some 10 miles on either side, embracing parts of Virginia and Maryland.

In June, 1831, the area's two most influential families were united in a marriage that would change the course of Virginia's history. Mary Ann Randolph Custis married Robert Edward Lee, the son of the famous Henry "Light Horse Harry" Lee, and so Robert E. Lee became the master of Arlington House. For 30 years the great house was home to the Lees. Then, one dark day in 1861, on the eve of war, Robert E. Lee declined the US Army's offer to lead it against the forces of the fledgling Confederacy. He chose instead to follow his home state into secession and lead Virginia's forces in the Confederate Army. Mrs. Lee and her family moved out of the house only one step ahead of the Union Armies preparing for the defense of Washington.

During the years of war that followed, Arlington House served as a military headquarters, a hospital, a convalescent camp, and a cemetery: the beginnings of what would become the Arlington National Cemetery.

Finally, the Civil War ended and the area that is now Arlington returned to farming. Then, Fort Myer, the home of the US Army's famous 3rd Infantry, was established. It was there in 1908 that the first airplane passed its endurance test when Orville Wright circled the airfield 57 times.

In 1920, the Virginia General Assembly changed the name of the area from Alexandria County to Arlington County to honor the Custis and Lee family home, and to memorialize its greatest general, Robert E. Lee.

Arlington & Arlington County

From the end of World War I, the area grew in proportion to the federal government. New population transformed Arlington County from a rural farming community to a bedroom community for the nation's capital. The new residents stimulated housing, services, and business. Soon Arlington was connected to the great city by an electric trolley operated by the Washington Virginia Railway Company. And still Arlington continued to grow. For 20 years between 1920 and 1940 it was the fastest-growing county in Virginia.

From the opening of the Pentagon in 1942, Arlington has become the center of military power in the United States. Since that time, Arlington's economy has expanded to become a diverse and powerful force in the region based on industries predicted to dominate in the years ahead: telecommunications, information, defense, aerospace, computers, and travel.

> ❖ *On September 11, 2001, Arlington's peace was shattered when a passenger plane hijacked by terrorists flew into a wing of the Pentagon. When it was over, 184 people were lost.*

Sights

Arlington National Cemetery

The Arlington National Cemetery covers about 600 acres and, while it's not the largest cemetery in the country, it is the most famous.

More than 200,000 veterans and their dependents are buried at Arlington. From Pierre L'Enfant, George Washington's aide during the Revolution, and Johnny Clem, the Drummer Boy of Shiloh, to General Maxwell Taylor, Chairman of the Joint Chiefs of Staff during the Vietnam Conflict, there are veterans buried here representing every conflict in which the United States has fought.

The cemetery is the site of the John F. Kennedy, Jacqueline Kennedy Onassis and Robert Kennedy gravesites, as well as the Challenger Space Shuttle Memorial, the Tomb of the Unknowns, and the mast of the USS *Maine*.

Notable civilians buried in the cemetery include Heavyweight Boxing Champion Joe Louis, our 27th President William Howard Taft, and Abner Doubleday, who, in addition to inventing the game of baseball, is credited with having fired the first Union volley at Fort Sumter at the outbreak of the Civil War.

The Changing of the Guard at the Tomb of the Unknowns is conducted every hour on the hour from October 1st to March 31, and every half-hour from April 1st to September 30th. While guarding the tomb, the sentinels take 21 steps, before turning and facing the tomb for 21 seconds. This corresponds with America's highest military honor, the 21-gun salute.

Open daily, 8 a.m. until 7 p.m. April through September; and 8 a.m. until 5 p.m. October through April. ☎ 703-607-8000, www.arlingtoncemetery.net.

At the entrance to Arlington National Cemetery is the **Women in the Military Service for America Memorial**, which honors all women who have served in times of conflict and of peace. An education center and theater tells the history of women in the armed forces, dating from 200 years ago up to the present. ☎ 703-533-1155 or 800-222-2294, www.womensmemorial.org.

Arlington House, The Robert E. Lee Memorial

Arlington House is on the grounds of the National Cemetery and was the home of General Robert E. Lee, General of the Confederate Army during the Civil War.

The house was built by George Washington Custis, grandson of Martha Washington by her first marriage to Daniel Park Custis, and features pre-Civil War furnishings, many of which originally belonged to the mansion.

Robert E. Lee married Custis' daughter and lived in the house for more than 30 years. At the outbreak of the Civil War he took his family and left the estate to follow the fortunes of the Confederacy. Wartime law required that property owners in an area occupied by federal troops must appear in person to pay their taxes. Unable to comply with this rule, the Lees saw the estate confiscated in 1864. The land was immediately set aside as a military cemetery. In 1882, however, Robert E. Lee's grandson, George Washington Custis Lee, brought suit against the United States for the return of his property. The suit was successful. However, hundreds of graves covered the land, so he accepted the federal government's offer of $150,000 for the property.

Arlington House is open daily, 9:30 a.m. until 4:40 p.m., except Christmas and New Year's day. For more information, ☎ 703-557-0614, www.nps.gov/arho. Handicapped access is limited to the first floor of the house.

The US Marine Corps War Memorial

The US Marine Corps War Memorial, also known as *Iwo Jima*, is dedicated to all Marines who have given their lives in defense of the United States from 1775. It was officially dedicated by President Dwight D. Eisenhower on November 11, 1954, the 179th anniversary of the Marine Corps.

The Memorial is one of the largest cast-bronze statue in the world. It features 32-foot-tall figures erecting a 60-foot-tall bronze flagpole. The M-1 rifle and the carbine carried by two of the figures are 16 and 12 feet long, respectively. The cloth flag flies from the pole 24 hours a day in accordance with a presidential proclamation of June 12, 1961. The sculpture was designed by Felix W. De Weldon, then on duty with the US Navy, from a Pulitzer-prize-winning photograph taken by war correspondent and photographer Joe Rosenthal.

The Memorial is open 24 hours daily, and is on Marshall Drive between Route 50 and Arlington National Cemetery; ☎ 703-289-2500, www.nps .gov/gwmp/usmc.htm.

The Netherlands Carillon

The 49-bell carillon, located adjacent to the *Iwo Jima* memorial, was presented to the nation by the people of the Netherlands, in gratitude for US aid given during and after the World War II.

The bells are four-fifths copper and one-fifth tin. The largest has a diameter of six feet, nine inches and weighs 12,654 pounds. The smallest is nine inches in diameter and weighs only 37.5 pounds. Verses cast on each bell were written by Dutch poet Ben von Eysslesteijn. The bells are installed in an open steel tower designed by Dutch architect Joost W.C. Boks.

The carillon is tuned to a chromatic scale and covers one more note than four octaves. It is played with an automatic electronic system. Concerts are presented by carillonneurs from around the world on Saturdays and national holidays, April through August. The carillon is on Marshall Drive, next to the Iwo Jima Memorial, between Route 50 and Arlington National Cemetery. ☎ 703-285-2500, www.nps.gov/gwmp/carillon.htm.

The Pentagon

The Pentagon is the home of the United States Department of Defense. It is also one of the world's largest office buildings, encompassing some 6.5 million square feet and employing 23,000 people. The US Capitol would fit into any one of the five wedge-shaped sections, each of which has exterior walls 921 feet wide. The building was constructed in only 16 months and was completed on January 15, 1943, at a cost of about $83 million.

> ❖   *The Pentagon has 8,770 parking spaces in 16 lots, more than 17½ miles of corridors, 131 stairways, 19 escalators, 614 water fountains, 284 restrooms, and 7,754 windows.*

The Pentagon has been closed to the public since the terrorist attack of September 11, 2001, which killed 184 people. Schools, educational organizations and other select groups can tour by reservation only. ☎ 703-697-1776, www.defenselink.mil/pubs/pentagon.

Other Points of Interest

The Arlington Historical Society Museum is housed in a former schoolhouse, now museum, which features Civil War artifacts, 19th-century kitchenware, and ladies' fashions through the years. The museum is at 1805 S. Arlington Ridge Road, and is open Saturday and Sunday from 1:00 until 4:00, ☎ 703-892-4204.

The Old Guard Museum graphically tells the story of the oldest US Army infantry regiment from 1784 right up to the present, and is the only Army museum in the Washington DC, area. The museum is open Monday through Saturday, and on Sunday afternoons. ☎ 703-696-6670, www .mdw.army.mil/oldguard. The museum is in Building 249, Sheridan Avenue, Fort Myer, Arlington.

The Gulf Branch Nature Center is situated in a 37-acre wooded valley and offers interpretive exhibits that include an 1871 hand-hewn log house and a forge operated by the Blacksmith's Guild of the Potomac. The park is open from sunrise until a half-hour after sunset. For more information, contact the nature center at 3608 N. Military Road, Arlington, ☎ 703-228-3403.

The 100-acre **Potomac Overlook Regional Park** is located along the banks of the Potomac River. It offers visitors a quiet day out walking the nature trails through stands of towering oak trees and tulip poplars. The park's nature center features many archaeological and wildflower exhibits, as well as magnificent views of the nation's capital, its skyline, and the Washington Monument. The park is open daily from dawn until dusk, the nature center, Tuesday through Saturday, and on Sunday afternoons. ☎ 703-528-5406, www.nvrpa.org/potomacoverlook.html. The park is at 2845 N. Marcey Road (off Military Road), Arlington.

Theodore Roosevelt Island in the Potomac River is accessible by car from the northbound lane of the George Washington Memorial Parkway. Two-and-a-half miles of trails lead through the marsh, swamp and forest. ☎ 703-289-2500, www.nps.gov/this/index.htm.

Annual Events

Whatever time of year you decide to visit Arlington, there's always something interesting to see and do. The following is but a partial list of the traditional annual events. For a more complete list, including special events, contact the **Arlington Convention & Visitors Service**, ☎ 800-677-6267, www.stayarlington.com.

The US Army Band Concerts are held December through March on Tuesday and Thursday evenings at Brucker Hall, Fort Myer, Arlington. For a complete schedule of performances, ☎ 703-696-3399, www.army .mil/armyband or www.usarmyband.com.

The National Cherry Blossom Festival, held in early April celebrates the blooming of more than 6,000 Japanese cherry trees around Washington's monuments. Week-long activities include lantern lighting ceremonies, concerts, art exhibits, a 10K race, and a boat cruise and parade. ☎ 202-547-1500.

Arlington & Arlington County

Easter Sunrise Service is held in the Arlington National Cemetery Memorial Amphitheater. Free shuttle from the visitors center parking lot starting at 5:30 a.m. ☎ 703-607-8052.

Arlington Arts Al Fresco is a summer-long series of free arts performances. ☎ 703-358-6960 for schedules.

Marine Corps Tuesday Evening Sunset Parades are held from late May through late August at the *Iwo Jima* Memorial in Arlington. ☎ 202-433-4073.

Rosslyn Jazz Festival is held in Gateway Park in the Rosslyn section of Arlington in early September. ☎ 703-522-6628.

Tours

Tourmobile Sightseeing offers daily narrated tours authorized by the National Park Service. There are 21 stops in Washington DC, and four in Arlington National Cemetery. There are also tours of Arlington National Cemetery daily. Board at the red, white and blue signs along the route. ☎ 202-554-5100 or visit www.tourmobile.com.

Entertainment

The following is a partial list of venues in the area; for further information, visit www.arlingtonarts.org.

Arlington Center for Dance, 3808 Wilson Boulevard, ☎ 703-522-2414, www.arldance.com.

Classika Theatre, 4041 S. 28th Street, ☎ 703-824-6200, www.classika.org.

Lubber Run Amphitheatre is a 1200-seat outdoor facility with performances June to September. North 2nd and North Columbus Street, ☎ 703-228-1850, arlingtonarts.org.

Rosslyn Spectrum Theatre, 1611 North Kent Street, ☎ 703-228-1850, www.arlingtonarts.org.

Thomas Jefferson Theatre, S. 2nd Street, Arlington, ☎ 703-228-6960 or the Arts Hotline at ☎ 703-228-6966.

Gunston Arts Center, 2700 South Lang Street, Arlington, ☎ 703-228-1850.

Signature Theatre is at 3806 South Four Mile Run, Arlington, ☎ 703-820-6500, www.signature-theatre.org.

Teatro De La Luna is at 2700 S. Lang Street, Arlington, ☎ 703-548-3092. This is Arlington's Spanish-language theater. Performances are given in Spanish with simultaneous English translation at various locations; www.teatrodelaluna.org.

The Washington Shakespeare Company makes its home at the Clark Street Playhouse, 601 S. Clark Street, Arlington. ☎ 703-418-4808, www.washingtonshakespeare.org.

The John F. Kennedy Center for the Performing Arts includes the Opera House, Eisenhower Theatre, the Concert Hall, the Terrace Theatre, the Theatre Lab, and the American Film Institute. 2700 F Street, NW, Washington DC, ☎ 800-444-1324, 202-467-4600, www.kennedy-center.org.

The National Theatre is at 1321 Pennsylvania Avenue, NW, Washington DC, ☎ 800-447-7400, 202-628-6161, www.nationaltheatre.org.

The Shakespeare Theatre is at 450 7th Street, NW, Washington DC, ☎ 202-547-1122, www.shakespearedc.org.

Warner Theatre, 513 13th Street NW at E Street, Washington DC, ☎ 202-397-SEAT (7328), www.warnertheatre.com.

Shopping

The national capital area offers its visitors many fine malls, small boutiques, and splendid shops, along with upscale stores, outlet malls, and historic districts which George Washington is known to have frequented. But Arlington has some fine shopping of its own, with several large malls and dozens of small specialty shops.

Ballston Common, on North Glebe Road and Wilson Boulevard in Arlington, is just one block from the Metro's Ballston Station on the Orange Line. There are 100 specialty stores on four floors, and an international food court on the ground floor. ☎ 703-243-6346, www.ballston-common.com.

Crystal City Shops, 1608 Crystal Square Arcade in Arlington, ☎ 703-922-4636, www.thecrystalcityshops.com, features an underground plaza with a unique collection of more than 130 specialty shops and stores. The food court has cafés and restaurants offering a variety of fine food to suit every palate, all at reasonable prices. Take Metro's Blue and Yellow lines. Crystal City Arcade is a short walk from the Crystal City Station.

The Fashion Centre at Pentagon City is at 1100 S. Hayes Street, Arlington, on Metro's Blue and Yellow Lines, connected to the Pentagon City Station. This four-story shopper's extravaganza features 170 stores anchored by Nordstrom and Macy's. There's a sunlit food court and six movie theaters. ☎ 703-415-2400, www.simon.com.

The **Market Common at Clarendon** has shops and restaurants in a walkable, street-front setting. 2800 Clarendon Boulevard, ☎ 703-807-2922, www.arlingtonvirginia.com/market_clarendon.

Pentagon Row is a Main Street-style mall with shopping, restaurants, and the Arlington Visitors Center. Joyce Street and Army-Navy Drive, ☎ 301-998-8100, www.pentagonrow.com.

The **Village at Shirlington** is at 2700 S. Quincy Street in Arlington. This is a Main Street shopping area where you can spend the day wandering in and out of the stores, then catch a movie, followed by a wonderful meal at any one of the dozen or more restaurants that line the avenue. ☎ 703-379-0007.

Dining

The list of fine restaurants that follows is representative of the more than 500 in the area. For a complete listing, visit **www.stayarlington.com**, where you can search by cuisine or area. Unless otherwise noted, all restaurants are open for both lunch and dinner, but closed on major holidays.

Alpine, 4770 Lee Highway, Arlington, ☎ 703-528-7600, caters to a mature crowd and offers an Italian and continental menu. Offerings include veal, pasta, and seafood.

The Carlyle Grand Café, 4000 S. 28th Street, Arlington, ☎ 703-931-0777, serves seafood, steaks and pasta upstairs and in the more casual bar downstairs. Open daily for lunch and dinner; Sunday for brunch.

The Grill, at the Ritz Carlton in Pentagon City, Arlington, ☎ 703-415-5000, is open for dinner daily. Reservations are accepted, required on Friday and Saturday. The restaurant offers an American menu and features a bar and wine cellar; a pianist provides music on the weekends.

Fuji, 77 N. Glebe Road, Arlington, ☎ 703-524-3666, offers Korean dishes such as bibimbap, fried dumplings, and bul goki, and also has a sushi bar. Reservations are accepted, required on Fridays and Saturdays. Closed on January 1.

Layalina serves Syrian and Lebanese food, 5216 Wilson Boulevard, ☎ 703-525-1170.

La Côte d'Or Café is a classic French restaurant with game and seafood dishes on the menu. 6876 Lee Highway, ☎ 703-538-3033.

Queen Bee, 3181 Wilson Boulevard, Arlington, ☎ 703-527-3444, open daily for lunch and dinner, offers Vietnamese dishes such as Hanoi beef noodle soup and Hanoi-style grilled pork.

Ray's the Steaks is all about steak. Although the dining room is a tad small, the steaks are not. They are all-natural, lean and and cooked to order. 1725 Wilson Boulevard, ☎ 703-841-7297.

Red, Hot & Blue, 1600 Wilson Boulevard, Arlington, ☎ 703-276-7427, is open for dinner and has a bar. The restaurant specializes in Memphis pit barbecue dishes for carry-out or dining in.

The Tivoli, 1700 N. Moore Street, Arlington, ☎ 703-524-8900, offers an à la carte Italian menu and specializes in pasta and seafood. Open for lunch and dinner, closed Sunday; reservations suggested.

Tom Sarris Orleans House, 1213 Wilson Boulevard, Arlington, ☎ 703-524-2929, features prime rib, steak, and salad bar. The family-owned restaurant has a New Orleans atmosphere with fountains, iron railings and Tiffany lamps. Open for lunch Monday-Friday, for dinner daily.

Woo Lae Oak, 1500 Joyce Street, on the grounds of the River House complex in Arlington, ☎ 703-521-3706. Open for lunch and dinner daily. The menu offers Korean cuisine. Specialties of the house include barbecued dishes prepared at your table.

Accommodations

Arlington has more than 40 hotels. Here's a sampling. Most establishments offer both handicapped-accessible and non-smoking rooms, but be sure to ask when making reservations.

Hotels & Motels

Hilton Arlington & Towers, 950 N. Stafford Street, Arlington, ☎ 800-468-8357, 703-528-6000, www.hilton.com. 209 rooms. Among the amenities are room service, meeting rooms, a gift shop, luxury level, exercise room, café, pool with lifeguard, and parking. Complimentary continental breakfast. $$$$

Hilton Garden Inn Arlington/Courthouse Plaza,1333 North Courthouse Road, ☎ 800-445-2667, www.hiltongardeninn.com. 189 rooms in Pentagon City, near Reagan National Airport. Offers suites and an indoor pool. $$$

Best Western Key Bridge, 1850 Fort Myer Drive, Arlington, ☎ 800-KEYBRIDGE, 703-522-0400, www.bestwestern.com. 178 rooms. $$

Days Inn Pentagon-Cherry Blossom, 3030 Columbia Pike, Arlington, ☎ 703-521-5570. 76 rooms. Free continental breakfast. $$

Comfort Inn Ballston, 1211 N. Glebe Road, Arlington, ☎ 703-247-3399. 126 rooms. It offers room service, a restaurant, bar, meeting rooms, a gift shop and garage parking. $$

Crowne Plaza, 1489 Jefferson Davis Highway, Arlington, VA 22202. ☎ 800-483-7870703-416-1600. 308 rooms. The hotel has a pool with lifeguard, room service, meeting rooms, valet service, free airport transportation and parking. $$$

Crystal City Courtyard by Marriott, 2899 Jefferson Davis Highway, Arlington, ☎ 703-549-3434, www.courtyard.com. 272 rooms. It features an indoor pool with lifeguard, room service, a bar, a café, meeting rooms, an exercise room, free airport transportation and parking. $$

Crystal City Marriott, 1999 Jefferson Davis Highway, Arlington, ☎ 800-228-9290, 703-413-5500, www.marriott.com. 347 rooms. Amenities include a pool with lifeguard, room service, restaurant, meeting rooms, an exercise room, free airport transportation and parking. $$$

Crystal Gateway Marriott, 1700 Jefferson Davis Highway, Arlington, ☎ 800-228-9290, 703-920-3230, www.marriott.com. 700 rooms. It features a pool with lifeguard, meeting rooms, an exercise room, free airport transportation and parking. $$$

Doubletree Hotel National Airport, 300 Army/Navy Drive, Arlington, ☎ 800-222-8733, 703-416-4100, www.doubletree.com. 632 rooms. Complimentary continental breakfast. Features include an indoor pool with lifeguard, room service, a bar, two restaurants, meeting rooms, an exercise room, free airport transportation and parking. $$$$

Embassy Suites, 1300 Jefferson Davis Highway, Arlington, ☎ 703-979-9799, www.embassysuites.com. 267 suites. Among the amenities are a pool with lifeguard, room service, a bar, a café, meeting rooms, and an exercise room, and there is free airport transportation and parking. $$$

Hilton Crystal City at Reagan National Airport, 2399 Jefferson Davis Highway, Arlington, ☎ 800-445-8667, 703-418-6800, www.hilton.com. 386 rooms. Among the amenities are a pool with lifeguard, room service, meeting rooms, a luxury level, an exercise room, free airport transportation and parking. There is a complimentary continental breakfast. $$$

Holiday Inn National Airport, 2650 Jefferson Davis Highway, Arlington, ☎ 800-278-2243, 703-684-7200, www.hinationalairport.com. 280 rooms. There is room service, a bar, a restaurant, a gift shop, an exercise room, free high-speed Internet service, free airport transportation and parking. $$

Holiday Inn Rosslyn, 1900 N. Fort Myer Drive, Arlington, ☎ 800-368-3408, 703-807-2000, www.basshotels.com. 308 rooms. It has an indoor pool with a lifeguard, meeting rooms and parking. $$

Hyatt Arlington, 1325 Wilson Boulevard, Arlington, ☎ 800-233-1234, 703-525-1234, www.arlington.hyatt.com. 302 rooms. Amenities include free wireless Internet access, room service, a bar, a café, meeting rooms, valet service, an exercise room and parking. $$$$

Hyatt Regency Crystal City, 2799 Jefferson Davis Highway, Arlington, ☎ 800-233-1234, 703-418-1234, www.crystalcity.hyatt.com. 685 rooms. Among the amenities are a pool with lifeguard, room service, a restaurant, meeting rooms, valet service, free airport transportation and parking. $$$$

Key Bridge Marriott, 1401 Lee Highway, Arlington, ☎ 800-327-9789, 703-524-6400, www.keybridgemarriott.com. 585 rooms. This large luxury hotel features a pool with lifeguard, room service, meeting rooms, valet service, an exercise room and parking. $$$$

 Quality Hotel & Suites, 1200 N. Courthouse Road, Arlington, ☎ 800-228-5151703-524-4000. 392 rooms. The hotel offers a bar, pool with lifeguard, room service, meeting rooms, valet service, exercise room and parking. $$-$$$

Quality Inn Iwo Jima, 1501 Arlington Boulevard, Arlington, ☎ 800-424-1501, 703-524-5000, www.yourdchotels.com. 141 rooms. Features include a heated pool with lifeguard, poolside service, room service, bar, café, meeting rooms, valet service, gift shop and parking. $$

Ritz-Carlton Pentagon City, 1250 S. Hayes Street, Arlington, ☎ 800-241-3333, 703-415-5000, www.ritzcarlton.com. 366 rooms. Amenities include a café, pool with lifeguard, gift shop, luxury level, exercise room and parking. Complimentary continental breakfast and Metro service at front entrance. It's five minutes from Reagan National Airport. $$$

Sheraton Crystal City, 1800 Jefferson Davis Highway, Arlington, ☎ 800-627-8209, 703-486-1111, www.sheraton.com. 218 rooms. This Sheraton has a pool with lifeguard, cable TV, meeting rooms, valet service, exercise room and parking. $$

Sheraton National Hotel, Columbia Pike and Washington Boulevard, Arlington, ☎ 800-468-9090, 703-521-1900, www.sheraton.com. 417 rooms. Amenities include a pool with lifeguard, room service, meeting rooms, valet service, exercise room, free airport transportation and parking. $$

Tips For Visiting Sights in the DC Area

The following are some useful tips and information that should help make your visit to Arlington and the capital area more enjoyable.

The Smithsonian Institution museums: To avoid crowds at the museums on the Mall (Air and Space Museum, Natural History, etc.), try to visit just after they open at 10 a.m., or after 5 p.m. (depending on seasonal hours). The museums become very crowded from just before lunch through the afternoon. You might try museums that are not on the Mall (the National Building Museum, the National Portrait Gallery, etc.) during the afternoons. For a good introduction to the Smithsonian museums, visit the Castle, which opens at 8:30 a.m., before the museums.

Monuments and Memorials: Visit monuments and memorials in the evening. They are very attractive when lit up and are much less crowded. Arlington National Cemetery is open until 7 p.m., and is less crowded in the early evenings.

Transportation

❖ *We suggest you leave your vehicle at your hotel and take advantage of DC's mass transit system – one of the finest in the world. Metrorail and Metro bus offer the fastest, cheapest way to get around, and they allow you to avoid the hassles of traffic congestion and limited parking.*

The **Metrorail subway system**, ☎ 202-962-1234, www.wmata.com, is clean, safe, and efficient. The trains are quiet, comfortable, and reliable. There's a Metrorail station within an easy walk from all major points of interest in the DC area, including the White House, Arlington National Cemetery, the US Capitol, the Smithsonian Institution, the National Zoo, and more.

Metrorail stations are marked above ground with brown pylons bearing a white "M." Take the escalators below ground to the open areas where you can purchase your farecard (fares are determined by how far you travel). Use your farecard to pass through the faregates and onto the train platforms. All Metrorail stations and trains are handicapped-accessible.

❖ *Smoking is not permitted on escalators, elevators, in stations, on trains or buses.*

The trains follow various routes designated by color. On the front of the train you will be able to read what color line that particular train is following.

❖ ***Rush Hours:*** *To avoid crowded conditions, do not use the roads and Metrorail from 6:30 to 9 a.m., or from 3:30 to 6 p.m. on weekdays.*

The **Metro Bus system** is also easy and inexpensive. Check with the front desk of your hotel for schedules and bus numbers, or ☎ 800-523-7009, www.wmata.com, to find out how to get anywhere in the DC area.

❖ *During the summer, the city is filled with visitors on weekends. DC is much less crowded during January and February, when the weather is generally moderate and accommodations are offered at bargain prices.*

Information

For visitor and tourist information, contact the **Arlington Visitors Orientation Center** at 1301 S. Joyce Street, Arlington, ☎ 800-677-6267. It's located in Pentagon City and is open daily from 9 a.m. until 5 p.m. Be sure to ask for a free copy of the *Arlington and Washington DC Visitor's Guide,* or visit the Web site at www.stayarlington.com.

Culpeper & Culpeper County

Situated in the rolling hills of the Piedmont, Culpeper County rises from an elevation of 300 feet on the eastern side to 600 feet on the west. Bounded by the Rapidan River to the south, and the Rappahannock River to the north, the entire area is well served and watered by these and a multitude of other small rivers, creeks, and streams. The climate is moderate, with mean annual temperatures of 35° in January and a balmy 76° in July. The annual precipitation averages about 41 inches. As long ago as 1749, George Washington, during his survey of the area, declared Culpeper a "high and pleasant situation." It hasn't changed.

Culpeper is an area of great growth, but one that keeps an eye on its historical roots and lifestyle. Situated as it is, Culpeper is blessed with an excellent location in the middle of a box consisting of Virginia's four main interstate highways. US Highway 29 runs right through the town and county, and there are four airports, two of them international, within a hundred miles.

❖ *Author Norman Crampton listed Culpeper in his book,* The 100 Best Small Towns in America, *in 1993.*

Whatever your passion – the great outdoors, history, horses, or simply a quiet day or two away from the hustle and bustle of city life – you will find it in Culpeper.

History

Culpeper County is a large tract of land separated from Orange County by an Act of the Virginia House of Burgesses in 1748. Culpeper convened its first county court on May 17, 1749. The original county boundary included not only Culpeper as we know it today, but also Madison County, severed from Culpeper in 1792, and Rappahannock County, cut off in 1831.

The county was named for Lord Thomas Culpeper, the Colonial Governor of Virginia from 1680 until 1683. He inherited his rights from his father, Lord John Culpeper, to whom the English King Charles II had given a large land grant.

Culpeper

Thomas Culpeper's holdings, including all of the Northern Neck territory, were inherited by his daughter Catherine, who married Lord Thomas Fairfax. Their son, the sixth Lord Fairfax, inherited the property and it was for him that the town of Culpeper, first called Fairfax, was named. Lord Fairfax's Virginia estate, comprising some 5.2 million acres, was confiscated by the colonists when the Revolutionary War began.

In the Culpeper courthouse, on October 21, 1765, 16 of the 20 members of Culpeper County Court, all holding commissions as Justices of the Peace from King George III, resigned in protest of the Stamp Act. Nine years later the citizens of Culpeper held a mass meeting during which they fiercely condemned the English Parliament and pledged themselves to defend their rights with their "lives and fortunes."

At the Virginia convention held in May, 1775 in Richmond, the colony was divided into 16 districts. Each district was instructed to raise and discipline a battalion of men "to march at a minute's notice." The district, including Culpeper, Fauquier and Orange counties, raised a force of 350 men called the **Culpeper Minute Men**. They first organized on July 17, 1775, under a large oak tree in "Clayton's old field," and then took part in the Battle of Great Bridge, the first Revolutionary battle fought on Virginia soil. The Culpeper Minute Men battle flag is inscribed with the words, "Liberty or Death" and "Don't Tread on Me."

Eighty-five years later, as the nation moved toward civil war, the Culpeper Minute Men were reorganized under the rattlesnake flag. The company staff, in 1860, assembled under the same old oak tree as did the original Minute Men of 1775. When the Civil War broke out, the men of Culpeper were mustered into the Confederate army as Company B, 13th Virginia Infantry Regiment. Other Confederate Culpeper units included the Little Fork Rangers and the Brandy Rifles.

Culpeper County saw a great deal of action during the four years that the Civil War ravaged the Virginia countryside. Armies of both sides marched back and forth across the county, camped, and fought within the boundaries of the county line. Most notable of the many engagements fought on Culpeper soil were the great battles of Cedar Mountain, a resounding victory for Confederate General Robert "Stonewall" Jackson over General John Pope's Union Army of Virginia, and Brandy Station, the largest cavalry engagement on the North American Continent; more than 10,000 Union horse soldiers under the command of General Alfred Pleasonton engaged some 9,000 men of Confederate General James Ewell Brown "Jeb" Stuart's cavalry division. The Union army was eventually driven off after more than 12 hours of fighting, but it was the first time that Federal cavalry had been able to match the Confederate horsemen in skill and determination.

After the Civil War ended, and the troops of both armies had all gone home, Culpeper County returned to its sleepy ways, and life continued

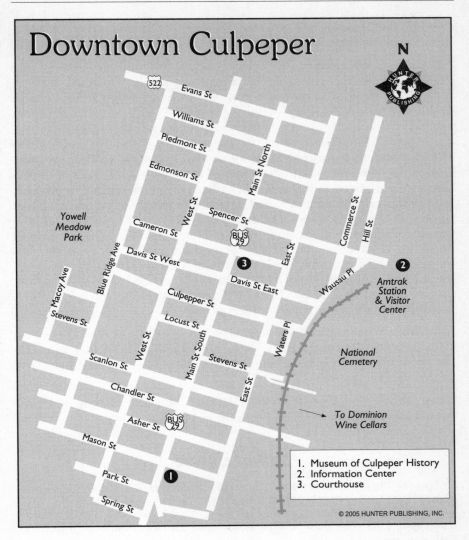

Downtown Culpeper

N

522
Evans St
Williams St
Piedmont St
Edmonson St
Main St North
Yowell Meadow Park
West St
Spencer St
Cameron St
Commerce St
Hill St
Blue Ridge Ave
Davis St West
BUS 29
East St
3
2
Davis St East
Macoy Ave
Wausau Pl
Amtrak Station & Visitor Center
Stevens St
Culpepper St
Locust St
West St
Main St South
National Cemetery
Scanlon St
Stevens St
Waters Pl
Chandler St
East St
To Dominion Wine Cellars
Asher St
BUS 29
Mason St
Park St
1
1. Museum of Culpeper History
2. Information Center
3. Courthouse
Spring St

© 2005 HUNTER PUBLISHING, INC.

much as it had for more than a hundred years. The first public school opened in 1871, the telephone arrived in Culpeper in 1891, and the population began to increase. In 1970, the census set the county population at 18,218; by 1996 it had grown to 31,700.

Sights

The current **Culpeper County Courthouse** was built in 1873 and is the third courthouse at this site at the corner of Main and Davis streets. It's been beautifully restored. Outside are a Civil War and a Vietnam Memorial. The courthouse can only be visited during the guided Civil War Walking Tours of Historic Old Town Culpeper, which are offered

Culpeper

through the Museum of Culpeper History (see below) every first and third Saturday from May to October; www.visitculpeper.com.

The **Culpeper National Cemetery** dates to 1867 and continues to hold burial services for veterans. It covers six acres. Entrance is from E. Stevens Street, downtown, across the railroad. Open from dawn to dusk daily. ☎ 540-825-0027.

The **Museum of Culpeper History**, located in downtown Culpeper, has brought together more than 250 years of Culpeper's past. Most of the exhibits were donated to the museum by local people dedicated to preserving the heritage of the town. Exhibits in the museum include a slab of stone with dinosaur tracks, Indian axes, Civil War memorabilia, and the Guinn collection of black and white photographs. The oldest house in town, the 1750 Burgandine House, is on the museum grounds. The museum is open year-round, Monday through Saturday, from 10 a.m. until 5 p.m.; and Sundays, May-October, 12:30-4 p.m. For more information, contact the museum at 803 S. Main Street, Street, Culpeper, VA 22701, ☎ 540-829-1749, www.culpepermuseum.com.

Dominion Wine Cellars are located on Winery Avenue, two miles south of Culpeper off Virginia Highway 3. Visitors can tour the facility and taste the wine. For more information, ☎ 540-825-8772, www.virginiawines-.org/wineries/dominion.

Gray Ghost, **Old House**, **Prince Michel**, **Rapidan River** and **Unicorn** wineries are near Culpeper; www.virginiawines.org.

Annual Events

Culpeper Day is held the first Saturday in May, ☎ 540-825-0764. Crafts, games, food and music on Davis Street in downtown Culpeper.

Culpeper Harvest Days Farm Tour, held the first weekend in October, features local farms and a farmer's market across from the Train Depot Visitor Center. ☎ 800-793-0631, www.culpeperag.org.

The **Bluemont Concert Series** is offered every Friday during July and August on the lawn of the Old County Courthouse, West Davis Street, ☎ 703-777-6303, www.bluemont.org. A variety of music – country, big band and folk – is performed.

The **Fourth of July Festival** is held July 4, ☎ 540-825-1093, www.culpeperva.us/july4. During the day, downtown Culpeper hosts sports tournaments, a car and motorcycle show and a parade. In the evening, the party moves to Yowell Meadow Park, with craft and food vendors, hot air balloon rides, dancing, live music and, of course, fireworks.

A **Holiday Open House** is scheduled for the Sunday before Thanksgiving at the shops and restaurants of historic downtown Culpeper. Street entertainment, caroling and carriage rides, all from noon to 5 p.m., ☎ 540-825-4416.

The **Christmas Tour of Homes** is the first Saturday in December, ☎ 540-825-8200, www.culpeperva.us/housetour. Privately owned homes in the historic district are open to ticket-holders for a Victorian Christmas celebration.

Recreation

Watersports – fishing, swimming, boating, water skiing, sailing, and canoeing – are all available on both the Rappahannock and the Rapidan rivers, and on Lake Pelham and Mountain Run Lake. Mountain Run Lake also offers hiking, picnicking, and a playground for the children.

Natural Areas

The Yowell Meadow Park, at Blue Ridge Avenue and Route 522 North, is one of the best-utilized recreational facilities in the Culpeper area. The well-maintained facility includes almost 20 acres of parkland and a plethora of amenities, including fitness trails, tennis and basketball courts, football, soccer and baseball fields, playgrounds and picnic areas. ☎ 540-727-3412.

Commonwealth Park is one of the finest equestrian centers in the Eastern United States. Horse Shows in the Sun is a summer series that draws competitors and spectators from all over the country. 13256 Commonwealth Parkway, Culpeper, ☎ 540-825-7469, www.hitsshows.com.

Mountain Run Lake Park in the western part of the county has views of the Blue Ridge Mountains, only 15 minutes from downtown. Picnicing, a fishing lake, and children's play area. Open from dawn to dusk. ☎ 540-727-3421.

Rappahannock River Campground offers primitive camping, whitewater adventures, canoeing, kayaking, tubing and fishing. 33017 River Mill Road, Richardsville, ☎ 800-784-PADL, www.canoecamp.com.

Hazel Lake Park, in Elkwood, is a privately-owned recreational park with a sandy beach, barbecues and special events, ☎ 540-399-1450.

Biking

Cyclists find the county's quiet roads most enjoyable. The Bike Stop rents road bikes and mountain bikes and offers information on routes. 120 W. Culpeper Street, ☎ 540-825-2105, www.rideva.com.

Culpeper

Golf

Golfers can play at **Meadows Farms Golf Course** in Locust Grove, ☎ 540-854-9890, www.meadowfarms.com/golf; and **South Wales Golf Course** in Jeffersonton, ☎ 540-937-3250.

Shopping

Culpeper also has some fine shops, and the local business community strives to please customers. The town has a thriving community of antique dealers, boutiques, tiny shops, a busy farmer's market, several department stores, and five shopping centers, including **MinuteMan Mall** with more than 200 dealers, and the **downtown district** of Culpeper itself.

Dining

Culpeper dining offers something tasty for just about everyone. Small cafés, delis, and restaurants, many located in downtown Culpeper, offer plenty of choices, from elegant restaurants to family-style dining.

Here is a sampling:

Aberdeen Barn, **Holiday Inn**, Business 29 South, Culpeper, ☎ 540-825-1037. Open seven days a week for breakfast, lunch and dinner. Steakhouse, seafood, lunch and breakfast buffet.

Baby Jim's Snack Bar is an old-fashioned outdoor snak bar serving burgers and milkshakes. 701 N. Main Street, ☎ 540-825-9212.

Travel back to the 1950s at the **Frost Café**, where the booths have individual jukeboxes. 101 E. Davis Street, ☎ 540-825-9212.

Hazel River Inn, 195 East Davis Street, Culpeper, ☎ 540-825-7148, www.hazelriverinn.com. Open for lunch and dinner, and Sunday brunch. Located in a 1750s building that has housed a hardware store, tobacco barn and stables during different eras. The basement pub was used as a jail in the Civil War. Continental cuisine with a Viennese flair. Decorated with antiques and local artwork, all of it for sale.

It's About Thyme,128 East Davis Street, Culpeper, ☎ 540-825-4264. Serves lunch and dinner in a historic building from Tuesday through Saturday. European country cuisine.

Lord Culpeper Restaurant, 401 South Main Street, Culpeper, ☎ 540-829-6445. In the old Culpeper Hotel. Lunch and dinner seven days a week; Sunday brunch. Caribbean cuisine.

Luigi's Italian Restaurant uses fresh ingredients in its pasta, meat and seafood dishes. 235 Southgate Shopping Center, ☎ 540-829-4688.

Serendipity Grill, 609 Meadowbrook Shopping Center, Culpeper, ☎ 540-825-5659. Open for lunch and dinner Monday through Saturday, serving sandwiches, hamburgers and salads.

Accommodations

Most establishments offer both handicapped-accessible and non-smoking rooms, but be sure to ask when making reservations.

Hotels & Motels

The Comfort Inn, 890 Willis Lane, Culpeper, ☎ 540-825-4900, is a modern, two-story motel. 49 rooms. Pets are allowed, and there's a swimming pool. Free continental breakfast. $

The Holiday Inn, US Business 29, Culpeper, ☎ 540-825-1253, www.holiday-inn.com/culpeperva. 158 rooms. There is a dining room and café, entertainment, swimming pool, wading pool, several meeting rooms and a coin-operated laundry. $

Bed & Breakfasts / Inns

The Fountain Hall Bed and Breakfast is at 609 S. East Street, ☎ 540-825-8300, www.fountainhall.com. This Greek-revival house in the downtown historic district has been converted into an exclusive bed and breakfast inn that offers an intimate, homey experience in a non-smoking atmosphere. The house is handicapped-accessible, has four guest rooms and two suites, all with private bath. A free continental breakfast is provided, which includes fresh-baked croissants. $$

Hazel River Inn, 11227 Eggbornsville Road, Culpeper, ☎ 540-937-5854, www.hazelriverinn.com, has three guest rooms, one with private bath. This 100-year-old home offers fine dining and lodging in a romantic setting. There is an outdoor pool, spa, sunroom and fireplaces. $$

Inn at Kelly's Ford in Remington is a luxurious inn on the grounds of the Kelly's Ford Civil War Battlefield. The main house has two rooms, another is in a silo, and three cottages house six large suites with Jacuzzi, fireplace and patio or balcony. There's a heated pool, outdoor Jacuzzi, and fine dining in a 30-seat restaurant. ☎ 540-399-1779, www.innatkellysford.com $$$

The Suites at Prince Michel Vineyard, US Route 29, Leon, ☎ 800-800-WINE, www.princemichel.com, offers four suites, breakfast included, right on the grounds of the vineyard. $$$$

Camping

Cedar Mt. Campground, 20114 Camp Road, Culpeper, ☎ 540-547-3374 or 800-234-0968, www.cedarmtn.com. Open year-round with 61 RV and

Culpeper

tent sites. There is a pavilion, store with propane and firewood, game room, stocked fishing pond and playing fields.

Rappahannock River Campground, 33017 River Mill Road, Richardsville, ☎ 540-399-1839 or 800-784-PADL, www.canoecamp.com, has primitive camping only. Canoe and tube rentals and kayaking.

Transportation

Culpeper is well served by four **interstate highways**: I-95, I-64, I-81, and I-66. US Highway 29 runs north and south through the town, connecting Culpeper with Manassas to the north and Charlottesville to the south.

By rail, the town is served by **Amtrak** (☎ 800-872-7245), and bus service is offered by **Greyhound** (☎ 800-231-2222, www.greyhound.com).

Culpeper Regional Airport, ☎ 540-825-8280, www.culpepercounty.gov/airport.sop.asp, has a paved runway of 4,000 feet.

Information

More information about the area can be obtained from the following:

The **Culpeper Visitors Center** and the **Chamber of Commerce** are located in the renovated 1904 Historic Train Depot at 109 SOUTH Commerce Street. A restored red caboose sits outside. Amtrak makes daily stops at the Depot, which houses visitor information and some historical displays. Pick up one of the walking tour brochures and stroll through this pedestrian-friendly historic city. Open 8:30 a.m. to 5 p.m. Monday through Friday; 9 a.m. to 5 p.m. weekeends. ☎ 888-CULPEPER, www.visitculpeperva.com.

Virginia Morton, author of the Civil War novel *Marching Through Culpeper* conducts **tours of the county's battlefields**: Cedar Mountain, Brandy Station, and Kelly's Ford (groups of 2 or more, price varies according to number). For rates on half-day or full-day tours or to make an appointment, ☎ 540-825-9147, www.edgehillbooks.com.

Fairfax County

*O*nce a farming community serving the nation's capital, Fairfax County has evolved into a major business center and one of the most desirable residential communities in the metropolitan Washington area. Tysons Corner, the county's downtown, has more office space than many large cities, and has one of the largest concentrations of retail shopping space in the nation.

Visitors to Fairfax County will enjoy a broad spectrum of communities, from the preserved turn-of-the century town of Clifton to the lakes and golf courses in the planned community of Reston.

More than 30,000 acres of park land and numerous recreational facilities beckon visitors. Over 100 miles of back-country trails are available for hiking, biking, and horseback riding. Tourists can travel back in time by visiting one or more of the county's many historical landmarks, including Mount Vernon, the estate of George Washington, and Gunston Hall, the home of George Mason.

World-class entertainment is presented year-round at Wolf Trap Farm Park for the Performing Arts and the George Mason University Center for the Arts. Programs presented by local performing arts and symphony groups are found in the communities throughout the county.

History

The recorded history of Fairfax County, Virginia, is an important part of the history of all Americans. Although the county wasn't formally established until 1742, the history of English settlement on the land spans 350 years from the early 1600s to the present.

One of the first men to record life in the area was the English explorer **Captain John Smith**. In 1608, Smith sailed up the Potomac River as far as present-day Arlington County. During his journey, which he undertook in order to draw a map of Virginia, he had many exciting encounters with Indian warriors, explored mighty forests teeming with wildlife, and crystal streams laden with fish, beaver and otter.

In 1694 the English king, Charles II, granted all the land between the Rappahannock and the Potomac Rivers, from the Chesapeake Bay to the headwaters, to a group of seven English noblemen. In 1719, however, all of that land came into the possession of Thomas, the sixth **Lord Fairfax**, after whom the county was named. By 1732, attempts had been made to form the land into a county, but it wasn't until 1741 that the Virginia assembly established Fairfax County with its courthouse located near present day Tysons Corner.

When the Fairfax County Courthouse was moved to its present location in Alexandria in 1751, the county was still very much a wilderness area. There were few roads and virtually no industry. The only wealth and commerce during the 18th century came from tobacco cultivation. Indeed, tobacco notes were the main form of monetary exchange for paying debts. In the end, however, the tobacco industry, due to poor land management practices and over use, ruined the soil in Fairfax County and helped to hasten an economic decline.

From the mid-1700s to the end of the 18th century, there were many changes in the lifestyle and character of Fairfax County. Forests were cleared, roads were built, mills sprang up everywhere, and other forms of industry grew.

During the last half of the 18th century, two of the county's most prominent residents, **George Washington** and **George Mason**, became the chief forces behind the formation of the new American nation. Both were businessmen and farmers who believed strongly in commercial enterprise and the accumulation of capital. In 1784, George Washington presided over the first corporate venture in America, the **Patowmack Canal Company**. The company was formed to construct a canal around the Falls, on Virginia's northern border, to make the Potomac River navigable, and stimulate trade between the East Coast and the Ohio Valley.

Washington went on to become Commander-in-Chief of the Continental Army. Later, in 1786, he became the nation's first president.

While Washington was the chief physical force behind the American Revolution, Mason was the chief intellectual force. Along with fellow Virginian Thomas Jefferson, Mason's ideas on the rights of man surfaced in such important documents as the Virginia Declaration of Rights and the Virginia Constitution of 1776, both of which were authored by him. The **Virginia Declaration of Rights** served as the model for both the American Bill of Rights and the French Declaration of Rights of Man and the Citizen, which was issued after the French Revolution.

As the 19th century dawned, it appeared that Fairfax County would continue to have economic prosperity and gain national recognition, especially with the new capital located just next door. Instead, the years from 1800 to 1850 were harsh ones. By then, the county's soils had been laid waste by the over-planting of tobacco, and the most prosperous economic area in the county, Alexandria City, had been ceded to the federal government. Moreover, the county's two most prominent citizens, Washington and Mason, had both died during the 1790s, leaving it virtually leaderless.

The decline of the population during this period reflects the harsh economic conditions of the area. At the turn of the 19th century there were more than 13,300 people living in the county; by 1830 that number had declined to around 9,200. The migration was due mainly to farmers leaving the depleted land in search of something better farther west in Kentucky and Ohio. The level of population in the county didn't rise above 10,000 again until after 1850.

The economic turnaround in Fairfax County began sometime in the mid-1840s. People from the northeastern part of the nation began to move into the area, bringing with them sorely needed new farming techniques that allowed them to use the impoverished land.

During the **Civil War**, Fairfax County became a wasteland. Confederate troops were located in the western area, while Union troops were positioned in the northern and eastern areas near Alexandria. Troops of both

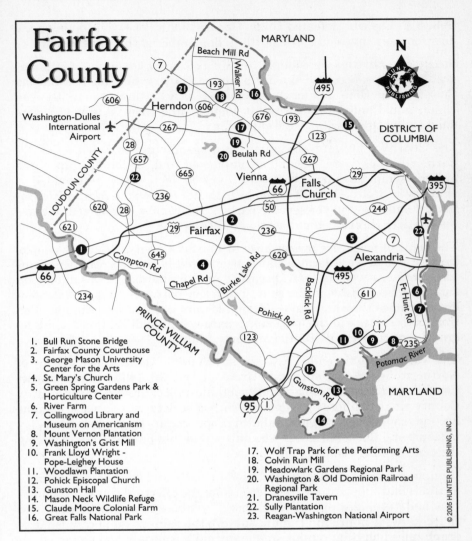

Fairfax County

MARYLAND

DISTRICT OF COLUMBIA

N

Washington-Dulles International Airport

Herndon

Vienna

Falls Church

Fairfax

Alexandria

LOUDOUN COUNTY

PRINCE WILLIAM COUNTY

MARYLAND

Potomac River

Beach Mill Rd
Walker Rd
Beulah Rd
Compton Rd
Chapel Rd
Burke Lake Rd
Backlick Rd
Pohick Rd
Gunston Rd
Ft. Hunt Rd

1. Bull Run Stone Bridge
2. Fairfax County Courthouse
3. George Mason University Center for the Arts
4. St. Mary's Church
5. Green Spring Gardens Park & Horticulture Center
6. River Farm
7. Collingwood Library and Museum on Americanism
8. Mount Vernon Plantation
9. Washington's Grist Mill
10. Frank Lloyd Wright - Pope-Leighey House
11. Woodlawn Plantation
12. Pohick Episcopal Church
13. Gunston Hall
14. Mason Neck Wildlife Refuge
15. Claude Moore Colonial Farm
16. Great Falls National Park
17. Wolf Trap Park for the Performing Arts
18. Colvin Run Mill
19. Meadowlark Gardens Regional Park
20. Washington & Old Dominion Railroad Regional Park
21. Dranesville Tavern
22. Sully Plantation
23. Reagan-Washington National Airport

Fairfax County

sides crisscrossed the county, often wreaking havoc and destruction on private property. Raiders from both sides, the most notable being the Confederate John Singleton Mosby, used the area as a staging ground for many a foray into enemy territory.

Two major battles, **1st and 2nd Manassas**, took place just to the south of and adjacent to Fairfax County. The first battle, in July 1861, was fought by inexperienced troops on both sides, and resulted in a rout for the Union Army under the command of General Irvin McDowell. This gave notice to the federal government that the war was going to last much longer than anyone had expected. The second battle, fought in late August, 1862, also resulted in a Confederate victory. This time it was General

Robert E. Lee who defeated Union General John Pope, thus opening the door for Lee's invasion of the north in September of the same year.

Seven minor battles were fought in Fairfax County. On June 1, 1861, several casualties occurred during a Union cavalry raid on the Fairfax County Court House. Later that month a bloody battle broke out between Union and Confederate forces at Vienna, and more skirmishes were fought near Dranesville and Centreville.

The Civil War brought disruption on a grand scale to Fairfax County. Farmer's crops were stolen and destroyed and, depending upon the owner's sympathies and the troops involved, businesses were raided or shut down. Railroads were seized by both sides. Even the *Alexandria Gazette,* a daily newspaper serving parts of the county, was forced to cease publication. It resumed publication after the war.

The signs of war were everywhere in Fairfax County. Destitute people, some of whom were former slaves, wandered hopelessly from one war-torn community to the next. Discarded military hardware was a common sight on any roadside in the county. Military patrols, Union and Confederate, roamed the countryside. Hospitals were jammed with the wounded from both sides, and the local mortuaries were filled. Railroad and telegraph services were disrupted and even halted.

The war in Virginia ended with the surrender of General Lee's Army of Northern Virginia to General US Grant on April 13, 1865 and reconstruction followed soon after. The traditional lifestyle of pre-Civil War Fairfax County was gone forever, replaced with a society where black citizens were given the right to vote and own property. The large plantations lay in ruins, and the northerners who had moved into Fairfax County during the 1840s and 1850s had fled.

Virginia was readmitted to the Union in 1870, and by then the county's fortunes had substantially recovered from the effects of war. The population had risen during the war years by almost 13,000. Schools and churches were flourishing again, as were the railroads and canals. Telegraph lines had been rebuilt, and many old businesses had reopened.

From 1930 onward, the county grew rapidly as people and businesses moved into the area. Between 1930 and 1950 the county's population quadrupled from 25,000 to 99,000. Today it is nearly one million.

Such rapid growth brought inevitable changes to the once-rural Fairfax County. The economy has changed from an agrarian one to one based upon the service industry, and while the lifestyle has altered, the standard of living has become higher.

Today, residents enjoy a collective income among the top in the nation. The new prosperity brought one of the best public school systems in the country, an international airport, many beautiful parks, and numerous recreational and cultural opportunities.

Fairfax County has come a long way since Captain John Smith sailed up the Potomac in the early 1600s.

The history of Fairfax County has been rich and fascinating, experiencing both war and peace, crashing economic depressions, and soaring economic expansions.

Sights

Fairfax County has preserved many of its historic sites for future generations to enjoy. Those that follow are but a sample.

Mount Vernon, the home of George Washington and one of the most visited historic homes in America, is first in popularity among visitors to the area. Washington's elegant mansion has been lovingly restored to its appearance in the last years of his life. The rooms, furnishings, handsome wood grainings, and satin window hangings all reflect the ambiance and the history of an exciting era in our nation's past.

Mount Vernon encompasses more than 30 acres of beautiful gardens and wooded grounds. The mansion's outbuildings reflect day-to-day life on the plantation much as it was in the late 1700s, and a short walk leads to the tomb where George and Martha Washington are buried.

The **Mount Vernon Inn**, ☎ 703-780-0011, offers lunch daily and candlelight dinners Monday through Saturday. Colonial cuisine is presented by costumed servers. There's also a food court for quicker meals. There's no need to buy a ticket to shop at Mount Vernon for gifts, jewelry, books, toys, gardening items, reproductions and furniture.

George Washington's Gristmill, three miles from the main estate, is operated by millers in Colonial costume. The site also has an excavation of Washington's whiskey distillery. The gristmill requires separate admission from Mount Vernon.

 Dogs on leashes are allowed at Mount Vernon during daytime hours. Gate attendants will even provide a bowl of water when needed! Mount Vernon is open daily year-round and is located 16 miles south of Washington, DC, and eight miles south of Old Town Alexandria, at 3200 George Washington Parkway. ☎ 703-780-2000, www.mountvernon.org.

Frying Pan Park and Kidwell Farm recreates the farming era from 1920 to 1940, which saw the advent of tractors, milking machines, and mechanical bailers. There are chickens, peacocks, rabbits, sheep, goats, pigs, cows and other livestock. The park is open from dawn to dusk; the farm from 10 a.m. to 6 p.m. 2709 West Ox Road, Herndon, ☎ 703-437-9101, www.fairfaxcounty.gov.

George Washington and George Mason attended **Pohick Episcopal Church**, which was completed in 1774 from plans drawn by Washington himself. It's still an active parish, with Sunday services at 7:45, 9 and 11:15 a.m. Call ahead for other times to see the church. Ask to see the Civil War soldier graffiti on the sandstone walls. 9301 Richmond Highway, Lorton, ☎ 703-550-9449, www.pohick.org.

Green Spring Gardens is a 27-acre park, demonstration garden and horticulture center. The former plantation has a restored historic manor house open for tours, English teas, and educational programs on gardening and history. 4603 Green Spring Road, Annandale, ☎ 703-642-5173, www.greenspring.org.

The Fairfax Museum is housed in an 1873 brick schoolhouse and includes exhibits on the county's history, including the Battle of Chantilly, fought nearby in September 1862. Open 9 a.m. to 5 p.m. daily. Admission is free. 10209 Main Street, Fairfax, ☎ 703-385-8414.

Fairfax Station Railroad Museum houses railroading memorabilia in a reconstruction of the 1858 Civil War field hospital and railroad depot that served the city until 1973. Open Sundays 1-4 p.m. and by appointment. 11200 Fairfax Station Road, ☎ 703-425-9225, www.fairfax-station.org.

Freeman House Museum is a restored 1859 home providing visitor information about the town of Vienna. Open weekend afternoons. 131 Church Street, NE, Vienna, ☎ 703-938-5187.

Gum Springs Historical Society and Museum celebrates the continuity of the Gum Springs community, which was founded by West Ford, a slave freed by George Washington. The free men and women worked in the trades they had learned on estates. Today many residents are descendants of the original families. Open Monday through Saturday afternoons and by appointment. 8100 Fordson Road, Alexandria, ☎ 703-799-1198, www.gshsfcva.org.

The **Herndon Depot Museum** houses artifacts from the town's history. Open daily. 717 Lynn Street, Herndon, ☎ 703-787-9879.

The **National Air and Space Museum's Udvar-Hazy Center** is home to some of the world's most famous craft, including the *Enola Gay*, Space Shuttle *Enterprise*, and a Concorde jet. Open 10 a.m. to 5 p.m. daily. Admission is free, but there is a charge for parking. 14390 Air & Space Museum Parkway, Chantilly, ☎ 202-357-2700.

The **Reston Museum** offers historial information on this unique community, along walking tours, children's art workshops every Saturday morning, and a gift shop. Open noon to 6 p.m. Wednesday-Sunday. Lake Anne Village Center, Reston, ☎ 703-709-7700, www.restonmuseum.org.

U.S. Geological Survey Visitor Center features natural science exhibits and the history of the nation's primary water and earth mapping agency. Open 8 a.m. to 6 p.m. weekdays. 12201 Sunrise Valley Drive, Reston, ☎ 703-648-4748, mac.usgs.gov/visitors.

Gunston Hall was the home of George Mason, father of the *Bill of Rights*. The magnificent house has undergone extensive archaeological and architectural studies that have inspired major changes to its plan, color schemes, and the carved wood trim. The porch of Gunston Hall overlooks the riverfront and its magnificent formal garden. The English boxwood alley was planted by George Mason. The house is 20 miles south of Washington on the Potomac River. From the north it can be reached via I-95 at Exit 55, or the George Washington Parkway to US 1. From the south take Exit 54 on I-95 to US 1 and follow the signs. Gunston Hall is open daily, year-round. ☎ 703-550-9220, www.gunstonhall.org.

Colvin Run Mill is a working 19th-century grist mill that processed grains and flours for use both at home and abroad. The gears and machinery are made almost entirely of wood and the milling technique was quite revolutionary for the early 1800s. The miller's house, along with a general store and a dairy barn, are also on the grounds. The park is open daily except Tuesday, with guided tours. The mill is five miles west of Tysons Corner at 10017 Colvin Run Road, Great Falls. ☎ 703-759-2771.

The Claude Moore Colonial Farm at Turkey Run is an 18th-century working farm. The farm has been restored to depict the lifestyle of the small farmer with a poor family in Colonial times. Of the farm's 100 acres, 12 are planted with corn, tobacco, wheat, kitchen gardens, and an orchard. The fields are tilled and planted by hand, using the basic principles of hoe agriculture. The farm is open April through mid-December, Wednesday through Sunday. 6310 Georgetown Pike, McLean. ☎ 703-442-7557, www.1771.org.

The Sully Historic Site looks much as it did when it was built in 1794, complete with Federal-period antiques. The estate includes a kitchen-laundry, smokehouse, stone dairy, formal gardens, and schoolhouse store. Sully is in Chantilly on Route 28, less than a mile north of US 50, and four miles south of the Route 267, the Dulles Access Road. The plantation is open daily except Tuesdays. ☎ 703-437-1794.

The Mason Neck Wildlife Refuge was the first federal refuge established for the endangered bald eagle. It provides more than 2,000 acres of habitat for the 200 animal species that live on Belmont Bay. The refuge is four miles south of Richmond Highway on Gunston Road. ☎ 703-490-4979, northeast.fws.gov/va/msn.htm.

The Mason Neck State Park is next door to the wildlife refuge. It provides 1,800 acres of magnificent parklands, with nature trails, picnic areas, and an abundance of wildlife, including deer, beavers, turtles and heron. ☎ 703-550-0960, www.dcr.state.va.us (select #24 on the map for this park).

Annual Events

George Washington's Birthday is celebrated in mid-February at Mount Vernon, ☎ 703-780-2000 or 703-799-8604, www.mountvernon.org.

The **Chocolate Lovers Festival** is held the first weekend in February in Old Town Fairfax. ☎ 703-385-1661, www.chocolatefestival.net.

The **Northern Virginia Fine Arts Festival** is held in Reston in May, ☎ 202-263-8543, www.restontowncenter.com.

The **International Children's Festival** is held in mid-September at Wolf Trap National Park for the Performing Arts, Vienna. ☎ 703-218-6500, www.artsfairfax.org/icf.shtml.

A **Wine Tasting Festival and Sunset Tour** takes place twice a year, in May and in October, at Mount Vernon, ☎ 703-780-2000 or 703-799-8604, www.mountvernon.org.

Celebrate Fairfax is in early June at the Fairfax County Government Center, ☎ 703-324-5392, www.celebratefairfax.org.

Taste of the Town is in late June at Reston Town Center, featuring food from dozens of restaurants, ☎ 202-263-8543, www.restontowncenter.com.

Fourth of July Celebrations are held at Mt. Vernon (☎ 703-780-2000), in Lee District Park (☎ 703-922-9841), at Lake Fairfax (☎ 703-471-5414) and there's a Fairfax parade (☎ 703-385-7858).

Reston Town Center Holiday Celebration begins the Friday after Thanksgiving with a holiday parade and tree lighting, and lasts the entire month of December, ☎ 202-263-8543, www.restontowncenter.com.

A variety of Fall and Christmas holiday events are held each year at Mount Vernon, Gunston Hall, Sully and Woodland plantations and Frank Lloyd Wright's Pope-Leighey House. Call those locations for more information.

Arts & Entertainment

Although Washington DC offers visitors an abundance of cultural attractions just a short distance away – such as The Kennedy Center for the Performing Arts, The National Theater, Arena Stage, Ford's Theater, the Corcoran Gallery of Art, the National Gallery of Art, the Smithsonian Institution – Fairfax County has a unique cultural community all its own. For a complete list of theaters and arts venues, see www.visitfairfax.org/entertainment.php.

Wolf Trap Park for the Performing Arts is the nation's only national park for the performing arts. The park consists of three separate facilities: the Filene Center, an open-air pavilion which seats 3,000 under roof and 4,000 on the lawn; The Barns, a 350-seat indoor theater used primarily in the fall and winter; and Children's Theater-in-the-Woods, a facility devoted to performances for and by children. Events are scheduled year-round. For more information and schedules, ☎ 703-255-1900, www.wolftrap.org.

The George Mason University Center for the Arts offers programs in ballet, dance, opera, symphony, jazz and theater. The season runs from September through April. For more information and schedules, ☎ 703-993-8888, www.gmu.edu.

Recreation

Several park systems, including some 35 parks, offer abundant recreational opportunities on more than 30,000 acres.

Parks

The **National Park Service**, www.nps.gov.parks, operates six parks in Fairfax County. Recreational activities in the parks include fishing, boating, rafting, hiking, rock climbing, and wildlife and nature photography.

The most notable of the area's National Park Service facilities is the **Great Falls National Park**, part of the George Washington Memorial Parkway. It is favorite of rock climbers, kayakers, hikers and picnickers. Features include a 76-foot waterfall on the Potomac River, and such historic sites as the nation's first canal system, designed by George Washington, and the ruins of Matildaville, built in 1790. Georgetown Pike, Great Falls, ☎ 703-285-2966, www.nps.gov/gwmp/grfa.

The **Fairfax County Park Authority**, www.co.fairfax.va.us/parks, manages four marinas, five nature centers, and eight recreation centers. Nature centers include the Hidden Oaks Nature Center at Annandale, the Hidden Pond Park at Springfield, the Huntley Meadows Park near Mount Vernon, the Riverbend Nature Center at Great Falls (see above), and Riverbend Park, also at Great Falls.

The **Fairfax County Department of Recreation**, ☎ 703-324-8700, www.co.fairfax.va.us/parks, also provides a wide variety of recreational programs year-round. These programs include arts and crafts, music, dance, martial arts, aerobics, and horseback riding.

Huntley Meadows Park is the county's largest, with 1,425 acres of wetlands, meadows and mature forest, provide great wildlife viewing. There's a half-mile wetland boardwalk trail, observation tower, and more than 200 bird species. 3701 Lockheed Boulevard, Alexandria, ☎ 703-768-2525, www.fairfaxcounty.gov/parks.

The **Northern Virginia Regional Park Authority** (☎ 703-352-5900, www.nrvpa.org) operates nine parks in Fairfax County. Activities include a wide variety of outdoor sports and recreation including golf, boating, fishing, swimming and camping. Trap and skeet shooting are available at the Bull Run Regional Park's public shooting center (7700 Bull Run Drive, Centreville, ☎ 703-631-0550), the only public shooting range in Northern Virginia.

Meadowlark Gardens Regional Park is a 95-acre garden park with three lakes surrounded by cherry trees. 9750 Meadowlark Gardens Court, Vienna. ☎ 703-255-3631, www.nvrpa.org/meadowlark.html.

Reston Town Center has an outdoor ice skating rink and a multi-plex cinema. ☎ 703-689-4699, www.restontowncenter.com.

The Washington & Old Dominion Railroad Regional Park is long and narrow, stretching the length of the county along the former railroad bed. Walk, run, bike or horseback ride the route. 21293 Smiths Switch Road, Ashburn. ☎ 703-729-0596, www.nvrpa.org/wod.html.

Golf

There are more than a dozen public golf courses in Fairfax County, as well as a wide range of other recreational facilities. For a complete list, ☎ 800-732-4732, 703-324-8700, or www.visitfairfax.org/recreation.php.

Shopping

With more than 200 shopping centers, Fairfax County is a mecca for shoppers. Shopping areas range in size from small specialty centers with 10 or fewer stores to super regional malls with more than 150 stores. The county boasts four of the latter, with national anchors such as Neiman Marcus, Macy's, Nordstrom, Bloomingdale's, and Lord & Taylor.

Tysons Corner in McLean has one of the largest concentrations of retail space on the East Coast, with two super malls, more than five million square feet of shopping area and 355 stores, ☎ 703-893-9400, www.shoptysons.com.

Other popular shopping spots include the **Springfield Mall**, which has 250 stores; **Fair Oaks Mall** with 210 stores; the **Reston Town Center**, with some 40 specialty retail shops and an 11-screen cinema; and **Potomac Mills** outlet extravaganza, with scores of shops and an 18-screen theater.

Antique stores and other specialty shops can be found in the towns of Clifton, Vienna, Herndon, and at the Great Falls Village Center and the Lake Anne Plaza in Reston.

Dining

For those who enjoy dining, Fairfax County offers thousands of choices; everything from traditional American food to the best ethnic delights can be found in the county's restaurants. For more information, contact the Fairfax County Convention and Visitors Bureau, ☎ 703-790-3329 or www.visitfairfax.org.

Colonial foods and historic settings are the specialties of such fine restaurants as the **Mount Vernon Inn**, on the grounds of the Mount Vernon estate, ☎ 703-780-0011; the **Cedar Knoll Inn**, overlooking the Potomac River, also at Mount Vernon, ☎ 703-799-1501; and the **Heart in Hand** in the Town of Clifton, ☎ 703-830-4111, www.heartinhandrestaurant.com.

Colvin Run Tavern in Vienna serves excellent and imaginative cuisine, 8045 Leesburg Pike, ☎ 703-356-9500.

At **Bombay Bistro**, regional fare like rockfish gets the Indian tandoori treatment, 3570 Chain Bridge Road, Fairfax, ☎ 703-359-5810. Also serving Indian fare in Fairfax, **Jaipur** is decorated with puppets and birds, 9401 Lee Highway, ☎ 703-766-1111. **Nizam's Restaurant** serves Turkish fare at 523 Maple Avenue W., in Vienna (☎ 703-938-8948).

In Falls Church, **Duangrat's** is an elegant Thai restaurant (5878 Leesburg Pike, ☎ 703-820-5775); **Four Sisters** has a large Vietnamese menu (6769 Wilson Boulevard, ☎ 703-538-6717); **Mark's Duck House** serves Hong-Kong-style Cantonese food (6184-A Arlington Boulevard, ☎ 703-532-2125); and **2941**'s view is stunning from a 30-foot high wall of windows (2941 Fairview Park Drive, ☎ 703-270-1500).

The Italian fare is highly acclaimed at **Maestro** in the Tysons Corner Ritz-Carlton. 1700 Tysons Boulevard, McLean, ☎ 703-917-5498. **Tachibana** is an excellent Japanese restaurant in McLean, 6715 Lowell Avenue, ☎ 703-847-1771.

Patrons have long enjoyed the unique cuisine at such restaurants as the **Hermitage Inn** (French) in Clifton, ☎ 703-266-1623, www.hermitage-innrestaurant.com; **L'Auberge Chez François** (French) in Great Falls, ☎ 703-759-3800, www.laubergechezfrancois.com; the **Russia House** in Herndon, ☎ 703-787-8880, www.russiahouserestaurant.com; **Paolo's Ristorante** (Italian) in Reston, ☎ 703-318-8920, www.paolosristorante.com; and **Pierre et Madeleine** (French) in Vienna, ☎ 703-938-4379.

Dozens of national and regional chains, wonderful local mom-and-pop cafés and restaurants, and hundreds of fast-food eateries provide endless possibilities for dining out, whatever your budget.

Fairfax County

Accommodations

This is just a sample of the more-than 80 hotels in Fairfax County. Most establishments offer both handicapped-accessible and non-smoking rooms, but be sure to ask when making reservations.

Mount Vernon/Springfield

See also Accommodations in Alexandria, page 32.

 Comfort Inn-Gunston Corner, 8180 Silverbrook Road, Lorton, ☎ 703-643-3100, has 129 rooms with coffee maker, iron and hair dryer. Pool, fitness center. $$

Best Western Springfield, 6721 Commerce Street, ☎ 703-922-6100. 179 rooms and suites, restaurant, outdoor pool, fitness center. $$$

 Hampton Inn-Springfield, 6550 Loisdale Court, adjacent to Springfield Mall, ☎ 703-924-9444, www.hamptoninnwashingtondc.com. The hotel has 153 rooms and suites. Restaurant, outdoor pool, airport shuttle, continental breakfast. $

Holiday Inn Express Springfield, 6401 Brandon Avenue, ☎ 703-644-5555, www.holidayspringfield.com. 194 rooms and suites, outdoor pool. $$

Hilton Springfield, 6550 Loisdale Road, adjacent to the Springfield Mall, ☎ 703-971-8900, www.hilton.com. 246 rooms and suites, restaurant, fitness center, business center, high-speed Internet access, outdoor pool. $$

Falls Church

Best Western Falls Church Inn, 6633 Arlington Boulevard, ☎ 703-532-9000. 105 rooms and suites, restaurant, outdoor pool. $

Fairview Park Marriott, 3111 Fairview Park Drive, ☎ 703-849-9400. 398 rooms and suites. Restaurant, spa, indoor and outdoor pools, exercise room. $$

Quality Inn Governor, 6650 Arlington Boulevard, Falls Church, ☎ 703-532-8900. 121 rooms and suites, restaurant, outdoor pool. $

Fairfax

Hilton Garden Inn Fairfax has a pool, fitness and business centers. 3950 Fair Ridge Drive, ☎ 703-385-7774. $$

Courtyard Marriott Fair Oaks, 11220 Lee Jackson Highway, ☎ 703-273-6161, www.marriott.com, has 144 rooms and suites, restaurant, spa, indoor pool, exercise room. $$

Hyatt Fair Lakes, 12777 Fair Lakes Circle, ☎ 703-818-1234. 316 rooms and suites. Full-service restaurant, spa, indoor pool, exercise room. $$

Tysons Corner

 Best Western Tysons Westpark Hotel, 8401 Westpark Drive, McLean, ☎ 703-734-2800. 301 rooms and suites, restaurant, spa, indoor pool, exercise room. $

Comfort Inn Tysons Corner, 1587 Springfield Road, Vienna. ☎ 703-448-8020, www.comfotinntysons.com. 250 rooms and suites, restaurant, spa, outdoor pool. $

Doubletree Hotel at Tysons Corner, 7801 Leesburg Pike, Falls Church, ☎ 703-893-1340. 405 rooms and suites. Restaurant, spa, indoor pool, exercise room. $

Embassy Suites Hotel Tysons Corner, 8517 Leesburg Pike, Vienna, ☎ 703-883-0707. 232 suites, restaurant, spa, indoor pool, exercise room. $$$

Holiday Inn Tysons Corner, 1960 Chain Bridge Road, McLean, ☎ 703-893-2100. 316 rooms and suites. Restaurant, spa, indoor pool, exercise room, free high-speed Internet access. $

McLean Hilton at Tysons Corner, 7920 Jones Branch Drive, McLean, ☎ 703-847-5000. 458 rooms and suites, restaurant, indoor pool, exercise room. $

The Ritz-Carlton, Tysons Corner, 1700 Tysons Boulevard, McLean, VA 22102. ☎ 703-506-4300. 400 rooms and suites, restaurant, spa, indoor pool, exercise room. $$$

Sheraton Premiere at Tysons Corner, 8661 Leesburg Pike, Vienna. ☎ 703-448-1234. 437 rooms and suites, restaurant, spa, indoor pool, outdoor pool, exercise room. $

Tysons Corner Marriott Hotel, 8028 Leesburg Pike, Vienna, ☎ 703-734-3200. 390 rooms and suites, including handicapped-accessible and non-smoking rooms. Restaurant, spa, indoor pool, exercise room. $

Vienna Wolf Trap Motel, 430 Maple Avenue West, Vienna. ☎ 703-281-2330, www.viennawolftrapmotel.com. 116 rooms and suites. $

Reston/Herndon/Dulles

Comfort Inn Herndon Dulles, 200 Elden Street, Herndon, ☎ 703-437-7555. 103 rooms and suites. Exercise room, free airport transportation. $$

Courtyard by Marriott-Dulles, 3935 Centerview Drive, Chantilly, ☎ 703-709-7100. 149 rooms and suites, restaurant, spa, indoor pool, exercise room. $

Courtyard By Marriott Herndon/Reston, 533 Herndon Parkway, Herndon, ☎ 703-478-9400. 146 rooms and suites, a restaurant, spa, indoor pool, exercise room. $

Days Hotel & Conference Center at Dulles, 2200 Centreville Road, Herndon, ☎ 703-471-6700, www.dullesdaysinn.com. 205 rooms and suites, spa, indoor pool, exercise room. $

 Hilton Washington Dulles Airport, 13869 Park Center Road, Herndon, ☎ 703-478-2900. 349 rooms and suites, restaurant, spa, indoor and outdoor pools. $

 Holiday Inn Express -Dulles East, 485 Elden Street, Herndon, ☎ 703-478-9777. 115 rooms/suites, free high-speed Internet, fitness center. $

Hyatt Dulles, 2300 Dulles Corner Boulevard, Herndon, ☎ 703-713-1234. 317 rooms and suites, full-service restaurant, spa, indoor pool, exercise room. $$

Hyatt Regency Reston, 1800 Presidents Street, Reston, ☎ 703-709-1234, has 514 rooms, and is adjacent to the "Main Street." There is a restaurant, sauna, whirlpool, heated indoor pool. $$

Marriott Suites Washington Dulles, 13101 Worldgate Drive, Herndon. ☎ 703-709-0400. 253 suites, spa, indoor pool, exercise room. $$

 Staybridge Suites Hotel-Dulles, 13700 Coppermine Road, Herndon, ☎ 703-713-6800. 112 suites, spa, indoor pool, exercise room. $$

Sheraton Reston Hotel, 11810 Sunrise Valley Drive, Reston, ☎ 703-620-9000. 310 rooms and suites, restaurant, spa, outdoor pool, exercise room. $

Westfields Marriott, 14750 Conference Center Drive, Chantilly, ☎ 703-818-0300. 340 rooms and suites, restaurant, spa, indoor pool, exercise room. $$$

Transportation

Fairfax County is served by **Washington Dulles** and **Reagan National** airports, **Greyhound**, ☎ 800-231-2222 or 703-569-6755, www.greyhound.com, and the Washington, DC **Metro**, ☎ 202-637-7000, www.wmata.com.

Amtrak has stations at Dulles International Airport and Franconia-Springfield (6880 Frontier Drive). In Lorton is the stop for the Amtrak

Auto Train, a high-speed non-stop sleeper train from Virginia to Florida, ☎ 800-USA-RAIL, www.amtrak.com.

Information

Fairfax County Visitors Center, located at the Comfort Inn Guston Corner, 8180-A Silverbrook Road, in Lorton, open daily, 9 a.m. to 5 p.m. ☎ 703-550-2450 or 800-732-4732. www.visitfairfax.org.

Fauquier County

*F*auquier County is a tiny swatch of green and pleasant Virginia countryside less than an hour's drive from the nation's capital, but far enough from the hectic pace of city life. You can relax, become one with nature, and enjoy the peaceful small-town atmosphere of the historic villages unique to Northern Virginia.

Although its history is a long and turbulent one, Fauquier has retained all the charm and beauty of its agricultural heritage. Scenic vistas, rolling hills and countryside, dotted here and there by picturesque working farms, historic landmarks, craft fairs, Civil War re-enactments, horse shows, steeplechases, and a rich variety of outdoor recreational opportunities are only a few of the many delights and attractions.

History

Prior to 1670, the only inhabitants of the land between the Falls of the Rivers and the Blue Ridge Mountains, now Fauquier County, were Native Americans. For a thousand years or more the mighty tribes had roamed the hills and valleys of Northern Virginia, hunting the deer and other game so abundant in the area.

Then the peace, unbroken for thousands of years, was shattered. Change came when the first white man, John Lederer, a German pioneer, arrived in what is now Fauquier County. Land undisturbed almost since the dawn of time would never be quite the same again.

Lederer wrote, *To heighten the beauty of the parts, the first springs of most of these great rivers which run into the Atlantic Ocean or the Chesapeake Bay, do here break out, and in various branches interlace the flowery meads, here luxurious herbage invites herds of red deer to feed*. The tourist industry describes the natural beauty of Fauquier County in much the same way today.

By 1722, the first efforts to settle the area were already under way. A treaty had been signed with the Iroquois who agreed to use the trails of the Shenandoah Valley for their excursions south into North Carolina rather than the long-established woodland trails of the Piedmont.

The first settlers began moving into the county by way of Thoroughfare Gap in the Bull Run Mountains to the north, and before the end of the 1720s the first settlement, now called **The Plains**, was situated at the very edge of the civilized world.

In 1736, Lord Fairfax established **Leeds Manor**, the first of the great homes, but later sold the property, comprising 160,382 acres of prime real estate, to John Marshall, James Markham Marshall and Rawleigh Cowlston for the princely sum of 14,000 pounds sterling – a great deal of money in those early times. But the gentlemen-entrepreneurs who had invested so heavily in the property had no intention of leaving behind the rich and gay society of civilized Colonial Virginia for the backwoods. Instead, they installed an overseer, erected two tobacco houses, and effectively blocked any further settlement of the land in upper Fauquier County until well after the Revolution.

During the Civil War the area became the center of Mosby's Confederacy. Colonel John Singleton Mosby organized his Rangers in 1863, and from then on his command gave conspicuous service to the Southern cause. For more than two years Mosby's men ranged far and wide, almost at will, causing havoc and destruction in the Union-occupied territories. Although there were no major battles fought in Fauquier, the county was pretty well devastated by the Union occupation. Crops and livestock were stolen and the land left uncultivated. Most of the churches, those that weren't gutted, were defaced.

When the war ended, however, life slowly returned to normal. By the end of September, 1865, the Orange and Alexandria Railroad was running again, and making stops at Catlett and Rappahannock Station. The soil was tilled, crops sown, and in the spring of 1866 a whole new generation of livestock was born. By the turn of the century, Fauquier County ranked third in the state for wheat production, and sixth for corn.

Today, the beauty of the countryside remains much the same in many places as it was when John Lederer first set foot in the area in 1670. The agricultural economy thrives, and the local people welcome visitors to this tiny corner of what they regard as paradise.

Sights

Kelly's Ford Equestrian Center, 16589 Edwards Shop Road, Remington, ☎ 540-399-1779, www.innatkellysford.com, offers trail rides, lessons, canoeing, biking & fishing, 9am to 5pm daily.

Monroe Park & Gold Mining Museum, 14421 Gold Dust Parkway, Goldvein, ☎ 540-752-5330, www.goldvein.com. Fourteen-acre park with museum housing artifacts and gold mining history. Playgrounds, soccer

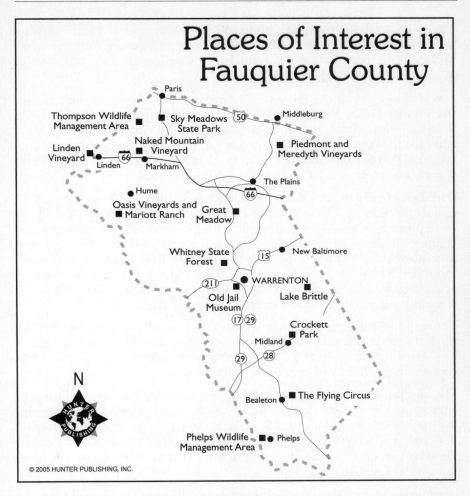

Places of Interest in Fauquier County

Paris

Thompson Wildlife Management Area

Sky Meadows State Park

50

Middleburg

Linden Vineyard

Naked Mountain Vineyard

66

Linden   Markham

Piedmont and Meredyth Vineyards

Hume

The Plains

66

Oasis Vineyards and Mariott Ranch

Great Meadow

Whitney State Forest

15

New Baltimore

211

WARRENTON

Old Jail Museum

Lake Brittle

17 29

Crockett Park

Midland

29   28

N

Bealeton

The Flying Circus

Phelps Wildlife Management Area   Phelps

© 2005 HUNTER PUBLISHING, INC.

& softball fields, pond & walking path. Park open Tuesday, Wednesday. Friday and Saturday, 9 a.m. to 5 p.m.

Old Town Warrenton is a Virginia and National Historic District, established and incorporated in 1810 on 71 acres of land donated by Richard Henry Lee, the father of the Declaration of Independence. The city was named for General Joseph Warren, who fought in the Revolutionary War at Bunker Hill.

During the early years, the old town achieved a reputation for its "salubrious climate and pleasant social life." After the Civil War it became a mecca for horse lovers. The Warrenton Hunt was established in 1888, the Warrenton Horse Show in 1900, and the first Virginia Gold Cup Race was run in 1922. Later, Warrenton became something of a resort, famous for its fine Warren Green Hotel and Fauquier White Sulpher Springs.

The sleepy country town has changed over the years but still retains an old-world atmosphere that belies the bustling community Warrenton has

The sleepy country town has changed over the years but still retains an old-world atmosphere that belies the bustling community Warrenton has become. The shaded streets and the historic buildings of the town center are reminders of more leisurely times.

A **walking tour** of the Historic District includes the Old Court House, the County Office Buildings, the California Building, the Old Jail, the Warren Green Hotel, the old Warrenton Library, Culpeper Street, Main Street, and Winchester Street. For a brochure and walking tour map, contact the Warrenton-Fauquier County Visitor Center at 33 N. Calhoun Street, Warrenton, ☎ 540-341-0988 or 800-820-1021.

Old Jail Museum. The Warrenton jail was built in 1779 and was still in use as recently as 1965. Today the jail is a Virginia Landmark and the headquarters of the County Historical Society. The jail also houses a museum with an assortment of exhibits and artifacts that reflect the long and interesting history of the area from the earliest times when Indians inhabited Fauquier, through Colonial times, the Civil War, and up to the present day. In its day the Old Jail was home to an assortment of drunks, runaway slaves, thieves, murderers, and drug abusers.

The original building was fairly small, with two cells downstairs and two upstairs. Over the years the building has been modified and repaired. A kitchen wing, added in 1824, has been fully restored to its original condition and is used for historical demonstrations.

The new building held four more cells, beyond which was an exercise yard surrounded by a high stone wall. It was here, until 1896, that the condemned felons mounted the 13 "unlucky steps" to the gallows. The Old Jail is at the Fauquier County Courthouse Square; it is open to the public Tuesday through Sunday year-round, from 10 a.m. until 4 p.m. For more information, ☎ 540-347-5525.

Brochures are available for **driving tours** of Fauquier County from the Warrenton-Fauquier County Visitor Center. The **Northern Tour** begins in Warrenton and takes in Payne Memorial in Orlean; the Smallest Post Office in Hume; the Marriott Ranch; the Oasis Vineyard; the Linden Vineyards; the Thompson Wildlife Management Area; the Naked Mountain Vineyard; Sky Meadows State Park; and several more stops of interest. The **Southern Tour** also starts in Warrenton and takes in a variety of interesting stops and recreation areas, including Neavil's Mill; Casanova Junction; the Weston Wildlife Area; Crockett Park and Germantown Lake; and the Warren Green Hotel (see below).

A **Virginia Civil War Trails** brochure is also available at the Visitors Center, and details a self-guided driving/walking tour of 12 area sites.

The Warren Green Hotel on Hotel Street, now a county office building, once welcomed generations of summer visitors, including General Lafayette, President Monroe, and General George Brinton McClellan, commander of the Union Army of the Potomac during the Civil War.

The California Building is "a mellow brick relic of the last century," built by Governor "Extra Billy" Smith with profits from the California Gold Rush. The old house, once a family residence, is now a county office building and a part of the walking tour of Warrenton's Historic District.

Afro-American Historical Association, 4243 Loudoun Avenue, The Plains, ☎ 540-253-7488, www.afro-americanofva.org, features historical and genealogical displays. Open Monday-Friday, 10 a.m. to 3 p.m., and Saturdays from 1 to 5 p.m.

Fauquier Veterans Memorial, Hospital Hill, Warrenton, honors citizens who died in military service during the 20th century. The bronze railing features marching soldiers by sculptor Fredrick Hart.

Annual Events

The **Upperville Garden Club Daffodil Show** is held the second week in April at Trinity Parish House. ☎ 540-554-8816.

Archwood Green Barns Farmers & Gardeners Market is open on Sundays, April through November in The Plains. ☎ 540-253-5289.

Warrenton Farmers' Market is held on Wednesdays and Saturdays, April through December. ☎ 540-347-2405.

The Virginia Gold Cup Races are held the first Saturday in May and the third Saturday in October at Great Meadow Race Course in The Plains. For tickets and more information, ☎ 540-347-2612, www.vagoldcup.com.

Warrenton Spring Festival is the third Saturday in May, Main Street, Warrenton, ☎ 347-4414, www.fauquierchamber.org.

The Strawberry Festival is held Memorial Day Weekend at Sky Meadows State Park, Delaplane. ☎ 540-592-3556.

Twilight Polo is held Friday evenings June through September at Great Meadow. ☎ 540-253-5156, www.greatmeadow.org.

A **Fourth of July Celebration** is held at Great Meadows, The Plains. ☎ 540-253-5001, www.greatmeadow.org.

The Fauquier County Fair is held in Warrenton the third weekend in July. ☎ 540-341-7950.

The Warrenton Horse Show is Labor Day week and weekend at the Warrenton Horse Show Grounds. ☎ 540-347-9442.

Leeds Jousting Tournament & BBQ is held the first Saturday in October in Hume. ☎ 540-364-4242.

Christmas in Old Town Warrenton features a parade on the first Saturday in December, beautiful lights and a variety of special activities throughout the holiday season. ☎ 540-349-3089.

First Night Warrenton is held in historic Old Town Warrenton on New Year's Eve. It's a non-alcoholic, family-oriented celebration of the arts. ☎ 540-341-0988, www.bluemont.org.

Vineyard Tours

Pearmund Cellars, 6190 Georgetown Road, Broad Run, ☎ 540-347-3475, www.pearmundcellars.com, offers tours and tastings Thursday through Monday.

Rogers Ford Farm Winery is open Friday through Monday, year-round. 14674 Rogers Ford Road, Sumerduck, ☎ 540-439-3707, www.rogersfordwine.com.

Stillhouse Vineyards, 4366 Stillhouse Road, Hume, ☎ 540-364-1203, www.stillhousevineyards.com, in the foothills of the Blue Ridge offers tours and tastings weekends mid-February to mid-December.

Linden Vineyards is two miles from Linden on Harrels Corner Road (Route 638). The winery offers tours, tastings, and a spectacular mountain view. Open April through December. ☎ 540-364-1997, www.linden-vineyards.com.

The Naked Mountain Vineyard is near Markham on Route 688. There's a picnic area with a panoramic view of the vineyard. Open weekends from 11 a.m. until 5 p.m. ☎ 540-364-1609, www.nakedmtn-.com.

Oasis Winery is on Route 635 near Hume, set among some of the most spectacular country in Northern Virginia. The vineyard and farm shop are open to the public daily from 10 a.m. until 5 p.m. ☎ 540-635-7627, www.oasiswine.com.

Piedmont Vineyards and Winery are on Route 626 near The Plains. Piedmont is located on a pre-Revolutionary farm. The vineyard, farm shop, and picnic areas are open to the public from 10 a.m. until 5 p.m. daily. ☎ 540-687-5528, www.piedmontwines.com.

Recreation

Parks

Well known for its equestrian sports, the area's parks and wildlife management areas abound with all sorts of natural life and scenic vistas. There are plentiful opportunities for fishing, boating, canoeing, hiking, bicycling, horseback riding, or simply an afternoon picnic under the trees.

There are public **tennis courts** at Cedar-Lee Middle School in Bealeton; Taylor Middle School, Warrenton Middle School, and Fauquier High School in Warrenton; and at Marshall Middle School in Marshall.

C.M. Crockett Park on Route 603 near Midland is 100 acres where popular activities include fishing and boating, hiking along the woodland nature trail, birdwatching and nature study. Among the facilities are a boat ramp, boat rentals, a comfort station, a couple of playgrounds for the kids, three picnic shelters, a concession stand and a 300-seat amphitheater; there's even a cross country ski trail. For more information, ☎ 540-788-4867.

Eva Walker Park, at the edge of Old Town Warrenton, is a nice place to take the kids for an afternoon of fun and relaxation. It features a children's park with playground equipment, horseshoe pit, a basketball court, and picnic area.

Lake Brittle is a state-owned tract of 77 acres that provides a variety of outdoor activities, including fishing, boating, hiking and picnicking. The park is in New Baltimore just of Route 600. Boat rentals are available, ☎ 540-347-6888.

Chester A. Phelps Wildlife Management Area, on Route 651 between Sumerduck and Remington, is a 4,540-acre park near the Rappahannock River. Recreational facilities include horseback riding, hiking and nature trails. Hunting and fishing is permitted in season and the park has handicapped-accessible trails. ☎ 540-899-4169.

Sky Meadows State Park, on Route 17 in Delaplane, is an 1,800-acre park that offers a great many outdoor recreational opportunities. It's a peaceful getaway close to the Blue Ridge Mountains. Easy access to the Appalachian Trail is available via four hiking trails within the park. Facilities include a number of woodland and parkland trails, riding trails, picnic areas, and several primitive campgrounds. A variety of supervised programs are available during the summer months, including Civil War re-enactments and farm heritage programs for the children. ☎ 540-592-3556.

The Richard Thompson Wildlife Management Area, on Route 688 near Hume, is a 4,000-acre wilderness area that extends through Fauquier County into Warren and Clark Counties. The park's biggest attraction is its lake, which is well stocked with smallmouth bass, sunfish, and channel catfish. The Appalachian Trail passes through the park, and there are several hiking and horseback riding trails. Open daily, sunrise to sunet; for more information, contact the Virginia Department of Game & Fisheries, ☎ 540-899-4161, www.dgif.virginia.gov.

Rady Park, off Route 17 at the north edge of Warrenton, has a one-mile paved hiking/biking trail and a picnic shelter along a stream.

Fauquier County

Marriott Ranch-Guided Trail Rides in Hume, ☎ 540-364-2627, offers trail riding on a 4,500-acre Texas longhorn cattle ranch. Reservations required, www.marriottranch.com.

Golf

Fairview Golf Center, 5020 Lee Highway, New Baltimore, ☎ 540-349-9761, has a driving range, putting green and pro shop.

Fairway Golf Center (practice range) is at 11435 Lucky Hill Road, Remington, ☎ 540-439-9305.

Fauquier Springs Country Club, 9236 Tournament Drive, Warrenton, ☎ 540-347-4205, www.fauquiersprings.com.

Kastle Greens Golf Club, 11446 Rogues Road, Midland, ☎ 540-788-3144, has an 18-hole golf course, driving range, pro shop and grill and bar.

Antiquing

If antiquing is your passion, you're in luck! You will find more than 50 dealers in a variety of interesting and fascinating buildings and malls, on side roads, main roads, and shady city streets. Collectors can enjoy a weekend with a difference digging around inside the many shops as they travel the back-country roads from one tiny community to the next.

Old Town Warrenton has more than 80 shops, boutiques, galleries and restaurants where you can pop in for a bite between shopping.

Entertainment

The Fauquier Community Theatre, a well-established performing arts organization at the Theater at Vint Hill, offers a variety of productions throughout the year. For schedules and ticket information, ☎ 540-349-8760.

The Bluemont Concert Series brings a variety of music to Northern Virginia each year during the summer. Programs ranging from big band to folk, and from country to gospel, begin in June and run through August. People bring picnic suppers and blankets to spread on the grass, and people of all ages get together each week to celebrate the music and the summer. Homemade refreshments are sold during the intermission. Saturdays, 7:30 p.m., Culpeper Street, Warrenton, ☎ 703-777-6306, www.bluemont.org.

The Flying Circus Airshow features precision aerobatics, wing walking, skydiving and rides in antique airplanes. Airshows are held on Sundays at 2:30 p.m., May through October. Located at Routes 17 and 644, Bealeton, ☎ 540-439-8661.

Dining

There are more than 40 restaurants and cafés in Fauquier County and Warrenton. Here is a just a sampling. See also the 1763 Inn and Ashby Inn & Restaurant under *Accommodations*, below.

Betty's Ben & Mary's Steak House, 6806 James Madison Highway, Warrenton, ☎ 540-347-4100. Specialties include filet mignon and prime rib, and they have an extensive wine list.

The Depot Restaurant, 65 S. Third Street, Warrenton, ☎ 540-347-1212, www.warrentondepot.com, is located in a turn-of-the-century train station and serves Mediterranean and American cuisine.

Fantastico-Ristorante Italiano & Inn, located at 380 Broadview Avenue, Warrenton, ☎ 540-349-2575, www.fantastico-inn.com, is open for lunch and dinner. Reservations recommended. The restaurant offers Northern Italian cuisine, with seafood, veal, and pasta dishes. The restaurant is handicapped-accessible.

Foster's Grille, 20 Broadview Avenue, Warrenton, ☎ 540-349-5776, www.fostersgrille.com, is open daily for lunch and dinner serving burgers, salads, beer and handmade milkshakes.

Frogs & Friends, 7391 John Marshall Highway, Marshall, serves French cuisine and is open for dinner Tuesday through Sunday.

The Frost Diner, 55 Broadview Avenue, Warrenton, ☎ 540-347-3047, is an historic silver diner open 24 hours.

Granpa Groovy's Seafood and More, 573 Frost Avenue, Warrenton, ☎ 540-347-5757, serves, seafood, prime rib and has a full bar.

Hunter's Head Tavern, 9048 John Mosby Highway, Upperville, ☎ 540-592-9020, is a traditional English pub open daily.

Legends Restaurant, 67 W. Lee Street, Warrenton, ☎ 540-347-9401, is open for lunch and dinner. The menu is continental; specialties of the house include filet mignon and Jack Daniel's shrimp. The restaurant is handicapped-accessible.

Main Street Bistro, 32 Main Street, Warrenton, ☎ 540-347-0550, serves American cuisine daily and has a lounge.

Molly's Irish Pub, 36C Main Street, Warrenton, ☎ 540-349-5300 serves lunch and dinner daily and Irish breakfast on Sunday.

Napoleon's Restaurant, 67 Waterloo Street, Warrenton, ☎ 540-347-4300, www.napoleonsrestaurant.com, is open for lunch and dinner. It offers continental cuisine and dining on the outdoor terrace or by the cozy fireplace, and live music on weekends. Specialties include veal, fresh fish, and seafood. The restaurant is handicapped-accessible.

Fauquier County

Osaka Japanese Steak & Seafood Restaurant, 139 W. Lee Highway, Warrenton, ☎ 540-349-5050. Food prepared before your eyes on Teppanyaki table by skilled hibachi.

Red Hot & Blue, 360 Broadview Avenue, Warrenton, ☎ 540-349-7100, serves Memphis-style barbecue daily. www.redhotandblue.com

The Rail Stop, 6478 Main Street, The Plains, ☎ 540-253-5644, is a small-town restaurant with a railroad theme. Closed Monday.

Town 'n Country Restaurant, 5037 Lee Highway, New Baltimore, ☎ 540-347-3614, is open for lunch and dinner. Cuisine is continental, with emphasis on steak, seafood, and pasta dishes. The restaurant is handicapped-accessible.

Accommodations

Hotels & Motels

Comfort Inn, 7379 Comfort Inn Drive, Warrenton, ☎ 540-349-8900, has 97 rooms, all with refrigerator and coffee maker. There is a guest laundry, fitness room, picnic tables, grills and an outdoor pool. Complimentary continental breakfast. $$-$$$

The Hampton Inn, 501 Blackwell Road, Warrenton, ☎ 540-349-4200, has 100 rooms, complimentary continental breakfast, meeting rooms, a coin laundry, an exercise room, an outdoor swimming pool, and several picnic tables and a grill. $$

 Holiday Inn Express Hotel & Suites, 410 Holiday Court, Warrenton, 540-341-3461, has an outdoor pool, guest laundry and fitness center. $

Howard Johnson, 6 Broadview Avenue, Warrenton, ☎ 540-347-4141, has 79 rooms, an outdoor swimming pool and adjacent restaurant. $

Rip Van Winkle, 184 Broadview Avenue, Warrenton, ☎ 540-347-7272, has 28 rooms. $

Bed & Breakfasts / Inns

The Ashby Inn & Restaurant, 692 Federal Street, Paris, ☎ 540-592-3900, www.ashbyinn.com. The inn has 10 guest rooms, four in a one-room schoolhouse. The inn will take children over the age of 10; no pets. The acclaimed restaurant serves dinner Wednesday through Saturday, and Sunday brunch, with contemporary American cuisine. Specialties include game pies, gumbo, venison and seafood. $$$

B&B at Foxgloves, 11221 Crest Hill Road, Marshall, ☎ 540-364-4499, www.foxgloves.net, has three guest rooms, all with private baths. A full breakfast is served. The Williamsburg Colonial home is elegantly decorated with some antiques in a peaceful, stately setting on a 90-acre farm. No children or pets allowed. $$$

Black Horse Inn, 8393 Meetze Road, Warrenton, ☎ 540-349-4020, www.blackhorseinn.com, has eight rooms with private baths, and stables for guests' horses. Full breakfast and dinner on request. Children 12 and older. $$

 Greenwich Inn, 4301 Bludau Drive, Warrenton, ☎ 540-428-3001, has 10 efficiencies and suites with high speed Inernet. www.greenwich-inn.com $

 The Grey Horse Inn, 4350 Fauquier Avenue, The Plains, ☎ 540-253-7000, has six rooms with private baths and furnished with antiques. Full breakfast. Weekday $105-195/night. Weekend $115-195/night. Children over 12 only; well-behaved pets allowed in the Garden Room. www.greyhorseinn.com $$$

Highland Farm & Inn Bed & Breakfast, 10981 Lee's Mill Road, Remington, ☎ 540-439-0088, www.highlandfarminn.com, has two rooms with private baths. Full breakfast on weekends; continental during the week. No children, pets or smoking. $$

Inn at Fairfield Farm, 5305 Marriott Lane, Hume, ☎ 540-364-3221, 877-324-7344, has 10 rooms, seven with private baths. Full breakfast; children permitted. It is located on the 4,500-acre Marriott Ranch (see page 78), which offers trail rides. $$$

1763 Inn, 10087 John S. Mosby Highway, Upperville, ☎ 540-592-3848, www.1763inn.com. The inn, once owned by George Washington, has 18 guest rooms in several buildings, all with private baths, TV, phone, refrigerators and coffee makers. There's a tennis court, a pool, and a fishing pond. Their dining room serves German-American food in an elegant atmosphere. $$$

Day-trip to Little Washington

Rappahannock County, at the edge of the Blue Ridge Mountains, may be tiny – with barely 7,000 residents – but it's big on scenery, history and celebrity.

The county "star" is the village of Washington, dubbed "Little" to avoid confusion with the nation's capital. George Washington himself, then a young surveyor, laid out the street plan in 1749. True to its name, Little Washington has never outgrown this 10-block grid.

Today, movie stars and newsmakers are drawn to the superb dining and lodging at the Inn at Little Washington. Shiny black limos pull up on the shady street in front of the modest-looking country inn that holds splendor inside. Guests have included the likes of Barbara Streisand and Alan Greenspan.

Fauquier County

Walk the quiet streets, pop into some artisan shops, or visit a nearby farm or winery. If you have the means to splurge at the inn, you won't be disappointed.

The **Inn at Little Washington** is five-star accommodtion in a country village. The 15 bedrooms and suites were sumptuously decorated, each in a unique way, by a London stage designer. In the dining room, fresh flower arrangements adorn every table. Luxurious fabrics hang from the ceilings, fringed silk-shaded lamps over each table. The wine cellar boasts 14,000 bottles. Breakfast is served in the glassed-in porch looking out onto a courtyard of water gardens and gazebo. Corner of Middle and Main streets, ☎ 540-675-3800, www.innatlittlewashington.com $$$$

For a more casual, less expensive getaway, the **Gay Street Inn B&B** welcomes children and pets with advance notice. The restored 1860s stucco farmhouse has four guest rooms with views of the Blue Ridge. It's furnished with some pieces made by the innkeeper, Robin Kevis, who's also a carpenter. Donna Kevis, a graduate of Johnson & Wales College of Culinary Arts, prepares the breakfasts. 160 Gay Street, ☎ 540-675-3288, www.gaystreetinn.com $$

Transportation

Interstate 66 runs east and west through the county, linking Fauquier with Northern Virginia and Washington DC. Other primary highways include US Highways 15, 17, 29, 50 and 211, and State Routes 28 and 55.

The county is served by **Greyhound Lines**, ☎ 800-231-2222, www.greyhound.com.

Air transportation is available through **Washington Dulles**, about 30 miles away, and **Reagan National**, 40 miles from Fauquier County.

Information

For tourist information, contact the **Warrenton-Fauquier County Visitor Center** at 33 N. Calhoun Street, Warrenton, VA 20186, ☎ 800-820-1021, 540-341-0988, www.fauquierchamber.org, www.fauquiertourism.com. The Visitor Center is open seven days a week from 9 a.m. until 5 p.m., except major holidays, and provides comprehensive information about local, regional and state attractions.

For the **Town of Washington**, ☎ 540-675-3128, www.town.washington.va.us.

Fredericksburg, Spotsylvania County & Stafford County

Spotsylvania County and the city of Fredericksburg have been entertaining travelers for more than three centuries. Today, much as in the
past, this historic region of Northern Virginia offers the chance to savor a
delightful combination of history, shopping, dining and recreational activities.

Throughout Stafford and Spotsylvania counties, and particularly in Fredericksburg, you'll discover exciting chapters in our nation's history. To
stroll the streets and the country lanes is to follow in the footsteps of the
patriots who helped found our country. Men like George Washington,
James Monroe, and Thomas Jefferson either lived or spent much of their
time in Fredericksburg. Here you can experience all the drama of the
Civil War, for Fredericksburg and its surrounding area was the scene, not
of one major battle in the War Between the States, but four. Crucial military engagements were fought at Fredericksburg, Chancellorsville, at
Spotsylvania Court House, and in The Wilderness.

Fredericksburg's downtown historic district offers the opportunity to
wander the age-old streets or browse the shop windows in some 350 original 18th- and 19th-century buildings. Eat lunch or dine in any one of a
dozen or more quaint, out-of-the-way cafés and restaurants.

Spend a day at beautiful Lake Anna, a 13,000-acre recreation area surrounded by gently rolling hills and meadows. Water-ski, fish, swim or sail
away the hours in an atmosphere of peace and tranquillity.

Throughout the region, expect to find a variety of comfortable lodgings,
fine restaurants and many unique shopping opportunities. In
Fredericksburg, past and present come together in perfect harmony to
provide for a memorable vacation.

History

The area around Fredericksburg and Spotsylvania has been inhabited for
thousands of years. To the Indians, the lands where the river waters fall
were favorite fishing and hunting grounds. To Virginia's early settlers,
the fall line of the Rappahannock River was a strategic location perfectly
situated to serve both as a frontier settlement and a river port.

In 1719, the English Crown appointed **Alexander Spotswood** governor,
and he served until 1722. Today, he is generally remembered as the architect of the new Colonial capital, Williamsburg.

Spotswood obviously enjoyed his term as governor, for he spent a great deal of time wandering the far reaches of the colony.

In 1713, a large deposit of iron ore was discovered near the Rapidan River west of present day Spotsylvania County. Spotswood was quick to seize the opportunity. Taking advantage of the license provided by his public office, he made arrangements to acquire 85,000 acres of land in the area. In 1720, the Assembly made Spotswood's acquisition a new county and called it Spotsylvania in his honor.

Spotswood was replaced as governor in 1722, but by then his fortune was secure. His extensive mining empire, perhaps one of the earliest industrial ventures in Colonial America, included a furnace and wharves on the Massaponax Creek. By the time he had established an elaborate home at Germanna, his enterprise was thriving. By 1728, his operations employed more than 1,600 workers. Unfortunately, Spotswood's magnificent home was destroyed by fire in 1750.

Soon the settlers, planters and homesteaders began arriving in Spotswood's county in ever-increasing numbers. **Tobacco** was the crop from which most of them derived their living. And their successful endeavors created new needs. The tobacco they grew had to be transported eastward, but the riverfront land at the falls had all been claimed more than a half-century earlier. At first, the settlers were permitted to use Spotswood's facilities and wharves, but that arrangement soon created problems. Friction between Spotswood and the planters was, however, alleviated when the Assembly once again obliged the former governor, designating another site as a port for the settlers.

Today, the town of **Fredericksburg** lies where the first wooden buildings were raised on a 50-acre site in 1728. The tiny town was named for Prince Frederick, the son of King George II. Frederick didn't live to become king. Instead, his son George became the third English king of that name, and the last king of the colonies in the New World. All of the streets that made up the original town are still in place, and all bear names honoring Frederick's family: George, Caroline, Sophia, Princess Anne, Hanover, Charlotte, William and Amelia.

During its formative years, Fredericksburg was little more than a raunchy little frontier river port, similar to the frontier cow towns of the far west. But slowly the town began to grow. The tiny population swelled as tradesmen, merchants, companies and an assortment of immigrants came to live and then prospered. By 1730 the English Crown had established more than 70 tobacco shipping and receiving centers in the colony. It was at these centers that quantities were controlled and taxes collected. When Fredericksburg was designated the official shipping and receiving center for Spotsylvania County in 1730, things really began to boom. Thousands of barrels of tobacco were brought to the inspection station on Wolfe Street. They were then transferred into the warehouse and stored until they could be placed on board ship for England and Europe.

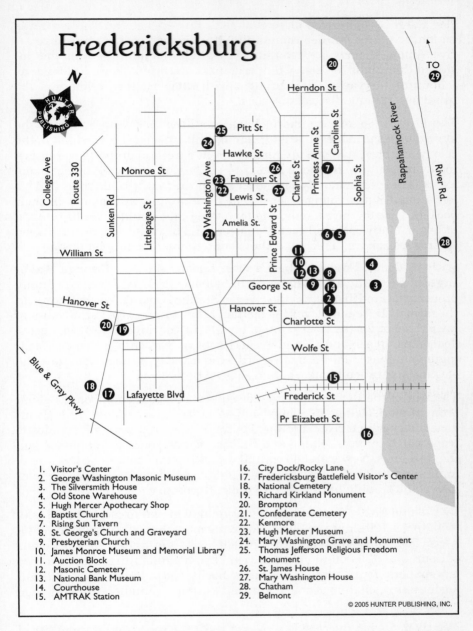

Fredericksburg

N

Herndon St

TO
29

Pitt St

Hawke St

Monroe St

Fauquier St

Lewis St

Amelia St.

William St

George St

Hanover St

Hanover St

Charlotte St

Wolfe St

Lafayette Blvd

Frederick St

Pr Elizabeth St

College Ave · Route 330 · Sunken Rd · Littlepage St · Washington Ave · Prince Edward St · Charles St · Princess Anne St · Caroline St · Sophia St · Rappahannock River · River Rd. · Blue & Gray Pkwy

1. Visitor's Center
2. George Washington Masonic Museum
3. The Silversmith House
4. Old Stone Warehouse
5. Hugh Mercer Apothecary Shop
6. Baptist Church
7. Rising Sun Tavern
8. St. George's Church and Graveyard
9. Presbyterian Church
10. James Monroe Museum and Memorial Library
11. Auction Block
12. Masonic Cemetery
13. National Bank Museum
14. Courthouse
15. AMTRAK Station
16. City Dock/Rocky Lane
17. Fredericksburg Battlefield Visitor's Center
18. National Cemetery
19. Richard Kirkland Monument
20. Brompton
21. Confederate Cemetery
22. Kenmore
23. Hugh Mercer Museum
24. Mary Washington Grave and Monument
25. Thomas Jefferson Religious Freedom Monument
26. St. James House
27. Mary Washington House
28. Chatham
29. Belmont

Fredericksburg

In 1732, the county court was moved from Germanna to a new building on Princess Anna Street in Fredericksburg. There it remained for more than 100 years until it was moved into the present building. Apparently the court in Fredericksburg which met monthly must have been an interesting and somewhat lively place. Thousands of lawsuits, some serious, many trivial, were heard by justices appointed by the governor.

The 1740s brought even more change to Fredericksburg. The town was no longer a tiny frontier community. New immigrants continued to arrive. Among them was a diversity of no-goods and ne'er-do-wells that included hundreds of convicted criminals exported from England as indentured servants. They brought with them poverty, crime and the usual assortment of social diseases.

The 1750s brought even more change, as Fredericksburg attracted the attention of the moneyed aristocracy. By this time most of the land in the colony had been snapped up. Already great parcels of property were passing by inheritance from one generation of landed gentry to the next and, as was the tradition, only the eldest son of the family could inherit. This left a great many younger sons wandering around with money in their pockets, time on their hands, and ambitions that would never be fulfilled at home. Many of them became pioneers and headed west. Some arrived in Fredericksburg, liked what they found there, and decided to stay.

Without doubt, Fredericksburg's most famous son was **George Washington**. From the age of six until 16 he lived at Ferry Farm, the family property located just across the river in Stafford County. Washington sold the farm in 1774 and moved his mother, Mary, to a cottage in the center of town. Except for the final years of his life, he continued to spend a great deal of his time in and around Fredericksburg. The cottage George Washington purchased for his mother still stands today, as does Kenmore, the elegant plantation home where his sister Betty lived.

The War of the Revolution and subsequent independence from England brought more change to Spotsylvania County. International trade dwindled, but the great river continued to serve as a major artery for domestic trade north to Philadelphia and Baltimore, and south to Tennessee and the Carolinas. New warehouses and wharves were built along the waterfront and Fredericksburg continued its role as a regional center for commerce and trading until well into the 19th century.

By the mid-1830s, the area's population had grown to more than 3,000, including 1,100 slaves, and was exporting more than 400 hogsheads of tobacco, 500,000 bushels of corn, 150,000 bushels of wheat, 75,000 barrels of flour, and $75,000 in gold per year. The town had five churches, two newspapers, four taverns, a dozen schools, and a hundred or so small businesses, including tanners, gunsmiths, ship's chandlers, and carriage builders.

And then, during the closing weeks of 1862, the peace and tranquillity of the region was shattered. Fredericksburg became the center of the deadly conflict that was the **Civil War**. Great battles were fought within the city limits and on Marye's Heights above Fredericksburg, at Chancellorsville, Spotsylvania Court House, and in the Wilderness. Confederate General Robert E. Lee and his Army of Northern Virginia successfully fought a succession of Union generals to a standstill. For many months the Confederate Army held the high ground outside Fredericksburg while the

Union Army was headquartered at the Chatham Plantation just across the Rappahannock in Stafford County. The scars of battle remain on the city streets and buildings, and in the cemeteries where more than 17,000 soldiers who died during those terrible times lie buried.

Today, much of Fredericksburg's past remains visible. The charming 18th- and 19th-century buildings have been maintained in much the same condition as when they were built. As you stroll the historic streets of the 40-block National Historic District, or walk the nave of Stafford County's beautiful old Aquia Church, you'll feel that you have indeed taken a step back in time.

Sights

The Belmont Estate, with its fine 18th-century mansion, was the home of renowned American artist Gari Melchers from the early 1900s until his death in 1932. Melchers and his wife modernized the old house and built the large stone studio and gazebo that overlooks the Rappahannock River. The house is furnished with many antiques and paintings the Melchers collected during their travels throughout the United States and Europe. The gardens include plantings of spring flowers, azaleas, wisteria, and an assortment of old hardwood trees. The studio contains a selection of the Melchers' works. The house is open daily except Thanksgiving, New Year's Day, and December 24, 25 and 31. The Gari Melchers Estate and Memorial Gallery, 224 Washington Street, Falmouth (just outside Fredericksburg), ☎ 540-654-1015, www.umw.edu/belm.

Chatham is a magnificent Georgian mansion built sometime between 1768 and 1771 by William Fitzhugh. It was the site of one of the best known plantations in the Fredericksburg area. During the Civil War Battle of Fredericksburg the great house served as General Burnside's Union headquarters. Today, it is owned and operated by the National Park Service and is a part of the Fredericksburg/Spotsylvania National Military Park. The grounds at the rear of the mansion have been restored to resemble their Colonial appearance. The mansion is across the river from Fredericksburg on Chatham Lane in Stafford County. The house is open daily, 9 a.m. to 5 p.m. except on Christmas and New Year's. For more information, contact the Fredericksburg/Spotsylvania National Battlefield Park Headquarters, Chatham House, Chatham Lane, Falmouth, VA, or ☎ 540-373-4461.

Civil War Life Museum houses extensive displays and rare artifacts. Located next to the Spotsylvania County Visitor Center, 4712 Southpoint Parkway, Fredericksburg, ☎ 540-834-1859, www.civilwar-life.com.

At the **Confederate Cemetery**, the bodies of more than 2,000 Confederate soldiers who died in the Fredericksburg/Spotsylvania area lie buried in the hallowed ground here. Most of them are unknown. Just after the end of the Civil War in 1865, a group of local women formed the Ladies

Memorial Association of Fredericksburg. They did so in order to raise money to buy land where they could inter the bodies of the Confederate dead. In 1867, their dream became a reality when land adjoining the Fredericksburg Cemetery was purchased and the two cemeteries were enclosed within a brick wall. Six Confederate generals rest, along with those who served them so well, within the walls of the cemetery: Seth Barton, Daniel Ruggles, Carter Stevenson, Dabney Maury, Abner Perrin, and Henry H. Sibley. The cemetery is on Washington Avenue at Amelia Street in Fredericksburg, ☎ 540-373-6122.

Ellwood is a once-prosperous antebellum farm that became a Union headquarters during the Battle of the Wilderness. Located on Route 20, just off State Route 3, in Orange County. To visit, sign in at the Chancellarsville Visitor Center. Open weekends late May to early October. Grounds and cemetery open year-round.

The Fredericksburg Area Museum & Cultural Center, 907 Princess Anne Street, Fredericksburg, is located in the Old Town Hall and Market House. Six permanent galleries tell the story of the city's past from prehistoric times through the 20th century. Exhibits include items from the days of slavery: chains and musical instruments; antique furniture and silverware; Confederate memorabilia; an assortment of china, snuff boxes, evening bags, and much more.

The town hall building that stands today on Princess Anne Street was completed in 1816. It replaced an earlier town hall located on the Caroline Street side of two lots set aside by the trustees for use as a market. The original building was torn down and the site parceled out to local merchants, leaving the inner market square much as it is today, with access via a narrow avenue from Caroline Street.

The new building was the site of a reception given for General Lafayette when he visited Fredericksburg in 1824 during his tour of America. It also housed the city government until 1982, making it one of longest continually used city halls in America. The center is open daily, year-round, except Thanksgiving, December 24 and 25, and New Year's Day; for hours and other information, ☎ 540-371-3037, www.famc.org.

Fredericksburg/Spotsylvania National Military Park: The National Battlefield Park encompasses four major Civil War battlefields in the Fredericksburg area, and is dedicated to the more than 17,000 young men who died on those four great fields of glory. Visitors can retrace some of the history of the Battles of Fredericksburg, where Robert E. Lee's army smashed General Burnside's Grand Divisions from strategic positions behind the Stone Wall and on Marye's Heights; Chancellorsville, where Confederate General Stonewall Jackson lost his life to friendly fire, but where Lee was able to defeat a supremely overconfident Union General Fighting Joe Hooker; Spotsylvania Court House, the site of the "Bloody Angle," an intense engagement of bloody hand-to-hand combat between Union and Confederate armies; and the terrible Battle of the

Wilderness that saw General Lee pitted against Union General US Grant for the first time. It ultimately turned the tide of war as Grant continued his march to Richmond.

The two visitor centers at Fredericksburg and Chancellorsville help interpret the four battlefields with audio-visual presentations and museum exhibits, including Civil War memorabilia, maps, and photographs. During the summer, Civil War living history is presented at several sites operated by the Park Service and guided walking tours led by knowledgeable park historians are also available in certain locations.

Be sure also to visit the **Stonewall Jackson Memorial Shrine**. From Fredericksburg, go 12 miles south on Interstate 95 to the Thornburg Exit, then five miles east on VA 606. There you will find the plantation office where Jackson, ill with pneumonia and his shattered left arm amputated, looked up and whispered, "Let us cross the river, and rest under the shade of the trees." Then he died.

The battlefields are open from dawn until dusk, and the visitor centers are open year-round from 9 a.m. until 5 p.m., except for Christmas and New Year's Day. Visitor center hours are extended during the summer. Fredericksburg Battlefield Visitor Center, 1013 Lafayette Boulevard, Fredericksburg, ☎ 540-373-6122. Chancellorsville Battlefield Visitor Center, Route 3 West, ☎ 540-786-2880; www.nps.gov/frsp.

Fredericksburg Baptist Church, 1019 Princess Anne Street, traces the origins of its congregation to 1767 and the beginning of the Baptist movement in Spotsylvania. The church itself, built in the Gothic Revival style, was completed in 1855 and is still in use today. But, like many other public buildings during the Civil War, it was used as a Union hospital and was heavily damaged by artillery fire. Open daily.

George Washington's Ferry Farm, Route 3 East, across the river from Fredericksburg, is where the boy George Washington lived and grew, from 1738-1752. This is the setting for the story of the Cherry Tree. Open daily, March-December, and weekends only, January and February. ☎ 540-373-3381, www.kenmore.org/visiting_ferry_farm.html.

The Hugh Mercer Apothecary Shop. Hugh Mercer was a political refugee from Scotland who emigrated first to Pennsylvania, and then, in 1761, to Fredericksburg. After distinguishing himself fighting during the French and Indian War, he established his apothecary shop and doctor's office at the corner of Caroline and Amelia Streets in 1771.

From the very beginning, Mercer's life – both personal and business – was one of success and contentment. He married George Gordon's daughter – Gordon was the town's most popular tavern keeper – and in 1774 he bought Ferry Farm from his good friend, George Washington. Unfortunately, Mercer was mortally wounded at the Battle of Princeton in January, 1777. His five children were raised by George Weedon, his brother-in-law.

Fredericksburg

Today, the old apothecary shop, restored to its original condition, presents a living history presentation of 18th-century medicines and surgical procedures within the setting of an old-time doctor's office. These procedures included bloodletting, toothdrawing, and the removal of cataracts as attempted by Doctor Mercer.

The shop is located at 1020 Caroline Street, Fredericksburg, ☎ 540-373-3362. It is open daily except Thanksgiving, Christmas and New Year's Day.

The James Monroe Museum. James Monroe was 28 years old when he moved to Fredericksburg to practice law under the guidance of his uncle, Judge Joseph Jones. For the first three years Monroe lived at the Jones home at 301 Caroline Street, a fine old house that still stands on lower Caroline Street, just blocks from the museum.

The museum is filled with all sorts of interesting artifacts and memorabilia. These include furniture and antiques purchased in Paris while Monroe was emissary to France, and used in the White House during his presidency. The collection also includes Monroe's elegant Louis XVI desk, many pieces of fine china, porcelain, silver, and jewelry, as well as articles of clothing and thousands of books, documents, maps, manuscripts and newspapers dating from the early 17th century.

The museum is at 908 Charles Street, Fredericksburg, and is open daily except Thanksgiving, Christmas and New Year's Day. ☎ 540-654-1043.

Kenmore. It was in 1747 that a young Fielding Lewis arrived with his new bride in Fredericksburg. His wife, Catherine Washington, was a first cousin of George Washington. Catherine Lewis died three years later in 1750 and Fielding Lewis married George's only sister, Betty, a few months later.

During the years that followed his second marriage, Lewis' enterprises prospered and he became a force in the local community. His magnificent mansion on Washington Avenue was completed in 1775 and contains three of the most elaborately decorated rooms of the period, including one featured in Helen Comstock's book, *The 100 Best Rooms in America*. Today, visitors can enjoy the elegant surroundings, a cup of spiced tea and a piece of gingerbread, and perhaps get a feel for the elegant life led by a gentleman and his family during the late Colonial period.

Kenmore is at 1201 Washington Avenue, Fredericksburg, and is open daily, March-December, and Saturdays only in January and February; closed Thanksgiving, Christmas Eve, Christmas Day, and New Year's Day. ☎ 540-373-3381, www.kenmore.org.

The Mary Washington House. For the last 17 years of her life, Mary Ball Washington lived in the home that her son, George, had bought for her in 1773. Her daughter, Betty, resided nearby at Kenmore. And so the venerable Mrs. Washington was able to live out her remaining years in comfort, close to the people she loved and amid the hustle and bustle of the busy downtown streets. Today, her home offers a glimpse into the life of one America's most famous citizens. The old house is filled with all sorts of memorabilia, period furnishings, antiques, and many of her personal possessions, including her "best dressing glass," which she willed to her son, George. The house is at 1200 Charles Street, Fredericksburg, and is open daily except Thanksgiving, Christmas Eve, Christmas Day, and New Year's Day. ☎ 540-373-1569, www.apva.org (look under "Properties").

Mary Washington Monument & Meditation Rock. Mrs. Washington came here often to rest and pray and, at her request, was buried here when she died in 1789 at the age of 81. The monument is on Washington Avenue at Pitt Street.

Masonic Lodge No. 4 A.F. and A.M. Located at Princess Anne and Hanover Streets in Fredericksburg, the lodge is where George Washington was initiated into the order on November 4, 1752. The building, dating from 1812, contains relics of his initiation and membership, an authentic Gilbert Stuart portrait and the 300-year-old Bible on which Washington took his Masonic obligation. The lodge is open daily, but is closed Thanksgiving and Christmas day. ☎ 540-373-5885.

National Bank Museum, A Bank for Fredericksburg. This building at 900 Princess Anne Street, ☎ 540-899-3243, houses more than 200 years of banking history. The structure has served continuously as a bank since 1820. Open Monday through Friday, 9 a.m. until 1 p.m.; closed all federal holidays.

Old Slave Block. This piece of pre-Civil War memorabilia, at the corner of William and Charles Streets, is a circular block of sandstone about three feet high, from which ladies mounted their horses and slaves and property were auctioned in antebellum days.

The Old Stone Warehouse, on Sophia Street at William Street, was constructed around the beginning of the War of 1812, possibly as a fortified building to defend the river landing and to store arms and ammunition. The old building has four floors, three of which are visible from the rear. Because the level of Sophia Street was raised between 1939 and 1941 to accommodate the new Chatham Bridge, only the second floor is accessible from the street.

During the Battle of Fredericksburg in December, 1862, the building was hit at least five times by Federal artillery. After the battle the warehouse served as a temporary morgue for some of the thousands of casualties.

From the end of the Civil War the warehouse played many roles in Fredericksburg's history. Today, the one-time warehouse, brewery, and fish curing house is owned by the city, administered by the Historic Fredericksburg Foundation, and leased to the Fredericksburg Area

Chapter of the Archaeological Society of Virginia. There is a sign at the entrance giving information about designated tours.

Old Town Fredericksburg consists of 18 blocks of historic buildings housing boutiques, restaurants, galeries and antique shops. Get a free parking pass at the Fredericksburg Visitor Center. ☎ 540-373-1776, 800-678-4748, www.oldtownfredericksburg.com

The Presbyterian Church. The church is a Greek Revival building, circa 1833, located at the southwest corner of Princess Anne and George Streets. Damage sustained by artillery fire during the Battle of Fredericksburg can still be seen in the front pillar. After the battle the church pews were torn loose and made into coffins for soldiers. Clara Barton, founder of the American Red Cross, is said to have nursed the wounded here. A plaque to her memory is in the churchyard. ☎ 540-373-7057.

The Rising Sun Tavern was built as a private residence in 1760 by Charles Washington, George Washington's youngest brother. Charles lived in the house for 20 years before moving westward to establish the town we know today as Charles Town, West Virginia.

The house was leased to one John Frazer in 1792, who opened it as the Golden Eagle Tavern. The tavern prospered, serving merchants and sailors who worked in the bustling wharves and warehouses on the riverfront. Over the years the tavern, known to those who frequented it either as the Eagle or the Golden Eagle, saw many new owners come and go. Then, in 1821, it was renamed the Rising Sun, and it continued under that name until 1827, when it once again became a private residence.

Today the old tavern, restored and refurbished to its 18th-century appearance, offers a tiny window on what tavern life in the 1700s might have been like. The "tavern wenches" of today treat visitors just as they would have back in the days when John Frazer was "Mine Host."

The Rising Sun Tavern, a National Historic Landmark and a Virginia Historic Landmark, is at 1304 Caroline Street, Fredericksburg, ☎ 540-371-1494. It is open daily except Thanksgiving, Christmas Eve, Christmas Day, and New Year's Day. For tour information, www.apva.org ("Properties").

Saint George's Church. The first town church, located on the site of the present church next to the market square lots, was a small frame building completed in 1734. It was the local center for the Anglican Church in Colonial Virginia. In 1786, the Anglican Church became the Protestant Episcopal Church and Saint George's continued under that banner for another 30 years or so. As the town's population continued to grow, so did the congregation. Soon it had outgrown the tiny frame building, and a new church was built in 1816. It, too, was soon outgrown and a third church, the one that stands today, was completed and consecrated by Bishop William Meade in 1849. The town clock was installed in the church tower in 1850 and is maintained by the City of Fredericksburg.

During the Civil War the church was used by General Lee's troops for their services. Unfortunately, it was heavily damaged in 1862 during the Battle of Fredericksburg, and was used as a hospital during the Battle of the Wilderness. The church has three priceless Tiffany windows. A silver communion set, which was stolen in 1862, was gradually recovered, piece by piece, over a period of some 70 years. The fine box pews survived the Civil War. The original clear diamond-shaped glass panes have been replaced by stained glass; the Mary Ball Washington stained glass window is of special interest.

Spotsylvania Court House Historic District. Here you will find several interesting sites, many reconstructed after the Civil War. Sites include the **Spotsylvania Court House, the Spotswood Inn, Christ Episcopal Church, the Confederate Cemetery**, and the **old jail. The Spotsylvania County Museum** houses local artifacts and genealogical records in the Old Berea Church, which dates to 1856. It is open year-round. ☎ 540-891-8687.

White Oak Museum, six miles east of Fredericksburg, houses Civil War artifacts from battle sites in the area. Open Wednesday through Sunday. 985 White Oak Road, Falmouth, ☎ 540-371-4234.

Annual Events

Unless otherwise noted, contact the **Fredericksburg Department of Tourism** (☎ 800-678-4748) for more information on the events below.

Washington's Birthday in February is celebrated in a big way in Fredericksburg, with Colonial games, tours, crafts, and entertainment at various locations.

George Washington's Birthday Celebration at George Washington's Ferry Farm, Falmouth, is highlighted by a Stone Toss Across the Rappahannock River. ☎ 540-370-0732, www.ferryfarm.org.

Many of Fredericksburg's private homes are open to the public during **Historic Garden Week**, usually held during the last week in April. For information, www.gardenweek.org.

The Virginia Renaissance Faire is held on weekends from mid-May through mid-June (see page 95). ☎ 703-508-5036, www.varf.org.

Fredericksburg Area Civil War Weekend, Memorial Day weekend, 800-654-4118, www.fredericksburgvirginia.net

The **Fredericksburg Heritage Festival** on July 4th is a city-wide, day-long celebration of Fredericksburg's rich and varied Colonial, Revolutionary, and Civil War past, featuring live entertainment, the Great Rappahannock River Raft Race, a Chili cook-off and much more. The fun begins at 8 a.m. and continues until 10 p.m. on July 4th. ☎ 540-373-9400.

Fredericksburg

Fredericksburg Agricultural Fair is the nation's oldest, dating to 1738. It is held at the end of July through the first week of August at the Fredericksburg Fairgrounds, 2400 Airport Avenue off Route 2/17, ☎ 540-373-1294, www.fredfair.org.

Fredericksburg Welsh Festival in mid-September celebrates the heritage of James Monroe, 900 block of Charles Street, Fredericksburg, www.welshfred.com.

The **Fredericksburg Area Wine Festival** is a popular day of wine tasting in early Ocotber, seminars, music, food, crafts, grape stomping, and children's activities. It's held the second week in August, ☎ 540-371-6522, 800-786-4192, www.fredericksburgwine.com. The event is held at Spotsylvania County's Izaac Walton League Park, ☎ 866-339-9463.

The **Black Arts Festival** showcases African-American art, entertainment and vendors in mid-September at Walker-Grant Educational and Cultural Center on Gunnery Road in Fredericksburg, ☎ 540-361-4000.

The **Fredericksburg Dog Mart** was originally a day of trading between the Indians and the settlers. Today, it has evolved to become a day of crafts, Indian events, rides, and a dog show – America's oldest, more than 300 years in the running. The event is held at Izaac Walton League Park, the first week in October, ☎ 540-786-5117.

The **Fredericksburg Dog Festival**, also on the first weekend on October, brings a parade of pooches through Old Town, followed by events and contests at Hurkamp Park. ☎ 540-372-1086.

The Annual Christmas Parade through Old Town Fredericksburg is the first Saturday in December, ☎ 800-678-4748.

During the **Christmas Candlelight Tour**, Fredericksburg's historic homes and public buildings are open to the public and are decorated for the holiday season. The event, held in mid-December, features carriage rides, Christmas carolers, decorations, costumed hostesses and musicians, as well as refreshments of the Colonial period. ☎ 800-678-4748.

First Night Fredericksburg rings in the New Year in Old Town Fredericksburg on December 31. More than 20 venues feature visual and performing arts. ☎ 800-678-4748.

Wineries

Hartwood Winery, 345 Hartwood Road, Hartwood, ☎ 540-752-4893, offers free tours and tastings, and a gift shop. Open Wednesday through Sunday.

Lake Anna Winery, 5621 Courthouse Road, Spotsylvania, ☎ 540-895-5085, www.lawinery.com. Open Wednesday-Sunday in summer; free tours and tastings of award-winning wines in a renovated barn.

Spotted Tavern Winery & Cider Mill, Hartwood Road at Dodd's Corner, Hartwood, ☎ 540-752-4453. Open weekends April-December for tours and tastings; the winery offers a selection of wine and cider for sale in season.

Entertainment

The Fredericksburg area offers a lively and diverse range of nightlife. Live music, from rock to jazz, country to zydeco, blues to bluegrass and soft piano to disco is available in many establishments.

Riverside Dinner Theater, 95 Riverside Parkway, Falmouth, ☎ 540-370-4300, www.riversidedt.com, features live Broadway musicals and dining. Shows and dinner Wednesday through Sunday.

The Virginia Renaissance Faire re-creates 16th-century England on weekends from mid-May through mid-June. In addition to costumed re-enactors, there is continuous entertainment on seven stages, games, food and shopping. For information, ☎ 703-508-5036, www.varf.org.

Recreation

There are dozens of lakes, streams, rivers, wildlife management areas, natural areas, preserves and mountains all within a short drive of Fredericksburg.

Abel Reservoir is a long, 185-acre lake with fishing and a boat ramp (power on the lake is restricted to electric motors only). The lake is open year-round. Take US 17 north to State Route 616 north and then 651 east, ☎ 540-752-5632.

Aquia Landing is a public beach on State Route 608 in Stafford. Picnicking, fishing and swimming with a lifeguard, Memorial Day through Labor Day.

Belvedere Plantation, 1601 Belvedere Drive, Spotsylvania, offers hayrides, pony rides, hot dog roasts, a petting zoo, and pick-your-own pumpkins and vegetables in season. Seven miles southeast of Fredericksburg on Route 17, ☎ 540-371-8494, www.belvedereplantation.com.

Central Park Funland, 1351 Central Park Boulevard, Fredericksburg, has bumper boats and cars, race cars, climbing wall, and miniature golf. Indoors are laser tag, an arcade, a carousel and batting cages. Open daily, ☎ 540-785-6700, www.cpfunland.com.

Lake Anna is a magnificent 13,000-acre water park. Several marinas provide access to the lake via boat ramps and boat rentals. Fishing tackle and bait are also available at the marinas. Activities include sailing, water-skiing, hiking, boating, picnicking and fishing. Take US 1 south to

State Route 208 west, and then go to State Route 601 north. ☎ 540-854-5503.

Lake Anna State Park. While you will surely enjoy your visit to Lake Anna, you will also enjoy the beach facilities at this beautiful park. The visitor center offers many interpretive exhibits, including a complete history of gold mining in the area, after which you too can try your luck panning for gold. Or you might like to spend a little time close to nature picnicking in the park, soaking up the sun on the beach, or strolling the park's more than eight miles of trails. The park is adjacent to Route 601 off State Route 208. ☎ 540-854-5503, 800-933-7275, www.dcr.state.va.us.

Lake Curtis is a 91-acre lake with a boat ramp, and lots of fish. The lake is open from 8 a.m. until dusk. Electric power only is allowed on the lake. The lake is adjacent to Curtis Memorial Park, with tennis, a pool, picnic areas and a golf course. Take US 17 north to State Route then 616 north to 662 west, ☎ 540-688-4871.

Motts Run Reservoir offers 160 acres of outdoor enjoyment. Facilities and activities include a boat ramp, boat rentals, picnicking and hiking, and fishing. The lake is open daily from 6 a.m. until 7 p.m. Electric power only is allowed on the lake. Take State Route 3 west to Route 639 north to State Route 618 west, ☎ 540-786-8989.

Ni Reservoir is a 411-acre lake where you can enjoy hiking, boating, picnicking and fishing. There's a boat ramp, and boat rental is available. The lake is open daily from 6 a.m. until 8 p.m. or 30 minutes before sunset, whichever is earlier. Take State Route 3 west, and then State Route 627 south, ☎ 540-898-7529.

The Rappahannock River runs from the Blue Ridge Mountains down to the Chesapeake Bay. Public access to the river is available in Fredericksburg at Motts Landing, River Road, Telephone and City Dock. Parking is available at Falmouth Beach in Stafford County.

The Rapidan River runs from the Blue Ridge Mountains into the Rappahannock River. Public access for canoe launching is available at Eley's ford, just off State Route 610 (Eley's Ford Road) in Spotsylvania, or at Germanna Ford off State Route 3.

Golf

Quality golf is available year-round in the Fredericksburg area. For golf packages, ☎ 877-PUTT-133, www.golffred.com.

Augustine Golf Club, 76 Monument Drive, Stafford, ☎ 540-720-7374, www.augustinegolf.com, is an 18-hole, par-71 championship course. There is a clubhouse and pro shop.

Cannon Ridge Golf Club is a new course, with a total of 36 holes. 475 Greenbank Road, Fredericksburg, ☎ 540-735-8000. www.cannon-ridge.com.

The Gauntlet at Curtis Park, 10 miles from Exit 133-B of I-95, ☎ 540-752-0963, www.gauntletgolfclub.com, is an 18-hole, par-72 championship course.

Lee's Hill Golfer's Club, 10200 Old Dominion Parkway, Spotsylvania, ☎ 800-930-3636, www.leeshill.com, is an 18-hole, par-72 championship course with a full clubhouse and practice facilities.

Meadows Farm Golf Course, 4300 Flat Run Road, Locust Grove, ☎ 540-854-9890, www.meadowsfarms.com/golf, has three separate nines, for a total of 27 holes.

Somerset Golf Club has 18 holes on the Rapidan River. 35448 Somerset Ridge Road, Locust Grove, ☎ 540-423-9300, www.leeshillgc.com.

Indoor Recreation

Cavalier Family Skating Center, 1920 Jefferson David Highway, ☎ 540-657-0758, offers roller skating and blading, rentals, and a video arcade.

Fredericksburg Ice Park has indoor ice skating, 1400 Central Park Boulevard, Fredericksburg, 540-785-1423, www.fipskate.com.

Slapshotz Indoor Recreation has indoor skating, 12220 Five Mile Road, Fredericksburg, ☎ 540-785-4625, www.slapshotz.com.

Shopping

The Fredericksburg area abounds with shopping opportunities. For visitors interested in local arts and crafts, there are more than 100 shops selling everything from pottery to copper goods, from basketry to weaving, and from jewelry to brass rubbings.

For the antique collector, the city and the surrounding area offer over 65 tiny shops, galleries, and stores, as well as several antique malls.

Or you can visit one of the area's shopping malls, including the **Spotsylvania Mall**, **Central Park**, the **Massaponax Outlet Mall**, and the **Aquia Towne Center**.

Dining

There are more than 100 locally owned and operated dining establishments in the Fredericksburg area. They offer a variety of menus from traditional American fare to a wide range of ethnic delights at prices that range from ridiculously cheap to fairly expensive. The following is only a small sample of what you can expect to find. All are in Fredericksburg, unless otherwise indicated.

2400 Diner serves Italian, American and Greek fare, 2400 Princess Anne Street, Fredericksburg, ☎ 540-373-9049.

six-twenty-three is contemporary dining in an historic landkmark, 623 Caroline Street, Fredericksburg, ☎ 540-361-2640.

Andrew's Mediterranean Bounty, 600 William Street, Fredericksburg, ☎ 540-370-0909, offers fine Mediterranean cuisine.

Claiborne's Restaurant, 200 Lafayette Boulevard, Fredericksburg, ☎ 540-371-7080, www.claibornesrestaurant.com, serves steaks and chops in the renovated 1910 train station.

The Garden Terrace at the Ramada Inn South, 5324 Jefferson Davis Highway, ☎ 540-898-1102. The restaurant offers indoor and poolside dining, and features fresh seafood, choice steaks and country cooking. Open for breakfast, lunch and dinner.

The General Store, 2018 College Avenue, Fredericksburg, ☎ 540-371-4075, specializes in pasta, burgers and sandwiches.

La Petite Auberge, 311 William Street, Fredericksburg, ☎ 540-371-2727. The restaurant offers fine French cuisine and fresh seafood. Open for lunch and dinner.

The **Log Cabin** specializes in seafood and steaks, 1749 Jefferson Davis Highway, Stafford, ☎ 540-659-5067.

Merriman's, 715 Caroline Street, Fredericksburg, ☎ 540-371-7723, www.merrimansrestaurant.com, offers innovative seasonal dishes.

The Olde Towne Steak and Seafood, 1612 Caroline Street, Fredericksburg, ☎ 540-371-8020, specializes in fresh seafood and prime rib. Open daily for dinner.

The **Parthenon** serves Greek and Italian cuisine, 2024 Augustine Avenue, Fredericksburg, ☎ 540-373-3898.

Renato Italian Restaurant, 422 William Street, Fredericksburg, ☎ 540-371-8228. Open for lunch and dinner, the restaurant offers authentic Italian cuisine, plus steaks and fresh seafood.

Sammy T's, 801 Caroline Street, Fredericksburg, ☎ 540-371-2008, serves vegan and vegetarian fare, homemade soups, salads and sandwiches.

Smythe's Cottage and Tavern, 303 Fauquier Street, Fredericksburg, ☎ 540-373-1645. Smythe's is set in an early 1800s cottage, and offers candlelight or outdoor dining. The cuisine is American, including beef, chicken, pot pies, roast pork and fresh seafood. Open for lunch and dinner.

Zum Rheingarten Restaurant serves German and Continential cuisine, 3998 Jefferson Davis Highway, Stafford, ☎ 703-221-4635. Reservations recommended.

Accommodations

Hotels & Motels

There are more than 40 in the area. Here is a sampling of those closest to Fredericksburg; for a complete listing, ☎ 800-678-4748, www.fredericksburgvirginia.net.

Best Western Central Plaza, 3000 Plank Road, ☎ 540-786-7404. This small motel has 76 rooms. Free continental breakfast. Small pets. $

Days Inn North, 14 Simpson Road, ☎ 540-373-5340, has 120 rooms. Free continental breakfast; on-site restaurant. $-$$

Hampton Inn Fredericksburg, 2310 William Street, ☎ 540-371-0330, has 166 rooms; pets accepted in smoking rooms. Free continental breakfast. $$

Holiday Inn/Fredericksburg North, 564 Warrenton Road, ☎ 540-371-5550, has 150 rooms, a swimming pool, a wading pool, a café, a bar and entertainment and dancing on Friday and Saturday. There's also a coin laundry and several meeting rooms. $-$$

Holiday Inn Select, 2801 Plank Road, ☎ 540-786-8321, has 200 rooms, a swimming pool with a lifeguard on duty, a wading pool and poolside service. There are also two restaurants, tennis courts and an 18-hole golf course for guest use. Free airport transportation. $$

Quality Inn Fredericksburg, 543 Warrenton Road, ☎ 540-373-0000, has 80 renovated rooms, an outdoor swimming pool and a playground. $$

Ramada Inn-Spotsylvania Mall, 2802 Plank Road, ☎ 540-786-8361, has 129 rooms, a pool, a café, room service, pets accepted. $$

Sleep Inn, 595 Warrenton Road, ☎ 540-372-6868, has 68 rooms. Free coffee in the lobby, and free continental breakfast. $

Wingate Inn & Conference Center specializes in the business traveler. Exit 133-B, 20 Sanford Drive, Fredericksburg, ☎ 540-368-8000, www.wingateinns.com. $

Wingate Inn is a new hotel with 99 rooms, indoor pool, fitness center and conference center. I-95, Exit 143-B, 15 Salisbury Drive, Stafford, ☎ 540-659-3600, www.wingateinns.com. $$

Fredericksburg

Bed & Breakfasts / Inns

Courthouse Road Bed & Breakfast has four rooms in the main house and a two-bedroom suite, all decorated with antiques. 2247 Courthouse Road, Stafford, ☎ 540-720-3785, 800-720-3784, www.courthouseroadbandb.com. $$

Fredericksburg Colonial Inn, 1707 Princess Anne Street, Fredericksburg, ☎ 540-371-5666, www.fci1.com. This two-story inn has 30 rooms. It was built in 1928 and offers guests an antebellum atmosphere and rooms individually decorated with antiques. Complimentary coffee and continental breakfast. $$

The Guest House at Walnut Grove, 7508 Belmont Road, Spotsylvania, ☎ 540-854-7993, is a circa-1730 home in a rural setting. $$

The Kenmore Inn, 1200 Princess Anne Street, Fredericksburg, ☎ 540-371-7622. The two-story structure in the historic district of Fredericksburg was built in the late 1700s. There are 12 rooms, four with fireplaces, some with canopied beds, all with antiques and reproduction furniture. TV is available in the lounge. The dining room is open for dinner Thursday-Saturday, and there is an English-style pub. Room service is available. Parking is on the street. Free coffee and continental breakfast. $$

La Vista Plantation Bed and Breakfast, 4420 Guinea Station Road, Spotsylvania, ☎ 800-529-2823, www.lavistaplantation.com, has rooms with fireplaces decorated with antiques in a country setting. Children welcome. $$

Littlepage Inn, 15701 Monrovia Road, Spotsylvania, ☎ 800-248-1803, www.littlepage.com, is an 1811 plantation home that has been in the family for six generations. There are nine guest rooms, and an outdoor pool and hot tub. $$

On Keegan Pond Bed and Breakfast, 11315 Gordon Road, Fredericksburg, ☎ 888-785-4662, is located between two Civil War battlefields. Private baths and full breakfast. $$

Richard Johnston Inn, 711 Caroline Street, Fredericksburg, ☎ 540-899-7606 or 877-557-0770, www.therichardjohnstoninn.com. The elegant inn, an 18th-century townhouse near the Fredericksburg Visitor Center on the banks of the Rappahannock River, features antiques and period furnishings, and offers an old-world atmosphere of gentility and Southern hospitality. Seven rooms and two suites. Free high-speed wireless Internet access; children and pets welcome by special arrangement. $$

Rockland Farm Retreat is a 4,000-acre historic plantation offering six rooms, near Lake Anna, 3609 Lewiston Road, Bumpass, ☎ 540-895-5098. $

Roxbury Mill Bed and Breakfast was the circa-1720 mill for Roxbury Plantation. There's a suite, two guestrooms and a children's room, all furnished with antiques. Located 20 minutes south of Fredericksburg at 6908 Roxbury Mill Road, Spotsylvania, ☎ 540-582-6611, http://members.aol.com/Roxburymil. $$

Camping

Aquia Pines Camp Resort, 3071 Jefferson Davis Highway, Stafford, ☎ 540-659-3447, has 125 sites, 75 with full hookups, and 31 with cable TV and optional telephone hookups. There are five rental cabins and group sites for tents and RVs. They have flush toilets, hot showers, sewage disposal, laundry, pool, game room and a grocery store where campers can purchase RV supplies and ice. Open year-round.

The **Dukes Creek Marina Campground**, 3631 Breaknock Road, Mineral, ☎ 540-895-5065, is on beautiful Lake Anna and offers 50 sites, boat launching facilities, and a store selling supplies and food. Rental boats, fishing tackle and bait are available at the marina. Activities at Dukes Creek include sailing, water-skiing, hiking, boating, picnicking and fishing. Open April-October.

Fredericksburg KOA Campground, a semi-wooded campground south of Fredericksburg on Highway 607, ☎ 540-898-7252, www.fredericksburgkoa.com, has 115 sites, some with full hookups; there are also several pull-throughs and nine one-room cabins. Other facilities include group sites for tents and RVs, flush toilets, hot showers, sewage disposal, laundry, grocery store, recreation hall, game room, a swimming pool, paddleboat rentals, a well-stocked fishing pond, bike rentals, a playground, planned group activities on weekends, horseshoes, volleyball, hayrides, and local tours. The campground is open all year. Credit cards are accepted.

The Rocky Branch Marina and Campground is on Lake Anna at 5153 Courthouse Road, ☎ 540-895-5475. Facilities include 38 sites with water and electric hookups, 25 tent sites, five boat ramps, a bathhouse with flush toilets and showers, and a store where campers can obtain boat rentals, fishing tackle and bait. Activities at Lake Anna include sailing, water-skiing, hiking, boating, picnicking and fishing. Open year-round.

Transportation

Fredericksburg is served by several trains daily by **Amtrak**, ☎ 800-872-7245, and commuter trains to Washington DC. The station is at Caroline Street and Lafayette Boulevard.

Greyhound, ☎ 800-231-2222, serves the city daily from 1400 Jefferson Davis Highway.

Fredericksburg

Local and area bus routes are served by **Fredericksburg Regional Transit** (FRED); for schedules and maps, ☎ 540-372-1222, www.fredericksburgva.gov/transit.

Information

The **Fredericksburg Visitor Center**, 706 Caroline Street, ☎ 540-373-1776 or 800-678-4748, www.fredericksburgvirginia.net, is a great place to begin your visit, and is an interesting site in itself. Built in 1824 by a local confectioner, Anthony Kale, it was first used as his shop and residence. During the Civil War, Union soldiers used the house as a holding area for local prisoners. There is an audio-visual orientation, and much information on lodging, dining and attractions. It is open daily from 9 a.m. until 5 p.m.

The Spotsylvania County Visitor Center, is at 4704 Southpoint Parkway, Spotsylvania, ☎ 540-891-8687 or 877-515-6197, www.spotsylvaniava.us/departments/tourism. There is a 10-minute video on the entire region, maps, brochures and discount tickets available. Open daily 9 a.m. to 5 p.m., with extended summer hours.

Stafford County Information Center is located in Belmont's Stroh Visitor Center, 224 Washington Street, Falmouth, ☎ 540-654-1015, http://co.stafford.va.us/visitor.

Tours

There are several guided and self-guided sightseeing tours of Fredericksburg and Spotsylvania County.

African American History of Fredericksburg is a self-guided walking and dirving tour. A **Children's Walking Tour of Historic Fredericksburg** is a self-guided walking tour created by a class of 4th graders. Brochures for both tours are available at the visitors center, 706 Caroline Street, Fredericksburg, ☎ 540-373-1776, 800-678-4748.

The *Civil War Walking Tour* is a two-part brochure available at the Fredericksburg visitors center and at www.fredericksburgvirginia.net. It includes sites in the Battle of Fredericksburg.

Living History Walking Tour, ☎ 540-899-1776, www.historyexperiences.com, offers costumed actor/historians as guides to the city, battlefield and phantoms of Fredericksburg.

River Cruise *City of Fredericksburg*, ☎ 800-598-2628, offers lunch and dinner cruises on the Rappahannock River daily except Mondays, April through November.

Trolley Tours of Fredericksburg, ☎ 540-898-0737, offers daily 60-minute tours of the historic district, departing from the Fredericksburg Visitor Center.

Leesburg & Loudoun County

L eesburg was originally named Georgetown for the English king, George III. It was later renamed Leesburg, most probably for Francis Lightfoot Lee, one of the signers of the Declaration of Independence and a respected local landowner. Leesburg is the seat of Loudoun County amid rolling hills and exceptional natural beauty. It's an area where picturesque country towns and Thoroughbred horse farms are scattered from one end to the other, and where fox hunting, point-to-point horse racing, steeplechasing, and horse shows are extremely popular.

Middleburg is the nation's horse and hunt capital, drawing celebrities and millionaires to this small town. The quaint downtown is lined with antique shops, galleries and eateries, many with an equestrian theme. The **Red Fox Inn** is an historic landmark, serving travelers since 1728. Confederate General John S. Mosby used Middleburg as a base camp from which to raid the region during the Civil War, and both sides skirmished here on their way to Gettysburg.

Sights

Aldie Mill, on Route 50 in Aldie, ☎ 703-327-9777, www.virginiaoutdoorsfoundation.org, was built around 1807. It's a grist mill powered by twin-shot water wheels. Open weekends, late April through October.

Ball's Bluff Regional Park, north of Leesburg on US Highway 15, features a small national cemetery and marks the site of a Civil War battle that took place on October 21, 1861. The battle resulted in a devastating defeat for four Union regiments by an overwhelmingly superior Confederate force. By the end of the fighting the Federal forces had been driven back to the banks of the Potomac River, where many of them were killed, drowned, wounded or captured as they tried to escape across the river. The Union general commanding the Federal forces, a US Senator, was among those killed. Oliver Wendell Holmes, who was wounded in the action, was one of the most prominent names in a list of casualties that numbered more than half of the Union force. Ball's Bluff Battlefield is open daily except for Thanksgiving, Christmas Day, and New Year's. ☎ 703-779-9372, www.nvrpa.org.

Fox Chase Farm is a riding complex offering stablesand riding, 23323 Foxchase Farm Lane, Middleburg, ☎ 540-687-5255, www.foxchase-farm.net.

John S. Mosby Heritage Area, ☎ 540-687-6681, www.mosbyheritagearea.org, near Middleburg, was commonly known as "Mosby's Confederacy." Three driving tours take in the historic, cultural and natural sights in the area.

Lanesville Heritage Area, in Claude Moore Park, Sterling, is 357-acre park with an 18th-century house. Open April-October; ☎ 703-444-1275.

Loudoun Heritage Farm Museum is an 18th-century farm that portrays 300 years of rural life. Open Tuesday through Saturday. 21668 Heritage Farm Lane, Sterling, ☎ 703-421-5322, www.loudounfarmmuseum.org.

The Loudoun Museum, 16 Loudoun Street in Leesburg, is a century-old restored building containing a number of interesting exhibits and memorabilia. There's also an audio-visual presentation that interprets life in the Loudoun County area. The museum is open daily but closed Thanksgiving, Christmas Eve, Christmas Day and New Year's. ☎ 703-777-7427, www.loudounmuseum.org.

Morven Park, Governor Westmoreland Davis Mansion, 17263 Southern Planter Lane, Leesburg, was originally the home of Thomas Swan, a former governor of Maryland. The estate was enlarged and improved by Westmoreland Davis, governor of Virginia from 1918 to 1922. Today, the 1,200-acre park includes the 28-room mansion, beautiful boxwood gardens, the Windmill Carriage Collection with its more than 100 horse-drawn carriages, the Museum of Hounds and Hunting, which features a video presentation and a variety of artifacts depicting the history of fox-hunting through the ages, and the Morven Park International Equestrian Institute. Morven Park is open Friday-Monday, April through October. ☎ 703-777-2414, www.morvenpark.org.

The **National Sporting Library** houses more than 11,000 books on equestrian sports dating back 500 years. 301 Washington Street, Middleburg, ☎ 540-687-6542, www.nsl.org.

Oatlands Plantation, on Route 15 six miles south of Leesburg, is a Greek-Revival mansion built in 1803 by George Carter on a 260-acre estate. The mansion and park were once the center of a 5,000-acre plantation. The house was extensively remodeled in 1827; the front portico was added during that time. Most of the building materials, including the bricks and wood, came from or were manufactured on the estate. The antique furnishings are American, English and French, collected mostly during the years 1897 to 1965 when the property was owned by Mr. and Mrs. William Corcoran Eustis of Washington. The estate has its own equestrian center, where horse shows and racing events are held. The formal gardens feature one of the finest displays of boxwood in the US. Oatlands is open daily late March through December and may also be booked for private functions. ☎ 703-777-3174, www.oatlands.org.

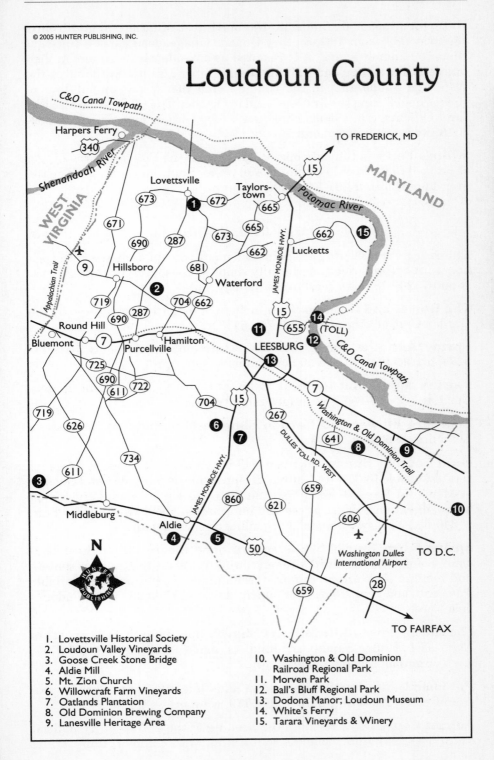

© 2005 HUNTER PUBLISHING, INC.

Loudoun County

Leesburg & Loudoun County

C&O Canal Towpath

Harpers Ferry
340

Shenandoah River

WEST VIRGINIA

Appalachian Trail

TO FREDERICK, MD

15

MARYLAND

Potomac River

Lovettsville

Taylors-town

JAMES MONROE HWY.

673   672   665
671   665
690   287   673   665
9   681   662
Hillsboro   Lucketts
2   Waterford
719   704   662
690   287
Round Hill   15   655   14 (TOLL)
Bluemont   7   Hamilton   11   12
725   Purcellville   LEESBURG   13
690   C&O Canal Towpath
611   722
719   704   15   7
626   Washington & Old Dominion Trail
734   267
611   DULLES TOLL RD. WEST   641   8   9
3   6   7
JAMES MONROE HWY.   659
860   621   10
Middleburg   606
Aldie   4   5   50   Washington Dulles   TO D.C.
International Airport
659   28
TO FAIRFAX

N
HUNTER PUBLISHING

1. Lovettsville Historical Society
2. Loudoun Valley Vineyards
3. Goose Creek Stone Bridge
4. Aldie Mill
5. Mt. Zion Church
6. Willowcraft Farm Vineyards
7. Oatlands Plantation
8. Old Dominion Brewing Company
9. Lanesville Heritage Area

10. Washington & Old Dominion
    Railroad Regional Park
11. Morven Park
12. Ball's Bluff Regional Park
13. Dodona Manor; Loudoun Museum
14. White's Ferry
15. Tarara Vineyards & Winery

Waterford, about five miles to the northwest of Leesburg on Virginia Highway 662, is an 18th-century Quaker village, designated a National Historic Landmark, and fully restored as a residential community. Visitors can take self-guided walking tours – brochures are available at the Waterford Foundation in the village – and there's an Annual Tour of Homes held during the first weekend in October. The celebration also features exhibits, crafts demonstrations, and traditional music. ☎ 540-882-3018, www.waterfordva.org.

White's Ferry is the only operating ferry on the Potomac, providing a shortened route from Leesburg to Maryland. Rent canoes or picnic on the Maryland shore. ☎ 301-349-5200.

Annual Events

Leesburg First Friday are held each month except January, with open houses at art galleries and specialty shops in Leesburg's historic district. ☎ 800-752-6118, www.leesburgfirstfriday.com.

The Homes and Gardens Tour, held in mid-April, is sponsored by the Garden Club of Virginia. ☎ 800-752-6118.

Spring Antiques Fair, Oatlands Plantation, Leesburg, ☎ 703-771-3174, attracts more than 200 exhibitors in late April.

Fairfax Hunt Point-to-Point, Belmont Country Club, Leesburg, mid-April, ☎ 703-787-6673, www.fairfaxhuntraces.org.

Leesburg Flower and Garden Show, held in mid-April in Historic Leesburg, ☎ 800-752-6118.

Hunt Country Stable Tour is a self-driven tour of famous stables and estates, hosted by Trinity Church in Upperville on Saturday and Sunday of Memorial Day Weekend. See the Web site for full details including hours, directions, ticket prices and information about the Country Fair. ☎ 540-592-3711, www.middleburgonline.com/stabletour.

Spring Farm Tour of two dozen farms and wineries throughout Loudoun County on the third weekend in May. Farms, equestrian centers and historic sites are on this free, self-guided tour. Brochure available from the Loudoun Tourism Council, ☎ 703-777-0426, www.loudoun-farms.org.

The annual juried **Aldie Mill Art Show** brings more than 70 artists to Aldie each Friday-Sunday in June, 11 a.m.-6 p.m., ☎ 703-327-9777, www.virginiaoutdoorsfoundation.org.

Potomac Celtic Festival is held in mid-June at Morven Park Equestrian Center, Leesburg, ☎ 703-938-9779, www.pcfest.org.

August Court Days re-enact the opening of the 18th-century judicial court. The festivities include a country fair with exhibits, stalls, crafts demonstrations, games and music. The event is held during the third weekend in August. ☎ 800-752-6118, www.preserveloudoun.org.

Annual Waterford Homes Tour & Crafts Exhibit is Virginia's oldest juried crafts fair, held in a National Historic Landmark Village the first weekend of October, ☎ 540-882-3018, www.waterfordva.org.

Glenfiddich Farm Pottery Fall Studio Show & Sale is the first weekend in October on a former dairy barn on Catoctin Mountin in Loudoun County, just west of Leesburg. 17642 Canby Road, Leesburg, ☎ 703-771-3329, www.glenfarmpottery.com.

Aldie Harvest Festival in mid-October features crafts, antiques, entertainment, blacksmithing demonstrations and Civil War re-enactments. ☎ 703-327-9777, www.virginiaoutdoorsfoundation.org.

Fall Farm Tour is a self-guided tour of private farms throughout Loundon County, with pumpkin-picking and hayrides, the third weekend in October. For brochure, call ☎ 703-777-0426, www.loudounfarms.org.

Christmas at Oatlands, held mid-November through December, features candlelight tours and 1800s decorations. ☎ 703-777-3174, www.oatlands.org.

Wineries and Breweries

Get a **Loudoun Wine Trail** guide from www.visitloudoun.org/winecountry.

Breaux Vineyards, 36888 Breaux Vineyards Lane, Hillsboro, ☎ 540-668-6299, www.breauxvineyards.com, has a tasting room with views of the winery operation and the Blue Ridge Mountains. Light gourmet fare is served on the patio.

Chrysalis Vineyards specializes in the Norton grape and award-winning Viognier. Open daily, year-round. 23876 Champe Ford Road, Middleburg, ☎ 540-687-8222, www.chrysaliswine.com.

Hidden Brook Winery is seven miles north of Leesburg, off Route 15, offering tours and tastings daily in a log winery. 43301 Spinks Ferry Road, Leesburg, ☎ 703-737-3935, www.hiddenbrookwinery.com.

Lost Creek Vineyard & Winery's tasting room on a hill overlooking the vineyards, offers gourmet cheese and bread. 43277 Spinks Ferry Road, Leesburg, ☎ 703-443-9836, www.lostcreekwinery.com.

Loudoun Valley Vineyards & Winery, 516 Charleston Pike, Waterford, ☎ 540-882-3375, www.loudounvalleyvineyards.com, has a glass-walled tasting room and decks with views of the Blue Ridge Mountains. Enjoy freshly baked bread and imported cheeses with wine tastings. Open year-round.

Leesburg & Loudoun County

Old Dominion Brew Pub, 44633 Guilford Drive, Ashburn, ☎ 703-724-9100, www.olddominion.com, offers more than 20 beers and free tours of the micro-brewery.

Swedenburg Estate Vineyard, Winery Lane, Middleburg, ☎ 540-687-5219, www.swedenburgwines.com, is located on the circa-1762 Valley View Farm, which is still in operation. Open daily.

Tarara Vineyard and Winery, 13648 Tarara Lane, Leesburg, ☎ 703-771-7100, www.tarara.com, features wines aged in a 6,000-square-foot cave overlooking the Potomac River. Tours and tastings offered daily.

Windham Winery is a 300-acre farm offering tastings Friday through Monday, and picnicing by the pond. 14727 Mountain Road, Hillsboro, ☎ 540-668-6464, www.windhamwinery.com.

Willowcroft Farm Vineyards, 38906 Mt. Gilead Road, Leesburg, ☎ 703-777-8161, www.willowcroftwine.com, is Loudoun County's oldest winery. Located on Mount Gilead, with views of Loudoun Valley. Open year-round.

Recreation

Parks & Natural Areas

Algonkian Regional Park, 47001 Fairway Drive, Sterling, ☎ 703-450-4655, www.nvrpa.org, is an 800-acre riverfront park with an 18-hole golf course, cottages, outdoor pool, boat launch and nature trails.

Red Rock Wilderness Overlook Regional Park, 43098 Edwards Ferry Road, Leesburg, ☎ 703-779-9372, www.nvrpa.org/redrock, has nature trails with views of the Potomac River.

Washington & Old Dominion Railroad Regional Park, ☎ 703-729-0596, www.wodfriends.org, is a 45-mile-long trail for walkers, joggers and bikers, with an adjacent bridle path.

Fitness Centers

Ida Lee Park Recreation Center, 50 Ida Lee Drive, Leesburg, ☎ 703-777-1368, is an indoor facility with a 25-meter pool, gym and weight room, located within a 138-acre park.

Farms

For more farms in the area, see www.visitloudoun.org/farms.cfm.

Patowmack Farm, 42461 Lovettsville Road, Lovettsville, ☎ 540-822-9017, www.patowmackfarm.com, is an organic farm that offers tours, luncheons and dinners; open May-November.

Field of Flowers, 37879 Allder School Road, Purcellville, ☎ 540-338-7231, www.field-of-flowers.com, is a farm where you can cut your own flowers and shop for crafts in The Barn Shop. The farm is open mid-April through October, Wednesday-Sunday.

Golf

Algonkian Regional Park & Golf Course, 47001 Fairway Drive, Sterling, ☎ 703-450-4655.

Brambleton Regional Park Golf Course, 42180 Ryan Road, Ashburn, ☎ 703-327-3403.

Dulles Golf Center & Sports Park, 21593 Jesse Court, Sterling, ☎ 703-404-8800, www.dullesgolfcenter.com.

Goose Creek Golf Club, 43001 Golf Club Road, Leesburg, ☎ 703-729-2500, www.goosecreekgolf.com.

Lansdowne Golf Club & Resort, 44050 Woodridge Parkway, Leesburg, ☎ 703-729-8400, www.lansdowneresort.com/golf.

Raspberry Falls Golf & Hunt Club, 41601 Raspberry Drive, Leesburg, ☎ 703-779-2555, www.raspberryfalls.com.

South Riding Golf Club, 43237 Golf View Drive, South Riding, ☎ 703-327-6660, www.southridinggc.com.

Shopping

Shopping in Loudoun County can mean browsing through antique shops and country stores, or heading for a large department store or outlet mall.

Dulles Town Center, 21100 Dulles Town Circle, Dulles, www.shop-dullestowncenter.org, at the intersection of Routes 7 and 28, has 125 shops, a food court and a theater complex.

Leesburg Corner Premium Outlets, 241 Fort Evans Road NE, Leesburg, ☎ 703-737-3071, www.premiumoutlets.com/leesburg, is a shopping village at the intersection of Route 7 and Route 15 Bypass.

Dining

Ball's Bluff Tavern, 2-D Loudoun Street SW, Leesburg, ☎ 703-777-7757, is where past meets present and north meets south. Open daily for lunch and dinner; live bands Tuesday-Saturday.

Bella Luna Restaurant is in the Leesburg Colonial Inn, 21 S. King Street, Leesburg, ☎ 703-777-5000, www.leesburgcolonialinn.com. The dining room is open for lunch and dinner.

Eiffel Tower Café has a real French chef, and serves lunch and dinner Tuesday through Sunday. 107 Loudoun Street, SW, Leesburg, ☎ 703-777-5142, www.eiffeltowercafe.com.

The Green Tree Restaurant, 15 S. King Street, Leesburg, ☎ 703-777-7246, www.leesburgcolonialinn.com, has been ranked among the best restaurants in the metropolitan Washington area. Specialties of the house include Robert's Delight (a beef dish), Jefferson's Delight (calves' liver soaked in milk), bread pudding, and in-house baking. On the weekends, 18th-century music is offered. Open for lunch and dinner.

The King's Court Tavern, 2-C Loudoun Street SW, Leesburg, ☎ 703-777-7747. Dine as travelers did in Colonial days, with a good meal, a glass of spirits and a good story.

Lansdowne Grill at Lansdowne Resort is a premier steakhouse also offering live Maine lobster, and fine wines, scotches, bourbons and cigars. 44050 Woodridge Parkway, Leesburg, ☎ 703-729-4073, www.lansdowne-resort.com/dining.cfm

Lightfoot Restaurant serves seasonal American cuisine in a restored 1900s bank building. 11 N. King Street, Leesburg, ☎ 703-771-2233, www.lightfootrestaurant.com

The Red Fox offers fine dining for lunch and dinner in seven cozy dining rooms, six of which have working fireplaces and hand-hewn beams. 2 E. Washington Street, Middleburg, ☎ 540-687-6301, www.redfox.com.

Tuscarora Mill, 203 Harrison Street SE, Leesburg, ☎ 703-771-9300, www.tuskies.com, offers fine dining, seasonal specials and an extensive wine and microbrew list. Open for lunch and dinner daily.

Accommodations

Hotels & Motels

Best Western Leesburg Hotel & Conference Center, 726 E. Market Street, Leesburg, ☎ 703-777-9400, www.bestwesternleesburg.com, has 99 rooms, an outdoor heated pool and picnic area, and wireless Internet access. $$

Fairfield Inn-Dulles Airport, 23000 Indian Creek Drive, Sterling, ☎ 703-435-5300, has 106 guest rooms, free continental breakfast, high-speed Internet access, airport shuttle and an indoor pool. $

Hampton Inn & Suites Leesburg is a new hotel with 101 rooms and suites one mile from historic district and across from the Leesburg Corner Premium Outlets. 117 Fort Evans Road NE, Leesburg, ☎ 703-669-8640. $$

Hampton Inn Dulles, 45440 Holiday Drive, Dulles, ☎ 703-471-8300, www.hamptondulles.com, has 127 rooms, and offers a complimentary continental breakfast. $$

Hampton Inn Dulles Cascades has 152 rooms, indoor pool, fitness center, business center, and complimentary airprot transportation. 46331 McClellan Way, Sterling, ☎ 703-450-9595, www.hamptoninndullescascades.com $

Holiday Inn Washington Dulles has nearly 300 rooms and suites, business center, restaurant, indoor pool, sauna and fitness center. 1000 Sully Road, Dulles, ☎ 703-471-7411, $

 Holiday Inn at Historic Carradoc Hall is a Colonial mansion at 1500 East Market Street, Leesburg, VA 22075, ☎ 703-771-9200, www.leesburgva.holiday-inn.com. The hotel has 122 rooms. Facilities include an outdoor swimming pool, The Mansion House Restaurant, and The Light Horse Tavern. Children stay free and pets are allowed; free airport shuttle. $

Resort

Lansdowne Resort, 44050 Woodridge Parkway, Leesburg, ☎ 703-729-8400, www.lansdowneresort.com, has 305 guest rooms and 14 suites with views of the Potomac River. There is a championship golf course, spa, health club and children's programs. $$$$

Bed & Breakfasts / Inns

There are more than two dozen inns and bed and breakfasts in the area. Following is just a sampling, featuring at least one from each part of the county. For a complete list, contact the **Loudoun County Bed & Breakfast Guild**, ☎ 800-752-6118, www.vabb.com.

Buckskin Manor, 13452 Harpers Ferry Road, Purcellville, ☎ 540-668-6864, www.buckskinmanor.com, has three guest rooms with private baths and a self-contained cottage. There is a pool and a pond. $$

Goodstone Inn & Estate, 36205 Snake Hill Road, Middleburg, ☎ 540-687-4645, www.goodstone.com, is a world-class country inn on 265 acres. There are 13 rooms with private baths, a stone swimming pool, hot tub, massage, canoes, mountain bicycles, hiking and birdwatching. Horses welcome. Golf and the Washington & Old Dominion Trail (see page 108) are nearby. $$$

The Leesburg Colonial Inn, 21 S. King Street, Leesburg, ☎ 703-777-5000, www.leesburgcolonialinn.com, offers guests a choice of 10 well-appointed rooms and suites, some with whirlpools and wet bars, cable TV and fireplaces. There's also a dining room and a café. The inn features lots of antiques and an old-world atmosphere. A complimentary full breakfast is served. $$

The Middleburg Country Inn at 209 E. Washington Street, Middleburg, ☎ 800-262-6082, is a former Episcopal parsonage built of brick. Guests have a choice of five guest rooms, and three suites, some with Jacuzzi and fireplace. Free airport transportation. $$$

The **Norris House Inn** is an elegant 1760 landmark in the historic district with six bedrooms, wireless Internet, gourmet breakfasts and a veranda. Children age seven and over are welcome. 108 Loudoun Street SW, Leesburg, ☎ 703-777-1806, www.norrishouse.com. $$

The Red Fox Inn, 2 E. Washington Street, Middleburg, ☎ 540-687-6301, www.redfox.com. This fine old establishment full of charm and antique furnishings has operated as an inn since 1728. There are 23 guest rooms, some with private patios and balconies, some with fireplaces, and a nationally acclaimed restaurant. $$$

Serene Acres is a Victorian country estate in the historic village of Bluemont offering two guest rooms and a studio cottage. Riding lessons, trail rides and summer pony camps offered. 19312 Walsh Farm Lane, Bluemont, ☎ 540-554-8618, www.sereneacres.com. $$

Transportation

Washington Dulles International Airport is located on the eastern edge of Loudoun County, 14 miles from Leesburg, and provides a full range of domestic and international flights. The stunning landmark structure was designed by Eero Saarinen. ☎ 703-471-7596, www.metwashairports.com/Dulles/

Greyhound also provides service to Leesburg (☎ 800-231-2222), and there is a **commuter bus** running between Washington and Leesburg (☎ 703-771-5665).

Information

Loudoun County Visitors Center, 222 Catoctin Circle SE, Suite 100, Leesburg, open daily from 9 a.m. to 5 p.m. ☎ 703-771-2617 or 800-752-6118, www.visitloudoun.org.

In Middleburg, look for the **Pink Box Information Center** housed in a small brick building on Mason Street. A self-guided walking tour booklet titled *Destination Middleburg: A Walking Tour Into the Past* is available. ☎ 540-687-8888, www.middleburg.com.

Manassas & Prince William County

A visit to Prince William County wouldn't be complete without touring the Manassas National Battlefield, and that's exactly why many people come. But the area has developed into a diverse tourist spot, with a 17,000-acre natural area (Prince William National Park), 46 miles of waterfront, and one of the world's largest outlet malls, Potomac Mills. Add to the mix the delightful quaint shops and streets of Old Town Manassas and Occoquan, and top it all off with a tour down the "antique shopping corridor."

Prince William County and the City of Manassas are near Washington DC, and many other travel destinations in both Virginia and Maryland.

History

The Prince William County of today is far different from the one that was formed way back in 1730 from Stafford and King George Counties. It offers the traveler an extraordinary pilgrimage into the past. Its old towns, historic sites and national battlefield provide a historical backdrop to a modern community rich in opportunity. The once-vast tract of land included areas that are now a part of Fairfax, Arlington, Alexandria, Loudoun, and Fauquier, but it was reduced to its present size and shape in 1759. Its first courthouse was built in 1731 on the banks of the Occoquan River at Woodbridge. Since then it has been moved from one site to another until, in 1893, it was finally relocated to the present county seat of Manassas.

Of the several small towns and villages that were chartered during Colonial times, only three remain: Dumfries, Haymarket, and Occoquan. Quantico owes its existence to the creation of the Quantico Marine Corps Base; Manassas and Manassas Park withdrew from the county in 1975 and became independent cities.

From Prince William's earliest times the **Potomac Path**, or King's Highway, was a major artery linking North and South. Men like Washington, Rochambeau, and Lafayette traveled the road, stopping along the way at George Mason's Woodbridge Plantation, Rippon Lodge, the home of Colonel Richard Blackburn, and the old Stagecoach Inn at the port of Dumfries. One of Virginia's most famous citizens' roots lie deep in Prince William's soil. Henry Lee III, "Light Horse Harry," the father of Confederate General Robert E. Lee, lived on the Leesylvania Plantation just to the north of the port city of Dumfries.

As the difficult situation between England and her colonies in the New World moved inexorably to a head, the citizens of Prince William County assembled at Dumfries on June 6th, 1774 and adopted the **Prince Wil-**

liam County Resolves. Later that year, one of the first companies of Minutemen in Virginia was organized. A native son of the county, William Grayson, became Virginia's first United States Senator.

The **Civil War** brought havoc and destruction on a grand scale to Prince William County. Two great battles, First and Second Bull Run, were fought at Manassas, and the small community, an important railroad junction and supply center, changed hands repeatedly throughout the war years. Today, those momentous days and the battles that were fought at Manassas are memorialized at the Manassas National Battlefield Park just northwest of the city.

Prince William County's rich history has been extensively documented and most of the important places and events are indicated on interpretive roadside markers throughout the county.

Historic Dumfries

Dumfries, a bustling Colonial tobacco port chartered in 1749, is the oldest continuously-chartered town in Virginia. It was named for the small Scottish town of Dumfries by John Graham, upon whose land the town was founded. During those early years the town had a number of hotels and stores, all run by Scottish merchants. There was also a dance hall, a theater, a race track and jockey club, a bank, a newspaper, and a courthouse. Cock fighting was a popular sport of the times, hence the nearby Cockpit Point. There was also an academy, a brick factory and several tobacco warehouses, along with the requisite tobacco inspector. Unfortunately, heavy silting and poor farming ruined the town and its industry.

The **Reverend Mason Locke Weems**, George Washington's first biographer, had a bookstore and warehouse in Dumfries. Weems is responsible for the story of Washington cutting down the cherry tree. He also wrote biographies of founding fathers Marrion, Penn, and Franklin. In 1802, the Weems property was sold to Benjamin Botts, who turned it into a law office. Botts became well known as the youngest defense attorney at the treason trial of Aaron Burr. He and his wife were killed in the Richmond Theater fire in 1811. The property changed hands several times after Botts died. Eventually it came into the possession of the Merchant family, and there it remained until the death of Miss Merchant at the age of 82 in 1968. For seven years following Miss Merchant's death the property lay abandoned to vagrants and vandals – until it was purchased by the city of Dumfries in 1974. The building, now one of the oldest structures in the town, has been completely restored. Today, the property that once housed Parson Weems' bookshop and the Botts' law office is a museum dedicated to the memory of the two famous men.

Manassas

Prior to the Civil War, Manassas was a rural community of small farms and holdings. By the late 1850s, however, things had changed. The com-

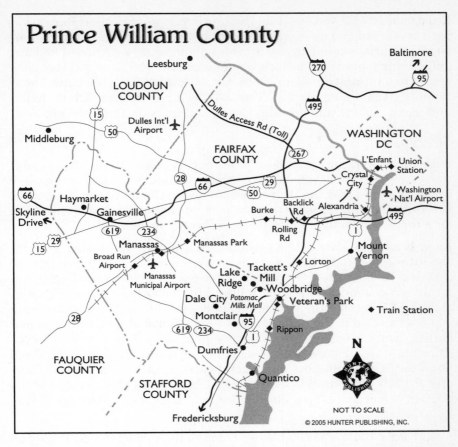

Prince William County

Leesburg

LOUDOUN COUNTY

Baltimore

270

95

Dulles Access Rd (Toll)

495

15

Dulles Int'l Airport

WASHINGTON DC

Middleburg

50

FAIRFAX COUNTY

267

L'Enfant   Union Station

28   66

29

Crystal City

66   Haymarket

50

Backlick Rd   Alexandria

Washington Nat'l Airport

Skyline Drive

Gainesville

Burke

495

619   234

Rolling Rd

15   29

Manassas

Manassas Park

Mount Vernon

Broad Run Airport

Lorton

1

Manassas Municipal Airport

Lake Ridge

Tackett's Mill

Woodbridge

28

Dale City   Potomac Mills Mall

Veteran's Park

Montclair

95

◆ Train Station

619   234

1

Rippon

FAUQUIER COUNTY

Dumfries

N

STAFFORD COUNTY

Quantico

HUNTER PUBLISHING

NOT TO SCALE

Fredericksburg

© 2005 HUNTER PUBLISHING, INC.

ing of the Orange and Alexandria and Manassas Gap Railroads had turned the area into the bustling hamlet of **Manassas Junction**. And it was the railroads that made the junction so important as a supply depot to both Confederate and Union armies. During the four years of strife the little community saw two major battles fought upon its soil, and dozens of smaller skirmishes, along with an assortment of military camps and field hospitals.

When the war ended in 1865, things in the tiny community at first began to return to normal. Then, with the rebuilding of the railroad and the return of interstate commerce, Manassas began to grow. By 1873 it had been chartered as a town. As money continued to pour into the coffers of local merchants and landowners, the architectural growth of the city began to reflect the Victorian era in which it was born. The old buildings and structures in the downtown historic district are fine examples of the times.

Today, the tidy little city is a fast-growing community only 30 minutes from downtown Washington DC, and 45 minutes from the heart of Virginia's beautiful Shenandoah Valley. The historic downtown area, now listed on the State and National Historic Registers of Historic Places, has been preserved and developed into one of Prince William County's most popular tourist sites. The city provides a number of self-guided walking and driving tours of the historic homes and Civil War sites and the many quaint and interesting shops. Opportunities for antique collecting, entertainment and dining abound. The Old Town has several historic museums and buildings, and provides a variety of festivals, fairs, and jubilees.

Occoquan

Occoquan is a Dogue Indian word that roughly translates to "at the end of the water." It is believed, because of the abundance of fish and ease of travel by canoe, that the Dogue once inhabited the Occoquan River area. It was for the same reasons that the pioneers found it to be a natural site for a community and a center for water-borne commerce.

As early as 1736, colonists had established a tobacco warehouse. By 1750, the little community had seen the beginnings of a thriving industrial complex. By the turn of the century, Occoquan had developed forges, water-driven grist mills, saw mills, tolling mills, and a bake house. The Merchant's Mill became the first automated grist mill in the nation. Grain was transported to the mill by water, then off-loaded from the ships and barges, transported into the plant for processing, and returned to the ships. It was all done with machinery operated by one man. From Occoquan it was transported to markets around the world. The mill operated for 175 years until it was destroyed by fire. All that remains of the original structure is the miller's office, now a museum operated by Historic Occoquan.

A mail stage route was established through the community in 1805. The cotton industry arrived in Occoquan when one of the first cotton mills in Virginia opened there in 1828. By the late 1850s, the timber, fish, and ship building industries, along with the first commercial ice storage house, had joined King Cotton in Occoquan. They turned the little riverside community into a thriving industrial complex.

The Civil War came and went, leaving Occoquan little changed and continuing to grow. By the turn of the century it had become a town with all the popular amenities, including a theater and an opera hall. Occoquan had become a cultural as well as a commercial center for the area. It was an idyllic time in the little community's history.

The good times came abruptly to an end in 1916, when much of the town was destroyed by fire. In 1928, Route 1 opened for interstate travel and Occoquan no longer stood astride the main artery between North and South. Things deteriorated even further when the railroad and over-the-road transport systems replaced the water-borne traffic. Even so, the good folk of the city made adjustments and it continued to thrive. But Occoquan's misfortunes were not yet over. Supermarkets outside of town began to take business from the small stores in town and the center began to die. Finally, in 1972, Hurricane Agnes paid a visit, destroying buildings, streets, sidewalks, and even the old iron truss bridge that crossed the river. The people of Occoquan began to rebuild, repair, and restore. Today the mills, the lumber yards, and the old ice houses are all gone, but in their place is a historic little riverside town that offers visitors a unique experience. There is fine dining in exquisite little restaurants and cafés, and unusual shops where you can browse for antiques, fine arts, needlework, crafts, collectibles, and fashions.

Almost as old as Virginia itself, Occoquan has evolved through the years into a unique blend of the old and the new.

Sights & Attractions

Manassas National Battlefield Park. In the early hours of July 21, 1861, the Civil War began in earnest as Union General Irvin McDowell hurled his army against that of Confederate General Pierre Gustave Toutant Beauregard's much smaller army. At first, the event was treated as something of a holiday. Dignitaries and celebrities came from Washington with their ladies to enjoy a picnic and watch the action as General McDowell put an end to the war before it had begun. At least, that was the way it was supposed to have gone. In reality, the fighting raged throughout the day. It was attack and counterattack until at last General Beauregard's army emerged victorious, sending a severely defeated Union army back toward Washington through the rain and in deep despair. Left behind were almost 4,700 casualties. The idea that the war would be a glorious affair, over in a matter of weeks, had been dispelled for good.

War came again to Manassas during the three days of August 28-30, 1862. This time General Robert E. Lee was at the head of the victorious Confederate army. The two battles cost both sides dearly. The Confederacy had 11,456 men wounded, missing, and killed; the Union losses were even higher at 17,170.

Today, the great field of war is a lush, green park dedicated to the men of both sides who gave their lives for one cause or the other. The park is dominated by the great equestrian statue of Confederate General Thomas J. "Stonewall" Jackson on Henry Hill.

The park is open daily. The visitor center is accessible to the handicapped but the actual battlegrounds are not. The visitor center also offers an interpretive slide show, an electric battle map, and a bookstore where a variety of Civil War books, maps, and tapes are on sale. There are several self-guided walking tours. The shortest is only about 30 minutes, while the longest takes more than 2½ hours. There is also a self-guided driving tour that includes 12 stops, two of which are optional walking tours, and covers 12 miles. Guided tours take place during the summer months, while in the winter they are by reservation only.

Manassas & Prince William County

For more information, contact the Manassas National Battlefield Park, 6511 Sudeley Road, Manassas, ☎ 703-361-1339, www.nps.gov/mana. The park is located at 12521 Lee Highway, off I-66 at Exit 47B.

Old Town Manassas. Old Town Manassas demonstrates how the struggle for the control of the major railroad junction led to the first major land battle of the Civil War. There are a number excellent shops and restaurants. The **Manassas Railroad Depot** off I-66 at Exit 47, built in 1914, contains railroad exhibits as well as the **Historic Manassas Visitor Center**, ☎ 703-361-6599, www.visitmanassas.org. You can pick up brochures for a self-guided walking tour here, or at the Manassas Museum.

The **Manassas Museum**, 9101 Prince William Street, offers an exciting journey through the history of the city and the Northern Virginia Piedmont region through a variety of interpretive video programs and exhibits that include Civil War memorabilia, antique furniture, maps, and photographs. The museum is open Tuesday through Sunday from 10 a.m. until 5 p.m. ☎ 703-368-1873.

Manassas Volunteer Fire Company Museum, 9322 Centreville Road in Old Town Manassas, ☎ 703-368-6211, displays antique fire apparatus and memorabilia used during the past 100 years. Open when the Volunteer Fire Department is open.

The Manassas Industrial School/Jennie Dean Memorial, 9601 Prince Williams Street, Manassas, is a school founded in 1894, where young African-American men and women learned marketable trades. It was founded by Jennie Dean, who was born a slave in 1852. The outdoor memorial and exhibit are open daily, year-round. ☎ 703-368-1873.

The **Mayfield Civil War Fort** is the last remaining Confederate earthwork in the City of Manassas. Open from dawn to dusk. Orientation and directions available at the Manassas Museum. ☎ 703-368-1873.

Mill House Museum highlights the history of Occoquan. Open daily year-round. 412 Mill Street, Occoquan, ☎ 703-491-7525.

Ben Lomond Historic Site and Old Rose Garden, 10311 Sudley Manor Drive, Manassas, is believed to have been occupied by both Confederate and Union soldiers as a hospital. The walls bear the signature of Union soldiers. On the grounds is one of the largest collections of antique roses. Grounds open daily. ☎ 703-792-4060.

Confederate Cemetery, Center Street in Manassas, is the burial sites of more than 250 Confederate soldiers. The public library has a list of those buried there. ☎ 703-361-6599.

Historic Occoquan. Occoquan is an original 18th-century mill town nestled on the banks of the picturesque Occoquan River. The town is neither a restoration nor a museum; rather it's a thriving artists' community filled with more than 100 shops, an enchanting village that has successfully linked more than 200 years of history with all the modern amenities, losing none of its charm in the process. Occoquan is on the National Register of Historic Places and hosts annual craft shows and other events.

There's plenty to see and do. Popular pastimes include taking a walking tour, dining out at one or more of the fine restaurants, and shopping for everything from antiques to hand-made quilts, and from fine arts to fashions. Most of the shops are open seven days a week from 10 a.m. until 5 p.m.

A self-guided tour takes about 45 minutes and guided tours are available by reservation. For more information, contact the Prince William County Visitor Information Center at 200 Mill Street, ☎ 703-491-4045, or the Occoquan Merchants Association, PO Box 606, Occoquan, VA 22125.

Occoquan Harbor River Cruises offers a 40-minute excursion cruise departing from 201 Mill Street, Dock A, in Occoquan. ☎ 703-385-9433.

Quantico National Cemetery is 725 wooded acres where veterans of America's armed conflicts are buried. Open Monday-Friday year-round, 18424 Joplin Road, Triangle. ☎ 703-221-2183, www.cem.va.gov/quantico.

The Marine Corps Air-Ground Museum. This museum is explored through a series of interpretive exhibits that span the history of the Corps from the end of the Spanish-American War to the end of the Korean War. Exhibits encompass a whole range of heavy equipment that includes field artillery, machine guns, 11 wheeled and tracked vehicles, eight armored fighting vehicles, and 19 aircraft. A number of cased exhibits contain small exhibits highlighting particular themes and weapons, and mannequins in historical settings wear the historical uniforms and equipment of the day. Exhibits are arranged in chronological order for a self-guided tour and are housed in vintage aircraft hangers.

The museum is located on the Quantico Marine Corps Base. It is handicapped-accessible and open April through mid-November, Tuesday through Sunday. Groups should plan to arrive at the museum no later than 3 p.m. Take I-95, Exit 150A, Triangle/Quantico. Follow the signs and enter the main gate at routes 1 and 619 near the Iwo Jima statue. Stop at the gate and be prepared to show photo ID. Follow the signs to the museum, which is at the end of Turner Field. For information, ☎ 703-784-2606, or contact the Officer-in-Charge, Marine Corps Air-Ground Museum, Bldg. 2014, MCB, Quantico, VA 22134-5001.

Freedom Museum at Manassas Regional Airport displays artifacts of US military involvement in 20th-century wars. 10400 Terminal Road, Manassas, ☎ 703-393-0660, 877-393-0660.

The **Weems-Botts Museum** covers the history of Dumfries and Prince William County. Guided tours available. Open year round, Tuesday through Sunday. 3914 West Duke Street, Dumfries, ☎ 703-221-2210.

Annual Events

There are dozens of unique and fun events held in Prince William County throughout the year. For a full calendar, call The Prince William County/ Manassas Conference and Visitors Bureau, ☎ 800-432-1792.

The Cherry Jubilee at Dumfries Community Center celebrates Washington's birthday in February. ☎ 703-221-2218.

Manassas St. Patrick's Day Parade in mid-March features fife and drum corps, Irish pipe bands, marching bands, Irish dance troops, and Irish heritage groups marching down Center Street. ☎ 703-368-1754.

The Manassas Railway Festival is held in Old Town Manassas the first Saturday in June. ☎ 703-361-6599.

The **Occoquan Spring Arts & Crafts Show** is in June, and the fall show is in September. ☎ 703-491-2168.

Anniversary of the Battle of Manassas in late July takes places at the Ben Lomond Manor House, which was used as a Civil War field hospital. 10311 Sudley Manor Drive, Manassas, ☎ 703-792-4060.

Prince William's County Fair, Virginia's largest county fair, is held each August, south of Manassas on Route 234. It offers nine days of fun. ☎ 703-368-0173.

A Civil War Weekend commemorating the second Battle of Manassas is held in August at the Ben Lomond Historic Site, Manassas. ☎ 703-792-4060.

The **Sugarloaf Crafts Festival** in mid-September attracts 300 of the nation's finest artists and craft designers to Prince William County Fairgrounds, 10624 Dumfries Road, Manassas. ☎ 703-368-0173.

Haymarket Days are held in mid-September with arts & crafts, food and a parade. ☎ 703-753-2600.

The **Manassas Fall Jubilee** and **Early American Craft Fair** is held in October in Old Town Manassas. ☎ 703-361-6599.

The **Festival of Freedom** takes place mid-October at the Freedom Museum with vintage aircraft, tanks, music and re-enactors. Manassas Regional Airport, 10400 Terminal Road. ☎ 703-393-0660.

Fall Gallery Walk in early November highlights art in Historic Old Town Manassas. ☎ 703-365-8558, www.artbeatgallery.org

Merry Old Town Manassas, the first weekend in December, features open houses, candlelight tour, tree-lighting, gingerbread contest, and a parade. ☎ 703-361-6599.

Dumfries Town Christmas Parade, December, ☎ 703-221-3400, ext. 133.

Entertainment

Hylton Memorial Chapel and Conference Center hosts Christian artists, concerts, speakers and events with seating for 4,000. Located at 14640 Potomac Mills Road, Woodbridge. ☎ 703-590-0076.

Lazy Susan Dinner Theater offers outstanding food, an informal atmosphere and memorable theatrical performances, making it one of the most popular evening spots in Northern Virginia. The evening begins with cocktails at 6 o'clock, followed by a buffet featuring salads, relishes, home baked breads, and Pennsylvania Dutch hot entrées, all prepared from scratch, including roast beef, chicken, fish, and home-made desserts for an endless bounty of delicious treats. Then, sit back and relax as you watch a full-scale Broadway production performed by a company of experts. For more information and prices, ☎ 703-550-7384.

The Virginia Shakespeare Company performs year-round at **The New Dominion Shakespeare Festival** in historic downtown Manassas in May and June. ☎ 703-365-0240, www.vashakes.org.

Loy E. Harris Pavilion in Old Town Manassas has ice skating in winter, concerts and other events the rest of the year. ☎ 703-361-9800, www.harrispavilion.com

Manassas Dance Company showcases award-winning choreography and international dancers. ☎ 703-257-1811, www.manassasdance.org

The Nissan Pavilion at Stone Ridge is an outdoor pavilion that offers concerts by well-known and emerging artists of every musical variety. There is reserved seating for 10,000, and lawn seating for another 15,000. The season runs spring through fall. Located at 7800 Cellar Door Drive, Bristow. ☎ 800-455-8999.

Old Dominion Speedway offers NASCAR, Winston Cup, drag racing and car shows. For more information and racing schedules, contact the office at 10611 Dumfries Road, Manassas, VA 22111. ☎ 703-361-RACE.

The **Potomac Nationals**, formerly the Potomac Cannons, is the Carolina League affiliate of the Washington Nationals. Barry Bonds, Bobby Bonilla, and Stump Merrill head the list of former Cannons players and managers in the major leagues. The Nationals offer great baseball in a traditional and exciting atmosphere, April through September at the Richard Pfitzner Stadium in Woodbridge. For more information, game schedule, and current prices, ☎ 703-590-2311, www.potomacnationals.com.

The **Prince William Symphony Orchestra** offers a five-concert series by leading musicians at various venues throughout the state. ☎ 703-580-8562, www.pwso.org.

Recreation

Parks & Natural Areas

Hemlock Park, on the Occoquan River, and **Meadowlark Botanical Gardens**, are two wonderful places for a leisurely stroll.

Leesylvania State Park is on 500 acres on the banks of the Potomac River. It's the site of the birthplace of "Light Horse" Harry Lee, the father of Robert E. Lee. Features include a visitor center, store, boat ramp, sandy beach, fishing, hiking, and the ruins of the Lee home and Civil War battlements. Wildlife, including nesting bald eagles, can be seen. 16236 Neabsco Road, Woodbridge. ☎ 703-670-0372, www.dcr.state.va.us.

Locust Shade Park is 400 acres with mini-golf, playgrounds, hiking trails and an amphitheater hosting evening concerts. 4701 Locust Shade Drive, Triangle, ☎ 703-221-8579.

Neabsco Creek has served as a waterway for trade since the 1700s. Today it's busy with recreational boaters who use the many marinas along Neabsco Road in Woodbridge.

Occoquan Bay National Wildlife Refuge, part of the Potomac River NWR network, is 643-acre site on the banks of the Occoquan and Potomac rivers. See tidal shorelines, marshes, meadows, woodlands and wildlife including nesting ospreys and bald eagles. Open Thursday-Saturday; Dawson Beach Road, Woodbridge, ☎ 703-490-4979, www.refuge.fws.gov.

Prince William Forest National Park. The land now occupied by the park has, from prehistoric times, been used to provide food and shelter. American Indians were probably the first to settle the land along Quantico Creek. Scottish immigrants established the port city of Dumfries at the estuary of the creek in 1756, and land to the west of the settlement was quickly cleared and planted with cotton and tobacco. The years that followed brought prosperity to the area, but poor land management caused severe soil erosion and extensive silting turned the once-thriving harbor into desolate marshlands. The mismanagement continued well into the 20th century. The land was depleted of its nutrients to the point where local farmers were barely able to make a living. Then, in 1933, the Resettlement Administration acquired the land and established the Chopawamsic Recreation Demonstration Area. The Civilian Conservation Corps went to work reclaiming the old and devastated farmland, overgrown and abandoned. New growths of hardwoods, pines, blackberries and blueberries were established. Wildlife returned to the one-time farmlands – white-tail deer, wild turkey, beaver, raccoon, and a variety of smaller animals. Gradually, the land recovered and blossomed.

Today, Prince William Forest Park has become one of Virginia's finest centers for outdoor recreation. It encompasses 17,000 acres of national forest, with streams, ponds, waterfalls, a nature center and more than 35 miles of nature trails. Popular activities in the park include hiking and bicycling on the park roads, fishing for bass, bluegill, perch and catfish in the lakes and streams; picnicking and orienteering. Camping is available either at the Oak Ridge Campground, where there are 113 sites, or at the Travel Trailer Village, which is operated by a park concessionaire. Group camping facilities are also available in the park, offering sites for groups of 50 or more, and five cabin camps with facilities ranging from restrooms to kitchens, and campfire grills to sleeping cabins.

The park is located on State Route 619, to the west of Dumfries off I-95. Take the Triangle exit and follow the signs a short distance west to the park entrance. ☎ 703-221-7181, www.nps.gov/prwi.

Fitness Centers

Chinn Aquatics and Fitness Center offers two pools, youth rooms, whirlpools, a sauna, a weight and exercise room, and racquetball courts. Daily admissions and plans available. Located at 13025 Chinn Park Drive, Prince William. ☎ 703-791-2338.

Dale City Recreation Center features an indoor pool, spa, cardio-fitness and weight rooms, racquetball and a batting cage. Daily admissions and plans available. Located at 14300 Minnieville Road, Dale City. ☎ 703-670-7113.

Freedom Aquatics and Fitness Center has two pools, water slide, whirlpool, jogging track and more. 10900 University Boulevard, Manassas, ☎ 703-993-8478.

Family Fun

Laser Quest Potomac Mills offers live-action laser tag for the entire family. Immerse yourself in this adventure game which features fog, music and entertainment. Located at 14517 Potomac Mills Road. For hours of operation, special events and other information, ☎ 703-490-4180, www.laserquest.com.

Old Mine Ranch is a hands-on pony ranch and working farm. There are pony and hay rides, a petting farm and a guided river hike. Open April through October, ending the season with a pumpkin patch and haunted hayrides. ☎ 703-441-1382.

Magic Putting Place is a unique miniature golf facility with two courses, 26 holes, featuring waterfalls, fountains and a magical atmosphere. Open daily and nightly April through October. ☎ 703-369-9299.

Signal Bay Waterpark is a 27,000-square-foot aquatic play park. 9300 Signal View Drive, Manassas Park. ☎ 703-335-8874.

Skate Quest-Prince William features a National Hockey League arena and an Olympic-sized arena. 5180 Dale Boulevard, Dale City. Open for year-round, indoor public skating, lessons and leagues. ☎ 703-730-8423, www.skatequest.com.

SplashDown Waterpark is more than 11 acres of water fun, with tube and cannonball slides, volleyball and more. Located at 7500 Ben Lomond Drive, Manassas. ☎ 703-361-4451.

WaterWorks Waterpark features water sprays and slides, as well as other sports fields and courts. Located at 5301 Dale Boulevard, Dale City. ☎ 703-680-7173.

Golf

Bristow Manor Golf Club is a par 72 course of more than 7,000 yards surrounding Bristow Manor, a historic Southern mansion. There is a pro shop, practice facility, professional teaching staff and a restaurant. 11507 Valley View Drive, Bristow. ☎ 703-368-3558, www.bristowmanor.com.

Broad Run Golf & Practice Facility offers golf for the entire family, with an 80-station practice range and 24 covered and heated stations. There is a nine-hole, par 35 course. Golf Academy Drive, off Route 28. ☎ 703-365-2443.

Bull Run Country Club offers pro-link GPS-based electronic yardage and course information available from each golf cart. Designed by Rick Jacobson, with bent grass greens, tees and fairways. Located at Route 15, four miles from I-66, Exit 40. ☎ 703-753-7777, www.bullruncc.com.

Forest Greens Golf Club is on gently rolling terrain and woodlands, and is home to the Mark Moseley P.L.A.Y. Foundation Golf Tournament. There is a restaurant, PGA staff, pro shop, practice putting green and driving range. Adjacent to Quantico National Cemetery and Prince William Forest Park in Triangle. ☎ 703-221-0123.

General's Ridge Golf Course is a championship course surrounded by rolling hills and hardwood forests on the site where Confederate General Richard S. Ewell built his winter encampment. There is a clubhouse, restaurant with patio dining, pro shop, practice holes and driving range. 9701 Manassas Drive, Manassas Park. ☎ 703-335-0777, www.manassasparkgolf.com.

Lake Ridge Park Golf Course is a nine-hole executive course on the banks of the upper Occoquan River. Designed to improve a short game, it has wide greens and challenging terrain. There is a driving range, clubhouse, lessons, snack bar and miniature golf. 12350 Cotton Mill Drive, Woodbridge. ☎ 703-494-5564.

The **Manassas Hills Golf Academy** is a nine-hole course with a discount golf shop, and a driving range. The short holes make it ideal for beginners or those who want just a quick game. The course is open from dawn until dusk. 7800 Willow Pond Court, Manassas, ☎ 703-368-2028.

The Ospreys at Belmont Bay is a par 70 course offering views of the Occoquan and Potomac Rivers and protected wetlands. 13401 Potomac Path Drive in Woodbridge. ☎ 703-497-1384.

The **Prince William Golf Course** is a challenging par 70, 18-hole course with a pro shop, a driving range, motorized carts, and Pro-Am Tournaments. The facility is open from dawn until dusk; 14631 Vint Hill Road, Nokesville, ☎ 703-754-7111.

Sunnybrook Golf Practice Range is one of the premier driving ranges in Northern Virginia, featuring 60 lighted tees, 16 elevated tees, and 16 covered and heated tees. There is PGA staff on hand, a pro shop and lunch specials. 8535 Sudley Road, Manassas, ☎ 703-369-0070.

Virginia Oaks Golf Course was built around Lake Manassas, offering outstanding golf and natural beauty. There is a pro shop, grass driving range, chop and putting greens. 7950 Virginia Oaks Drive, Gainesville. ☎ 703-754-7977.

Shopping

Historic Old Town Manassas offers art galleries, antiques, crafts, dining and 1900s artchitecture. There's a bustling farmer's market Thursday and Saturday at Church Street and Quarry Road, May through October. ☎ 703-361-6599.

Historic Occoquan is tiny, but boats more than 100 shops, eateries, coffeehouses, and scenic river views. Mill Street, Occoquan, ☎ 703-491-5984.

Dealers of all varieties line the **Antique Corridors** along Route 28 to Manassas, and Route 1 to Woodbridge.

Potomac Mills, one of the largest outlet malls in the US, has become a destination in itself. There are more than 220 well-known manufacturers' outlets. Reductions of 20-60% off the recommended retail prices on goods ranging from home furnishings to children's fashions, toys to women's clothing, and electronics to men's fashions and accessories are not unusual. There is also a 20-screen cinema and a food court with more than 20 vendors.

The mall is located off I-95, 30 minutes from downtown Washington DC, 60 minutes from Baltimore, MD, and 90 minutes from Richmond, VA. From I-95, take Exit 158 (southbound), or Exit 156 (northbound); open Monday through Saturday from 10 a.m. to 9:30 p.m., and from 11 a.m. to 6 p.m. on Sundays. For more information, contact Potomac Mills Mall, 2700 Potomac Mills Circle, Suite 307, Prince William, VA 22192, ☎ 800-VA-MILLS, www.potomac-mills.com.

Manassas Mall features specialty shopping with offerings like Chesapeake Knife and Tool, Bath and Body Works, and more. There is a seven-screen movie theater and a food court. Located at 8300 Sudley Road, Manassas, ☎ 703-368-0181, www.manassasmall.com.

Dining

Manassas

Carmello's & Little Portugal, Old Town Manassas at 9108 Center Street, ☎ 703-368-5522, www.carmellos.com, specializes in Northern Italian and Portuguese gourmet food. Open for lunch Monday-Friday, and for dinner seven days a week. Closed major holidays.

Casa Chimayo, 8209 Sudley Road, ☎ 703-369-2523, is a family-style Mexican restaurant with good food and moderate prices.

Chez Marc's namesake, proprieter Marc Fusilier, passed away in 2003, but the outstanding French cuisine is carried on. A prix fixe dinner is served Monday-Wednesday. Open for dinner Monday-Saturday and lunch Thursday and Friday. 7607 Centreville Road, Manassas, ☎ 703-369-6526, www.chezmarc28.com.

The China Jade Restaurant, 8423 Sudeley Road, ☎ 703-361-5764, is a fine Chinese restaurant specializing in Hunan and Szechuan seafood. Open for lunch and dinner.

Panino Ristorante, 9116 Mathis Avenue, ☎ 703-335-2560, is one of the top upscale restaurants in the area, serving regional Italian dishes of veal, poultry, seafood and pasta.

The Yorkshire Restaurant, 7537 Centerville Road, ☎ 703-368-4905, is a family-style restaurant specializing in seafood, steaks, and subs. Breakfast is served all day.

Woodbridge

Damon's Clubhouse, 14595 Potomac Mills Road, ☎ 703-492-6337, is a casual restaurant with a sports theme, serving specialties like Alaskan salmon, Chesapeake crab cakes and barbecued ribs. Open for lunch and dinner.

Gecko's, 13188 Marina Way, ☎ 703-494-5000, specializes in American food and seafood. Open for lunch and dinner. Handicapped-accessible.

Pilot House Restaurant & Marina, 16216 Neabsco Road, ☎ 703-221-1010, has a marina view and offers fine seafood and steaks. Open for dinner only.

Occoquan

The Garden Kitchen, 404 Mill Street, ☎ 703-494-2848, offers gourmet sandwiches, quiche and baked specialties for breakfast, lunch and dinner.

The Occoquan Inn, 301 Mill Street, ☎ 703-491-1888, specializes in traditional Virginia country cuisine. Open for lunch and dinner.

Sea, Sea & Company, 201 Mill Street, ☎ 703-494-1365, is a nautical-themed restaurant overlooking the Occoquan River. Open for lunch and dinner.

Accommodations

Most establishments offer both handicapped-accessible and non-smoking rooms, but be sure to ask when making reservations.

Near I-95

 Quality Inn is at 1109 Horner Road, Woodbridge, ☎ 800-221-2222. The hotel has 94 rooms including handicapped-accessible and non-smoking rooms. There's also a meeting room, two Jacuzzi suites, a guest laundry, a games room and an outdoor pool. Complimentary continental breakfast. $

Best Western Potomac Mills, 14619 Potomac Mills Road, Woodbridge, ☎ 703-494-4433, has 176 rooms, a guest laundry, a games room and an outdoor pool. Complimentary continental breakfast. $

Dumfries Econo Lodge, 17005 Dumfries Road, Dumfries, ☎ 800-424-4777, has 134 rooms, efficiencies, a full-service restaurant. A complimentary continental breakfast are provided. $$

Woodbridge Econo Lodge, 13317 Gordon Boulevard, Woodbridge, ☎ 703-491-5196 or 800-424-4777, has 65 rooms, an indoor pool and an exercise room. Complimentary continental breakfast. $$

 The Holiday Inn Express, 17133 Dumfries Road, Dumfries, ☎ 703-221-1141 or 800-HOLIDAY, has 187 rooms, a game room, an exercise room and an outdoor pool. Complimentary continental breakfast. $$

Ramada Inn-Quantico, 4316 Inn Street, Triangle, ☎ 703-221-1181, has 134 rooms, restaurant, lounge, outdoor pool and banquet facilities for 250. $$

Manassas

 Best Western Battlefield Inn, 10820 Balls Ford Road, ☎ 703-361-0221, has 120 rooms, full-service restaurant, meeting room, a lounge and an outdoor pool. $$

The Best Western Manassas, 8640 Mathis Avenue, ☎ 703-368-7070, has 60 rooms. There's also a restaurant, Jacuzzi suites, a fitness room and a lounge with live entertainment. $$

The Courtyard by Marriott, 10701 Battleview Parkway, ☎ 703-335-1300, has 149 rooms, including 12 suites, banquet facilities, indoor swimming pool, exercise room, whirlpool and guest laundry. $$

Days Inn, 10653 Balls Ford Road, ☎ 703-368-2800, has 120 rooms and a swimming pool. $

The Hampton Inn, 7295 Williamson Boulevard, ☎ 703-369-1100 or 800-HAMPTON, has 125 rooms, several Jacuzzi rooms, an exercise room and an outdoor pool. Complimentary continental breakfast. $

Holiday Inn Manassas, 10800 Vandor Lane, ☎ 703-335-0000, has 158 rooms, full-service restaurant, a meeting room, fitness room, lounge and an outdoor pool. $$

Old Towne Inn, 9403 Main Street, ☎ 703-368-9191 or 888-869-6446, offers 56 rooms, an outdoor pool, a restaurant and lounge in the heart of Old Town Manassas. $$

 Red Roof Inn, 10610 Automotive Drive, ☎ 703-335-9333, has 119 rooms. Complimentary coffee is available in the lobby. $

Super 8, 8691 Phoenix Drive, ☎ 703-369-6323 or 800-800-8000, has 78 rooms, including handicapped-accessible and non-smoking rooms, a restaurant next door, a fitness room and an indoor pool. $$

Super 8 , 7249 New Market Court, ☎ 703-369-1700 or 800-800-8000, has 150 rooms, Jacuzzis and a guest laundry. $$

Bed & Breakfasts / Inns

Bennett House, 9252 Bennett Drive, Manassas, ☎ 703-368-6121, www.virginia-bennetthouse.com, has two guest rooms in a Victorian country inn in historic Old Town. There are porches, patios, and four-poster beds. Breakfast and afternoon tea are served to guests. $$

Shiloh Bed and Breakfast, 13520 Carriage Ford Road, Nokesville, ☎ 703-594-2664, www.shilohbb.com, is a Georgian-style home on a 150-acre plantation overlooking a lake. There are two suites, each with private bath, kitchen and entrance. Full gourmet breakfast provided, and a hot tub and gazebo are available. $$$

Sunrise Hill Farm, 5590 Old Farm Lane, Manassas, ☎ 703-754-8309, has two guest rooms and is located in the heart of the Manassas Battlefield. The home is furnished with European and American antiques. A full gourmet breakfast is served. Horseback is a popular way to see the battlefield, and the inn offers boarding for horses. $$

Camping

Greenville Farm Campground is 43 wooded acres on a 200-acre working farm. There are 150 sites, some with full hook-ups. There is fishing and planned activities. Open year-round, limited in winter. 14001 Shelter Lane, Haymarket. ☎ 703-754-7944.

Hillwood Camping Park has 140 sites, all with full hook-ups. Route 295, Gainesville, open year-round. ☎ 703-754-4611.

Mountain View Campground has 125 sites, some with full hook-ups. There are boat rentals, fishing and swimming on Silver Lake, picnic areas, bathhouse, and sewage disposal. Located off Route 681 on Silver Road, Haymarket. ☎ 703-753-2267.

Prince William Forest Park has 75 sites, some with full hookups, plus tent campsites and cabins. There is a swimming pool, playground, laundry and it's open year-round. Located on Route 234 South. ☎ 703-221-1181, www.nps.gov/prwi.

Transportation

Prince William County is served by **Washington Dulles International** (☎ 703-582-2700) and **Reagan Washington National** airports (☎ 703-417-8000, www.metawashairports.com).

Manassas Municipal Airport (☎ 703-361-1882, www.manassas-city.org) is the number one relief airport for both.

Amtrak stops at Manassas, Quantico and Woodbridge. For schedules and fare information, ☎ 800-872-7245, www.amtrak.com.

The Virginia Railway Express is Northern Virginia's commuter rail service to and from Union Station in Washington, DC. For information, ☎ 703-497-7777, www.vre.org.

Greyhound buses stop at two eastern county locations, neither of which are full-service terminals: **Triangle**, 18518 Jefferson Davis Highway, ☎ 703-221-4080; and **Woodbridge**, 14010 Jefferson Davis Highway, ☎ 703-494-6718.

A **Greyhound Suburban Bus Station** is located north of Woodbridge in Springfield near I-95 at 6583 Backlick Road. For schedule information and fares, ☎ 800-231-2222 or 703-451-5801, www.greyhound.com.

Information

The **Prince William County Visitor Information Center**, ☎ 703-491-4045, is located at 200 Mill Street, in Occoquan.

Manassas & Prince William County

The **Manassas Visitor Center** is in the Railroad Depot, 9431 West Street off I-66 at Exit 47, ☎ 703-361-6599, www.visitmanassas.com.

The **Prince William County/Manassas Conference and Visitors Bureau**. Write the bureau for information at 14420 Bristow Road, Manassas, VA 20112-3932, ☎ 800-432-1792, www.visitpwc.com.

The Coastal Region

Virginia's wide, flat coastal region slopes gently from the Chesapeake Bay, rising no more than a hundred feet or so between the shoreline and the fall line, a geologic formation that signals the beginning of Virginia's Piedmont. Through this coastal plain flow several mighty rivers, including the James, the Potomac, the Rappahannock and the York. The major landforms are two peninsulas that jut out into the Chesapeake Bay – the Middle Peninsula and Northern Neck. The rivers and the peninsulas provide a water wonderland for recreation and watermen alike.

Besides fishing, antiquing is probably one of the most popular activities on both Peninsulas. The quaint "court houses" – or county seats – provide hours of browsing through curio shops. Take a break at any one of a plenitude of fine seafood restaurants to sample the harvest of the Chesapeake Bay, North America's largest estuary.

Hampton Roads

Hampton Roads, one of the world's finest and largest natural harbors, is a wide, deep channel in southeastern Virginia through which the James River flows into Chesapeake Bay.

The term is the old seafaring name given to the water "roads" around the mouth of the Chesapeake, and has, since Colonial days, been a key factor in the defense of the United States.

It was here, where southeastern Virginia meets the sea, that dawn's early light broke on the opening act in American history. Here the first permanent English-speaking settlers made their home, and the deciding battle of America's war for independence was staged.

On the shores of the bay and along the banks of the fast-flowing rivers which spilled into it grew the towns and cities of the New World. On the north side of Hampton Roads the Colonial towns of Jamestown, Yorktown and Williamsburg, and the cities of Hampton and Newport News – locally known as "the Peninsula" – sprang up and prospered. On the south side, Norfolk emerged as a powerful seaport and staging area for America's naval might.

Hampton Roads is the home of the Atlantic Fleet and the largest naval installation in the world. Here astronauts trained for moon missions, and aircraft carriers are commissioned and sent around the world.

Virginia Beach is the most populated city in the Commonwealth, Suffolk the largest in land area, and Chesapeake one of the fastest-growing. These changes have made Hampton Roads the 27th largest metropolitan area in the nation, the fastest growing in Virginia and a great place to visit.

The Weather

Mild winters make Hampton Roads a year-round destination. Since the Virginia Beach oceanfront is one of the East Coast's busiest resorts, the "shoulder seasons" of spring and fall mix still-pleasant weather with low humidity and fewer crowds. Hurricanes and tropical storms are possible June through September. Ice storms are occasional, but the average annual snowfall is less than eight inches. July is the warmest month, with a daily high temperature averaging near 90 degrees. January is the coolest month, with a normal high of 50 degrees.

Getting Here & Getting Around

Norfolk International Airport and the **Newport News-Williamsburg Airport** provide service to major cities. **Hampton Roads Transit** (☎ 757-222-6100, www.hrtransit.org) provides bus, trolley and ferry service as well as sightseeing tours.

Water is everywhere, which adds a special challenge to getting around Hampton Roads. "Tunnel traffic" is a term visitors should come to know and manage. For delays, call ☎ 757-640-0055, or tune to AM 530. Bridge-tunnel systems connect Southside (Norfolk and Virginia Beach) to the Peninsula (Hampton and Newport News). The Chesapeake Bay Bridge-Tunnel, 17 miles in length, is the largest bridge-tunnel complex in the world. Carrying a $12 toll each way, it connects Southside to the bucolic Eastern Shore, home of the famed Chincoteague ponies. Call ahead in severe weather for travel restrictions (☎ 757-331-2960; www.CBBT.com).

Hampton

Nearly four centuries ago the Kecoughtan Indians welcomed the first settlers on the shores of Hampton. Today, Hampton continues the welcoming tradition by hosting visitors from around the world.

Hampton's heritage encompasses the traditions of the military, the beginnings of free education, the downfall of Blackbeard the pirate, the Civil War and the training of America's first astronauts.

Today, Hampton is a unique combination of small-town charm and big city amenities. On the city's revitalized waterfront, visitors can board a

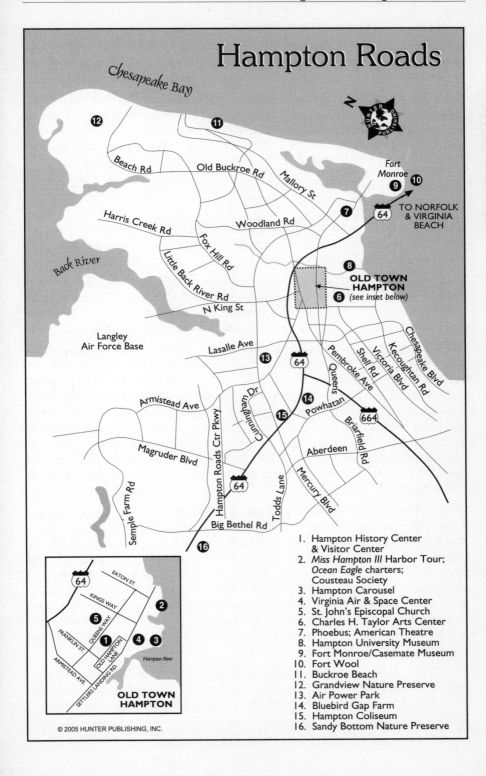

Hampton Roads

Chesapeake Bay

Beach Rd

Old Buckroe Rd

Mallory St

Harris Creek Rd

Woodland Rd

Back River

Fox Hill Rd

Little Back River Rd

N King St

Langley
Air Force Base

Lasalle Ave

Armistead Ave

Cunningham Dr

Magruder Blvd

Hampton Roads Ctr Pkwy

Semple Farm Rd

Big Bethel Rd

Todds Lane

Mercury Blvd

Aberdeen

Powhatan

Queens

Pembroke Ave

Shell Rd

Victoria Blvd

Kecoughtan Rd

Chesapeake Blvd

Briarfield Rd

Fort
Monroe

TO NORFOLK
& VIRGINIA
BEACH

OLD TOWN
HAMPTON
(see inset below)

1. Hampton History Center
   & Visitor Center
2. *Miss Hampton III* Harbor Tour;
   Ocean Eagle charters;
   Cousteau Society
3. Hampton Carousel
4. Virginia Air & Space Center
5. St. John's Episcopal Church
6. Charles H. Taylor Arts Center
7. Phoebus; American Theatre
8. Hampton University Museum
9. Fort Monroe/Casemate Museum
10. Fort Wool
11. Buckroe Beach
12. Grandview Nature Preserve
13. Air Power Park
14. Bluebird Gap Farm
15. Hampton Coliseum
16. Sandy Bottom Nature Preserve

EATON ST.

KINGS WAY

QUEENS WAY

FRANKLIN ST.

ARMISTEAD AVE.

SETTLERS LANDING RD.

OLD HAMPTON LANE

Hampton River

OLD TOWN
HAMPTON

boat for a narrated tour of the Chesapeake Bay, and explore space age artifacts in the world-class Virginia Air and Space Center and. They can experience the thrill of a giant-screen IMAX movie or take a spin on an antique carousel.

Hampton also offers two Civil War forts, African-American heritage sites, Bay-front beaches, self-guided walking and driving tours, great seafood restaurants and a choice of moderately priced hotels. Plus, Hampton's central location makes it the perfect base for day-trips to Colonial Williamsburg and Virginia Beach.

History

It was on July 9, 1610, almost two years after Captain John Smith's epic voyage of discovery, that English colonists founded the settlement that would eventually become Hampton.

Less than 10 years after the settlement was established, the first African slaves to arrive in North America stepped ashore from a Dutch ship at Old Point Comfort. Thus began a chain of events that would last for more than 240 years and end only with the defeat of the Confederacy in 1865.

The years that followed the settlement on Hampton Roads brought prosperity to the area. Unfortunately, that was not all it brought. Privateering and piracy had been a well established source of riches for a number of years beginning with the royal-sanctioned voyages of **Captains John Hawkins** and **Francis Drake** during Queen Elizabeth's reign in the late 1500s. By the early 1700s, piracy had become the scourge of the seas. As in the Civil War days yet to come, merchant ships had to run the gauntlet of dozens of fast predator ships in order to make safe haven in Hampton Roads. The most famous of those predators was Edward Teach – **Blackbeard**.

In 1718, **Governor Alexander Spotswood** decided that something had to be done. During the fall of that year he sent an expedition to capture Teach. On November 21, Lieutenant Robert Maynard cornered Blackbeard and his crew among North Carolina's barrier islands and engaged them in a fierce battle. During the fray Blackbeard received some 20 sword and five pistol wounds, but he fought on until he finally dropped dead. His head was severed from his body and, along with his surviving crew members, was carried back to Hampton, where it was stuck on a pole and raised at the entrance to the harbor – a grim warning to other pirates.

For almost 150 years after Blackbeard's death, Hampton's fortunes continued to improve and the community grew. Then, on May 2, 1861, the city ratified a vote to secede from the Union and join the Confederacy.

On March 9, 1862, the most famous naval action of the Civil War, the conflict between the Confederate ironclad CSS *Virginia* and the USS *Moni-*

tor took place in Hampton Roads harbor. The battle between the two behemoths lasted for more than four hours, only to end in a stalemate. Neither ship sustained any serious damage during the action, but the concept of naval warfare had changed forever.

It wasn't too long after the famous naval battle that Norfolk fell to Federal forces. From then on, the area remained in Union hands until the end of the war. **Fort Monroe** in Hampton was the jumping-off point for General George B. McClellan's ill-fated Peninsula Campaign of 1862, and the place where Jefferson Davis and several members of his cabinet were incarcerated at the end of the war. Many influential members of the Federal government wanted the Confederate president executed for war crimes, but eventually he was released; he left Fort Monroe on May 13, 1868.

Langley Field opened as the National Advisory Committee for Aeronautics on August 17, 1917. It was the beginning of a new era of prosperity for Hampton; America was about to take to the skies in earnest. By 1935, Langley Field had become the center of tactical aviation for the US Army. On October 4, 1956, the first truly supersonic fighter airplane, the Super Saber, was christened *Miss Hampton.*

With the advent of supersonic flight it seemed to be only a small step for man to achieve the velocity needed to escape the earth's atmosphere and venture off into the last great unknown – space. And so it was, on October 1, 1958, the National Advisory Committee for Aeronautics became the National Aeronautics and Space Administration – **NASA**.

America's first astronauts were chosen on April 1, 1959, and the "magnificent seven" arrived at Langley to embark upon one of the toughest training programs ever devised. The result of that program was the epic flight into space made by Marine **Colonel John Glenn** on February 20, 1962. Glenn orbited the earth three times in the Mercury capsule *Friendship 7,* and so became the first American in orbit.

Today, Hampton is a prosperous port city proud of its contribution both to aerospace and to the history of the nation. Fortunately for visitors to Hampton, much of its history lives on through its attractions, museums and historic sites.

Sights

Exploring historic Hampton is easy. The city's **Circle Tour** – you can start your tour wherever you see one of the blue and white tour signs – will guide you to a turn-of-the-century carousel, a modern air and space center, an outstanding ethnic museum, a moat-encircled pre-Civil War fortress, and many other interesting sites. Visitors can tour downtown Hampton either on foot or by car. The walking tour of all the suggested stops will take a morning or an afternoon. The driving tour will take about 3½ hours. Add a boat trip and your tour of the city will take about three hours more. So, put on your walking shoes, start your engines, and take the plunge.

The **Hampton History Museum** opened in 2003 in a new state-of-the-art Colonial-style downtown building, giving a permanent home to thousands of artificats of this oldest continuous English-speaking settlement in America. The museum's nine galleries chronicle the city's 400-year history from its first inhabitants, the Kecoughtan Indians, to the founding of the space program at Langley. The exhibits flow chronologically with interactive features like sound and lighting effects, and tactile exhibits, like the one that allows visitors to lift a musket. The Confederate burning of Hampton is brought to life by the sounds of voices and crackling fire, lighting simulating flames, and burned-out shells of buildings. Costumed interpretors appear to describe events. Open Monday-Saturday, 10 a.m. to 5 p.m., and Sunday 1 to 5 p.m. Admission $5 for adults, $4 for seniors, children under 12 and active military personnel. 120 Old Hampton Lane, ☎ 757-727-1610, www.hampton.gov/history_museum.

The **Art Market** in downtown Hampton is an outdoor gallery of original sculpture, mosaics and other durable art pieces that change annually. The two dozen pieces, located along Queens Way between Eaton and Franklin streets, are for sale and on display for one year, at which time a new call for artists is issued; ☎ 757-727-1271, www.downtownhampton.com/artmarket.

The **Cousteau Society's** headquarters are located in a replica lighthouse on the Hampton riverfront. Offices occupy the second and third floors, while the first floor is open to the public to showcase the life and work of the late famed undersea explorer Jacques-Yves Cousteau. There's a photo gallery, gift shop, a shark cage and other diving equipment from Cousteau expeditions, and models of the famous research vessels, *Calypso* and *Alcyone*. Kids can climb into a hovercraft and have their photos taken, while videos of the award-winning Cousteau films and television specials play continuously. Admission is free. 710 Settlers Landing Road, ☎ 757-722-9300, www.cousteausociety.org.

The Hampton Carousel. Built in 1920, this antique merry-go-round features 48 intricately carved horses and two stately chariots. Restored in 1991 to its original beauty, the carousel was a featured attraction at Hampton's Buckroe Beach Amusement Park for nearly 65 years. It is now housed at the city's downtown waterfront. Stop in for a ride or just listen to the original calliope. Tickets ($1 per ride) can be purchased at the Virginia Air & Space Center (see below). The carousel is open April through October, Monday through Saturday from 10 a.m. until 5 p.m., and on Sunday from noon until 5 p.m. ☎ 757-727-6381, www.hampton.gov/parks.

The **Virginia Air & Space Center** is at 600 Settlers Landing Road in downtown Hampton. Opened in 1992, this $29 million facility serves as the official visitors center for the NASA Langley Research Center and houses some dramatic objects related to the space program. There is a three-billion-year-old moon rock that was collected during the *Apollo 17* mission, the *Apollo 12* command module that journeyed to the moon and back, and a replica of the Lunar Orbiter that mapped the moon's surface for future landings. The center's open-air observation deck overlooks the Hampton River and offers a bird's-eye view of the river and Hampton Roads Harbor. Inside the center is a five-story IMAX theater. The center is open from 10 a.m. until 5 p.m., Monday through Wednesday, and from 10 a.m. until 7 p.m., Thursday through Sunday, Memorial Day through Labor Day; after Labor Day, 10 a.m. to 5 p.m. daily; admission charged (see Web site for details). ☎ 757-727-0900, www.vasc.org.

Fort Monroe and the Casemate Museum. Named in honor of President James Monroe, this is the largest stone fort ever built in the United States and the only moat-encircled fort still in active use. The fort, a National Historic Landmark, is home to the Army's Training and Doctrine Command.

Visitors to Fort Monroe can walk along the fortress ramparts just as Abraham Lincoln did as he watched his forces capture the city of Norfolk during the Civil War. Inside Fort Monroe is a series of caverns that house the Casemate Museum. These caverns were originally built to house the fort's guns. Today, they contain exhibits of weapons, Civil War memorabilia and uniforms. The cell in which Confederate President Jefferson Davis was imprisoned after the Civil War is preserved as a part of the museum.

❖ *Writer Edgar Allen Poe served at Fort Monroe as an enlisted man before pursuing his writing career.*

Other historic sites inside Fort Monroe include the Seacoast Batteries, built between 1891 and 1920, overlooking Hampton Roads harbor and Fort Wool; and the Lincoln gun, the first 15-inch Rodman gun ever made. Fort Monroe is open daily year-round from 10:30 a.m. until 4:30 p.m. ☎ 757-727-3391. Fort Monroe is accessed via Mercury Boulevard and Mellen Street through Hampton's Phoebus District.

St. John's Church, 100 W. Queens Way, downtown Hampton, was established in 1610. It is the oldest continuous English-speaking parish in the United States. Its tree-lined churchyard holds graves dating back to 1701 and includes a memorial to Virginia Laydon, the first surviving child born in the New World. The parish's most cherished possession is the communion silver made in London in 1618 – the oldest communion silver in continuous use in an area originally settled by the English. Another prized feature at St. John's is a stained-glass window depicting the baptism of the Indian princess, Pocahontas. The church is open Monday through Friday year-round from 9 a.m. until 3 p.m., and on Saturday 9 a.m. until noon. No tours on Sunday due to services. ☎ 757-722-2567.

Little England Chapel is a landmark to the religious lives of post-Civil War blacks. The sanctuary has an exhibit that includes a video, photographs, 19th-century religious books and Sunday school lessons. Call for a tour. Admission is free. 4100 Kecoughtan Road, ☎ 757-722-4249.

The **Hampton University Museum** is located in the Huntington Building at Ogden Circle on the Hampton University Campus. Founded in 1868, the museum is the second-oldest in Virginia. Its collection includes art and artifacts from cultures and nations worldwide, focusing on African, African-American and Native American, and includes Henry O. Tanner's famous painting *The Banjo Lesson*. In addition, the campus is the site of six national historic monuments, including the Emancipation Oak where President Abraham Lincoln's *Emancipation Proclamation* was first read to Hampton's newly-freed people. The campus is open daily until dusk. Admission is free; the museum is open Monday through Friday 8 a.m. until 5 p.m., and Saturday from noon until 4 p.m. ☎ 757-727-5308 or www.hamptonu.edu/museum.

Air Power Park is home to one of the largest civilian-owned collections of aircraft and missiles in the United States. Surrounding the park's information center are aircraft from the nation's various military services. These include a Nike surface-to-air missile, a P-1127 Kestrel vertical-lift jet, and an F-110D Super Sabre, the first Air Force fighter with true supersonic performance. The park, located at 413 W. Mercury Boulevard, Hampton, is open daily from 9 a.m. until 5 p.m., admission free. ☎ 757-727-1163, www.hampton.gov/parks.

Bluebird Gap Farm, a unique city park designed to resemble a working farm, provides children with an opportunity to see and touch the resident pigs, horses, cows and goats. Admission is free; the farm is open Wednesday through Sunday year-round, from 9 a.m. until 4:30 p.m. It's at 60 Pine Chapel Road, near the Coliseum area of Hampton. ☎ 757-727-6739, www.hampton.gov/parks.

The Charles H. Taylor Arts Center, 4205 Victoria Boulevard, showcases changing exhibits of work by regional artists. Admission free; the center is open Tuesday through Friday, 10 a.m. to 6 p.m., and on weekends, 1-5 p.m. ☎ 757-727-1490, www.americantheatre.com/taylor.

The ***Miss Hampton II*** is a two-decker, 65-foot tour boat that carries visitors from the Hampton Visitor Center dock out into Hampton Roads harbor. As it cruises past the world's largest naval base, the boat provides spectacular views of aircraft carriers, nuclear submarines, destroyers and frigates.

Before the boat returns to Hampton, it docks at **Fort Wool**, an island fortress, for a 45-minute guided tour that covers the fort's role during the Civil War. Cruises depart the dock at the Hampton Visitors Center twice daily at 10 a.m. and 2 p.m., Memorial Day through Labor Day.

Fort Wool is located on an artificial island in the middle of Hampton Roads harbor. Abandoned by the army in 1967, the fort's remaining fortifications include cannon casemates dating back to the Civil War. Constructed partially under the direction of Robert E. Lee, it offers spectacular views of the harbor, Chesapeake Bay and ships departing and arriving from around the world. For cruise and tour information, ☎ 888-757-BOAT or www.misshamptoncruises.com.

Events

Downtown Queens Way is blocked to traffic for a street party every Saturday, mid-April to early September for the popular **Saturday Night Block Parties**. ☎ 757-727-1570, www.hamptoneventmakers.com.

The **Hampton Blackbeard Festival** takes place at the waterfront the first weekend in June and includes mock sea battles, a pirate parade and ball. Admission is free. ☎ 757-727-1570, www.downtownhampton.com/blackbeard.

The **Hampton Jazz Festival**, held at the Coliseum in late June attracts America's most successful jazz and contemporary musicians. ☎ 757-838-5650 for the featured artists and tickets.

The **Afrikan American Festival**, held in conjunction with the Hampton Jazz Festival in June, is a family-oriented event that offers live music, ethnic food, and African and African-American arts and crafts. Held at Mill Point Park in downtown Hampton. ☎ 800-800-2202.

The **Hampton Cup Regatta** is the largest in-board hydroplane race in the United States. This mid-August event draws some of the fastest inboards and hydroplanes to the East Coast for the three-day race series. Boaters race at Mill Creek near Fort Monroe. ☎ 800-800-2202.

Hampton Bay Days, held in September, is one of Hampton Roads' premiere festivals, with national recording acts, seafood and exhibits relating to the ecology of the Chesapeake Bay. There's a midway with rides, and the city's downtown streets become pedestrian concourses packed with arts and crafts booths and a juried art show. ☎ 757-727-1641, www.baydays.com.

Phoebus Days are held every October. This three-day block party has music, tournaments, a parade and seafood. ☎ 757-727-0808, www.phoebus.info.

Hampton Holly Days. Hampton's historic downtown and waterfront districts provide the staging area for the city's annual Christmas holiday celebration. This includes the lighting of the official city Christmas tree, a lighted boat parade, a downtown street parade, romantic horse-and-carriage rides and a children's "Breakfast with Santa Claus." The popular

Parade of Sail culminates with arrival of Santa and Mrs. Claus by boat. ☎ 800-800-2202 for details.

Entertainment

The **American Theatre** is a recently restored historic gem in the Phoebus section of Hampton. The acoustics are wonderful is this 400-seat venue, where no seat is more than 75 feet from the stage. Performances include nationally-acclaimed jazz, dance, classical and international entertainers. 125 East Mellen Street, ☎ 757-722-2787, www.theamericantheatre.com.

The **AMC 24**, ☎ 757-896-2330, at Hampton Towne Centre on Big Bethel Road, is one of Virginia's largest theaters, with an amazing 24 screens.

The Hampton Coliseum is an architectural jewel, circa 1970's, placed among 75 acres of landscaped parkland with a 14-acre fresh-water lake. The Coliseum, at 1000 Coliseum Drive, is equipped with a large portable stage and a fully-equipped sound system. For more information and a schedule of events, ☎ 757-838-5650, www.hamptoncoliseum.org.

The new **Hampton Roads Convention Center** opened in 2005 next to Hampton Coliseum, with 344,000 square feet of exhibit space, meeting rooms, banquet space for 3,500 and two ballrooms. The nautical-themed design features billowing canvases over the entrance and winding canals through the property. The 300-suite John Q. Hammons Embassy Suites Hotel will be connected to the center by a covered walkway. ☎ 800-487-8778, www.hrcc.com.

Several **music series** take place June though August. Friday evenings feature jazz at Mill Point Park (☎ 757-727-1570, www.hamptoneventmakers.com), and Groovin' by the Bay features live big band and beach music Sunday evenings at Buckroe Beach (☎ 757-727-6348, www.hampton.gov/parks).

Langley Speedway, 3165 N. Armistead Avenue, hosts NASCAR Winston Series racing series and local stock races on a classic short track. Races are every weekend from April through October. ☎ 757-865-1100.

Shopping

For more than 200 years, merchant ships sailing into Hampton Roads from exotic places around the world stopped first at the Royal Customs House in Hampton. There the great ships unloaded their cargoes of tea, spices, silk, tools, furnishings and other items. It was a time for excitement and celebration, because the colonists flocked into the city to purchase the latest imports and hear the news from their homelands.

Today, Hampton is still a great place to shop. **Historic Downtown Hampton**, www.downtownhampton.com, incorporates the site of the old seaport, and is sprinkled with restaurants, art galleries, antique shops and boutiques, including a wine shop and VIrginia products store. Its cobblestone streets are lined with red brick sidewalks and crape myrtle trees.

Phoebus, a few miles from downtown, is a charming, turn-of-the-century neighborhood with a Victorian feel, antique and curio shops and seafood restaurants. ☎ 757-727-0808, www.phoebus.info.

At **Coliseum Central**, along Hampton's busy Mercury Boulevard, you'll find bustling shopping centers, Coliseum Mall, and the Power Plant, where where Outdoor World is a mecca for sportsmen, anglers and adventurers. In this giant Bass Pro Shop, visitors can try fly-casting and rock-climbing.

Recreation

Buckroe Beach, at the end of Pembroke Avenue, is the place to relax and enjoy some fun in the sun, sand and waves. Bordering the Chesapeake Bay, Buckroe's clean sand and gentle surf are ideal for children. Lifeguards are always on duty during the season, and the pavilion hosts big-band concerts and other events during the summer. Picnic shelters are available for a nominal fee. The beach is open daily year-round.

Sandy Bottom Nature Preserve opened in 1996 and represents the reclaiming of 450 acres once used to mine sand. Now a city-owned park, Sandy Bottom is a sanctuary for animals and humans amidst a growing metropolitan area. The nature center continues to evolve, with well-presented exhibits on the animals and plants in the region. There are nature trails, camping and two lakes – remnants of the sand excavation – for fishing and boating. The nature center is open daily except Monday, and park is open daily from sunrise to sunset. ☎ 757-825-4657.

Grandview Nature Preserve is a pristine waterfront preserve and estuary ideal for observing the local wild and marine life, hiking and birdwatching. The 578-acre preserve includes a 2½-mile stretch of bayfront beach and a six-mile path. ☎ 757-727-8311, www.hampton.gov/parks.

For the angler there are **fishing piers** at Grandview and Buckroe beaches, and **charter fishing boats** depart from Hampton's downtown waterfront for excursions on the Chesapeake Bay.

Boat ramps are available at **Dandy Point Boat Ramp** on Dandy Point Road on Back River (☎ 757-253-7072), **Sunset Boat Ramp** on State Park Drive on the Hampton River (☎ 757-850-5116), and at **Gosnold's Hope Park** on Little Back River Road (☎ 757-850-5116), which also has picnic facilities and a fitness trail.

Transient boat slips are available at the **Downtown Public Pier** (☎ 757-727-1276), along with several marinas on the Hampton River and Sunset Creek.

Golfers can chose from two public 18-hole golf courses, the **Hamptons Golf Course** on Butler Farm Road, ☎ 757-766-9148, www.hampton.gov/ thehamptons, and **The Woodlands** on Settlers Landing Road, ☎ 757-727-1195.

Dining

As one might imagine, this city offers an abundance of seafood restaurants. If it's a quick breakfast on the way to the boat or the beach, or an evening of fine dining that you're looking for, you'll find plenty to suit your taste, with more than 130 eateries.

Anna's Italian Restaurant serves up hearty portions of home-cooked traditional Italian fare. 555 Settlers Landing Road, ☎ 757-727-7707.

Bahir Dar adds some African adventure to the Hampton dining scene. Meals are family-style with an Ethiopian twist: The main course is served to the entire table on a platter atop a large, flat piece of bread. Instead of forks, diners pinch off pieces of the bread to pick up the food. Open for lunch and dinner every day but Monday. 17 E. Queens Way, ☎ 757-723-0100.

Diners at **Buckroe Beach Grille** have a bird's eye view atop Salt Ponds Marina. Eat seafood, pasta, burgers indoors or out on the deck. Open for dinner Tuesday-Sunday with a Sunday brunch buffet from 9 a.m. to noon. 1 Ivory Gull Crescent (off N. Main Street), ☎ 757-850-6500.

Tucked into a typical-looking shopping center, **Delargy's Bistro** defies the expected with imaginative Italian specialties and attentive service. Closed Sundays. 1814 Todds Lane, ☎ 757-825-1450, www.delargysbistro.com

The Grey Goose, 101-A W. Queens Way, ☎ 757-723-7978, is a quaint Southern-style tea room that serves ample portions of Virginia's stews and chowders. Specialties include crab soup, Virginia ham biscuits and delicious desserts. Open for lunch Monday-Saturday.

La Bodega Hampton, 22 Wine Street, ☎ 757-722-VINO, offers a world-class selection of fine wines, imported beers, gourmet sandwiches on fresh-baked bread and outdoor café-style seating. Box lunches are available.

Marker 20 is in a refurbished row building on downtown Hampton's historic Queens Way. It's a lively seafood restaurant, where you can watch sports at the bar and order shrimp and oysters by the bucket, listen to live music on the deck, or sit in the dining room where the walls are decorated with nautical charts. Open daily for lunch and dinner. 21 E. Queens Way, ☎ 757-726-9410, www.marker20.com.

Musasi Restaurant, 49 W. Queens Way, ☎ 757-728-0298, is a sushi bar and sit-down restaurant in the heart of downtown. The cuisine and hospitality are authentic Japanese.

Oyster Alley, in the Radisson Hotel at 700 Settlers Landing Road, ☎ 757-727-9700, offers seasonal outdoor, waterfront dining. Specialties include fresh seafood, salads and sandwiches.

Pier 21, also in the Radisson Hotel at 700 Settlers Landing Road, ☎ 757-727-9700, offers more formal indoor dining with a view of the marina. Specialties include fresh seafood and delicious desserts.

The new **Power Plant of Hampton Roads** has themed restaurants like Five, Jake's Garage, Johnny Carino's Country Italian, Joe's Crab Shack, Funky Parrot, McFaddens and the Cactus Café. To top off a great meal, there's the Coldstone Creamery.

Sam's Seafood Restaurant, 23 Water Street, ☎ 757-723-3709, is located among the fishing docks of the Phoebus neighborhood and offers a spectacular view of the Chesapeake Bay. Fried seafood is the specialty.

Siren in Phoebus adds steaks and Japanese fare to the traditional seafood line-up. Closed Sundays. 33 E. Mellen Street, ☎ 757-722-9842.

One in a local chain of five restaurants, **Surf Rider** is a lively place to gather for fresh seafood, steaks and barbecue. Warm weather brings live music out on the riverfront deck. Open daily for lunch and dinner. 1 Marina Road, ☎ 757-723-9366.

Nearly half a century old, **Smitty's Better Burger** is an institution. The waitstaff brings the food out to hang on the car window, just like the old days. And just like the old days, it's "cash only." Open daily until 9:30 p.m. 1313 N. King Street, ☎ 757-723-0661.

Victoria Station serves lunch and afternoon tea in the antique-filled dining rooms of a Victorian home. Open Tuesday-Saturday, 11 a.m. to 4 p.m. Tea is served 2-4 p.m. 36 N. Mallory Street, ☎ 757-723-5663.

Accommodations

Most establishments offer both handicapped-accessible and non-smoking rooms, but be sure to ask when making reservations.

Hotels & Motels

Best Western, 2000 W. Mercury Boulevard, ☎ 757-825-3398, www.bestwesternhamptonroads.com, is recently renovated with 142 guest rooms, including some handicapped-accessible. Free continental breakfast, in-room coffeemakers, cable, outdoor pool and fitness center. Suites have microwaves and refrigerators. $$

Courtyard by Marriott, 1917 Coliseum Drive, ☎ 757-838-3300, has 146 guest rooms, a full-service restaurant, a café, coffee in the rooms, a heated swimming pool, meeting rooms, free high-speed Internet service and an exercise room. $$

Hampton Inn, 1813 W. Mercury Boulevard, ☎ 757-838-8484, has 132 rooms, pool privileges and a free continental breakfast. $$

Holiday Inn Hampton Hotel & Conference Center, 1815 Mercury Boulevard, ☎ 757-838-0200, www.hamptonva.holiday-inn.com, has 321 rooms, restaurant, a bar, two pools, meeting rooms, free high-speed Internet service, an exercise room and free airport transportation. $$

 Quality Inn Suites, 1809 W. Mercury Boulevard, ☎ 757-838-5011, www.qualityinnsuites.com, has 179 rooms, a full-service restaurant, room service, a bar, a café, coffee in the rooms, and an indoor pool. $$

Radisson Hotel Hampton, 700 Settlers Landing Road, ☎ 757-727-9700, www.radisson.com, has 172 rooms, a full-service restaurant, room service, a bar, a café, coffee in the rooms, a swimming pool, pool-side service, a shopping arcade, meeting rooms and free airport transportation. Some rooms have river and marina views and whirlpool tubs. $$

Ramada Inn, 1905 Coliseum Drive, ☎ 757-827-7400, has 134 guest rooms, an outdoor pool, and free continental breakfast. $

Bed & Breakfasts / Inns

Lady Neptune Bed & Breakfast at Buckroe Beach began life miles away at Hampton Point. Scheduled for demolition in 1988 to make way for new development, the owners had it moved by barge to its present location. The 1930 Victorian now overlooks the Chesapeake Bay and hosts guests in its four bedrooms. Children are welcome, and the owner, Shirley McQueen, will even babysit for an extra charge. There's a Louis XV sitting room with fireplace, an outdoor spa, and full southern breakfast buffet that may include anything from catfish and grits to Crab Eggs Benedict and Virginia ham. 507 N. First Street, ☎ 800-693-6568, 757-850-6060, www.ladyneptuneinn.com. $$

Little England Inn is a charming Victorian in a historic neighborhood within walking distance of the downtown waterfront. Completely renovated with modern conveniences for its 100ˈ birthday in 2002, the rooms feature private baths, queen-sized beds, fine linens, private phones, televisions, and individual temperature controls. Children over 12 welcome. Pets are not allowed, but the Armistead Animal Inn (☎ 757-723-5118) is just a few blocks away. 4400 Victoria Boulevard, ☎ 800-606-0985, 757-722-0985, www.littleenglandinn.com. $$

Victoria House, on Hampton's historic Victoria Boulevard, ☎ 800-201-4642, www.victoriahousebb.com, is a late-1800 Queen Anne-style house. There are four rooms, each with a private bath, air conditioning, cable, VCR and laptop hook-ups. Two sitting rooms are nicely decorated with antiques. Rooms are non-smoking with either queen or king-size beds. One room has a two-person Jacuzzi. There is a wrap-around porch, a deck and gardens outside. $$$

Transportation

The **Newport News/Williamsburg International Airport** and the **Norfolk International Airports** are both within 30 minutes of downtown Hampton. Ground transportation is available through a variety of taxi and rental car companies.

Amtrak, ☎ 800-872-7245, serves nearby Newport News. **Greyhound Lines**, ☎ 800-231-2222, serves the city at 2 West Pembroke Avenue, Hampton.

Hampton Roads Transit provides bus and trolley service, ☎ 757-222-6100, www.hrtransit.org.

Information

Downtown Hampton Development Partnership, 756 Settlers Landing Road, ☎ 757-727-1271, www.downtownhampton.com.

Hampton Convention & Visitor Bureau, 2 Eaton Street, Hampton, VA 23660. ☎ 757-722-1222 or 800-487-8778, www.hamptoncvb.com.

Hampton Visitor Center, 120 Old Hampton Lane, inside Hampton History Museum, ☎ 800-800-2202.

Newport News

*L*ocated between Colonial Williamsburg and Norfolk-Virginia Beach, Newport News stretches 25 miles along the mighty James River. It is the home of the Newport News Shipbuilding, one of the world's largest shipyards and one of Virginia's largest employers.

A vacation in Newport News will take you through more than 250 years of maritime heritage and military history with nearly a dozen museums and historic sites. Fine dining is available in a variety of traditional and ethnic restaurants.

Newport News

History

On a balmy day in May, 1607, three small wooden ships sailed quietly into Hampton Roads and disappeared up the James River to land their passengers at Jamestown.

To the 143 men aboard those three ships that sailed around the point under the command of **Captain Christopher Newport** in 1607, the land here was a garden of Eden, a great mantle of deep green foliage, ancient trees, and sandy bluffs rolling down to the banks of the James River. Newport stopped at present-day Newport News point, calling it Point Hope. The idyllic shoreline had been discovered and would never be the same again, for within 10 years the first settlers had established the first small communities in the area.

During the late 18th century, the fortunes of the local planters and the burgeoning tobacco industry continued to grow throughout Warwick and other Tidewater counties. Dirt roads were carved through the virgin forest to connect Newport News, Hampton, Yorktown and Williamsburg.

Realizing the strategic importance of the point at the entrance to the James River, Major General Benjamin F. Butler fortified the area, and Camp Butler was quickly established northward along the river from the present Chesapeake and Ohio terminals.

On hearing of Butler's intrusion into Newport News, Confederate General Robert E. Lee was quick to respond. On June 10, 1861, some 1,400 Confederates clashed with a large force of more than 3,500 Federal troops at Big Bethel. The result was a decisive victory for the smaller Confederate army.

Camp Butler served throughout the war as a staging area for Union forces under the command of Fort Monroe, a role that the City of Newport News would continue through the Spanish American War and two World Wars.

Almost a year after Big Bethel, Newport News was witness to the naval battle that would change the course of history. In March, 1862, at the Gosport Navy Yard near Norfolk, Confederate engineers raised the sunken Union frigate *Merrimac* and went to work refurbishing it, sheathing her deck with four inches of iron plate, and fitting a great iron ram to the bow. Renamed the *Virginia,* she targeted the Union warships *Cumberland* and *Congress*, which were blockading the mouth of the James River under the guns of Camp Butler.

The *Congress* fired a broadside at the strange-looking ship, only to see the cannon balls bounce off the iron upper works. The *Virginia*'s powerful rifled guns smashed into the *Cumberland's* wooden hull, and then the iron ram burst through the ship's sides, tearing a hole that sent the doomed ship to the bottom.

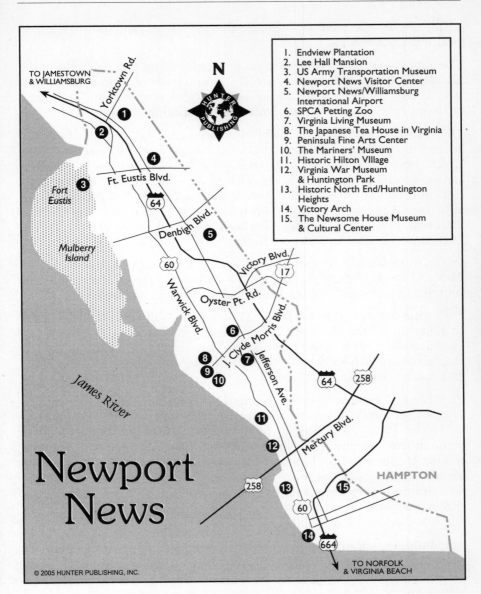

1. Endview Plantation
2. Lee Hall Mansion
3. US Army Transportation Museum
4. Newport News Visitor Center
5. Newport News/Williamsburg International Airport
6. SPCA Petting Zoo
7. Virginia Living Museum
8. The Japanese Tea House in Virginia
9. Peninsula Fine Arts Center
10. The Mariners' Museum
11. Historic Hilton Village
12. Virginia War Museum & Huntington Park
13. Historic North End/Huntington Heights
14. Victory Arch
15. The Newsome House Museum & Cultural Center

N

TO JAMESTOWN & WILLIAMSBURG

Yorktown Rd.

Ft. Eustis Blvd.

Fort Eustis

Mulberry Island

Denbigh Blvd.

Warwick Blvd.

Oyster Pt. Rd.

Victory Blvd.

J. Clyde Morris Blvd.

Jefferson Ave.

James River

Mercury Blvd.

Newport News

HAMPTON

© 2005 HUNTER PUBLISHING, INC.

TO NORFOLK & VIRGINIA BEACH

By this time the *Virginia* had taken more than 100 hits from the federal cannon, but remained virtually unscathed. The *Congress*, in a desperate attempt to escape the iron monster, beached herself on Newport News Point, where the *Virginia* bombarded her into a blazing wreck. It was a time of jubilation for the Confederacy, and one of great consternation for the Union. Help, however, was close at hand.

The following morning, the *Virginia* returned to deal the Union steam frigate *Minnesota* a similar fate, when the crew saw a strange craft lying alongside. It was another ironclad, the USS *Monitor*. The world's first battle of ironclads began.

For almost four hours the two great ships ranged up and down Hampton Roads, fighting at close quarters, firing hundreds of rounds from their great guns, all to no avail. By mid-day neither ship had suffered more than superficial damage, and both retired claiming victory.

On April 11, the *Virginia* sallied forth once again, but this time her challenge remained unanswered. The *Monitor* stuck close to shore under the protection of Fort Monroe's seacoast guns. It was to be the last serious outing for the *Virginia*, for on May 11, in an effort to deny the Federals her capture, her crew scuttled her off Craney Island. The *Monitor* fared little better, for she sank some seven months later in heavy seas off Cape Hatteras. Portions of the ship have been recovered and can be seen at the Mariners' Museum in Newport News.

In the wake of the ironclads, came the 1862 Peninsula Campaign. Union Major General George B. McClellan's advance against Richmond was halted by Confederate Major General John Bankhead Magruder.

Following the end of the Civil War, it soon became obvious that the world in general, and the Hampton Roads area in particular, had changed forever. Industry, both in the north and in the south, was booming, and at the forefront, with its deep waters ideally suited to the new ocean-going steamships, was Newport News.

First the railroads came to the area and Newport News was chosen as the Atlantic terminal for a continental rail system that would link the Atlantic to the Pacific. By May 1, 1882, the C&O line had begun regular through-train service from Newport News to the midwest. And with the coming of the railroads, Newport News began to grow and to take on the air of a booming frontier town. Saloons and bordellos catered to the dock workers and stevedores who frequented Hell's Half Acre around 18th Street. Railroad crews and the men who worked at the docks were billeted in dormitories and rail cars.

Shipbuilding had arrived in Newport News when the Chesapeake Dry Dock and Construction Company opened for business in 1886. By 1890 the name had been changed to the Newport News Shipbuilding and Dry Dock Company, and it was well on its way to becoming the largest and most efficient shipyard in the United States.

Together the railroads and the shipyard attracted other business to the area and Newport News became a Mecca for the skilled of the world.

By 1914 and the outbreak of the First World War, the area's population had grown to more than 35,000, and great steel battleships were being built at Newport News.

In 1918, the nation's first federal housing development, Hilton Village, was built for shipyard workers.

The end of the First World War also saw the end of Hell's Half Acre. The C&O finally acquired the land and used it to expand their coal-dumping facilities.

With World War II and the need for carriers and battleships, shipbuilding was again underway in earnest. By 1943 the payroll at the shipyard had grown to more than 31,000, and the population of the area had reached 189,000. As the main Port of Embarkation, 730,000 service men and women said good-bye from Newport News during the four years the United States was involved in the World War II.

By war's end, the city had far outgrown its original boundaries, and in 1958, Newport News and Warwick county merged to become greater Newport News. Old port facilities and downtown buildings were torn down to make way for modern stores and offices. Pier B was completed in the autumn of 1967 and replaced the outmoded port facilities. A new City Hall was built at the south end of Washington Street and completed in 1972. It became the core of a new civic center which embraced the nearby courthouse, the Federal Building, and the new Victory Arch.

Sights

The **Mariners' Museum** introduces visitors to the lore of the sea and man's maritime adventures over the past 3,000 years. Galleries include the new International Small Craft Center, showcasing 75 examples of watercraft from 310 countries, Defending the Seas, Age of Exploration, the Chesapeake Bay, the Crabtree Collection of Miniature Ships and the Great Hall of Steam. Together, they contain the most extensive international collections of objects gathered together by mariners, including paintings, maps, scrimshaw, coins, models, unique watercraft, hand-crafted figureheads, audio-visual displays, a working steam engine and more. The museum's Research Library and its more than 70,000 volumes and 350,000 photographs is open to the public. The museum is open daily, except for Thanksgiving and Christmas Day. The Research Library is open Monday through Saturday. There is also a gift shop. The USS *Monitor* Conservation Center, due to open in 2007, will house the remains of the famous ironclad.

The museum is set in a 550-acre park at the junction of Warwick and J. Clyde Morris boulevards that also features the five-mile Noland Walking Trail; it's three miles south of Interstate 64, Exit 258-A. For more information, ☎ 757-596-2222 or visit www.mariner.org.

Peninsula Fine Arts Center, located in The Mariners' Museum park, brings the finest of the art world to the Peninsula: collections from Virginia and other institutions, combined with national traveling exhibitions and works by exceptional regional artists, supplement the center's permanent collections of paintings, sculpture, prints and drawings, ceramics and photography. The center is open Tuesday-Saturday, 10 a.m.-5 p.m. and for a Thursday night music series in the Arts Café. Admission is charged.

The center is at the junction of Warwick and J. Clyde Morris boulevards, about three miles south of Interstate 64, Exit 258-A. ☎ 757-596-8175 or visit www.pfac-va.org.

Virginia War Museum. Here the fascinating saga of military history unfolds. This museum has more than 50,000 artifacts, including uniforms, posters, documents, photographs, insignia, vehicles, weapons, accouterments, an 1883 brass Gatling Gun, a World Way I Renault Tank, a Civil War blockade runner's uniform, and a wall from the infamous Dachau Concentration Camp. It brings to life and documents America's involvement in wars dating from 1775 to the present. The museum also features a gift shop, educational programs, a military history film collection, and a research library and archive which is available for public use by appointment.

Open Monday through Saturday from 9 a.m. until 5 p.m., and from 1 p.m. until 5 p.m. on Sundays, closed major holidays; admission is charged. The museum is at 9285 Warwick Boulevard in Huntington Park, near the James River Bridge. ☎ 757-247-8523, www.warmuseum.org.

Lee Hall Mansion. This circa-1858 Italianate mansion was the headquarters for two Confederate generals – John Bankhead Magruder and Joseph E. Johnston – during the initial stages of the 1862 Peninsula Campaign. It is one of the few 19th-century plantation houses remaining on the Peninsula. Restored to is former glory, the home features six period rooms and an exhibit on the Peninsula Campaign. It is located at 163 Yorktown Road and is open Monday through Saturday. Open Monday and Wednesday through Saturday, 10 a.m. to 4 p.m.; and Sunday 1 to 5 p.m. Guided tours by costumed interpretors every half hour. Admission charged; closed on major holidays. ☎ 757-888-3371 or visit www.lee-hall.org.

Endview Plantation. This 1760 farmhouse has been used in three wars: As a stopover for the Virginia Militia during the Revolution, as a training ground during the War of 1812, and as a Confederate captain's home and a hospital for both sides during the Civil War. Living history, archeological and restoration projects. Located at 362 Yorktown Road. Open Monday, Wednesday through Saturday from 10 a.m. until 4 p.m., and Sunday from 1 until 5 p.m. Closed Wednesdays, January-March. Admission charged. ☎ 757-887-1862, www.endview.org.

Virginia Living Museum, 524 J. Clyde Morris Boulevard, is a combination wildlife park, science museum, aquarium, botanical preserve, and planetarium. The numerous indoor and outdoor exhibits provide carefully protected natural environments for a variety of plant and animal life designed to let you explore bird, marine, mammal, reptile and insect life native to America's Eastern Shore and Coastal Plain.

A new 62,000-square foot exhibit features two unique two-level walk-through habitats, a 30,000-gallon Chesapeake Bay Aquarium and four exhibit galleries with numerous hands-on activities. The new ¾-mile outdoor boardwalk and Coastal Plain Aviary complete the $22.6 million project.

Summer hours, 9 a.m. to 6 p.m. daily. The rest of the year, hours are Monday through Saturday, 9 a.m. to 5 p.m., and Sunday, noon to 5 p.m. Admission charged. ☎ 757-595-1900 or visit www.valivingmuseum.org.

The **Peninsula SPCA/Petting Zoo** features puppies and kittens, farm animals, llamas and birds. The exotic area has big cats, a kangaroo, otters and alligators. 523 J. Clyde Morris Boulevard. Open Monday through Friday from 10 a.m. until 5 p.m., Saturday from 10 a.m. until 4:30 p.m., and Sunday from noon until 5 p.m. Admission charged. ☎ 757-595-1399, www.peninsulaspca.com.

The US Army Transportation Museum at Fort Eustis has a truck that walks and a ship that flies. Visitors explore the world of motion, from the mighty steam locomotives of yesteryear to the world's only captive flying saucer. Exhibits include the first helicopter to land at the South Pole, a vertical landing and take-off aircraft, the "Flying Crane," the world's largest helicopter, and more than 200 years of army transportation history. Outdoor displays include many of the actual vehicles in use by the army of yesterday, today, and tomorrow. All visitors must show ID to enter the base. The museum is open Tuesday through Sunday from 9 a.m. until 4:30 p.m., and is closed all major holidays; admission free. ☎ 757-878-1115, www.eustis.army.mil. From Williamsburg, take I-64 east to Fort Eustis, Exit 250A.

The Newsome House Museum and Cultural Center, an historic home built in 1899, was the one-time home of Joseph Thomas Newsome, a prominent black attorney. Newsome was the editor of a black newspaper and co-founder of the Newport News Church, and he formed the Colored Voters League of Warwick County. Today, the restored Victorian home is a landmark which continues Newsome's devotion to the expression of black culture and history through changing exhibits by African-American artists. The Center is open Monday and Wednesday through Saturday from 10 a.m. until 4 p.m., and Sunday from 1-5 p.m. Admission free. 2803 Oak Avenue. ☎ 757-247-2360, www.newsomehouse.org.

Victory Arch. Since Hampton Roads was the World War II port of embarkation, returning men and women of the armed forces marched through a wooden arch during their homecoming. Today, the stone arch that replaced it serves as a memorial with an eternal flame for all the men and women who have served their country. Located at 25th Street and West Avenue in downtown Newport News.

Historic Hilton Village is a neighborhood of English cottage-style homes, the nation's first ever federal housing development. Built from

1918 to 1920 for shipyard workers, it is on the National Registry of Historic Places. Many homes are still residences, while those facing Warwick Boulevard now house specialty shops.

Historic North End-Huntington Heights, between Huntington Avenue and Warwick Boulevard, is an early 1920s neighborhood listed on the National Register of Historic Places.

Entertainment

Cozzy's Comedy Club offers live comedy Friday and Saturday, music and karaoke Tuesday through Thursday. 9700 Warwick Boulevard, ☎ 757-595-2800, www.cozzys.com.

The new **Ferguson Center for the Arts** at Christopher Newport University, ☎ 757-594-7448, houses three performing arts spaces: a 460-seat music and theater hall and an intimate 200-seat studio theater, both of which opened in 2004, and a 1,700-seat concert hall, which will open in September 2005.

Peninsula Community Theatre, located in Historic Hilton Village at the corner of Warwick Boulevard and Main Street, hosts concerts, musical, comedies, dramas and children's theater. The box office number is ☎ 757-595-5728, www.peninsulacommunitytheatre.org.

Yoder Barn Heritage Theatre, a restored 1935 dairy barn at 660 Hamilton Drive, hosts Broadway-style shows, concerts and symphonies. ☎ 757-249-4187, www.yoderbarn.com.

Annual Events

The **Battle of Hampton Roads**, first weekend in March at The Mariners' Museum (see page 149), commemorates the historic clash of the the ironclads USS *Monitor* and CSS *Virginia*. 100 Museum Drive, ☎ 757-596-2222, www.mariner.org

The Children's Festival of Friends is entertaining as well as educational for the entire family. The event is held in early May at Newport News Park. ☎ 757-926-1400.

The Annual Fourth of July Party celebrates Independence Day on the Superblock at 26th Street in Downtown Newport News. All sorts of lively entertainment and a fireworks display. ☎ 757-926-1400.

The **Biennial**, held at the Peninsula Fine Arts Center beginning the first week in September, is one of the best established juried shows in the state. ☎ 804-596-8175, www.pfac-va.org.

The Annual Fall Festival of Folklife, more than 25 years in the running, is held in Newport News Park the first weekend in October. It is a weekend of traditional crafts set among the fall foliage in the 8,000-acre park where more than 200 crafts people display and sell their works, many of them creating right before your eyes. ☎ 757-926-1400.

The Virginia Living Museum Art Show and Sale, held in November, is a gathering of East Coast artists to celebrate, demonstrate, display and sell works in a variety of media. The event is sponsored by the Virginia Living Museum. For the location and more information, ☎ 757-595-1900, www.valivingmuseum.org.

Artful Giving, early-November through the first week in January, at the Peninsula Fine Arts Center, is an art show and sale for the holidays. ☎ 757-596-8175, www.pfac-va.org.

The Star of Wonder is an annual holiday presentation by the Planetarium which explores the many theories behind the famous Star of Bethlehem. The event is held from Thanksgiving through January 1 at the Virginia Living Museum. ☎ 757-595-1900, www.valivingmuseum.org.

Celebration in Lights runs from Thanksgiving through January 1. The celebration is a spectacular two-mile tableau of seasonal scenes created with freestanding displays of more than two million lights and enhanced by a rainbow of floodlights. ☎ 757-926-1400.

Annual Holiday Open House, the Newsome House Museum & Cultural Center, the month of December. ☎ 757-247-2360.

Antebellum Holidays at Lee Hall Mansion, throughout December, ☎ 757-888-3371, www.leehall.org.

Christmas at Endview, December, ☎ 757-887-1862, www.endview.org.

Recreation

Fishing

The **James River Fishing Pier**, ☎ 757-247-0364, offers sportsmen and women the chance to "hook the big one," while the **Bay Charter Service**, ☎ 757-930-8768, offers deep-sea fishing trips for striper, menhaden, flounder, croaker, scup and sea trout, into the Chesapeake Bay and beyond from early May through late summer. Bank fishing is also available on the many backwater creeks and streams that abound in and around Newport News.

Parks & Preserves

Huntington Park overlooks the James River and features Fort Fun, a playground for the kids, a sandy beach area, a public boat ramp, a volleyball area, rose garden, a snack bar and covered grills. Located at the James River Bridge on Warwick Boulevard. There is a fishing pier with a seafood restaurant for waterfront dining. ☎ 757-886-7912.

Newport News Park, 13564 Jefferson Avenue, is an 8,100-acre woodland park which offers a wide variety of family fun and outdoor recreation. There are two 18-hole golf courses and a disc-golf course, paddleboating, canoeing, and fishing on a reservoir, archery, picnicking at the sheltered picnic areas, 30 miles of hiking and bike trails, camping, wildlife and bird study programs, a playground and the Nature and Historical Interpretive Center. ☎ 757-886-7912, www.newport-news.va.us/parks.

Newport News Golf Club at Newport News Park is a 36-hole golfing complex encompassing two wooded championship courses. The 6,757-yard Cardinal Course is designed for golfers at all levels of skill, while the 7,000-yard Deer Run Course will test even the most experienced golfer. You will see wildlife of all sorts, shapes and sizes here and the course is listed on the National Audubon Society Register. After a round of golf, you can relax at the Deer Run Club House and Restaurant. ☎ 757-886-7925.

Harwood's Mill, located in the southeast end of Newport News in York County, is a 265-acre reservoir with boat rentals for fishing and fun. There is a network of hiking and bike trails, and a picnic shelter. ☎ 757-886-7912.

Mariners Museum Park is 550 acres of wooded rolling hills, fields, tranquil Lake Maury and the five-mile Noland Trail. Rowboat and canoes rentals and fishing. ☎ 757-596-2222, www.mariner.org.

Shopping

In the **Patrick Henry Mall** area are all sorts of major retail stores and eateries (www.shoppatrickhenrymall.com), and **Hilton Village** has a variety of antique and specialty shops.

The **museum shops** at The Mariners' Museum, Peninsula Fine Arts Center, US Army Transportation Museum, Virginian Living Museum and Virginia War Museum offer one-of-a-kind shopping, from fine art prints to military memorabilia.

Dining

Newport News offers a wide variety of dining options with dozens of restaurants and cafés with varied ethnic and American menus.

99 Main, at 99 Main Street (of course!), ☎ 757-599-9885, excellently serves light, European-influenced meals. Open for dinner Tuesday-Saturday.

As its name suggests, there's outdoor dining at **Al Fresco**, 11710 Jefferson Avenue, ☎ 757-873-0644. The menu is Italian based with vegetarian specials. Open for lunch and dinner; closed Sundays.

Amadeus Café, Spanish Restaurant & Lounge, 13144 Jefferson Avenue, ☎ 757-833-3779, doesn't have much connection to its Austrian composer namesake, but there is live music Friday and Saturday, which along with the food, is Latin. Open for lunch and dinner; closed Monday.

Barclay's, 943 J Clyde Morris Boulevard, ☎ 757-952-1122, is an elegant bistro with chandeliers, upholstered chairs, a double-sided fireplace and the art of namesake Barclay Sheaks, all in a surprising location inside the Hoilday Inn. Open daily for lunch and dinner.

Bill's Seafood House, 10900 Warwick Boulevard, ☎ 757-595-4320, serves up seafood, steak and barbecue in a family atmosphere. No alcohol is served, but other drinks come with unlimited refills. Open for lunch and dinner; closed Sunday.

Blue Cactus Café, 10367 Warwick Boulevard, ☎ 757-596-7372 is a Tex-Mex diner in Hilton Village. Open for lunch and dinner; closed Sunday and Monday.

Blue Star Diner, 9955 Warwick Boulevard, ☎ 757-595-6782, is one of the last real diners, where two people can eat for under $10. The homemade rolls are to die for. Open daily 6 a.m. to 10 p.m.

Boxwood Inn, 10 Elmhurst Street, ☎ 757-888-8854, offers lunch and dinner.

Cities Grille, 605 Pilot House Drive in Oyster Point, ☎ 757-595-6085, is sophisticated and upbeat. Open for lunch and dinner daily.

Cowboy Syd's, 3150 William Styron Square North, ☎ 757-599-5800, in the new Port Warwick section serves American cuisine with Cajun and Creole influences. The wine list is huge (view the glassed-in wine room), with many available by the glass. Open for lunch and dinner daily.

The Crab Shack, ☎ 757-245-2722, is located on a pier jutting out into the James River at the James River Bridge, offering seafood, spectacular water views, and outdoor deck dining (weather permitting).

Danny's Deli Restaurant, 10838 Warwick Boulevard, ☎ 757-595-0252, serves up free dill pickles when you sit down to eat. This alcohol-free, family-oriented place is a favorite among locals. Serves lunch and dinner until 7 p.m.

Can't make up your mind? The dinner special at **El Mariachi Mexican Restaurante**, 660 J. Clyde Morris Boulevard, ☎ 757-596-4933, allows you to sample five different items. Great Margaritas and fried ice cream. Open for lunch and dinner daily.

Kappo Nara, 550 Oyster Point Road, ☎ 757-249-5395, has a full Japanese menu and sushi bar.

At **Nara of Japan Steak and Seafood Restaurant**, 10608 Warwick Boulevard, ☎ 757-595-7399, chefs prepare – or rather perform – the meal right at your tabletop grill, with fancy knife-work and vegetable tossing. Open for dinner nightly.

At **Nawab Indian Cuisine**, 11712 Jefferson Avenue, ☎ 757-591-9200, exotic music, spices and aromas blend for a delightful dining experience. Open for lunch and dinner daily.

Manhattan's N.Y. Deli, 601 Thimble Shoals Boulevard, ☎ 757-873-0555, offers New York-style deli sandwiches and daily hot specials served in a casual atmosphere.

Mitty's Ristorante, in the Omni Hotel, 1000 Omni Boulevard, ☎ 757-873-6664, offers fresh-baked Focaccia bread, views of the open kitchen, and a wood-burning pizza oven.

The Red Maple Inn, 202 Harpersville Road, ☎ 757-596-6333, is located in a converted two-story home and has a contemporary regional menu.

Schlesinger's Chop House, 1106 William Styron Square South, ☎ 757-599-4700, brings fine dining to the new Port Warwick community. In addition to beef, there's veal, seafood and chicken. The service and fare are stupendous, with prices to match. Open for lunch and dinner daily and Sunday brunch.

Schlotsky's Deli, 11831 Jefferson Avenue, ☎ 757-591-8800, serves great sandwiches and other deli foods.

Sushi Yama Japanese Restaurant, 11745-2 Jefferson Avenue, ☎ 757-596-1150, has a tatami room for traditional seating.

At **Tapas Lounge**, 141 Herman Melville Avenue in Port Warwick, ☎ 757-594-9484, the offerings are appetizer-sized, so go crazy and try several from the diverse ethnic menu. Open for lunch and dinner daily except Monday. Stays open until 2 a.m. on weekends and midnight during the week.

Tropical Smoothie Café, 4191 William Styron Square North, ☎ 757-595-0600, serves deli food.

Tuscany Ristorante Italiano, 12638 Jefferson Avenue, ☎ 757-989-0731, in Turnberry Shopping Center serves Italian food for lunch and dinner; closed Sunday.

Accommodations

Hotels & Motels

Comfort Inn, 12330 Jefferson Avenue, ☎ 757-249-0200, 800-368-2477, has 124 guest rooms and a Colonial décor. Pets are allowed, and there is a free continental breakfast, an airport shuttle, and a pool and fitness room. $$

Days Inn Newport News, 14747 Warwick Boulevard, ☎ 757-874-0201. The hotel has 112 guest rooms, cable TV, a swimming pool and a playground. Free coffee is provided in the guest rooms and some rooms have kitchens. There's a coin laundry, restaurant, and a picnic area. $

 Days Inn Oyster Point, 11829 Fishing Point Drive, ☎ 757-873-6700 or 800-873-2369, has 125 guest rooms, a fitness center and an outdoor pool. Visit www.daysinnoysterpt.com. $

Hampton Inn - Victory Boulevard, 151 Ottis Street, ☎ 757-989-8977, 800-426-7866, www.hampton-inn.com, has 80 rooms, an indoor pool and fitness center. $$

Hampton Inn & Suites, 12251 Jefferson Avenue, ☎ 757-249-0001, has 120 guest rooms, 30 of them suites, some with gas-lit fireplaces and kitchens. Pool, fitness center, and coffee-makers in each room. $$

Hilton Garden Inn, 180 Regal Way, ☎ 757-947-1080, has 122 rooms, an indoor pool, spa and fitness center. Each room has refrigerator, microwave, a desk with two phones and free high-speed Internet. There are also larger executive guestrooms and a 24-hour business center. Visit www.hiltongardeninn.com. $$

Holiday Inn Hotel & Suites, 943 J. Clyde Morris Boulevard, ☎ 757-596-6417, is a 122-room hotel with an indoor pool, fitness center, and an excellent on-site restaurant, Barclay's. All rooms have a granite vanity in the bath, coffee maker, safe, high-speed Internet, and two-line phones. Suites have separate living and dining areas, microwave, refrigerator and fax machine. $$

Holiday Inn & Efficiencies Express, 16890 Warwick Boulevard, ☎ 757-887-3300, has 57 guest rooms. Free breakfast, and coffee-makers in the rooms, outdoor pool and fitness canter. $

 Host Inn, 985 J. Clyde Morris Boulevard, ☎ 757-599-3303, 888-599-3303, has 50 guest rooms, a swimming pool, cable TV, free coffee in the lobby. $

The Mulberry Inn, 16890 Warwick Boulevard, ☎ 800-223-0404 or 757-887-3000, www.mulberryinnva.com, has 100 guest rooms, some of them efficiencies, complimentary continental breakfast, coffee-makers in the rooms, outdoor pool, fitness center, and guest laundry. $

Omni Newport News Hotel, 1000 Omni Boulevard, ☎ 757-873-6664, 800-843-6664, has 183 guest rooms, a heated indoor pool, cable TV, and an exercise room, restaurant and lounge. $$

Point Plaza Suites and Conference Hotel is at 950 J. Clyde Morris Boulevard, ☎ 757-599-4460, 800-841-1112, www.newportnewspointplazasuitehotel.com. The hotel has 214 guest rooms, a swimming pool, cable TV, restaurant and bar. $$

Bed & Breakfasts / Inns

The Boxwood Inn, 10 Elmhurst Street in Lee Hall Village, ☎ 757-888-8854, www.boxwood-inn.com, is the former home of Simon Curtis, "bossman" of Warwick County. The inn has four suites and a restaurant, is handicapped-accessible, and serves a full breakfst. No children or pets. $$-$$$

Information

The Newport News Tourism Development Office, 2400 Washington Avenue, Newport News, VA 23606-2998, ☎ 888-493-7386, www.newport-news.org, will send information to potential visitors, and assist with travel plans to the Peninsula. Group tour itineraries are also available.

The Newport News Visitor Center is at Newport News Park, I-64 Exit 250-B. Maps, local and state information, and tickets to attractions are available at the center, which has a gift shop open 9a.m. to 5 p.m. daily. ☎ 757-886-7777 or 888-493-7386.

Transportation

The **Newport News/Williamsburg International Airport** serves Southeastern Virginia with several major airlines. The airport is 15 minutes from downtown Newport News, and 25 minutes from Williamsburg. Ground transportation is available through a variety of taxi and rental car companies. ☎ 757-877-0221, www.nnwairport.com.

The city is served by **Amtrak**, ☎ 800-872-7245, www.amtrak.com, with a station at 9304 Warwick Boulevard, and **Greyhound Lines**, ☎ 800-231-2222, www.greyhound.com.

Norfolk

*I*f you ask a native of Norfolk what the city means to him, he might cock his head to one side, think for a moment, and then tell you it's the toots of the tugboats pushing the barges; the crack of ball against bat at the riverfront baseball stadium; the sound of music at Town Point Park; and the cheers of the waiting crowd as another Navy ship comes home.

The people who live in and around this great city-by-the-sea are proud of their hometown and the magnificent panorama that is Hampton Roads harbor, one of the world's greatest natural harbors. Sailors know it as Mile Marker Zero on the Intracoastal Waterway.

Norfolk began as the most prosperous town in Colonial Virginia and has grown to be one of the leading trading ports on the East Coast. Visitors today find Norfolk a bustling cultural and historical center with a newly revitalized and hip downtown, an international airport and one of the nation's busiest harbors, now a year-round port for cruise ships.

Norfolk is also the location of two of the nation's most important naval and air bases, and is the home port of the United States Atlantic Fleet. Its strategic mid-Atlantic location also makes it the perfect home base for enjoying nearby ocean beaches, amusement parks and rich historical sites like Jamestown, Yorktown and Colonial Williamsburg.

Just across the Elizabeth River, Portsmouth rose to prominence as the nation's shipyard, while Suffolk grew from a Colonial township bordering the Great Dismal Swamp into a sprawling, rural Eden famed for its forests and peanut crops.

Norfolk offers visitors a surprise package of fun, history and cultural attractions. You can take a harbor cruise for a close-up view of a working and recreational waterfront, from industrial shipyards and busy tug boats to sleek yachts. You can sail the harbor on a tall-masted ship, enjoy a relaxing dinner cruise, or tour the sights on a replica of a Mississippi riverboat. And you can see the Navy's powerful fleet with a tour of the Naval Station Norfolk, the world's largest. After all that, you can relax and unwind on more than seven miles of sandy beach right on the Chesapeake Bay.

Norfolk has several fine museums and art galleries, including the world-renowned Chrysler Museum of Art, and NAUTICUS, the National Maritime Center.

Norfolk also boasts its own a symphony orchestra and the Virginia Opera, which is the official opera company of the Commonwealth. Venues for various events and performances include the massive Norfolk Scope arena, the fabulous Harrison Opera House, Wells Theater, and the newly restored Attucks Theatre, and African-American landmark. The city is also the home of Old Dominion and Norfolk State universities, Eastern Virginia Medical School and Virginia Wesleyan College.

Norfolk

History

Greater Norfolk's dramatic history began in 1607 when three ships, the **Discovery**, the **Susan Constant** and the **Godspeed** landed on the southern shores of the Chesapeake Bay at Cape Henry. The ships, under the command of Captain John Smith, took on fresh water and food, then sailed onward up the James River and founded the first permanent English settlement in America, Jamestown.

In 1673, the House of Burgesses authorized a fort on Four Farthing Point (now **Town Point Park**) to protect the harbor from the Dutch, and later from pirates. In 1680, storehouses were built for imported goods and the export of tobacco from the Virginia Colony.

The "Towne of Norfolk" was established in 1682 on land bought with 10,000 pounds of tobacco. In the early days it was a trade center where tar, hides, and lumber were brought in from North Carolina and distributed to all points of the compass. Soon the great natural harbor expanded its activities into the shipbuilding and iron working industries. This led to vigorous trade between the city and Great Britain, as well as the West Indies. By 1775, Norfolk was called the colony's most prosperous city.

Norfolk has seen many setbacks during its long and turbulent past. War ravaged the area from its very beginnings. During the **Revolutionary War**, Lord Dunsmore's bombardment of the city in 1776 led to a fire that virtually destroyed it, displacing most of the populace.

Borough Church (built in 1739), though damaged, was virtually the only structure left standing. Renamed and rebuilt in 1827, **St. Paul's Church** still stands, complete with an English cannonball in its wall. Residents returned to the city, constructing notable homes like the **Moses Myers** and **Willoughy-Baylor** houses, both of which are still standing.

During the War of 1812, **Fort Norfolk** was built on the Elizabeth River to protect the harbor from the British. The war ended with the Treaty of Ghent, a copy of which was brought to Norfolk by Richard Drummond, who renamed his property Ghent, now one of the city's most fashionable and trendy neighborhoods. After its incoporation as a city in 1845, a new city hall was built. The spectacular classical revival building now houses the **MacArthur Memorial**.

The Civil War once again brought turmoil to the city, which was occupied by federal troops for much of the war. But once again, the city recovered and prospered. Railroads opened, and together with the rich farmlands and waterways, the port of Norfolk grew into one of the busiest in the world. In 1907, the city hosted the World's Fair, known as the Jamestown Tercentennial Exposition. Speakers included President Theodore Roosevelt, Mark Twain and Booker T. Washington. Many elaborate buildings were constructed on the fairgrounds. About 17 still stand and are known as "Admirals' Row," housing officers at **Naval Station Norfolk**, the world's largest naval installation.

The 20th century brought great new advances and prosperity to Norfolk. Trade and industry boomed. During the Second World War, the city's population doubled. In 1976, Norfolk's first major waterfront renovation project opened on the banks of the Elizabeth River. The renovation continued on into the 21st century and today the entire waterfront area is an aggregation of upscale attractions, hotels, restaurants and unique shops.

The last decade has witnessed Norfolk's metamorphosis from "old Navy town" to the "New Norfolk." Urban redevelopment has preserved the past while celebrating the present. In 2004, Norfolk received a Virginia Gover-

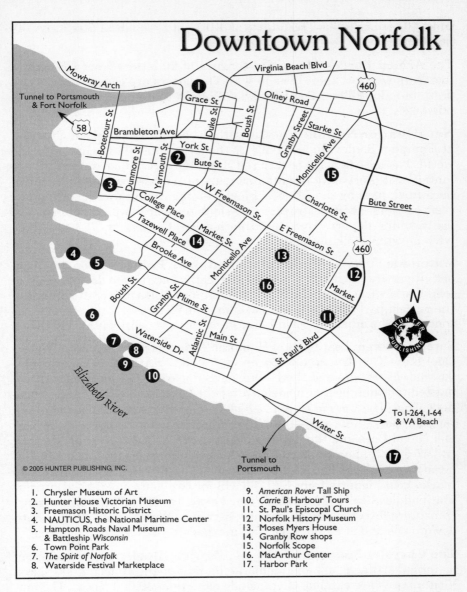

Downtown Norfolk

Virginia Beach Blvd

Mowbray Arch

Tunnel to Portsmouth & Fort Norfolk

58

Grace St

Olney Road

460

Brambleton Ave

Botetourt St

Duke St

Boush St

Granby Street

Starke St

York St

Dunmore St

Yarmouth St

Bute St

Monticello Ave

College Place

W Freemason St

Charlotte St

Bute Street

Tazewell Place

Market St

E Freemason St

460

Brooke Ave

Monticello Ave

Market

Boush St

Granby St

Plume St

Waterside Dr

Atlantic St

Main St

St. Paul's Blvd

Elizabeth River

N

To I-264, I-64 & VA Beach

Water St

Tunnel to Portsmouth

© 2005 HUNTER PUBLISHING, INC.

1. Chrysler Museum of Art
2. Hunter House Victorian Museum
3. Freemason Historic District
4. NAUTICUS, the National Maritime Center
5. Hampton Roads Naval Museum & Battleship *Wisconsin*
6. Town Point Park
7. *The Spirit of Norfolk*
8. Waterside Festival Marketplace
9. *American Rover* Tall Ship
10. *Carrie B* Harbour Tours
11. St. Paul's Episcopal Church
12. Norfolk History Museum
13. Moses Myers House
14. Granby Row shops
15. Norfolk Scope
16. MacArthur Center
17. Harbor Park

nor's Conference Award for promoting itself as an African American destination, and *Money* magazine called Norfolk "The South's #1 Big City." This vibrant cultural and historic city has the unique dining and entertainment offerings to satisfy even the most discriminating visitor.

Sights

The self-guided **Cannonball Trail** is a pedestrian introduction to the city's 400-year history. Granite sidewalk inlays mark the route which links 40 historic sites. Trail starts at 401 East Freemason Street, ☎ 800-368-3097.

The **Armed Forces Memorial** consists of 20 letters from US service members who lost their lives in war. The letters are cast in bronze and scattered along Town Point Park as if blown there by the wind. ☎ 757-664-6620.

Naval Station Norfolk, together with the **Norfolk Naval Air Station**, at Hampton Boulevard and I-564, is the largest naval installation in the world. The base is home port to the ships and aircraft carriers of the Atlantic Fleet. Forty-five minute bus tours of the base, narrated by naval personnel, pass by the Atlantic Fleet training center, awe-inspiring aircraft carriers, swift destroyers and sleek nuclear-powered submarines. Daily tours depart from the Information Center, ☎ 757-444-7955, www.navstanorfolk.navy.mil.

Waterside Festival Marketplace and Town Point Park on the Elizabeth River are the center of tourist and festival activity in downtown Norfolk. Visitors can watch the Navy, merchant and pleasure crafts ply one of the busiest ports on the East Coast, shop at Waterside, catch an outdoor concert at the adjacent Town Point Park, or visit nearby NAUTICUS.

Several different boat tours of Hampton Roads harbor leave from Waterside daily. The *American Rover* (☎ 757-627-SAIL, www.americanrover.com) gives two- and three-hour tours aboard a 149-passenger three-masted topsail schooner modeled after the Chesapeake Bay cargo schooners of old. The *Carrie B* (☎ 757-393-4735, www.carriebcruises.com) is a reproduction Mississippi-style paddlewheeler that gives tours of the Norfolk Naval Base and the nation's oldest drydock. The *Spirit of Norfolk* (☎ 757-627-7771, www.spiritofnorfolk.com), offers elegant lunch and dinner-dance cruises. The *Victory Rover* (757-627-7406, www.navalbasecruises.com) departs from NAUTICUS for two-hour naval base cruises. The paddlewheel *Elizabeth River Ferry*, (☎ 757-222-6100, www.hrtransit.org/ferry) provides service between Norfolk and Portsmouth downtowns and at $1.00 is a great, inexpensive way to see the harbor.

The Chrysler Museum of Art, 245 W. Olney Road, has a collection of historical artifacts, art and memorabilia that spans almost 4,000 years. Visitors can view exhibits that include more than 30,000 pieces. The museum's holdings include a world-renowned Tiffany glass collection, Art Nouveau furniture, pre-Columbian art and collections from Africa, Egypt, Islam, Europe and America. The museum is open Wednesday through Sunday. Admission charged. ☎ 757-664-6200, www.chrysler.org.

The Norfolk Botanical Garden, located on Azalea Garden Road adjacent to Norfolk International Airport, encompasses 155 acres of botanical beauty. The garden boasts one of the largest collections of azaleas, camellias and roses on the East Coast, and 25 theme gardens. Visitors can tour the more than 12 miles of garden walks and pathways on foot or by trackless train, take a canal boat tour and enjoy a delightful culinary experience in the café. The Botanical Garden is open daily year-round. Admission charged. ☎ 757-441-5830, www.norfolkbotanicalgarden.org.

The Virginia Zoological Park, 3500 Granby Street, sits on 53 beautifully landscaped acres on the Lafayette River. It is home to more than 350 animals, from elephants and rhinos, to reptiles and nocturnal species. Two Siberian tigers are among visitors' favorite residents. The Okavango Delta exhibit features exotic African species. ☎ 757-441-2706, www.virginiazoo.org.

The **Hermitage Foundation Museum**, 7637 North Shore Road, is in a Tudor-style riverside mansion built by William and Florence Sloane in 1908. The museum features an outstanding collection of Eastern and Western art, and 12 acres of beautiful grounds open to walkers and picnickers. The museum is open Monday through Saturday. ☎ 757-423-2052, www.hermitagefoundation.org.

St. Paul's Episcopal Church, 201 St. Paul's Boulevard, was the only building to survive the burning of Norfolk in 1776. Even so, the church did not go undamaged. A cannonball fired at the city during Lord Dunsmore's bombardment remains lodged in the southern wall. The church's tree-lined cemetery is dotted with 17th- , 18th- and 19th-century tombstones. The church, which features a fine Tiffany stained-glass window, is still in use. The public is welcome to visit the churchyard any time and may visit the interior of the church Tuesday through Friday. ☎ 757-627-4353.

The **Moses Myers House**, 331 Bank Street, is an excellent example of Federal architecture. The house, built in 1792 by one of America's first millionaires, is now dedicated to interpreting the traditions of early Jewish immigrants. Seventy percent of the current collection of furnishings is original to the first generation of Myers and reflects the French influences prevalent during the period. The house is open Tuesday through Saturday. ☎ 757-441-1546, www.chrysler.org.

The **Hunter House Victorian Museum**, 240 W. Freemason Street, is located on a cobblestone street in Norfolk's historic Freemason neighborhood. The house, built in 1894, once belonged to Dr. J.W. Hunter, Jr. and today displays the Hunter family's Victorian furnishings. These include a nursery of children's playthings and a collection of early 20th-century medical equipment. The house is open April through December, Wednesday through Saturday, and on Sunday afternoons. Admission charged; group tours for 12 or more available year-round. ☎ 757-623-9814, www.hunterhousemuseum.org.

The **Willoughby-Baylor House** is undergoing renovation, and will house the new **Norfolk History Museum**. The elegant Georgian-style home was built in 1794 by William Willoughby on the original plot of land that became the "Towne of Norfolk" in 1682. 601 East Freemason Street, ☎ 757-664-6200, www.chrysler.org.

The **General Douglas MacArthur Memorial**, on City Hall Avenue and Bank Street, is located in the restored former city hall, and is where MacArthur is buried. Eleven galleries contain the memorabilia of his life and military career. There are three other buildings on MacArthur Square: a theater where a film biography is shown, a gift shop and the Library/Archives. The complex is open daily. ☎ 757-441-2965, www.macarthurmemorial.org.

NAUTICUS, The National Maritime Center, on the downtown waterfront, is a spectacular multi-level entertainment and educational attraction dedicated to maritime technology. Through a series of ingenious interactive exhibits, shows and theaters, you can try your hand at such tasks as landing a jet fighter on the deck of an aircraft carrier, loading container cargo, navigating an ocean-going vessel and participating in a very realistic naval combat situation aboard an Aegis class destroyer. NAUTICUS also features films such as *The Living Sea*, shown in stunning 70mm format, the Hampton Roads Naval Museum and the Battleship *Wisconsin* (see below). Open daily in summer, closed Mondays the rest of the year; admission charged. ☎ 800-664-1080, www.nauticus.org.

The **Hampton Roads Naval Museum at NAUTICUS** is officially operated by the US Navy, and highlights the naval battles and events that took place in the Norfolk area, many of which changed US history. From the Battle of Virginia Capes during the American Revolution, through the clash of the first ironclad ships during the Civil War, to World War II and Desert Storm, turning-point battles are illustrated and interpreted through detailed model ships, naval artwork, underwater artifacts and traditional exhibits. For more information, ☎ 757-322-2987, www.hrnm.navy.mil. Open daily, 10 a.m. to 6 p.m. in summer. The rest of the year it's open Tuesday through Saturday 10 a.m. to 5 p.m., and Sunday noon to 5 p.m. Admission is free.

Battleship USS *Wisconsin*, the last and largest battleship built in the US, is berthed next to NAUTICUS at Town Point Park. The deck is open to the public the same hours as the Hampton Roads Naval Museum. Entrance is through the NAUTICUS lobby; admission is free. ☎ 757-322-3108, www.hrnm.navy.mil.

The **Tugboat *Huntington*** is a floating museum docked at NAUTICUS. Built in 1933 by Newport News Shipyard Apprentices, the tugboat helped dock and launch hundreds of aircraft carriers, submarines and passenger liners during its 50-year career. It is restored so visitors can see crew and captain's quarters, galley, wheelhouse, and a massive power plant. There are photographs, exhibits and a video. ☎ 757-627-4TUG, call for hours.

Fort Norfolk, on the banks of the Elizabeth River at 810 Front Street near Ghent, is called one of the best-preserved War of 1812 sites in America. It is the only surviving fort of the 19 that George Washington commissioned to be built in 1794. For more information or to schedule a visit, ☎ 757-625-1720, www.norfolkhistorical.org/fort.

Entertainment

The 1919 **Attucks Theatre**, once the cultural center of the city's vibrant African-American community, reopened in 2004 after an extensive renovation. The grand opening featured the Preservation Hall Jazz Band. The state-of-the-art theater brings concerts, theater, speakers, educational programs, and arts groups. 1010 Church Street, ☎ 757-623-1111.

The **NorVa** brings top-name musical performers to this intimate converted warehouse in Norfolk's hip downtown. The two-level concert hall holds only 1,500 people and features a separatre smoking area. Past performers have included Ringo, Stone Temple Pilots, the Cowboy Junkies and the Neville Brothers. 317 Monticello Avenue, ☎ 757-622-9877, www-.thenorva.com.

Ted Constant Convocation Center opened in 2002 on the campus of Old Dominion University offering athletic and concert events. Hampton Boulevard and Monarch Street, ☎ 757-683-3462, www.constantcenter-.com.

Hurrah Players is a youth theater group at 935 Woodrow Avenue (☎ 757-627-5437, www.hurrahplayers.com), and the **Generic Theatre** on 21st Street brings new and off-beat theater to Ghent (☎ 757-441-2160, www.generictheater.org).

The **TCC Roper Performing Arts Center** originally opened as a movie palace in 1926. The former Loew's State Theater has been lovingly restored by Tidewater Community College and now hosts concerts, ballet and theater. 340 Granby Street. ☎ 757-822-1450, www.tcc.edu/roper.

The **Virginia Opera**, the official opera company of the Commonwealth, stages its productions in the dazzling **Harrison Opera House**, on Boush Street. The company was called by *NBC Nightly News* "... one of the nation's very best regional companies." It has earned international recognition for the American and world premiers of four major operas: *Mary, Queen of Scots; Harriet, the Woman Called Moses; A Christmas Carol*; and *Simon Bolivar*. For information, schedules and tickets, ☎ 757-623-1223, www.vaopera.org.

The Virginia Stage Company (VSC) is the premier fully professional theater in the region, offering dynamic productions in the historic **Wells Theatre** at 110 E. Tazewell Street. Artists from across the country conceive, design and rehearse VSC productions. For information, schedules and tickets, ☎ 757-627-1234, www.vastage.com.

Norfolk

The Virginia Symphony is the oldest such musical group in the Southeast. This nationally acclaimed symphony offers a classical masterworks series, pop series, family series, casual classics and dance series, performing more than 140 concerts each year. Outdoor concerts are scheduled throughout the spring and summer months. Special holiday performances take place in December. For information, schedules and tickets, ☎ 757-892-6366, www.virginiasymphony.org.

The **Norfolk Scope** and **Chrysler Hall** comprise Norfolk's cultural and convention center. Scope's domed arena accommodates as many as 11,300 people for concerts, circuses, ice shows, professional ice hockey matches and other entertainment programs. Its exhibition hall houses conventions, trade shows and various special events. Chrysler Hall, a 2,500-seat luxury theater in the Scope Plaza, serves as a forum for symphonies, ballets, Broadway shows and concert artists. 201 East Brambleton Avenue. For information, schedules and tickets, ☎ 757-664-6464 or 800-736-2000, www.norfolkscope.com.

The Norfolk Admirals provide championship-caliber hockey from October to mid-March. Members of the American Hockey League and affiliated with the Chicago Blackhawks, they play at home in the Scope Convention Center. For information, schedules and tickets, ☎ 757-640-1212, www.norfolkadmirals.com.

The Norfolk Tides is the top farm team for the New York Mets. The Tides provide economical, family-oriented entertainment from May to September in Norfolk's waterfront stadium, Harbor Park. The Tides are members of the AAA International League. For information, schedules and tickets, ☎ 757-622-2222, www.norfolktides.com.

Events

Stockley Gardens Arts Festivals take place in spring and fall in Ghent. Fairfax Avenue, ☎ 757-625-6161.

The **Virginia Arts Festival** is a month-long festival held from late April to late May in locations throughout Hampton Roads, and showcasing world-class art and performances by regional artists and from around the world. The festival has gained a national reputation for drawing renowned artists in music, dance and theater. The signature event is a performance by the Virginia International Tatoo. ☎ 757-282-2800 or visit www.virginiaartsfest.com.

The International Azalea Festival in late April celebrates Norfolk's role as headquarters of the North Atlantic Treaty Organization's (NATO) Supreme Allied Commander Atlantic. The festival features a grand parade through downtown Norfolk, an air show, music and arts, and the Azalea Queen's coronation amid the beauty of the Norfolk Botanical Garden. ☎ 757-282-2801, www.azaleafestival.org.

The **Afr'am Festival** draws more than 200,000 people to downtown Norfolk on Memorial Day weekend for a celebration of cultural diversity. African-American art, food and entertainment, sponsored by the Southeastern Virginia Arts Association. ☎ 757-216-7518, www.sevaa.org.

Harborfest began in 1976 and has grown steadily in popularity ever since. Today, hundreds of thousands of people attend this annual three-day waterfront celebration held in June at the downtown Waterfront and Town Point Park. The celebration features fireworks, nationally known entertainers, the best in Chesapeake seafood, sailboat races and a visit by tall sailing ships from around the world. ☎ 757-441-2345, www.festeventsva.org.

Town Point Festivals are held throughout the summer season at Town Point Park. The weekend-long celebrations of food and music include the Bayou Boogaloo in June, Norfolk Jazz Festival in July, the Children's Festival in September, and the Virginia Wine Festival in October. ☎ 575-441-2345, www.festeventsva.org.

The Great American Picnic & Independence Day Celebration takes place each July 4 at Town Point Park. It features old-fashioned games, live music, great food, and fireworks over the Elizabeth River. ☎ 757-441-2345, www.festeventsva.org.

Norfolk Botanical Garden is illuminated Thanksgiving through New Year's Eve, presenting the Garden of Lights, a 2.5-mile driving route. ☎ 757-441-5830, www.nbgs.org.

Holidays in the City celebrates Thanksgiving, Christmas, Hanukkah, Kwanzaa and New Year's Eve in both Norfolk and across the river in Portsmouth. Downtown skyscrapers are decorated with nearly 10 miles of white lights. The glittering profiles of the buildings are visible from many miles away. The six-week celebration, which begins in November, includes the Grand Illumination Parade, the Lighted Boat Parade, the Olde Towne Music Festival, trolley tours of the bedecked downtown area and decorated ships at the Norfolk Naval Base. ☎ 757-623-1757, www-.downtownnorfolk.org.

Norfolk

Shopping

The **MacArthur Center** (300 Monticello Avenue, www.shopmacarthur-.com) is the showplace of downtown Norfolk's shopping district. The city gambled on this downtown gem – and won. Nordstrom and Dillard's anchor the three-story, 17-acre complex, helping draw thousands of visitors to the city. The 150 shops inside run the gamut, from cosmetics to hip West Coast-influenced clothing and trendy eateries.

Military Circle Mall (880 North Military Circle) has the major department stores like Leggett, Hecht's and JC Penney, as well as the Cinemark Military Circle, an 18-theater cinema.

The **Waterside Festival Marketplace** (333 Waterside Drive, www.watersidemarketplace.com) offers a unique shopping experience on the Elizabeth River, with shops, restaurants and nightclubs.

Shops in the **Ghent** historic district feature everything from antiques to gifts, and from clothing to kitchenware. The Ghent Market and Antique Center on Granby Street features 100 dealers on one block.

Recreation

Boating & Sailing

The Chesapeake Bay, Elizabeth River and Lafayette River provide ample recreational opportunities for motorboat and sailboat enthusiasts alike. The marina at **The Waterside**, at Mile Marker Zero on the Intracoastal Waterway, is a popular stop for boating enthusiasts.

Fishing & Crabbing

The Chesapeake Bay, Elizabeth River and Lafayette River also provide great opportunities for fishing and crabbing. Blue crabs, croaker, spot fish, bluefish, sea trout and many other species of fish can be caught from piers, head boats and bay beaches. Fishing piers, charter fishing, and head boats are available in Ocean View and Willoughby Bay.

Golf

Public golf courses include: **Lake Wright Golf Course** on Northampton Road, ☎ 757-459-2255, and the **Ocean View Golf Course** on Norfolk Avenue, ☎ 757-480-2094.

Swimming

Norfolk's Ocean View beaches on the **Chesapeake Bay** provide miles of sand and gentle surf. There are lifeguards, picnic shelters and fishing piers.

Dining

The Greater Norfolk rea has long been famous for its fresh seafood, including flounder, crab, scallops and oysters, but lately there's been an explosion of eclectic restaurants. Dozens of fine restaurants, some with wonderful waterfront views, offer everything from delicate French entrées and spicy ethnic fare to the regional and local specialties. The Ghent neighborhood has long been the in-place to eat and be seen in Norfolk, but now Granby Street's restaurant row is just as popular.

4-5-6 Fish – the name says it all. Located at 456 Granby Street, seafood is the specialty. The elegant interior features lots of mahagony and a glass-enclosed waterfall (☎ 757-625-4444).

Amalfi Ristorante features outdoor dining in fashionable Ghent, an Italian market, espresso bar, and vegan dishes to round out the Italian menu. 2010 Colley Avenue, ☎ 757-625-1262.

Aroma Café & Grill is in yet another great old resurrected building on Granby Street with soaring ceilings, marble floors and lots of warm wood tones. While the menu is American, Aroma has the feel of a European bistro, with a long bar and sidewalk tables. 233 Granby Street, ☎ 757-625-4888.

Azar's Natural Foods Market & Café offers delicious and authentic Mediterranean and Middle Eastern fare with friendly service in Ghent. 2000 Colley Avenue, ☎ 757-664-7955, www.azarfoods.com.

Located behind the NorVa theater, **Backstage Café** is a popular place to go before or after a show. The theme is rock and roll, with a light, pub menu. Open late. 312 Granby Street, ☎ 757-622-5915.

Baker's Crust, 330 W. 21st Street in Ghent, ☎ 757-625-3600, serves European breads, eclectic pasta and fish dishes. Finish an evening on the town with an excellent dessert and cappuccino, or stop by the crêpe bar. Open for lunch and dinner daily.

Bangkok Garden serves authentic Thai food from Pad Thai to Drunken Noodles. 339 West 21st Street in Ghent, ☎ 757-622-5047, www.bangkok-garden.com.

Bardo Edibles & Elixirs has a Zen theme and the deécor is very Feng Shui. The fun menu includes offerings like Buddha Buns, Sushi of the Moment and Pomegranite martinis. 430 W. 21st Street in Ghent, ☎ 757-622-7362.

The Blue Hippo, 147 Granby Street, ☎ 757-533-9664, is small but sophisticated, serving up an imaginative menu and nightly specials. It is open for lunch Monday through Friday, dinner Monday through Saturday, and Sunday brunch.

Bodega is a lively tapas bar with a Mediterranean atmosphere and menu. 442 Granby Street, ☎ 757-622-8527.

Café Nordstrom is a great place for lunch or light supper after shopping in MacArthur Center. ☎ 757-314-1111.

Castaldi's Market & Grill, in the spectacular new MacArthur Center, serves an Italian menu for lunch and dinner daily. ☎ 757-627-8700.

Charlie's Café is an all-American diner, a popular breakfast spot that makes great omelettes. Open daily, 7 a.m. to 3 p.m. 1800-A Granby Street, ☎ 757-625-0824.

Norfolk

Club Soda's stylish and sexy atmosphere is something you'd expect in Manhattan. It has an innovative menu and cocktail list. 111 Tazewell Street, ☎ 757-200-SODA.

Cobia Grille offers seafood with a New American flair. 117 W. Tazewell Street, ☎ 757-640-8000.

Doumar's at 20th Street and Monticello Avenue, ☎ 757-627-4163, is an attraction in itself, a drive-in with car service. The menu features barbecue, burgers and ice cream.

Fellini's is a popular gathering spot for gourmet pizza and homemade pasta. 40th and Colley Avenue, ☎ 757-625-3000.

Freemason Abby, 209 West Freemason Street, ☎ 757-622-3966, offers a traditional American menu in a very non-traditional setting, a 19th-century church. Open for lunch and dinner daily.

Havana American Café serves up Cuban and other Spanish dishes in a lively atmosphere with a vibrant nightlife. 255 Granby Street, ☎ 757-627-5800.

Kincaid's Fish, Chop & Steak House at 300 Monticello Avenue in MacArthur Center, ☎ 757-622-8000, is an up-scale chain that specializes in grilled meat and seafood and has an extensive menu. There is a lighter menu for the lounge and a large imported beer selection. Open daily for lunch and dinner.

At **Kotobuki Japanese Restaurant and Sushi Bar** the shoes come off when you sit down to eat at the sunken tables. 721 W. 21st Street, ☎ 757-628-1025.

La Galleria Ristorante, 120 College Place, ☎ 757-623-3939, offers a Northern Italian menu with a wood-burning pizza oven and breads and sauces for retail sale. There is an exciting piano lounge and excellent desserts. Open for lunch and dinner.

Magnolia Steak serves it creatively and in large portions. 749 W. Princess Anne Road, ☎ 757-625-0400.

The Monastery, 443 Granby Street, ☎ 757-625-8193, offers a Czech and east European menu, and the specialties of the house include delicious breads, roast duck, steak tartare, Wienerschnitzel and goulash. The décor features antique mirrors and original works by local artists. Open for lunch and dinner.

New Belmont features fine American dining downstairs, and an upstairs pub that attracts nightlife for live music. 2117 Colonial Avenue, ☎ 757-623-4477.

No Frill Grill serves up burgers, ribs and chicken. There's an outside patio and nightly specials. 806 Spotswood Avenue, ☎ 757-627-4262.

Housed in a pair of brightly-painted Victorian beauties, **The Painted Lady** serves steak and seafood, and afternoon tea. 112 E. 17th Street, ☎ 757-623-8872, www.thepaintedlady.com.

Rajput Indian Cuisine offers authentic dishes for lunch, dinner and an all-day Sunday buffet. 742 E. 21st Street, ☎ 757-625-4634.

Rom Thai, 7512 Granby Street, ☎ 757-480-7900, serves great Thai food. Vegetarians will find plenty of choices. It is open for lunch Monday through Friday, and dinner nightly. Thai dancing on some weekends.

The menu at **Scotty Quixx** blends gourmet burgers with sophisticated entrées like quail Santorini. 436 Granby Street, ☎ 757-625-0008.

Todd Jurich's Bistro, 150 Main Street, ☎ 757-622-3210, serves adventurous dishes along with light and healthy fare. There's an extensive wine list.

The 219, appropriately located at 219 Granby Street, serves lunch and dinner. The food at the atmosphere are eclectic and the large windows look out onto the busy street, ☎ 757-627-2896, www.the219.com.

Uncle Louie's, 132 East Little Creek Road, ☎ 757-480-1225, has a full-service deli up front, and a sophisticated art-deco restaurant in the rear.

Wild Monkey, 1603 Colley Avenue, ☎ 757-627-6462, is a fun eatery in Norfolk's historic Ghent district where the no-frills menu is written on the walls. It is open for lunch and dinner Monday through Saturday, and Sunday brunch.

Accommodations

Hotels & Motels

Best Western Center Inn has 152 guest rooms, newly renovated, an indoor pool and Olympic-sized outdoor pool, a restuarants serving award-winning steak, and seven lodges in a shady, country club setting. 235 North Military Highway, ☎ 757-461-6600, www.bestwestern.com. $$

Comfort Inn-Naval Station Norfolk, 8051 Hampton Boulevard, ☎ 757-451-0000, has 120 rooms, a swimming pool, and free continental breakfast. $$

Courtyard by Marriott is a new facility in the center of downtown, designed for the business traveler. The large rooms have work desks, free high-speed Internet and voicemail. There is an indoor swimming pool, hot tub and exercise room. Special rates for extended stay available. 520 Plume Street, ☎ 757-963-6000, www.marriott.com. $$$

 Days Inn Marina has 116 rooms all overlooking the Chesapeake Bay, a marina with sail and fishing boats, picnic area,

Olympic-sized pool, and private sandy beach. The Fisherman's Wharf Retaurant is next door. 1631 Bayville Street, ☎ 757-583-4521, 800-329-7466, www.daysinn.com. $$

 Days Inn, Military Circle has 161 guest rooms, a restaurant, outdoor pool and guest laundry. 5701 Chambers Street, ☎ 757-461-0100, 800-DAYS-INN, www.daysinn.com. $

DoubleTree Hotel Norfolk Airport, 880 N. Military Highway adjacent to Military Circle Mall, ☎ 757-461-9192, www.doubletreehotels.com, has 200 rooms, a full-service restaurant, a pool, meeting rooms, business center and fitness center. $$$

Econo Lodge Military Circle accommodates pets under 20 pounds and is convenient to the airport, restaurants and Military Circle Mall. 865 North Military Highway, ☎ 757-461-4865, 800-424-4777, www.choice-hotels.com. $

Econo Lodge, East Ocean View is just yards from the Chesapeake Bay beach. 1111 East Ocean View Avenue, ☎ 757-480-1111, 800-360-3529. $

Econo Lodge-West Ocean View, 9601 4th View Street, ☎ 757-480-9611, 800-768-5425, is a small motel close to the Chesapeake Bay. $$

Hampton Inn-Naval Station Norfolk, 8501 Hampton Boulevard, ☎ 757-583-2621 or 800-426-7866, has 119 rooms, 28 of them efficiencies. There is a heated indoor pool. $$

Hilton Norfolk Airport, 1500 North Military Highway, ☎ 757-466-8000 or 800-422-8000, www.norfolkhilton.com, is a large hotel with 249 rooms and striking modern architecture. There are three restaurants, gift shop, beauty salon, a bar, a café, coffee-makers in the rooms, high-speed Internet, a pool with poolside service, two tennis courts, entertainment and dancing, meeting rooms, a grand ballroom, an exercise room, sauna and airport transportation. $$

Holiday Inn Select Airport has 147 large rooms and suites with refrigerator, microwave, coffee maker, two-line phones and high-speed Internet. There is a restaurant with a veranda, business center, recreation center with pool and whirlpool. Located at Lake Wright Executive Center, 1570 North Military Highway, ☎ 757-213-2231, www.ltdmanagement.com/portfolio.htm. $$

Best Western Holiday Sands, 1330 East Ocean View Avenue, ☎ 757-583-2621 or 800-525-5156, www.holidaysands.com, is on seven miles of beach on the Chesapeake Bay. There are 96 rooms, with efficiencies and two-room apartments offered. There is a swimming pool, fitness room, airport shuttle, free high-speed Internet access and continental breakfast. $$

 Clarion Hotel James Madison, Granby and Freemason Streets, ☎ 757-622-6682, www.clarionhotel.com, is an updated historic downtown boutique-style hotel with 124 rooms, a full-service restaurant, ballroom, and health club. $$$

Norfolk Marriott Waterside Hotel, 235 E. Main Street, ☎ 757-627-4200 or 800-228-9290, is a 23-story luxury hotel overlooking the waterfront with 405 rooms. There is garage parking, a full-service restaurant, an indoor pool with poolside service, health club, entertainment, meeting rooms, an exercise room, a gift shop, airport transportation and continental breakfast. $$$

Quality Suites & Sleep Inn Lake Wright, 6280 Northampton Boulevard, ☎ 757-461-6251 or ☎ 800-228-5157, www.lakewrighthotel.com, is two hotels. There are a full-service restaurant, free coffee in the rooms, a pool, meeting rooms, and free airport transportation. Other facilities include a beauty shop, tennis courts and the adjacent Lake Wright Golf Course, which is operated by the city of Norfolk. $$

Radisson Hotel Norfolk is in the heart of the city's culture, across the street from Norfolk Scope and Chrysler Hall. Broadway show packages available (www.broadwaypackage.com) 700 Monticello Avenue, ☎ 757-627-5555, 800-333-3333, www.radisson.com/norfolkva. $$

Ramada Limited is at Ocean View Beach, adjacent to golfing and public beaches. 719 East Ocean View Avenue, ☎ 757-583-5211, 800-734-0208, www.ramada.com. $

Ramada Limited Norfolk has an outdoor pool and is adjacent to Military Circle Mall. 515 North Military Highway, ☎ 757-461-1880, 800-272-6232, http://www.ramadamilitarymallnorfolk.com. $

Sheraton Norfolk Waterside Hotel, 777 Waterside Drive, ☎ 757-622-6664 or 800-325-3535, www.sheraton.com/norfolk, is a large, luxury hotel on the Norfolk waterfront with 446 guest rooms, including 20 suites with balconies and river views. Garage parking, two restaurants, outdoor swimming pool, entertainment and dancing, meeting rooms and a health club. $$$

Tazewell Hotel & Suites, 245 Granby Street, ☎ 757-498-1000 or toll-free 877-623-6200, www.thetazewell.com, is a century-old hotel with a $7 million facelift. There are 60 studio and two-room suites, all with microwave, refrigerator, coffee-makers, VCR and CD players. There is a business center, fitness room, three adjacent restaurants, and a martini bar in the lobby. Full breakfast buffet. $$$

Tides Inn has 105 rooms, large efficiencies with full kitchen, an outdoor pool, and is two blocks from Little Creek Amphibious Base. 7950 Shore Drive, ☎ 757-587-8781, 800-480-6071, www.tidesinnbythebay.com. $

Bed & Breakfasts / Inns

Freemason Inn is a recently renovated Victorian home in the historic Freemason District. The four rooms, including one honeymoon suite, are decorated in an elegant English style. All have gas fireplaces, poster beds and Jacuzzis. Fine linens and bath products, terry robes and slippers are provided. Breakfast is a three-course, gourmet, candlelight affair. No pets; children over 12 only. Smoking is allowed in the courtyard only. 411 West York Street, ☎ 757-963-7000, 866-388-1897, www.freemason.com. $$$

The Page House Inn, 323 Fairfax Avenue, ☎ 757-625-5033, 800-599-7659, www.pagehouseinn.com, is a bed and breakfast in a Georgian Revival mansion in the historic Ghent district of the city. Four large rooms and three suites, some with whirlpools, all non-smoking. Gourmet breakfast served. Near the Chrysler Museum of Art. $$$

Day-trip to Smithfield & Isle of Wight County

As you approach Smithfield on Rte. 10, where the highway crosses the Pagan River, keep a sharp lookout for a white iron historical marker. Closer inspection reveals its defiant message, declaring this the "one Southern town that refused to surrender" during the Civil War.

Keep going and a real treat awaits: a Southern town that is nothing but welcoming.

A half-hour drive from the urban centers of Hampton Roads, Smithfield and Isle of Wight County rise upon the bluffs of the James and Pagan rivers. Here, small river towns still welcome fishing boats, as they have for centuries. Inland, farmlands stretch to the horizon, miles-upon-miles of peanuts, corn and soybeans.

Smithfield is the commercial and political center of the county. Arthur Smith IV founded the city in 1750 on the Pagan River, where it formed a natural basin deep enough for ships to moor. Smithfield soon thrived as a trading center. Its prosperous years remain on display amid the fine homes lining **Church Street** or tucked along riverside neighborhoods: Homes decked with scalloped eaves, turrets, stained glass windows, rambling porches and arching windows with views of marshes stretching out to the James.

Downtown Smithfield has recaptured some of that historical atmosphere with old-fashioned street lamps, brick pavers and neatly trimmed storefronts. It's a nice setting for a stroll and Smithfield promotes a self-guided **Historic Walking Tour** as the best way to see and learn about its past.

Out into the countryside, inspiring little surprises await the visitor willing to take an unbidden turn. **Rescue** and **Battery Park** are small communities where boatloads of oysters and fish once passed through the local custom house and wharves.

For a real sense of history, visit **Fort Boykin**. Built in 1623, it witnessed action during the Revolutionary War and the War of 1812. Today, it is a park. **St. Luke's Church**, in Benns Church near the intersection of Routes 10 and 258, is the oldest church of brick foundation in the United States. It was built in 1632.

And finally, south of Smithfield, past farm towns like Foursquare and Bethel Church, stands **Boykins Tavern**. This vintage 1762 inn sums up the spirit of Smithfield and Isle of Wight. A fundraising effort by private citizens raised almost $1 million needed to restore its stately two-tier porch, columns, brickwork, wood floors and furnishings.

It seems the town that "refused to surrender" is equally stubborn about not letting its history, or its charm, slip away.

For a unique dining experience, try **Smithfield Station Waterfront Inn, Restaurant & Marina**, which resembles a lighthouse on the Pagan River (☎ 757-357-7700). Top it off at the old-fashioned **Smithfield Ice Cream Parlor** (☎ 757-357-6166). Washington really did dine at **The Smithfield Inn**, where the menu features regional fare and there are five one-bedroom suites to stay in (☎ 757-357-1752, www.smithfield-inn.com). **The Mansion on Main** is an 1889 Victorian in the historic district with four guestrooms and a tea room (☎ 757-357-0006, www.mansion-on-main.net).

For more information about visiting Smithfield and Isle of Wight County, contact the **Isle of Wight Tourism Bureau**, PO Box 37, Smithfield, VA 23431, ☎ 800-365-9339, www.smithfield-virginia.com. There is a **visitors center** at 335 Main Street in Smithfield, ☎ 757-357-5182, and a **museum** at 103 Main Street in Smithfield, ☎ 757-357-7459.

Transportation

Norfolk International Airport (☎ 757-857-3351, www.norfolkairport.com) recently underwent a massive expansion. The airport is seven miles from downtown Norfolk, and is served by several major and several regional carriers with more than 200 flights daily. Call individual carriers for information. Ground transportation is available through a variety of taxi and rental car companies.

Hampton Roads Transit (HRT) offers public transportation by bus and by ferry, as well as sightseeing tours by bus and trolley of downtown Norfolk, Norfolk Naval Base, Olde Towne Portsmouth and Oceana Naval Air Station. Tours depart from Norfolk's Waterside, Portsmouth Visitors Center, the Virginia Beach Oceanfront and the Naval Base. Tours of the world's largest Naval installation have an official Navy guide on board.

Norfolk

Schedules are available at visitors centers, by calling ☎ 757-222-6100 or visiting www.hrtransit.org.

Gray Line Tours, ☎ 757-853-6480. Norfolk is the hub for tours of the city's historic districts and museums, and for day trips to nearby cities, Colonial Williamsburg and Busch Gardens.

The area is served by **Amtrak**, ☎ 800-872-7245, www.amtrak.com, with service to major cities on the East Coast, and by **Greyhound Lines**, ☎ 800-231-2222, with a terminal at 701 Monticello Avenue.

Norfolk is connected to Interstate 95 at Richmond via Interstate 64, thus providing a link with Florida and the south. It connects to the Eastern Shore via Route 13 and the Chesapeake Bay Bridge-Tunnel. Norfolk has the only permanent customs facility between Washington DC and Atlanta, Georgia.

❖   *The Atlantic Intracoastal Waterway officially begins in the Norfolk Harbor.*

Information

The Norfolk Convention and Visitors Bureau is at 232 E. Main Street, Norfolk VA 23510, ☎ 757-664-6620 or toll-free 800-368-3097.

The Norfolk Visitor Information Center is on 4th View Street in Ocean View, off Interstate 64, Exit 237, ☎ 757-441-1852 or 800-368-3097.

Portsmouth

*P*ortsmouth is a historic seaport town on the Elizabeth River, the world's deepest natural harbor. The city is 29 square miles in size and is located within the Norfolk-Virginia Beach Metropolitan Area. Portsmouth is bordered by five neighboring cities that comprise a region referred to as **Southside Hampton Roads**.

Whether on land or on the water, cultural and recreational opportunities abound in and around Portsmouth. The area boasts several museums, including the Children's Museum of Virginia, and a waterfront pavilion drawing the best in entertainers. Opportunities for fishing, swimming, boating and sailing can be found on the multitude of rivers surrounding the city on nearly all sides.

History

Once again it was the erstwhile Captain John Smith who first surveyed the Portsmouth area during his epic voyage of 1608. In 1620, Englishman John Wood petitioned King James for a land grant upon which to build a shipbuilding site, and the site was patented on June 15, 1659, by William Carver. Carver, a patriot in Bacon's Rebellion, was hanged for treason in 1676.

Portsmouth itself was established on February 27, 1752 by an act of the General Assembly, and named for Portsmouth, England, by its founder Colonel William Crawford. The Gosport shipyard, adjoining Portsmouth, was established on November 1, 1767 by Andrew Sprowle.

The Revolutionary War saw Lord Dunsmore, the last Royal Governor of Virginia, driven from Williamsburg into refuge with Sprowle in Gosport. They were finally driven from the harbor in 1776 when Portsmouth was occupied by the 4th Virginia Regiment and Fort Nelson was built at Hospital Point.

In 1779, an English fleet under the command of Sir George Collier invaded Portsmouth, captured Fort Nelson and burned 137 vessels as well as the Gosport Shipyard. By 1780, the city had been fortified and garrisoned by General Leslie with 3,000 English soldiers and 60 ships.

General Lord Cornwallis assumed command of the troops in Portsmouth and in August, 1781 evacuated the city for Yorktown where he surrendered on October 19, thus bringing the war to an end.

Unfortunately, war came again to Portsmouth when the city and Navy Yard were attacked by the British under Admiral Sir John Warren during the War of 1812, and again by Union forces in 1862 during the Civil War. Confederate forces burned Portsmouth and the Navy Yard when they abandoned it to Federal forces on May 10,1862, thus beginning eight years of Union occupation.

With the end of the Civil War, Portsmouth's economy slowly began to get back on its feet. By the beginning of the First World War in 1914 the Navy Yard was undergoing expansion; by the end of the war three new dry docks and 24 ships were built.

By 1940, the Naval Shipyard had doubled in size and peak employment of 42,000 had been reached. During the war years the yards produced some 101 new ships. The end of the Cold War and military downsizing have reduced employment at the shipyard and sent Portsmouth leaders on a mission to redefine the city.

Today, Portsmouth is a bustling port city with a population of about 100,000. It has a strong African-American community making up about 51% of the population. The city's waterfront along the Elizabeth River hosts festivals and concerts from April through October. A ferry terminal

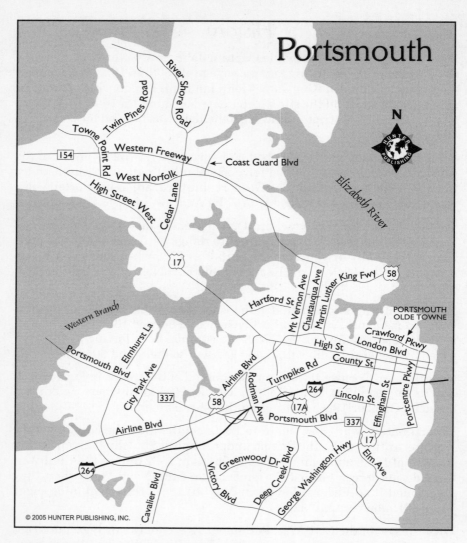

Portsmouth

River Shore Road
Twin Pines Road
Towne Point Rd
Western Freeway
154
West Norfolk
← Coast Guard Blvd
High Street West
Cedar Lane
Elizabeth River
17
N
HUNTER PUBLISHING
Hartford St
Mt Vernon Ave
Chautauqua Ave
Martin Luther King Fwy
58
PORTSMOUTH OLDE TOWNE
Crawford Pkwy
London Blvd
Western Branch
Elmhurst La
Portsmouth Blvd
City Park Ave
High St
County St
Turnpike Rd
Airline Blvd
Rodman Ave
264
Lincoln St
Effingham St
Portcentre Pkwy
337
58
17A
Portsmouth Blvd
337
Airline Blvd
17
Greenwood Dr
Deep Creek Blvd
George Washington Hwy
Elm Ave
Victory Blvd
264
Cavalier Blvd
© 2005 HUNTER PUBLISHING, INC.

at High Street Landing makes it even easier to get to Norfolk's downtown waterfront, just a few minutes away. A major hotel and conference center graces the waterfront and High Street is an antiquing mecca.

The area is steeped in more than 300 years of history. Portsmouth itself has five historic districts with a rich diversity of architectural styles, and an Olde Towne that resembles the city's English namesake. The harbor, one of the oldest working facilities of its kind in the country, is a place where you can spend hours watching the ships come and go, take a relaxing harbor cruise, or watch the sunset.

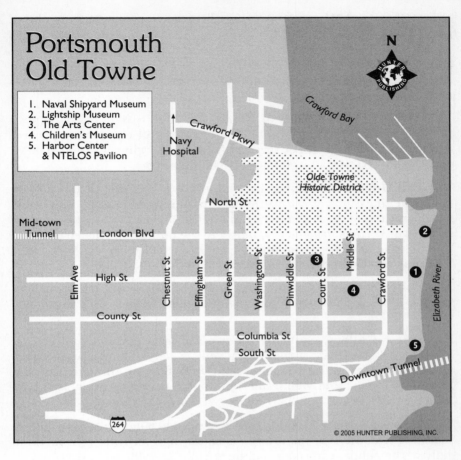

Portsmouth Old Towne

1. Naval Shipyard Museum
2. Lightship Museum
3. The Arts Center
4. Children's Museum
5. Harbor Center
   & NTELOS Pavilion

Crawford Bay

Crawford Pkwy

Navy Hospital

Olde Towne Historic District

North St

Mid-town Tunnel

London Blvd

Elm Ave

High St

Chestnut St

Effingham St

Green St

Washington St

Dinwiddle St

Court St

Middle St

Crawford St

Elizabeth River

County St

Columbia St

South St

Downtown Tunnel

264

© 2005 HUNTER PUBLISHING, INC.

Sights

The Courthouse Galleries, in the 1846 Courthouse at Court and High streets, features the works of international and regional artists. Open daily in summer, closed Monday the rest of the year. ☎ 757-393-8543, www.courthousegalleries.com.

The Children's Museum of Virginia, 221 High Street, has 80 interactive exhibits including a rock climb, bubble room, art moves, planetarium and other galleries. The second floor houses the magnificent Lancaster train exhibit. Admission charged. Open daily in summer, closed Monday the rest of the year. ☎ 757-393-5258, www.childrensmuseum.com.

The Lightship Museum, at the foot of London Boulevard, is an authentic restored 1915 lightship and National Historic Landmark. See how the men of the Lightship Service lived during their many months at sea on this lightship-turned-museum. Open daily in summer, closed Monday the rest of the year. ☎ 757-393-8741, www.portsnavalmuseums.com.

Portsmouth

Naval Shipyard Museum, at 2 High Street on the waterfront, is a log of naval history dating back to the 1700s. Exhibits include model ships and memorabilia from the nation's oldest shipyard, along with more that portray the lifestyle of 18th- and 19th-century Portsmouth. Open daily in summer, closed Monday the rest of the year. ☎ 757-393-8591, www.portsnavalmuseums.com.

The Virginia Sports Hall of Fame, 420 High Street, offers inspirational displays depicting Virginia's best athletes. It also honors those of outstanding achievement or service to sports in Virginia. Closed Monday. ☎ 757-393-8031, www.virginiasportshalloffame.com.

The Hill House, Olde Towne Portsmouth, is a four-story English basement dwelling containing the original furnishings and antiques collected by generations of the Hill family. Built in the 1800s, it is the only home of its kind in Portsmouth open regularly to the public. The house is at 221 North Street and is open for tours April through October, on Wednesday, Saturday and Sunday from 1 until 5 p.m. ☎ 757-393-0241.

The Pokey Smoky is a small-scale replica of a 19th-century steam locomotive; it takes passengers on a ride through Portsmouth's City Park. ☎ 757-465-2937.

Riverview Gallery, featuring the work of local and national artists, offers an artistic feast for the eyes, a wide variety of handcrafted items, affordable prices and a friendly staff. Open Sunday through Tuesday, 11 a.m. to 5 p.m., and Wednesday through Saturday, 11 a.m. to 8 p.m. 1 High Street. ☎ 757-397-3207, www.riverviewgallery.com.

Visual Arts Center – TCC at Olde Towne, 340 High Street, is a gallery space for Tidewater Community College's high-tech art school. Open daily to the public; admission is free. ☎ 757-822-6999, www.tcc.edu.

The Olde Towne Walking Tour lasts about an hour and takes in 45 historic sights and places of interest. Pick up your map and tour itinerary from the Portsmouth Visitor Information Center at 6 Crawford Parkway, or ☎ 800-PORTS-VA to have it mailed to you.

The Lantern Tour begins in the lobby of the Holiday Inn-Olde Towne at 8:30 p.m. on Tuesdays from June through September, and features costumed guides. Olde Towne Portsmouth is beautiful in the evenings; the lights twinkle on the boats in Crawford Bay and lanterns give a warm glow to the cobblestone streets. ☎ 800-PORTS-VA.

Olde Towne Trolley Tours depart from the Visitor Information Center at North Landing. The one-hour narrated tour is offered from Memorial Day through Labor Day and during the Christmas season. ☎ 757-393-5111 or 800-PORTS-VA.

***Carrie B* Harbor Cruise**. The *Carrie B* is a reproduction of a 19th-century Mississippi river boat; cruises are run by the nation's oldest naval shipyard and largest naval base. It is a great way to see the waterfront landmarks of the historical area. Cruises depart from North Landing twice daily, June through Labor Day. For schedules and more information, ☎ 757-393-4735, www.carriebcruises.com.

The Elizabeth River Ferry, operated by HRT between Norfolk and Portsmouth, ☎ 757-222-6100, www.hrtransit.org, and the **Ocean Marine Water Taxi**, ☎ 757-391-3000, are other fun ways to see the Portsmouth waterfront area.

Events

For dates and information concerning the following events, call the **Portsmouth Convention & Visitors Bureau** at ☎ 800-PORTS-VA.

A Taste of Portsmouth features the best of Portsmouth restaurants. Held in February.

The **Crawford Bay Crew Classic** is an intercollegiate rowing regatta held in March.

Virginia Waterfront International Arts Festival is a month-long affair featuring world-class performances throughout the 50-mile region of the Virginia waterfront. For locations of Portsmouth performances, ☎ 757-664-6492 or visit www.vaintlartsfest.com.

Memorial Day Remembrance features the nation's oldest continually-running Memorial Day Parade.

The **Seawall Festival** is a family festival featuring a children's park, food, crafts, golden oldies and beach music. Held in early June.

The **Cock Island Race**, held in late June, has become one of the largest sailing events on the East Coast. More than 100 sailboat race on the Elizabeth River.

The **Eastern Amateur Golf Tournament**, held in July, attracts the top 150 amateur golfers in the US and internationally.

A Faire For the Arts, known for years as the Seawall Art Show, is an outdoor juried show emphasizing visual and performing arts in late August.

Rendezvous, **Mile Marker Zero**, is a social event held in September, for owners of powerboats and yachts.

The **Umoja Festival** in mid-September is an African-American celebration of music, dance and art. The weekend features an African marketplace, children's activities, food and exhibits.

Olde Towne Ghost Walk is held in late October. Costumed re-enactors tell tales of the ghosts and haunted houses on a walking tour of Olde Towne.

Portsmouth

Olde Towne Arts & Antiques Festival is an "open house" by antique shops and art galleries in mid-November.

The **Lighted Boat Parade and Fireworks** take place in late November on the Portsmouth and Norfolk waterfronts.

December features the **Olde Towne Historic Holiday Trolley Tours**, home tours of **Olde Towne** and **Port Norfolk**, and the **Olde Towne Holiday Music Festival**.

Entertainment

At The **Commodore Theatre**, 421 High Street, visitors can take in a first-run movie on a 42-foot screen while having dinner and drinks in this 1945 art deco-style movie theater. ☎ 757-393-6962, www.commodoretheatre.com.

NTELOS Pavilion at Harbor Center is a 6,500-seat outdoor theater and festival park for cultural events, entertainment and city festivals. There are 3,500 covered seats and 3,000 lawn seats. Entertainers have ranged from Tony Bennett to Widespread Panic. ☎ 757-391-3260, www-.harborcenter.com.

Willett Hall, 3701 Willett Drive, presents regionally and nationally known entertainment and seats 2,000 people. For a schedule of events, tickets, or more information, ☎ 757-393-5144, www.willetthall.com.

Shopping

Olde Towne Portsmouth and the waterfront area offer a great many unique shopping opportunities. The historic district abounds with tiny shops and stores, antique shops, crafts and fine art shops, and stores where you can find custom-made jewelry and ceramics. For the mall shopper, there's **Tower Mall**, the nearby **Chesapeake Square Mall**, and **Norfolk's Waterside**, only a five-minute ferry ride away.

Recreation

Parks & Preserves

Portsmouth City Park is a beautifully landscaped 93-acre facility overlooking the Western Branch of the Elizabeth River and Baines Creek. Activities and facilities include boating, tennis, workshops, programmed activities and live entertainment. There is also a nine-hole golf course. ☎ 757-465-2937.

Hoffler Creek Wildlife Preserve, 4510 Twin Pines Road, is the last viable wilderness area in Portsmouth, and was saved from development by a group of volunteer residents. Now, the 142-acre site consists of wetlands, wooded forest and a unique saltwater lake. There are hiking trails and demonstration areas, including a butterfly garden, a backyard habitat and an oyster garden, guided bird walks and a nature center. Open Saturdays, 10 a.m. to 4 p.m.; no pets. ☎ 757-398-9151, www.hofflercreek.org.

Golf

Bide-A-Wee, on Bide-A-Wee Lane, is an 18-hole championship course renovated in 1999 with PGA tour consultant Curtis Strange. The layout has bent grass greens and Bermuda fairways. There are two practice putting greens, a golf range and chipping green, restaurant, lounge and meeting rooms. ☎ 757-393-8600.

The Links at City Park, 140 City Park Avenue, offers a challenging layout for novice and expert golfer alike. Par for the nine-hole executive course is 31, with five par-3 holes and four par-4. There is also an 18-hole putting course and 30-station lighted driving range. Facilities include PGA instruction, a pro shop and concessions. ☎ 757-465-1500.

The Sleepy Hole Golf Course is owned by the city of Portsmouth, but is located in Suffolk, overlooking the Nansemond River. The brisk winds that blow in off the river make the course something of a challenge for golfers at all levels of skill. Facilities at the course include a PGA professional, club fitting and repairs and an excellent driving range. The golf shop offers an outstanding selection of golf equipment, clothing and gifts. ☎ 757-538-4100.

Boating

Portsmouth is Mile Marker Zero on the Intracoastal Waterway and attracts thousands of boats each year, of every shape and size. There are deep-water slips for boats from 20 to 100 feet, free two-hour docking at High Street Landing and North Harbor, and several marinas offering reasonable rates. Portsmouth is a walking city, with restaurants, museums and historic sites all with easy striking distance of the waterfront, and downtown Norfolk is just minutes away on the Elizabeth River Ferry. Call ☎ 800-PORTS-VA for a *Boaters Guide*.

Dining

Alice Mae's Soul Food Café, 515 Washington Street, ☎ 757-399-7091, serves up comfort foods like chitterlings, pig's feet and collards.

Baron's Pub, 500 High Street, ☎ 757-399-4840, is locally famous for the ½-pound Baron Burger and acoustic entertainmnet at night.

The Bier Garden, 434 High Street, ☎ 757-393-6022, serves authentic German cuisine and offers more than 100 beers from around the world.

Brutti's, 467 Court Street, ☎ 757-393-1923, is a European bistro specializing in beef and seafood, and creative martinis. Serves great omelets for breakfast and gourmet sandwiches for lunch.

Café Europa, 319 High Street, ☎ 757-399-6652, is open for lunch and dinner. The restaurant offers a continental menu served in an intimate European atmosphere. Specialties of the house include seafood gazpacho, veal dishes, and fabulous desserts.

The China Garden, 301 High Street, ☎ 757-399-8888, serves a Chinese buffet that is a favorite among locals. It's conveniently located near the Children's Museum and The Commodore Theatre.

Eaton Gogh, 440 High Street, ☎ 757-397-3752, serves regional specialties for lunch and dinner.

Foggy Point Bar & Grill, 425 Water Street, ☎ 757-673-3032, www-.portsmouthrenaissance.com/dining.html, in the new Renaissance Portsmouth Hotel, features an elegant nautical décor and views of the river.

Fusion 440, 467 Dinwiddie Street, ☎ 757-398-0888, www.fusion440-.com, is eclectic, artistic and top-notch.

Island Grill, 8 Crawford Parkway, ☎ 757-393-2573, has a waterfront view from the Holiday Inn Portsmouth Waterfront.

La Tolteca serves authentic Mexican cuisine at two locations: 6031 High Street West, ☎ 757-484-8043, and High Street Landing, ☎ 757-391-2828.

The **Lobscouser Restaurant**, 337 High Street, ☎ 757-397-2728, offers seafood dining in casual elegance in the heart of Olde Towne Portsmouth.

Market Fare, 2622 Detroit Street, ☎ 757-397-0900, is a European bistro in Port Norfolk with an adventurous menu, extensive wine list, fresh-baked breads and in-house desserts.

Paddy O'Brian's, 612 Court Street, ☎ 757-399-6120, is a fun, neighborhood pub featuring American food and live music.

Roger Brown's Restaurant and Sports Bar, 316 High Street, ☎ 757-399-5377, is the brainchild of Portsmouth native and NFL legend Roger Brown. Casual, American dining with a 50-seat bar, several large-screen televisions and volume controls in the booths.

Sassafras, 606 High Street, ☎ 757-399-4480, is southern eclectic serving creative regional fare.

Thumpers, 600 Court Street, ☎ 757-399-1001, serves Cajun fare like fried gator bites, crawfish pasta and jambalaya.

Whistle Stop, 509 Middle Street Mall, ☎ 757-393-3747 or 757-399-9206, is a sandwich and ice cream shop.

Accommodations

Hotels & Motels

Best Value Inn and Suites, 333 Effingham Street, ☎ 757-397-5806, is close to all the major attractions. There is a restaurant, free continental breakfast, and an outdoor pool. $$

Comfort Inn-Olde Towne, 347 Effingham Street, ☎ 757-397-7788, has 62 guest rooms, suites with Jacuzzi and fully-furnished efficiencies, an outdoor pool and exercise room. $$

Days Inn, 1031 London Boulevard, ☎ 757-399-4414, offers fully furnished studio suites, a free continental breakfast, and an exercise room. $$

 Holiday Inn-Portsmouth Waterfront, 8 Crawford Parkway, ☎ 757-393-2573, 800-456-2811, www.portsmouthva.holiday-inn.com, has 221 guest rooms including non-smoking and handi-capped-accessible rooms. The hotel is on the Elizabeth River waterfront. Facilities include an outdoor swimming pool, exercise room, dockage, a lounge with a riverfront deck, meeting rooms, guest laundry, valet and room service. Rooms have coffee makers, hairdryers, iron and ironing boards. $$

The **Renaissance Portsmouth Hotel & Waterfront Conference Center**, 425 Water Street, ☎ 757-673-3000, www.renaissanceports-mouth.com, is the centerpiece of Portsmouth's revitalized waterfront. There are 250 guest rooms, all with water views, a 144-seat restaurant, two ballrooms, a marina, amphitheater, indoor pool, and meeting rooms. $$$

Super 8 Motel, 925 London Boulevard, ☎ 757-398-0612, offers afford-able accommodations with 56 guest rooms. $

Bed & Breakfasts / Inns

Glen Coe Bed & Breakfast Inn at 222 North Street, ☎ 757-397-8128, www.glencoeinn.com, is an 1890s Victorian home in Olde Towne Ports-mouth. It has three guest rooms. $$

The **Golden Goose Resort at Sea**, 10 Crawford Parkway, ☎ 757-489-7073, 757-576-9085, www.golden-getaway.com, is a 43-foot motor yacht that can accommodate four people, operating from the Tidewater Yacht Marina May through February. $$

The **Patriot Inn Bed & Breakfast**, 201 North Street, ☎ 757-391-0157, www.bbonline.com/va/patriot, is a 1784 Colonial home in the Olde Towne historic district. No children under 12. $$

Portsmouth

Day-trip to The Great Dismal Swamp

Spanish moss drips from twisted trees and the distinctive knees of the cypress jut up from inky swamp water along the edges of mysterious Lake Drummond. This beautiful yet unwelcoming environment of the Great Dismal Swamp was encountered by runaway slaves who hid here and attempted to forge a living. For this reason, the swamp is a stop on the National Park Service's Underground Railroad Network to Freedom Program.

Today the 111,000-acre National Wildlife Refuge harbors creatures like black bear, bobcat, river otter, and birds of prey. Explore by foot, bike or kayak, or take a narrated bus tour arranged by the Suffolk Visitor Center.

Trails begin on Washington Ditch Road off Route 642 on the western edge of the refuge. Hike through a southern swamp forest of maple, tupelo, bald cypress and pine. The 4.5-mile Washington Ditch Road leads to Lake Drummond, one of only two natural lakes in all of Virginia. The Dismal Town Boardwalk Trail is a much shorter and accessible trail at just under a mile. Paddlers can access the lake from the eastern side of the swamp, where there is a visitor center (☎ 757-986-3705, http://greatdismal-swamp.fws.gov).

After your swamp adventure, explore Suffolk's historic downtown, and perhaps stay at the new **Hilton Garden Inn** overlooking the Nansemond River. For more information, contact the Suffolk Division of Tourism, ☎ 757-923-3880, www.suffolk-fun.com.

Transportation

Portsmouth is located in the heart of Hampton Roads and is easily accessible from all directions. It is dissected by four major highways: **Interstate 264** and **Highway 58** run east and west; **Routes 17** and **164**, the Western Freeway, run north and south. All four highways connect to the **Interstate 64/664** Beltway. By water, Portsmouth is located at the Zero Mile Marker of the Intracoastal Waterway, with quick and inexpensive ferry service to Norfolk's waterfront. The ferry docks at North Landing, and three blocks south at the new High Street Landing ferry terminal.

Norfolk International Airport is a 30-minute drive from Portsmouth and serves both commercial and passenger air traffic.

Information

For visitors guides, brochures and information, contact the **Portsmouth Convention & Visitors Bureau**, 505 Crawford Street, Portsmouth,

Virginia 23704. ☎ 757-393-5327 or 800-PORTS-VA, www.portsmouth-.va.us/tourism.

The Portsmouth Visitor Information Center is at 6 Crawford Parkway at the North Landing ferry dock, ☎ 757-393-5111 or 800-PORTS-VA.

Virginia Beach

The famous three-mile boardwalk and amusement rides, 35 miles of Atlantic and Chesapeake Bay beaches, spectactular fishing and golfing, and myriad dining and entertainment options make Virginia Beach a premier vacation spot. On the off-chance the weather doesn't cooperate, there are fine museums, world-class shopping venues, and fine historic homes to visit.

As well as being one of the East Coast's best resorts, Virginia Beach is also the state's most populous city, with nearly a half million residents and growing by the minute. A new Town Center provides first-rate dining and shopping, a $202 million convention center is scheduled for completion in 2007, and many more millions are going into continued redevelopment of retail and commercial areas near the oceanfront.

Despite all this activity, there are still several large undeveloped tracts of public land where recreation, solitude and wildlife can be found. And then there's the expansive Atlantic Ocean, where bottlenose dolphins and humpback whales can be seen from shore or on a sightseeing cruise. More than a cliche, Virginia Beach truly is a destination that "has it all."

History

The first English settlers to land in America, did so at Cape Henry on April 29, 1607, 13 years before the Pilgrims landed at Plymouth Rock. Those first settlers, led by Captain John Smith, then moved inland to found the first permanent English settlement at Jamestown.

Cape Henry lies on the northern tip of Virginia Beach at the mouth of the Chesapeake Bay where, during bad weather, the seas can be treacherous and unpredictable. In 1720, Virginia's governor requested that a lighthouse be built on Cape Henry. At first the English King refused, but finally agreed and work began only to be halted in 1774 by the outbreak of the Revolutionary War. The lighthouse was finally completed in 1791 and still stands to this day. In 1962 it became Virginia Beach's official symbol.

It wasn't until the 19th century that Virginia Beach gained its reputation as a popular vacation spot. The coming of the railroad brought easy access to the oceanfront from the bustling port city of Norfolk. Hotels began to spring up and the waterfront area went through various stages of construction and development. Back in those days, the great Princess Anne Hotel, a self-contained vacation paradise, occupied more than two oceanfront blocks and was served by a railroad link that ran almost to the lobby.

The boardwalk and the Cavalier Hotel were completed in the late 1920s and together they ushered in a new era of gaiety and prosperity. Since then, the resort has continued to increase in popularity and is one of the East Coast's premiere vacation spots.

Sights

The **Association For Research and Enlightenment**, 67th Street and Atlantic Avenue, is the international headquarters for the work of psychic Edgar Cayce. Open daily, admission free. There are self-guided tours and a gift shop. ☎ 757-428-3588, www.edgarcayce.org.

Atlantic Wildfowl Heritage Museum, 1113 Atlantic Avenue, is in the DeWitt Cottage (ca. 1895), one of the oldest buildings on the oceanfront. It is dedicated to the wildfowl of the Atlantic Flyway and features decoy exhibits and carving demonstrations. Open daily in summer, closed Monday the rest of the year. ☎ 757-437-8432, www.awhm.org.

The **Christian Broadcasting Network** at Regent University, 977 Centerville Turnkpike, was founded by Pat Robertson, as was the University. The public is invited to tapings of the broadcasts; tours are given Monday through Friday. ☎ 757-226-2745, www.cbn.com.

The Contemporary Art Center of Virginia, 2200 Parks Avenue, is a 32,000-square-foot facility devoted to the presentation of 20th-century art through exhibitions, education and the performing arts. The center is open daily except Monday. ☎ 757-425-0000, www.cacv.org.

The **Farmers Market**, 3640 Dam Neck Road in Princess Anne Commons, is the place to buy local and organic produce, plants, flowers, preserves, dairy and gifts. There's also a restaurant. Open year-round, with special events and music on weekends. ☎ 757-427-4395.

Fort Story off Route 60 is an active military base and a treasure of historic landmarks. The First Landing Cross marks the area where the first English settler touched shore in the New World in 1607 – 13 years before Plymouth. A monument pays tribute to the Battle Off the Capes, an important event of the Revolutionary War. The **Old Cape Henry Lighthouse** at Fort Story is the oldest government-built lighthouse in the nation, dating back to 1791. It's also the city's traditional symbol. Open daily; admission charged. Photo ID required to enter the fort's main gate. ☎ 757-422-9421, www.ava.org.

Hunt Club Farm at 2388 London Bridge Road, offers a playground, petting farm, seasonal produce market, crafts, Christmas tree sales, and a

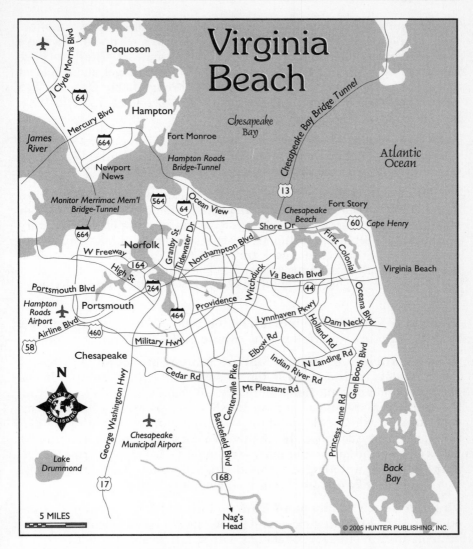

Virginia
Beach

Poquoson

Chesapeake
Bay

Atlantic
Ocean

Hampton

Fort Monroe

James
River

Hampton Roads
Bridge-Tunnel

Newport
News

Monitor Merrimac Mem'l
Bridge-Tunnel

Ocean View

Chesapeake
Beach

Fort Story

Cape Henry

Shore Dr

Norfolk

W Freeway

Northampton Blvd

Virginia Beach

High St

Va Beach Blvd

Portsmouth Blvd

Portsmouth

Providence

Hampton
Roads
Airport

Airline Blvd

Lynnhaven Pkwy

Dam Neck

Chesapeake

Military Hwy

Elbow Rd

Indian River Rd

N Landing Rd

Cedar Rd

Mt Pleasant Rd

N

Chesapeake
Municipal Airport

Lake
Drummond

Back
Bay

5 MILES

Nag's
Head

© 2005 HUNTER PUBLISHING, INC.

haunted hayride in October. Open daily. ☎ 757-427-9520, www.hunt-clubfarm.com.

Motor World at 849 General Booth Boulevard. has go-kart tracks, bumper boats, kiddy rides and mini-golf. ☎ 757-422-6419, www.vbmotorworld.com.

The **Naval Amphibious Base-Little Creek** on Shore Drive is the major operating base for the amphibious forces of the United States Atlantic Fleet. ☎ 757-462-7923.

Norwegian Lady Statue at 25th Street on the Boardwalk was a gift from the people of Moss, Norway, and commemorates a tragic 1891 wreck off the Virginia Beach coast.

The **Ocean Breeze Fun Park** at 849 General Booth Boulevard offers family fun on the Wild Water Rapids, a waterpark with slides, a wave pool, and an assortment of children's water amusements. They also have the MotorWorld driving park, miniature golf, batting cages and whole lot more. The park is open daily, Memorial Day through Labor Day; see Web site for schedule and admission prices. ☎ 757-422-4444, 757-425-1241, www.oceanbreezewaterpark.com.

At **Oceana Naval Air Station** you can watch the Navy's most advanced aircraft take off and land from Jet Landing Observation Points on Oceana Boulevard and London Bridge Road. ☎ 757-433-3131.

The **Old Coast Guard Station** at 24th Street and Atlantic Avenue is a former 1903 US Life Saving Station. It houses visual exhibits of a number of shipwrecks along the Virginia coastline that tell the story of bravery and disaster. You'll see artifacts, rescue equipment, photographs and models. Visitors can take a peek through the TOWERCAM mounted on the roof that zooms in on passing ships. The museum is open daily, year-round; admission charged. ☎ 757-422-1587, www.oldcoastguardstation-.com.

Tidewater Veterans Memorial, on the 1000 block of 19th Street, is a modern sculpture waterfall paying tribute to the area's military forces.

The **Virginia Aquarium and Marine Science Museum**, 717 General Booth Boulevard, is one of the top 10 aquariums in the country. It has 800,000 gallons of aquariums, more than 100 hands-on exhibits depicting the marine environment, and an IMAX 3-D theater. Housed here are sharks, sea turtles, seals, dolphins, sea otters, and even a stingray petting tank. An outdoor boardwalk takes visitors through a salt marsh for views of waterfowl and other marine animals. Seasonal boat trips for dolphin and whale watching are offered. The museum is open daily; admission charged. ☎ 757-425-FISH or visit www.vmsm.com.

Virginia Beach Amusement Park at 15th and Atlantic Avenue at the oceanfront has thrilling rides and games for all ages. Open March-November, daily in summer; weekends only in fall. ☎ 757-422-2307.

Virginia Legends Walk at the 13th Street Park on Atlantic Avenue honors important Virginians, from Thomas Jefferson to Patsy Cline, on a self-guided tour. ☎ 757-491-7866, www.va-legends.com.

Historic Homes

The **Adam Thoroughgood House**, 1636 Parish Road, is one of the oldest remaining brick houses in the United States. Built in 1680 and restored and remodeled in 1745, the house is reminiscent of an old English cottage. A feature here is the fine 17th-century "gentlemen's pleasure garden." The house is open daily except Monday; admission charged. ☎ 757-431-4000.

The **Francis Land House** at 3131 Virginia Beach Boulevard once was the residence of a prominent family of planters. The 18th-century Dutch gambrel-roofed house represents the architecture and lifestyle enjoyed by the gentry of Colonial Virginia. The house is furnished with period antiques and is open Tuesday through Sunday; admission charged. ☎ 757-431-4000.

The **Ferry Plantation** at 4136 Cheswick Lane dates to 1642, when Adam Thoroughgood began a ferry service to connect plantations. The current dwelling was built in 1830 to replace the 1740 house that was destroyed by fire. The 10-room Federal house faces the Western Branch of the Lynnhaven river. Open Tuesdays and Thursdays. Admission charged.

Lynnhaven House at 4405 Wishart Road is a stately, well-preserved example of 18th-century architecture. The house was built in 1725 and is open daily except Monday, May to October; admission charged. ☎ 757-460-1688, www.apva.org.

Upper Wolfsnare at 2040 Potters Road is a brick country home built by Thomas Walke III in 1759. Walke was a ratifier of the US Constitution. Features of the home include period furniture, china, Walke family portraits and an authentic 18th-century herb garden. The house is a private residence, but is open to the public on Wednesdays in July and August; admission charged. ☎ 757-491-3490, www.virginiabeachhistory.org.

Annual Events

Spring comes early to the Virginia Beach Pavilion for the **Virginia Flower & Garden Show** in mid-January (☎ 757-853-0057, www.vafgs-.org), and arrives again in late March for the **Mid-Atlantic Home & Garden Show** (☎ 757-420-2434, www.tbaonline.org).

In early February, nearly 10,000 hardy swimmers jump into the Atlantic for the **Polar Plunge** to benefit Special Olympics Virginia. ☎ 877-874-7462, www.polarplunge.com.

The **Mid-Atlantic Sports and Boat Show** is held at the Virginia Beach Pavilion in February. ☎ 757-437-7600.

Players from around the world vie in the **Millennium Chess Festival** in early April. ☎ 757-491-SUNN, www.beacheventsfun.com.

Spring Wine Festival features an international sampling of wines in mid-April. ☎ 757-491-SUNN, www.beacheventsfun.com.

The last weekend in April and the first weekend in May bring classic and custom cars, ATVs and monsters trucks to the beach for the **Cruisin' Virginia Beach Auto Super Show**, **Extreme Weekend ATV Wars**, and **Monsters on the Beach**. ☎ 757-491-SUNN, www.beacheventsfun.com.

Beach Music Weekend and National Shag Championship takes places in the sand in May and features lots of grooving to the city's official dance: the Shag. ☎ 757-491-SUNN, www.beacheventsfun.com.

The **Pungo Strawberry Festival** takes place over two days in late May in one of the city's farming communities. ☎ 757-721-6001, www.pungo-strawberryfestival.org.

North American Sand Soccer Championships take place in the sand in early June. ☎ 757-368-4600.

The **Boardwalk Art Show & Festival**, held over four days in June, showcases works by hundreds of artists from around the United States. Paintings, ceramics, fine crafts, sculpture and photography are shown – many for sale – along the 14-block stretch of the Virginia Beach Board-walk. ☎ 757-425-0000, www.cacv.org.

Viva Elvis is a tribute to Rock 'n Roll and The King, held in late June. Features Elvis impersonators and food vendors offering Elvis' favorites. ☎ 757-491-SUNN, www.beacheventsfun.com.

The **Hampton Roads Shakespeare Festival** takes place in summer at various outdoor and indoor locations. Performances are free. ☎ 757-425-1154, www.summershakes.com.

Many music and ethnic festivals take place throughout the summer. The **PANorama Caribbean Music Fest** is in early May, followed by the **Latin Festival** in early June, the **Soul Music Beachfest** in late August, and the **Blues at the Beach** in mid-September. ☎ 757-491-SUNN, www.beacheventsfun.com.

Stars & Stripes Explosion is a spectacular July 4th celebration at the oceanfront. ☎ 757-491-SUNN, www.beacheventsfun.com.

The **East Coast Surfing Championship** is the oldest surfing contest in the nation. It draws hundreds of the world's top professionals, and is held over five days in late August. ☎ 800-861-SURF, www.surfecsc.com.

In early September, the **Rock 'n Roll Half Marathon** draws 15,000 runners, walkers and wheelchairs who are cheered along the 13-mile course by rock bands. ☎ 757-491-SUNN, www.beacheventsfun.com, or www-.RnRHalf.com

The **American Music Festival** is held in early September at several stages along the oceanfront. It is billed as the largest musical event on the East Coast. ☎ 757-491-SUNN, www.beacheventsfun.com.

The **Neptune Festival**, one of the top 10 festivals in the Northeast, celebrates the final days of summer. Held during the last two weeks in September, the festival features an air show, sand-castle competition, music, a parade and a ball. ☎ 757-498-0215, www.neptunefestival.com.

Holiday Lights at the Beach is a driving tour through 250 dazzling and animated light displays along the oceanfront from mid-November through New Year's. ☎ 757-491-SUNN, www.beacheventsfun.com.

Entertainment

Virginia Beach is a resort town, so it comes as no surprise that the entire city is dedicated to the entertainment of its visitors. Music and dance clubs abound and there's something available for everyone, from jazz to country and from reggae to golden oldies and beach music. For the young at heart, the sophisticated, or people simply looking for a casual night out on the town where blue jeans and tank-tops are the accepted mode of dress, it's all there in Virginia Beach.

There are so many nightclubs and other opportunities it's impossible to list them all here. Once you arrive, you'll find up-to-date listings in the local newspapers or at the Visitor Information Center. ☎ 800-VA BEACH.

Verizon Wireless Virginia Beach Amphitheater is a dazzling, 20,000-seat outdoor concert venue that attracts major rock, country and jazz artists from April through October. ☎ 757-368-3000. For tickets, ☎ 757-671-8100, www.verizonwirelessamphitheater.com/vabeach, or www.ticketmaster.com.

The **Thoroughgood Inn Comedy Club**, 4801 Shore Drive, offers top entertainment with nationally known comedians in a full-service restaurant. ☎ 757-460-8399, www.tgicomedyclub.com.

The Little Theatre of Virginia Beach, at 24th Street and Barberton Drive, showcases local talent performing a variety of theatrical productions from drama to music. For more information and schedules, ☎ 757-428-9233.

The Virginia Beach Convention Center, 1000 19th Street, hosts major shows, conventions and events. A major, $200 million expansion due to be completed in 2007 will triple the existing pavilion. ☎ 757-437-4774 for a recording of the schedule, or 757-437-7629 for the box office.

Virginia Beach Pavilion Theater, 1000 19th Street, ☎ 757-437-4747, hosts dance, musicals and theater productions; the Virginia Musical Theatre stages productions here. ☎ 757-340-5446, www.vmtheatre.org.

The **Virginia Beach Sportsplex** is a three-level, 6,000-seat stadium that opened in 1998 as the home of the Hampton Roads Mariners professional soccer team. The adjacent Hampton Roads Soccer Complex features 19 multi-sport playing fields. ☎ 757-430-8873.

The Virginia Symphony Orchestra performs in Virginia Beach. Call for information and schedules at ☎ 757-671-8611, www.vbso.org.

Virginia Beach

Shopping

The shopping opportunities in Virginia Beach are virtually boundless. Stores in the resort areas, in the malls and in the shopping centers are open seven days a week and provide just about everything you might want.

Town Center is Virginia Beach's new "main street," a combination business, residential, dining, retail and government complex at Virginia Beach and Independence boulevards. The 24-story office tower is the city's newest landmark, visible for miles. Retailers include a giant outdoor retailer, fine men's and women's clothiers, music and bookstores, a day spa, and restaurants ranging from the casual to the upscale. It's all connected by brick-paved sidewalks and open green spaces with fountains. There's also free parking in a secure garage; ☎ 757-366-4000, www.vabeachtowncenter.com.

The **Resort Area**, which encompasses 2nd Street through 40th Street, is an extravaganza of souvenir shops, surf shops, art galleries and craft shops.

The **Hilltop Area** at Laskin and First Colonial Roads consists of Hilltop East, North and West; Hilltop Square, Regency Hilltop; and La Promenade. These are all shopping centers offering everything from the best in haute couture and fine jewelry to discount merchandise. ☎ 757-428-2224, www.hilltopshops.com.

Loehmann's Plaza, at Virginia Beach Boulevard and Stepney Lane, features Loehmann's, Lillian Vernon and Linens 'N Things outlets.

Lynnhaven Mall at 701 Lynnhaven Parkway is one of the largest shopping malls on the East Coast, with several large department stores and many small shops and restaurants. ☎ 757-340-9340, www.lynnhaven-mall.com.

The **Pembroke Mall** at Virginia Beach and Independence boulevards is the first mall ever built in Virginia Beach. It features several large department stores, along with a variety of specialty shops and restaurants. ☎ 757-497-6255, www.pembrokemall.com.

Recreation

Virginia Beach has recreational opportunities aplenty. From surfing to deep-sea fishing, windsurfing to golf, and from jet skiing to scuba diving, whatever your fancy you'll find it somewhere in Virginia Beach.

Parks & Natural Areas

Throughout the city, a number of parks provide a variety of recreational facilities and activities. These include play areas, ball fields, picnic areas, and lakes. For more information, call the Department of Parks, ☎ 757-563-1100.

Back Bay National Wildlife Refuge, 4005 Sandpiper Road, ☎ 757-721-2412, www.backbay.fws.gov, is a 7,700-acre refuge of beach, woodland and marsh in southern Virginia Beach. The park provides natural habitats for migratory waterfowl. The best months to visit are December and January, when you can see whistling swans, bald eagles and peregrine falcons. Biking and hiking are available.

False Cape State Park is five miles south of the Back Bay Refuge at 4001 Sandpiper Road. The park is one of the few remaining undeveloped areas along the Atlantic coastline, and is accessible only by foot, boat, bike or guided tram tour. No private vehicles are allowed. The park offers a unique opportunity to see marine birds and animals like pelicans and dolphins in their native habitat, along with a variety of marine plants, forests and dunes. Camping is allowed in the park at designated sites, but all water and gear must be carried in, and it's a five-mile trek. ☎ 757-426-7128, 800-933-7275, www.dcr.state.va.us/parks/falscape.htm.

First Landing State Park, 2500 Shore Drive, encompasses almost 3,000 acres of some of Virginia's finest parkland. Its salt marshes, lagoons, Chesapeake Bay beach and woodlands provide diverse natural habitat for many species of wild birds and animals. Facilities at the park include the Chesapeake Bay Center, an interactive educational center with aquariums and touchtanks, 27 miles of hiking and bike trails, picnic areas and boat ramps. Guided walks and kayak rentals are available. Camping facilities include cabins and full-service campsites. Open daily; parking fee. ☎ 757-412-2300, www.dcr.state.va.us/parks/1stland.htm.

Mount Trashmore, 300 Edwin Drive, is a former landfill transformed into a playground for old and young alike. Fly a kite from the highest point in the city or take a stroll around the man-made lake. ☎ 757-497-2157.

Fishing

The **Virginia Saltwater Fishing Tournament** is a Commonwealth of Virginia-sponsored event held year-round and open to everyone who fishes in the tournament waters and complies with the rules. For information and rules, contact the Virginia Saltwater Fishing Tournament, 968 S. Oriole Drive, Suite 102, Virginia Beach, VA 23451, ☎ 757-491-5160.

Charter a private boat to try your luck at catching large game fish, or join a group on board a party boat for a half-day or full-day excursion out of the Lynnhaven Inlet on the Chesapeake Bay or Rudee Inlet off the Atlantic. Party boats leave from the **Lynnhaven Seafood Marina**, ☎ 757-481-4545; or the **Virginia Beach Fishing Center**, ☎ 757-422-5700, www.virginiafishing.com.

Virginia Beach

You can also fish from the **Virginia Beach Fishing Pier** at 15th Street.

Back Bay and **Lake Smith** provide the best opportunities for freshwater fishing in the area. If you're fishing from a commercial pier or with a licensed fishing charter, you don't need a license. Otherwise, temporary fishing licenses can be obtained at the Virginia Beach Municipal Center, corner of Princess Anne and James Madison boulevards, Building 10B, thrid floor, ☎ 757-427-8822, or at any store that sells fishing tackle, such as Wal-Mart or Bass Pro Shops.

Eco-Tours & Kayaking

With more than 120 miles of scenic waterway, Virginia Beach offers paddling opportunities galore. Local outfitters and guides include **Adventure Alternatives**, ☎ 757-468-4669, www.adventurealternatives.com; **Wild River Outfitters**, ☎ 757-431-8566, www.wildriveroutfitters.com; **Tidewater Adventures Kayak Eco Tours**, ☎ 757-480-1999 or 888-669-8368, www.tidewateradventures.com; **Back Bay Getaways** for eco-adventures, ☎ 757-721-4484, www.backbayadventures.com; and **Chesapean Kayak Tours**, ☎ 757-287-0938, www.chesapeankayak.com, which specializes in dolphin watching.

The *Miss Virginia Beach* offers sightseeing and seasonal whale-watching and dolphin cruises along the oceanfront. ☎ 757-422-5700.

Golf

Nearly year-round mild weather makes Virginia Beach a popular place to tee off. There are 11 courses open to the public in the immediate Virginia Beach area. Several participate in the city's Golf Package Program and all are willing to arrange golf outings for groups. For the *Golf Vacation Guide,* ☎ 866-4-VB-GOLF, www.vbgolf.com.

Bow Creek Municipal Golf Course, 3425 Clubhouse Road. ☎ 757-431-3763, www.vbgov.com/dept/parks/golf. The par-70 course measures 5,917 yards.

Cypress Point Country Club, 5340 Clubhead Road. ☎ 757-490-8822. Par 72; 6,740 yards.

Hell's Point Golf Club, 2700 Atwoodtown Road. ☎ 757-721-3400, www-.hellspoint.com. The course measures 6,766, with a par of 72.

Heron Ridge, 2973 Heron Ridge Drive, ☎ 757-426-3800, www.heron-ridge.com, is a 7,010-yard, par-72 public course.

Honey Bee Golf Club at 2500 S. Independence Boulevard, ☎ 757-471-2768, is a 6,005-yard, par-70 course.

Kempsville Greens Municipal Golf Course at 4840 Princess Anne Road, ☎ 757-474-8441, www.vbgov.com/dept/parks/golf, is a 5,500-yard, par-70 course.

Owl Creek Golf Course at 411 S. Birdneck Road, ☎ 757-428-2800, measures 3,793 yards, with a par of 62.

Red Wing Lake Golf Course at 1080 Prosperity Road, ☎ 757-437-4845, www.vbgov.com/dept/parks/redwing, is a 7,080-yard, par-72 course.

Signature at West Neck, 3100 Arnold Palmer Drive, ☎ 757-721-2900, www.signatureatwestneck.com, has lakes and gardens, and is a par 72 Championship course designed by Arnold Palmer.

Stumpy Lake Golf Course at 4797 E. Indian River Road, ☎ 757-467-6119, measures 6,846 yards, with a par of 72.

Tournament Players Club of Virginia Beach, 2500 Tournament Drive, ☎ 757-563-9440, www.playatpc.com, a championship par-72 public course has 7,000-plus yards. PGA pros are available for lessons.

Tennis

Virginia Beach has nearly 200 public tennis courts – most of them lighted and all free. Just south of the resort area, the Parks and Recreation Department operates the **Owl Creek Municipal Tennis Center** at 938 S. Birdneck Road, ☎ 757-437-4804. The Center offers tennis lessons and tournaments with seating for 1,300 persons, and charges a nominal court fee.

Dining

With more than 100 restaurants to choose from, eating out in Virginia's oceanfront city offers everything from come-as-you-are barbecue to elegant French dining. It's impossible to list them all, but here is a sampling. For more information, contact the Virginia Beach Convention & Visitors Bureau at ☎ 800-VA-BEACH or visit www.vbfun.com.

Alexander's On The Bay, at the foot of Fentress Street, ☎ 757-464-4999, has a spectacular view of the Bay from every table. It is located at the foot of the Chesapeake Bay Bridge-Tunnel and decorated in a nautical theme. Specialties of the house include veal Oscar, chateaubriand, lobster and their own desserts. Open for dinner only.

The Beach Pub, 1001 Laskin Road, ☎ 757-422-8817, isn't fancy, but locals rave about the weekend breakfasts which are served until 2 p.m. Where else can you order crab cakes and clam fritters with your eggs? The Sunday clientele ranges from those coming straight from church to those heading for their surfboards. Open daily for breakfast, lunch and dinner.

Blue Pete's Seafood & Steak Restaurant, 1400 Muddy Creek Road, ☎ 757-426-2005, is open for dinner, closed Mondays. Specialties include fresh seafood, sweet potato biscuits and their own desserts. The restaurant is located on a creek in a wooded area.

Captain George's Seafood Restaurant has two locations at 2272 Pungo Ferry Road, ☎ 757-721-3463, and 1956 Laskin Road, ☎ 757-428-3494. Both are open for dinner only, offering a multitude of fresh seafood choices, generously served. It's hard, but try to save room for their dessert favorites that include strawberry shortcake and baklava.

The Coastal Grill, 1427 Great Neck Road, ☎ 757-496-3348, is open for dinner. Specialties include fresh fish and roast chicken in light and airy surroundings and a totally non-smoking atmosphere.

Frankie's Place For Ribs, has two locations at 408 Laskin Boulevard, ☎ 757-428-7631, and 5200 Fairfield Shopping Center, ☎ 757-495-7427. If you're someone who can never get enough ribs, Frankie's is the place. Beef or pork, rack or half-rack, they're served up no-nonsense style. Utensils are optional. Frankie's is open for lunch and dinner.

Henry's Planet Seafood, 3319 Shore Drive, ☎ 757-481-7300, is open for lunch and dinner with plenty of fresh seafood specialties. The restaurant has a cylindrical aquarium in the middle of the two-story lobby, a raw bar, and views of busy Lynnhaven Inlet. Open for lunch and dinner daily.

La Caravelle Restaurant at 1040 Laskin Road, ☎ 757-428-2477, is open for dinner only, offering a French-Vietnamese menu. Specialties include Vietnamese Imperial Rolls, Le Crab en Chemise, daily lobster specials, and vegetarian dishes. The restaurant features romantic French country décor and a pianist in the evenings.

Le Chambord and **The Bistro**, 324 N. Great Neck Road, ☎ 757-498-1234, are actually two restaurants in one location, offering lunch and dinner. Le Chambord has a French continental menu, with specialties of seafood, beef and duck, served with pampered elegance. The pastry car is to die for. The Bistro offers more affordable, casual dining. Both are located in an old post office building featuring modern Mediterranean-style décor and fireplaces.

The Lynnhaven Fish House, 2350 Starfish Road, ☎ 757-481-0003, is open for lunch and dinner. Specialties are fresh seafood and Belgian whiskey pudding. The restaurant is on Lynnhaven fishing pier and has a live lobster tank and a raw bar.

The Pungo Grill, 1785 Princess Anne Road, ☎ 757-426-6655, is open for lunch and dinner and offers a regional American and Continental menu. Specialties include Cajun soups, home-made desserts and French roast coffee.

Rudee's On The Inlet, 227 Mediterranean Avenue, ☎ 757-425-1777, is open for lunch and dinner. Specialties are fresh seafood, steamed shrimp and handcut steak. The restaurant features outdoor dining, a raw bar, nautical décor and a casual atmosphere.

San Antonio Sam's Ice House Café, 604 Norfolk Avenue, ☎ 757-491-0263, is open for dinner and offers Tex-Mex cuisine. Specialties include fajitas, enchiladas and chili.

Tandom's Pine Tree Inn, 2932 Virginia Beach Boulevard, ☎ 757-340-3661, is open for lunch and dinner and offers a Continental menu. Specialties of the house include fresh seafood, prime rib and veal Oscar.

Waterman's, 415 Atlantic Avenue, ☎ 757-428-3644, is open for lunch and dinner daily and Sunday brunch, specializing in seafood and beef. The restaurant features four dining areas, all with a view of the ocean.

Accommodations

As one of the most popular resorts on the East Coast, Virginia Beach offers just about any type of lodging, and over 11,000 hotel rooms. A sampling from the affordable to the luxurious follows. For more information, contact the Virginia Beach Convention & Visitors Bureau at ☎ 800-VA-BEACH or visit www.vbfun.com.

Hotels & Motels

Alamar Resort Inn, 311 16th Street near the boardwalk, ☎ 800-346-5681, 757-428-7582, www.va-beach.com/alamarresort, has deluxe rooms and suites decorated with Queen Anne-style furnishings, a large heated pool and a rooftop sundeck. $$$

Ambassador Suites, 2315 Atlantic Avenue, ☎ 800-554-5560, www.vb-hotels.com/ambassador, offers 54 luxurious oceanfront apartments and an outdoor pool. $$$

Barclay Towers Resort Hotel, 809 Atlantic Avenue, ☎ 800-344-4473, www.vbhotels.com/barclay-towers, is a luxury all-suite accommodation right on the boardwalk. $$$

Beach Carousel, 1300 Pacific Avenue, ☎ 757-425-1700 or 800-813-7692, www.beachcarousel.com, is a small family motel with a heated pool. $$

Belvedere Motel, 36th Street at the oceanfront, ☎ 800-425-0612, has 50 guest rooms, many with balconies. There is a swimming pool and bicycle rentals. $$

Best Western Beach Quarters Inn, 300 Atlantic Avenue, ☎ 800-645-8705, www.beachquartersinn.com, has 62 spacious rooms and efficiencies with oceanfront balconies, and an outdoor pool. $$

Best Western Oceanfront, 11th and Atlantic Avenue, ☎ 866-829-2326, www.bwocean.com, has 110 guest rooms, all with ocean views. There is a bar, meeting rooms, a pool and an oceanfront diner. $$$

Boardwalk Resort Hotel, 1601 Atlantic Avenue, ☎ 800-317-9432, www.theboardwalkresort.com, has 106 sleek, modern rooms and suites, private balconies overlooking the Atlantic, and an indoor swimming pool. $$$

The Breakers Resort Inn, 1503 Atlantic Avenue, ☎ 800-237-7532, www.breakersresort.com, has 56 guest rooms with private balconies. There are 15 suites, a heated pool, an exercise room, a free breakfast, and free bicycle rentals. $$$

Capes Resort Hotel, 2001 Atlantic Avenue, ☎ 877-956-5421, www.capes-hotel.com, has 59 rooms, all with oceanfront balconies and an indoor pool. $$$

Captain's Quarters Resort Hotel, 304 28th Street, ☎ 800-333-6020, is a block from the oceanfront. The hotel has 75 guest rooms, a heated pool, and a whirlpool. $$$

The Cavalier, 42nd Street at Atlantic Avenue, ☎ 800-446-8199, www-.cavalierhotel.com, is an historic beauty with 384 guest rooms, five restaurants, lighted tennis, two olympic-sized pools, a health club, a private beach and a unique "sunshine guarantee." $$$

Clarion Beach Quarters Resort, 501 Atlantic Avenue, ☎ 800-345-3186, www.virginiabeachclarion.com, has oceanfront rooms and suites with private balconies, rooftop pool and tennis courts, a heated indoor pool and health spa. $$

Colonial Inn, 2809 Atlantic Avenue, ☎ 800-344-3342, www.col-inn.com, has oceanfront rooms, a heated indoor pool and outdoor pool, and an on-site restaurant. $$

Comfort Inn-Oceanfront, 20th and Atlantic Avenue, ☎ 800-443-4733, www.virginiabeachcomfort.com, has 83 newly renovated oceanfront suites with balconies and kitchenettes. There are meeting rooms, an indoor pool and spa, fitness center and a free continental breakfast. $$$$

Comfort Inn-Virginia Beach, 2800 Pacific Avenue, ☎ 800-441-0684, www.comfortinn.com/hotel.va448, has 137 guest rooms with refrigerator and microwave, indoor and outdoor pools, an exercise room, free bike rentals, and a free continental breakfast. $$$

Courtyard by Marriott, 5700 Greenwich Road, ☎ 800-321-2211, www-.courtyard.com, has 134 guest rooms. There are meeting rooms, a heated pool, an exercise room and hot breakfast buffet. $$$

The **Crowne Plaza Hotel**, 4453 Bonney Road, ☎ 800-847-5202, www.ic-hotelsgroup.com, near the new Town Center, has 149 newly renovated rooms, an indoor pool, health club, and full-service restaurant and lounge. $$

Cutty Sark Motel, 3614 Atlantic Avenue, ☎ 757-428-2116, www.cuttysarkvb.com, is a quiet, family-owned motel across the street from the beach. Also has weekly cottage rentals. $$

Days Inn Airport, 5708 Northampton Boulevard, ☎ 757-460-2205, is a motel with 148 guest rooms, located near Norfolk International Airport. $$

Days Inn at the Beach, 1000 Atlantic Avenue, ☎ 800-843-7096, www.the.daysinn.com/virginiabeach09178, has 113 rooms, most with balconies, an outdoor pool and hot tub. $$

 Days Inn-Oceanfront, 32nd Street and Atlantic Avenue, ☎ 800-292-3297, has 120 guest rooms, all with balconies overlooking the oceanfront, including handicapped-accessible and non-smoking rooms. $$$

 DoubleTree Hotel Virginia Beach, 1900 Pavilion Drive, ☎ 800-222-8733, www.doubletree.com, is a large luxury hotel with 292 guest rooms. There is a restaurant, a pool, and tennis. $$$

Econo Lodge Oceanfront, 2109 Atlantic Avenue, ☎ 800-999-3630, is an oceanside motel with 55 guest rooms, some with ocean views. $$$

Founders Inn, 5641 Indian River Road, ☎ 800-926-4466, www.founders-inn.com, has 240 guest rooms. This four-diamond Colonial-style hotel is on the campus of Regent University. Amenities include a full-service restaurant, lighted tennis, two pools, an exercise room, free airport and local transportation and golf privileges. $$

Hampton Inn, 5793 Greenwich Road, ☎ 800-426-7866, www.hamptoninnvirginiabeach.com, is a motel with 122 newly renovated guest rooms, a pool, and exercise room. $$

Hilton Garden Inn at Virginia Beach Town Center, 252 Town Center Drive, ☎ 800-445-8667, www.hiltongardeninn.com, opened in 2003 with 176 luxury rooms, free high-speed Internet, business and fitness centers, indoor pool and breakfast buffet. $$

 Holiday Inn Executive Center, 5655 Greenwich Road, ☎ 757-499-4400, www.vabeach-execctr.holidayinn.com, has 331 guest rooms, a full-service restaurant, bar, indoor and outdoor pools. $$

Holiday Inn-Oceanside, Atlantic Avenue and 21st Street, ☎ 800-882-3224, has 138 guest rooms. There is a full-service restaurant, a bar, and an indoor pool. $$$

Holiday Inn Sunspree Resort, 39th Street and Oceanfront, ☎ 800-942-3224, has 266 guest rooms and suites, a full-service restaurant, a bar, meeting rooms, a heated indoor pool and an outdoor pool in a tropical setting. $$$

Howard Johnson Oceanfront South, 18th and Atlantic Avenue, ☎ 800-258-1878, has 107 guest rooms with private balconies, an indoor pool, rooms with whirlpool, microwave and refrigerator available, and a guest laundry. $$$

Newcastle Hotel, 12th Street and Atlantic, ☎ 800-346-3176, www.newcastlehotelvb.com, has 83 guest rooms, including some suites with whirlpool tub and fireplaces. There is a heated, indoor pool and an oceanfront restaurant. $$$

The **Oceanfront Inn**, 2901 Atlantic Avenue, ☎ 888-VA-OCEAN, www.oceanfrontinn.com, has spacious oceanfront rooms with private balconies, and an oceanfront restaurant. $$$

Ramada On the Beach, 615 Atlantic Avenue, ☎ 800-888-4111, www.virginiabeachramadainn.com, has oceanfront rooms with private balconies, a seafood restaurant and sushi bar, indoor heated pool and fitness center. $$$

Ramada Plaza Resort Oceanfront, 57th Street and Atlantic, ☎ 800-365-3032, www.ramadaplazavabeach.com, is a large vacation hotel with 246 guest rooms, some with ocean views. There is a restaurant, bar, a pool with a swim-up bar and a swimming beach. $$$$

Sandcastle Oceanfront Resort Hotel, 1307 Atlantic Avenue, ☎ 757-428-2828, 800-233-0131, www.sandcastle-vabeach.com, has 150 oceanfront and oceanview rooms with private balconies, indoor heated pool, fitnes room, and a mini-mall with restaurant, lounge and gift shops. $$

Sea Gull Motel on the Beach, Atlantic Avenue at 27th Street, ☎ 888-871-4855, www.seagullmotel.com, has 51 guest rooms, an indoor pool, and a rooftop deck. $$

Surfside Oceanfront Inn & Suites, 1211 Atlantic Avenue, ☎ 800-437-2497, www.surfsideinn.com, has oceanfront rooms with balconies, two-room suites, an indoor pool and on-site restaurant. $$$

Turtle Cay Resort, 600 Atlantic Avenue, ☎ 888-989-7788, www.turtlecayresort.com, has luxurious villas, a spa, two outdoor pools and a cascading waterfall. $$$

Virginia Beach Resort Hotel & Conference Center, 2800 Shore Drive, ☎ 800-468-2722, www.virginiabeachresort.com, is a large luxury hotel with 295 suites, including handicapped-accessible and non-smoking rooms, overlooking the Chesapeake Bay. Restaurant, indoor and outdoor pools, tennis, golf privileges, a private beach, boat and jet ski rentals. $$$

Bed & Breakfast

Angie's Guest Cottage, 302 24th Street, ☎ 757-428-4690, www.angiescottage.com, was built in the early 1900s and has a colorful history as a rooming house and home for Coast Guardsmen. It has eight rooms, is located a block from the ocean, and offers a unique alternative to the high-rise hotels on the boardwalk. $$

Barclay Cottage Bed & Breakfast, 400 16th Street, ☎ 757-422-1956, www.barclaycottage.com, is an 1895 Victorian cottage, one of only two left in the entire city. It has five rooms furnished with antiques and hand-made quilts. It's two blocks from the beach, and provides complimentary beach chairs, umbrellas, towels and boogie boards. $$

 ## Camping

Leashed pets are allowed at all of the following campgrounds.

First Landing State Park at 2500 Shore Drive, ☎ 757-412-2300 or 800-933-7275 (reservations), www.dcr.state.va.us/parks/1stland.htm, has 222 sites and 20 cabins. Cabins are available year-round; camping is open March through November. None of the sites has hookups, but there are flush toilets, hot showers and sewage disposal. There is a beach on the Chesapeake Bay for swimming and fishing, picnic areas, boat ramps, hiking and biking trails, a camp store and a visitor's center.

Holiday Trav-L-Park at 1075 General Booth Boulevard, ☎ 757-425-0249 or 800-548-0223, www.htpvabeach.com, is a large, wooded campground with 900 sites and 44 cabins, open year-round. Full-hookups, pull-throughs, and phone hookups are available. There are group sites, cabins, hot showers and sewage disposal. There's also a full-service store where RV supplies, groceries, ice and LP gas are available. Facilities include a recreation hall, a pavilion, four swimming pools, a wading pool, a fishing pond and bike rentals. There is a recreation director, planned activities, and a number of hiking and nature trails.

North Bay Shore Campground, 3257 Colchester Road, ☎ 757-426-7911, has 140 sites with water and electric, and five cabins. Open April 15 through October 1. Facilities include flush toilets, hot showers, sewage disposal, a coin laundry, a grocery store, and public telephone. There is salt water swimming and fishing, a playground, a sports field, a tennis court and a volleyball court.

North Landing Beach Riverfront Campground & Resort, 161 Princess Anne Road, ☎ 757-426-6241, has 200 sites, full hook-ups, nine cabins, and is open all year. There is a pool, boat ramp and store.

Outdoor Resorts Virginia Beach, 3661 S. Sandpiper Road, ☎ 800-333-7515, has 250 waterfront sites, all with water, electric and cable hookups, open year-round. Facilities include hot showers, sewage disposal, and public telephone. Recreational facilities include salt water swimming and fishing, a playground, bike rental and planned activities during the summer.

Virginia Beach KOA Campground, 1240 General Booth Boulevard, ☎ 757-428-1444 or 800-562-4150, www.koa.com, is a semi-wooded campground with 350 sites with full hookups, and 13 cabins, open year-round. Facilities include pull-throughs, phone hookups, group sites, cabins, hot showers and sewage disposal. There's also a full-service store where RV supplies, groceries, ice and LP gas are available. Facilities include a recreation hall, a pavilion, two swimming pools, a wading pool, mini-golf and basket ball hoops. There are planned activities during the summer season.

Transportation

Virginia Beach is served by **Norfolk International Airport**, ☎ 757-857-3351, www.norfolkairport.com, a 20-minute drive from the oceanfront. Major airlines offer daily service connecting to all major hubs and most major cities in the US and overseas.

Amtrak, ☎ 800-321-8684, serves Newport News, 45 minutes away, with bus service from there to 19th Street and Pacific Avenue in Virginia Beach.

Greyhound Lines also serves Virginia Beach from 1017 Laskin Road. ☎ 757-422-2998 for schedule information.

By road, Virginia Beach is accessed via **Interstates 64** and **264**, and is linked to **Interstates 85** and **95** via **US Highways 13 and 17**.

Information

The Virginia Beach Department of Convention and Visitor Development is at 2101 Parks Avenue, Suite 500, Virginia Beach, VA 23451, ☎ 757-437-4700. The Visitor Information Service number is 800-VA BEACH, www.vbfun.com.

The Historic Triangle

Jamestown, Williamsburg, and Yorktown – collectively known as Virginia's Historic Triangle – represent the beginning, middle and end of the Colonial period. Here the first English-speaking people settled and stayed, established a Colonial government, and fought the deciding battle in the War for Independence.

Just a few miles south of **Williamsburg** on the banks of the James River visitors will find Jamestown Island where, in 1607, a few brave men and boys founded the first permanent English settlement in the New World. East of Williamsburg, on the banks of the York River, lies **Yorktown**. It was there that George Washington accepted the surrender of General Lord Cornwallis in 1781, and thus won the nation's freedom.

Not only is the area steeped in history, it is also home to the Mid-Atlantic's largest water play park and a theme park with one of the largest roller coasters in the world. The shopping – from Colonial crafts to outlet shopping – is among the best in the southeast.

Charles City County, to the west of Williamsburg, has nine plantations that tell the history of Colonial life and offer a wonderful driving tour along the James River.

Williamsburg

A vacation in and around Williamsburg can find one strolling down the streets of a restored 18th-century village, shopping in a modern outlet mall, dining in an elegant restaurant, golfing one of the East Coast's best courses, or screaming upside down on one of the world's scariest roller coasters at Busch Gardens. The College of William and Mary, founded in 1693, is the second-oldest in the nation, and counts three presidents in its alumni, including Thomas Jefferson.

Other modern-day attractions make Williamsburg a timeless destination. Water Country USA is the Mid-Atlantic's largest water theme park. Busch Gardens is a wonderland of wild rides and live shows set on 360 acres. Outstanding shopping, dining, golf and entertainment help make a visit to Colonial Williamsburg unforgettable.

History

Williamsburg, which celebrated its 300th anniversary in 1999, was one of America's first planned cities. Laid out in 1699 as a model capital, the Middle Plantation took Jamestown's place as the seat of Colonial government in 1699.

From 1699 to 1780, Williamsburg was the political, social and cultural capital of a land that stretched west to the Mississippi and north to the Great Lakes. It was at Williamsburg that patriots developed the fundamental concepts of the new republic – responsible leadership, public duty, self-government and freedom of conscience. And it was at Williamsburg that lesser-known men and women became distinctly American citizens.

A visit to the restored Colonial Williamsburg is a step back in time to a thriving 18th-century community. It's a theater of living history where merchants sell their wares, craftspeople ply their trades and patriots sit in dark corners and whisper of revolution.

Restoration of the old capital began in 1926 when John D. Rockefeller Jr., inspired by the imagination of the Reverend W.A.R Goodwin of Bruton Parish Church, decided to return Williamsburg to its former glory. Rockefeller led, financially supported and remained closely involved in the project until his death in 1960.

The Historic Triangle

Today, Colonial Williamsburg, with its authentic character and baroque town plan, is the pride of the nation. The historic area covers 301 acres and includes 88 original buildings as well as hundresds that have been faithfully reconstructed on their original sites. The Colonial Williamsburg of today is a bustling community of homes, shops, taverns and exhibition buildings along with a hundred gardens and greens. The Historic Area interprets the life and excitement of Colonial times.

Sights

Colonial Williamsburg

Perhaps nowhere else in America does the exciting story of the nation's past come to life more vividly than at Colonial Williamsburg, the restored capital of Colonial Virginia.

Inside exhibition buildings, historic interpreters use collections of 18th-century English and American furnishings and artifacts to teach social, cultural and political history.

Although the buildings and collections are among the finest in America, they cannot convey the full meaning of 18th-century Williamsburg. To portray the life and times of those early patriots, Colonial Williamsburg presents a program of living history that includes the practice of more than 40 Colonial crafts and trades. These activities range from apothecary to wigmaking. The exhibitions are brought to life through a series of presentations and narrations by skilled interpreters and historians.

Among the programs are the participatory mock 18th-century trials conducted in the renovated Courthouse. Visitors help conduct the court's business, play the parts of defendants and plaintiffs, and sit as jurors. The cases are taken from the court records of the 1700s.

Market Square at the center of the town comes to life several days each week on "Market Days." Hawkers at outdoor stalls offer Colonial crafts, foods and wares and generally enliven the town's central green.

Other programs include first-person portrayals by African-American interpreters of the lives of slaves in a wealthy Colonial household. They share with visitors the black perspective on the master of the house and the great questions of the Revolution.

As you stroll through Colonial Williamsburg, you'll meet outspoken patriots, shopkeepers, and others who enlighten visitors about the time period and their daily life. You may even meet the likes of Thomas Jefferson or Patrick Henry, catch a street performance, or run into the Colonial Williamsburg Fifes & Drums who perform daily.

Children can take part in Colonial games, enjoy a story hour, explore hands-on museum activities, or help tend a garden. To really play the

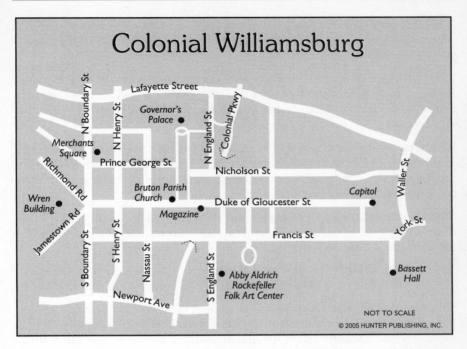

Colonial Williamsburg

NOT TO SCALE
© 2005 HUNTER PUBLISHING, INC.

part, rent a Colonial costume at Market Square or the Visitor Center. All ages delight in taking a turn posing in the stocks and pillories for a photo.

Start your visit at the Visitor Center on the Colonial Parkway at VA 132, ☎ 800-HISTORY, www.colonialwilliamsburg.com, open daily, 9 a.m. to 5 p.m. Daily and annual passes can be purchased here. Be sure to pick up a copy of *This Week at Colonial Williamsburg*, which includes a map, guide and schedule of events.

❖ **VISITORS WITH DISABILITIES:** *Every effort is made to accommodate those with restricted mobility while still retaining the authenticity of Colonial life. Many of the buildings have wheelchair access once inside, but be aware that most buildings are reached via steps. The Visitor Center can provide a detailed listing of accessible buildings. Wheelchair ramps may be made available with advance notice. Wheelchair parking and rental is also available. A hands-on tour of several exhibits may be arranged for the visually impaired, and licensed guide dogs are permitted in all buildings. Sign language tours are also available with two weeks advance notice.* ☎ *800-HISTORY.*

The Exhibition Buildings

The Capitol, at the east end of Duke of Gloucester Street, is where the House of Burgesses met from 1704 until 1779. It is also the scene of Patrick Henry's stirring speech against the Stamp Act.

The Public Gaol, to the north of the Capitol across Nicholson Street, is where debtors, criminals and pirates – including Blackbeard's crew – were imprisoned.

The Raleigh Tavern, on Duke of Gloucester Street, was a frequent meeting place for Thomas Jefferson, Patrick Henry and many other Revolutionary patriots. The tavern was one of the capital's most popular social centers.

The Governor's Palace, at the north end of Palace Green, was the official residence of the Royal Governor of Virginia. The palace, one of the most elegant in Colonial America, is set in 10 acres of restored ornamental gardens.

The Peyton Randolph House, built in 1716, was the home of the president of the first Continental Congress, and Rochambeau's headquarters prior to the Yorktown Campaign.

The James Geddy House was the home of a prominent silversmith. The property features a working brass, silver, bronze and pewter foundry.

The George Wythe House, was the home of America's first law professor – he taught Jefferson, Clay and Marshall. The house was also George Washington's headquarters before the siege of Yorktown, and Rochambeau's afterward. The house, outbuildings and gardens form a miniature plantation layout.

The Magazine, located on Duke of Gloucester Street, one block east of Palace Green, was the arsenal of the Virginia colony. The exhibit features a fine collection or arms.

The Historic Trades are living history exhibits where tradesmen and women dressed in authentic 18th-century costumes pursue many of the trades that were practiced in Colonial Williamsburg. These include an apothecary, printer, bookbinder, silversmith, wigmaker, shoemaker, blacksmith, harnessmaker, cabinetmaker, miller, milliner, gunsmith, wheelwright, cook, cooper and carpenter.

The Public Hospital is a faithful reconstruction of the first public institution in the English colonies devoted exclusively to the treatment of mental illness. It serves as the entrance to the DeWitt Wallace Decorative Arts Museum.

The Bruton Parish Church, on Duke of Gloucester Street, is one of America's oldest Episcopal churches, in continuous use since 1715. Organ recitals are given July through September and in December on Tuesday, Thursday and Saturday; in January and February on Saturdays; and during the other months on Tuesday and Saturday. The church is open daily.

The Courthouse, on Duke of Gloucester Street, east of Palace Green, is where the county and city business was conducted from 1770 until 1932.

The interior has been carefully restored to its original appearance. Visitors participate in scheduled re-enactments of court sessions.

Bassett Hall, an 18th-century frame house on 585 acres, was the home of Mr. and Mrs. John D. Rockefeller Jr. After a two-year renovation it opened to the public in December 2002. Exhibits and tours integrate the life of the Rockefellers with the early years of Colonial Williamsburg Restoration.

Ludwell-Paradise House was the first property John D. Rockefeller purchased in 1926. The elegant townhouse was built by Philip Ludwell II around 1755. At one time the *Virginia Gazette* was printed here.

Museums

The **Abby Aldridge Rockefeller Folk Art Museum**, a half-block southeast of the old section on York Street, houses an outstanding collection of American folk art. Items in the collection were created by artists not trained in studio techniques, but who faithfully recorded the aspects of everyday life through paintings, sculpture, needlework, ceramics, toys and other media. 301 South England Street, ☎ 757-220-7698.

The **DeWitt Wallace Decorative Arts Museum** is a modern museum adjoining the public hospital. The gallery features exhibits, lectures, films and related programs that depict English and American decorative arts made and used in Williamsburg and other colonies during the 17th, 18th and early 19th centuries. Corner of Francis and South Henry streets, ☎ 757-220-7724.

Carter's Grove reopens in 2005 after a two-year renovation. Located eight miles southeast of the Historic Area on the James River, Carter's Grove plantation spans nearly 400 years of Virginia history. The Georgian mansion was built in the 1750s by Carter Burwell and has been called "the most beautiful house in America." A reconstructed slave quarter interprets the lives of 18th-century enslaved field workers. Also on the property is **Wolstenholme Towne**, a reconstructed settlement, and the underground **Winthrop Rockefeller Archeology Museum** with exhibits of early American artifacts.

Other Sights

The **College of William and Mary**, at the west end of Duke of Gloucester Street, was constructed in 1693. It is America's second oldest college – only Harvard is older. William and Mary initiated the honor system and the elective system of studies. The Phi Beta Kappa Society was founded here in 1776.

A number of campus buildings are open to the public, including the **Muscarelle Museum of Art** (☎ 757-221-2710), the **Wren Building**, the country's oldest academic building in continuous use, and the **Swem Library**.

Presidents Park, 211 Water Country Parkway, is an outdoor educational museum featuring 18-20 foot busts of all 43 United States presidents. Open daily, year-round. ☎ 757-259-1121, 800-588-4327, www.PresidentsPark.org.

The **Williamsburg Pottery Factory** sells pottery, furniture, china, glass, stemware, wines, cheeses, plants and many unique items. The Pottery has been family-owned for 50 years, when Jimmy Maloney first set up a kiln on the side of the road. There are now more than 50 factory outlets on more than 200 acres. The Pottery is open daily except Christmas, and is located on Richmond Road (Route 60 West), about seven miles west of Williamsburg. For information and a brochure, ☎ 757-564-3326, www-.williamsburgpottery.com.

The **Williamsburg Soap & Candle Company** has an observation booth where visitors may watch candles and soap being made. Founded in 1964 as a family business, the factory now produces six million candles a year. Shoppers will find plenty of bargains, including factory seconds at reduced prices. The Candle Factory Restaurant serves breakfast and lunch. Located at 7521 Richmond Road, six miles west of Williamsburg. Open daily except Thanksgiving, Christmas and New Year's Day. ☎ 757-564-3354 or visit www.candlefactory.com.

The **Williamsburg Winery**, located in an 18th-century-style winery building some two miles from the restored area at 5800 Wessex Hundred, is surrounded by more than 50 acres of vineyards. Professional guides conduct tours through the underground barrel cellars and explain the wine-making process. You can try a taste of five different wines in the shop, and have lunch in the Gabriel Archer Tavern. The Winery is open year-round. ☎ 757-229-0999, www.williamsburgwinery.com.

Theme Parks

Water Country USA is the Mid-Atlantic's largest water play park. Located on 40 acres, Water Country offers water rides, slides, pools, shows, and a special children's area. You can take a nostalgic trip back to the 1960s surfing scene with a ride on the Malibu Pipeline, lunch at Daddy-O's, and shopping at W.C. Duds surf shop. The park is open from mid-May through mid-September. ☎ 757-253-3350 or 800-343-7946, www.watercountryusa.com.

Busch Gardens Williamsburg, three miles east of Williamsburg, is a European-themed park nestled on 360 acres of Virginia woodland. Highlights are Alpengeist, one of the top roller coasters in the country, and the new Apollo's Chariot, with more vertical drops than any other steel roller-coaster in the world. There are 40 more thrilling rides, a cornucopia of food, entertainment, shops and exhibits are featured in nine authentically detailed 17th-century hamlets. These include Banbury Cross and Hastings from England, Heathersdown from Scotland, Aquitaine from France, Rhinefeld and Oktoberfest from Germany, San Marco and

Festa Italia from Italy and New France from Canada. In-between the action, catch a live show or a 4-D film. The park is closed during the winter months. For operating hours, admission prices and a comprehensive brochure, ☎ 757-253-3350 or 800-343-7946, or visit www.buschgardens.com.

Annual Events

Each year, Colonial Williamsburg hosts a full schedule of interesting and themed events. For a full calendar, ☎ 800-HISTORY, www.colonialwilliamsburg.com.

Historic Garden Week in April open Williamsburg's historic homes to the public, ☎ 804-644-7776, www.vagardenweek.org.

Colonial Williamsburg hosts an annual **Garden Symposium** on historic gardens, ☎ 800-603-0948.

Thousands come to Merchants Square in late April for the **Annual Art on the Square**, a juried art show featuring original and diverse art media. The Junior Woman's Club of Williamsburg, www.williamsburgjuniors.org.

Independence Day Celebration in Colonial Williamsburg features fifes and drums, a reading the Declaration of Independence, fireworks and more. ☎ 800-HISTORY, www.colonialwilliamsburg.com.

The **Virginia Shakespeare Festival** takes place during July and August at the College of William and Mary. ☎ 757-221-2674 (box office), www.vsf.wm.edu.

Early October brings **An Occasion for the Arts** to Merchants Square, an annual juried festival of nationally acclaimed artists, music and stage performances. ☎ 757-259-1206.

The month of October is **Howl-O-Scream** at Busch Gardens Williamsburg, ☎ 800-343-7943, www.buschgardens.com.

Christmas in Colonial Williamsburg kicks off with the Grand Illumination, a gala of fife and drum tattoos, musket and artillery salutes, caroling, dancing, music, fireworks and the illumination of buildings. It is traditionally held the first Saturday in December.

The first Saturday in December is also the date of the **Williamsburg Area Community Christmas Parade**, which starts at 9 a.m. at Merchants Square, ☎ 757-229-6511, and the **Christmas Homes Tour** in the Historic Area, ☎ 757-565-7844.

Williamsburg's **First Night Celebration** on December 31 is a non-alcoholic, family-oriented celebration with entertainment at Colonial Williamsburg and the College of William and Mary, with a grand finale fireworks display at midnight. ☎ 800-965-4827, www.firstnightwilliams-burg.org.

Entertainment

The Original Ghosts of Williamsburg Tour blends history with scary folklore on a candlelit walking tour of Williamsburg's Historic Area. The tour is based on *The Ghosts of Williamsburg* by L.B. Taylor, and features a certified historical interpreter. Tours are offered year-round. ☎ 757-565-4821, www.wmbggrouptourservices.com.

Mystery Dinner Playhouse is a dinner comedy in which the audience participates in solving the murder mystery. Performs weekly, year-round. Located in the Ramada Inn & Suites at 5351 Richmond Road. ☎ 888-471-4802, www.mysterydinner.com.

At Rosie Rumpe's Regal Dumpe you become part of a bawdy 16th-century London pub. Sing along and enjoy a huge feast in the tradition of King Henry VIII. Located in the Quality Inn Historic, 1402 Richmond Road. ☎ 888-767-9767 or visit www.rosierumpes.com.

The Williamsburg Players is the area's oldest continuous community theater. Professional-quality theater performed at 200 Hubbard Lane, where every seat has a great view of the stage. Season runs September through June. ☎ 757-229-0431, www.williamsburgplayers.org.

Haunted Dinner Theater is a family-friendly mystery show accompanied by a 70-item all-you-can-eat buffet. June through Christmas at Capt. George's Restaurant, 5356 Richmond Road, ☎ 757-258-2500, www-.haunteddinnertheater.com.

Pirate's Cove Adventure Golf is miniature golf with pirate scenes for all ages open March through November. 2001 Mooretown Road, ☎ 757-259-4600, www.piratescove.net.

Recreation

Golf

Colonial Golf Course was named one of the top 10 new courses in 1996 by *Golf Magazine*. This championship course has five sets of tees, the Colonial Golf Academy, three-hole practice course, indoor and outdoor practice areas, and a full-service club house and restaurant. Located at 8285 Diascund Road. ☎ 757-566-1600, www.golfcolonial.com.

Colonial Williamsburg: The Golden Horseshoe Gold and Green Courses, designed by Robert Trent Jones, and his son, Rees, have been rated among the "Best of the Best" by *Golf Magazine*. Golf equipment and accessories are available in both pro shops, and both courses have restaurants. The resident professional offers a full-service, year-round program. Located at 401 South England Street. ☎ 800-HISTORY.

Ford's Colony Country Club has three courses featuring rolling hills, lush woodlands and lots of water . The course is the home of the Virginia State Open, and is consistently ranked as one of the top courses in Virginia. There is a fitness center, pro shop, banquet facilities, an award-winning wine cellar, and The Dining Room, a five-star restaurant. Located on Longhill Road, three miles west of Williamsburg. ☎ 757-258-4100, www.fordscolony.com.

Kingsmill Resort offers three golf courses overlooking the James River: the 18-hole River Course; the 18-hole Plantation Course, designed by Arnold Palmer; and the Woods Course, designed by Curtis Strange. Kingsmill also offers 15 tennis courts, including six Hydro Courts. Kingsmill Road off Route 60. ☎ 757-253-3906, www.kingsmill.com.

Kiskiack Golf Club is a championship course, set on scenic rolling hills and lakes. There is a large driving range, sheltered hitting stations, practice putting green, and bunkered chipping area. Located at exit 231B off I-64. ☎ 800-989-4728.

The Tradition Golf Club at Stonehouse utilizes the natural terrain of forests, creeks, ravines and meadows. The course can accommodate all levels of play. Located at exit 227 off I-64, on State Highway 30. ☎ 757-566-1138.

Williamsburg National Golf Club is a Nicklaus-designed course, voted one of the 10 best courses in Virginia by *Golf Digest*. There are junior and twilight rates, and rental clubs are available. Located at 3700 Centerville Road. ☎ 800-826-5732 or visit www.wngc.com.

Parks & Beaches

The **Colonial National Historic Park** offers a number of locations for fishing, biking, hiking and picnicking from Jamestown to Yorktown along the 23-mile Colonial Parkway. ☎ 757-898-3400, www.nps.gov/colo.

The **York River State Park**, east of Croaker on the York River, is known for its rare and delicate estuarine environment, where fresh and saltwater meet to create a habitat rich in marine and plant life. The visitor Center, and the activities within the park, focus on the history, use and preservation of the York River and its marshes. Popular activities at the park include hiking, boating, fishing and picnicking. Facilities include a network of nature trails, a fitness trail, picnic areas, a playground for the children and a shelter. ☎ 757-566-3036, www.dcr.state.va.us/parks/york-rive.htm.

Shopping

Shopping in and around Williamsburg is as diverse as it gets. Within Colonial Williamsburg you can purchase the 18th-century-style items that you see being made there by artisans. Outside the historic district, outlet shopping malls and the famous Williamsburg Pottery have made the area a mecca for bargain-hunters.

Most of the goods you will see being made in **Colonial Williamsburg** are for sale. Nine of the shops have been restored to recreate the world as it was back in Colonial times, and stepping into any one of them is to walk through a portal into the past.

The stores contain an assortment of merchandise typical of the 18th century. Three cornered hats, jewelry, tea services, pottery and old maps and prints are only a few of the goodies found in the quaint little shops and stores.

Each shop has a history all its own. Jewelers at the Golden Ball once fashioned a pair of earrings for George Washington's daughter. The Greenhow Store sold china to Patrick Henry.

In the Crafthouses you can find a variety of beautiful reproduction furnishings, flatware, bedding and unique gifts for all occasions.

Step out of the 18th and into the 21st century at **Merchants Square**, a Colonial-revival village of 40 shops and restaurants located just steps from Colonial Williamsburg. Here you'll find a wide variety of fine goods, including fashions, Christmas decorations, candles, books, leather goods and handmade candies; ☎ 800-447-8679.

Travel west from Williamsburg on Richmond Road and you'll find **The Prime Outlets** of more than 80 designer stores, **Patriot Plaza Premium Outlets**, **The Williamsburg Outlet Mall**, **Basketville of Williamsburg**, and **The Williamsburg Pottery Factory**, a marketplace of several hundred acres that's become a phenomenon and destination in itself.

Dining

A. Carroll's Bistro, 601 Prince George Street, ☎ 757-258-8882, www.a-carrolls.com, serves seafood and beef in an elegant atmosphere. Live jazz on Friday nights.

The **Aberdeen Barn**, 1601 Richmond Road, ☎ 757-229-6661, www.aberdeenbarn.com, is open for dinner and is accessible to the handicapped. Specialties are roast prime rib, seafood and barbecue baby-back ribs. There's also a bar and an open-hearth grill.

Berret's Seafood Restaurant & Raw Bar, 199 S. Boundary Street, ☎ 757-253-1847, www.berrets.com, is open for lunch and dinner and is accessible to the handicapped. The restaurant offers a regional American menu, with specialties from the waters of the Chesapeake Bay and the Atlantic. There is a raw bar, outdoor dining and a variety of Virginia wines and micro-brewed beers available.

Bray Dining Room, at Kingsmill Resort & Conference Center in James City County, ☎ 757-253-3900, serves regional foods in a formal setting overlooking the James River.

The **British Corner Shoppe & Café**, 603 Prince George Street, ☎ 757-645-3100, serves individually-made subs on fresh-baked bread.

Captain George's Seafood Buffet, 5363 Richmond Road, ☎ 757-565-2323, www.captaingeorges.com, is open for dinner and is famous for its all-you-can-eat buffet, with more than 70 items. You can dine by the 12-foot waterfall and the 300-foot stream.

Chowning's Tavern, on Duke of Gloucester Street, ☎ 757-229-2141 or 800-TAVERNS, is open for continental breakfast, lunch and light pub fare and is operated by Colonial Williamsburg. Specialties are Brunswick stew and prime rib. The restaurant features an 18th-century tavern atmosphere, a vine-covered garden, strolling musicians and a Tap Room with a variety of draft beers. No reservations are taken.

Christiana Campbell's Tavern, on Waller Street, ☎ 757-229-2141 or 800-TAVERNS, is open for lunch and dinner and is within Colonial Williamsburg. The restaurant features period décor with antique and reproduction furnishings, and serves seafood, mixing contemporary and 18th-century dishes.

Cities Grille and Wine Shop, 4511-C John Tyler Highway, ☎ 757-564-3955, is a fun American-style bistro where you can select your wine from the extensive shop next door.

The **Dining Room at Ford's Colony Country Club**, 240 Ford's Colony Drive, ☎ 757-258-4107, www.fordscolony.com, is open for dinner (the Grille Room serves lunch). One of the area's finest and most elegant restaurants, with specialties including game and seafood, and there is usually one four-course meal on the menu. There is an up-close view of the kitchen, a wine cellar, a bar and traditional décor with Georgian-style paneling, beamed ceilings and a fireplace.

Fat Canary, 410 Duke of Gloucester Street at Merchants Square, ☎ 757-229-3333, is a new, lively restaurant open for dinner nightly serving contemporary Asian-influenced cuisine.

Huzzah! is at the Woodlands Hotel & Suites adjacent to the Colonial Williamsburg Visitor Center complex, 800-TAVERNS, www.colonialwilliamsburg.com. It's a new, casual eatery with a Colonial flair. Wondering about the name? "Huzzah" was the Colonial shout for "hooray."

The Jefferson Inn Restaurant, 1453 Richmond Road, ☎ 757-229-2296, has been family-operated since 1956. The restaurant is open for dinner, with regional favorites including Virginia peanut soup, Southern fried chicken, Virginia ham, stuffed pork chops, as well as steak, fresh seafood and Italian dishes.

The **King's Arms Tavern** on Duke of Gloucester Street, ☎ 757-229-2141 or 800-TAVERNS, is open for lunch and dinner within Colonial Williamsburg. The restaurant offers a Colonial American menu, with specialties like game pie, peanut soup, Virginia ham, and filet mignon stuffed with oysters. The restaurant is set in a restored 18th-century tavern with Colonial décor and balladeers. Reservations are recommended.

The Regency Room, at the Williamsburg Inn in Colonial Williamsburg, ☎ 757-229-2141 or 800-TAVERNS, is open for breakfast, lunch and dinner and is accessible to the handicapped. The elegant, formal restaurant offers a continental menu, served on white tablecloths with fresh flowers and silver, live music every night and dancing on Friday and Saturday. Leave the denim at home – jacket and tie are requred for dinner. Specialties include Caesar salad tossed table-side, plenty of seafood, veal and their own splendid desserts and pastries. Sunday brunch features Champagne and live music. The **Terrace Room** serves a traditional afternoon Tea.

The Seafare of Williamsburg, 1632 Richmond Road, ☎ 757-229-0099, is open for dinner and is accessible to the handicapped. Specialties include seafood, steak and veal, served in style by tuxedoed waiters. There is a nautical décor, a salad bar and warm rum bread to start the meal.

Shields Tavern, on Duke of Gloucester Street in Colonial Williamsburg, ☎ 757-229-2141 or 800-TAVERNS, is open for lunch, dinner, and Sunday brunch. The seasonal menu reflects the harvest of local farms, rivers and the Chesapeake Bay. The restaurant is a restored Colonial tavern built in 1745 and features balladeers at dinner. Garden seating is available, weather permitting. Dinner reservations recommended.

The Trellis Restaurant, 403 Duke of Gloucester Street in Merchant's Square, ☎ 757-229-8610, is open for lunch and dinner. Specialties of the house include fresh seafood and decadent chocolate desserts. Outdoor dining is available.

The Whaling Company, 494 McLaws Circle, ☎ 757-229-0275, www-.whalingcompany.com, is open for lunch and dinner. House specialties include fresh seafood, choice steaks and chicken. The dress is casual, with décor suggesting an old-fashioned fishing village.

The Whitehall Restaurant, 1325 Jamestown Road, ☎ 757-229-4677, www.thewhitehall.com, is fine European dining at its best. Located in a late-1800s farmhouse with five dining rooms and a huge wine cellar, visible through a glass floor. Great German food.

Accommodations

With nearly 70 hotels and motels, and two dozen bed & breakfast inns in Williamsburg, there's a lodging for every taste and budget. Here is but a sampling. For more, see www.visitwilliamsburg.com.

Historic Area

Accommodations in the Historic Area include these five properties. For additional information, ☎ 800-HISTORY.

Colonial Williamsburg's Colonial Houses offer immersion in the period within a number of Colonial houses and taverns. Facilities and services include dining privileges at the Williamsburg Inn, free airport transportation and use of the recreational facilities at the Colonial Williamsburg Inn. $$$$

Colonial Williamsburg Governor's Inn, is three blocks from the Historic Area, has 200 affordable guest rooms and an outdoor pool. Guests have free use of the recreational facilities at the nearby Woodlands Hotel & Suites. $

Colonial Williamsburg Inn, 136 Francis Street in the Historic Area, is a small luxury hotel with 62 suites. The hotel features a restaurant, a swimming pool with a lifeguard and poolside service, an exercise room, tennis courts, golf, lawn games, several meeting rooms and gift shop. It is furnished in the style of a country estate, and features spacious lounges and a shaded terrace. $$$$

Colonial Williamsburg Lodge, 310 S. England Street, has 323 rooms. The hotel is decorated with American folk art and has a swimming pool with poolside service and a lifeguard, a beauty shop, tennis courts, golf, and a new spa across the street. An all-new conference center and restaurant is scheduled for completion in late 2006. $$$

Williamsburg Woodlands, 102 Visitor Center Drive, offers 300 rooms and suites in a casual retreat hotel on 44 wooded acres adjacent to the Historic Area. There are two outdoor pools, golf, miniature golf, badminton, and a restaurant. $$

Hotels & Motels

 Best Western Patrick Henry Inn, York and Page streets, Route 60 East, ☎ 757-229-9540, www.patrickhenryinn.com, has 301 rooms and whirlpool suites, an outdoor pool, and is a half-block from the Hisoric Area. $$

 Clarion Hotel & Conference Center, 500 Merrimac Trail, ☎ 800-666-8888, www.williamsburgclarion.com, has 250 newly renovated room and suites, an Olympic-sized indoor pool, a restaurant and business center. $$

There are three **Comfort Inn** properties in Williamsburg: a 157-room motel close to the Historic District, ☎ 800-358-8003, www.comfortinnhistoric.com, $; an 80-room motel adjacent to Prime Outlets, ☎ 800-964-1774, $; and **Comfort Inn and Suites** in the heart of Williamsburg, ☎ 800-444-4678, $$.

Country Inn & Suites by Carlson, 400 Bypass Road, ☎ 757-259-7990, www.countryinns.com/williamsburgva_historicarea, is a new lodging with 66 rooms and suites, an indoor heated pool and fitness room. $$

Courtyard By Marriott, 470 McLaws Circle, ☎ 800-321-2211, www.courtyard.com/phfwb, has 151 rooms, a full-service restaurant, an indoor pool, free high-speed Internet and an exercise room. $$

Days Hotel Busch Gardens, 201 Water Country Parkway, ☎ 800-635-5366, is an upscale hotel with 202 rooms, a full-service restaurant, an outdoor pool, exercise room, sand volleyball court, jogging trail and picnic area. $-$$

Days Inn Historic Area, 331 Bypass Road, ☎ 800-759-1166, has 120 rooms, a heated outdoor pool, sand volleyball, a lobby with fireplace and a verandah. $$

Econo Lodge-Colonial, 216 Parkway Drive, ☎ 757-253-6450, is small motel (48 rooms) within walking distance of the Historic Area. $

Embassy Suites Williamsburg, 3006 Mooretown Road, ☎ 800-333-0924, www.embassysuites.com/es/williamsburg, has 168 suites, a nightly reception and complimentary made-to-order breakfast, indoor pool and spa and fitness center. $$$

Great Wolf Lodge-Indoor Waterpark Resort, 555-559 E. Rochambeau Drive, ☎ 800-551-9653, http://williamsburg.greatwolflodge.com, is a gigantic family resort with an indoor water park. The Northwoods-themed resort has 301 suites, a restaurant, spa and arcade. Rates include waterpark passes for a family of four. It's located just north of Williamsburg in York County. $$$$

Hampton Inn & Suites Historic Area, 1880 Richmond Road, ☎ 800-346-3055, has 100 rooms and suites with kitchens. $$

Hilton Garden Inn, 1624 Richmond Road, ☎ 877-609-9400, www.williamsburg.gardeninn.com, has 119 rooms and suites, a pool, business center and fitness center. $$

Holiday Inn Downtown and Holidome, 814 Capitol Landing Road, ☎ 800-368-0200, has 137 rooms with a Colonial décor, a full-service restaurant, golf privileges, an exercise room and convention facilities. The 10,000-square-foot Holidome has in indoor heated pool, shuffleboard, putting green, whirlpool, exercise room and sauna, and is handicapped-accessible. $-$$

Holiday Inn Patriot, 3032 Richmond Road, ☎ 757-565-2600, www.holidayinnpatriot.com, has 160 rooms, indoor and outdoor pools, restaurant, lounge, fitness center, and conference facilities. $$

Kingsmill Resort, 1010 Kingsmill Road, ☎ 800-832-5665, www.kingsmill.com, is a large resort complex with 405 rooms. The hotel offers a range of services and facilities that include golf and tennis, two 18-hole golf courses, marina privileges, meeting rooms, a spa with an exercise instructor, and indoor and outdoor pools. There are complimentary shuttles to Colonial Williamsburg and Busch Gardens. $$$$

The Marriott Hotel-Williamsburg, 50 Kingsmill Road, ☎ 800-442-3654, www.marriotthotels.com/phfcw, has 295 rooms. The hotel features a full-service restaurant, heated indoor/outdoor pool, health club, tennis courts, sauna, whirlpool, convention facilities, a shopping arcade, tennis courts, several meeting rooms, entertainment and dancing. $$$

Quality Inn Lord Paget, 901 Capitol Landing Road, ☎ 757-229-4444, is a 94-room motel in a quiet, wooded setting with a duck pond and outdoor pool. Several adjoining suites for families are available, with full kitchens, living areas and patios. $

Radisson Fort MaGruder Hotel & Conference Center, 6945 Pocahontas Trail, ☎ 800-333-3333, www.radisson.com, has 303 rooms and is built around an original redoubt from the Civil War. The hotel features a full-service restaurant, indoor and outdoor swimming pools, lighted tennis courts, golf privileges, an exercise room and convention facilities. $$

 Ramada Inn 1776, 725 Bypass Road, ℅ 757-220-1776, one mile from the Historic Area, has 202 Colonial-style rooms. The 42 landscaped acres have five duck ponds, a playground, tennis, volleyball and an outdoor pool. $

Ramada Inn Outlet Mall, 6493 Richmond Road, ☎ 800-524-1443, has 128 rooms and is adjacent to the Williamsburg Outlet Mall. There is a complimentary continental breakfast, full-service restaurant, and an outdoor pool. $

Williamsburg Hospitality House, 415 Richmond Road, ☎ 800-932-9192, has 295 rooms and suites, located two blocks from the Historic Area. There are two restaurants, a swimming pool, golf privileges, entertainment and dancing and complimentary afternoon tea. $$-$$$

Bed & Breakfasts / Inns

A Boxwood Inn of Williamsburg, 708 Richmond Road, ☎ 888-798-4333, www.boxwoodinn.com, is a renovated 1928 inn with four luxurious King/Queen suites and a lovely porch, within walking distance of Colonial Williamsburg. No smoking, pets or children. $$

A Primrose Cottage B&B, 706 Richmond Road, ☎ 800-522-1901, www.primrose-cottage.com, has four antique-filled guestrooms, each with a television and private bath. Guests can play the harpsichord build by the innkeeper. No smoking, pets or children. $$

A Williamsburg White House, 718 Jamestown Road, ☎ 866-229-8580, www.awilliamsburgwhitehouse.com, takes the presidential theme to the fullest. There are four presidential bed chambers, cocktails are served in the Diplomatic Reception Room, and breakfast in the Kennedy Library. And of course, there's a Rose Garden outside! Smoking area outside. No pets, no children under 14. $$$

An American Inn B&B-Williamsburg Manor, 600 Richmond Road, ☎ 757-220-8011, www.williamsburg-manor.com, is a family-friendly 1927 inn with five rooms, just three blocks from the Historic Area. $$

Cedars of Williamsubrg B&B, 616 Jamestown Road, ☎ 800-296-3591, www.cedarsofwilliamsburg.com, was built in the 1930s during Williamsburg's reconstruction by craftsmen trained in Colonial building techniques. It has nine guest rooms and candlelight breakfast is served on the Tavern porch. No pets; well-behaved children by pre-arrangment. $$$

Colonial Capital B&B, 501 Richmond Road, ☎ 800-776-0570, www.ccbb-.com, is a 1926 antique-filled Colonial three blocks from the Historic Area. The five guestrooms have canopy beds and private baths. Children over eight are welcome. $$$

Fife and Drum Inn, 441 Prince George Street, ☎ 888-838-1783, www.fifeanddruminn.com, is a small hotel in downtown Williamsburg with nine rooms. It is still owned by teh descendents of A. Webster Hitchens, who built it as a commercial building in 1933. Children six and older welcome. $$$

Fox & Grape B&B, 701 Monumental Avenue, ☎ 800-292-3699, www.foxandgrapebb.com, is a two-story Colonial with four guest rooms.The innkeepers make and sell unique Noah's Ark folk art. $$

Governor's Trace B&B, 303 Capitol Landing Road, ☎ 800-303-7552, www.governorstrace.com, is just one door away from the Historic District and George Washington's favorite tavern. Three guestrooms, two with private screened porches. $$$

Legacy of Williamsburg B&B, 930 Jamestown Road, ☎ 800-962-4722, www.legacyofwilliamsburgbb.com, offers a choice of four rooms and two suites in a contemporary inn with period antiques and furnishings, including six fireplaces and canopy beds. $$$

Liberty Rose B&B Inn, 1022 Jamestown Road, ☎ 800-545-1825, www-.libertyrose.com, offers four rooms in a romantic hilltop estate. Full breakfast served at "tables for two" on the morning porch. There are gardens, courtyards, a grand piano and fireplaces. $$$$

Magnolia Manor B&B, 700 Richmond Road, ☎ 800-462-6667, www-.magnoliamanorwmbg.com, has four rooms and suites, all with king canopy beds. Suites have fireplaces. Well-behaved children by prior arrangement. $$$

War Hill Inn, 4560 Longhill Road, ☎ 800-743-0248, www.war_hill_inn.com, offers a choice of five rooms and two suites in a large country manor, built in 1969 under the guidance of a Colonial Williamsburg architect. $$

Williamsburg Sampler B&B Inn, 922 Jamestown Road, ☎ 800-722-1169, www.williamsburgsampler.com, has four rooms located in a plantation-style house with Colonial-style furnishings. $$-$$$

Camping

Anvil Campground, 5243 Mooretown Road, ☎ 800-633-4442, www-.anvilcampground.com, has 60 shaded sites and full hook-ups, a store, three playgrounds, pool, and game room.

Carter's Cove Campground, 8758 Pocahontas Trail, ☎ 757-220-0386, has 75 shaded, quiet sites, full hook-ups, pull-through sites. There's a playground and public transportation to major attractions.

Colonial Campgrounds, 4712 Lightfoot Road, ☎ 800-336-2734, is a fairly large campground with about 200 grassy and semi-wooded sites; most are pull-throughs and have hookups. Facilities include tenting, flush toilets, hot showers, sewage disposal, a laundry, public telephone and a store where you can obtain LP gas, RV supplies, ice and groceries. There is a recreation room, a pavilion, coin-operated games, a swimming pool, lawn games and a playground.

Jamestown Beach Campsites is located on the James River near Jamestown Settlement, ☎ 800-446-9228 or 757-229-7609. This large, wooded campground has 600 sites, many wooded and with fill hookups. There is a camp store, game room, and pavilion. Swimming, boating and fishing on the shores of the James River.

Williamsburg & Colonial KOA Resorts, 4000 and 5210 Newman Road, ☎ 800-KOA-1733, www.williamsburgkoa.com, has 150 open and shaded sites, most with full hookups. There are camping cabins, tenting, flush toilets, hot showers, sewage disposal, a laundry, public telephone and a store where one can obtain RV supplies, ice and groceries. There is a recreation room, a pavilion, a heated swimming pool, pond fishing, coin-operated games, lawn games, a playground and a shuttle to Colonial Williamsburg.

Transportation

Williamsburg is 150 miles south of Washington DC, and roughly midway between Richmond and Norfolk off Interstate 64.

Newport News/Williamsburg Airport is 20 minutes from downtown Williamsburg. **Richmond International Airport** and **Norfolk International Airport** are about 50 minutes from Williamsburg.

AMTRAK, ☎ 800-872-7245, offers direct service to Williamsburg from major East Coast cities. The station is at 468 N. Boundary Street.

Greyhound Lines, ☎ 800-231-2222, also serves the area at 468 N. Boundary Street.

Williamsburg Area Transport serves the Williamsburg Pottery Factory, Colonial Williamsburg, Busch Gardens, Water Country USA, Prime Outlets and key points in between from Memorial Day weekend through Labor Day, seven days a week. ☎ 757-259-4093 during business hours, or 757-259-4111 after hours and on weekends, www.williamsburgtransport.com.

Ground transportation is available through **Carey VIP Chauffeured Services** at ☎ 757-220-1616, www.careyvip.net.

Information

For information regarding the Historic Triangle area, contact the **Williamsburg Area Convention & Visitors Bureau**, 201 Penniman Road, Williamsburg, VA 23185. ☎ 757-253-0192 or 800-368-6511, or visit www.visitwilliamsburg.com.

For information on **Colonial Williamsburg**, call 800-HISTORY or visit www.colonialwilliamsburg.org.

For information regarding the Colonial Parkway, contact **The Colonial National Historic Park**, PO Box 210, Yorktown, VA 23690. ☎ 757-898-3400.

Charles City County

There's no city in Charles City County, and its unique location between the James and Chickahominy Rivers makes it one of those rare places where you can leave the stress and pressure of business life far behind.

History

Residents of this area have, for thousands of years, represented a diverse cross-section of humanity: Native Americans, English colonists, planters, slaves and free blacks. Presidents, signers of the Declaration of Independence, emancipators and fierce Confederate patriots, educators and agronomists were either born, lived or worked in Charles City County. Many of their descendants still live there today. The third-oldest organized black church and one of the first free black communities were located in the county.

The area's first inhabitants were the **Chickahominy Indians**, whose population numbered about 1,000 in 1607, but by 1705 had all but disappeared. At the beginning of the 20th century, tribe members made diligent efforts to renew the population, and today they are one of the largest tribes remaining in Virginia.

The English established Charles City County in 1616, and westward expansion began. Those early settlers, sustained by the burgeoning tobacco industry, prospered and grew rich, though at great cost to the Indians. Plantations and farms sprang up all along the James River. Against all odds, the gracious homes and mansions survived the rigors of the Revolutionary War, the War of 1812 and the Civil War that devastated the area around Richmond and Petersburg to the west.

Today, many of the old stately homes are open for visitors. The county's extensive timberlands, tidal waters and thousands of acres of richly cultivated farmland are also preserved in this historic rural community.

As there is no city, the heart of Charles City County is its early 18th-century courthouse – a cultural link between past and present.

Sights

Take a trip along Route 5, one of America's most scenic highways, and you can visit eight historic plantation properties, spend the day savoring the lush gardens and historic houses, enjoy a wonderful meal, stay the night in one of the magnificent historic homes, rise to a hearty country breakfast and then do it all over again.

Belle Air Plantation, 11800 John Tyler Highway, is a 17th-century house built around 1670. Massive heartpine timbers and beams form the structure and much of the interior decoration of the mansion. The old home features one of America's finest Jacobean staircases and it overlooks acres of landscaped gardens and rolling farmlands. Open by appointment. ☎ 804-829-2431, www.jamesriverplantations.org.

The Berkeley Plantation is the site of the first official Thanksgiving in 1619. It is also the birthplace of Benjamin Harrison, a signer of the Declaration of Independence; of William Henry Harrison, the ninth president

Charles City County

of the United States; and the ancestral home of Benjamin Harrison, the 23rd president. *Taps* was composed at Berkeley in 1862. Today, the plantation remains in its traditional state, furnished with authentic antiques and surrounded by boxwood gardens. ☎ 804-829-6018, www.berkeley-plantation.com.

Schedule a visit to **Clearview Farm Alpacas**, 18310 The Glebe Lane, to see these magical animals. ☎ 804-829-5092, www.clearviewfarmalpacas.com.

The **Edgewood Plantation**, famous for its Gothic Revival architecture, features 7,000 square feet of antiques, charm, romance and history. Built in 1849, the house has served as a church, a post office and as a signal post for the Confederacy – Cavalry General J.E.B. "Jeb" Stuart stopped at the plantation in 1862 – and today is a bed & breakfast. The old house proudly features cozy fireplaces, a free-standing double spiral staircase and magnificent formal gardens. The Edgewood Plantation is at 4800 John Tyler Highway, and is open for special events and for Garden Week in April; tours are available be reservation. ☎ 804-829-2962 or 800-296-3343, www.edgewoodplantation.com.

Fort Pocahontas at Wilson's Wharf, Route 5, on the James River, was the transportation center for local tobacco, and was seized as a Union fort during the Civil War. It was the site of one of the greatest victories won by a force of nearly all African Americans, the US Colored Troops. Restoration and archeological work is being conducted at the fort, which is privately owned.

At the **North Bend Plantation**, 12200 Weyanoke Road, one can enjoy the hospitality of one of Virginia's oldest families. Built in 1819 for Sarah Harrison – the sister of the ninth US president, William Henry Harrison – Union General Philip "Little Phil" Sheridan made it his headquarters in 1864. Large rooms with private baths, beautifully appointed with period antiques, make North Bend a bed & breakfast with a real difference. The grounds are open daily, and house tours can be arranged for groups. ☎ 804-829-5176, www.northbendplantation.com.

Piney Grove at Southall's Plantation, 16920 Southall Plantation Lane, was established in the 18th century as the country home of the prominent Southall family. The original 1790 portion is a rare survival of early Tidewater log architecture. The grounds also include **Ashland** (1835), **Duck Church** (1917) and **Dower Quarter** (1835). Today the Gordineer family offers historic bed & breakfast accommodations in the 1857 Ladysmith House. Guests will enjoy mint juleps, star-filled skies and candlelight breakfasts. The gardens and grounds are open daily for a self-guided tour and guided group house tours are available by appointment (Motorcoach tours welcome). ☎ 804-829-2480 or visit www.pineygrove.com.

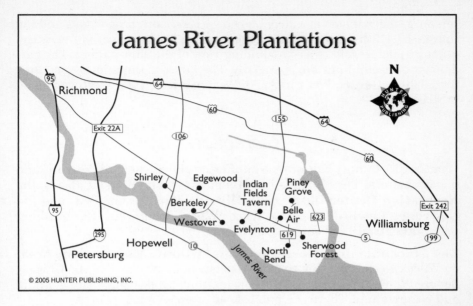

James River Plantations

© 2005 HUNTER PUBLISHING, INC.

At **Renwood Fields**, 17575 Sandy Point Road, explore the The Amazing Maize Maze, a maze in a cornfield, and **A Glimpse into the Past Farm Museum**. Open July through October. ☎ 804-829–5399, www.renwood-fields.com.

The Sherwood Forest Plantation, 14501 John Tyler Highway, was the home of John Tyler after he served as president of the United States from 1841 until 1845. The house, built in 1730, has been lovingly restored and furnished with the possessions of President Tyler and his young bride, Julia Gardener. Still occupied by the president's grandson, the house's original outbuildings still stand among more than 80 varieties of trees and landscaped grounds. The museum shop features many items of presidential memorabilia and a variety of fine gifts. The plantation is open daily, except Thanksgiving and Christmas Day. ☎ 804-829-5377, 804-282-1441, www.sherwoodforest.org.

The Shirley Plantation, settled in 1613 by Sir Thomas West, is the oldest one in Virginia. The mansion, built by Edward Hill in 1723 for his daughter Elizabeth and her husband John Carter, is presently occupied and operated by the 11th generation of the Carter family, making it the oldest family business in America. Many original portraits, antiques and items of fine silver grace the magnificent old house, characterized by its unique square flying staircase. The plantation is open daily from 9 a.m. until 5 p.m., closed Thanksgiving and Christmas days. The gift shop offers a wide variety of unusual decorative and gift items. The Shirley Plantation is at 501 Shirley Plantation Road, ☎ 800-232-1613; or visit www.shirleyplantation.com.

Westover is one of the most elegant Colonial plantations in Virginia. Built around 1730 by William Byrd II, the founder of Richmond and Petersburg, the mansion is widely known for its superb proportions and the finest early 18th-century gates in the country. The lawn, with its century-old tulip poplars, offers a commanding view of the James River. The gardens and outbuildings are open daily. The house is sometimes open during Historic Garden Week in April. Westover is at 7000 Westover Road. ☎ 804-829-2882.

Recreation

Charles City County has four parks offering playing fields, bike trails and picnic shelters. They include the **Harrison Park** (Wayside Road), the **Recreation Center** (Route 612), **Hillside Park** (Route 664) and the **Lawrence Lewis Jr. Park** on Wilcox Wharf Road, which has a fishing pier, hiking trails and observation decks.

The Chickahominy Recreational and Wildlife Management Area, on Wilcox Neck Road (Route 623), consists of 5,300 acres on the Chickahominy River. It is open to the public for hunting, boating, fishing, hikng and nature study. There is a public boat ramp on Morris Creek.

Annual Events

Many of the James River Plantations participate jointly in special events throughout the year. There is an autumn festival, ghost tours, and Progressive Dinners around most holidays, from President's Day to Christmas. Visit www.jamesriverplantations.com/events.htm.

James River Plantations Garden Week. House tours are held the last full week in April, ☎ 804-644-7776 or www.jamesriverplantations.com.

The **Shirley Polo Cup** takes place in mid-June at Shirley Plantation. ☎ 804-643-7407, www.shirleypolocup.com.

The Charles City County Fair is held in mid-September with arts and crafts competitions, recipe contests, carnival rides and a midway. ☎ 804-829-9241.

Chickahominy Fall Festival & Pow-wow, held by the Chickahominy tribe on the fourth weekend in September, features Native American dancing, music, food, and crafts. ☎ 804-829-2186 or 804-829-6333. It's free and open to the public.

The First Official Thanksgiving at Berkeley Plantation features a play re-enacting the historic event. ☎ 804-829-6018 for ticket information.

A **Christmas Parade** is held the day after Thanksgiving featuring bands, floats and contests. ☎ 804-829-9227.

Christmas is a particularly special time at the James River Plantations. The month of December is **Christmas in Plantation Country**, and feature tours, teas, progressive candlelight dinners, caroling and historical interpretations. Contact plantations individually, or visit www.james-riverplantations.com/events.htm.

Dining

The **Coach House Tavern**, 12602 Harrison Landing Road, is a critically acclaimed restaurant housed in a restored outbuilding on the grounds of the Berkeley Plantation – just a hundred yards from the manor house where the first 10 US presidents dined with the Harrisons. Open for lunch daily, dinner on Friday and Saturday by appointment. Offers elegant candlelit dining overlooking the magnificent English gardens. ☎ 804-829-6003 for information and reservations.

Indian Fields Tavern, 9220 John Tyler Highway, is a turn-of-the-century farmhouse which has been turned into one of Charles City County's most exciting and acclaimed restaurants. Indian Fields is open for lunch, dinner and Sunday brunch. Enjoy the region's finest foods while surrounded by some of Virginia's most beautiful countryside. ☎ 804-829-5004, www.indianfields.com, for information and reservations.

Accommodations

These historic mansions offer lodging to guests. All are located within a half hour west of Williamsburg, along Route 5 and overlook the James River.

Edgewood Plantation Inn B&B, 4800 John Tyler Memorial Highway, ☎ 800-296-3343, www.edgewoodplantation.com, offers eight rooms to overnight guests in the 1849 historic mansion. There are English gardens, a pool, grist mill, gazebos and horseback riding packages. Children over 12 only. $$

North Bend Plantation, 12200 Weyanoke Road, ☎ 804-829-5176, www.northbendplantation.com, has large guestrooms with fireplaces, canopy beds, private baths, and antiques. A full breakfast is served with heirloom china and silver. The extensive grounds include a pool, volleyball, croquet. Children welcome. $$

Piney Grove at Southall's Plantation, 16920 Southall Plantation Lane, ☎ 804-829-2480, www.pineygrove.com, has three rooms and three suites in the 1857 Ladysmith House, filled with antiques, fireplaces, and private baths. A hearty plantation breakfast is served by candlelight in the 1790 Log Room. Outside are gardens, a pool and nature trail. $$$

Charles City County

Hotels & Motels

River's Rest Motel & Marina, 9100 Wilcox Neck Road, ☎ 804-829-2753, has 20 rooms, some with water views of the Chickahominy River. There are boat slips, canoe rentals, and a restaurant serving breakfast, lunch and dinner. Close to all the plantations. $

Bed & Breakfasts / Inns

Orange Hill Bed & Breakfast, 18401 The Glebe Lane, ☎ 888-501-8125, www.orangehillbb.com, is a Victorian-era farmhouse with two guest-rooms. No credit cards. $$

Red Hill Bed & Breakfast, 7500 John Tyler Memorial Highway, ☎ 804-829-6045, is a Colonial home with four guestrooms. No children or pets. Smoking in designated areas. $.

Information

Charles City County Department of Development, PO Box 66, Charles City, VA 23030, ☎ 804-829-9217, www.co.charles-city.va.us.

Jamestown & Yorktown

The Colonial National Historical Park incorporates two of America's most historic sites, Jamestown and Yorktown, which have major anniversaries this decade. Located on the Virginia peninsula between the York and James rivers, each site has its own story to tell. They are connecting stories, for the events that took place at Jamestown led inevitably to those at Yorktown. The Colonial Parkway, 23 miles of scenic roadway that links the two sites, makes it easy to follow the sequence of events from the nation's Colonial beginnings at Jamestown in 1607 to their conclusion with the surrender of General Cornwallis at the Battle of Yorktown in 1781. The Colonial Parkway is, in itself, well worth a visit. It's a scenic route that provides access to many other historic spots while showing off the area's spectacular natural beauty.

Historic Jamestowne, The Original Site

Jamestown Island lies at the western end of the Colonial Parkway. The town itself is an archeological dig in progress. Even so, it's not difficult to imagine life as it must have been during those first days.

It was on May 13, 1607, that 104 Englishmen and boys stepped ashore on the banks of the James River, established the first permanent English-speaking settlement in North America, and so set in motion a series of events that would change the world. During its brief lifetime, the tiny settlement became Virginia's first capital and the place where representative legislative government in America began on June 30, 1619.

The story of Jamestown is still a mystery that continues to unfold even as the 400th anniversary of the settlement approaches in 2007. Extensive archeological excavations since the turn of the century have uncovered more than 500,000 artifacts and numerous building foundations, but failed to provide all the answers. But just in the last few years, archaeologists have made some exciting discoveries, namely the remains of the 1607 James Fort, as well as evidence of manufacturing by the early colonists. Visitors can view the Jamestown Rediscovery Archaeological Project in progress. It is sponsored by the Association for the Preservation of Virginia Antiquities, which jointly operates Historic Jamestowne along with the National Park Service.

Touring Historic Jamestowne

Historians and archaeologists have worked closely together to provide a picture of what life must have been like for the early settlers who landed on the island back in 1607. Excavations have uncovered foundations, innumerable artifacts and burial grounds. Visitors are welcome to watch current digs.

Whether you take a tour with a costumed interpreter, a park ranger, or on your own, a tour of the site will take you through the old town, where exhibits, statues and memorials interpret the historic events. There is also a five-mile driving tour that takes in the entire island, with paintings and signs at pull-offs along the route that describe the struggles of the early settlers.

Begin your self-guided walking tour at the visitor center. Take plenty of time, stroll for an hour or two, and let your imagination wander. Before you move on, however, be sure to see the 15-minute orientation film and the exhibits in the center's museum.

The first stop on your tour after you leave the visitor center is the **Tercentenary Monument**. From the terrace, you can see the foundations of the town site. The 103-foot-high granite shaft, erected in 1907, commemorates the 300th anniversary of the founding of Jamestown.

Next is the **Statue of Pocahontas**, the daughter of Chief Powhatan. Her marriage to John Rolfe in 1614 helped to improve relations between the local Indians and the English.

The **Old Church Tower** is the only 17th-century structure still standing. The tower is an addition to the first brick church built in 1639. In 1907, the 300th anniversary of the founding, a memorial church was built over the foundations of the 1639 brick church and an earlier frame church built in 1617. It was here on July 30th in 1619 that the first representative legislative assembly in North America convened to lay out the

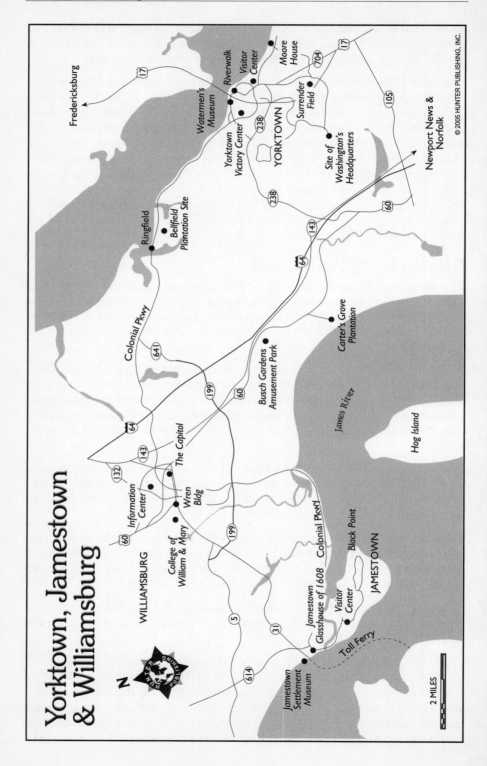

Yorktown, Jamestown & Williamsburg

foundations for the representative style of government that we enjoy today.

Just down the road, close to the banks of the James River, you'll find the **Statue of John Smith**. John Smith is a historical character who must have been a legend in his own lifetime. Explorer, soldier, author and president of the Virginia Council in 1608-1609, he instituted a policy of rigid discipline with the admonishment, "He who will not work, will not eat." It was largely because of him and his strong leadership that the colony survived, prospered and grew.

The location of the 1607 **James Fort** was a mystery for nearly four centuries. Within days of their arrival, the settlers were attacked by Indians. They hastily constructed a palisaded fort of upright log timbers, choosing a spot on high ground behind a bend in the river as the best defense against their other enemies, the Spanish. The precise location of the fortification was not known, and historians speculated that its remains must have been eroded by the mighty James River. But in 1996 archaeologists found the east corner of the fort and have been working on tracing its outline ever since. In 2004 they discovered a brick-lined wine cellar with 300-year-old intact glass bottles made in England between 1680 and 1700. Also discovered in 2004 is a later building, dating from around 1693, positioned diagonally across the fort which, by then, was no longer in use. It's believed to have been the governor's house, or a residence for high-ranking colonists.

a little farther on along the road, the **Robert Hunt Shrine** is dedicated to the colony's first Anglican minister. The Reverend Hunt played a key role in the colonists' spiritual life and their efforts to survive.

The **Dale House**, near the sea wall, is named for Sir Thomas Dale, governor of Virginia from 1611 to 1616. It now serves as the Jamestown Rediscovery Archeological Laboratory. There is a viewing area where visitors can see artifacts from the dig.

The **Memorial Cross** marks some 300 shallow graves hastily dug by the colonists during the winter of 1609-1610 – the period known as the "Starving Time."

At the west end of the settlement, is the location of the **Third and Fourth Statehouses**. Representative government grew and developed in these buildings. The Third Statehouse was burned by Nathaniel Bacon during his ill-fated rebellion against the royal government in 1676. The Fourth Statehouse was built upon the foundations of the Third, but the structure accidentally burned in the fall of 1698, thus sparking the movement by the General Assembly to relocate the capital from Jamestown to Williamsburg.

New Towne was developed sometime soon after 1620. It's a section of Jamestown where wealthy colonists built more substantial homes. The foundations of many of the homes and other buildings were excavated by archaeologists during the 1930s and 1950s. Later these excavations were covered with white bricks to protect them. Take your time, stay on the pathways and off the ruins, and try to imagine those far off days. It's not difficult to picture how tough it must have been for the first settlers to survive the rigors of the uncivilized New World, especially during the first and second winters.

Return along the road toward the park and visit the **Glasshouse**. There you can watch artisans demonstrate the art of glassblowing – one of Virginia's first industries – as it was done in the 17th century.

The entrance station to the park is open daily from 8:30 a.m. until 4:30 p.m. Once admitted, visitors may remain in the park until dusk. The visitor center is open daily from 9 a.m. until 5 p.m. The Glasshouse is open daily 8:30 a.m. until 5 p.m. Admission charged. For information on Historic Jamestowne, ☎ 757-229-1733, www.historicjamestowne.org, or www.nps.org/colo/jamestown/jamestown.htm.

Jamestown Settlement

Just outside the National Historic Park boundary on the Colonial Parkway is the Jamestown Settlement, a state-operated museum. While not on the actual settlement site, it brings history to life through replicas of the three ships that sailed from England to Virginia in 1607, a recreated fort and Powhatan Indian village.

The new visitor welcome area is a spectacular 45-foot high rotunda. There is an extensive gift shop and a large café with outdoor seating. Further enhanced visitor facilities, new indoor and outdoor exhibits, and a new documentary film will be ready for the 400th anniversary of the founding of Jamestown in 2007, which coincides with the museum's own 50th anniversary. James Fort, Powhatan Village and the English ships will undergo significant changes to incorporate recent discoveries at actual archaeological sites in Virginia.

Your visit starts with a 15-minute documentary film shown inside the new theater, which opened in 2004. The film chronicles the struggle of the colonists to survive in their new and strange home. The museum has several galleries that detail the conditions in Europe that motivated travel to the New World, the lives of the Powhatan Indians who inhabited coastal Virginia at the time of English arrival, the origins of Africans brought to Virginia, and the history of the colony's first 100 years.

Next, visit the outdoor living history areas, where historical interpreters demonstrate the Powhatan way of life and life within the stockaded walls of James Fort. Then board replicas of the *Susan Constant*, *Godspeed* or *Discovery* docked at a pier on the James River. Under the decks you can see where passengers lived during the four-month crossing of the Atlantic. Two of the ships are being redesigned for the 2007 anniversary to more accurately reflect their actual size.

Jamestown Settlement is open daily, 9 a.m. to 5 p.m. Admission charged. ☎ 888-593-4682, www.historyisfun.org, or write to the Jamestown-Yorktown Foundation, PO Box 1607, Williamsburg, VA 23187.

Yorktown

Yorktown is a charming riverfront village with many homes and shops surviving from the Colonial period. Art galleries, antique and curio shops line the narrow, quiet streets – it's a town best experienced on foot. The $10 million **Riverwalk Landing** (www.riverwalklanding.com) has waterfront dining, a dozen shops, a performance stage, piers for cruise ships, recreational and sightseeing boats, and much-needed parking. The complex, a project of York County, is anchored by the historic **Frieght Shed**, which served as a steamship terminal from 1935 to 1952. The adjacent **Yorktown Beach** is a scenic place for a swim or a walk along the York River.

Surrounding the village is the **Yorktown Battlefield**, part of the Colonial National Historical Park. These serene fields witnessed a bloody three-day seige that would prove to be the last major battle of the American Revolution.

During the summer of 1781 the British Army, under General Cornwallis, began fortifying Yorktown and Gloucester Point in order to establish a naval base. At the end of August, a French fleet blocked the York River to prevent Cornwallis' escape. Meanwhile, General George Washington moved 17,600 American and French forces from New York to surround Cornwallis' 8,300 troops. On October 19, 1781 Cornwallis surrendered, effectively ending the war.

Close to Yorktown lie the remains of the English earthworks of 1781 as modified and strengthened by Confederate forces during the Civil War. A little further out are the reconstructions of the French and American lines. George Washington ordered the original allied works leveled immediately after the siege. The reconstruction of the more significant sections is the result of careful archaeological investigation and documented research.

Yorktown Battlefield

Begin your visit to Yorktown by stopping in at the **National Park Service Visitor Center**, at the end of the Colonial Parkway.

The events of the siege and the story of the town are set forth in a theater program and exhibits in the visitor center. Among the items on display are tents used by Washington during the Yorktown campaign, part of a reconstruction of an English frigate and artifacts recovered from the York River. The **Siege Line Overlook** on the roof of the center offers a panoramic view of strategic points on the battlefield.

Take a ranger-guided walking tour, watch an artillery demonstration or drive the seven-mile **Battlefield Tour Road**, which takes visitors near the American and French siege lines. On display are the various types of artillery used to defeat the British. **Surrender Field** was the site of the ceremonies ending the siege. There is an overlook and a recorded message about the event. **Moore House**, site of the negotiations leading to the surrender, is open every afternoon in the summer and weekends in the spring and fall.

The nine-mile **Encampment Tour Road** visits the locations of the allied encampments during the siege, including Washington's Headquarters. A trail connects it to the Newport News park trail system for additional biking, hiking, and jogging.

The historic earthworks are tangible evidence of the significant events of the Battle of Yorktown, but are subject to erosion. Be sure to walk only in designated areas. Yorktown Battlefield is open daily; admission charged. ☎ 757-898-2410, www.nps.gov/colo/Yorktown/ythome.htm.

Yorktown Victory Center

The Yorktown Victory Center, just beyond Highway 17, tells the story of the American Revolution through a stirring documentary and many unique interpretive exhibits. *A Time of Revolution* is an 18-minute film depicting a night during the Yorktown siege. The Witnesses to Revolution Gallery is a fascinating interpretation of sight and sound from the perspectives of 10 diverse people affected by the war. Another exhibit, Yorktown's Sunken Fleet, recreates the bow of the *Betsy,* one of the many ships lost during the seige. In the recreated Continental Army camp, costumed interpreters play out their everyday lives as members of George Washington's army. They demonstrate cooking, musketry, military drills, music and 18th-century surgery. At the center's farm, they interpret Virginia farm life as it might have been in the late 18th century, and invite visitors to lend a hand. Open daily from 9 a.m. until 5 p.m., except for Christmas and New Year's Day.

Other Sights

A self-guided walking tour of the town begins just over Tobacco Road from the visitor center, past the Yorktown Victory Monument to Main Street.

The Yorktown Victory Monument was authorized by the Continental Congress in 1781. Construction began 100 years later during the Centennial Celebrations of the Allied Victory over the English. The monument was completed in 1884.

If you're lucky, you may catch a performance of the **Fifes & Drums of York Town**, a youth corps that performs in Colonial garb several times a week at the Victory Monument and the Yorktown Visitor Center. ☎ 757-898-9418, www.fifes-and-drums.org.

The Hornsby House is the first house on the left on Main Street as you leave the Park Service walkway. The stately Georgian-style house was designed by Joseph Geddy for Mr. and Mrs. J.W. Hornsby in 1933 and built in a Flemish bond brick pattern. The house is still owned by the Hornsby family.

The Digges House is a little farther along the street to the right. Once the home of Dudley Digges, an attorney who served as a member of the Colonial legislature, it was built around 1760 and still carries the scars of 1781.

The Sessions House is a few yards farther to the left. The Sessions House is thought to be the oldest house in Yorktown.

The Nelson House, an 18th-century Georgian-style structure, was built by "Scotch Tom" Nelson and eventually became the home of Thomas Nelson Jr., one of the signers of the Declaration of Independence. The house was restored in the 1970s, and retains its scars from the siege of 1781. It is open to the public during the spring, summer and fall. ☎ 757-898-2410 for hours.

The Customs House was built in 1721 and was the storehouse and office of Richard Ambler while he served as Collector of Ports in Yorktown during the Colonial period. It is believed to be the oldest customs house in the United States. ☎ 757-258-0519.

The Burcher Cottage was constructed in the 1800s and is a gift shop operated by a Park Service concessionaire.

The Pate House, located across the street from the Customs House, was built by Thomas Pate in the early 1700s.

The Somerwell House, a little farther down on the same side of the street, was built around 1707 by local ferryman Mungo Somerwell. Today it houses Period Designs, featuring an assortment of household furnishings inspired by 17th and 18th-century antiques.

The Medical Shop is a reconstruction of an 18th-century medical shop. It was re-built by the National Park Service in 1936.

The Swan Tavern is a reconstruction of a popular Yorktown tavern built originally on the site by "Scotch Tom" Nelson and Joseph Walker in 1722. The original structure was destroyed by an ammunition explosion during the Civil War.

❖ *For more information, ☎ 888-593-4682 or write to the Jamestown-Yorktown Foundation, PO Box 1607, Williamsburg, Virginia 23187; or visit www.historyisfun.org.*

The Watermen's Museum, 309 Water Street, interprets the story of Virginia's watermen who, for centuries, have worked the rivers, tributaries, and the Chesapeake Bay. The museum is open April 1 to Thanks-

Jamestown & Yorktown

giving, Tuesday through Saturday, and on weekends the rest of the year. ☎ 757-887-2641, www.watermens.org.

The Archer House, on Water Street not far from the town pier, was used as a home and store by the Archer family for more than a hundred years. The old building is typical of a Colonial waterfront dwelling.

The Cornwallis Cave was not, contrary to local legend, the headquarters of the English general during the siege. Most likely it was used by other English officers and civilians.

Return to the visitor center by turning right onto Comte de Grasse Street, then left on Main Street and left again onto the Park Service walkway, past the Victory Monument on your left and over Tobacco Road, a trail once used by plantation workers to roll the hogsheads of tobacco down to the warehouses on the waterfront.

Annual Events

Military Through the Ages in mid-March features re-enactors and modern-day veterans demonstrating camp life, military tactics and weaponry at Jamestown Settlement, ☎ 888-593-4682.

Jamestown Landing Day in mid-May is celebrated at both Jamestown Settlement, ☎ 888-593-4682, www.historyisfun.org; and at Historic Jamestowne, ☎ 804-648-1889, www.historicjamestowne.org.

First Assembly Day commemorates the nation's first legislative assembly at Jamestown in 1619. Held in late July/early August. ☎ 757-898-3400, 757-229-1733.

Bacon's Rebellion Weekend in mid-September features living history programs on the 1676 rebellion, evening walking tours, and a symbolic burning of the town site at Historic Jamestowne. ☎ 757-229-1733 or 757-898-2410.

September and October bring the **Annual Jamestown Lecture Series**, featuring the director of archaeology for Jamestown Rediscovery Project and other scholars. ☎ 757-229-0412.

Yorktown Day in mid-October includes ceremonies, a parade and tactical demonstrations at the Yorktown Visitor Center (at the battlefield). ☎ 757-898-2410.

Yorktown Victory Weekend is an encampment at Yorktown Victory Center in October marking the anniversary of America's victory at Yorktown, ☎ 888-593-4682.

Foods & Feasts of Colonial Virginia is a three-day Thanksgiving event exploring the cuisine of the early Virginia colony. Held at Jamestown Settlement and Yorktown Victory Center, ☎ 888-593-4682.

Yorktown Celebrates Christmas is held the first Saturday night in December and features a Holiday Tree Lighting & Procession of Lights, and a Lighted Boat Parade on the York River. There's entertainment by the Fifes & Drums, caroling, and hot cider on the beach. ☎ 757-890-4970.

A Colonial Christmas, mid-December to the end of the month, allows visitors to experience 17th- and 18th-century holiday traditions at Jamestown Settlement and Yorktown Victory Center, ☎ 888-593-4682.

Dining

The Café at the Duke overlooks the York River at the Duke of York Motel. Breakfast and lunch are served in the River Room daily; dinner is served on Friday and Saturday. ☎ 757-898-3232, www.dukeofyorkmotel.com.

Carrot Tree Kitchens (corner of Read and Main streets, ☎ 757-246-9559, www.carrottree.com) is a new lunch spot in a very old location, the house Cole Digges built in 1720. Everything is made from scratch, and the carrot cake is the specialty. Located in the historic district, the menu is as American as the setting: Brunswick Stew, crab cakes, pulled pork sandwiches, country ham and biscuits. Open daily 10 a.m. to 4 p.m.

The new **Riverwalk Landing**, on Water Street, has a large waterfront restaurant with a marina theme, fine dining indoors, casual outdoors. ☎ 757-890-3525, www.riverwalklanding.com.

Waterstreet Landing is a casual spot across the street from the beach with great gourmet pizza and ice cream. Open for lunch and dinner daily. ☎ 757-886-5890, www.waterstreet-landing.com.

The **Yorktown Pub**, 540 Water Street, ☎ 757-886-9964, www.yorktown-pub.com, overlooks the York River and is open for lunch, dinner and nightlife. For a fun, casual meal with a great view, this is the place. Specialties include the Pub Burger and prime rib sandwiches. It's a favorite of the biker crowd.

Accommodations

Hotels & Motels

Duke of York Motel, 508 Water Street, ☎ 757-898-3232, www.duke-ofyorkmotel.com, overlooks the York River opposite the Town Beach. The motel has 57 rooms, shady lawns, a swimming pool and a café. $-$$

Yorktown Motor Lodge is at 8829 George Washington Highway (Route 17), ☎ 800-950-4003, is just three miles from Yorktown Battlefield. There are 42 rooms, free morning coffee, an outdoor pool and a playground. $

Bed & Breakfasts / Inns

 Marl Inn B&B at 220 Church Street, Yorktown, ☎ 757-898-3859 or 800-799-6207, www.marlinnbandb.com, has four guest rooms with private baths and entrances. There is a fireplace in the parlor and bicycles available for guests. Children and pets welcome. $$$

Rogers House Bed & Breakfast, 114 Church Street, ☎ 757-898-4852, www.rogershousebandb.com, has two rooms and a suite in a recently renovated early-20th-century house. The property has been in the owners' family since at least 1691. Front porches overlook the York River, and a rear deck is attached to an above-ground pool. $

York River Inn B&B at 209 Ambler Street, Yorktown, ☎ 800-884-7003, overlooks the water and is furnished with Virginia antiques and collectibles. There are three rooms with private baths. The Inn serves a full gourmet breakfast, and is a non-smoking facility. $$

The Eastern Shore

Accomack & Northampton Counties

Virginia's Eastern Shore encompasses the southernmost tip of the Delmarva Peninsula, which forms the eastern boundary of the Chesapeake Bay.

The peninsula is a quiet place of solitude and rich natural settings, colorful waterfowl, rustic workboats and scenic islands, where the pirate Blackbeard once sought refuge.

Numerous undeveloped islands off the ocean side of the shore form one of the last unspoiled barrier island ecosystems on the East Coast.

Hikers can roam the miles of unspoiled, uncrowded beaches of Assateague National Wildlife Refuge and see the famous Chincoteague wild ponies. The migration of tens of thousands of shorebirds each year makes birding popular. Fishing opportunities are some of the best on the East Coast, either in the Chesapeake Bay, the Atlantic Ocean, or dozens of tidal creeks in-between. Hunters will find many species of wildlife and waterfowl. For shoppers, the many quaint seaside villages offer numerous antique and gift shops.

Getting Around

The **Yorktown Trolley** operates April through October, making eight stops every 40 minutes. ☎ 757-890-3300.

Sightseeing cruises include the *Miss Yorktown* and *Yorktown Lady* (☎ 757-229-6244, www.yorktowncruises.com), and **Yorktown Hauntings Cruise** (☎ 800-378-1571, www.yorktownhauntingscruise.com) There's also a **Ghosts of Yorktown** candlelight walking tour (☎ 888-474-4788, www.theghosttour.com).

Information

York County Tourism, 224 Ballard Street, ☎ 757-890-3300, www.york-county.gov/tourism

The **Gallery at York Hall** serves as an informal welcome center for the town. Located in a historic building at Main and Ballard streets, the Gallery displays and sells local artwork and handcrafts, and has themed exhibits throughout the year. Open Tuesday through Saturday, 10 a.m. to 4 p.m. and Sunday 1-4 p.m. ☎ 757-890-4490.

History

The first recorded account of a visit by white men to the Eastern Shore was written in 1603 by Thomas Canner. Canner was a member of a landing party led by Captain Gilbert, a nephew of Sir Walter Raleigh who, following orders from his uncle, was searching for traces of the colony that had vanished from Roanoke Island some 15 years earlier. The landing party was ambushed by hostile Indians. Only two men survived the attack. One of them was Thomas Canner.

In 1608, that much-traveled English captain, John Smith, came ashore with a party of 32 men to explore and map the area.

The first permanent white settler, Thomas Savage, arrived in 1614 and, to this day, his descendants are among the Shore's most prominent families. Other settlers followed and a county government was soon established.

Englishman John Rolfe set the course of Eastern Shore agriculture with cultivation of a weedy plant called tobacco. Eastern Shore landowners, like others around the Chesapeake Bay, built small kingdoms based on royal land grants, tobacco and slave labor. When tobacco became unprofitable, their loamy, fertile soil supported crops of potatoes, feed corn and vegetables.

Even today, three-quarters of the vegetables produced in Virginia grow on Northampton and Accomack county farms. Road signs on the main highway, Route 13, advise motorists to watch out for slow-moving tractors. Farm stands selling freshly picked produce are plentiful. With the decline of oyster harvesting, aquaculture has become Virginia's fastest growing crop.

The Eastern Shore

Prior to the construction of the **Chesapeake Bay Bridge-Tunnel** in 1964, the only link to the mainland was a long ferry ride to Hampton Roads. Today, new retirement communities and golf courses are signs of things to come, while residents strive to maintain their traditional life-styles and environmentalists seek to preserve America's last coastal wilderness.

The **Virginia Coastal Reserve**, created through 50 years of land purchases by the Nature Conservancy, preserves the Atlantic side of the Eastern Shore. This important habitat is comprised of 14 islands and 45,000 acres of beach, marsh and maritime forest. Migrating songbirds congregate here in droves every spring and fall, and waterfowl inhabit the marshes year-round.

Even as the outside world "discovers" the Eastern Shore, the region's geographic isolation still maintains a quiet gem of close-knit communities surrounded by productive farmland and one of the last undeveloped coastlines on the east coast.

Sights

Towns and points of interest are listed south to north.

The Chesapeake Bay Bridge-Tunnel. You can't visit the Eastern Shore and not visit Virginia's man-made wonder. Go north through the peninsula from Virginia Beach, or south from Philadelphia via US 13, and you have to drive the 17.6-mile passage that are the world's largest bridge-tunnel complex. The toll is $12 each way, but it is discounted if the return trip is made within 24 hours.

Construction of the bridge-tunnel complex required the building of 12 miles of trestled roadway, two mile-long tunnels, two bridges, almost two miles of causeway, four man-made islands and 5½ miles of approach roads, for a total length of almost 23 miles. A second parallel bridge span was recently completed in 1999, easing traffic and safety problems.

Be sure to make a stop at the **Sea Gull Fishing Pier and Restaurant** on the first of the Bridge-Tunnel's four man-made islands 3½ miles from Virginia Beach. Cast your line from the free 625-foot pier and you might catch any one of a variety of species of fish, including bluefish, flounder, croaker, trout, and shark. Or you might like to take time out and enjoy a great meal in one of the unique dining spots of the world. The restaurant is open for breakfast, lunch and dinner, and serves a variety of foods and wines, from sandwiches to fresh seafood.

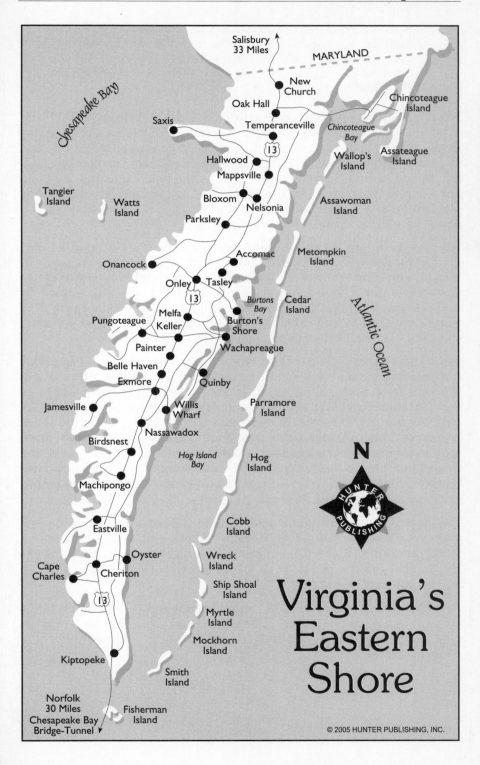

Salisbury
33 Miles

MARYLAND

Chesapeake Bay

New
Church

Oak Hall

Chincoteague
Island

Saxis

Temperanceville

Chincoteague
Bay

13

Hallwood

Wallop's
Island

Assateague
Island

Mappsville

Tangier
Island

Watts
Island

Bloxom

Nelsonia

Assawoman
Island

Parksley

Accomac

Metompkin
Island

Onancock

Onley   Tasley

13

Burtons
Bay

Cedar
Island

Melfa

Atlantic Ocean

Pungoteague

Keller

Burton's
Shore

Painter

Wachapreague

Belle Haven

Exmore

Quinby

Jamesville

Willis
Wharf

Parramore
Island

Nassawadox

Birdsnest

Hog Island
Bay

Hog
Island

Machipongo

N

Eastville

Cobb
Island

Oyster

Wreck
Island

Cape
Charles

Cheriton

Ship Shoal
Island

13

Myrtle
Island

Mockhorn
Island

Kiptopeke

Smith
Island

Norfolk
30 Miles
Chesapeake Bay
Bridge-Tunnel

Fisherman
Island

Virginia's
Eastern
Shore

HUNTER PUBLISHING

© 2005 HUNTER PUBLISHING, INC.

❖ *It's a good idea to call ahead in severe weather. In heavy winds, vehicles with cargo carriers and bike racks may not be allowed to cross. Ask at the toll booth if a shuttle van is available to transport such items. For more information,* ☎ *757-331-2960, www.cbbt.com.*

Eastern Shore of Virginia National Wildlife Refuge, ☎ 757-331-2760, www.fws.gov, is at the northern terminus of the Chesapeake Bay Bridge-Tunnel. The visitor center houses an extensive collection of waterfowl carvings and exhibits on the migratory birds that pass through each fall, including endangered species such as the bald eagle and the peregrine falcon. Hiking trails on the 752-acre refuge and an elevated viewing platform atop a World War II bunker make this a bird-watcher's paradise. There's even a butterfly trail!

Kiptopeke State Park, three miles north of the Chesapeake Bay Bridge-Tunnel, ☎ 757-331-2267, is one of Virginia's newest state parks. It is located on the site where the ferries to the mainland once docked before the bridge-tunnel was constructed. An artificial bay was formed by sunken, concrete-filled ships that can still be seen from the beach. The waters are shallow and calm enough for safe swimming, even for small children. Fishing, birdwatching, and camping are available.

Cape Charles (☎ 757-331-2304, www.ccncchamber.com) is a sleepy little town on the western shore near the southern tip of the peninsula that is enjoying a renaissance. It's small enough to remain friendly, but large enough to maintain a business community for visitors as well as the increasing number of residents in the new Bay Creek community, which boasts two PGA golf courses. Shops and antique stores, quaint inns, marinas, boat ramps, charter fishing, a mile-long beach, fine old homes and tree-shaded streets are just a few of the attractions. At the old-fashioned **Watsons Hardware**, folks still gather to chat around the pot-bellied stove, and at **Rayfield's Pharmacy** there's a jukebox and soda fountain.

The **Cape Charles Museum and Welcome Center** is a great place to start your visit. It opened in 1996 in a former building of Delmarva Power, circa 1947. Exhibits change each year, but typically highlight the life, industry and history of the Eastern Shore. Open Friday through Sunday afternoons. ☎ 757-331-1008.

Arts Enter Cape Charles, 305 Mason Avenue, ☎ 757-331-ARTS (2787), www.artsentercapecharles.org, offers dance and art workshops as well as several musical, dance and theater performances each month in the restored Palace Theatre.

❖ *Cape Charles also has one of the few public beaches in Northampton County. The broad expanse of white sand is perfect for sunbathing and the mile-long sea wall promenade, "The Boardwalk," is a great place for a stroll in the sunshine or the moonlight. There's a gazebo where you can relax, chat, and enjoy spectacular sunsets over the sparkling waters of the Chesapeake Bay.*

Eastville was established as the Northampton County seat in 1631 and has remained the seat of government ever since. The Northampton County Courthouse contains the oldest continuous set of court records in the country, dating from 1632. Many of the old homes in Eastville have survived from Colonial times. Several of them are open to the public during Garden Week. The Debtors' Prison, old Clerk's Office and an ancient whipping post beside the prison are at the old county seat.

The **Barrier Islands Center** in Machipongo is located on an old almshouse farm. The large, airy house includes displays and artifacts from the harsh life on the barrier islands. ☎ 757-678-5550, www.barrierislandscenter.com.

The quiet little village of **Willis Wharf** is vital to the Shore's aqauculture industry, with two companies spawning clams and oysters here. **E.L. Willis & Co. Store and Restaurant**, in business since 1850, serves lunch Monday-Saturday, ☎ 757-442-4225. **Broadwater Bay Ecotours** depart Willis Wharf for trips to the barrier islands for sightseeing, clam-digging and seafood roasts with Capt. Rick Kellam, whose family lived on the now-deserted Hogg Island for five generations. ☎ 757-442-4363, www.broadwaterbayecotours.com.

One of the largest villages on the Shore, **Exmore** is the commercial center of Northampton County with a healthy row of antique and curio shops, a recently renovated streetscape, the famous Exmore Diner, and New Ravenna, where upscale mosaic tiles are created.

Wachapreague, the Little City by the Sea, is a scenic fishing village on the Eastern Shore. Known also as the Flounder Fishing Capital of the World, it's a great place to enjoy a quiet afternoon on the waterfront. Or, if that's not to your taste, you can embark upon a deep-sea fishing trip on one of the many charter boats that leave the harbor daily for the fishing grounds offshore and the tiny inlets of the Atlantic coast. For more information and complete listing of charter boats, call the Eastern Shore Tourism Commission, ☎ 757-787-2460.

Onancock's "isolated charm" is fast becoming discovered. This 300-year-old fishing village has a new, cosmopolitan feel with eclectic eateries, stylish B&Bs and upscale boutiques. Yet the town's past is well-preserved at places like **Kerr Place**, home of the **Eastern Shore of Virginia Historical Society** (☎ 757-787-8012, www.kerrplace.org), and **Hopkins & Bros. General Store and Restaurant**, one of the oldest on the East Coast. From the wharf you can catch a cruise to Tangier Island, or sit on the "Liar's Bench" where old men have been known to tell a tall tale or two about fish they've caught. For more information, ☎ 757-787-3363, http://onancock.org.

Pam Barefoot has made her **Blue Crab Bay Co.** specialty food products famous, starting as a cottage industry whose products were seen in the Julia Roberts movie *Sleeping with the Enemy*. If you haven't tried the Sting Ray Bloody Mary Mixer or Barnacles Snack Mix with the characteristic light blue crab labels, you're in for a treat. Go to their Web site, or visit the gift shop, four miles south of Onley on Route 13 in the Accomack Airport Industrial Park (☎ 800-221-2722, www.bluecrabbay.com).

Tangier Island is a quaint mix of old and new cut off from the mainland by the waters of the Chesapeake Bay. The island, first discovered by Captain John Smith in 1608, wasn't settled until 1686. During the war of 1812, the British Navy landed troops on the island and used it to prepare for the assault of Fort McHenry. To visit the island you'll take an exciting cruise down Onancock Creek and across the open water of the Chesapeake Bay. You'll find a handful of shops, B&Bs and a vibrant soft-shell crab industry. For more information and cruise schedules, ☎ 757-891-2240, http://tangierisland-va.com. Seasonal.

Accomac is a good place to take a sidewalk tour, with an astounding amount of historic architecture within a short radius of the town center.

The Debtor's Prison in Accomac. Built in 1784 as the jailer's residence and adapted as a debtor's prison in 1824, the old building is a fine example of an 18th-century tradesman's residence and remains essentially unchanged since 1784. The structure has two rooms on the first floor and two more in the loft. The heavy doors and bars were added in 1824. The old prison contains many relics and memorabilia from Colonial times, including the bell from the Accomac church, some books written and donated by President Woodrow Wilson and an old ledger from the store at Drummond's mill. There's also a map of the Chesapeake Bay dated November 30, 1781. To arrange a visit, ☎ 757-787-3436.

The Eastern Shore Railway Museum, located in Parksley, two miles west of Route 13, stands on the site of the original Parksley Station and preserves the Golden Age of the Railroad on the Delmarva Peninsula. The museum is open daily year-round, Monday through Saturday from 10 a.m. until 4 p.m., and on Sundays from 1 until 4 p.m. Closed Wednesdays, November through March. ☎ 757-665-RAIL.

Bloxom Vineyard and Winery opened in 2004 as the Eastern Shore's first winery open for tours and tastings. Robert and Francesca Giardina believe the Shore's unique microclimate, framed by the Chesapeake Bay and the Atlantic Ocean, give their wines, which include Chardonnay, Merlot, Cabernet Sauvignon and Cabernet Franc, a dinstinctive flavor.

Open May-October, Wednesday-Sunday noon to 6 p.m. Mason Road, Bloxom, ☎ 757-665-5670.

At **Turner Sculpture** on Route 13 in Melfa, you can view the bronze sculptures of world-renowned artists William and David Turner. See miniature and life-sized sculpture of wildlife and waterfowl. Open daily. ☎ 757-787-2818, www.turnersculpture.com.

The Locustville Academy opened in 1859 in Locustville and operated for 20 years. It is the only survivor of at least a dozen schools of higher learning that served the Eastern Shore during 1800s. Today, the museum offers visitors a look at the way college level education was conducted more than a century ago. The museum is open by arrangement. ☎ 757-787-7480 or 757-787-2460.

In summer, **Chincoteague** is a hopping resort town, with seafood restaurants galore, boutiques and nightlife, made famous by its namesakes, the wild ponies who live on the island next door. After Labor Day it becomes a quiet coastal town again. Rent a bike to explore the village and the **Chincoteague Wildlife Refuge** or visit one of the museums that chronicle life on and near the sea. Chincoteague Chamber of Commerce, ☎ 757-336-6161, www.chincoteaguechamber.com.

The Oyster and Maritime Museum, 7125 Maddox Boulevard in Chincoteague, tells the story of the oystering and seafood business, once the major industry of the island. Exhibits include live marine animals, shell specimens, historical and marine artifacts and implements used in the seafood industry. ☎ 757-336-6117, www.chincoteaguechamber.com/oyster/omm.html.

The Refuge Waterfowl Museum, 7089 Maddox Boulevard in Chincoteague, offers a unique look at wildlife through a number of interpretive exhibits and displays. These include carved waterfowl, antique decoys and art, boats, weapons and traps. Open daiy, 10 a.m. to 5 p.m. (call for winter hours), ☎ 757-336-5800.

The Chincoteague National Wildlife Refuge, on Assateague Island, is the home of the famed Chincoteague ponies and an area of great natural beauty set aside to protect wildlife and its habitat. Beyond that, the refuge is a fine place to spend a day enjoying the great outdoors. Activities such as hiking, bicycling and driving are allowed only in designated areas. Fishing and crabbing are permitted in Toms Cove, Swans Cove and other specified areas. Pets are not allowed in the refuge – not even in the car. ☎ 757-336-6577, http://chinco.fws.gov.

The Assateague Island National Seashore is a narrow, 37-mile barrier island that parallels the shore of Maryland and Virginia. It is a wild and remote region, and from the Virginia side, it is accessible only by foot or by a guided tram tour. The shoreline changes constantly as the offshore winds and storms drive the sand into a wonderland of dunes and quiet beaches. The island provides natural habitats for a variety of wild animals, birds and marine life, including the great blue heron, black-crowned heron, snowy egret, dunlins, American widgeon, the peregrine falcon, and the famed Chincoteague ponies.

The island is also a refuge for humans who need to get right away from the stress of city life. Three areas are available on the island for public use: the **National Seashore**, the **Chincoteague National Wildlife Refuge** and Maryland's **Assateague State Park** at the northern end of the island. Hiking, bicycling, backpacking, fishing, boating, birdwatching and camping are only a few of the activities available. For more information, call the National Park Service at the Barrier Island Visitor Center in Berlin, Maryland, ☎ 410-641-3030, www.nps.gov/asis. For information on tours entering from the Virginia end, ☎ 757-336-6155.

The NASA/Wallops Flight Facility Visitor Center is the place to see an assortment of space-flight vehicles, equipment and exhibits on America's space flight program. The visitor center is open daily, 10 a.m. to 4 p.m. Closed in December and January, and closed Tuesday and Wednesday in the spring. ☎ 757-824-1344, www.wff.nasa.gov/~wvc.

The Decoy Factory at Oak Hall is the world's largest. Watch as the workers carve and paint wooden ducks, geese and other native waterfowl, and then visit the gift shop for a souvenir made right there on the premises. The factory is open daily from 9 a.m. until 5 p.m. ☎ 757-824-5621.

Recreation

Fishing

The opportunities for fishing are nearly endless on the Eastern Shore. You can charter a deep-sea fishing boat from one of the villages, or try surf fishing off one of the barrier islands. Then there's the expansive Chesapeake Bay and its many inlets to explore.

The major ports for charter fishing trips are **Cape Charles**, **Wachapreague** and **Chincoteague**, with a handful of boats leaving from Quinby, Onancock, Cheriton, Oyster and Willis Wharf. Rent a small boat from marinas in Chincoteague and Wachapreague, or from Cherrystone Campground in Cape Charles. Or launch your own boat at one of the Eastern Shore's 30 public boat ramps.

For a full list of charter boat companies and captains, request a copy of the *Hunting & Fishing Guide* from the Eastern Shore of Virginia Tourism Commission (757-787-2460, www.esvatourism.org).

Watersports

The Eastern Shore boasts some of the best flatwater **kayaking** in the United States. Paddling among Atlantic barrier islands through tall grass marshes allows an intimate glimpse of the Shore's natural beauty.

Just minutes from the Chesapeake Bay Bridge-Tunnel, **Southeast Expeditions** sits next to Sunset Beach Resort. They can provide boats, lessons, gear and transportation to the water. (☎ 888-62-MARSH, www-.sekayak.com).

Further north in Chincoteague are several outfitters (☎ 757-336-6161, www.chincoteaguechamber.com). One of these, **Wildlife Expeditions**, rents canoes and sea kayaks and takes visitors on guided sunrise, sunset and eco-tours (☎ 757-336-6811, www.intercom.net/~cptkyak).

Golf

Bay Creek's Arnold Palmer course near Cape Charles sits along the Chesapeake Bay and Old Plantation Creek waterfront. The **Jack Nicklaus Signature Course** is another 18 holes scheduled for completion in Fall 2005. Be sure to ask for the "local discount" for Virginia residents. ☎ 757-331-9000, www.bay-creek.com.

Birdwatching

The **Eastern Shore Virginia Birding and Wildlife Trail** is a driving route that runs the length of the Eastern Shore, noting prime viewing areas on and off Route 13. A map is available from the Eastern Shore Tourism Commission (☎ 757-787-2460).

Shopping

Forget the giant malls of the big city with their hundreds of specialty shops and department stores; you won't find them on the Eastern Shore. What you will find is a delightful variety of artists' galleries, antique stores and gift shops. Visit the quaint little coastal towns and villages so typical of old-world Virginia, spend endless hours browsing the shaded streets and waterfronts, and then take time out for a quiet moment with a cup of coffee or a seafood meal in one of the many restaurants along the way.

Watch artisans at work in the famous bronze foundry at **Turner Sculpture**, Route 13 in Melfa (☎ 757-787-2818, www.turnersculpture.com), creating mosaic tile at **New Ravenna** in Exmore (☎ 757-442-3379, www.newravena.com), painting historic barrier islands at **Seaside Gallery** in Cheriton (☎ 757-331-2583, www.thelmapeterson.com) or carving decoys at **Stoney Point Decoy Factory**, the world's largest, in Oak Hall (☎ 757-824-5621).

African-American folk artist Danny Doughty displays his folk art paintings at the **Folk House in Painter**, along with the craft and art of 30 others who work in metal, fiber, pottery and sculpture (☎ 757-442-2224, www.thefolkhouse.com). **Mary "Mama-Girl" Onley** welcomes visitors to her home studio in Painter (☎ 757-442-4885).

There are also art galleries in Painter (**The Painter Gallery**, ☎ 757-442-9537), Cape Charles (**The Arts Enter**, ☎ 757-331-2787), and Northampton (the **Northampton Gallery**, ☎ 757-678-5151). Along the way, keep your eyes open for antique treasures, from small junk shops to large indoor malls, scattered up and down Route 13.

Annual Events

The Annual Seafood Festival, held early in May at Toms Cove Campground at Chincoteague, has become something of a ritual for seafood lovers from around the country. Every year, thousands make the trek to the island to enjoy this harvest of the sea. ☎ 757-787-2460, www.esva-chamber.org.

Art in the Park, held on July 3 at the Barrier Islands Center, is an outdoor celebration of local artisans who demonstrate theirs skills and sell their work. ☎ 757-787-2460, www.esvachamber.org.

The Annual Pony Swim and Penning, held in late July, is, without question, the most popular event for visitors to the Eastern Shore. Although the origin of the ponies is unknown, they have become the object of local legend. The story is that they descend from survivors of a 16th-century shipwreck. Today, the excitement of Pony Penning Week is felt all over the island. To control the number of ponies, a certain number are auctioned off each year to benefit the Chincoteague Volunteer Fire Department, which owns the herd. Firemen and volunteers round up the ponies for a swim from the island to the mainland. ☎ 757-336-6161, www.chincoteaguechamber.com.

Family Fun Day on the Bay in late September is the only day of the year that bicycles and pedestrians are allowed on the Chesapeake Bay Bridge-Tunnel. The southbound span is closed to vehicular traffic, while the northbound remains open. The event attracts about 7,000 people who bring food donations for the Foodbank of Southeastern Virginia as their entry fee. ☎ 757-331-2960, www.cbbt.com.

The Eastern Shore Harvestfest, held in early October, is a celebration of the foods that made Virginia's Eastern Shore famous. Visitors enjoy a variety of local foods and cuisine, including seafood, sweet potatoes and chicken, along with all sorts of entertainment and exhibitions. ☎ 757-787-2460, www.esvachamber.org.

The Eastern Shore Birding Festival, held in October at Sunset Beach Resort just north of the bridge-tunnel, is a one-of-a-kind event celebrating the peak of the fall bird migration. Thousands upon thousands of birds congregate here in preparation for their annual flight to the tropics. Activities include tours, presentations, exhibits and workshops. ☎ 757-787-2460, www.esvachamber.org/festivals/birding.

Dining

Opportunities for fine dining on local produce from the land and sea exist in all sorts of locations the length and breadth of the peninsula. Visitors to the Eastern Shore can enjoy a variety of local foods and cuisine, including fresh seafood, beef, sweet potatoes, chicken and much, much more.

Armando's Restaurant, on North Street in Onancock, ☎ 757-787-8044, is a true gem of the Eastern Shore. Armando Suarez, owner and chef, is a native of Argentina who came to the shore in 1988. Armando creates his own eclectic originals combining the freshest seafood and meats with the diverse tastes of Italian, Japanese, Cajun, Indian, Chinese and European cooking. He calls it "New American" cuisine. Fine wines and nightly specials served. Open for dinner only, 5 to 9 p.m. Tuesday through Sunday, and until 10 p.m. Friday and Saturday.

From **AJ's on the Creek**, 6585 Maddox Boulevard, Chincoteague, ☎ 757-336-5888, www.chincoteague.com/rest/AJS.html, you can watch wildlife on Eel Creek, and dine on seafood. Open daily for lunch and dinner.

The **Bay Creek Community** near Cape Charles has two restaurants: the **Cabana Bar** and **Aqua** at Bay Creek's Marina Village. ☎ 757-331-9000, www.bay-creek.com.

At **Bizotto's Gallery and Café**, 41 Market Street, Onancock, ☎ 757-787-3103, you can shop for fine leathergoods, crafted by the owner, while you wait for your food – which will undoubtedly be a delicious and imaginative meal.

Captain's Deck Restaurant, on Route 13 south in Nassawadox, is open for breakfast, lunch and dinner. If it's seafood that delights you, you'll find it here. And, if you're a fisherman, they'll prepare your catch and include two vegetables and cornbread, all for the price of a couple of hamburgers. There's also a weekend breakfast buffet, and breakfast is served all day long. ☎ 757-442-7060.

Charlotte Hotel and Restaurant opened in 2004, resurrecting the hospitality of the 1907 White Hotel on North Street, Onancock. Serves New American cuisine in a cozy, farmhouse-style dining room. Lunch and dinner Wednesday through Sunday ☎ 757-787-7400, www.thecharlottehotel.com.

The Eastern Shore

The Chesapeake, A Seafood Bistro and Wine Bar, 307 Mason Avenue, Cape Charles, ☎ 757-331-3123, has sidewalk tables and elegant décor inside. Open for dinner; closed Mondays. Call for winter hours.

Chincoteague Inn, 6262 Main Street, Chincoteague, has been serving Eastern Shore cooking for more than 30 years. Large windows give views of the Intracoastal Waterway and spectacular sunsets. **PT Pelican's**, the inn's outdoor bar, provides a casual dining experience, often with live entertainment. ☎ 757-336-6110, www.chincoteague.com.

The **Eastville Inn** serves lunch and dinner in an historic inn at 16422 Courthouse Road, Eastville. ☎ 757-678-5745, www.eastvilleinn.com.

Etta's Channel Side Restaurant, on East Side Drive in Chincoteague overlooking the channel and the lighthouse, is open for lunch and dinner on weekends and dinner only Monday through Thursday. Specialties include local seafood dishes. It has a pleasant family atmosphere. ☎ 757-336-5644.

Harbor Grille in Cape Charles has sidewalk tables and serves lunch and dinner, 203-05 Mason Avenue, ☎ 757-331-3005.

Inn and Garden Café, 145 Market Street, Onancock, is a gourmet restaurant in a quaint old inn serving up "southern hospitality with a twist." Open for dinner Wednesday-Saturday. ☎ 757-787-8850.

Island House Restaurant in Wachapreague, ☎ 757-787-4242, offers dining on fresh local seafood and Black Angus steaks overlooking the waterfront.

Little Italy Ristorante on Route 13 in Nassawadox, ☎ 757-442-7831, www.francolittleitaly.com, features stromboli, calzone and pizza for lunch and dinner; take-out available.

Mariah's at Tower Hill B&B is on Kings Creek near Cape Charles, 3018 Bowden Landing, ☎ 757-331-1700, www.towerhillbb.com. Dinner is served Tuesday-Saturday. There are two dining rooms, a pub, and a wine cellar with private romantic seating. The menu features local seafood delicacies with Asian flair. The sunset views are gorgeous.

Pelican Pub is on Sunset Beach Resort's beach, just north of the Chesapeake Bay Bridge-Tunnel. Enjoy casual fare, great sunsets and live entertainment. ☎ 800-899-4SUN, www.bwsunsetbeachresort.com.

Sting-Ray's Restaurant, on Route 13 near Capeville, ☎ 757-331-2505, is open for lunch and dinner. Don't let the gas station outside deter you – the food is gourmet, the wine list extensive, and the crème brûlée to die for.

The Trawler Restaurant, on Route 13 in Exmore, is open for lunch and dinner. It offers a variety of specialties which include the host's sweet potato biscuits, she crab soup and an assortment of local seafood dishes. Call for reservations, ☎ 757-442-2092.

Wright's Seafood Restaurant features The Crab Galley, an all-you-can-eat buffet featuring steamed crabs, steamed shrimp, Alaskan crab legs and barbecue ribs. The restaurant is located in Atlantic overlooking Watts Bay. Dinner only; closed Mondays. ☎ 757-824-4012, www.wrights-restaurant.com.

Accommodations

Most establishments offer both handicapped-accessible and non-smoking rooms, but be sure to ask when making reservations.

Hotels & Motels

Anchor Inn, 3775 Main Street in Chincoteague, ☎ 757-336-6313, has several efficiencies, waterfront apartments, and a cottage. Facilities include a boat launching ramp, fish cleaning tables, freezers for storing your catch, a recreation room for your own private crab steaming party, and a meeting room. $$

 Best Western Eastern Shore Inn, ☎ 757-442-7378, in Exmore, has a heated pool, in-room coffee, free continental breakfast, HBO and laundry facilities. $

 Best Western Sunset Beach Resort, near the entrance to the Chesapeake Bay Bridge-Tunnel in Cape Charles, ☎ 800-899-4786 or 757-331-1776, www.bwsunsetbeachresort.com, has 74 rooms, a restaurant, a beachside bar, a pool, a wading pool, and a private beach. $$-$$$

Birchwood Motel at 4650 Main Street, Chincoteague, ☎ 757-336-6133, has 41 guest rooms, a swimming pool, cable TV, a dock and crabbing pier and rooms with water views. Free coffee is provided in the guest rooms. $$

The **Cape Charles Hotel**, 235 Mason Avenue, Cape Charles, is the renovated 1884 McCarthy Hotel with 18 rooms with private baths. ☎ 757-331-4816, www.capecharleshotel.com. $$

The **Charlotte Hotel** is Onancock's former White Hotel, now a three-story boutique-style gem decorated in a whimsical, farmhouse theme by the artistic proprietress. Here past and present mingle: Antique stained glassed windows in the sparkling white bathrooms; DVD players in old barnboard hutches. On-site restaurant. 7 North Street, Onancock, ☎ 757-787-7400, www.thecharlottehotel.com. $$

Comfort Inn on Route 13 at Onley, ☎ 757-787-7787, www.comfortinn-onley.com, has 80 guest rooms and 10 suites, including handicapped-accessible and non-smoking rooms. There is an outdoor pool, exercise room and data-port telephones. Restaurants and shopping nearby. A free continental breakfast is included in the rate. $

The Eastern Shore

Comfort Suites – Chincoteague, 4195 Main Street, Chincoteague, is waterfront hotel where the outdoor pool and balconied rooms all have gorgeous views of the water. ☎ 757-336-3700, www.comfortsuites.com. $$

Days Inn Cape Charles is three miles north of the Bridge-Tunnel on Route 13, ☎ 800-331-4000. It has more than 100 rooms, truck and boat parking, a restaurant and pool. $$

Driftwood Lodge 7105 Maddox Boulevard, Chincoteague, ☎ 800-553-6117, www.driftwoodmotorlodge.com, offers 52 spacious guest rooms overlooking the wildlife refuge, handicapped facilities and a swimming pool. Every room has a refrigerator, private balcony and patio. Several restaurants nearby. $$

At **Hampton Inn & Suites**, on the waterfront in Chincoteague, all rooms and suites have balconies with water views. Indoor heated pool, business center and free high-speed Internet. 4179 Main Street, ☎ 757-336-1616, www.hamptoninnchincoteague.com. $$

Refuge Inn, 7058 Maddox Boulevard, Chincoteague, ☎ 757-336-5511, www.refugeinn.com, is within walking distance of the wildlife refuge; amenities include a hot tub, indoor-outdoor pool, laundry facilities and bike rentals. $-$$$

Wachapreague Motel is a short walk from the marina and Island House Restaurant at 17 Atlantic Avenue, Wachapreague, ☎ 757-787-2105. The hotel has 30 comfortable rooms, efficiencies and two-bedroom apartments. Small boat rentals are available. $$

Waterside Motor Inn, 3761 S. Main Street in Chincoteague, ☎ 877-891-3434, has 45 rooms, four condos, and private balconies overlooking the Chincoteague Channel, panoramic sunsets, a waterfront swimming pool, a fishing pier, a tennis court and a marina. $$

Bed & Breakfasts / Inns

76 Market Street Bed & Breakfast, located at the same address as its namesake in Onancock, has featherbeds and complimentary wine and cheese hour at 5 p.m. ☎ 888-751-7600, www.76marketst.com. $$

1848 Island Manor House Bed and Breakfast, 4160 Main Street, Chincoteague, has eight guest rooms, spacious public rooms and a courtyard with a fountain. Children age 10 and older welcome. ☎ 757-336-5436, www.islandmanor.com. $$

Bay View Waterfront B&B, 35350 Copes Drive, Belle Haven (near Exmore), is an 1800 home built in the Eastern shore "big house-little house" style on 140 acres. It overlooks Occohannock Creek with views the Cheseapeake Bay and has three guestrooms and an outdoor pool. ☎ 757-442-6963, www.bayviewwaterfrontbedandbreakfast.com. $$

Cape Charles House Bed and Breakfast at 645 Tazewell Avenue, Cape Charles, is a 1912 Colonial revival home with five spacious rooms with private baths. A gourmet breakfast is served. ☎ 757-331-4920, www.capecharleshouse.com. $$

The **Fisherman's Lodge** on Route 182 in Quinby, is a relaxed, 1930s lodge. There are 10 rooms, six with private baths. ☎ 888-442-7133, www.fishermanslodge.com. $

Garden and the Sea Inn in New Church, ☎ 757-824-0672, began as a tavern in 1802. Six rooms and French dining in an elegant European country inn. Dinner is open to the public on Friday and Saturday. $$-$$$

Garrison Bed and Breakfast, 34000 Seaside Road in Painter, is a Southern Colonial home with four bedrooms. A big southern breakfast is served and dinner is available Thurday through Saturday in the formal dining room. Spacious grounds, screened-in gazebo. Children age six and over are welcome. ☎ 866-777-9446, http://garrisonbandb.com. $$

Gladstone House Bed & Breakfast at 12108 Lincoln Avenue in Exmore, is a stately Georgian brick home on a former estate. There are three guestrooms with private baths. Business services include copying, printing, faxing and free wireless Internet (they'll even lend you a PC card). There's an elevator and a player piano. ☎ 800-262-4837, www.gladstonehouse.com. $$

Harborton House, 28044 Harborton Road, Harborton, is a charming Victorian in a charming little fishing village. There are three guestrooms, beautiful gardens, and bicycles to borrow. ☎ 757-442-6800, www.harbortonhouse.com. $

 Pickett's Harbor Bed & Breakfast is a beautiful home on the Chesapeake Bay in a secluded setting. Children and pets welcome. Nottingham Ridge Lane, near Cape Charles, ☎ 757-331-2212, www.pickettsharbor.com. $$

Shirley's Bay View Inn is in one of the oldest houses on Tangier Island – and operated by one of the oldest families, the Pruitts. There are rooms in the main house and in seven cottages. Guests get both sunrise and sunset views from the beautiful grounds. Breakfast is served on Grandma's antique china and transportation to and from the boat is provided. ☎ 800-330-3554, www.tangierisland.net. $$

Sterling House is a craftsman-style bungalow three doors from the Cape Charles beach. The four guestrooms are named after historic ships that plied the waters between Norfolk and Cape Charles. ☎ 757-331-2483, www.sterling-inn.com. $$

Tower Hill B&B is a five-bedroom waterfront inn on Kings Creek near Cape Charles. Several rooms have fireplaces and electric wood-burning stoves. Two rooms are located in a tower that was added during the home's 2002 renovation. There's a fine dining restaurant, game room, fishing, and kayaks you can borrow. 3018 Bowden Landing, ☎ 757-331-1700, www.towerhillbb.com. $$

Camping

Cherrystone Family Camping Resort in Cheriton is on VA 680, off US 13, 11 miles north of the Chesapeake Bay Bridge-Tunnel, ☎ 757-331-3063, www.cherrystoneva.com. It is set on 300 acres of Chesapeake Bay waterfront. Facilities include 700 sites, flush toilets and hot showers, a restaurant, four piers, boat rentals, cruises, mini-golf, playgrounds, and four pools. You can also rent a camping trailer or deluxe cabin. There is fishing, crabbing, boating, and various planned activities and live entertainment.

Inlet View Campground on Chincoteague Island offers 414 waterfront sites, full hookups, a grocery store, public phones, flush toilets and hot showers, sewage disposal, a laundry and LP gas is available. Recreation room, go-carting, saltwater fishing, a boat launching ramp, playground. ☎ 757-336-5126, www.happysnails.com/inletview.

Kiptopeke State Park, three miles north of the Chesapeake Bay Bridge-Tunnel on Kiptopeke Drive, just off US 13, ☎ 757-331-2267, has 141 sites, hot showers, and electric hookups. Also has hiking and bicycle trails, a boat launch, fishing and a beach on the Chesapeake Bay.

Maddox Family Campground on Chincoteague Island offers 550 sites with full hookups, a grocery store, public phones, flush toilets and hot showers, sewage disposal, a laundry and LP gas is available. Facilities include a recreation room, pavilion, swimming pool, mini-golf, playground, volleyball and horseshoes. ☎ 757-336-3111, www.chincoteague.com/maddox.

Pine Grove Campground on Chincoteague Island offers 150 sites with full hookups, a grocery store, public phones, flush toilets and hot showers, a swimming pool and a playground; sewage disposal, laundry and LP gas available. ☎ 757-336-5200, www.pinegrove-campground.com.

Tall Pines Harbor Campground in Sanford, near Crisfield, Maryland, has more than 80 spacious, shaded sites, some with full hook-ups and some for primitive tenting. There's a dump station, outdoor pool, and a sandy swimming beach on Pocomoke Sound. ☎ 757-824-0777, www.tallpinesharbor.com.

Toms Cove Park on Chincoteague Island offers 875 sites with full hookups. There is a full-service store, public phones, handicapped facilities, flush toilets and hot showers, sewage disposal, a laundry and LP gas. A recreation room, bicycle rentals, pool, a boat ramp and dock, water skiing, saltwater fishing, and a playground are also available. ☎ 757-336-6498, www.tomscovepark.com.

Information

Eastern Shore of Virginia Tourism Commission, PO Box 460, Melfa, VA 23410. ☎ 757-787-2460, www.esvatourism.org.

The Chincoteague Chamber of Commerce, PO Box 258, Chincoteague, VA 23336. ☎ 757-336-6161, www.chincoteaguechamber.com.

Chesapeake Bay's Northern Neck

Nestled between the Rappahannock and Potomac Rivers, Virginia's Northern Neck is a narrow, picturesque peninsula as beautiful and unspoiled as it was when Captain John Smith first visited in 1608. Visitors can explore local historic sites, sail, cruise, fish or simply relax and enjoy the scenery. Here you can visit the birthplaces of George Washington and Robert E. Lee, as well as two signers of the Declaration of Independence.

Located less than two hours from the nation's capital, the Northern Neck peninsula encompasses five counties: **King George**, **Westmoreland**, **Richmond**, **Northumberland** and **Lancaster**.

History

The area was first settled by Europeans more than 300 years ago, but Native Americans had lived on the peninsula for more than 10,000 years. Many of the rivers on the Northern Neck such as the Wicomico, Coan, and Nomini are named for Indian tribes.

As the colony grew, so did the Northern Neck. Settlers established farms and towns on the rivers. Great Americans, taken with the natural beauty of the area, made their homes and fortunes by the waters of the Chesapeake and the great tidal waterways. Three presidents – George Washington, James Monroe and James Madison – were born on the peninsula.

By the 1880s the Northern Neck economy was booming. Steamboats out of Baltimore and Norfolk plied the Chesapeake Bay from one end to the other, stopping at the wharves in the tiny river ports to drop off supplies and pick up a variety of local products from the farms and canneries headed for markets in the big cities.

Fortunately, the Northern Neck's growing economy did little to spoil its great natural beauty. Today, the tiny towns and villages have changed little with the years. The peninsula has retained all its old-world appeal.

This is a place where the charm and quality of everyday country life leaves a lasting impression. Its bustling county fairs and town market days, local arts, crafts and music, seafood fresh from the waters of the rivers and bay, home-grown produce, friendly people, and fresh sea air make a visit here one you will never forget.

Touring

Take your time on a tour of Virginia's Northern Neck. Rush it and you'll miss the little things – the tiny corner shops and cafés, the coves and bays and the small local museums.

If you arrive on the peninsula from Washington or Baltimore, you can follow the loop road, routes 3, 202, and 360 paralleling the Potomac from Oak Grove through Montross to Burgess. From Burgess, take Route 200 along the Chesapeake Bay to Kilmarnock, then turn west and follow Route 3 up the Rappahannock through Lancaster, Farnham and Warsaw, back to Montross.

From Williamsburg, Norfolk, Virginia Beach, Richmond and the South, you'll arrive on Route 17 north. Cross the Rappahannock by the Downing Bridge on Route 360 at Tappahannock and drive to Warsaw. From there you can turn east or west and follow the loop road until it brings you back again to Warsaw.

Whichever route you decide to take, don't be afraid to wander off the beaten path. The side roads and byways often lead to magnificent views, quaint little restaurants, old country churches and secluded spots.

If arriving from the north, you'll want to begin your tour in **King George County**. A good place to start is the **Potomac Gateway Welcome Center**, at Route 301 near the Potomac River Bridge, which provides information on the Northern Neck, Middle Peninsula and Fredericksburg regions. Open daily, 9 a.m. to 5 p.m. ☎ 540-663-3205.

The **King George County Museum and Research Center** is located in the Old Jail at the County Courthouse at 9483 Kings Highway. Open year-round, except for major holidays and two weeks at Christmas. ☎ 540-775-9477. Nearby, the **Caledon Natural Area** is a bald eagle summer foraging area.

Next is **Westmoreland County**, east of Oak Grove and bounded by the Rappahannock and Potomac Rivers. There you'll find several interesting and historic sites.

Colonial Beach is a resort town on the Potomac with a fascinating history told at the **Colonial Beach Museum**, 128 Hawthorn Street, ☎ 804-224-3379 (open weekends only). Have a seafood dinner overlooking the water or take a walk along the beach.

Near Colonial Beach, on Leedstown Road, is the **Ingleside Plantation Winery**, which is open for tours and tastings year-round, ☎ 804-224-8687, www.wine.com; and the **Westmoreland Berry Farm** where you can pick your own fruit, ☎ 800-997-2377, www.westmorelandberryfarm-.com.

The **George Washington Birthplace National Monument**, off Route 3 on Route 204 near Oak Grove, is the site where our first president was born. The original house is no longer there. The Memorial House and farm you see today are reconstructions that depict and interpret the everyday life on an 18th-century plantation. Costumed guides and inter-preters till the fields, tend the animals, and demonstrate weaving, spin-ning and candle-making as it was done by the early settlers. Food is prepared in the Colonial kitchen. During the summer months, special activities include a Colonial Crafts show, Indian and Black Heritage His-tory days, a Gentry Weekend, and Colonial Medicine days, all of which provide glimpses of the lifestyle of the early colonists. The park is a great place for a family outing. There are picnic areas, nature walks and even a place to go fishing. The park is open daily from 9 a.m. until 5 p.m. except for Christmas Day and New Year's Day. ☎ 804-224-1732, www.nps.gov/gewa.

From the George Washington Birthplace, return to Route 3, go east to Route 347 and turn north to **Westmoreland State Park.** This is your opportunity to enjoy an afternoon of fun and sunshine. If you feel so in-clined, you can spend the night in one of the park's overnight cabins. There's plenty to do, from swimming in the Olympic-sized pool to fishing the tidal waters of the Potomac. There are several hiking, bicycle and bri-dle trails, a sandy beach, a playground for the kids, a snack bar, a restau-rant, and a visitor center. Boats and bicycles are available for rent, and the camping facilities include electric and water hookups. ☎ 804-493-8821, www.dcr.state.va.us/parks/westmore.htm.

The Stratford Hall Plantation is just east of Westmoreland State Park off Route 3 on Route 214 near Montross. Stratford Hall was the birth-place of Confederate General Robert E. Lee. The house, built in 1738 by Thomas Lee, was also home to two signers of the Declaration of Inde-pendence, Richard Henry Lee and Francis Lightfoot Lee. The "H-shaped" manor house is constructed entirely from bricks made on the estate and timber hewn from its own forests. The great hall at the center of the house measures 29 feet square with a 17-foot-high ceiling, and is consid-ered one of the most architecturally significant structures to survive from Colonial times. Today, the 1,600-acre estate is managed as a working farm. Costumed guides lead tours through the house and you can wander through meadows, wildflowers and a beautiful boxwood garden, then walk the woodland trail to the bluffs overlooking the Potomac River. There's also a museum, a collection of 18th- and 19th-century carriages, a working mill and a log cabin dining room in a wooded setting. Lunch is served daily in the log cabin, and there are two guesthouses for overnight

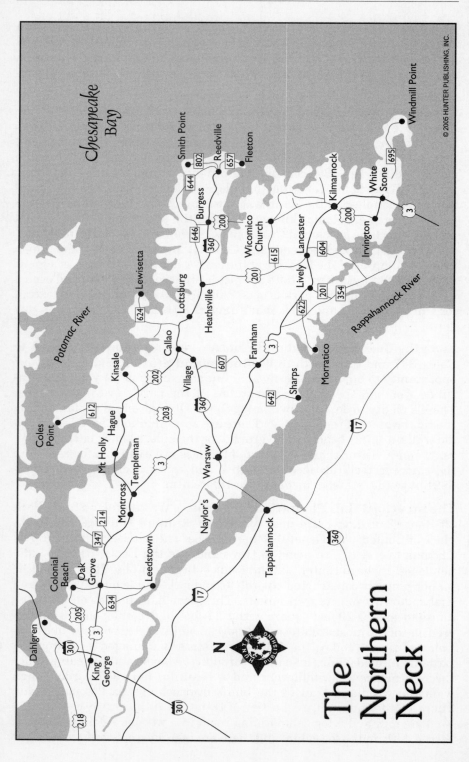

stays. The house and grounds are open daily from 9:30 a.m. until 4:30 p.m. ☎ 804-493-8038, www.stratfordhall.org.

The **Armstead Tasker Johnson High School Museum**, 18849 King's Highway, Montross, ☎ 804-493-7070, preserves the history of African American education in Westmoreland County.

From Stratford Hall, return to Route 3 and turn east to **Montross**, a quaint little place with an old-world character all its own. Drop in at the visitor center at the Westmoreland County Museum and pick up a walking tour map. Be sure to visit the old courthouse and, if you have time, have lunch or dinner at the Inn of Montross.

The Westmoreland County Museum, located on Courthouse Square in Montross, highlights Westmoreland County history and culture from its beginnings to the present. Special exhibits and facilities include a library with extensive historical and research materials, and a beautiful brick-walled garden, created by the Westmoreland Garden Club to honor the three US Presidents born on the Northern Neck. Open Monday through Saturday, ☎ 804-493-8440.

From Montross, continue east along Route 3 to the intersection with Route 202 and then turn left toward Mount Holly and continue on to **Kinsale**. Interesting side trips along the way include **Coles Point**, **Kinsale** and **Lewisetta**. All offer magnificent views across the Potomac River and are well worth a visit.

Kinsale was an active steamboat landing during the late 19th century. The **Kinsale Museum**, housed in an 18th-century pub, tells the story through exhibits, and offers a walking tour. It is open Friday through Sunday. ☎ 804-472-3001.

At **Heathsville**, you'll enter Northumberland County, the first county established on the Northern Neck in 1648, and the "mother county" from which all the others on the Northern Neck were formed. **Rice's Hotel/ Hughlett's Tavern** in Heathsville was built in 1795 behind the Northumberland County Courthouse. The original three-room tavern has been expanded over the years to its present 24-room, two-story structure. The building is listed on the National Register of Historic Places and includes exhibits, a gift shop and a Colonial-style restaurant and pub. Tours can be arranged by calling ☎ 804-580-3377. There is a gift shop next door in the Old Jail.

From Heathsville, take Route 360 to the junction of Route 604 and the **Scenic Byway**. The Scenic Byway offers a pleasant drive, views of the Chesapeake Bay and Smith Point Lighthouse, and is a fun trip across the water by way of the Sunnybank Ferry. From the ferry, follow the signs along the route to **Reedville** and the Fisherman's Museum.

The **Reedville Fishermen's Museum** is composed of two buildings. The Walker House is interpreted as a fisherman's home at the turn of the century. The Covington Gallery features the permanent menhaden industry exhibits and three special exhibits each year. There is also a heritage boat collection, which includes the *Elva C.*, a restored 1922 workboat.

By the early 1900s the fishing industry had been so good to Reedville it was reputed to be the richest town per capita in the United States. Reedville's opulent era and its history are interpreted through the many interesting exhibits in the museum, and through the fine old Victorian mansions on Main Street. For information on the museum, ☎ 804-453-6529, www.rfmuseum.org; open daily, May to October; weekends the rest of the year.

On your return trip to **Burgess**, take the scenic byway by following Route 644 through nice farmland and cross the Little Wicomico River on the Sunnybank Ferry, a free two-car shuttle that operates Monday through Saturday.

From Burgess, turn south on Route 200 and follow it through **Kilmarnock**, where you may want to stop and browse through the gift and antique shops or the Kilmarnock Museum (76 Main Street, ☎ 804-435-0874), which is open Thursday through Saturday. Continue to **Irvington** and Christ Church. If you'd like to enjoy some wonderful scenery along the may, you might take the scenic detour which begins just south of Wicomico Church and rejoins Route 200 just outside Kilmarnock.

Historic Christ Church in Irvington, dating from 1735, is perhaps the best example of a virtually unchanged Colonial church in America. The church is built of brick in the form of a cross, with walls three feet thick; the floors of the nave and transepts are the original limestone slabs. The church's original three-decker pulpit dominates the choir, congregation and the individually enclosed high-backed pews. The 18th-century structure is a masterpiece of religious architecture and well worth a visit. A video presentation in the Carter Reception Center, narrated by Roger Mudd, interprets the church's history and prepares you for the tour. The reception center is open daily, April to November; ☎ 804-438-6855, www-.christchurch1735.com.

Also in Irvington, the **Steamboat Era Museum**, opened in 2004, celebrating the steamboats that plied the Chesapeake Bay, stopping at many Northern Neck communities, between 1890 and 1935. 156 King Carter Drive, ☎ 804-438-6888.

From Irvington, take Route 200 north to the junction with Route 3 in Kilmarnock; turn west on Route 3 and drive on into **Historic Lancaster**, a tiny town with a population of only 150. The family of Mary Ball Washington, George Washington's mother, was among the early settlers in the Lancaster area. Mary Ball Washington herself was born nearby at Epping Forest, and many of Washington's maternal ancestors are buried in the churchyard of **St. Mary's Whitechapel Church** (☎ 804-462-5908), five miles west of Lancaster on Route 622. Lancaster's **County Court-house**, in the historic district and surrounded by sycamore trees, was built just prior to the Civil War, in 1860. The marble obelisk is one of the first monuments erected to Confederate soldiers.

The **Mary Ball Washington Museum and Library** is also in Lancaster's historic district. **Lancaster House**, which houses the museum, was built in 1800 and is part of a complex that also contains the **Old Clerk's Office** and the **Old Jail**. The many exhibits featured in the museum include artifacts and memorabilia from the Ball family history, watermen's tools of the trade, archaeological artifacts, paintings, pictures, quilts, costumes and children's toys. Of special interest are the recently restored Civil War flags and banners that once belonged to the Lancaster County unit of the Confederate army. The Old Clerk's Office, built in 1797, and the Old Jail, built in 1820, are also open to the public. The Old Jail is maintained as a living history museum. It contains a criminal cell along with the living quarters of a jailer in the early 19th century. The museum complex is open Tuesday through Friday; the library, Wednesday through Saturday. ☎ 804-462-7280, www.mbwm.org.

From Lancaster, continue westward along Route 3 to Warsaw, the final stop on your tour of Virginia's Northern Neck. The **Richmond County Museum** has recently relocated to the Old Jail on Courthouse Green. The museum offers a small glimpse into Richmond County's past. The displays of domestic and agricultural memorabilia depict and preserve the rural lifestyle that has characterized Richmond County since its earliest days. Warsaw, originally named Richmond Court House, has been the county seat for more than 150 years. It was renamed in 1831 in sympathy with the Polish struggle for liberty. Today, located as it is on one of the Northern Neck's busiest highways, Warsaw has become something of a commercial center for a variety of shops, stores and restaurants. The old courthouse, also located on the Courthouse Green, was built in 1748 and is still in use to this day. The museum is open February 1 through mid-December, Wednesday through Saturday, from 11 a.m. until 3 p.m. ☎ 804-333-3607.

If you'd rather have someone else do the driving, check out the offerings of **Northern Neck Heritage Tours**, ☎ 804-580-6336, www.NNHT.com.

Annual Events

For a complete listing and more details, visit www.northernneck.org.

George Washington's Birthday is celebrated in February with ranger programs and costumed interpreters at George Washington Birthplace, ☎ 804-438-6855, www.nps.gov/gewa.

The Northern Neck

The **Historic Garden Week Northern Neck Tours**. Held the third week in April and organized by the Garden Club of Northern Neck. ☎ 800-393-6180.

The **Blessing of the Fleet** in May is the annual dedication of the Menhaden Fishing Fleet at Reedville. The celebration includes a parade of boats and the Reedville Chantey Singers. ☎ 804-453-6529.

The **Annual Reedville Bluefish Derby**, the second weekend in June, includes a fishing tournament, nightly activities, arts & crafts, food, and nightly entertainment. ☎ 804-453-5325.

The **Annual Potomac River Festival** is held in mid-June at Colonial Beach. Fireman's parade, boat parade and fireworks. ☎ 804-224-0732.

There are **Fourth of July** celebrations in Colonial Beach, Reedville, at Stratford Hall Plantation and George Washington's Birthplace. For details, www.northernneck.org/events.htm.

The **Richmond County Fair**, held on the Richmond County Fairgrounds at the end of August, features demonstrations, livestock, farm produce, and a variety of competitions. ☎ 804-333-3420.

The **Boardwalk Arts & Crafts Show** is held along the Colonial Beach Boardwalk in mid-September, ☎ 804-224-8145.

October brings the **Northern Neck Seafood Extravaganza** to Ingleside Plantation Vineyards, ☎ 804-224-8687.

Christmas on Cockrell's Creek is held in mid-December at the Reedville Fishermen's Museum (see page 259). Features special displays, activities and a house tour with transportation by boat shuttle. ☎ 804-453-6529, www.rfmuseum.org.

Recreation

The Northern Neck is a boating and fishing paradise. Wherever you go, you're not far from a marina or boat landing. Surrounded on three sides by water, the Northern Neck offers endless possibilities for boating, fishing or cruising. Bring your own canoe, sailboat, motor boat, or fishing boat and make use of any number of public launching ramps for a day on the bay, rivers, streams and creeks. You don't own a boat? Don't worry, there are dozens of friendly charter boat captains ready and willing to see to your every water-borne need, from deep-sea fishing to simply cruising the Chesapeake Bay. For more information, contact the **Northern Neck Tourism Council**, ☎ 800-393-6180, www.northernneck.org/recreation-.htm.

Boat Cruises

Tangier Island Cruise and **Rappahannock River Cruises** leave from Reedville, operating May through mid-October. Reservations are required. ☎ 804-453-2628, www.tangiercruise.com.

Smith Island Cruise operates from Reedville May through mid-October. ☎ 804-453-3430, www.cruisetosmithisland.com, for reservations.

Fishing

Fishing opportunities on the Northern Neck are exciting. The great variety and quality of the available species make it one of the finest fishing areas on the East Coast. Every year, anglers from across the United States make their way to the peninsula to try their luck, either in the tidewater rivers or on the Chesapeake Bay. No matter what your level of skill, you're sure of a great experience.

During April and May, the striped bass move up the bay to spawn. The once depleted stock has recovered and more and more large catches are reported every year. The striped bass also runs during the fall and winter months from October through December.

By May the "chopper" bluefish will be running. Anglers enjoy great sport as fish of up to 20 pounds slam into their tackle and fight every inch of the way into the boat. By June the smaller, but no less aggressive "taylor" bluefish will have arrived in the Bay. The action continues from May through November when the last "choppers" leave. Pound for pound, the bluefish ranks among the top of the world's gamefish.

May also brings the beginning of bottom fishing to the Bay. Good fishing spots can be found close in as well as offshore. The near-shore locations are especially well suited for smaller boats. Anglers can expect to catch a variety of species, including croaker, spot, trout and flounder.

By mid-summer the action includes the Spanish mackerel, a beautifully colored fish given to leaping gracefully from the water. The Spanish mackerel offers good sport and fine eating. For a list of marinas and charter boats, ☎ 877-285-4593, www.northernneck.org/boatingfishing.htm.

Swimming

If you're looking for a vacation of fun in the sun, a secluded sandy beach on the warm waters of the Chesapeake Bay, or a rocky outcrop where you can toast your body on a warm afternoon, you should check out the many coves and inlets on the eastern shore of the Northern Neck.

There are **public beaches** at Colonial Beach, Hughlettt's Point Natural Area, VirMar Beach in Northumberland County, Westland Beach in Lancaster County, and Westmoreland State Park.

The Northern Neck

Natural Areas

There's something about a day out in the country exploring the tiny back roads and bays along the river banks and the shores of the Chesapeake Bay. The days are warm and still, the air alive with the sounds and fragrance of spring and early summer. A brook trickles among the wildflowers in a country meadow. A songbird trills high in an old oak tree, and the dull buzz of insects can be heard. Add an afternoon at a country fair, followed by a stop at the Ingleside Plantation Winery for a tour of the vineyard and a taste of the local product, and you're sure of an experience you will never forget.

The Northern Neck has hundreds of hiking trails that meander through the woods, fields and marshes, along the river banks and the shores and inlets of the Chesapeake Bay. **Westmoreland** and **Belle Isle State Parks** have a number of interesting trails, as do **George Washington's Birthplace** near Oak Grove and **Stratford Hall** in Stratford.

The Caledon Natural Area, just off Highway 301 in King George County, is one of the best places in the United States to observe the bald eagle and one of the most significant eagle summering areas on the East Coast. You can take a ranger-led eagle-watching tour and observe the birds in their native habitat, feeding, soaring or perching high in the treetops along the banks of the Potomac River. Tours are available by reservation only, June through September. Be sure to bring your camera. ☎ 540-663-3861.

Hughlett Point Natural Area on the Chesapeake Bay offers trails, a woodland boardwalk and wildlife viewing platforms. ☎ 804-684-7577.

Golf

Millers Glen Golf Course, in Mt. Holly, ☎ 804-472-2602, is a small nine-hole public country club.

Golf at the Tides Inn in Irvington has two different courses to suit your style of play: the Golden Eagle, ☎ 804-438-5501; and the Par 3, ☎ 804-438-4454; www.the-tides.com/golf.

Quinton Oaks Golf Course, in Callao, ☎ 804-529-5367, www.quinton-oaks.com, has 18 holes, a driving range and a practice green.

Shopping

You won't find any shopping malls on Virginia's Northern Neck, but the small country towns and villages, the resorts, and the highways and byways abound with tiny shops and stores to delight even the most discerning taste.

Dining

Bambery's Restaurant & Lounge in Heathsville is upscale, yet casual. 8200 Northumberland Highway, Heathsville. ☎ 804-580-8181, www.bamberys.net.

The **Crazy Crab**, at the foot of Main Street on Cockrell's Creek in Reedville, ☎ 804-453-6789, is a fun place for lunch or dinner, and offers a panoramic water view. It is closed Mondays.

Dockside Restaurant and Blue Heron Pub is on the Potomac in Colonial Beach, in a 1930s oyster house and British-style pub. ☎ 804-224-8726, www.dockside-blueheron.com.

Good Eats Café, Route 202 and 203 in Kinsale, ☎ 804-472-4385, features Chesapeake classics and new dishes served in a casual atmosphere. Dinner is served Thursday through Sunday.

The **Inn at Montross** is a 1790s historic inn serving French-inspired cuisine. ☎ 804-493-0573, www.innatmontross.com.

Lee's is a family-style restaurant serving breakfast, lunch and dinner every day but Sunday. 34 Main Street, Kilmarnock, ☎ 804-435-1255.

Mount Holly Steamboat Inn in Mount Holly serves Chesapeake favorites from the historic home and large deck overlooking Nomini Bay. ☎ 804-472-9070, www.mthollysteamboatinn.com.

The Pilots Wharf serves fresh fish with river views in Coles Point. ☎ 804-472-3955, www.colespoint.com.

Rice's Hotel/Hughlett's Tavern in Heathsville serves Progressive American Cuisine in an historic inn, one of the oldest surviving wood structures in the Northern Neck. Open for lunch and dinner; closed Sunday and Monday. ☎ 804-580-7900, www.hughlettstavern.com.

Stratford Hall Plantation Dining Room, Route 214, Stratford, ☎ 804-493-8119, serves gourmet food in the birthplace of Robert E. Lee.

The Tides Inn has elegant dining overlooking Carter's Creek. Reservations required. Irvington, ☎ 804-438-4427, www.the-tides.com/dining.

Trick Dog Café in Irvington is hip and fun, as is the food. Tidewater Drive, ☎ 804-438-1055.

Willaby's, on Route 3 in White Stone, ☎ 804-435-0044, www.willabys.com, features daily specials, gourmet burgers and homemade desserts and special sauces. Lunch is served Monday through Saturday.

The Northern Neck

Accommodations

Hotels & Motels

Best Western Warsaw, 4522 Richmond Road, Warsaw, ☎ 804-333-1700, www.bestwestern.com/warsaw, has 38 rooms and an outdoor swimming pool.

 Colonial Beach Days Inn, Colonial Beach, ☎ 804-224-0404, overlooks the Potomac River and has 60 guest rooms. $

Holiday Inn Express has 68 rooms and luxury suites, a swimming pool, 5334 Mary Ball Road (Route 3), Kilmarnock. ☎ 804-436-1500 $$

 St. Andrew Motel at 226 Methodist Church Road, White Stone, ☎ 804-435-1101, has 30 guest rooms and a swimming pool in a wooded setting. $$

The Tides, on King Carter Drive and historic Carter's Creek in Irvington, ☎ 800-843-3746 or 804-438-5000, www.the-tides.com, is a resort that offers just about everything for an all-inclusive vacation, from supervised children's activities to golf, tennis, boating, yachting, canoeing and cruising. It sits on a hill on 25 landscaped acres, surrounded by water on three sides. The inn has 106 newly renovated and enlarged rooms and suites, two restaurants, a private beach, a walking trail, bicycles and paddleboats, two pools (one saltwater and one heated), lighted tennis courts, 45 holes of some of the best golf in Virginia, and a marina. $$$$

Windmill Point Resort and Marina, 56 Windjammer Lane, Windmill Point, ☎ 804-435-1166, www.windmillpointresort.com, offers 52 waterfront rooms, a marina, two swimming pools, three tennis courts, golf and a mile of sandy beach. $$$

Bed & Breakfasts / Inns

The Bell House is a beautiful old Victorian, once the summer home of Alexander Graham Bell. Credit cards not accepted. 821 Irving Avenue, Colonial Beach, ☎ 804-224-7000, www.thebellhouse.com. $$

Chestnut Cove B&B is a unique getaway where you can take a workshop in the Zekiah stained glass studio. The waterfront contemporary lodging sits on 15 acres. ☎ 804-394-3142, www.zekiahglass.com. $$$

Fleeton Fields B&B is a brick Colonial-style B&B on the Chesapeake Bay. Furnished in antiques; kayaks and canoes available. Children welcome by prior arrangement. 2783 Fleeton Road, Reedville. ☎ 804 453-5014 or 800-497-8215, www.fleetonfields.com. $$$

 Hope and Glory Inn is in a delightfully restored old schoolhouse in Irvington that's received many awards for its romantic accommodations. Children and pets welcome in the four guest cottages. ☎ 800-497-8228, www.hopeandglory.com. $$$

 The Inn at Montross is on Courthouse Square in Montross, ☎ 804-493-0573, www.innatmontross.com. This small hotel was originally built in 1683. Facilities include five guest rooms with four-poster beds, decorated with original antiques and primitive and modern art; the inn has a restaurant. $$

 Mt. Holly Steamboat Inn, on Nomini Creek in Mt. Holly, ☎ 804-472-9070, www.mthollysteamboatinn.com, features outdoor patio dining, weekend brunches and lodging packages. There are eight rooms with waterfront views. Kids welcome. $$

The Plaza Bed & Breakfast is a beautifully renovated 1903 Victorian house on Potomac River beach. Full breakfast, afternoon tea, pool/spa, gardens and wraparound porch. Weems Street. Colonial Beach. ☎ 804-224-1101, www.colonialbeachplaza.com. $$

The Skipjack Inn at Port Kinsale Marina & Resort, Kinsale, ☎ 804-472-2044, www.portkinsale.com, has four rooms and a swimming pool. Continental breakfast; dining is offered at the Mooring Restaurant. $$

Stratford Hall Plantation offers a unique overnight option on an historic plantation, the birthplace of Robert E. Lee. Twenty rooms are available in two guesthouses with full kitchens and private baths. ☎ 804-493-8038, www.stratfordhall.org/overnight.html. $$

The Gables, 859 Main Street in Reedville, just off Cockrell's Creek, ☎ 804-453-5209, www.thegablesbb.com, is a unique Victorian brick mansion with a fascinating history. The five-level home was built in 1909 by a sea captain who brought the bricks in on his three-masted schooner to build the house and the bank across the street. When he retired, the schooner was built into the top two levels of the home, with the mast through the center of the home. There are two guest rooms with water views, and bathrooms across the hall from each. The Coach House has four rooms, an ice-cream parlor and a patio. No pets or children. $$-$$$

The Inn at Levelfields, Route 3 in Lancaster, ☎ 804-435-6887 or 800-238-5578, www.innatlevelfields.com, features antiques, a gourmet breakfast, four rooms, all with private baths and fireplaces. $$

Flowering Fields Bed & Breakfast, 232 Flowering Field, White Stone, ☎ 804-435-6238, has six rooms and offers a full breakfast with crab cakes and omelets on the menu. $-$$

Camping

Cole's Point Plantation, on Route 728 in Cole's Point, ☎ 804-472-3955, 804-472-4761 (restaurant), www.colespoint.com, has a marina, restaurant and campground. There is a swimming pool, rental cottages and boat rentals. $$

Monroe Bay Campground in Colonial Beach, ☎ 804-224-7418, is a bayside campground with 350 sites – 92 with full hookups. Facilities include flush toilets, hot showers, a grocery store, and sewage disposal. There is a recreation room, a pavilion, saltwater swimming, saltwater and pond fishing, boating, boat ramps, a basketball court and a playground. April through October.

Westmoreland State Park in Montross, ☎ 804-493-8821, has 98 camp sites, about half with hookups. Facilities include flush toilets, hot showers, and sewage disposal. There is a pavilion, swimming, lake fishing, boating, boat ramps, boat rentals, and hiking trails.

Heritage Park Resort, on Newland Road on Cat Point Creek in Warsaw, ☎ 804-333-4038, has an Olympic-sized swimming pool, canoeing, fishing, full hookups and is open year-round.

The Chesapeake Bay/Smith Island KOA and Marina, Reedville, ☎ 804-453-3430, is a riverside campground with 70 semi-wooded sites – some with full hookups, and some on the waterfront. Facilities include pull-throughs, cabins, flush toilets, hot showers, a limited grocery store, and sewage disposal. There is a recreation room, a pavilion, a swimming pool, boat rentals, river swimming, fishing, boat ramps, mini-golf and a playground.

Information

For assistance planning your visit to the Northern Neck, or for further information and brochures, you can contact any of the following organizations.

The Northern Neck Tourism Council, PO Box 1707, Warsaw VA 22572, ☎ 800-393-6180, www.northernneck.org.

The Potomac Gateway Welcome Center, 3540 James Madison Parkway, King George VA 22485. ☎ 540-663-3205.

The Westmoreland County Visitor Center on Courthouse Square, Montross VA 22520. ☎ 888-733-9288, www.wcchamber.org.

The Colonial Beach Visitor Center, on the Boardwalk, Colonial Beach VA 22443. ☎ 804-224-8145, www.colonialbeach.org.

The Lancaster County Visitors Center, 453-A N. Main Street, Kilmarnock, ☎ 804-435-6092, www.lancasterva.com.

Warsaw-Richmond County Chamber of Commerce, PO Box 1141, Warsaw, VA 22572, ☎ 804-333-3737, www.warsaw-rcchamber.com.

Chesapeake Bay's Middle Peninsula

*T*he name says it all. The Middle Peninsula, or "Mid-Pen" to locals, is the finger of land located between the Virginia Peninsula (Hampton and Newport News) and the Northern Neck. This rural area, still largely agricultural, features meandering back roads, miles and miles of coastline, and a rich Colonial history. Follow these back roads and you'll find gorgeous river plantations, historic sites and delicious seafood restaurants. The waters of the Chesapeake Bay and the York and Rappahannock rivers still provide a livelihood for many, while the "courthouses" of Gloucester, Tappahannock and the city of West Point are growing yearly. The Mid-Pen includes the counties of Essex, Middlesex, Gloucester and King William.

Essex County & Tappahannock

*E*ssex County is on the southern shore of the Rappahannock River in the heart of the Middle Peninsula. It's an area that depends upon the waters of the Rappahannock and the Chesapeake Bay, as recreation, fishing and tourism account for much of its income. Although its population is relatively small, Essex County and its seat, Tappahannock, have much to offer. For the outdoor lover there's fishing, boating, cruising, hunting, and golf. For the antique buff, there are numerous antique shops located both in Tappahannock and surroundings. The people are friendly and outgoing, and visitors are always welcome.

History

Although there is archaeological evidence of human occupation as far back as 12,000 BC, Essex County's recorded history dates from around the time of Captain John Smith's epic voyage of the winter of 1607-08. Since that time the area has seen a number of changes, not the least being its constantly changing name.

In 1645, Bartholomew Hoskins patented the Tappahannock site, which became known at first as Hobbs His Hole (or deep anchorage). That name was later shortened to Hobbs's Hole. Next it was called New Plymouth, but not for long. Finally, it became Tappahannock,meaning "place of tidal waters."

Essex County, named for the English Earl of Essex, is the result of the division of the Old Rappahannock County made in 1692. Back then,

Rappahannock County encompassed territory that today includes some 50 modern counties in Virginia and West Virginia. The division was made along the river. The northern side became Richmond County on the Northern Neck; the southern side became Essex County.

Bacon's rebellion against the Colonial governor in 1676 brought armed conflict to the area. Nathaniel Bacon was a young English planter who was outraged at the way the new colony was being misgoverned by Sir William Berkeley. When Berkeley refused to take measures to stop the Indian attacks, Bacon decided to take on the task himself. But Bacon's movement soon broadened into open rebellion against the local aristocracy as dissatisfaction with Berkeley grew. Bacon's men defeated Governor Berkeley's cavalrymen, first at Picataway Creek, and then in the Dragon Swamp. The rebellion ended suddenly when Bacon died soon after his followers had burned Jamestown and driven Berkeley and his followers into refuge on board an English man-o'-war.

Bacon's rebellion was followed by the French and Indian War of the 1750s. The men of the Essex Militia, many of them gentlemen officers, including Colonel Joshua Fry who preceded George Washington as commander of Virginia's forces, were sent off to fight for king and colony.

The Stamp Act of 1765 led ultimately to the American Revolution and one of its first confrontations in Tappahannock. On the evening of February 27, 1766, gentlemen from nine counties gathered at Leedstown to draft the resolutions that led Virginians to disobey the English Parliament. They also resolved to publicly humiliate one of the community's leading merchants and staunch supporters of the Stamp Act, Archibald Ritchie. Richard Henry Lee called Ritchie "the greatest enemy of his country." These momentous events all took place some seven years before the Boston Tea Party.

During the Civil War years Tappahannock was the training post for the 55th Virginia Infantry Regiment.

After the Civil War, the present Essex County and Tappahannock resumed their quiet rural existence and the area soon became one of those sleepy little backwaters where the pace is a little slower and the quality of life a little better.

Sights

There are dozens of historic houses and interesting places to visit within the boundaries of Essex County. Tappahannock's historic district alone has 15. The half-dozen attractions listed here represent only a small portion of what awaits. For more information and a complete listing, contact the Tappahannock-Essex County Chamber of Commerce, PO Box 481, Tappahannock, VA 22560. ☎ 804-443-5241, www.essex-virginia.org.

Essex County Museum, 227 Prince Street, Tappahannock, ☎ 804-443-4690, exhibits artifacts of local history from the last 300 years. Open Friday-Sunday. Start your self-guided walking tour here; guided tours are given Saturday mornings.

Essex County Courthouse, built in 1848 to replace the old courthouse, now the Beale Baptist Church, is a construction of largely Greek Revival design incorporating some Federal features. For many years the courthouse has housed the largest collection of portraits in the county. Unfortunately, the collection suffered many losses during a fire in 1965. Even so, dozens of portraits of Essex County leaders over the past 200 years still remain for all to enjoy.

The Beale Memorial Baptist Church, on Church Street, is a Greek Revival structure incorporating the wall of the original county courthouse. The old building has a long and interesting history. Built in 1728, it was the center of justice in the county for 120 years until the new courthouse was built in 1848. For a while the building was little used. Then, in 1874, the Tappahannock Baptists organized the Centennial Baptist Church. The Reverend Frank Beale, the son of Colonel Beale of the 9th Virginia Cavalry, was named the new church's first pastor and the congregation moved into the old courthouse in 1878. Frank Beale led the Centennial Church for more than 30 years so it was no real surprise when, only weeks after his death in 1908, it was renamed in his honor.

The Customs House, close to waterfront on the Rappahannock River at the foot of Prince Street, is now a private home. The house was built in the early 1800s on a lot once owned by Archibald Ritchie, and was the original location of Whitlock's Ordinary, a popular gathering place for the local gentry.

The Scots Arms Tavern, on Prince Street, was built in 1680 and has been owned and maintained by the Derieux family for more than a century. Today, the old tavern is a private residence.

The Ritchie House, at the corner of Prince and Cross Streets, is one of the oldest buildings in Tappahannock. It's a wonderful old property that faithfully reflects the times when Archibald Ritchie played out his role in the American Revolution. The original, ornate paneling was removed in the 1930s and can be seen on display in the Tappahannock and Essex rooms at the Winterhur Museum in Wilmington, Delaware. The Ritchie House is now a private law office, open by appointment, ☎ 804-443-3368.

Wheatland and its gardens overlook Saunder's Wharf, the only steamboat landing remaining on the Rappahannock River. The old house was built sometime during the early 1800s and characterizes the transition between the Federal and Greek Revival styles of architecture. The two-story porticos at the front and rear of the large rectangular frame provide the old house with a somewhat stately appearance. Wheatland is a private residence, not open to the public.

The Middle Peninsula

Shopping

Tappahannock and Essex County offer a number of shopping opportunities, especially antique shops. Although there are no alls or department stores, the Rappahannock Shopping Center provides most local needs. Beyond that, the quaint little country stores of the area, so much associated with rural Virginia, provide an old-world ambiance most people find hard to resist.

Dining

Lowery's Seafood Restaurant, on Church Lane (US 17), has offered good food at reasonable prices in a quiet family atmosphere since 1938. The restaurant specializes in local seafood and is open for breakfast, lunch and dinner seven days a week. ☎ 804-433-2800.

Moo's River's Edge Eatery serves ice cream, hot dogs and BBQ in Essex Square Shopping Center. They even deliver. ☎ 804-445-9005, www.riverfoods.com.

Roma's Italian Restaurant, in the Rappahannock Shopping Center, offers "Italian food at its best," along with daily specials and a Thursday Italian and American buffet. ☎ 804-443-5240.

Accommodations

Hotels & Motels

Days Inn at Tappahannock, at the junction of US Highway 17 and Route 360, ☎ 800-325-2525 or 804-443-9200, has 60 rooms. Rates include a free continental breakfast. $

The Super 8 Motel, at the junction of US Highway 17 and Route 360, ☎ 804-443-3888, has 43 rooms. Rates include coffee in the lobby, a continental breakfast and cable TV. $

Bed & Breakfasts / Inns

The **Essex Inn** is an elegant country inn at the corner of Water Lane and Duke Street in Tappahannock. There are four rooms and two fully-equipped apartments. ☎ 866-377-3982 or 804-443-9900, www.essex-virginia.org/esx_inn.htm. $

The Linden House B&B Plantation, on Route 17 north of Tappahannock in Champlain, ☎ 866-887-0286 or 804-443-1170, www.linden-plantation.com, is a restored planter's home built around 1750. The inn has three guest rooms and one suite, each individually named and decorated with country furnishing and antiques. All have private baths and are non-smoking. Set on more than 200 acres of Virginia's most beautiful countryside, it has a magnificent English Garden, five porches and a gazebo where guests can enjoy the view sipping a glass of lemonade or a cup of coffee. A full plantation breakfast is served. Children over 12 are permitted. No pets. $$-$$$

Recreation

The Woodside Country Club, four miles north of Tappahannock on Route 17, offers guests a small, but challenging nine-hole course set in the midst of some of Virginia's most beautiful wooded terrain. There is a pro shop and a snack bar with a view. ☎ 804-443-4060.

Hobb's Hole is an 18-hole championship course just south of Tappahannock, with a restaurant. ☎ 804-443-4500, www.hobbshole.com.

Garrett's Marina, on Route 17 at Bowler's Wharf, provides access to the Rappahannock River for anglers and boaters. Facilities include a boat ramp, boat rentals, a snack bar, restrooms, gas and fuel service and a ship's store. ☎ 804-443-0190.

June Parker Marina is also on the Rappahannock River, ☎ 804-443-2131.

Rappahannock River Cruises, a Reedville-based company on the Northern Neck, offers daily cruises on the Rappahannock, departing from Hoskin's Creek, Tappahannock, at 10 a.m., and returning at 5 p.m. The cruise takes in all the sights and sounds along the river. Stops along the way include the Ingleside Winery, for a tour and wine tasting, and Wheatland, the only remaining steamboat landing on the Rappahannock. For more information and reservations, ☎ 804-453-2628, www.tangiercruise.com.

Information

Tappahannock-Essex County Chamber of Commerce, Courthouse Square, PO Box 481, Tappahannock, VA 22560. ☎ 804-443-5241, www.essex-virginia.org. The Chamber is open weekdays from 8:30 a.m., until 4:30 p.m.

Gloucester & Mathews Counties

Gloucester County, on the tip of the Middle Peninsula, is where Pocahontas saved the life of Capt. John Smith; where Dr. Walter Reed, conquerer of yellow fever, was born; and where a visitor can sense the long-ago life of a gentle leisure class peculiar to this region of Virginia.

The Middle Peninsula

It can't be proven conclusively whether Pocahontas was born in Gloucester County. She did, however, live here as a young girl. Her father,
Powhatan, and the tribe spent much of their time at what was then
known as Werowocomico on Timberneck Creek.

There are numerous historic sites and markers throughout Gloucester
County's bucolic countryside. The key to getting around is learning the
different place names – and being sure to pronounce it "Gloss-ter" should
you get lost and need directions. The "Courthouse" is the county's historic
district, with a Court Green dating to the mid-1700s, and quaint shops
lining the main street. In White Marsh, you can see the large old tobacco
estates that made the fortunes of early settlers. In insulated communities like Guinea, people have been harvesting the waters for generations.

Gloucester Point's location at the mouth of the York River has made it a
strategic point in American history. French warships once moored offshore, enforcing an embargo that eventually forced British General
Cornwalis to surrender, ending the Revolutionary War. Today, the Point
is home to the Virginia Institute of Marine Science, a ground-breaking institution affiliated with the College of William & Mary.

While farming and fishing remain important vocations in Gloucester
County, the area is increasingly becoming a bedroom community to the
growing Hampton Roads area, with lots of houses where farms once stood
and shopping centers springing up along the main highway, Route 17.

For most residents, however, the quiet rural life is still the norm. Visitors
can tap into it by taking their time meandering throughout the countryside.

Neighboring Mathews County is further off the beaten track, but well
worth the scenic drive. It's fast becoming a haven for artists who sell their
wares in quaint local shops. There's a walking and driving tour, a bike
tour, and a Blueways guide detailing 90 miles of waterways to explore by
kayak or canoe.

Routes 643 and 14 in Mathews County form a 14-mile horseshoe-shaped
scenic drive with expansive Chesapeake Bay views at either end, and
Mathews Courthouse in the middle serving the needs of this rural county
since Colonial times.

Route 643 ends at windswept Haven Beach, a good place to cool toes in
the surf, while Route 14 leads to a scenic overlook for far-off New Point
Comfort Lighthouse. On a spit of sand that was separated from the mainland by the 1933 hurricane, the early-1800s, 63-foot-tall structure lit the
entrance to Mobjack Bay until the 1960s.

If it's Saturday night, end your day at Donk's "Lil Ole Opry" for live country and bluegrass music.

Sights

Abingdon Episcopal Church, on Route 17 near White Marsh is one of the oldest parishes in the state. The original church was built about 1655, the present church in 1755. Many of Gloucester's early prominent residents are buried in the cemetery, which is open daily to the public. ☎ 804-693-3035, www.abingdonchurch.org, for opening hours of the church.

Every other Saturday night, Virginia's Li'l Ole Opry comes alive at **Donk's Theater** in Mathews. Hometown favorites and Nashville stars perform country, bluegrass and gospel for an evening of toe-tapping family entertainment. ☎ 804-725-7760. Doors open at 7:30; show at 8 p.m.

Gloucester Courthouse is the local term for the county seat, and also refers to the 1766 courthouse complex. The preserved brick Colonial buildings and are surrounded by a low brick wall and the main street which encircles it. There is a debtor's prison, tavern, and county museum. Nearby is a statue of Princess Pocahontas. ☎ 804-693-2355.

Gloucester Museum of History, ☎ 804-693-1234, located in the Botetourt Building, once a tavern and later called the Botetourt Hotel, at 6539 Main Street. The muséum is open Monday through Saturday.

Gwynn's Island Museum details this remote island's fascinating history, from 10,000-year-old Indian artifacts. Open May-October, Friday-Sunday, 1-5 p.m. (804-725-7949).

The **Rosewell Ruins** are the skelatal remains of a 1725 manor home that burned in 1916. It is said the architecture and grandeur of Rosewell rivaled the Governor's Palace in Williamsburg; it was definitely considered one of the finest examples of Georgian architecture in the colonies. Today the site, four miles off Route 7 near White Marsh, is undergoing archeological excavation and restoration, and there is a new visitors center. Call The Rosewell Foundation for visiting hours, ☎ 804-693-2585, www.rosewell.org.

Mathews County Historical Society has exhibits in **Tompkins Cottage**; open April-October, Friday and Saturday, 10 a.m. to 1 p.m., and by appointment (804-725-9743).

Virginia Institute of Marine Science, at the base of the Coleman Bridge off Route 17, is a research facility of the College of William & Mary. Waterman's Hall features aquariums of indigenous fish and endangered sea turtles. There is also a touch tank with shellfish. Open 8 a.m. until 5 p.m., Monday through Friday. Closed major holidays. ☎ 804-684-7000, www.vims.edu/aquarium.

Walter Reed's Birthplace is a tiny, unassuming one-room farmhouse on Belroi Road in Gloucester, but the man born here certainly went on to bigger things – namely freeing mankind of the yellow fever scourge. Dr. Reed's experiments in Cuba in 1900 proved that yellow fever was carried by mosquitoes. The house is open during Daffodil Festival, Garden Week and by appointment. ☎ 804-693-7452.

Annual Events

The Daffodil Festival, the first Saturday in April, celebrates Gloucester's world-famous daffodils. Call Gloucester Parks and Recreation, ☎ 804-693-2355.

Mathews Market Days are the Friday and Saturday after Labor Day on the historic courthouse district's village green..

The Guinea Jubilee, held in late September at the Abingdon Ruritan Fair Grounds on Route 216 (Guinea Road), celebrates the harvest of Gloucester's waters with a carnival, oyster-shucking contests and plenty of seafood.

Recreation

With 100 miles of shoreline, you're never more than a few minutes from the water in Gloucester County. The county's five rivers, dozens of tidal creeks, and the nearby Chesapeake Bay provide opportunities for fishing, boating and swimming. There are 14 public boat landings, five marinas, five parks, a public beach and two campgrounds.

Beaverdam Park, 8687 Roaring Springs Road, ☎ 804-693-2107, has freshwater lake fishing, boat ramps and rentals, hiking trails and picnicking. Open daily.

Dragon Run is a swampy river that provides an interesting and unique canoe or kayak trip of about 25 miles. Call the Friends of Dragon Run, ☎ 804-693-5246, www.dragonrun.org.

Gloucester Point Beach Park, on the York River at the base of the Coleman Bridge, ☎ 804-693-2355, has a fishing pier, beach swimming, boat ramps, a shelter and a playground.

Gloucester Point Campground, 3149 Campground Road (follow signs from Route 17), ☎ 804-642-4316, has 235 sites with full hookups, a boat ramp, store, game room, two swimming pools, bathhouses and a playground. It is open year-round.

Shopping

Whether you are looking for flea market finds or rare 18th-century treasures, Gloucester and Mathews counties are an antique-hunter's bonanza.

Up to 75 indoor and outdoor vendors set up at dawn every Saturday and Sunday at **Stagecoach Antiques and Flea Market** on Route 17 in Gloucester. The 15-acre complex is about eight miles north of the Coleman Bridge and is the place to find old tools, country primitives, and every kind of self-proclaimed "junk," both old and new. It's open weekends 6 a.m. to 5 p.m., and there's even a food vendor for when you get hungry.

While driving Route 17, keep an eye out for two large antique malls and several shops. **Marketplace Antiques** is a gigantic former furniture store in the White Marsh Shopping Center. Individual vendor areas are easy to navigate through and pleasantly arranged. There are many nautical antiques, primitives, books, jewelry, military items, decorative pieces, and antique cars and wagons. It's open daily.

A few miles north is **Plantation Antiques Mall**, two floors of antiques and collectibles from around the world; open daily. **Preston House Antiques** is in the same building, offering furniture, ceramics and lots of flow blue china.

Main Street in **Gloucester Courthouse** has half a dozen small antique and curio shops to peak inside. Take Route 14 east towards Mathews, but stop first at the **Peace Frog** outlet. The cute little froggy icon is world-famous, but its home is right here in Gloucester. An outlet store features seconds, discontinued clothing and perfectly new items real cheap (☎ 800-44-PEACE, www.peacefrogs.com).

Further along Route 14, **Holly Hill Antiques** is a former daffodil farm and still has chickens and other small animals. The Victorian house, built by a freed slave in 1880, and no fewer than 10 barns and outbuildings overflow with primitives, furniture, garden items, glassware, you name it. If you don't see it, ask Pop Weller and he can probably find it. Open Friday-Sunday, 10 a.m.-5 p.m. (for more information, visit www.gloucesterantiques.com).

In Mathews Courthouse, clever shops occupy recycled buildings from another time: the **Dilly Dally Emporium** in the old gas station, a new lunch counter in **Richardson's Old Reliable Drug Store**, and **Annie Rooney's** antiques, where, as recently as 2003, folks bought cod fish and cheddar cheese in Sibley's General Store.

Across the street, the **Mathews Visitor Center** shares space with Maggie's Boutique. Maggie herself is often behind the counter, knitting stylish shawls for the upscale shop. Find local art at **The Gallery** or the **Bay School of the Arts**.

Dining

El Ranchito Mexican Restaurant, 7313 Main Street, Gloucester. The name means "small ranch," and that's just what this pleasant building resembles. Authentic, fresh food. Closed Mondays. ☎ 804-694-8003, www.lranchito.com.

Goodfellas, on Route 17 in White Marsh, ☎ 804-693-5950, offers prime rib, seafood and pasta. It is open for dinner Tuesday through Saturday and Sunday from 11:30 a.m. until 10 p.m.

The **Irish Cottage Pub and Eatery**, Main Street, Mathews, is a family restaurant with bar in the back. Open daily. ☎ 804-725-7900.

Kelsick Gardens, 6604 Main Street, Gloucester Courthouse, ☎ 804-693-6500, www.kelsickgardens.com, features daily lunch specials, gourmet sandwiches, wine and gifts. It is closed Sundays.

Nick's Spaghetti & Steak House, 1440 George Washington Memorial Highway (Route 17), Gloucester Point, ☎ 804-642-2330, is open daily for lunch and dinner, serving Italian dishes and seafood.

The River's Inn, 8109 Yacht Haven Drive near Gloucester Point, is at a marina and most tables offer a view of Sarah's Creek. Outside there is a seasonal crab deck; inside the atmosphere is elegant, yet casual. Specialties include seafood, duck, pork and other dishes. ☎ 804-642-9942.

Rosalia's Italian Pizza and Restaurant, 6545 Market Drive, in the Winn-Dixie shopping center on Route 17 in Gloucester, ☎ 804-693-7960, is one of those great local Italian restaurants, short on formality and long on great food.

Seawell's Ordinary, on Route 17, about five miles north of the Coleman Bridge in Gloucester, ☎ 804-642-3635, carries on the tradition in a 1712 building that became a public eating place or "ordinary" in 1757. Seafood and homemade desserts are its specialties.

Southwind Café on Church Street in Mathews Courthouse, is an eclectic eatery in a 1921 general store. Serves lunch and dinner; closed Sunday and Monday. ☎ 804-725-2766.

Stillwaters on Main, 6553 Main Street, Gloucester, ☎ 804-694-5618, is a new restaurant in Gloucester Courthouse, offers a creative regional menu. It is open for lunch and dinner Tuesday through Saturday.

Accommodations

Hotels & Motels

 Comfort Inn, on Route 17, one mile south of Gloucester Courthouse, ☎ 804-695-1900, has 79 rooms and offers a free continental breakfast. Pets welcome. $

Gloucester Inn Motel, 1408 George Washington Highway (Route 17), ☎ 804-642-3337, has 16 rooms, all with microwave and refrigerator. There is a restaurant next door and a beach and boat ramp a quarter-mile away. $

Tidewater Motel, 3666 George Washington Memorial Highway (Route 17), Gloucester, ☎ 804-642-2155, has 38 rooms, 14 with kitchenettes. $

Bed & Breakfasts / Inns

The **Mathews County Visitor & Information Center** has developed a network of guest cottages and tourist homes among private homeowners. See www.visitmathews.com, ☎ 804-725-4BAY, 877-725-4BAY (725-4229), Tuesday-Saturday, 10 a.m.-4 p.m.

Airville Plantation, 6423 T.C. Walker Road, Gloucester, ☎ 804-694-0287, has three rooms, one with private bath. This plantation is on 200 acres and is decorated with period furniture. Full breakfast served. There is a cottage, pool, beach, fishing and a dock. $$

Buckley Hall Inn B&B, on Route 198 near Mathews Courthouse, has four rooms, a wrap-around porch, and bicycles to lend. ☎ 888-450-9145, www.buckleyhall.com. $$

The **Inn at Warner Hall** is a fabulously restored historic home on a 1642 plantation that is the ancestral home of George Washington. Seven guestrooms and two suites are appointed with every convenience. Located on expansive grounds on the Severn River in Gloucester County. ☎ 804-695-9565, 800-331-2720, www.warnerhall.com. $$$

Kingston Plantation on Route 658 in Mathews County is an expansive property on the North River offering three suites, two bedrooms and a separate carriage house for guests. There are six fireplaces, a pool, tennis court and dock. ☎ 804-725-5831, www.kingston-inn.com. $$

The North River Inn, 8777 Toddsbury Lane, Gloucester, ☎ 804-639-1616, 877-248-3030, www.northriverinn.com, has two rooms and three suites, all with private baths. The 100-acre 17th-century family-owned estate is on the water, and has a dock. A full breakfast is available on weekends. $-$$$

The Willows B&B, 5344 Roanes Wharf Road, Gloucester, ☎ 804-693-7575, has four room with private baths in a country setting; breakfasts are wonderful. $$

The Middle Peninsula

Information

Contact the **Gloucester Parks, Recreation & Tourism**, ☎ 804-693-2355, 866-VISITUS, www.co.gloucester.va.us.

For **Mathews County**, ☎ 877-725-4BAY, www.visitmathews.com.

Middlesex County

*T*he Rappahannock and Piankatank Rivers form rural Middlesex County, with the tip extending into the Chesapeake Bay. This location made it a favorite of marauding pirates, and today among boaters, with more than 20 marinas in the county. The population centers include the county seat of **Saluda**, plus **Deltaville** and **Urbanna.**

Urbanna was one of the nation's first planned communities, laid out in 1681 and designated by the Colonial government as one of 20 ports through which all tobacco and imported goods would pass. Even though it was pillaged during the Revolution and attacked during the War of 1812 and the Civil War, there are many historic buildings left to see. Today fishermen still unload their catch as they have for centuries in the protected harbor which has become popular with recreational craft. Visitors can browse the antique shops and tour the historic sites and stay in a quaint old inn.

Sights

There are more than a dozen historic sites in Urbanna, which are detailed in the brochure *A Self-Guided Walking Tour of Urbanna, Virginia*, available at the Town of Urbanna office at 45 Cross Street, ☎ 804-758-2613.

The Old Tobacco Warehouse and Visitor Center, constructed in 1766, houses an exhibition area on the history of Urbanna. For more information, call the Town of Urbanna, ☎ 804-758-2613.

The **R.S. Bristow Store** on Cross Street, Urbanna, ☎ 804-758-2210, first opened in 1876 and is still a general store, selling "a little bit of everything," including clothes, shoes, housewares and gifts.

The Old Courthouse on Virginia Street is the oldest building left in Urbanna, built in 1748. It now houses the headquarters of the Middlesex County Women's Club.

The Middlesex County Museum, in Saluda, ☎ 804-758-3663, houses exhibits on the history of the county.

Virginia Motor Speedway in Saluda showcases racing the way NAS-CAR used to be. Root for local boys racing on the half-mile dirt track under the lights. Late model races every Saturday night at 6 p.m. May-October. ☎ 804-758-1867, www.virginiamotorspeedway.com.

Dining & Accommodations

Atherston Hall B&B, 250 Prince George Street, Urbanna, ☎ 804-758-2809, has four rooms, two with private baths. A full breakfast and afternoon tea is served. No pets are allowed. Children are welcome with advance notice. Complimentary bikes are available. $$

Café Mojo in Urbanna, serves fresh local seafood in a funky atmosphere. Closed Mondays. ☎ 804-758-4141.

Debbie Hall, on Fishing Bay Trace, Deltaville, ☎ 804-776-6800, has four condos that sleep up to six people each. Visit www.fishingbay.com for more information. $$$

Eckhard's, on Route 3 in Topping, ☎ 804-758-4060, serves classic German food, including schnitzel.

Edentide Inn is a restored farmhouse with wide views of the Piankatank River, near Deltaville. ☎ 804-776-9616,www.edentideinn.com. $$

Marshall's Drug Store has an old-fashioned lunch counter and soda founation at 50 Cross Street in Urbanna. Open Monday-Friday, 8 a.m. to 6 p.m. and Saturday 8 a.m. to 3 p.m. ☎ 804-758-5344.

The **Sanderling House B&B** offers three guestrooms and a cottage near Deltaville. It has it's own marina, so you can even arrive by boat. ☎ 804-776 0970, www.sanderlinghouse.com $$

Virginia Street Café, at Virginia & Cross streets in Urbanna, serves three meals daily. ☎ 804-758-3798.

Camping

Bethpage Camp-Resort, ☎ 804-758-4349, www.bethpage.com, has 600 sites on Robinson Creek.

Bush Park Camping Resort, ☎ 804-776-6750, has 400 sites on Bush Park Creek, near Urbanna.

Cross Rip Campground, ☎ 804-776-9324, named for a lightship that was once stationed off the coast of Massachusetts, is near Deltaville and has 44 sites. Open May-September.

The Middle Peninsula

Annual Events

The Urbanna Oyster Festival is a celebration of the harvest of the bay, held annually since 1958 on the first weekend in November. Oysters are served in every conceivable fashion, and a highlight is the Virginia State Oyster Shucking Contest. In 1988 the event was designated the "official" state oyster festival. ☎ 804-758-0368, www.urbannaoysterfestival.com.

A Christmas Parade and Home Tour is held in Urbanna the first weekend in December.

Information

Deltaville Community Association, www.deltavilleva.com.

The Town of Urbanna, ☎ 804-758-2613, www.visiturbanna.com.

Middlesex County, ☎ 804-758-4330, www.co.middlesex.va.us.

The West Point Area

West Point and its contiguous counties are about 45 minutes east of Virginia's capital, Richmond, and about an hour from the military and port complexes on the Chesapeake Bay. The West Point area consists of the town itself, King William, King and Queen, and New Kent Counties, and lies on a small peninsula at the head of the York River between the Pamunkey and Mattaponi Rivers.

Residents of the West Point area enjoy an uncrowded, unhurried, friendly environment that includes the one small town, West Point, surrounded by many outlying villages.

Those accustomed to the heavily urbanized parts of the United States are pleasantly surprised by the many attractions and amenities in and around West Point, and many more within a short drive. Colonial Williamsburg and the cities of Richmond, Hampton, Newport News, Norfolk, Virginia Beach, and the Eastern Shore are all within easy driving distance.

History

In 1653 a settler on the lower York, John West, patented 3,000 acres around the site of the now-abandoned Cinquoteck, and the neck of land thereafter known as West Point. West was the grandson of Thomas West, second Earl de la Warr, who had been governor of the first English settlement in early days.

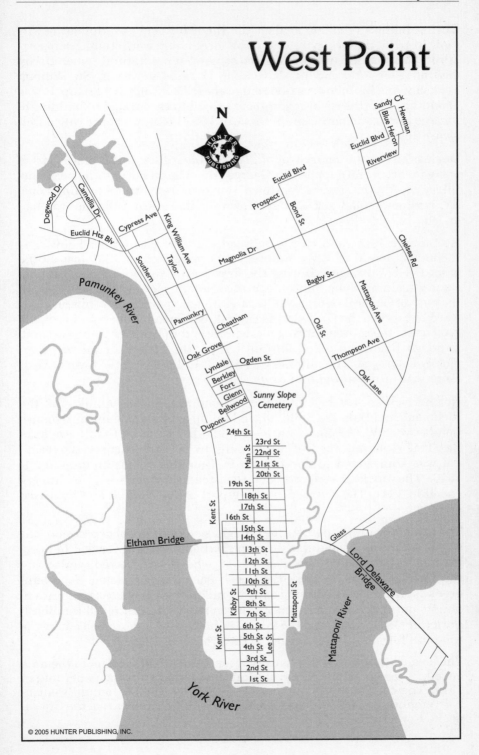

West Point

The Middle Peninsula

During Bacon's rebellion against the English Royal government of Virginia in 1676, the local planters on the three rivers were staunch supporters of the cause. The rebellion ended somewhat prematurely when Bacon died of fever after having driven the Colonial governor, Sir William Berkeley, and his followers into refuge aboard an English warship. It was about that time the royal government sought to encourage the building of tobacco towns and ports; one of them, at West Point, was to be called Delaware Town.

During the Revolutionary War of 1775-83, the little town became a port of entry for arms and supplies for George Washington's army. The heavy artillery used in the siege of Yorktown, sent over from France by King Louis XV, was assembled at Delaware Town for its return after the war had ended.

By the mid-19th century, the railroad had arrived in West Point. The Richmond and York River Railroad was completed in 1861 just as the great Civil War began. During the first year of the war, West Point became a training camp for Confederate soldiers. However, it was right in the path of General George McClellan's invading army on its march westward to capture the Confederate capital, Richmond. Robert E. Lee made good use of the railroad during his defense of the Confederate capital and, although Richmond didn't fall until 1865, the little railroad was completely destroyed. The railroad was rebuilt in 1870, and the town of West Point was incorporated that same year.

Northern financiers took over the railroad, established a link with the Richmond and Danville Railroad, and set up a regular steamship connection between West Point, Baltimore and other ports on the Chesapeake Bay. Unfortunately, the traffic soon outgrew the little port and the terminal was transferred to Portsmouth in Hampton Roads on January 1, 1896. The railroad remains, but the steamship service to Baltimore ended in 1941. The railroad is now a part of the Norfolk and Southern system.

The loss of the town's port status brought several years of depression, but a new source of income was developed when investors decided to bring the tourist industry to West Point. A large hotel was erected overlooking the York River and, in 1900, the Beach Park was completed. Soon hundreds of visitors were arriving daily by rail to enjoy the pleasant location, dining, dancing and many other amusements. Fire destroyed the Beach Park complex in 1910, and the tourist industry had almost died out by the time the Terminal Hotel burned to the ground in 1926.

The downturn in the local economy after the death of tourism in the area ended, however, with the arrival of an Ohio-based pulp and paper mill in 1914. The company was purchased in 1918 by Elis Olsson, a Swedish-born engineer, and continues to flourish to this day as a part of the Chesapeake Corporation.

Today, West Point is not one of the places you'll find at the top of the nation's lists of holiday resorts. But it's a place where you can enjoy a quiet vacation, while still close enough to the action for a night of fine dining and entertainment.

Sights

The landscape around the West Point area abounds in historic sites, and the three counties have more surviving Colonial churches than any others in Virginia.

Colonial Downs, in New Kent County, is Virginia' first horse race facility since the 1800s and features harness and thoroughbred racing, and polo. It is located at Exit 214 off I-64. ☎ 804-966-7223, www.colonialdowns.com.

Courthouse Green Historic District, on Routes 681 and 655 at King and Queen Courthouse, ☎ 804-785-4420, dates back to 1690 and features a 19th-century tavern, jail, courthouse and other buildings.

Historic Chelsea Plantation, 874 Plantation Lane, Providence Forge, ☎ 804-843-2386, www.webcentre.com/usr/chelsea, is open Thursday through Sunday from 10 a.m. until 4:30 p.m.

J.C. Graves Historic Museum, ☎ 804-769-2357, is located in the New Mt. Zion Baptist Church, Route 633 near Walkerton. There are African-American and military history exhibits, and genealogical research. Open by appointment.

King William Courthouse, circa 1725, is the oldest continually used courthouse in the nation.

Mattaponi Indian Reservation, two miles east of Route 30, near West Point, King William County, ☎ 804-769-2229. There is a museum; call ahead.

Pamunkey Indian Reservation is eight miles from Route 30 on Route 633 near West Point in King William County, ☎ 804-843-4792. It holds events throughout the year and the museum is open Tuesday-Sunday.

Powhatan's Legacy: Pamunkey-Mattaponi Trail is a self-guided driving tour of 14 King William County historic homes, churches and buildings that are listed on the National Register of Historic Places. Brochures are available through the West Point Chamber of Commerce (☎ 804-843-4620), or King William County Offices (☎ 804-769-4927).

The West Point Historic District is a waterfront community of Victorian homes. For more information, contact the West Point Area Chamber of Commerce, ☎ 804-843-4620.

The Middle Peninsula

Annual Events

The **Crab Carnival** draws thousands of people from all over Virginia to West Point the first full weekend in October. The event is a crab-lover's gourmet feast and a time for family fun that has grown increasingly popular over the years. From boats and from docks, everybody puts out crab lines or a crab pot. The event is a tribute to the "beautiful swimmers" that are the Chesapeake Bay blue crabs, and is staged by the West Point Chamber of Commerce with a great many volunteers. ☎ 804-843-4620.

Recreation

Located as it is on the three rivers – the York, the Pamunkey and the Mattaponi – West Point is something of an outdoor and sportsman's paradise. The three counties are famous for deer, quail and a variety of other game. Several thousand acres of privately owned hunting land are open to the public on payment of a small charge for the season's hunting privilege.

Vast marshes and backwaters furnish a natural habitat for migrating ducks and geese. The three rivers provide anglers with many opportunities to pursue their sport. Species available in the rivers include bass, pike, bream and shad.

A privately operated marina on the Mattaponi in West Point provides fuels and service, and public boat launching ramps and fueling stations are available.

King William Park County Recreational Park, ☎ 804-769-4280, has a playground, basketball courts, and several playing fields.

The New Kent Nature Trail helps to develop public appreciation for the area's natural resources. The trail passes through portions of a 565-acre forestry complex owned and managed by the Chesapeake Forest Products Company. Various species of plans and points of interest are marked with numbered stakes and the location of each is shown on a map in a booklet available from the West Point Chamber of Commerce. The total length of the trail is about 2½ miles and it may comfortably be hiked in about 3½ hours. However, the trail is divided into sections so you can return to the parking lot from either of two places without hiking the entire length of the footpath or retracing your footsteps. The sections vary in difficulty – the easiest and shortest is the red section. For more information and a descriptive booklet, contact either the Chesapeake Forest Products Company, ☎ 804-843-5402, or the Chamber of Commerce, 804-843-4620.

New Kent County has a fine and challenging 18-hole golf coursethe **Brookwood Golf Course**, ☎ 804-932-3737, 7325 Club Drive, off Highway 60 in Quinton. And the **West Point Country Club** has a nine-hole golf course, a swimming pool, picnic area, tennis courts and a 10-acre boating lake.

The **Middle Peninsula Regional Airport** in Shacklefords is home to one of the oldest skydiving clubs in the country – great fun to watch. There's a jumping event every Halloween. ☎ 804-785-9725, www.sky-divethepoint.com.

Dining & Accommodations

Anna's Italian Restaurant is on King William Avenue in West Point, ☎ 804-843-4035.

The Jasmine Plantation Bed & Breakfast Inn is between Williamsburg and Richmond in historic New Kent County, ☎ 804-966-2159, www.jasmineplantation.com. The inn is a fully restored 18th-century house built in 1750 and located on 47 acres of beautiful Virginia countryside. The Jasmine has six guest rooms decorated in various period antiques. Guests who are situated in rooms without connecting bathrooms are provided with plush terry robes. Visitors enjoy peace and quiet and a full country breakfast, served outdoors on the deck if weather permits. $$-$$$

LasTuna's is a Mexican restaurant at 614 Main Street, West Point, ☎ 804-843-3955.

Nick's Spaghetti and Steakhouse in Shackelford, about five minutes from West Point on Route 33, ☎ 804-785-6300.

Retta's B&B is an 1830 Greek Revival home at 403 Main Street, West Point. Children six and older welcome. Choose the one- or the two-room suite. Smoking in designated areas. ☎ 804-843-9192, www.rettabb.com. $

Tony & George's Seafood Restaurant, 2880 King William Avenue, West Point, ☎ 804-843-4448, is open daily for lunch and dinner.

Victorian Pointe B&B, 115 Main Street, West Point, ☎ 804-843-3533, is located where the three rivers meet. Enjoy breezes or even breakfast on the wide verandah. There are three guestrooms. No pets; children by special arrangement. $

Information

For more information about the West Point area, contact the **West Point Tri-River Chamber of Commerce**, 618 Main Street, West Point, VA 23181, ☎ 804-843-4620, www.westpointva.com, www.westpointvirginia.org.

Central Virginia

Ashland & Hanover County

A shland, located in Hanover County just 10 miles from Richmond, is an ideal jumping-off spot when sightseeing around Richmond, Colonial Williamsburg, Petersburg, Charlottesville or Fredericksburg.

In Hanover, you can spend a day or two at Paramount's Kings Dominion – one of the nation's premiere theme parks – or visit the hallowed grounds at Scotchtown, the former home of Patrick Henry. You can also enjoy a leisurely stroll along the city streets of Ashland, take a side-trip to the Civil War battlefield at Cold Harbor, or simply relax for an afternoon's shopping and a quiet lunch far away from the strain and stress of big city life.

History

Ashland developed as a "child of the railroad." In 1836, the **Richmond, Fredericksburg & Potomac Railroad Company** laid a single track line from Richmond to the South Anna River, through what is now Ashland. The railroad purchased much of the forested land along its right-of-way as a source of fuel for its steam engines. In 1845, it erected "a long, low building with a large room suitable for balls, picnics, etc.," on the site of the present Randolph-Macon College "Old Campus." The railroad called the new facility Slash Cottage and began to run excursions out of Richmond to the resort and to sell lots on each side of the tracks.

Soon the area developed as a summer resort with hotels, minerals springs, a horse racing track, and charming Victorian homes built facing the railroad tracks. The new town was incorporated in 1858. After the Civil War, Randolph-Macon College relocated to Ashland.

But Hanover County's roots go much further back, to 1720. The County was named for King George I of England. Prior to English colonization, the Pamunkey Indians populated the area. The county's northern boundary, the Pamunkey River, carries their name and they maintain a reservation on the lower section of the river in neighboring King William County.

During the 18th century Hanover was the center of the "Great Awakening" in Virginia led by the Reverend Samuel Davis who founded the Hanover Presbytery. Hanover County is also the birthplace of two great American patriots, Patrick Henry and Henry Clay.

During the 19th century, Hanover played a major role in the Civil War. General Grant's Union Army crossed the Pamunkey River on its way to fight at Cold Harbor, and its strategic location just to the north of the Confederate capital of Richmond made it the site of numerous other battles and skirmishes.

Today, Hanover County is filled with reminders of its turbulent and often tragic past. Many 18th- and 19th-century homes have been preserved. Its historic sites and battlefields draw thousands of visitors to the area every year. But life in Hanover County continues much as it has for more than a century after the Civil War ended.

Sights

Ashland Farmer's Market is a growers-only market open every Saturday morning, May through November, in downtown Ashland. For information on produce markets throughout the county, contact the Hanover Extension Office, ☎ 804-752-4310.

Ashland/Hanover Visitors Center, 112 North Railroad Avenue, Ashland, ☎ 800-897-1479 or 804-752-6766, is located in the restored 1932 train station. Be sure to pick up the brochure, *Ashland Walking Tour,* a self-guided tour of sites including Cross Bros. Grocery; the Hanover Arts & Activities Center; the Ashland Presbyterian Church; the Masonic Hall; the Washington Franklin Hall; the College Chapel and the Macmurdo Home. The visitor center is open daily from 9 a.m. until 5 p.m.

Hanover County Black Heritage Museum, 204 Virginia Street, ☎ 804-752-6110, explores the county's African-American heritage, with exhibits on family life and Black inventors.

Hanover Courthouse Complex, built in 1735, houses the courthouse itself, a tavern and the 19th-century jail to form a rare historical complex. It was at the old courthouse that Patrick Henry participated in the Parson's Cause case of 1763 and gave a first thrust toward the American Revolution. Then, in 1774, the citizens of Hanover assembled at the courthouse and adopted the Hanover Resolves. The courthouse is located on Route 301, southeast of Ashland, and is open by appointment. ☎ 804-537-5815.

Hanover Tavern, built in 1732, was owned by John Shelton, father-in-law of Patrick Henry, from 1752 until 1764. From 1785 until 1835 it was a stop on the northern stagecoach line. It is located on Route 301, across from the courthouse. ☎ 804-537-5050.

North Anna Battlefield Park has a self-guided walking tour of the battlefield where more than 150,000 Union and Confederate soldiers built fortifications along the North Anna River in May of 1864. Located on Verndon Road in Doswell, north of Ashland. ☎ 804-365-4695.

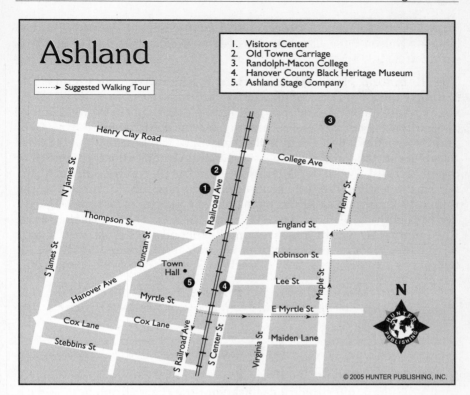

Ashland

Suggested Walking Tour

1. Visitors Center
2. Old Towne Carriage
3. Randolph-Macon College
4. Hanover County Black Heritage Museum
5. Ashland Stage Company

© 2005 HUNTER PUBLISHING, INC.

Ashland & Hanover County

Paramount's Kings Dominion, on Interstate 95 in Doswell, is a 400-acre family amusement park consisting of themed areas. Attractions include the Water Works Water Park, 12 world-class roller coasters, and a host of fun-filled rides, restaurants, fun houses, and live shows. Kings Dominion is open from mid-March through October. ☎ 804-876-5000, www.kingsdominion.com, for brochures and information.

Randolph-Macon College, built in 1830, is one mile west of Interstate 95 at Ashland. The historic buildings of the Methodist-affiliated college include the Washington-Franklin Hall, the Old Chapel and Pace Hall. The welcome center is at England and Henry streets. For information about campus tours, ☎ 800-888-1762, www.rmc.edu.

Scotchtown, **Home of Patrick Henry**, built in 1720 by Charles Chiswell, was the residence of Patrick Henry from 1771 until 1777. It was also, for a short period of time, the girlhood home of Dolly Madison. The house features fine examples of Colonial architecture and is listed on the National Register of Historic Places. Scotchtown is about 11 miles to the northwest of Ashland and is open Wednesday through Sunday, April through October, and by appointment. ☎ 804-227-3500.

The **Sycamore Tavern**, built in 1732, was the fourth stagecoach stop on the road from Charlottesville to Richmond. The building served as a tavern well into the 19th century. Today it houses the historical and genealogical Page Memorial Library, named for the wife of the noted author Thomas Nelson Page. The house is open on Wednesday, Friday and Saturday. ☎ 804-883-5355.

The **Richmond National Battlefield Parks** in Hanover County. The National Park Service has four units in Hanover County. Beaver Dam Creek and Gaines' Mill were a part of the Battles of the Seven Days of 1862 when Robert E. Lee successfully defended Richmond during General George McClellan's Peninsula Campaign. The Battle of Cold Harbor took place in 1864 and was a part of General Grant's all-out campaign to defeat and destroy the Confederate Army of Northern Virginia. Cold Harbor was a costly affair for General Grant, whose frontal attack on the well-entrenched Confederate forces of General Lee was repulsed with heavy casualties, leading him to break off the action and cross the James River to threaten the railroads around Richmond and Petersburg. To tour all four units, follow the signs from Mechanicsville along Route 156. All four parks are open daily. ☎ 804-226-1981, www.nps.gov/rich/home.htm.

❖ *Old Towne Carriage*, ☎ *804-227-3100, offers horse-drawn carriage rides through Ashland's historic district.*

Recreation

Ashland Berry Farm, Old Ridge Road, 10 miles northwest of Ashland, ☎ 804-227-3601, offers hayrides, pick-your-own berries and pumpkins, a petting zoo and Christmas shop.

All Golf Center, 11000 Washington Highway, Ashland, ☎ 804-550-2622, has heated tee boxes, miniature golf and batting cages.

The Hollows Golf Course, 15401 Greenwood Church, Montpelier, ☎ 804-798-2949, is a 12-hole public course, 12 miles west of Ashland.

James River Wine Cellars offers tours and tastings Wednesday-Sunday. Closed January and February. 11008 Washington Highway, Glen Allen. ☎ 804-550-7516, www.jamesrivercellars.com.

Overhill Lake, off Route 33, Ashland, ☎ 804-798-6819, www.overhill-lake.com, has a sandy beach and offers paddleboats on a five-acre lake.

RF & P Model Railroad Exhibit is on display the second Saturday of each month at the Ashland/Hanover Shopping Center, Ashland, ☎ 804-798-0250.

Town of Ashland Swimming Pool, 1112 Maple Street at Carter Park, Ashland, ☎ 804-798-2520.

Dining

Small as it is, Ashland, along with the other small communities in Hanover County, offers a wide variety of dining opportunities. Dozens of unique restaurants and cafés offer a variety of culinary experiences. For a full list call the Hanover Visitor Information Center at ☎ 804-752-6766.

Ashland Coffee & Tea, 100 N. Railroad Avenue, Ashland, ☎ 804-798-1702 is a cozy coffee house that serves both lunch and dinner. There is entertainment on weekends.

Baja Bean Company, 6233 Mechanicsville Turnpike, Mechanicsville, is a fun, lively place to dine on fresh, California-style Mexcian food. ☎ 804-257-5445, www.bajabean.com.

Henry Clay Inn, 114 N. Railroad Avenue, Ashland, ☎ 804-798-3100, serves brunch and dinner with porch dining in the summer. Open Friday through Sunday only.

Homemades by Suzanne, 102 N. Railroad Avenue, Ashland, ☎ 804-798-8331, serves lunch only, offering sandwiches, soups, salads and desserts. Closed Sunday.

Ironhorse Restaurant, 100 S. Railroad Avenue, Ashland, ☎ 804-752-6410, is a gourmet restaurant offering a new menu every month. Serves lunch and dinner; closed Sunday and Monday.

Smokey Pig, 212 S. Washington Highway, Ashland, ☎ 804-798-4590, is a specialty barbecue restaurant well known in the Ashland area. Closed Monday.

Accommodations

Hotels

Best Western Kings Quarters, off Interstate 95 at Paramount's Kings Dominion, ☎ 804-876-3321, www.bestwesternkingsquarters.com, is a large hotel with 248 rooms,a full-service restaurant and café, swimming pool, lighted tennis courts and an exercise room. $

Days Inn, 806 England Street at Interstate 95 and State Route 54 West, ☎ 804-798-4262, has 89 rooms, a full-service restaurant and café. $

Hanover House Motor Lodge, five miles south of Ashland on Interstate 95, ☎ 804-550-2805, is a medium-sized motor hotel with 90 rooms, including handicapped-accessible and non-smoking rooms. Facilities and services offered include a full-service restaurant and café, swimming pool, meeting rooms, valet service, golf privileges and an exercise room. Senior citizen discount. $-$$

Econo Lodge, on Interstate 95 and Virginia 54, ☎ 804-798-9221, has 87 rooms and a swimming pool. Discount for seniors. $

Hampton Inn, 705 England Street, ☎ 804-752-8444, www.hampton-inn.com, has 74 rooms, an exercise room, and outdoor pool. $$

The Henry Clay Inn, in the center of the town behind the train station, ☎ 804-798-3100, www.henryclayinn.com, is a small country inn with 15 guest rooms, restaurant, gift shop and art gallery. The building is a replica of a 1906 Georgian Revival structure that was destroyed by fire in 1946. $$

Quality Inn & Suites, 810 England Street, ☎ 804-798-4231, www.choicehotels.com, is a well-appointed hotel with 165 rooms, ia full-service restaurant and café, a swimming pool and an exercise room. $

Camping

Americamps Richmond-North, Exit 89 off I-95, ☎ 804-798-5298, www.americamps.com.

Paramount's King's Dominion Campground, Exit 98 off I-95, ☎ 804-876-5355. It has more than 300 sites, with water, sewer and electric hookups available, three cabins, a store with arcade games and groceries, a volleyball court, pool, miniature golf, and a free shuttle to and from Paramount's King's Dominion theme park.

Transportation

Hanover County is linked to the rest of Virginia by a network of highways that includes **Interstates 95** and **295**, **US Highway 1** and **SR 54**.

Ashland and Hanover County are served by the **Richmond International Airport** with direct flights to more than 55 cities and connecting flights to all national and international destinations.

Information

The **Ashland/Hanover Chamber of Commerce** and the **Hanover Visitor Information Center** are in the 1920s train station at 112 North Railroad Avenue, Ashland, VA 23005, ☎ 804-752-6766, 800-897-1479, www.town.ashland.va.us. Self-guided walking tours of the town and the African-American Heritage Trail are available.

Bedford & Bedford County

Strategically located between the metropolitan areas of Lynchburg and Roanoke, the Bedford area abounds with natural beauty and outdoor recreational opportunities.

Bedford County was established in 1754 and named for the fourth Duke of Bedford. In 1836, the Town of Liberty, now the city of Bedford, was established and thrived on an agrarian economy until Bedford's industrial development began in 1880. Since that time, industrial growth in the area has been consistent and often fostered by the involvement of local citizens. In the early 1980s the city undertook renovation of its historic downtown district and became one of Virginia's first Main Street Cities.

Bedford is located in the heart of the county on US Highway 460 and is bounded by the Blue Ridge Mountains to the west, the James River on the northeast, and Smith Mountain Lake to the south.

Winter is a time to spend cozy evenings by the fire at one of the county's many period bed and breakfast inns laden with heirlooms and friendly hospitality. When the snow arrives, there are ample trails and shelters in the high country that invite the hardy souls who enjoy winter hiking and camping.

The spring brings a breathtaking rebirth of nature among the overlooks of "America's most scenic drive." The **Blue Ridge Parkway** springs into vibrant color as the dogwoods, mountain laurel and rhododendron burst forth into the new season. Trails, self-guided wildflower walks, romantic picnic clearings, campgrounds, charming restaurants and lodging facilities all come together to provide one of the most entrancing vacation spots in all of Virginia.

In the summer, the focus of Bedford County shifts to the iridescent waters of **Smith Mountain Lake**. This beautiful 22,000-acre water park, with its more than 500 miles of shoreline, rimmed by mountains, is where the action is. Smith Mountain Lake is a haven for watersports enthusiasts from around the state. Boating, fishing, sailing, water-skiing, swimming and sunbathing are only a few of the exciting pastimes available on the water. Add a little golf, perhaps some tennis, and some of the finest lakeside dining in Virginia, and you have the makings of a fine, relaxing getaway.

The fall brings a new experience to Bedford County. All along the Blue Ridge Parkway, cascades of brilliant colors roll across the hills and valleys. Thousands of visitors flock to the area in search of the fall colors on the mountains. On the crystal water of Smith Mountain Lake, anglers seek the record-sized stripers and largemouth bass. Then hunting season arrives, and more than 18,000 acres of the Jefferson National Forest and dozens of private tracts open for deer, wild turkey and bear hunting.

Sights

Avenel, a manor house built in 1838 by William Burwell, was once the focal point of social, cultural and political life in Bedford. Each December, the legends of Christmas past are brought back to life in a series of traditional luncheons, dinners and entertainment by period actors and musicians. Tours by appointment. ☎ 540-586-1814.

Bedford City/County Museum is housed in an 1895 Masonic building at 201 East Main Street. Exhibits tell the history of the area going back to early Native Americans, and include a display honoring those who participated in D-Day. The museum is open Tuesday through Saturday, 10 a.m. to 5 p.m.; it has a genealogy library and is handicapped-accessible. ☎ 540-586-4520, www.bedfordvamuseum.org.

Bedford County Courthouse, the third to occupy the site, was built in 1930 in the Classic Revival style. ☎ 540-586-7632, www.co.bedford.va.us.

Bedford Farmer's Market on Washington Street offers fresh produce and local crafts Tuesday, Friday and Saturday during spring, summer and fall. ☎ 540-586-2148, www.centertownbedford.com.

Bedford Meeting House was built in 1838 as a Methodist meeting house, when the town was known as Liberty. Open by appointment. ☎ 540-586-9639, www.bedfordhistory.org.

Booker T. Washington National Monument honors the African-American leader who was born in slavery on this tobacco plantation in 1856. Exhibits, a film and living history farm interpret his life as educator, orator and founder of the Tuskegee Institute in Alabama. Open daily 9 a.m. to 5 p.m. Free admission. 12130 Booker T. Washington Highway, Hardy, 540-721-2094, www.nps.gov/bowa

No two hand-painted pieces are alike at **Emerson Creek Pottery**'s factory outlet, located in an 1825 log cabin built by blacksmith Silas Wade. Have lunch on the picnic tables in this country setting. 1068 Pottery Lane, Bedford, ☎ 540-297-7884, www.emersoncreekpottery.com.

Hickory Hill Winery is a small, family-owned winery two miles from Smith Mountain Lake. Open for tours and tastings in a renovated 1923 farmhouse, Friday through Monday, mid-March through mid-December. 1722 Hickory Cove Lane, Moneta, ☎ 540-296-1393, www.hickoryhillvineyards.com.

Historic Centertown Bedford along Main Street feaures shopping for antiques, art, jewelry, and gifts, as well dining. A walking tour and visitors guide are available for this National Historic District. ☎ 540-586-2148, www.bedfordmainstreet.org.

Holy Land USA, on Route 746, southwest of the city of Bedford, is a unique attraction on 400 acres that is a replica of the lands of Syria,

Israel and Jordan. There is primitive camping and picnic areas. ☎ 540-586-2823, www.holyland.pleasevisit.com.

James River Restored Canal Lock, at Battery Creek Lock, was part of the James River and Kanawha Canal System built in 1948-49. ☎ 540-586-4357.

Longwood Cemetery on Longwood Avenue, ☎ 540-586-7161, dates back to the Revolutionary War.

National D-Day Memorial, at the intersection of routes 122 and 450 in the city of Bedford, honors allied Armed Forces in the 1944 invasion of Normandy, and the town of Bedford which suffered the largest loss of life per capita of any community in the nation. Open daily, 10 a.m. to 5 p.m. ☎ 540-587-3619, www.dday.org.

Peaks of Otter Winery, 2122 Sheep Creek Road in Bedford County, offers fruit-of-the-farm wine tastings and tours. Open August through December or by appointment. ☎ 540-586-3707, www.peaksofotterwinery-.com.

Poplar Park, on Grand Arbre Drive in the city of Bedford, is the home of the largest yellow poplar tree in the US, ☎ 540-586-7161.

Thomas Jefferson's Poplar Forest, on Route 661 in Bedford County, is an octagonal house designed and built by Thomas Jefferson as his personal retreat. The house and an archaeological exhibit are open daily, April through November, ☎ 434-534-8118.

The **Wharton Garden** on North Bridge Street has brick walks and terraces through a mature boxwood maze. It's adjacent to the Bedford Central Library and the Wharton House.

Recreation

Adrenaline Air Sports offers sky diving at Smith Mountain Lake Airport, ☎ 540-296-1100, www.air-sports.com.

The Appalachian Trail passes through the county on its way from Georgia to Maine. It can be accessed at Mileposts 80.5, 90.9 and 92.5 on the Blue Ridge Parkway. ☎ 540-586-4357.

Blue Ridge Parkway. A portion of this 470-mile scenic drive passes through the northwest portion of the county. ☎ 540-586-4357.

Bridgewater Marina & Boat Rentals has parasailing, Moneta, ☎ 800-729-1639, www.bridgewaterplaza.com.

Endeavor Ballooning offers scenic balloon rides, ☎ 540-992-OFLY, www.endeavorballoon.com.

Liberty Lake Park is a 60-acre area on Burke's Hill Road that offers a stocked fishing lake, playing fields, playgrounds and a handicapped hiking trail. There is a holiday light display each December. ☎ 540-586-7161.

The Peaks of Otter can be seen from Milepost 86 on the Blue Ridge Parkway. These peaks, known as Sharp Top, Flat Top, and Harkening Hill, were once home to Native Americans of 10,000 B.C. Visitors can hike or take the guided bus tour to the peak of Sharp Top, where the wonderful stonework of the Civilian Conservation Corps can be seen. The restored Johnson Farm interprets southern mountain life during the 19th century. There are walking trails, a visitor center and an inn nearby.

Peaks of Otter Visitor Center at ☎ 540-587-4995 or 877-HI-PEAKS. **Peaks of Otter Restaurant and Lodge**, ☎ 800-542-5927, www.peaksofotter.com.

Reba Farm Inn offers horseback riding in the mountains and countryside, from a couple of hours to overnight camping trips. 1099 Reba Farm Lane, Bedford, ☎ 540-586-1905, 888-235-3574, www.rebafarminn.com.

Smith Mountain Lake State Park in Huddleston offers boating, hiking, camping and swimming with 16 miles of shoreline. Rental cabins are available. ☎ 540-297-6066, www.dcr.state.va.us.

Virginia's Explore Park is an outdoor living history museum with six miles of nature trails and 12 miles of mountain bike trails. Located at Milepost 115 on the Blue Ridge Parkway. ☎ 540-427-1880, 800-842-9163, www.explorepark.org.

Washington/Jefferson National Forests. These vast national forest lands offer a wealth of recreational opportunities. ☎ 540-291-2188, www-.southernregion.fs.fed.us/gwjnf.

Golf

Bedford Country Club, 3563 Peaks Road, Bedford, ☎ 540-586-8407.

Colonial Hills Golf Club, 1990 Gumtree Road, Forest, ☎ 434-525-3954.

Ivy Hill Golf Club, 1327 Ivy Hill Drive, Forest, ☎ 434-525-2680, www-.ivyhillgc.com.

London Downs Golf Club, 1400 New London Road, Forest, ☎ 434-525-4653, www.londondownsgolf.com.

Mariners Landing Golf and Lake Community, 1037 Whitetail Drive, Huddleston, ☎ 800-491-8491, www.marinerslanding.

Poplar Forest Golf Course, 960 Ramblewood Road, Forest, ☎ 434-534-9418.

Sycamore Ridge, 1270 Trails End Road, Goodview, ☎ 540-297-6490.

The **Westlake Golf and Country Club**, 360 Chestnut Creek Drive, Hardy, ☎ 540-721-4214, www.golfwestlake.com.

Entertainment

Bedford Council for the Arts, the cultural committee of Bedford Main Street, ☎ 540-586-2148, www.bedfordmainstreet.org.

Little Town Players, Elks National Home Theatre, award-winning community theater, ☎ 540-586-5881, www.littletownplayers.com.

The **Sedalia Center** hosts festivals and international talent under the outdoor pavilion, 1108 Sedalia School Road, Big Island, ☎ 434-299-5080, www.sedaliacenter.org.

The **Smith Mountain Lake Wine Festival** is in late September with 21 wineries, 55 craft vendors, food and live bands. ☎ 800-676-8203.

Dining

The **Cabana at Mariners Landing** is open Tuesday through Saturday for lunch and dinner and Sundays for brunch. 1037 Whitetail Drive, Huddleston, ☎ 540-297-3200, www.marinerslanding.com.

Forks Country Restaurant, 1619 Forest Road, Bedford, ☎ 540-586-9041.

The **Landing Restaurant** at Bernard's Landing Resort blends New York chic and Caribbean flair in its southern fare. 775 Ashmeade Road, Moneta, ☎ 540-721-3028, www.bernardslanding.com.

Mango's serves steaks and seafood with a tropical flair. Live entertainment. 16430 Booker T. Washington Highway, Bridgewater Plaza, Moneta, ☎ 540-721-1632, www.mangosbarandgrill.com.

Millstone Tea Room combines Mediterranean, Eastern European and Southern American fare in a roadside village tearoom. 9058 Big Island Parkway (Route 122 North), Sedalia, ☎ 540-587-7100, www.millstone-tearoom1939.com.

New London Steak House, 4312 New London Road, Forest, ☎ 434-525-3826, is open for dinner Wednesday through Sunday, serving steak, seafood, BBQ ribs, and chicken.

Olde Liberty Station, 515 Bedford Avenue, Bedford, ☎ 540-587-9377, www.oldelibertystation.com, offers seafood and prime rib. Closed Sunday.

Peaks of Otter Restaurant, Milepost 86 on the Blue Ridge Parkway, ☎ 540-586-1081. Open for breakfast, lunch and dinner, serving a variety of seafood, steaks and sandwiches.

Bedford County

R U Up, 140 West Main Street, ☎ 540-587-0145, offers homemade pastries, sandwiches and a variety of coffees.

The Sportsman is a lively seafood place at Smith Mountain Lake. 16111 Smith Mountain Lake Parkway, Huddleston, ☎ 540-297-7900, www.the-sportsman.us.

Accommodations

Hotels & Motels

Belvew Bay Condominiums, Smith Mountain Lake, Huddleston, ☎ 540-297-7532, has 22 units and two suites. There is a restaurant, pool and coffee shop. $$

At **Bernard's Landing Resort & Conference Center** every room has a lake view. There's tennis, volleyball, a health club, pool, Jacuzzi and restaurant. Full-equipped condos and townhomes. 775 Ashmeade Road, Moneta, ☎ 540-721-8870, www.bernardslanding.com. $$$

Campers Paradise is a lakefront motel, campground and restaurant. 1336 Campers Paradise Trail, Moneta, ☎ 540-297-6109, www.campersparadise.com. $

Days Inn has 75 rooms and serves a continental breakfast. 921 Blue Ridge Avenue, US 460 West, Bedford, ☎ 540-586-8286, www.daysinn.com. $

Days Inn, 921 Blue Ridge Avenue, Bedford, ☎ 540-586-8286 or 800-528-1234, is a pleasant motel with 78 rooms where pets are welcome. The hotel has a restaurant, a café, a bar and a pool. Discounts for senior citizens. $

The Peaks of Otter Lodge, at Mile Post 86 on the Blue Ridge Parkway close to Bedford, ☎ 540-586-1081, www.peaksofotter.com, may be one of the most perfect vacation inns in Virginia. Everything at Peaks of Otter is in harmony with nature. From the lakeside setting to the décor of natural woods and subtly blended textures, tones and colors, the hotel seems at one with its surroundings. You can enjoy the fresh air, nature trails, fishing and pioneer history. At the end of the day there's always a good meal and wonderful hospitality in the restaurant where a heaping plate and good service make you feel right at home. There are 60 lakefront rooms. Some special packages include meals. $$

Super 8 Hotel, Highway 460 West, Bedford, ☎ 540-587-0100, has 58 units and a pool. Free breakfast. $

Bed & Breakfasts / Inns

Liberty House B&B has two rooms and a suite in Bedford's Historic District. 602 Mountain Ave. ☎ 540-587-0966, www.wp21.com/liberty. $

Love Stone Inn Bed and Breakfast is a French Country retreat with four guest rooms and a cottage. Guests are greeted with a glass of Virginia wine and hors d'oeuvres on the deck overlooking Smith Mountain Lake. 100 Summer Lane, Huddleston. ☎ 540-296-0510, www.LoveStone-Inn.com. $$

Mariner's Landing Golf & Lake Community has condos, villas and townhomes, a pool, golf course, tennis course, restaurant and lakefront. 1037 Whitetail Drive, Huddleston, ☎ 540-297-3200, 800-491-8491, www-.marinerslanding.com. $$$

Otter's Den, Route 43, two miles south of Blue Ridge Parkway, ☎ 540-586-2204, www.ottersden.com, is a late-1700s renovated log cabin with two guest rooms and private baths. Outdoor hot tub and spectacular views. No children under 12. $$

Reba Farm Inn, 1099 Reba Farm Lane, Bedford, ☎ 888-235-3574, www.rebafarminn.com, has six guest rooms, including one suite, all with private baths, in a 200-year-old farmhouse; amenities include horseback riding and a pool. Children are welcome and a full three-course breakfast is included. $$-$$$

Vanquility Acres Inn Bed and Breakfast is a modern home on 10 acres offering two suites and one guest room. 105 Angus Terrace, Bedford. ☎ 540-587-9113, www.vanquilityacresinn.com. $$

West Manor is a restored 1820 manor house with several restored cottages available to guests. 3594 Elkton Farm Road, Forest. ☎ 434-525-0923, www.westmanorbb.com. $$$

Camping

Blue Ridge Campground, 8131 Burnt Chimney Road, Wirtz, ☎ 540-721-3855.

 Campers Paradise, 1336 Campers Paradise Trail, Moneta, ☎ 540-297-6109, www.campersparadise.com.*

Eagles Roost, 15335 Smith Mountain Lake Parkway, Huddleston, ☎ 540-297-7381.

Otter Creek, Milepost 61, Blue Ridge Parkway, Big Island. No hook-ups. ☎ 434-299-5862.

Peaks of Otter, Milepost 86, Blue Ridge Parkway, Bedford, ☎ 540-586-7321, 877-HI PEAKS.

Smith Mountain Lake State Park, 1235 State Park Road, Huddleston, ☎ 540-297-6066.

Wildwood Campground, Blue Ridge Parkway between Mile Posts 61 & 62, Monroe, ☎ 434-299-5228.

Bedford County

Transportation

The **Roanoke Regional Airport** is served by most major and regional carriers with direct or connecting flights to all major domestic and international destinations. There is also an airport at Smith Mountain Lake.

Information

The new **Bedford Area Welcome Center**, 816 Burke's Hill Road, Bedford, VA 24523, ☎ 877-HI-PEAKS, 540-587-5681, www.visitbedford.com, has exhibits, a picnic area, and views of the Peaks of Otter. It is open daily, from 9 a.m. until 5 p.m., year-round.

Charlottesville & Albemarle County

History

*P*erhaps Thomas Jefferson's own words best describe the panoramic vistas and rolling hills of Albemarle County. He wrote, "These mountains are the Eden of the United States."

The Eden where Mr. Jefferson was born, where he made his home and that inspired him to write those words, has changed somewhat with the times, but the historic streets of Charlottesville, the spectacular beauty of the Blue Ridge and the country lanes of Albemarle County remain.

Charlottesville, set almost in the center of the state, is the trading center for a widespread area. In Colonial times tobacco was the premiere product. Today, the county's output is far more diverse. Wheat, peaches, frozen foods, electronic products, beef and dairy cattle, race horses, light industry, apple-growing and wine-making continue to stimulate an already lively economy. The University of Virginia (and its related enterprises), however, remains Charlottesville's biggest employer.

Albemarle County's history began with its founding in 1744, when it was named in honor of **William Ann Keppel**. Keppel, the second earl of Albemarle and governor general of the colony of Virginia, never set foot in the county.

The county seat was moved from Scottsville to Charlottesville in 1762. Charlottesville took its name from Queen Charlotte, the wife of King George III.

In 1769 at the age of 26, Thomas Jefferson began the design and construction of his beloved mountain-top estate, **Monticello**. The house was built and subsequently remodeled over a period of some 40 years, reflecting Jefferson's fondness for architecture and the amusement he found, as he put it, in "... putting up and pulling down." Jefferson returned to his "little mountain" home when he retired from the presidency in 1809. He founded the University of Virginia at Charlottesville in 1817.

Our nation's fifth president, James Monroe, also lived in Albemarle County. On a mountain top, only a couple of miles or so from Monticello, lies **Ash Lawn Highland**, Monroe's 550-acre estate. Monroe was a good friend of Thomas Jefferson. In fact it was Jefferson who personally selected the site where Monroe built his house. James and his wife, Elizabeth, moved into Highland on November 23, 1799.

Today, history comes to life in Charlottesville and Albemarle County. Jefferson's Monticello, Monroe's Ash Lawn Highland, the old country homes, inns, mills and Charlottesville's historic downtown district, offer visitors a unique view of one of Virginia's most beautiful and historically significant locations.

❖ *Charlottesville has been ranked as one of the best places to live in the country, and it boasts numerous writers among its former and present citizens.*

Sights

A Sightseeing Tour of Historic Charlottesville and Albemarle County takes in most of the places of interest in and around the city. A map and detailed information are available at the Convention and Visitors Bureau on Virginia Highway 20S. ☎ 434-977-1783.

Albemarle County Court House, on Court Square in Charlottesville, was once used as a "common temple." It was shared by Episcopalians, Methodists, Presbyterians and Baptists – one Sunday per month designated for each denomination, though all were welcome to attend each Sunday. Open Monday through Friday, 8:30 a.m. to 4:30 p.m. ☎ 434-972-4083.

Ash Lawn-Highland: Home of James Monroe is on County Highway 795 and built upon a site personally selected by Thomas Jefferson. The 535-acre estate was the home of President James Monroe. It is owned today by Monroe's old college, William & Mary. The early 19th-century working estate offers visitors a look at what life must have been like on the plantation. Guided tours of the house and gardens show many of Monroe's possessions, spinning and weaving demonstrations, and the magnificent boxwood gardens complete with peacocks. Special events at the estate include a summer festival of operas, children's shows, spring and Christmas programs and a Colonial crafts weekend. The estate is open daily except for Thanksgiving, Christmas and New Year's Day. ☎ 434-293-9539, www.ashlawnhighland.org.

Charlottesville & Albemarle County

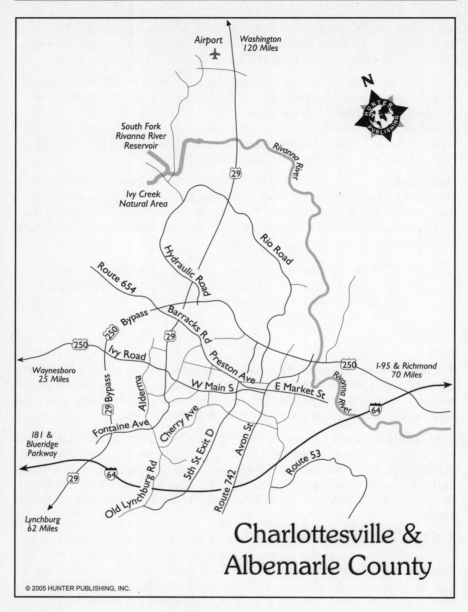

Charlottesville &
Albemarle County

Kluge-Ruhe Aboriginal Art Collection is part of the University of Virginia and is one of the foremost private collections of Australian Aboriginal art in the world. 400 Worrell Drive, Charlottesville, ☎ 434-244-0234, www.virginia.edu/kluge-ruhe.

McGuffey Art Center is located in a former elementary school with 40 studios, three galleries and a gift shop. 210 Second Street, NW, Charlottesville, ☎ 434-295-7973, www.mcguffeyartcenter.com.

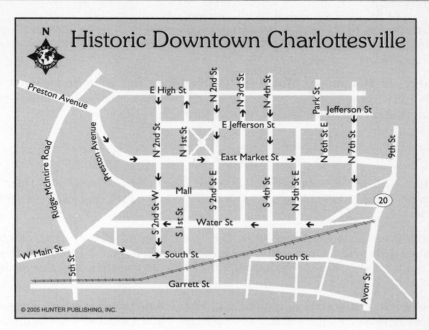

Michie Tavern, three miles south of Charlottesville on VA 53, is built upon land granted to Patrick Henry's father and later bought by John Michie. It was built in 1784, has been lovingly restored and contains many fine antiques. The old outbuildings, also extensively restored, include a kitchen, smokehouse, springhouse and a wine museum. The Michie Tavern is open daily except Christmas and New Year's Day. Lunch is served, and there's a gift shop. ☎ 434-977-1234, www.michietavern-.com.

Monticello is two miles west of Charlottesville on VA 53. Set on a mountaintop overlooking the city, it is one of the most beautiful estates in Virginia. Considered a classic of early American architecture, the house was designed by Thomas Jefferson and built over a period of more than 40 years. It symbolizes the pleasure Jefferson found in putting things up and pulling them down. Most of the furnishings are original. Start at the Visitor Center, then tour the restored orchard, vineyard, vegetable garden and Mulberry Row, the site of the old plantation workshops. Monticello is open daily except Christmas Day. ☎ 434-984-9800, www.monticello.org.

The **University of Virginia** in Charlottesville, founded in 1819 by Thomas Jefferson, was built according to his designs. The university's red brick buildings form the center of Jefferson's "academical village." Smooth green lawns, ancient oak trees, Jefferson's famous serpentine walls and the room where Edgar Allen Poe lived as a student are only a few of the features on display for visitors to enjoy. Free guided walking tours year-round except for three weeks during mid-December and early January. ☎ 434-924-7969, www.virginia.edu/exploring.html.

University of Virginia Art Museum shows art from ancient times to the present, 155 Rugby Road, Charlottesville, ☎ 434-924-3592, www.virginia.edu/artmuseum.

Virginia Discovery Museum, east end of the Historic Downtown Mall in Charlottesville, ☎ 434-977-1025, www.vadm.org, is a hands-on museum for children. Open Tuesday through Sunday.

Wineries

First Colony Winery is open daily for tours and tastings. 1650 Harris Creek Road, Charlottesville, ☎ 434-979-7105, www.firstcolonywinery.com.

Jefferson Vineyards includes the land where Jefferson first established a vineyard. Open daily for tours and tastings. 1353 Thomas Jefferson Parkway, Charlottesville, ☎ 800-272-3042, www.jeffersonvineyards.com.

Keswick Vineyards is located on historic 400-acre Edgewood Estate. Nearby Keswick Hall offers daily tastings while a tasting room is under construction. 1575 Keswick Winery Drive, Keswick, ☎ 434-244-3341, www.keswickvineyards.com.

King Family Vineyards is in Crozet, 15 minutes west of Charlottesville. 6550 Roseland Farm, ☎ 434-823-7800, www.kingfamilyvineyards.com.

Kluge Estate Winery and Vineyard is one of Virginia's newest wineries. There's a Farm Shop offerings tastings, gourmet fare, Virginia products and plants. Open Tuesday through Sunday, 10 a.m. to 5 p.m. 3550 Blenhiem Road, Charlottesville. ☎ 434-977-3895, www.klugeestate.com.

Oakencroft Vineyard & Winery, 1486 Oakencroft Lane (3½ miles west of Route 29 on Barracks Road), Charlottesville, ☎ 434-296-4188, www.oakencroft.com. Open for tours and tastings, April through December.

White Hall Vineyards, Sugar Ridge Road, White Hall, ☎ 434-823-8615, www.whitehallvineyards.com, is 13 miles from Charlottesville.

Wintergreen Winery is nestled on the edge of the Blue Ridge mountains. Tours and tastings are offered in a 19th-century farm building. Light gourmet picnic fare is available. Open daily year-round. 462 Winery Lane, Nellysford, ☎ 434-361-2519, www.wintergreenwinery.com.

Recreation

Skating

Charlottesville Ice Park, 230 West Main Street, ☎ 434-817-2400, www.icepark.com, on the Historic Downtown Mall, has public skating.

Golf

The City of Charlottesville owns two courses, **McIntire Park Golf Course**, 250 Bypass, ☎ 434-970-3589; and **Meadow Creek Golf Course**, Pen Park Road, ☎ 434-977-0615.

Albemarle County also has the **Keswick Hall Golf Club**, ☎ 434-923-4363, 701 Club Drive in Keswick, and the **Birdwood Golf Course** at Boar's Head Inn, 200 Ednam Drive, Charlottesville, ☎ 434-293-4653.

Outdoors

Within day-trip distance of Charlottesville are a myriad of opportunities, including the Shendandoah National Park, George Washington National Forest, and Old Rag Mountain.

Blue Ridge Parkway Visitors Center at Humpback Rocks is the first stop heading south on the parkway. It tells the story of one of the most successful public works projects under Roosevelt's New Deal. There's a collection of buildings recreating a typical 19th-century farm and a trail to the top of Humpback Mountain where spectacular views await. Milepost 5.8 Blue Ridge Parkway, Afton, ☎ 540-377-2377, www-.nps.gov/blri.

Ragged Mountain Natural Area is a 980-acre preserve owned by the City of Charlottesville. There's a reservoir and four miles of trails. ☎ 434-970-3589, http://monticello.avenue.org/icf/RMNA.html.

Rivanna River flows through Albemarle and Fluvanna counties offering fishing, canoeing and swimming. ☎ 434-293-6789.

Riverview Park & Rivanna Greenbelt is 26 miles along the river with picnic areas, fishing, hiking and biking on the Rivanna Greenbelt trail. ☎ 434-970-3589, www.charlottesville.org/parks.

Thomas Jefferson Parkway and **Kemper Park** are on Route 53. The parkway is actually a 3.2-mile round trip walking trail. Charlottesville, ☎ 434-984-9822, www.monticello.org/parkway.

Shopping

Charlottesville's pedestrian-only **Downtown Mall** has many distinctive boutiques, while nearby shopping malls in the Charlottesville/Albemarle area combine specialty shops with department stores. The **Corner**, on

Charlottesville & Albemarle County

University Avenue adjacent to the UVA campus, offers stylish boutiques and fun shops geared to student life.

Entertainment

Evening and weekend entertainment can range from the University of Virginia's Culbreth Theatre to a concert band performance on the Downtown Mall to 18th-century opera performed in the boxwood gardens of Ash Lawn-Highland. For information on weekly cultural events in and around Charlottesville, Call the **Arts Line**, ☎ 434-980-3366.

Ashlawn Opera Festival takes place from July through mid-August in the boxwood gardens of Ash Lawn-Highland, Route 795, featuring opera and musical theater. ☎ 434-293-4500, www.ashlawnopera.org.

The Charlottesville and University Symphony Orchestra, ☎ 434-924-3984, offers a free concert series at Cabell Hall Auditorium on the grounds of UVA, October through April, www.virginia.edu/music/ensembles/cuso.html.

Charlottesville Downtown Foundation, Downtown Amphitheater, ☎ 434-296-8548, hosts Fridays After Five, a free concert series showcasing local musical talent late April to Oct. 1.

Live Arts, 123 East Water Street, ☎ 434-977-4177, offers mainstream and experimental productions.

The **Paramount Theater** first opened as a movie house in 1931, and reopened in 2004, offering live art performances. 215 E. Main Street, Charlottesville, ☎ 434-979-1333, www.theparamount.net.

Piedmont Council of the Arts, ☎ 434-980-3366, http://avenue.org/pca, is the local arts agency serving Charlottesville, Albemarle and surrounding counties.

Prism Coffee House, Charlottesville, ☎ 434-977-7476, features live performances by local and national artists. Visit www.theprism.org.

University of Virginia has the Culbreth Theatre, ☎ 434-924-3376, and the Helms Theatre, ☎ 434-924-3376; www.virginia.edu.

Annual Events

Virginia Festival of the Book is a five-day series of readings, discussions and book signings held at various locations in mid-March. ☎ 434-924-3296, www.vabook.org.

The **Annual Dogwood Festival**, held over 10 days in mid-April, features a parade, queen's coronation and dance, lacrosse and golf tournaments, carnival and fireworks, ☎ 434-961-9824.

Foxfield Steeplechase Races take place in late April and late September. They're a staple of the Charlottesville social scene. ☎ 434-293-9501, www.foxfieldraces.com.

Historic Garden Week, held in mid-April, is a time when many of Albemarle County's fine private homes and gardens are open to the public. ☎ 804-644-7776, www.vagardenweek.org.

Crozet Arts and Crafts Festivals are held in May and October; ☎ 434-823-2211.

The **African-American Cultural Arts Festival** in late July celebrates this rich heritage at various venues throughout the city. 910 Rockcreek Road, Charlottesville, ☎ 434-979-0582, www.cvilleafrican-amfest.com.

The **Albemarle County Fair** takes place a week in early August, celebrating the area's agricultural heritage and economy. ☎ 434-293-6396, www.albemarlecountyfair.com.

The **Monticello Wine and Jazz Festival** is in early October. Admission charged; ☎ 434-296-4188 ext. 21.

Virginia Film Festival, the last week in October, features film screenings and discussions with leading film makers. It takes place at various locations throughout Charlottesville and on the University of Virginia campus. ☎ 800-UVA-FEST, www.vafilm.com.

Jeffersonian Thanksgiving Festival in mid-November at Charlottesville's Historic Court Square and Downtown Mall, ☎ 434-978-4466, www.jeffersonianthanksgiving.org.

Downtown for the Holidays kicks off at Thanksgiving and runs through December, featuring shopping, entertainment and decorations in downtown Charlottesville. ☎ 434-977-1812.

The Charlottesville Tradition is held the first weekend in December, offers arts, shopping, food and entertainment, starting on Friday with the grand illumination of the Downtown Mall. ☎ 434-961-5846.

First Night Virginia features fireworks, entertainment and food on New Year's Eve in downtown Charlottesville. ☎ 434-975-8269, http://monticello.avenue.org/firstnightvirginia.

Dining

Charlottesville and Albemarle County offer an extraordinary array of interesting dining possibilities, from simple, quick and economical to elegant or exotic. There are casual bistros, lively microbreweries and sophisticated eateries. Just a sampling of the more popular dining places are described below. For a complete listing, www.soveryvirginia.com.

Aberdeen Barn, 2018 Holiday Drive, ☎ 434-296-4630, www.aberdeen-barn.com, is open for diner nightly. The menu includes prime rib, steak and seafood.

Bang! serves Oriental tapas, has martini bar and outdoor dining, serving dinner Monday through Saturday. 213 Second Street, SW, Charlottesville, ☎ 434-984-2264.

Biltmore Grill, 16 Elliewood Avenue, ☎ 434-293-6700, is a very popular burger joint that serves pasta and salads too. Open daily for lunch, dinner and nightlife.

Bizou is a casual French bistro with outdoor dining, serving lunch and dinner Monday through Saturday. 119 W. Main Street, Charlottesville, ☎ 434-977-1818.

Buddhist Biker Bar & Grill, 20 Elliewood Avenue, ☎ 434-971-9181, dinner, and the bar is open until 2 a.m. Don't let the name fool you – it's not just a bar and it's not just for bikers. It's casual, but the food, wine and service are top-notch. There is patio dining.

C & O, 515 E. Water Street, ☎ 434-971-7044, is open for lunch and dinner. The menu offers French, Asian and American cuisine. The food and service are excellent.

Café Europa, 1331 W. Main Street, ☎ 434-295-4040, offers tasty Greek fare. Open daily.

The Continental Divide, 811 W. Main Street, ☎ 434-984-0143, serves up generous portions of good Mexican food and reasonable prices. Open daily.

The Court Square Tavern, 500 Court Square, ☎ 434-296-6111, offers a warm, English pub atmosphere. Closed Sunday.

Fleurie is an elegant French restaurant with an extensive wine list, serving dinner Monday through Saturday. Reservations recommended. 108 3rd Street NE, Charlottesville, ☎ 434-971-7800.

Inn at Court Square serves lunch in the oldest building in downtown Charlottesville. 410 E. Jefferson Street, ☎ 434-295-2800.

Ivy Inn Restaurant, 2244 Old Ivy Road, ☎ 434-977-1222, www.ivy-innrestaurant.com, is open for lunch and dinner. The menu includes seafood and steak.

Michael's Bistro & Taphouse, 1427 University Court, ☎ 434-977-3697, is a fun atmosphere with good food, open daily.

Mono Loco serves upscale Cuban and Spanish cuisine, open for lunch and dinner daily. 200 W. Water Street, Charlottesville, ☎ 434-979-0688.

Old Mill Room at Boar's Head Inn is a four-diamond gem serving imaginative cuisine and fine wines. Open daily. Route 250 West of Charlottesville, ☎ 434-972-2230, www.boarsheadinn.com.

OXO is a hip eatery in a warehouse-style setting. 215 W. Water Street, Charlottesville, ☎ 434-977-8111.

Rococo's, 2001 Commonwealth Drive, ☎ 434-971-7371, offers delicious Italian food. Open daily.

Starr Hill Restaurant & Brewery, 709 West Main Street, ☎ 434-977-0017, www.starrhill.com, is open for lunch and dinner. The setting is a brewery in a historic, turn-of-the century building. The menu includes smoked trout wontons, Caribbean marinated chicken, Pommery-herb pork loin and West Indian seafood sauté. The food is good and prices are reasonable.

Take It Away Sandwich Shop 115 Elliewood Avenue, ☎ 434-295-1899, has possibly the best sandwiches in town. Take-out only; closed Sunday.

Tiffany's Seafood Restaurant, 2171 Ivy Road, ☎ 434-293-5000, serves seafood and pasta.

Wild Greens is an American Grill open all day for lunch and dinner, brunch on Sundays. 2162 Barracks Road, Charlottesville, ☎ 434-296-9453.

Zocalo – meaning "center of town" in Spanish – offers patio dining on the downtown mall and a fireplace inside. 201 E. Main, Charlottesville, ☎ 434-977-4944, www.zocalo-restaurant.com.

Accommodations

More than 2,700 rooms are available in the Charlottesville area; from economy-style motel rooms to full-service inns and hotels.

Motels & Hotels

Best Western Cavalier Inn at the University, 105 Emmett Street, ☎ 888-882-2129, www.cavalier.com, has 118 rooms, a full-service restaurant and café, a swimming pool, and free continental breakfast. $

 Days Inn-University Area, 1600 Emmett Street, ☎ 804-293-9111, www.daysinn.com, 120 rooms. There is a full-service restaurant and café, and a swimming pool. $

DoubleTree Hotel Charlottesville, 990 Hilton Heights Road, ☎ 800-494-9467, www.charlottesville.doubletree.com, has 234 rooms. There is a full-service restaurant and café, a swimming pool with poolside service, tennis courts, an exercise room and convention facilities. $$

English Inn of Charlottesville, at I-64, Exit 23 and 5th Street, ☎ 434-971-9900, 800-786-5400, www.wytestone.com, has 90 units. There is a swimming pool, an exercise room, and a free continental breakfast. Smoking and handicapped-accessible rooms available. $$

Hampton Inn, 2035 India Road, ☎ 434-978-7888, has 123 rooms, a swimming pool, health club privileges, free continental breakfast and airport, railroad and bus depot transportation. $

Holiday Inn-University Area & Conference Center, 1901 Emmett Street, ☎ 434-977-7700, has 170 rooms, a swimming pool, and free continental breakfast. $

Holiday Inn Monticello, at I-64, Exit 23 and 5th Street, ☎ 434-977-5100, has 130 rooms, a full-service restaurant and café, a swimming pool and golf privileges. $

Omni Charlottesville, 235 West Main Street, ☎ 434-971-5500, has more than 200 rooms, a full-service restaurant and café, a swimming pool with poolside service, an exercise room, convention facilities, airport, railroad and bus depot transportation. $$

Red Roof Inn of Charlottesville, 1309 West Main Street, ☎ 434-295-4333, has 135 rooms, a full-service restaurant and café and a swimming pool. $

Bed & Breakfasts / Inns

200 South Street Inn, 200 South Street, Charlottesville, ☎ 800-964-7008, www.southstreet.com, is actually two elegant restored homes filled with period furniture and antiques. A free continental breakfast and evening wine are included in the rate. $$$

Clifton – The Country Inn, 1296 Clifton Inn Drive, ☎ 434-971-1800 or 888-971-1800, has 14 rooms, all with private baths. This elegant, 18th-century manor house renovated in 2005, is set on 40 acres and has a gourmet restaurant, wine cellar, and fireplaces. There is a pool, tennis, spa and private lake. www.cliftoninn.com. $$$$

Inn at Court Square, 410 East Jefferson Street, Charlottesville, ☎ 434-295-2800, www.innatcourtsquare.com, offers five guest rooms in the historic district, enticing common areas furnished with antiques, and whirlpool tubs. $$

Inn At Monticello, 1188 Scottsville Road, Charlottesville, ☎ 434-979-3593, www.innatmonticello.com, has five rooms, all with private baths, in an 1850 Southern manor two miles from Monticello. Bedrooms have antiques, canopy beds, down comforters and fireplaces. Children over 12 welcome. $$

Inn At Sugar Hollow Farm is 20 minutes from Charlottesville, near White Hall on Sugar Hollow Road, ☎ 434-823-7086, www.sugarhollow-

.com. There are five rooms, all with private baths, in a quiet country setting. Fireplaces, whirlpools and gardens. Children over 12 welcome. $$

Inn At The Crossroads, on Route 692 just south of Charlottesville, ☎ 434-979-6452, www.crossroadsinn.com, has five guest rooms and a cottage, all with private baths. The inn has been operating since 1820. There are panoramic mountain views and a full breakfast is served. $$

Foxfield Inn, 2280 Garth Road, eight miles from Charlottesville, ☎ 434-923-8892, www.foxfield-inn.com, has five rooms, all with private bath. Restored, gracious home; children over 14 welcome. $$

Keswick Hall at Monticello, 701 Club Drive, Keswick, ☎ 800-274-5391, www.keswick.com, is an Italianate mansion set on 600 acres of Virginia's rolling countryside. There are 48 lush guest rooms and a new fine dining restaurant. Outside is a golf course, formal gardens and a new, spectacular edgeless pool. $$$$

Prospect Hill Plantation Inn, 2887 Poindexter Road, Trevilians, just east of Charlottesville, ☎ 540-967-0844 or 800-277-0844, www.prospecthill.com. There are 10 rooms and three suites, all with private baths, in a 1732 manor house on 50 acres. A full breakfast in bed and a five-course candlelight dinner are served. $$$$

The Quarters, 611 Preston Place, ☎ 434-979-7264, offers a three-room suite in an 1830 dependency building. Suite has private entrance, sitting room with fireplace and a full breakfast is served. $$$

Silver Thatch Inn, 3001 Hollymead Drive, ☎ 800-261-0720, www.silverthatch.com, has seven rooms, all with private baths, and some have fireplaces and canopy beds. The inn dates to 1780. Children over 14 welcome. There is a restaurant with an extensive wine list. $$$

Resorts

Boar's Head Inn, 200 Ednam Drive, one mile west of US 29, ☎ 434-296-2181, 804-296-2181, www.boarsheadinn.com, is a full-service resort with 159 guest rooms and suites including handicapped-accessible units. There are four full-service restaurants, an outdoor swimming pool with poolside service and a lifeguard on hand, golf privileges, and exercise room, convention facilities and hot air ballooning. The management provides free airport, railroad and bus depot transportation. $$$

The Wintergreen Resort, 43 miles from Charlottesville at Nellysford on US 250, ☎ 437-325-2200, www.wintergreenresort.com, is a full-service resort complex. See page 340. $$

Camping

The Charlottesville KOA, on Route 708 between Routes 20 and 29, ☎ 800-562-1743, www.charlottesvillekoa.com, is the closest camping ground to Monticello. It offers 70 wooded sites, some with full hookups. Facilities also include 11 pull-throughs, three camping cabins, hot showers and flush toilets, sewage disposal, a laundry and a grocery store. There is a recreation room, a pavilion, a fishing lake a playground, planned group activities and weekend entertainment in season. Open mid-March to mid-November.

Transportation

The Charlottesville/Albemarle Airport has scheduled connections with several East Coast destinations.

Interstate 64 runs east and west intersecting with **Interstate 95** in Richmond, **Interstate 85** in Petersburg and **Interstate 81** in Staunton.

Information

Charlottesville/Albemarle CVB-Downtown Visitors Center, 100 5th Street NE, Charlottesville, ☎ 434-977-6100, www.SoVeryVirginia.com, is a great introduction to the historic district and beyond. Open daily, 10 a.m. to 5 p.m.

Charlottesville/Albemarle CVB-Main Visitors Center is at 600 College Drive, Charlottesville. ☎ 877-386-1102, www.SoVeryVirginia.com. Open daily, 9 a.m. to 5 p.m.

Danville & Pittsylvania County

*I*n Danville, in Pittsylvania County, the past still decorates its neighborhoods. It's a textile and tobacco center where the leisurely pace of the Old South blends with the modern tempo of commerce and industry. Until recently, Danville was one of the nation's largest bright-leaf tobacco auction markets. Danville became the last capital of the Confederacy when Jefferson Davis sought refuge at the Sutherlin House after the fall of Richmond in 1865. Danville is also the birthplace of Nancy Langhorne, who became Lady Astor and was the first woman to be seated in the British House of Commons.

Sights

AAF Tank Museum houses the most extensive international collection of tank and cavalry artifacts in the world, dating to 1509. Open Monday through Saturday, year-round. 3401 US Highway 29B, Danville, ☎ 434-836-5323, www.aaftankmuseum.com.

Carrington Pavilion is the city's outdoor amphitheater at 629 Craghead Street, ☎ 434-779-8961, www.rockinattheriver.com.

The **Crossing at the Dan** is a former railroad yard transformed into an entertainment and recreation complex. The 1899 Rail Station houses the Danville Science Center and AMTRAK station, and the Southern Railroad Warehouse houses the Community Market. There's also the relocated **Estelle H. Womack Museum of Natural History**, an outdoor amphitheater, festival area and Riverwalk biking and walking trail. 677 Craghead Street, Danville, ☎ 434-797-8961.

The famous auctions of the **Tobacco Warehouse District** are silent now, but visiting the 40-block heart of the city gives a glimpse into this city's mill-town past. The late-19th-century warehouses, factories and shops illustrate the city's role as one of the South's chief tobacco markets.

The **Dan River Mill Historic District** along both sides of the Dan River represents Danville's other major industry – textiles.

Danville Museum of Fine Arts and History is housed in the Sutherlin Mansion, The Last Capital of the Confederacy, at 975 Main Street. Confederate President Jefferson Davis, with his cabinet, fled Richmond only hours before it fell to Union forces under the command of Lieutenant General Ulysses S. Grant in April, 1865. He took refuge in the Sutherlin home and from there, for 10 days or so until Lee's surrender at Appomattox, directed the fortunes of the doomed Confederacy. Today, the old house is open to visitors and offers them a look at the parlor, library and bedroom where President Davis spent his final days in office. Other exhibits include a permanent collection of silver, textiles and costumes, and a rotating exhibition by national and regional artists. The Sutherlin House is open daily except Monday. ☎ 434-793-5644, www.danvillemuseum.org.

Danville Science Center, 677 Craghead Street, ☎ 434-791-5160, www.dsc.smv.org, features hands-on exhibits for all ages. It is housed in Danville's renovated train station. Open daily.

The Historic District of Danville, bounded by Jefferson Avenue and Greet Street, is listed on the National Register of Historic Places. The area is highlighted by **Millionaires Row** on Main Street, whose Victorian mansions abound with gables, gingerbread scrollwork, columns, porticos, cupolas and minarets.

The Wreck of the Old 97 Marker, on Riverside Drive between North Main Street and the Locust Lane overpass in Danville, identifies the site of the famous train wreck of September 27, 1903, made famous by the popular folk song of the same name. Listen to the ballad at www.visit-danville.com.

Pittsylvania County Courthouse, Chatham. This Greek Revival courthouse was built in 1853 and the clerk's office maintains records back

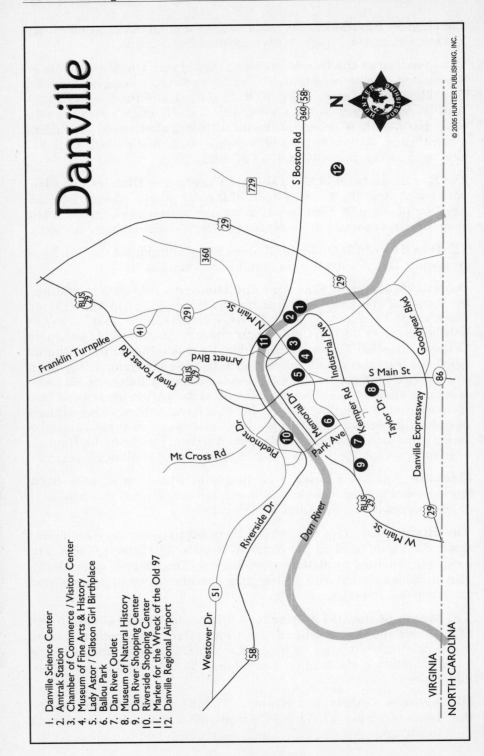

Danville

1. Danville Science Center
2. Amtrak Station
3. Chamber of Commerce / Visitor Center
4. Museum of Fine Arts & History
5. Lady Astor / Gibson Girl Birthplace
6. Ballou Park
7. Dan River Outlet
8. Museum of Natural History
9. Dan River Shopping Center
10. Riverside Shopping Center
11. Marker for the Wreck of the Old 97
12. Danville Regional Airport

VIRGINIA

NORTH CAROLINA

to 1747 with detailed genealogical records. Open Monday through Friday except when court is in session. ☎ 434-432-7887.

Streetcar Diners, Main Street, Chatham, ☎ 434-432-9626. The only two known streetcar diners in Virginia; there are only 20 left in the United States.

Tomahawk Mill Winery, Chatham, ☎ 434-432-1063, is open for tours and tastings Tuesday through Saturday, March 15 through December 15. There is a historic water-powered grist mill.

Town of Chatham Walking Tour. Brochures on the Victorian architecture of Chatham are available at a kiosk in town.

Historic Grist Mills. About 100 grist mills were built on Pittsylvania County waterways during the last two centuries. Three remain today. Contact the Danville Welcome Center for information, ☎ 434-793-4636.

Shopping

Danville's downtown has undergone a recent revitalization, with several antique shops, sidewalk cafés and specialty shops.

Three large malls – **The Piedmont Mall**, **The Riverside Shopping Center** and **The Ballou Park Center** – are other highlights of Danville's shopping world. Smaller, but no less interesting plazas house specialty stores and outlets, while the downtown area, the heart of Danville's business community, offers a wide variety of shops. **The Dan River Factory Outlet** is at 1001 W. Main Street, ☎ 434-799-5361.

The **Danville Community Market**, 629 Craghead Street, offers farm fresh produce, baked goods, crafts and a welcome center, Friday and Saturday from 8 a.m. until 5 p.m., and Sunday from noon until 5 p.m., April through December. ☎ 434-797-8961.

Annual Events

Tank Museum Military Extravaganza features radio-controlled tank battles and a military show in mid-March at the Tank Museum. ☎ 434-836-5323, www.aaftankmuseum.com.

Art on the Lawn takes place in late April on the grounds of Danville Museum of Fine Arts and History. ☎ 434-793-5644, www.danvillemuseum.org.

The Festival in the Park, held the third weekend in May at Ballou Park, West Main Street, Danville, features arts, crafts, music and entertainment. ☎ 434-793-4636.

The Annual 4th of July Celebration and Hot Air Balloon Rally, held over the 4th of July weekend, features an old-fashioned Fourth with games, contests, fireworks, entertainment and a hot air balloon rally with more than a dozen balloons. Call ☎ 434-793-4636 for information.

In late September, **Old 97 Rail Days** commemorate the fateful wreck of the Southern Railway train in 1903 that killed 11 people. The event inspired the famous ballad, *Wreck of the Old 97*. ☎ 434-793-4636.

Dining

Danville offers a wide variety of dining opportunities in more than 85 restaurants and cafés serving everything from fast food to ethnic cuisine.

Joe & Mimma's Italian Restaurant, 3336 Riverside Drive, Danville, ☎ 434-799-5763, offers traditional Italian fare in a casual atmosphere.

Libby Hill, 2105 Riverside Drive, Danville, ☎ 434-791-4680, www.libbyhill.com, serves daily seafood specials.

Purple Onion Restaurant and Tiki Bar, 215 Main Street, Danville, ☎ 434-791-3810, serves burgers and seafood.

Sir Richard's Steakhouse, US 58 East, Danville, ☎ 434-822-8444, offers everything from sandwiches to steaks and seafood. There is a buffet lunch, and a lounge with live entertainment on weekends. Open daily.

Accommodations

Hotels & Motels

 Comfort Inn & Suites, 100 Tower Drive, Danville, ☎ 434-793-2000, has 120 rooms, a pool, a bar, free breakfast and high-speed Internet. $

 Days Inn, 1390 Piney Forest Road, Danville, ☎ 434-836-6745, has 46 rooms and a free continental breakfast. $$

Economy Inn, 3050 West Main Street, Danville, ☎ 434-792-3622, has 52 rooms. $

Hampton Inn, 2130 Riverside Drive, Danville, ☎ 434-793-1111, has 59 rooms; some are whirlpool suites. There is a pool, fitness room, and a restaurant nearby. $

Holiday Inn Express, 2121 Riverside Drive, Danville, ☎ 434-793-4000, has 100 rooms, a swimming pool, meeting rooms and a free continental breakfast. $

The Innkeeper West, 3020 Riverside Drive, Danville, ☎ 434-799-1202, www.innkeepershotel.com, is a motel with 116 rooms, a pool and free continental breakfast. $

 The Innkeeper North, 1030 Piney Forest Road, Danville, ☎ 434-836-1700, has 121 rooms, a pool, fitness center and free continental breakfast. $

 Ramada Inn/Stratford Conference Center, 2500 Riverside Drive, Danville, ☎ 434-793-2500, www.stratford-inn.com, has 157 rooms, a pool, a bar, meeting rooms, an exercise room and full complimentary breakfast. $

Bed & Breakfasts / Inns

Fall Creek Farm Bed & Breakfast on a 50-acre farm, offers lodging in cabins made from century-old hand-hewn logs and furnished with antiques. 2556 Green Farm Road, Danville, ☎ 434-791-3297, www.fall-creek-farm.com $

Sims-Mitchell Bed & Breakfast offers two suites in the historic house, and a 1950s guest cottage. 242 Whittle Street SW, Chatham, ☎ 434-432-0595, www.victorianvilla.com $

Transportation

The nearest commercial airport is **Piedmont International Airport** in Greensboro, NC. Danville is served by **Greyhound** and **Amtrak**.

Information

Danville Welcome Center, 645 River Park Drive, ☎ 434-793-4636, www.visitdanville.com.

Historic Chatham Virginia, www.historicchatham.com, has links to a variety of activities and information sources.

Hopewell & Prince George County

*I*n the heart of the Williamsburg-Richmond-Petersburg triangle, the small port city of Hopewell stands as one of Virginia's truly undiscovered treasures.

Visit Hopewell and the quiet village of City Point for a few hours, an afternoon or even for a few days, and you will find yourself very close to American history and Americans who figured prominently in our nation's past.

Hopewell & Prince George County

You'll appreciate being only minutes away from the Lower James River Plantations, the Petersburg National Battlefield and the bosom of American military history. The excitement and desperation of the closing days of the Civil War can be relived right here in Hopewell.

History

City Point was the headquarters of the Army of the United States during the Civil War and, though few shots were ever fired at the city, it was here that the war was won. During the 10 months of the siege of Petersburg in 1864-65, City Point was one of the busiest seaports and supply depots in the world. President Lincoln visited City Point twice. It was during his second visit in March and April of 1865 that both Petersburg and the Confederate capital, Richmond, fell to General Grant's forces.

Founded in 1613, Hopewell was the second permanent English settlement in America. From the earliest times, it has been an important inland port, having a fine channel about 28 feet deep and 300 feet wide. It was the birthplace of Edmund Ruffin, who fired the first shot of the Civil War at Fort Sumter, and of the noted political leader John Randolph.

Hopewell's two plantations, Weston Manor and Appomattox Manor, offer excellent examples of plantation life, gardens and furnishings.

Sights

Appomattox Manor and Grant's Headquarters is located in City Point at the confluence of the James and Appomattox Rivers. The 23-room manor house and its outbuildings have survived the ravages of time as well as the devastation of war. It was from this old manor house that General Ulysses S. Grant directed the attack on General Lee's defenses around Petersburg during the 10-month siege that eventually resulted in Lee's surrender at Appomattox on April 12, 1865. The manor, now part of Petersburg National Battlefield, features General Grant's primitive T-shaped "Headquarters Cabin," and is open daily except Christmas and New Year's. ☎ 804-732-3531, www.nps.gov/pete.

The **City Point Early History Museum** houses artifacts and exhibits on Hopewell's Colonial, Civil War and early-20th-century history. Open 10 a.m. to 4:30 p.m., April through October. 609 Brown Avenue, ☎ 804-458-2564.

The **City Point Open Air Museum** is an outdoor tour featuring 25 points of interest and highlights the people and events of City Point during the Civil War. A walking tour brochure is available at the Visitor Center, ☎ 804-541-2461.

Weston Manor overlooks the Appomattox River. It was reputedly presented as a wedding gift to Christian Eppes and William Guilliam in

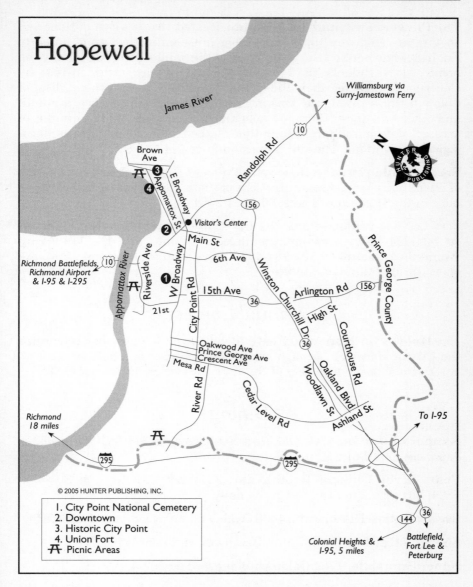

Hopewell

James River

Williamsburg via
Surry-Jamestown Ferry

Brown
Ave

10

Randolph Rd

E Broadway

156

② Visitor's Center

Main St

6th Ave

Winston Churchill Dr

Arlington Rd

156

Prince George County

Richmond Battlefields,
Richmond Airport
& I-95 & I-295

10

Appomattox River

Riverside Ave

W Broadway

City Point Rd

15th Ave

36

High St

36

Courthouse Rd

21st

Oakland Blvd

Oakwood Ave
Prince George Ave
Crescent Ave

Woodlawn St

Mesa Rd

River Rd

Cedar Level Rd

Ashland St

To I-95

Richmond
18 miles

295

295

144

36

Colonial Heights &
I-95, 5 miles

Battlefield,
Fort Lee &
Peterburg

© 2005 HUNTER PUBLISHING, INC.

1. City Point National Cemetery
2. Downtown
3. Historic City Point
4. Union Fort
⊼ Picnic Areas

1789. Christian was the daughter of Richard Eppes, the heir to the Appomattox Plantation. Her mother was the daughter of William Robertson, whose family was descended from Pocahontas. Listed on the National Register of Historic Places, Weston is considered notable because of its well preserved original interior. The manor's distinctive moldings are 85% original. During the Civil War it was home to 12-year-old Emma Wood, who wrote a journal of her wartime experiences. Weston Manor and its gardens, at Weston Lane and 21st Avenue, are open Monday through Friday, and on Sunday afternoons, April through October. ☎ 804-458-4682.

The Flowerdew Hundred Museum, located 10 miles east of Hopewell on Virginia Highway 10, is an outdoor museum at the site of an early English settlement on the south bank of the James River. Originally the home of local Indians, the Flowerdew Hundred was settled in 1618 by Governor George Yeardley. Today, the site offers a look at the earliest of Colonial times through a working replica of an 18th-century windmill and other buildings. There are also interpretive tours and thousands of artifacts dating from prehistoric times – the result of extensive archaeological excavations. The site is open daily. ☎ 804-541-8897.

Sears Catalog Homes. Hopewell's Crescent Hills neighborhood has one of the nation's largest concentrations of these quaint homes and cottages built in the 1920s and '30s. ☎ 804-541-2461.

Fort Lee has two museums: the **US Army Quartermaster Museum** (☎ 804-734-4203, www.qmmuseum.lee.army.mil/) and the **US Army Women's Museum** (☎ 804-734-4327, www.awm.lee.army.mil). Both are open Tuesday through Sunday.

Annual Events

The Hooray for Hopewell Festival, held in mid-September, celebrates the City of Hopewell through exhibitions of arts and crafts, good food, entertainment and a variety of children's activities. ☎ 804-541-0232.

Dining

Kanpai of Japan, 5303 Oaklawn Boulevard, ☎ 804-541-8853, serves Japanese food daily.

Pearl River Chinese Restaurant, 264 East Broadway, ☎ 804-452-5824, has an all-you-can-eat buffet daily.

Rosa's Italian Ristorante, 4098 Oaklawn Boulevard, ☎ 804-458-7844.

Sherry's Garden Café, 236 E. Broadway, ☎ 804-541-3200.

Silver Star Café, 2701 Oaklawn Boulevard, ☎ 804-458-7399.

Accommodations

Hotels & Motels

Comfort Inn, 5380 Oaklawn Boulevard, ☎ 804-452-0022, has 126 rooms, eight of them with whirlpool. There is a pool, fitness center, restaurant, and pets are allowed. $

Hampton Inn Hopewell, 5103 Plaza Drive, ☎ 804-452-1000 or 800-HAMPTON, has a pool, sauna, exercise room and a free continental breakfast. $

Quality Inn, 4911 Oaklawn Boulevard, ☎ 804-458-1500, has 115 rooms, a swimming pool, an exercise room, valet service and free continental breakfast. $

Transportation

Richmond International Airport is about 20 miles from Hopewell. **Amtrak** serves nearby Petersburg, about four miles away.

Information

City of Hopewell Visitor Center, Colonial Corner Shopping Center, 4100 Oaklawn Boulevard, Hopewell, VA 23860, ☎ 800-863-8687 or 804-541-2461 or visit www.ci.hopewell.va.us. Open daily 9 a.m. until 5 p.m., except major holidays.

Information on the City Point Open Air Museum Walking Tour, the African-American Heritage Tour and the Virginia Civil War Trails at City Point driving tour are available at the **Prince George Chamber of Commerce**, ☎ 804-458-5536.

Lynchburg & Amherst County

Nestled in the James River valley near the geographic center of Virginia and bordered by the eastern ridge of the Blue Ridge Mountains, Lynchburg is built upon seven hills that give the city a unique view over the surrounding countryside.

To the west is Bedford County, Thomas Jefferson's country retreat. To the south is Campbell County, one of central Virginia's most urbanized counties. To the north lie Amherst and Nelson Counties and the famous Virginia four-season resort at Wintergreen. And, only 20 miles to the east, is the reconstructed village of Appomattox Court House where, in April, 1865, the Civil War ended and the nation reunited.

Lynchburg is a city of trees, historic landmarks and recreation. It's a city proud of its culture and deeply committed to the arts. It's a city where quality of life is important, where life is a little slower, the scenery spectacular and outdoor recreation a way of life.

Lynchburg & Amherst County

History

Lynchburg was named for **John Lynch**, who began a ferry service across the James River in 1757. By the 1780s, a thriving community had grown up around Lynch's ferry. In 1786 the General Assembly granted Lynchburg its charter. The town was incorporated in 1805 and Lynchburg became a city in 1852.

Commerce has been crucial to the development of Lynchburg. For more than a hundred years tobacco was the product most important to the area. It was produced here, auctioned and made into cigarettes and plugs for chewing. Tobacco made the people of Lynchburg prosperous. So much so that, by the mid-1800s, the city was second only to New Bedford, Massachusetts in per capita income.

During the Civil War Lynchburg became a major storage depot, as well as a burial place for some 2,000 Civil War dead, including six Confederate Generals among whom Jubal Early is perhaps the most well known.

During the **Battle of Lynchburg**, fought over June 17th and 18, 1864, General Early is credited with having saved Lynchburg from Union forces. Early had his men run an empty train back and forth with great commotion, leading Union General David Hunter to believe massive Confederate reinforcements were arriving by rail. Early's breastworks can still be seen at Fort Early.

Sights

Amazement Square, The Rightmire Children's Museum, 27 Ninth Street, Lynchburg, is devoted to encouraging creativity in children and adults. Located in the historic J.W. Wood Building with four floors of interactive exhibits and workshops, all connected by pathways, tunnels and a glass elevator. Open daily. ☎ 434-845-1888, www.amazement-square.org.

The **Anne Spencer House and Garden**, 1313 Pierce Street, was the home of Anne Spencer, a noted poet whose works are included in the *Norton Anthology of Modern American and British Poetry*. "EdanKraal," Spencer's writing cottage, is on the grounds and there's a small museum with Spencer memorabilia, artifacts and antiques. The garden is open daily, the house by appointment only. ☎ 434-846-0517.

Legacy Museum of African-American History, 403 Monroe Street, Lynchburg, has exhibits and programs on all aspects of local black history and culture. Open Thursday through Sunday. ☎ 434-845-3455, www.legacymuseum.org.

Lynchburg Museum, 901 Court Street, in the Old Court House, is an excellent example of Greek Revival architecture. Built in 1855 and re-

Lynchburg

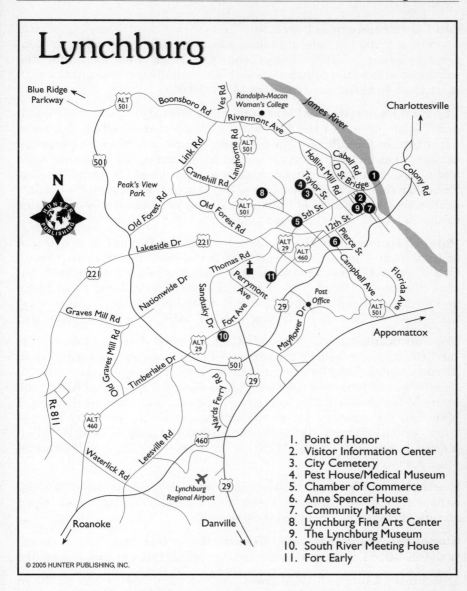

Blue Ridge Parkway

ALT 501

Boonsboro Rd

Ves Rd

Randolph-Macon Woman's College

James River

Charlottesville

Rivermont Ave

Link Rd

Langhorne Rd

ALT 501

501

N

HUNTER PUBLISHING

Peak's View Park

Cranehill Rd

Old Forest Rd

Hollins Mill Rd

Cabell Rd

D St Bridge

Colony Rd

Taylor St

❶

❹ ❸

❷
❾ ❼

❽

ALT 501

5th St

12th St

❺

Pierce St

Old Forest Rd

Lakeside Dr

221

ALT 29

ALT 460

❻

Campbell Ave

Florida Ave

221

Nationwide Dr

Thomas Rd

Perrymont Ave

Sandusky Dr

Graves Mill Rd

Fort Ave

❶❶

Post Office

29

ALT 501

Appomattox

Old Graves Mill Rd

Timberlake Dr

❿

ALT 29

Mayflower Dr

501

29

Rt 811

ALT 460

Wards Ferry Rd

Leesville Rd

460

Waterlick Rd

Lynchburg Regional Airport

29

Roanoke

Danville

1. Point of Honor
2. Visitor Information Center
3. City Cemetery
4. Pest House/Medical Museum
5. Chamber of Commerce
6. Anne Spencer House
7. Community Market
8. Lynchburg Fine Arts Center
9. The Lynchburg Museum
10. South River Meeting House
11. Fort Early

© 2005 HUNTER PUBLISHING, INC.

stored to its original appearance, the old building houses three galleries which interpret the early history of the Lynchburg area, including a restored courtroom from the mid-19th century. The Old Court House is open daily except Thanksgiving, Christmas and New Year's Day. ☎ 434-847-1459.

Miller Claytor House is the townhouse where Thomas Jefferson is believed to have proven that tomatoes were not poisonous by eating one. Interpretors teach about 19th-century life. The house was dismantled and rebuilt here at Riverside Park. ☎ 434-847-1459.

Old City Cemetery, at Fourth and Taylor Streets, is the resting place of more than 2,200 Confederate soldiers from 14 states, including six Confederate generals. The 500-foot-long "Old Brick Wall" bordering the southeast side of the cemetery features a magnificent rose garden with more than 60 varieties of roses. ☎ 434-847-1465.

The Pest House Medical Museum, in the Old City Cemetery at Fourth and Taylor Streets, is the 1840s white frame medical office of Quaker physician Dr. John Terrell. The museum features a number of interesting exhibits that include original medical instruments, an operating table and period furnishings. On one side is a duplicate of Dr. Terrell's office. The other side is a representation of the quarantine hospital for Confederate soldiers suspected of having smallpox. The museum is open daily. ☎ 434-847-1465, www.gravegarden.org.

Point of Honor, 112 Cabell Street, is a restored, Federal-style mansion on Daniel's Hill above the James River. It was built in 1815 by Dr. George Cabell, Patrick Henry's personal physician. The house features an unusual octagon-bay façade, finely crafted woodwork, antique furnishings and formal gardens. Point of Honor is open daily except Thanksgiving, Christmas and New Year's Day. ☎ 434-847-1459, www.pointofhonor.org.

The Randolph-Macon Woman's College, 2500 Rivermont Avenue, is the first Southern college for women to have been granted a Phi Beta Kappa chapter. The 100-acre campus is an interesting mixture of architecture that includes the Houston Chapel designed by Vincent Kling. The Maier Museum of Art, also located on campus, houses a fine collection of 19th- and 20th-century American paintings, including works by Thomas Hart Benton, Edward Hicks, Winslow Homer, James McNeil Whistler, Mary Cassatt and Georgia O'Keefe. ☎ 434-947-8136, www.maiermuseum.rmwc.edu.

South River Meeting House, 5810 Fort Avenue, ☎ 434-239-2548, www.qmpc.org/srmh.htm, is a restored Quaker meeting house. Open Monday-Friday, costumed guides give tours.

Stonewall Vineyards and Winery, Route 608 and 721, Concord, ☎ 434-993-2185, www.stonewallwine.com, offers tours and tastings daily.

Lynchburg Community Market has been in existence since 1783 in downtown. It features special events, food festivals, craft shows, collector's showcases and music competition all year long; ☎ 434-847-1499.

Entertainment

Academy of Fine Arts, 600 Main Street, Lynchburg, opened in 2004 in an historic theater offering performing arts and classes. ☎ 434-528-3256, www.afalynchburg.org

Shopping

Shops, stores and outlets scattered around the city offer everything from antiques to fine clothing, and from gifts to handicrafts. Shopping centers include the **River Ridge Mall**, **Candler Station** and **Waterlick Plaza**. **The Lynchburg Community Market** features restaurants, local handicrafts and fresh product year-round at 1219 Main Street, Lynchburg, ☎ 434-847-1499.

Recreation

Parks & Natural Areas

The Blackwater Creek Natural Area, located right in the heart of the city, offers a pleasant, open-air environment with 3½ miles of paved pathways for bikers and joggers, and nine more miles of woodland, creek-side nature trails. A map of the 300-acre area is available from the Lynchburg Chamber of Commerce, the Parks and Recreation Department and the Visitor Center. ☎ 434-455-5858, www.lynchburgva.gov.

The Blue Ridge Mountains, **the Blue Ridge Parkway** and several access points to the **Appalachian Trail** are only minutes away from Lynchburg. The Blue Ridge and the Greater Lynchburg area offer abundant opportunities for camping, hiking, backpacking, fishing, nature watching and wildlife photography.

Holliday Lake State Park, Route 2, Box 622, Appomattox, ☎ 434-248-6308.

James River State Park, on Route 1 in Gladstone, is one of Virginia's newest. Fifteen hundred acres of rolling countryside, forest and three miles along the James River provide hiking, biking, fishing, canoeing and primitive camping. There's an Environmental Education Center, picnic areas, boat rentals, boat launching, and fishing pier. Visitors can learn about the culture of settlers who lived aboard flat-bottomed boats. ☎ 434-933-4355, www.dcr.state.va.us/parks/jamesriv.htm. For camping reservations, ☎ 800-933-PARK.

Golf

The nearby community of Forest has the **Ivy Hill Golf Club**, ☎ 434-525-2680, and **London Downs**, ☎ 434-525-4653.

Annual Events

Antique Rose Festival and Cemetery Art Show celebrates the Old City Cemetery's famous roses at the peak of their bloom in mid-May. 401 Taylor Street, Lynchburg, ☎ 434-847-1465, www.gravegarden.org.

Cheers on the River kicks off in May and ends in August with the Friday Cheers Summer Season of music, food and beverage. Lynchburg Community Market, 12th and Main streets, ☎ 434-528-3950, www.downtownlynchburg.com.

The **Batteau Festival** takes place in mid-June at Wingina; it's an eight-day land and river festival celebrating the history of the batteau, a type of boat used to navigate the shallow waters of the James in the 18th and 19th centuries. Rte. 56 and Rte. 647, Wingina, ☎ 434-528-3950, www.batteaufestival.com.

Kaleidoscope is Lynchburg's fall celebration during the month of September. The event features activities, arts, entertainment and sports. ☎ 434-847-1811.

Lynchburg Art Festival is held in September. ☎ 434-528-9434.

Thousands flock to the **Virginia Garlic Festival** during the second week in October for a garlic cook-off, gourmet foods, wine tastings, music, arts and crafts. Rebec Vineyards, five miles north of Amherst on Route 29, ☎ 434-946-5168, www.rebecwinery.com.

The Historic Appomattox Railroad Festival in Appomattox Court House (about 20 miles east of Lynchburg) offers two days of fun in the fall, featuring food, crafts, music, antiques and dancing. ☎ 434-352-2621.

Downtown Lynchburg Holiday Traditions takes place Saturdays in December with free horse-drawn carriage rides, photos with Santa, strolling carolers, and a sidewalk Christmas sale. ☎ 434-528-3950, www-.downtownlynchburg.

Dining

Asian Café serves contemporary Chinese fare. Lunch buffet Monday through Friday. Open daily. 713 Main Street, ☎ 434-847-6886.

Babcock House Bed & Breakfast Inn and Restaurant, 106 Oakleigh Avenue, Appomattox, ☎ 800-689-6208 or 434-352-7532, www.babcockhouse.com, is open to the public for lunch, Tuesday-Friday, and dinner, Tuesday-Sunday.

The **Crown Sterling Steakhouse**, 6120 Fort Avenue, ☎ 434-239-7744, is open for dinner and specializes in beef and fine American dining. Reservations are recommended.

Granny Bees Restaurant serves homestyle cooking, real cheap. Open for breakfast daily, lunch Monday-Friday, and dinner Wednesday-Sunday. Main Street, Appomattox, ☎ 434-352-2259.

Jazz Street Grill, 3225 Old Forest Road, Lynchburg, ☎ 434-385-0100, serves lunch and dinner Monday-Saturday and its award-winning brunch on Sunday. Enjoy New Orleans cuisine while listening to live jazz. Open until midnight Friday and Saturday.

Main Street Eatery, 907 Main Street, Lynchburg, ☎ 434-847-2526, www.mainsteatery.com, serves lunch Monday-Friday and dinner Monday-Saturday in Lynchburg's downtown historic district. This casually elegant, brick-walled restaurant serves up Old World Mediterranean, Italian and German fare with a new American flare. But the menu is a "mere suggestion," as Chef Urs takes requests for favorite dishes he has created over the years. October features a special "Ocktoberfest" menu by this accomplished European chef. Extensive wine list and impeccable service. Save room for dessert.

Meriwether's Market Restaurant, 4925 Boonsboro Road, ☎ 434-384-3311, www.meriwethers.com, is a wine and specialty food shop and gourmet restaurant specializing in Southern regional fare, including rotisserie and wild game. Lunch and dinner, Monday-Saturday.

Sachiko's International Restaurant, 126 Old Graves Mill Road, ☎ 434-237-8260, is open for dinner and offers beef, chicken, lamb and seafood, plus assorted pastries baked in-house.

Accommodations

Most establishments offer both handicapped-accessible and non-smoking rooms, but be sure to ask when making reservations.

Hotels & Motels

Best Western 2815 Candler's Mountain Road, ☎ 434-237-2986, offers 87 rooms. The hotel has a restaurant and outdoor pool. $

 Comfort Inn, 3125 Albert Lankford Drive, ☎ 434-847-9041, has 120 rooms, a swimming pool, free continental breakfast, restaurant. $

Days Inn, 3320 Candler's Mountain Road, ☎ 434-847-8655, www.daysinnlynchburg.com, is within walking distance of the mall and movie theaters. There are 131 rooms. The hotel has a swimming pool, and offers a free full breakfast. $$

Hampton Inn, 5604 Seminole Avenue, ☎ 434-237-2704, has 65 rooms and offers guests a complimentary deluxe breakfast and a swimming pool. $

Holiday Inn Express, 5600 Seminole Avenue, ☎ 434-237-7771, www.hiexpress.com, has 104 rooms, a swimming pool and hospitality suites for special occasions. Free continental breakfast. $

Holiday Inn Select, 601 Main Street, ☎ 434-528-2500, www.hiselect.com/lynchburgva, has 243 rooms, a full-service restaurant and café, a swimming pool. $

Lynchburg Radisson Hotel, 2900 Candler's Mountain Road, ☎ 434-237-6333, www.radisson.com/lynchburgva, is a large, luxury hotel with 167 rooms, , ballroom, convention facilities and lounge. Other amenities include full-service restaurant and café, a swimming pool, meeting rooms, an exercise room and free continental breakfast. $$

Bed & Breakfasts / Inns

Babcock House Bed & Breakfast is an 1890 inn in the heart of historic Appomattox. There are six guest rooms and a restaurant. ☎ 800-689-6208, www.babcockhouse.com. $$

Federal Crest Inn B&B, 1101 Federal Street, ☎ 434-845-6155, has four guest rooms and one suite, all with private baths, fireplaces, down comforters, canopy beds and whirlpool tubs. Georgian Revival home surrounded by magnolias. www.federalcrest.com. $$

Ivy Creek Farm B&B is an elegant inn on an eight-acre country estate. 2812 Link Road, Lynchburg, 434-384-3802, www.ivycreekfarm.com. $$

Longacre Bed & Breakfast and Tea Room is a fabulous home reminiscent of an English tudor estate It has five unique guest rooms and a carriage. 107 South Church Street, Appomattox, ☎ 434-352-9251, 800-758-7730, www.longacreva.com. $

Norvell-Otey House, 1020 Federal Street, ☎ 434-528-1020, www.norvellotleyhouse.com, has four rooms, three with private bath, in an 1817 Federal-style manor house. They serve a full Southern breakfast; lunch and dinner are available. $$

The Residence B&B, 2460 Rivermont Avenue, ☎ 434-845-6565 or 888-835-0387, www.the-residence.com, has three rooms and one suite, three with private baths. It is a former Randolph-Macon Woman's College presidential home. $$

Spring Grove Farm Bed & Breakfast is an 1842 Virginia plantation on Route 613, about six miles northwest of Appomattox. There are 11 guest rooms and a cottage. ☎ 434-352-7429, www.springgrovefarm.com. $$

Camping

Wildwood Campgrounds, Route 130, Monroe, ☎ 434-299-5228, is a full-service facility, offering a pool, fishing, horseshoes, recreation room.

Paradise Lake Campground, US 460W, PO Box 478, Appomattox, VA 24522, ☎ 434-993-3332.

Day-trip to Appomattox

Just 20 miles east of Lynchburg is the quiet village of Appomattox Court House. Here, you can retrace the events of Lee's surrender to Grant, browse shops in the picturesque downtown, then stay in a comfortable historic inn.

After the fall of Petersburg and Richmond on April 2, 1865, Confederate General Robert E. Lee and his Army of Northern Virginia headed west from Petersburg toward Amelia Court House along the long road that would lead eventually to Appomattox Court House.

After the Civil War the tiny community of Appomattox Courthouse became something of a backwater and was finally abandoned altogether in 1892. Nearby Appomattox Station, on the other hand, grew and became prosperous due to its position on the railroad.

During the late 1880s, a group of Union veterans formed the Appomattox Land Company to develop the area. Their plans never came to fruition, and unfortunately, the little village was allowed to deteriorate. The old buildings either fell down or were plundered for their building materials. Then, in 1930, Congress passed a bill that provided for the building of a monument at the site of the old Appomattox courthouse. The monument was never built, but the idea had been kindled and, in 1934, it was suggested that the entire village be restored to its wartime condition. The idea was received with enthusiasm and a bill creating the **Appomattox Court House National Historic Park** was signed into law on August 3, 1935. The land was quickly acquired, but the project was interrupted by World War II. After the war, work on the project began in earnest and the park was opened to the public and dedicated on April 6, 1954.

The reconstructed village looks much the same today as it did in 1865. The old buildings on view today, all lovingly restored, include the McLean House, where the surrender took place, Meeks' Store, the Woodson Law Office, the Clover Hill Tavern, the jail, the Kelly House, the Mariah Wright House, the Isbell House, the Peers House, and the Surrender Triangle, where the Confederate regiments laid down their arms and furled their banners.

Before you leave Appomattox, you might like to visit the site of the Battle at Appomattox Station a few miles away in the modern city of Appomattox. Appomattox Station was where General Sheridan captured General Lee's supply trains, thus forcing him to surrender. ☎ 434-352-8987, www.nps.gov/apco.

Lynchburg & Amherst County

Transportation

The **Lynchburg Regional Airport** is served by several major airlines, with departures daily. **Greyhound Lines** provides passenger and parcel service. **Amtrak** offers passenger service.

Lynchburg is accessed by a network of highways that includes **US Routes 29, 460** and **501**.

Information

Lynchburg Regional Convention and Visitors Bureau, 12th & Church Streets, Lynchburg, VA 24504, ☎ 434-845-3966, www.discover-lynchburg.org. Also see www.downtownlynchburg.com.

Visitor Information Center, Appomattox Chamber of Commerce, 5 Main Street, in old train depot, ☎ 434-352-2621. Open daily 9 a.m. until 5 p.m. www.appomattox.com.

Appomattox Court House National Historic Park, PO Box 218, Appomattox, VA 24522. ☎ 434-352-8987, www.nps.gov/apco.

Nelson County

*E*xploring the natural beauty that is Nelson County could take some time. The Blue Ridge Mountains, George Washington National Forest, Crabtree Falls and the James River are only a few of the outstanding attractions. You won't see many traffic lights in Nelson County. You may, however, fish the quiet streams, rest at a country inn, tour a vineyard, visit a multitude of unique shops and, of course, enjoy the magnificent scenery. There's even a country resort where you can do everything from golf to skiing.

Rich in history, Nelson County is home to such 18th- and 19th-century treasures as Woodson's Mill and the elegantly restored Oak Ridge estate. And the county is within easy reach of many of Virginia's most celebrated historical sites, including the homes of four US presidents and several important Civil War landmarks.

History

Native Americans were the first settlers to arrive in what is now Nelson County. Ancestors of the **Algonquin, Sioux** and **Iroquois Indians** migrated to the area some 11,000 years ago in search of mammoths and mastodons. Not finding any, some of the tribes decided to stay to hunt, fish and gather the native plants.

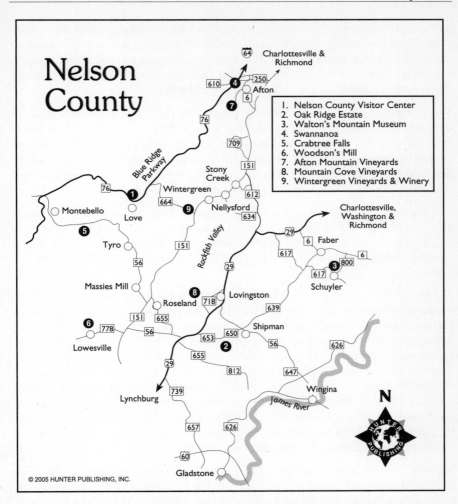

Nelson County

1. Nelson County Visitor Center
2. Oak Ridge Estate
3. Walton's Mountain Museum
4. Swannanoa
5. Crabtree Falls
6. Woodson's Mill
7. Afton Mountain Vineyards
8. Mountain Cove Vineyards
9. Wintergreen Vineyards & Winery

© 2005 HUNTER PUBLISHING, INC.

In the 17th and 18th centuries, thousands of English pioneers emigrated to the colonies, settling in Jamestown, filling the Tidewater area and then building settlements along the James River. By the late 1730s, the settlers had arrived with their slaves and indentured servants in what is present-day Nelson, Amherst and Albemarle Counties. They were tobacco growers, interested in acquiring the large tracts of frontier land they needed to grow the valuable cash crop.

During the same period, Scotch-Irish, Irish and German immigrants moved into the Shenandoah Valley from Pennsylvania and Northern Virginia looking for cheap land and the freedom to worship as "dissenters" from the Anglican religion. Many of them settled in the western part of present-day Nelson County. French Huguenots also brought their culture and skills to the area.

Nelson County was formed from parts of Amherst County in 1807, and named for **Thomas Nelson Jr.**, the third governor of Virginia.

In the 19th century, the western part of Nelson County became an important apple-producing region. Apples and other produce were shipped to markets by canal and railroad. Water-powered grist mills and logging operations employed the county's residents. Several mills were built along the canals and rivers, and villages grew up around them.

The eastern side of Nelson County prospered from the discovery of large deposits of soapstone, a metamorphic rock unaffected by acids and heat. It is used to build fireplaces, mantels and stoves. The **Virginia Soapstone Company** – it later became Alberene Soapstone – was founded in Schuyler and is today the New World Stone Company where talented sculptors produce fine works of art from soapstone.

The turn of the 19th century was the high point for Nelson County's economy. By the time the Great Depression arrived, the county had already experienced several years of recession, and the population dropped steadily from a high of 17,000 to 11,000, as young people left looking for jobs.

For the next 40 years or so, life continued quietly in Nelson County. Then disaster struck in the form of **Hurricane Camille**. The destruction in Nelson County was of a magnitude that has never occurred in Virginia before or since. Rivers and creeks burst their banks, exploding onto the countryside, gouging out huge new water courses, lifting houses off their foundations, crumbling roads and bridges. Huge chunks of mountain slid off the bedrock sending tons of mud, boulders and trees tumbling down into the valleys. Thirty inches of rain fell in a six-hour period – a phenomenon likely to happen only once in a thousand years. Hurricane Camille took the lives of 134 people and destroyed 300 buildings, 130 bridges and culverts and well over half of the county's roads.

Nelson County slowly recovered from the disaster that was Camille. The recovery included the development of Wintergreen Resort, the restoration of Oak Ridge, the development of the Walton's Mountain Museum, the resurgence of the apple industry, the maturing of new vineyards and the steady growth of Nelson County's tourism industry.

Sights

Nelson County offers a number of exciting attractions. These include panoramic views of the Blue Ridge Mountains, crystal rivers and streams, fabulous sunsets and the tiny communities that provide the county with a character all its own.

Crabtree Falls is the highest vertical-drop cascading waterfall east of the Mississippi. The three-mile Crabtree Falls Trail features a series of five major cascades and a number of smaller ones that fall a total of 1,200 feet. The area offers a feeling of isolation and freedom in a forest stream setting to both hikers and backpackers.

After crossing an arched wooden bridge spanning the Tye River, the trail wanders through rugged mountainside capturing scenic views of the magnificent waterfalls. The trail provides views of the falls from overlooks designed to accent the natural beauty of the valley. The first overlook is just 700 feet from the lower parking lot, making it an excellent stopover for travelers. More adventuresome hikers may continue on to the other overlooks, to Crabtree Meadows where the trail ends, or to the Appalachian Trail just a half-mile beyond Crabtree Meadows.

The peak season for viewing the waterfalls is from winter through spring when the water is at its highest. Good hiking boots or comfortable walking shoes are recommended. During the winter the trail may be covered with snow and ice, and so should be traveled with caution.

The trail is most easily reached from Route 56 near Montebello, just off the Blue Ridge Parkway in the Glenwood Pedlar Ranger District of the GW National Forest, ☎ 540-291-2188.

The Oak Ridge Estate is a plantation of some 5,000 acres that provides an unsurpassed combination of diverse architectural structures and expansive vistas.

The mansion, built in 1802, became the home of Thomas Fortune Ryan at the turn of the 20th century. Ryan's middle name, Fortune, was an appropriate one, for this Nelson County native of humble beginnings became one of the 10 wealthiest men in the country.

Ryan made a number of alterations to the original structure. He established a formal Italian garden and built more than 80 out-buildings, including a rotunda greenhouse, a carriage house, a railroad station, a dairy complex and a spring house. The remains of an abandoned airstrip, horse racing track and underground watering system that pre-dates any city water system may also be seen at the estate.

Take a self-guided tour of the grounds or two hour guided tour, which will take you through the first floor of the mansion as well as portions of the grounds. Call for hours, ☎ 434-263-8676, www.oakridgeestate.com.

Walton's Mountain Museum. Earl Hamner Jr. created the story behind *The Waltons* television series based on his own family's experiences growing up during the Depression era in the rural village of Schuyler. The school building he and his siblings attended has been converted to a museum, which contains nostalgic memorabilia, replicas of the sets created for the series (John-Boy's bedroom; the Walton's Kitchen, which features a long table and benches; the Walton's Living Room, a 1930s-style family room with period furnishings; and Ike Godsey's Store) and an audio-visual presentation. The museum is located at Routes 617 and 800 in Schuyler; open daily, March through November. ☎ 434-831-2000, www.waltonmuseum.org.

Woodson's Mill, on Route 778 in Lowesville, has been noted by historians as one of the finest examples of a 19th-century mill in the state. The old mill is not only intact, it is still operating much as it did in the early 1800s. All of the mill's machinery is powered by water, and some five tons of wheat, corn and other grain are ground each week just as they were almost 200 years ago.

The mill was originally built in 1794 by Guiliford Campbell. Back then it was called Big Piney Mill. The present structure, built on the foundations of the original mill and completed in 1845, is a fine example of four-story post-and-beam construction. The old mill was purchased in 1900 by Dr. Julian Woodson who, besides being a miller, was both a medical doctor and a dentist.

The mill is not open to the public; however, there are several picnic tables and a shelter on the grounds. For more information, call the **Nelson County Department of Tourism** at ☎ 800-282-8223, or see www.jb-woodson.com/woodsonsmill.

Recreation

Outdoor enthusiasts will enjoy the many hiking, fishing, hunting and boating opportunities available in Nelson County. More than 19,000 acres of the vast **George Washington** and **Jefferson National Forests** are within the county, and the Appalachian Trail passes through its northwest portion. For boaters and fishermen, there are public boat launches at **Tye River Park** and **Lake Nelson**. There's also the **James River Wildlife Management Area** on Route 626, offering wildlife viewing, fishing, hiking and biking trails.

There are five wilderness areas in the National Forests surrounding Nelson County: **St. Mary's**, **The Priest**, **Three Ridges**, **James River Face**, and **Thunder Ridge**, as well as the **Mount Pleasant National Scenic Area**. The 65-mile Glenwood Horse Trail provides a variety of experiences for the horse enthusiast, while the South Pedlar ATV Trail System is open to ATVs and dirt bikes. For more information, contact the Glenwood Pedlar Ranger District, ☎ 540-291-2188, www.fs.fed.us/r8/gwj/gp.

Several loops of the **Virginia Birding and Wildlife Trail** pass through Nelson County. It is a new driving trail that provides opportunities to see a wide variety of wildlife. To obtain a guide, ☎ 866-VA-BIRDS, www.dgif.state.va.us/wildlife/vbwt.

Apple Country

The **Apple Shed** sells produce and has an 1852 cidermill. On Route 29, one mile south of Route 6 West, ☎ 434-263-8843.

Dickie Brothers Orchard is on Route 666 off Route 56W in Roseland. The orchard is well known for its Red and Golden Delicious, Winesap, Rome, Stayman and Granny Smith apples, as well as for cider, apple butter and pumpkins. The farm is open seven days a week. ☎ 434-277-5866 or 434-277-5516, www.dickiebros.com.

Drumheller's Orchard is on Route 741 off US Highway 29 in Lovingston. Produce available to the public includes Red and Golden Delicious, Winesap, Rome, York, Stayman and Granny Smith apples, along with cider, apple butter, honey, baskets and pumpkins. ☎ 434-263-5036.

Fitzgerald's Orchard is on Route 682, off Route 56W, in Tyro. Produce available at the farm includes Red and Golden Delicious, Winesap, Rome, York, Stayman, Gala and Granny Smith apples. Fitzgerald's is open Monday through Saturday. ☎ 434-277-5798.

Flippin-Seaman Packing Shed are well known for their Empire, Jonathan, Red and Golden Delicious, Winesap, Rome, York, Stayman, Gala and Granny Smith apples; and for their apple butter, cider, baskets, honey, jellies, pumpkins, dried flowers and gifts. The packing shed is on Route 56W in Tyro, and is open Monday through Saturday. ☎ 434-277-5824, www.flippin-seaman.com.

Mountain Cove Orchard is on route 718 off Route 19 in Lovingston. ☎ 434-981-3091, www.mountaincoveapples.com.

Saunders Orchards, on Route 56W at Piney River, offer visitors a variety of fine produce including Red and Golden Delicious, Gala, Braeburn, Rome, York, Stayman, Gala and Granny Smith apples. ☎ 434-277-5455.

❖ *More than 40 varieties of apples are grown in Nelson County. In the spring the blossoms are something to see, and in the fall the harvest is in. To obtain a fact sheet and a driving tour map, call the Nelson County Department of Tourism,* ☎ *800-282-8223.*

Winery Tours

For information on Nelson County's seven wineries, ℅ 800=282-8223, www.nelsoncounty.com.

Afton Mountain Vineyards, located on a southeastern slope of the Blue Ridge Mountains at 960 feet, have a *terroir* especially suited to the growing of Europe's noble wine grapes and Afton Mountain wines have won awards in California as well as on the East Coast. The winery is open for tours, tastings and picnics daily, except Tuesday. The vineyard is located on Route 631 south. ☎ 540-456-8667, www.aftonmountainvineyards.com.

Nelson County

Cardinal Point Winery has Blue Ridge Mountain views and offers tastings and viewing of a documentary video on wine-making. 9423 Batesville Road, Afton, ☎ 540-456-8400.

Delfosse Winery is a brand new winery, opened in 2005. There are five miles of walking trails, lakes and picnic areas. Tours and tastings are given Thursday through Sunday. 500 DelFosse Winery Lane, Faber, ☎ 434-263-6100, www.delfossewine.com.

Hill Top Berry Farm & Wineryhas a picnic area, goft shop, historical tour, daily wine and food pairings, seasonal blackberry picking, and cabin-style lodging. Open Wednesday though Sunday. 2800 Berry Hill Road, Nellysford, ☎ 434-361-1266.

Mountain Cove Vineyards consists of 12 acres of vineyards planted to seven varieties of hybrid grapes. Visitors can tour the winery, taste the product, follow the process from vine to bottle and learn first-hand how wine is made. The winery is off Route 718 in Lovingston and is open for tours Wednesday through Sunday in the afternoons; closed January and February. ☎ 434-263-5392, www.mountaincovevineyards.com.

Veritas Vineyard & Winery offers tours and tastings Wednesday through Monday. 145 Saddle Farm, Afton. ☎ 540-456-8000, http://www.veritaswines.com.

The **Wintergreen Winery** is in the beautiful Rockfish Valley adjacent to the Blue Ridge Parkway. The vineyards and winery offer spectacular views during all seasons of the year. Part of the historic Highview Plantation built by the Rodes family, the vineyard sites are well-suited to the growing of hybrid and vinifera varieties that produce the finest wines. The vineyard is on Route 664 and is open every day. ☎ 434-361-2519, www.wintergreenwinery.com.

Shopping

Neat little shops and stores selling everything from antiques to fine jewelry, and from outdoor sportswear to hand-crafted curios are dotted here and there across the county and in a half-dozen or so tiny communities. And, as you travel the country roads from one shop to the next, you're sure of a smile and a welcome at every one.

Dining

Restaurants with quaint names like the Blue Ridge Pig, the Chicken Coop, and the Copper Mine offer everything from sophisticated smoked meat to seafood, and from burgers to home-made apple pie. The Wintergreen Resort alone has four fine restaurants that offer a range of dining, including an elegant gourmet experience or casual family dining with panoramic views of the Shenandoah Valley. For a complete list, call the Nelson County Department of Tourism at ☎ 800-282-8223.

Blue Ridge Pig, Highway 151, Nellysford, ☎ 434-361-1170, is rustic yet sophisticated, offering smoked-meat sandwiches.

Chicken Coop, Business Route 29, Lovingston, ☎ 434-263-5300, offers chicken and barbecue.

Copper Mine, Wintergreen Resort, ☎ 434-325-8090, offers breakfast, elegant gourmet dining, and Sunday brunch.

D'Ambola's serves Italian cuisine, all prepared fresh. Open for dinner Tuesday-Sunday. Route 151 in Afton. ☎ 540-456-4556

Devils Grill, ☎ 434-325-8100, is located on top of the mountain at Devils Knob golf course. Dinner Wednesday-Sunday, reservations required.

Dulaney's Steak and Seafood, located at The Inn at Afton. Breakfast, lunch and dinner with a view of Rockfish Gap; closed Tuesdays. ☎ 540-943-7167.

The Edge overlooks the ski slopes at Wintergreen Resort, ☎ 434-325-8080, offers casual family dining with view of the Blue Ridge.

Lovingston Café, 165 Front Street, Lovingston, ☎ 434-263-8000, serves up steaks, seafood and wholesome vegetarian meals.

Mossy Creek 2 (MC2) serves contemporary American cuisine with a southern twist. Open for lunch and dinner daily and Sunday brunch. Nellysford, ☎ 434-361-0231.

Stoney Creek Bar and Grill outdoor dining, American fare for lunch and dinner daily. Located on the Stoney Greek Golf Course at Wintergreen Resort, Nellysford. ☎ 434-325-8110.

Vito's Italian Restaurant, Highway 29, Lovingston, ☎ 434-263-8688.

Accommodations

You won't find any chain hotels in Nelson County, but you will find a variety of bed & breakfasts, country inns, cabins and a four-season resort. For a complete listing or accommodations in the area, www.nelson-county.com.

Bed & Breakfasts / Inns

The Acorn Inn, on Route 634 at Nellysford, ☎ 434-361-9357, www.acorninn.com, offers guests a choice of three accommodations. The Acorn Cottage, a cozy house with a kitchen, bathroom and queen bedroom, is popular with honeymooners and families with small children. The inn was, in years gone by, a horse stable that today offers comfortable, contemporary lodgings with the feel of an art gallery.

Each of its 10 bright, carpeted bedrooms has stable doors, a double bed, a writing desk and a big window. The Farmhouse has two queen guest rooms with hardwood floors, handsewn quilts and an eclectic mixture of South American art and photographs, as well as big windows that offer stunning views of the mountains and meadows. $

Dutch Haus Geselligkeit offers forest solitude, three guest rooms and a blend of Dutch and Pennsylvania German hospitality. Located three miles from the Blue Ridge Parkway at milepost 27, ☎ 800-341-9777

 The **Inn at Afton Banquet and Conference Center** is a 118-room motel atop Afton Mountain, adjacent to the Blue Ridge Parkway. Full restaurant and lounge with entertainment in season, and an outdoor heated pool. ☎ 800-860-8559, www.theinnatafton.com. $

Mark Addy, in Nellysford on Highway 151, ☎ 434-361-1101 or 800-278-2154, www.mark-addy.com, has been beautifully restored and lovingly appointed to recreate the richness and romance of a bygone era. The enchanting rooms and opulent suites give an atmosphere of luxury and relaxation rarely found in a commercial hotel. The nine guest rooms have private bathrooms and some offer magnificent views of the surrounding countryside. Guests can enjoy a quiet afternoon on one of five sunlit porches or take a ramble on the Mark Addy's 12½ acres. $$

The Meander Inn, Route 612 in Nellysford, ☎ 434-361-1121, www.meanderinn.com, is an 80-year-old Victorian farmhouse perfect for a relaxing vacation and refreshing change of pace. The inn sits on 50 acres alongside the Rockfish River and offers its guests the comfort of a rural working horse farm. There are five guest rooms, all with private bath. Enjoy spectacular views of the Blue Ridge Mountains, the soft sounds of the river, a glass of wine at sunset, a hot tub under the stars and a sense of well being. The inn serves a generous country breakfast. $$

Oakmoor Country Inn is a new log home on 13 acres with three suites. 98 Lobbans Lane, Afton, ☎ 540-456-6690, www.oakmoorinn.com. $$

Resort

The Wintergreen Resort is an 11,000-acre facility offering a variety of year-round recreational opportunities. The resort is high atop Virginia's Blue Ridge Mountains, with spectacular views of the surrounding valleys and ridges. Reach Wintergreen on Route 664 near Nellysford, one mile off the Blue Ridge Parkway.

Wintergreen can accommodate more than 1,000 guests in a variety of rental homes and condominiums ranging in size from studios to six bedrooms. Most of the units have fireplaces and fully-equipped kitchens. Some offer magnificent views of the mountains and valleys.

The Mountain Conference Center can accommodate groups from 10 to 500 people with more than 25,000 square feet of meeting and banquet space in 15 rooms.

Recreational facilities at the resort are both spectacular and extensive. Devils Knob 18-hole golf course is the highest in Virginia, and there's also the 18-hole Stoney Creek championship golf course.

Other facilities at Wintergreen include 20 composition clay and five all-weather, hard surface tennis courts; one indoor and five outdoor swimming pools; 17 ski slopes and trails; the 20-acre Lake Monocan for swimming and canoeing; an equestrian center and stables; the Wintergreen Spa-indoor/outdoor sports facility; and the Stoney Creek Fly Fishing stream. There is also a 30-mile network of marked hiking trails, an outdoor center and nature program and bicycles available for rent.

During the summer, Wintergreen offers special children's programs in a variety of fun-filled activities, as well as a special nature program that introduces the youngsters to the natural beauty and wildlife of the Blue Ridge Mountains.

Wintergreen has four full-service restaurants offering everything from fine continental cuisine to country-style family meals. Three lounges are good places to relax after a strenuous day in the outdoors; and two seasonal restaurants offer extra service for golfers and skiers.

The climate at Wintergreen provides cool mountain breezes and low humidity during the spring and summer; summer temperature rarely exceeds 85°. Colder temperatures in the winter, combined with the mountain elevation, provide excellent skiing from December through March.

Wintergreen is also home to the Outdoor Wilderness Leadership School, offering experiences in mountain biking, rappelling, rock climbing and kayaking.

For more information and reservations, contact the Wintergreen Resort, PO Box 706, Wintergreen, VA 22958, ☎ 800-266-2444 or 434-325-2200, or visit www.WintergreenResort.com.

Transportation

Nelson County is in Central Virginia and lies on the eastern slope of the Blue Ridge Mountains. It lies midway between the **Lynchburg Regional Airport** and **Charlottesville-Albemarle Airport**. **Greyhound** serves Lexington and the nearest **Amtrak** service is in Charlottesville.

Information

For more information and brochures, contact the **Nelson County Department of Tourism**, US Highway 29, PO Box 636, Nelson County, VA 22949, ☎ 804-263-5239 or 800-282-8223, www.nelsoncounty.com. The Visitor Center on US Highway 29, just south of Lovingston, is open daily.

Orange County

*O*range County is an inland paradise of gently rolling hills edged to the west by magnificent vistas of the Blue Ridge Mountains. Visitors to Orange enjoy warm summer days and an air of quiet country living far away from the busy life of the great cities.

The towns of Orange and Gordonsville provide a pleasing mixture of modern hospitality and old-world charm. It's one of those great places where one can enjoy a leisurely stroll through the historic district, browse the shops, and enjoy a quiet meal at a family-style restaurant or café.

History

Orange County came into being in 1734. It was named for William IV, Prince of Orange and husband of Anne, Princess Royal of England.

The first settlers of Orange County were a group of German immigrants. They were introduced to the area in 1714 by the Lieutenant Governor of Virginia, **Alexander Spotswood**. Twenty years after the first German settlers arrived he built for himself a palatial mansion. He called it, and the thriving new community of which it was a part, **Germanna**.

Germanna was at the far west of the English territories in the New World. Spotswood, however, was a restless man, an entrepreneur ever on the lookout for new opportunities. In 1716 he led an expedition from Germanna westward across the Blue Ridge Mountains in an effort to prove that the mountains were no barrier to the rich lands that lay beyond. Spotswood's expedition had just the desired effect. Soon a general expansion west of the Blue Ridge was under way.

The Revolutionary War with England came and went and, although men from the county played significant roles in the conflict, the hostilities, for the most part, bypassed Orange County. The only actions that took place within its boundaries seem to have been Lafayette's march through the county and an English raid that terrorized the area known as Antioch Church. Today, Lafayette's route is still known as the "Marquis Road."

Orange County's most famous resident, **James Madison**, had a historic meeting with Baptist Elder John Leland in Orange County that inspired

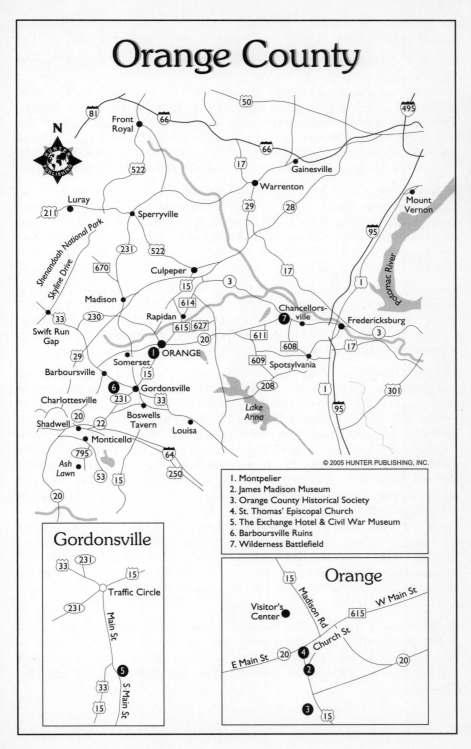

Orange County

1. Montpelier
2. James Madison Museum
3. Orange County Historical Society
4. St. Thomas' Episcopal Church
5. The Exchange Hotel & Civil War Museum
6. Barboursville Ruins
7. Wilderness Battlefield

© 2005 HUNTER PUBLISHING, INC.

Gordonsville

Orange

the language on religious freedom of the First Amendment. Madison served as President of the United States during the War of 1812.

The War of 1812 had little impact on the tranquillity of Orange County. When the Civil War broke out in 1861, however, it was a very different story. The area was the theater for many battles, engagements and skirmishes. The railroads were an important part of General Lee's lifeline. They brought him supplies, troops, and reinforcements throughout the war years. Many Confederate hospitals were established in and around the Town of Orange, and in 1862 the war came violently home to its residents when Union and Confederate troops clashed on the town's streets.

In November, 1863, General Lee's forces and sections of Union General George Gordon Meade's Army of the Potomac clashed when Meade crossed the Rapidan River at Mile Run. Lee and his army spent that winter in quarters along the banks of the Rapidan. While he was there, Lee and many members of his staff worshipped at St. Thomas' Episcopal Church in the town of Orange.

The year 1864 saw the fortunes of the Confederate army take a turn for the worse. In May, General US Grant crossed the Rapidan with a great army and succeeded in pushing Lee into the eastern section of Orange County. The resulting **Battle of the Wilderness** was one of the bloodiest encounters of the entire war.

Although the Battle of the Wilderness was a victory for Lee and his Confederate army, it was also the beginning of Grant's relentless campaign of attrition. He knew the Confederacy could not match the resources and numbers of reinforcements available to him. He also knew that if he could keep Lee on the run, force him into battle as often and as quickly as possible, he would reduce Lee's ability to wage an offensive war. Thus, he would slowly bring him to the point where he could resist no more and the war would be over. And Grant was right. First he forced Lee into the bloody Battle of the Wilderness on May 5th and 6th, and then the Battle of Spotsylvania Court House from May 8th through the 12th. Cold Harbor followed on June 1st through the 3rd and, although it was a Confederate victory, the cost was heavy, with both sides suffering enormous losses. Finally, Grant encircled Richmond and laid siege to the important railroad junction of Petersburg. Petersburg fell on April 2, 1865; the war, for all intents and purposes, ended a few days later on April 12th at Appomattox Court House.

With the end of the Civil War, peace and tranquillity returned once again to Orange County. The community soon recovered from those terrible days now so long ago. Today, it seems little has changed over the hundred and fifty years since General Lee sat and prayed in the little church of St. Thomas.

Sights

The **Barboursville Vineyard and Historic Ruin** are on the grounds of the old Barboursville Estate on Route 777. A crumbling ruin is all that's left of the home of Governor James Barbour. The house was designed by Barbour's good friend, Thomas Jefferson. The vineyards, some 126 acres set on an estate which incorporates 850 acres of beautiful rolling hillside close to the Blue Ridge Mountains, take great pride in their award-winning Chardonnays, Cabernets and other fine wines. The Barboursville Vineyards welcome visitors for tours of the ruins and wine tasting year-round, Monday through Saturday and on Sunday afternoons. The Vineyards are closed on major holidays, including Thanksgiving, Christmas and New Year's. There is a restaurant and a guest cottage. ☎ 540-832-3824, www.barboursvillewine.com.

Civil War Museum at The Exchange Hotel, in Gordonsville at 400 South Main Street, is a restored railroad hotel that served as a military hospital during the Civil War. Throughout the war years the old hotel received the wounded and the dying from a dozen major battlefields and a hundred or more skirmishes. In one year alone, 23,000 men were treated at the Exchange – 6,000 in one month alone. Today, the hotel houses one of the finest Civil War museums in the area. It also has rooms available for receptions and weddings and is open April through November, Tuesday. Contact the Exchange at ☎ 540-832-2944, www.hgiexchange.org.

Ellwood Manor is a 1790 plantation home on a knoll overlooking Wilderness Run. The land is the burial site of the arm of General Stonewall Jackson. Open weekends Memorial Day through Columbus Day, and operated by the National Park Service. Route 20, Locust Grove, ☎ 540-786-2880, www.fowb.org.

Horton Vineyards is charting new territory in Virginia wine-making, utilizing the French grape Viognier and other European varieties. 6399 Spotswood Trail, Gordonsville, ☎ 540-832-7440, www.hvwine.com

James Madison Museum, 129 Caroline Street, Orange, offers a unique glimpse into the life and times of our nation's fourth president. The building also houses the Hall of Agriculture; it is open daily except major holidays. ☎ 540-672-1776, www.jamesmadisonmus.org.

Montpelier, about four miles southwest of Orange on Route 20, was the life-long home of James Madison, the fourth president of the United States, and his wife, Dolley. Settled in 1723 by Madison's grandparents, Montpelier continued to prosper until after his death, when it was sold by Mrs. Madison to pay off her son's gambling debts.

After Madison's death, the house changed hands six times, eventually becoming the property of William and Ann Rogers Du Pont. The Du Ponts enlarged the old house, added horse barns, greenhouses, a dairy and even a railroad. Du Pont's daughter, Marion Du Pont Scott, took over the property in 1928 and continued to improve and restore it. Her contribution to the estate, which incorporates some 2,700 acres, includes a steeplechase course.

The property was deeded to the National Trust for Historic Preservation following Mrs. Scott's death in 1983. It was opened to the public in 1987.

A massive renovation will remove many of the alterations made to the mansion since the president's death, restoring it to the way James and Dolley Madison knew it in the 1820s. Even though the project will be on-going at least through 2007, portions of the home will be open to the public at all times.

The 200-acre old growth forest has been called the best example of old growth in the Piedmont and is a National Natural Landmark. A new system of trails now allows visitors to see tulip poplars that date to James Madison's lifetime. There's also a two-acre formal garden of walks, marble statues, flower beds and herbs. Montpelier is open daily, March through December, and on weekends during January and February. ☎ 540-672-2728, www.montpelier.org.

The **Orange County** and **African-American Historical Societies** are at 130 Caroline Street. Extensive research and archival collection of books, periodicals, maps, and files on local families, buildings and historic sites. Open 1-5 p.m. weekdays. Information and research materials are available, not only for Orange County, but for many of its neighboring counties, including Madison, Culpeper, and Greene. ☎ 540-672-5366, www.orangecovahist.org.

Rapidan Village, founded in 1772, is a small community with an interesting history. During the Civil War the village changed hands 15 times. After fighting all day, it has been said that members of both armies swam the Rapidan River at night to trade with each other. The **Waddell Memorial Church** in Rapidan is a fine example of carpenter Gothic architecture.

St. Thomas' Episcopal Church, 119 Caroline Street, was built during the years 1833 and 1834 at a cost of $3,500. During the Civil War, after the Battles of Cedar Mountain, Fredericksburg, Chancellorsville, the Wilderness and Spotsylvania Court House, the church saw extensive use as a Confederate hospital. During the winter of 1863-64 when the Confederate army occupied defensive positions along the Rapidan River, it was a principle place of worship for Confederate General Robert E. Lee and many members of his staff. Of special interest is the Tiffany window located on the left side of the church near the front. Tours of the church may be arranged by calling the church office, ☎ 540-672-3761.

The Wilderness Battlefield is where General Robert E. Lee's Army of Northern Virginia clashed with General Grant's Federal forces for the first time on May 5th and 6th, 1864. Self-guided tours of the battlefield begin at the National Park Service Exhibit Shelter on Route 20, one mile west of the intersection with Route 3. For more information, contact the Park Service at ☎ 540-373-4461, www.nps.gov

Entertainment

Four County Players give presentations throughout the year. This community theater group is housed in a converted, early 20th-century schoolhouse in Barboursville. ☎ 540-832-5355, www.avenue.org/fourep.

Shopping

For the discerning shopper on the hunt for that little something special, a number of antique stores and gift shops offer a variety of unusual gifts and memorabilia in Orange. Arts & crafts stores have an abundance of hand-crafted gifts, folk art and toys. Orange also has several galleries, an herb shop and a flea market where one can browse the stalls.

Recreation

Lake Orange is a 124-acre lake with a marina and a number of picnic areas where you can spend a quiet day out in the country fishing, hiking, boating, picnicking or simply relaxing in the sunshine. Only rowboats or boats with electric motors are allowed on the lake. ☎ 540-672-3997.

Lake Anna is a magnificent 13,000-acre water park. It has several marinas where boat ramps are available for public use, and boat rentals, fishing tackle and bait can be arranged for at the marina stores. Activities at Lake Anna include sailing, water-skiing, hiking, boating, picnicking and fishing for largemouth bass, smallmouth bass, yellow perch, bluegill, black crappie, pumpkinseed, walleye, pickerel, carp, striped bass, sunfish and channel catfish. Take US 1 south from Orange to State Route 208 west, and then go to State Route 601 north. For more information, Lake Anna State Park, ☎ 540-854-5503.

The Rapidan River offers scenic river rafting, tubing, canoeing and fishing. It flows through the heart of Orange County. From the town of Orange, take Route 15 North.

Oakland Heights Farm Horseback Riding, Route 15, Gordonsville, ☎ 540-832-3350, www.oaklandheights.ova.net.

Skydive Orange, offers skydiving at the Orange Airport, Route 20 South, ☎ 540-942-3871, www.skydiveorange.com.

Golf

Golfers can play at **Brownings Golf Course** in Locust Grove, ☎ 540-854-4454; **Meadows Farms Golf Course**, in Locust Grove, ☎ 540-854-

Orange County

9890, www.meadowsfarms.com; **Somerset Golf Club**, also in Locust Grove, ☎ 540-423-1500, www.somersetfarm.com; or **Shenandoah Crossing Resort** in Gordonsville, ☎ 540-832-9400, www.shenandoah-crossing.com.

Annual Events

For a complete listing of events, ☎ 877-222-8072, www.visitocva.com.

President James Madison's Birthday Celebration, held March 16 at Montpelier, ☎ 540-672-2728.

Montpelier Wine Festival, held the first weekend in May, is a two-day celebration held on the grounds of the Montpelier estate emphasizing local wines, crafts, food, music, and fun, ☎ 540-672-5216.

Dolley Madison Birthday Celebration, May 20 at Montpelier, ☎ 540-672-2728.

The Orange County Fair, held in July at Montpelier, is a real, old-fashioned country fair with all the sights and sounds associated with such an event, ☎ 540-672-2271, www.orangecountyvafair.com.

Shakespeare at the Ruins is held the last week in July through mid-August at the Barboursville Ruins, ☎ 540-832-5355.

The **Somerset Steam and Gas Pasture Party**, held the last weekend in August, offers demonstrations of working antique steam and gas driven tractors and automobiles, ☎ 540-672-2495.

Orange Street Festival, held the first weekend in September, offers visitors a wealth of arts, crafts, food, music, and fun for all. ☎ 540-672-5216.

Gordonsville Street Festival is on the first Saturday in October, ☎ 540-832-5853.

Montpelier Hunt Races, held on the Montpelier estate on the first Saturday in November, involves both steeplechasing and flat racing, ☎ 540-672-0027, www.montpelier.org/races.htm.

Christmas Open House, is held the first weekend in December throughout the Main Street business district of Orange, ☎ 540-672-2540.

Dining

Cape Porpoise Restaurant, 182 Byrd Street, Orange, ☎ 540-672-0800.

Country Cookin', 13246 James Madison Highway, Orange, ☎ 540-672-5353.

Dairy Korner Restaurant, Routes 15 and 20, Orange, ☎ 540-672-4797.

Happy Garden Chinese Restaurant, 130 East Main Street, Orange, ☎ 540-672-1044.

Inwood Restaurant, Route 15 North, Gordonsville, ☎ 540-832-3411.

Jean's Café, 152 Caroline Street, Orange, ☎ 540-672-5690.

Lake Izac Tavern at the Shenandoah Crossing lodge in Gordeonsville serves regional fare with a lake view. Open for breakfast weekends only, lunch and dinner Thursday through Monday. ☎ 540-832-9590, www.shenandoah-crossing.com

Mario's Pizzeria and Restaurant, 269 Madison Road, Orange, ☎ 540-672-3344.

Not the Same Old Grind, 110 E. Church Street, Orange, ☎ 540-672-3143.

Palladio Restaurant serves fine Northern Italian fare and Virginia wines at Bourboursville Vineyards, Route 777. Open for lunch Wednesday through Sunday and dinner Friday and Saturday. Reservations recommended. ☎ 540-832-7848, www.palladiorestaurant.com/index.php.

Tolliver House Restaurant, 209 North Main Street, Gordonsville, ☎ 540-832-3485.

Willow Grove Inn and Restaurant, 14079 Plantation Way, Route 15 North, Orange, ☎ 540-672-5982, www.willowgroveinn.com.

Accommodations

The Town of Orange offers plenty of places to stay, including a number of quiet country guest houses and bed & breakfast inns.

Greenock House, 249 Caroline Street in Orange, ☎ 540-672-3625, www.greenockhouse.com, offers a romantic Victorian atmosphere with private verandahs, canopied beds, fireplaces and individually decorated rooms. There are 10 rooms, all with private baths. A full breakfast and complimentary afternoon tea are included in the rate, and a gourmet dinner can also be had. $$

Holiday Inn Express has an outdoor pool and fitness center. 750 Round Hill Road, Orange, ☎ 540-672-6691, 800-HOLIDAY, www.holidayinnexpress.com. $$

The Holladay House, 155 West Main Street in Orange, ☎ 540-672-4893 or 800-358-4422, www.holladayhousebandb.com, is a restored Federal-style brick home. There are four guest rooms and two suites, all with private bath, each with their own sitting area, furnished with family pieces. Breakfast may be served in the guest rooms. $$

The Shadows, 14291 Constitution Highway in Orange, ☎ 540-672-5057, www.theshadowsbedandbreakfast.com, is a restored farmhouse built in 1923 and set on 44 beautiful acres. There are four rooms and two cottages, all with private baths. There is a large stone fireplace and guest rooms are filled with antiques. The Shadows offers its guests a romantic getaway in the country. Rates include a hearty gourmet breakfast. $$

Shenandoah Crossing offers rooms in a lodge as well as cabins and townhomes on wooded lots, some on the lake. There's also a 1742 manor house, RV and wilderness camping. There's an equestrian center and full-service restaurant. 10 Shenandoah Crossing, Gordonsville, ☎ 540-832-9400, www.shenandoah-crossing.com. $

Sleepy Hollow Farm, 16280 Blue Ridge Turnpike in Gordonsville, ☎ 540-832-5555, 800-215-4804, www.sleepyhollowfarmbnb.com, is an 18th-century house surrounded by all the sights and sounds of the Virginia countryside: cattle in the fields, extensive woodlands and a pond. Three guest rooms and three suites, all with private baths. There's also a gazebo and a children's play area with swings and a sandbox. The house is set amid flower and herb gardens. Rates include a full country breakfast. $

The **Vineyard Cottage** at Barboursville Vineyard is an 18th-century brick servants' quarters renovated to house guest suites with all the modern amenities. ☎ 540-832-7848, www.barboursvillewine.com. $$$

Willow Grove Inn & Restaurant, 14079 Plantation Way in Orange, ☎ 540-672-5982 or 800-949-1778, www.willowgroveinn.com, is a beautiful mansion set among 37 acres of formal gardens and sloping lawns. There are 10 rooms, all with private baths. The house features antique-filled rooms and a pub. The rate includes a full-course dinner and a hearty plantation breakfast. $$$$

Transportation

There are two airports: **Orange County Airport**, ☎ 540-672-2158, and **Gordonsville Airport**.

Information

Orange County Department of Tourism and Visitors Bureau is at 122 East Main Street, in the 1910 Orange Train Station, Orange, VA 22960. ☎ 540-672-1653 or 877-222-8072, or visit www.visitocva.com.

Germanna Visitors Center, Route 3, Locust Grove, houses memorabilia related to this early German settlement. ☎ 540-423-1700, www.germania.org.

Petersburg & Prince George County

*P*etersburg is in a tri-county area south of the James River. A visit to the old city is an experience that transcends more than 350 years of history, culture and American life. The city's past and present come together in Old Towne, a revitalized commercial district of restaurants and sidewalk cafés, boutiques, crafts and antique stores. Only 25 minutes south of Richmond, Petersburg is convenient to the Plantation Country on the James River, as well as the major historic destinations of Williamsburg, Jamestown and Yorktown.

Most visitors associate Petersburg with the closing days of the Civil War, and so they should. Petersburg was the subject of the longest siege in American history. But Petersburg has also been an important transportation and commercial center since before the Revolution.

History

Petersburg's history begins in 1845 when the General Assembly at Jamestown ordered a fort constructed at the falls of the Appomattox River. Fort Henry was built and Major General Abraham Wood installed as its first commander.

Nearly 100 years later in 1733, William Byrd II laid the foundations for two cities: Richmond and Petersburg. But it wasn't until 1748 that the General Assembly officially created the town of Petersburg. The towns of Blandford and Pocahontas were created at the same time. In 1784 all three towns, plus a fourth, Ravenscroft, were incorporated as the single town of Petersburg.

It 1781, English troops under the command of Generals Benedict Arnold and William Phillips occupied the town. That same year, English General Lord Cornwallis surrendered his army to George Washington at Yorktown and the War of the American Revolution ended.

The years following the Revolutionary War were years of growth and prosperity. The town became a popular watering hole with a social life that, for a time, eclipsed that of its neighbor to the north, Richmond. But the euphoric times ended with the advent of the Civil War. At first, Petersburg was little affected by the conflict raging around it. During the early years of the war, the city sent troops to fight for the Southern cause. But Petersburg was far too important to the Confederate war effort to escape attention for long.

By 1864 five railroads ran through the city from all points east, west and south, providing a vital line of supply to and from Richmond. And so it was that the sleepy little city on the river bank became the scene of one of the most extended and devastating sieges in American history. For al-

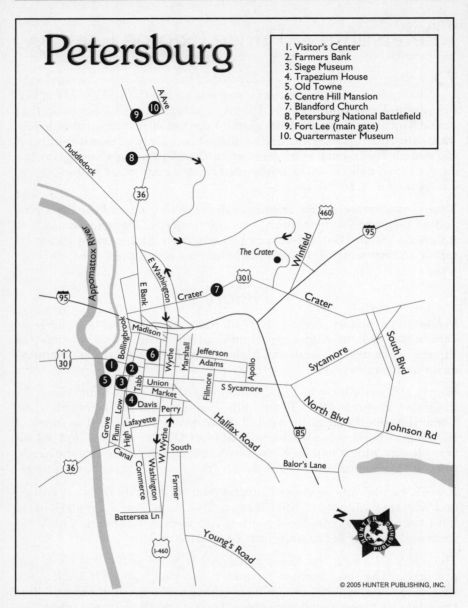

Petersburg

1. Visitor's Center
2. Farmers Bank
3. Siege Museum
4. Trapezium House
5. Old Towne
6. Centre Hill Mansion
7. Blandford Church
8. Petersburg National Battlefield
9. Fort Lee (main gate)
10. Quartermaster Museum

© 2005 HUNTER PUBLISHING, INC.

most 10 months Confederate forces held on in the face of insurmountable odds until at last, on April 3rd, 1865, General Lee withdrew from the beleaguered city and began his long march to Appomattox and surrender. During the siege more than 28,000 Confederate soldiers and 42,000 Union soldiers lost their lives. The earthworks of that fearful struggle remain today as reminders of a period in Petersburg's history that though long gone, will never be forgotten.

After the Civil War ended, the shattered city slowly recuperated. Today, besides being a museum of American history, Petersburg is a thriving commercial and industrial city with a bright future.

Sights

Battersea, Upper Appomattox Street and Battersea Lane, ☎ 804-733-2400, is a circa-1768 Palladian house built by John Banister, first mayor of Petersburg. The house is open by appointment.

Blandford Church, 111 Rochelle Lane, was built in 1735. The old parish church was restored in 1901 as a memorial to the Southern soldiers who died during the Civil War. In honor of the Confederate dead, the states each contributed a stained glass window designed by Louis Comfort Tiffany. The old tombstones in the churchyard date to the early 1700s. More than 30,000 Confederate soldiers are buried in the cemetery where the first Memorial Day was observed in June, 1866. Open daily, with guided tours every 45 minutes. ☎ 804-733-2396.

Centre Hill Museum, 1 Centre Hill Court, built in 1823 and remodeled in the 1840s and 1901, is the grandest old home in the city. The Federal-style building is a testament to the old Southern culture. Ornate woodwork, plaster motifs, antique furnishings and the 1886 inlaid grand piano are only a few of the wonders of Centre Hill. The mansion is at Centre Hill Court and is open daily except Thanksgiving, Christmas and New Year's Day; tours every hour. ☎ 804-733-2401.

The Farmers Bank of Virginia, 19 Bollingbrook Street, houses a fine collection of banking memorabilia. Built in 1817, the accommodations on the upper floors served the cashier and his family. The kitchen and laundry at the rear served as home for the bank's slaves. This is one of the oldest bank buildings in America. Visitors can see its heavy safe which was kept in the cashier's office during banking hours and lowered through the floor to the vault below at night. The bank is open by appointment. ☎ 804-733-2400.

Lee's Retreat is a 26-stop driving tour that traces General Robert E. Lee's retreat from Petersburg to Appomattox where he surrendered. Maps available at the Petersburg Visitor Center; ☎ 800-6-RETREAT.

Old Towne Petersburg is a historic district of antique galleries, boutiques, craft shops, restaurants and a diverse mixture of renovated residences and commercial buildings.

The Petersburg National Battlefield is a national park covering more than two square miles. It preserves many of the Confederate and Union fortifications, trenches and gun emplacements. The park is open daily and, during the summer months, features daily living history demonstrations. Access for the disabled includes several paved trails and ramps. For an interpretive brochure and tour map, contact the Superintendent,

Petersburg National Battlefield Park, 1539 Hickory Hill Road, Petersburg, VA 23803, ☎ 804-732-3531, www.nps.gov/pete/index.htm.

Pamplin Historical Park and National Museum of the Civil War Solider, 6523 Duncan Road, ☎ 877-PAMPLIN, 804-861-2408, or visit www.pamplinpark.org. This new, innovative museum tells the story of the battle. Tudor Hall is a plantation home that was used as a headquarters during the battle. Tours and costumed programs are offered daily.

The Siege Museum, 15 West Bank Street, houses the exhibits and memorabilia that interpret the 10-month Civil War siege of Petersburg. A film, *The Echoes Still Remain*, with Joseph Cotten, is shown every hour on the hour. The museum is open daily except Thanksgiving, Christmas and New Year's Day. ☎ 804-733-2404.

The Trapezium House is at 244 North Market Street. Eccentric Irish bachelor Charles O'Hara built this house in 1817. He built it in the form of a trapezium – without right angles or parallel walls – because he believed a story told to him by his West Indian slave that such a house could not harbor ghosts and spirits. Call for hours. ☎ 804-733-2400.

Recreation

Petersburg offers more than 400 acres of parkland. In addition, the Appomattox River and Wilcox Lake offer boating and great fishing, the local golf courses are challenging, and there are opportunities for tennis and hiking, as well as several fitness centers and health clubs. Petersburg is also rich in culture and entertainment opportunities ranging from a symphony orchestra and Art League to eight cinemas. A major arts festival is held each April, and the holiday "Lighting of Petersburg" is a special delight for visitors.

Annual Event

A **Commemorative Encampment and Reenactment** of the Revolutionary War battle is held in mid-April each year at Battersea Plantation on the West End of Washington Street; ☎ 804-733-2402.

Dining

Petersburg offers a number of fine restaurants and cafés, with all sorts of traditional American and ethnic cuisine available. Contact the Petersburg Visitor's Center at ☎ 800-368-3595 for a full list.

Alexander's, 101 W. Bank Street, ☎ 804-733-7134, serves Italian and Greek food.

Canton Restaurant, 950 S. Sycamore Street, ☎ 804-732-6441.

Dixie Restaurant, 250 N. Sycamore Street, ☎ 804-732-5761, serves lunch and dinner with daily specials such as salmon cakes.

High Street Bistro is at the Petersburg Regency Hotel & Conference Center, 380 E. Washington Street. ☎ 804-733-0000.

King's Barbecue, serves Virignia barbecue at two locations: 3321 W. Washington Street, ☎ 804-732-5861, and 2910 S. Crater Road, ☎ 804-732-0975.

Leonardo's Deli & Café, 7 Bollingbrook Street, ☎ 804-863-4830, serves lunch and dinner, with daily specials.

Mad Italian, 2545 S. Crater Road, ☎ 804-732-9268, specializes in Italian cuisine.

Accommodations

Petersburg offers a range of lodging, from large hotels to unique bed & breakfasts. Following is just a sampling. For a complete list, contact the **Petersburg Visitor Center** at ☎ 800-368-3595.

Hotels & Motels

Quality Inn, 405 East Washington Street, ☎ 804-733-1776, is a pleasant motor hotel with 120 rooms. Amenities include a restaurant and two cafés, a swimming pool, meeting rooms and valet service. The management provides free airport and rail station transportation and offers a senior citizen discount. $$

Comfort Inn, 11974 South Crater Road, ☎ 804-732-2000. 96 rooms. There is a swimming pool, meeting rooms and valet service. Free continental breakfast; senior citizen discount. $-$$

Days Inn, 12208 South Crater Road, ☎ 804-733-4400. 155 rooms. Features are a restaurant and café, swimming pool, a playground, an exercise room, meeting rooms and valet service. Pets are allowed in the rooms and there is a senior citizen discount. $$

Holiday Inn Express, 12001 South Crater Road, ☎ 804-732-2000, has 98 rooms, a putting green, pool, sauna and tennis courts. $$

Howard Johnson, ☎ 804-732-5950, 530 East Washington Street, has 160 rooms and an outdoor pool. $$

Best Western Steven Kent, six miles south of Petersburg on I-95 at Exit 45, ☎ 804-733-0600, has 138 rooms. There are handicapped-accessible and non-smoking rooms, a restaurant and café, a swimming pool, a playground, lighted tennis courts, an exercise room, meeting rooms and valet service. Pets are allowed in the rooms and the management offers a senior citizen discount. $$

Bed & Breakfasts / Inns

Folly Castle Inn, 323 West Washington Street, ☎ 804-861-3558, www-.follycastle.com, has three suites, all with private baths, in a restored 1763 Greek Revival home. Suites have fireplaces and guest kitchens. Full Southern breakfast served; no pets or children. $$

The High Street Inn, 405 High Street, ☎ 804-733-0505, is a well-appointed inn with six guest rooms. Located in the historic district of Old Towne, the Queen Anne mansion offers individually decorated rooms, antique furniture, complimentary afternoon tea and a free continental breakfast. $$

La Villa Romaine B&B, 29 South Market Street, ☎ 804-861-2285, www.lavilla.tierranet.com, has four rooms, two with private bath, in a pre-Civil War mansion furnished in French antiques. An elegant full breakfast is served. $$

Transportation

Petersburg is served by **Richmond International Airport** with direct service to more than 50 cities nationwide and with connections to world-wide destinations through all major US carriers.

Petersburg is also served by **Greyhound Lines** bus lines (☎ 800-231-2222) and by **Amtrak** (☎ 800-872-7245).

Information

The **Petersburg Visitors Center** is located in the McIlwaine House at 425 Cockade Alley, ☎ 800-368-3595 or 804-733-2400. Another location is at Carson on Interstate 95, ☎ 434-246-2145. For more information, visit the city's Web site at www.petersburg-va.org.

Richmond

Virginia's capital is a city of extraordinary contrasts, where Victorian opulence blends smoothly with Colonial simplicity. Grand estates and stylized townhouses, wrought iron and gingerbread, cobblestones, magnolias and boxwoods, and four centuries of history together with a modern skyline create a breathtaking blend of past and present.

Visitors to Richmond encounter Civil War battlefields, world-renowned museums, distinctive architecture, living history reenactments and magnificent gardens. From a sightseeing flight over the city to a riverboat trip or a stroll through the quaint and historic neighborhoods, there's always something interesting to do.

History

From the earliest days when a band of English explorers pushed westward from Jamestown in 1607, it would seem that Richmond has never known a dull moment. For years the settlers fought the Indians for the ground upon which the city now stands. In 1775 Patrick Henry stood in St. John's Church and made a speech that set the colony on the road to revolution. His stirring request for "Liberty or Death" was the beginning of the birth of a nation. Five years later Richmond was named Virginia's state capital.

Then came the great Civil War and Richmond took on a new role. It's ironic that the city became the capital of the Confederacy because Virginia, as a state, was against secession. But for four years the great city withstood one threat after another. For four years the battle cry of the United States was "On to Richmond." In 1862 General George McClellan landed a vast Union army at Fort Monroe and so began his Peninsula Campaign aimed at the capture of the city. Slowly but surely, one engagement after another, McClellan headed toward the Confederate capital. Yorktown fell to "Little Mac," and then he was at the gates of the city. The Confederate commanding general, Joseph E. Johnston, was severely wounded and had to be replaced. It was his replacement that saved the city. Robert E. Lee led the Army of Northern Virginia through the devastating battles of The Seven Days, during which Lee and McClellan fought six major battles at a combined cost of more than 36,000 casualties. Costly though the Seven Days were, they ended in victory for Lee. Slowly, but surely, he pushed McClellan back to Harrison's Landing on the banks of the James River where. McClellan then left the peninsula to fight again at the Battle of Antietam, the bloodiest single day of the Civil War.

Finally, in April, 1865, with General Grant's forces once again poised to take the city, Richmond was evacuated and abandoned. The retreating Confederate soldiers burned the government warehouse and headed west to join Robert E. Lee on his retreat from Petersburg along the road to Appomattox.

Richmond, however, survived. Today it exemplifies the modern South. It's a city very much aware of the past and its culture, but also a city with a view toward to the future. History and industry combine to provide a healthy and growing economy in one of the nation's great cities.

Sights

Richmond is known for its unique neighborhoods. Don't miss **Careytown's** shopping district, **Church Hill's** antebellum homes, the muse-

Richmond

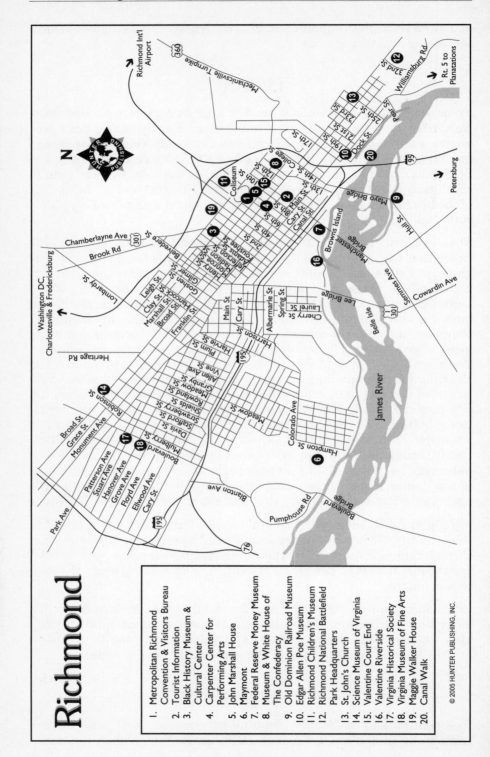

Richmond

1. Metropolitan Richmond Convention & Visitors Bureau
2. Tourist Information
3. Black History Museum & Cultural Center
4. Carpenter Center for Performing Arts
5. John Marshall House
6. Maymont
7. Federal Reserve Money Museum
8. Museum & White House of The Confederacy
9. Old Dominion Railroad Museum
10. Edgar Allen Poe Museum
11. Richmond Children's Museum
12. Richmond National Battlefield Park Headquarters
13. St. John's Church
14. Science Museum of Virginia
15. Valentine Court End
16. Valentine Riverside
17. Virginia Historical Society
18. Virginia Museum of Fine Arts
19. Maggie Walker House
20. Canal Walk

ums and historic homes of **Court End**, and **The Fan** district's Monument Avenue, with its many restaurants and turn-of-the-century townhomes. Then there's **Shockoe Bottom** and **Shockoe Slip**, where history meets eclectic in the many hangouts and boutiques housed in former warehouses and factories on cobblestone streets.

Agecroft Hall, 4305 Sulgrave Road, was rescued from destruction in England. Antique furniture and 23 acres of landscaped grounds and gardens reflect the style of a glorious age. Agecroft is open Tuesday through Sunday. ☎ 804-353-4241, www.agecrofthall.com.

The **American Historical Foundation Museum/US Marine Raider Museum**, 1142 West Grace Street, houses the personal artifacts of Jeb Stuart and John Singleton Mosby and the largest collection of military knives and bayonets in the United States. An exhibit chronicles the famous WWII Marine Raiders. The museum is open Monday through Friday. ☎ 804-353-1812.

Annabel Lee offers river cruises with dining and entertainment on the James River. 4400 East Main Street, ☎ 804-644-5700.

Beth Ahabah Museum & Archives, 1109 W. Franklin Street, ☎ 804-353-2668, chronicles Jewish American history. Open Sunday through Thursday.

The **Black History Museum & Cultural Center of Virginia**, at 00 Clay Street, interprets African-American life in Virginia from Jamestown in 1619 until today. The museum houses a collection of more than 5,000 artifacts and documents, limited editions, art and photographs. It is open Tuesday through Saturday. ☎ 804-780-9093, www.blackhistorymuseum.org.

Canal Walk is a 1.25-mile path along the James River and Kanawha and Haxall canals. These canals were first conceived in the late 1700s as a means of circumventing "The Falls," thereby linking the Atlantic Ocean and the Ohio River and establishing Richmond as a port. Markers and exhibits along the way interpret the area's history. It's accessible at 5th, 7th, Virginia, 14th, 15th and 17th streets, with handicapped access at 5th and 14th. Canal boat tours are also available. ☎ 804-648-6549, www.richmondriverfront.com.

The Chesterfield Museum Complex and Magnolia Grange are on Iron Bridge Road between Beach and Lori Roads. The Chesterfield County Museum, Old Courthouse and 19th-century jail make up a complex that interprets the rich history of Chesterfield County. Magnolia Grange, built in the 19th century, is a fully restored plantation house featuring period furnishings and decorative arts. The complex is open Sunday through Friday. ☎ 804-777-9663, www.chesterfieldhistory.com.

At the **Children's Museum of Richmond**, 2626 West Broad Street, children can touch, explore and experience through participatory exhibits, classes and workshops that introduce them to the arts, nature and more. The museum is open daily in summer, closed Mondays from September through May and on major holidays; see Web site for hours and admission. ☎ 804-474-2667, www.c-mor.org.

The **Edgar Allan Poe Museum**, 1914-16 East Main Street, honors the great American writer with five buildings surrounding an "enchanted garden." The museum houses the largest collection of Poe memorabilia and artifacts in the world. It is open Tuesday through Sunday. ☎ 804-648-5523, www.poemuseum.org.

The Henricus Historical Park is located in Chesterfield County. From Richmond, take Route 10 south to Old Stage Road. Established in 1611 by Sir Thomas Dale, Henricus was the second permanent English settlement in the country. The park is accessible by a mile-long path along the river; open daily. ☎ 804-706-1341, www.henricus.org.

The **Historic Jackson Ward Museum** preserves the history of the Jackson Ward neighborhood and African Americans in Richmond. Call for hours. 502-504 N. Third Street, ☎ 804-343-1825.

The Hollywood Cemetery, at Cherry and Albemarle Streets, was named for its multitude of holly trees. It is the resting place of more than 18,000 soldiers, Presidents Tyler and Monroe, Confederate President Jefferson Davis and the famed Confederate cavalry general, James Ewell Brown "Jeb" Stuart. ☎ 804-648-8501, www.hollywoodcemetery.org.

Virginia Holocaust Museum, 2000 East Cary Street is a tribute to Holocaust survivors, with 25 exhibit rooms. Open daily. ☎ 804-257-5400, www.va-holocaust.com.

The Lewis Ginter Botanical Garden, 1800 Lakeside Avenue, features the magnificent displays of the Flagler Perennial Garden, the Minor Garden, the West Island Garden and the Cottage Garden. Visitors can enjoy a meal at the Lora Robins Tea House, shop in the gift shop or eat in the Garden Café in the new E. Claiborne Robins Visitors Center. The Botanical Garden is open daily. ☎ 804-262-9887, www.lewisginter.org.

The John Marshall House, 818 East Marshall Street, is an outstanding example of Federal architecture and retains many of its original features and a rich collection of Marshall family memorabilia. The house is open Tuesday through Sunday. ☎ 804-648-7998, www.john-marshall.org.

The **Maggie Walker National Historic Site**, 110½ East Leigh Street, commemorates the life and time of a progressive and talented African-American woman. Despite many adversities, Maggie Walker achieved success in business and finance as the first woman in the United States to found a bank. The house, restored to its 1930s appearance, is furnished with Walker family pieces. The house is open Monday-Saturday. ☎ 804-771-2017, www.nps.gov/mawa.

Maymont, 1700 Hampton Street, is a 100-acre estate with a 33-room Victorian Romanesque Mansion. There is a new Visitor Center and high-tech Nature Center, featuring a 125-foot series of linked aquariums, a 3D model of the James River, and a 20-foot waterfall. The estate also features formal Italian and Japanese Gardens, antique carriage rides, and native animal habitats. The grounds are open daily. ☎ 804-358-7166, www.maymont.org.

The Meadow Farm Museum, at Mountain and Courtney Roads in Glenn Allen, is an 1860s living historical farm featuring a 19th-century farmhouse, barn, doctor's office, forge and smokehouse. Costumed interpreters perform the daily domestic and agricultural tasks throughout the year. Grounds are open daily; the museum is open Tuesday through Sunday. ☎ 804-501-5520.

Metro Richmond Zoo, 8300 Beaver Bridge Road, ☎ 804-739-5666, is the home of many exotic animals. Open Monday-Saturday.

The Money Museum, in the Federal Reserve Building at 701 East Byrd Street, has exhibits from throughout history. The museum is open by appointment Monday through Friday. ☎ 804-697-8108, www.rich.frb.org.

Monument Avenue, described as "one of the most beautiful streets in America" is a grand boulevard featuring impressive statues honoring tennis star Arthur Ashe and Civil War heroes. This breathtaking parade of impressive monuments and stately slate-roofed mansions features ancient oaks and maples, magnolias, boxwoods and wrought iron detail.

The Museum and White House of the Confederacy, 1201 East Clay Street, house the nation's most comprehensive collection of military, political and domestic artifacts and art associated with the period of the Confederacy. The White House, accurately restored to its mid-19th-century appearance, was the executive mansion of Confederate President Jefferson Davis and his family from 1861 until 1865. Now a National Historic Landmark, it is open daily for guided tours. ☎ 804-649-1861, www-.mdc.org.

The Old Dominion Railroad Museum, 102 Hull Street (in a restored Railway Express Agency car), features photographs and artifacts from the area's railroad history. The museum is open on Saturday and Sunday. ☎ 804-233-6237, www.odcnrhs.org.

The **Richmond National Battlefield Park and Visitor Center**, 470 Tredegar Street, present a comprehensive overview of the city's Civil War battlefields. The Chimborazo Visitor Center contains a museum and offers a 12-minute slide presentation and a 30-minute film on life in Richmond during the Civil War. The center also has brochures, handbooks and detailed maps for touring the battlefields. The Center is open daily. ☎ 804-771-2145, www.nps.gov/rich.

Richmond

St. John's Church, 2401 East Broad Street, is where Patrick Henry made his famous "Liberty or Death" speech. Built in 1714, St. John's is the oldest church in Richmond. Reenactments of the Second Virginia Convention of 1775 are held on Sundays during the summer. Open daily. ☎ 804-648-5015, www.historicstjohnschurch.org.

Science Museum of Virginia, 2500 West Broad Street and housed in the Old Broad Street Station, contains more than 250 hands-on exhibits on aerospace, astronomy, chemistry, electricity and physics. The museum also houses the Ethyl Universe Planetarium and Space Theatre, an IMAX theater offering fascinating films and multimedia planetarium shows. The museum is open daily. ☎ 804-864-1400, www.smv.org.

The **Three Lakes Nature Center and Aquarium**, 400 Sausiluta Drive, houses a 50,000-gallon freshwater aquarium. The center features wetland exhibits, aquatic animals and plant life, forest animals and more. The center is open Tuesday-Sunday. ☎ 804-261-8230.

Tuckahoe Plantation is the boyhood home of Thomas Jefferson. On Route 6 west of Richmond. Grounds open daily, tours available by appointment. ☎ 804-784-5736.

The Valentine Richmond History Center, 1015 East Clay Street, houses major exhibitions that explore American urban and social history by focusing on Richmond's past. The exhibits examine antebellum race relations, the concept of history and the rise of museums, and costumes and textiles through Virginia's past. The museum also includes Wickham House, a National Historic Landmark and outstanding example of Federal architecture. Built in 1812, the house has lovingly been restored to its former splendor featuring rare neoclassical wall paintings and antique furnishings. The Valentine is open Tuesday-Sunday. ☎ 804-649-0711, www.richmondhistorycenter.com.

The Virginia Aviation Museum, 5701 Huntsman Road, houses a number of vintage aircraft and aviation exhibits from World War II. The museum is open daily. ☎ 804-236-3622, www.vam.smv.org.

Virginia Executive Mansion, Capitol Square, ☎ 804-371-2642. The official residence of the governor has been restored to its 1830s appearance. Open by appointment only.

The Virginia Historical Society, at Kensington and Boulevard, houses seven galleries that exhibit rare Virginia-related treasures and changing exhibits on Virginia history, including collections of photographs, prints and art. The Society is open daily. ☎ 804-358-4901, www.vahistorical.org.

The Virginia Museum of Fine Arts, 200 N. Boulevard, has outstanding collections of art nouveau, art deco, Himalayan, contemporary, impressionist and British sporting art. The museum also houses a large collection of Fabergé Russian Imperial Easter eggs. It is open Wednesday through Sunday. ☎ 804-340-1400, www.vmfa.state.va.us.

Virginia State Capitol, at 9th and E. Grace Streets, ☎ 804-698-1788, is home of the oldest legislative body in the western hemisphere, and a marble statue of George Washington, the only piece he ever posed for. The building, designed by Thomas Jefferson, was inspired by a Roman temple; substantial renovations were done in 2005. Guided tours daily.

Walking Tours are available from the Old Dominion Railway Museum (☎ 804-231-4324, www.odcnrhs.org; the Valentine Richmond History Center (☎ 804-649-0711, www.richmondhistorycenter.com); the Historic Richmond Foundation (☎ 804-360-1701, www.lets-get-frank.com); Richmond Discoveries (☎ 804-222-8595, www.richmonddiscoveries.com); and Richmond Walks (☎ 804-673-WALK).

Entertainment

As Virginia's capital, Richmond offers a diverse selection of nightlife and entertainment. From elegant dinner theaters to family playhouses, and from classical theater to modern ballet, there's something to suit every taste.

Barksdale Theatre is the Richmond area's oldest theater company, performing at Willow Lawn, Broad Street and Staples Mill Road. The company performs a mix of comedies, drama and musicals year-round. ☎ 804-282-2620 for schedules and information.

The Byrd Theatre, 2908 West Cary Street in Carytown, is a restored 1838 movie palace that retains the lavish décor of the period, features pre-movie music on a vintage Wurlitzer organ and still shows movies. ☎ 804-353-9911 for schedules and information.

The Concert Ballet of Virginia performs at the Woman's Club auditorium, Bolling Haxall House, 211 E. Franklin Street, ☎ 804-798-0945.

Elegba Folklore Society and Cultural Center stages performances of traditional African American dance and music. 101 E. Broad Street, ☎ 804-644-3900, www.efsinc.org.

Mystery Dinner Playhouse, Best Western Governor's Inn, 9826 Midlothian Turnpike, ☎ 804-649-2583. The audience helps solve the mystery while dining on a four-course meal.

The Richmond Ballet. ☎ 804-344-0906 for schedule and information.

Richmond Landmark Theater, at Laurel and Main streets, is an unusual theater that dates to 1927 when the opulent, Near Eastern-style building was erected for the Shriners. The theater presents Broadway productions, concerts and lectures. ☎ 804-780-4213 for schedules and information.

Richmond Symphony. ☎ 804-788-1212 for schedule and information.

Theatre IV, 114 West Broad Street, is one of Richmond's most honored and creative professional theaters. ☎ 804-344-8040 for schedules and information.

The Virginia Opera presents most of its productions at the Landmark Theater, 6 N. Laurel Street. ☎ 804-644-8168 or 866-673-7282 for schedules, tickets and information.

Recreation

Spectator Sports

Whether it's a baseball game or a day at the track, the Richmond area has it.

Colonial Downs features harness and thoroughbred racing, and polo. Exit 214 off I-64, east of Richmond in New Kent County, ☎ 804-966-RACE (7223), www.colonialdowns.com.

The **Richmond Braves** play AAA professional baseball at The Diamond, 3301 N. Boulevard, ☎ 804-359-4444, www.rbraves.com.

The **Richmond River Dogs** play ice hockey at the Richmond Coliseum, October-April. ☎ 804-225-7825, www.riverdogshockey.com.

Richmond International Raceway, Laburnum Avenue, Strawberry Hill, hosts NASCAR racing on a ¾-mile track. ☎ 804-345-RACE, www-.rir.com.

Richmond Kickers play soccer at the University of Richmond during the summer, ☎ 804-644-5425, www.richmondkickers.com.

Southside Speedway, Genito Road between Midlothian and Hull Street, hosts stock-car racing. ☎ 804-763-3567, www.southside-speedway.com.

Golf

There are more than 20 public courses in the greater Richmond area. A complete listing is available at www.visitrichmond.com, or call ☎ 888-RICHMOND.

Water Sports

The **James River Park System** offers boating, tubing, kayaking and canoe landings, nature trails, and fishing along the river. Boating access is at Huguenot Woods and Pony Pasture Rapids, both off Route 147 on the south side of the James at the western end of Richmond. On the eastern end, access is at Ancarrow's Boat on Maury Street, Exit 73 off I-95. This is also a historic site, a former slave trading dock. ☎ 804-646-8911.

Richmond Raft Company, 4400 E. Main Street, offers trips on Class I through Class IV whitewater on the James River. ☎ 804-222-7238, www.richmondraft.com.

Adventure Challenge, 8225 Oxer Road, ☎ 804-276-7600, offers whitewater, kayaking, tubing and rafting.

Shopping

There are several malls in the Richmond area including the new **Stony Point Fashion Park** (Regency Square, 1420 Parham Road, ☎ 804-740-7467, www.shopstonypoint-regencysquare.com) and **Short Pump Town Center** (11800 West Broad Street, ☎ 804-360-1700, www.shortpump-mall.com).

The Shockoe Slip, on East Cary Street between 12th and 14th Streets in the historic downtown district, offers shopping among Richmond's historic buildings and gaslit cobblestone streets.

Carytown, on West Cary Street, provides some eight blocks of shops, stores, restaurants and theaters adjacent to the historic Fan District.

The 17th Street Market, on 17th Street, has been in existence for more than 300 years. It's a farmer's market built on the site of an old Indian trading community, with a wealth of seasonal produce and flowers. Open daily, April through early December.Shockoe Bottom, 17th and Main streets, ☎ 804-646-0477, www.17thstreetfarmersmarket.com.

Annual Events

There are hundreds of interesting events held throughout the year in the Richmond area. Listed below are just a few of the major annual events. For a complete calendar, call the Richmond Convention and Visitors Bureau, ☎ 800-370-9004.

Maymont Flower & Garden Show is held in February at the Greater Richmond Convention Center, ☎ 804-358-7166, www.maymont.org.

The Historic Garden Week in Virginia, held in mid-April, features many private houses and gardens of historic interest that open their doors for the public to enjoy. More than 200 homes and gardens participate throughout the state. ☎ 804-644-7776, www.vagardenweek.org.

Bizarre Bazaar Spring Market is in early April, attracting nationally known crafters and artists, gifts and plants. Richmond Raceway Complex. ☎ 804-673-7015, www.thebizarrebazaar.com.

The **French Film Festival** takes place in early April at Virginia Commonwealth University's Byrd Theatre. ☎ 804-357-3456, www.frenchfilm-.vcu.edu.

Strawberry Hill Races in mid-April feature steeplechase racing at Colonial Downs. ☎ 804-569-3238, www.strawberryhillraces.com.

The **Dogwood Dell Festival of Arts** takes place weekends, May through August, at an outdoor amphitheater in Byrd Park. ☎ 804-646-1437, www.dogwooddell.org.

NASCAR comes to Richmond International Raceway in May and September. ☎ 804-345-RACE, www.rir.com.

Shockoe Tomato is a food and entertainment celebration in July at 17th Street Farmers' Market. ☎ 804-646-0477.

Carytown Watermelon Festival in mid-August is a food and music festival with a watermelon theme. ☎ 804-353-1525.

Down Home Family Reunion celebrates African-American life, music, dance, crafts and food. Held in mid-August at Abner Clay Park in Jackson Ward. ☎ 804-644-3900, www.efsinc.org.

The Virginia State Fair, held the last week in September at Richmond Raceway, includes animal and 4-H contests, music and entertainment, a horse show and a carnival. ☎ 804-569-3200, www.statefair.org.

The **National Folk Festival** features musicians on seven stages, food and crafts. Held on Brown's Island the second weekend in October. ☎ 804-788-6466, www.citycelebrations.org.

Richmond Highland Games and Celtic Festival is in late October at Richmond Raceway Complex; it features the US Celtic Nationals Hevy Scottish Athletic Competition. ☎ 804-569-3221, www.richmondceltic.com.

Craftsmen's Christmas Classic Arts & Crafts Festival brings 500 exhibitors in late October to Richmond Raceway Complex. ☎ 888-96-CRAFT, www.CraftShow.com.

The Grand Illumination and **James River Parade of Lights** are held in December. ☎ 804-344-3232, 804-706-1340.

Dining

There are hundreds of excellent restaurants, cafés and eateries in and around Richmond. The sampling listed here is only a small representation, with at least one restaurant from each neighborhood of the city. Half the fun of a visit to Virginia's capital is walking the historic cobblestone streets in search of the dining experience with a difference. For a complete listing, call the Richmond Convention and Visitors Bureau, ☎ 888-RICHMOND (888-742-4666), www.richmond.com/visitors.

Acappella, in the Patrick Henry Inn, 2300 East Broad Street, ☎ 804-377-1963, offers continental fare in an 1850s row house in Church Hill.

Farouk's House of India, 3033 West Cary Street, ☎ 804-355-0378, is open for lunch and dinner, takes reservations and offers an interesting and comprehensive menu at reasonable prices. Specialties of the house include curries and tandoori.

The Halfway House, 10301 Jefferson Davis Highway about 12 miles south on the way to Petersburg, ☎ 804-275-1760, is open for lunch and dinner, takes reservations and offers good American fare at reasonable prices. Specialties of the house include lobster, Colonial chicken and beef pies. The restaurant is in a Colonial manor house that was a stagecoach stop until the late 19th century. George Washington, Lafayette, Patrick Henry and Thomas Jefferson are only a few of the notables that stopped by.

Kuba Kuba serves up Cuban coffee, roast pork and paella in the Fan district. 1601 Park Avenue, ☎ 804-355-8817.

La Petite France, 2108 Maywill Street in the West End, ☎ 804-353-8729, www.lapetitefrance.net, is open for lunch and dinner and offers a wonderful French menu. Specialties of the house include seafood and veal.

Linden Row Inn, 100 East Franklin Street, ☎ 804-738-7000, is Southern cuisine at its best. Patio dining is available at this downtown antebellum landmark.

Mamma 'Zu serves innovative Italian cuisine in Oregon Hill, 501 S. Pine Street, Richmond, ☎ 804-788-4205.

Ma-Musu's West African Cuisine serves authentic, spicy fare. 2043 W. Broad Street, Richmond, ☎ 804-355-8063.

Morton's Steak House is part of a nationwide chain of elegant steakhouses serving martinis and fine wines. 111 Virginia Street in Shockoe Slip, ☎ 804-648-1662, www.mortons.com.

Poe's Pub, 2706 East Main Street, ☎ 804-648-2120, has an Irish pub atmosphere, but specializes in catfish and ribs.

Old Original Bookbinders is an institution in Shockoe Bottom, 2306 E. Cary Street, ☎ 804-643-6900.

O'Toole's, 4800 Forest Hill Avenue, ☎ 804-233-1781, is open for lunch and dinner and offers good wholesome food in an Irish pub atmosphere. The restaurant specializes in seafood, steak and barbecued dishes.

Sam Miller's Warehouse, 1210 East Cary Street in Shockoe Slip, ☎ 804-644-5465, is open for lunch and dinner. Specialties of the house include seafood, lobster and prime Western beef.

The Tanglewood Ordinary, in the far West End at 2210 River Road West, Maidens, ☎ 804-556-3284, offers casual family dining in a log cabin. Specialties of the house include fried chicken, black-eyed peas and ham.

The Tobacco Company Restaurant, 1201 E. Cary Street, ☎ 804-782-9555, www.thetobaccocompany.com, is a converted tobacco warehouse in Shockoe Slip. Specialties of the house include prime rib, fresh fish and home baking.

Accommodations

Here is a sampling of the more than 150 lodgings in the RIchmond area. For more, see www.richmond.com/visitors.

Hotels & Motels

The Berkeley Hotel, 1200 East Cary Street, ☎ 804-780-1300, www.berkeleyhotel.com, is a European-style hotel with 55 rooms. The management offers pool privileges, health club privileges, free valet parking and free airport and local transportation; there is a restaurant and in-room high-speed wireless Internet service. $$$$

Best Western Airport Inn, 5700 Williamsburg Road, Sandston, ☎ 804-222-2780, has 122 units, a pool, and free airport transportation. $

Courtyard by Marriott, 6400 West Broad Street, ☎ 804-282-1881, has 145 rooms, a full-service restaurant and café, a pool with poolside service, and an exercise room. $$

Crowne Plaza Richmond, 555 East Canal Street, ☎ 804-344-2900, is a large luxury hotel with 300 rooms, a full-service restaurant, bar and café, indoor pool, convention facilities, a concierge, a gift shop and exercise room. Free transportation to the airport and railroad station. $$$

Days Inn, 2100 Dickens Road, ☎ 804-282-3300, has 180 rooms, a swimming pool, playground and free continental breakfast. $

DoubleTree Richmond Airport, 5501 Eubank Road, ☎ 804-226-6400, has 160 rooms, most of them suites, a full-service restaurant, a swimming pool with poolside service, a café and free airport transportation. $$

Embassy Suites, 2925 Emerywood Parkway, ☎ 804-672-8585, www.embassysuites.com, has 226 suites, a swimming pool, an exercise room and a gift shop. $$

Holiday Inn Airport, 5203 Williamsburg Road, Sandston, ☎ 804-222-6450, is a large hotel with 230 rooms, a full-service restaurant, bar and café, a swimming pool with a lifeguard on duty, and free airport transportation. $$

Sheraton Richmond West, 6624 W. Broad Street, ☎ 804-285-2000, is a large luxury hotel with 372 rooms, a full-service restaurant, bar and café, a swimming pool with poolside service, a playground, lighted tennis courts, a gift shop and an exercise room. $$

 The Jefferson Hotel, 101 W. Franklin Street, ☎ 804-788-8000, www.jeffersonhotel.com, is a recently renovated luxury hotel with 275 rooms. There is a full-service restaurant, bar and café and several meeting rooms. The hotel also has a shopping arcade, tennis and golf privileges, a new indoor swimming pool a spa, and a famous staircase and 70-foot rotunda. $$$$

Linden Row Inn, 100 E. Franklin Street, ☎ 804-783-7000, www.linden-rowinn.com, has 70 rooms in several renovated 1840s Greek Revival townhouses. Courtyard gardens and a restaurant. $$

Marriott Richmond, 500 East Broad Street, ☎ 804-643-3400, is a large luxury hotel with 400 rooms, a full-service restaurant, bar and café, a swimming pool with poolside service and a lifeguard on duty and convention facilities. $$

Omni Richmond, 100 South 12th Street overlooking the James River, ☎ 804-344-7000, www.omnihotels.com, is a large luxury hotel with more than 360 units, a full-service restaurant, bar and café, a swimming pool with poolside service, convention facilities, a concierge, a shopping arcade and an exercise room. $$

 Quality Inn West End, 8008 West Broad Street, ☎ 804-346-0000, is a large hotel with 193 rooms, a swimming pool and complimentary continental breakfast. $

 Wyndham Hotel Richmond Airport, 4700 South Laburnum Avenue, ☎ 804-226-4300, has 151 a full-service restaurant, an indoor swimming pool, an exercise room a gift shop, a bar and a café. Free airport transportation. $$

Ramada Inn West, 1500 Parham Road, ☎ 804-285-9061, has 91 rooms, a restaurant and a swimming pool. $$

Ramada Southeast, 4303 Commerce Road, ☎ 804-275-7891, has 166 rooms, a full-service restaurant, a bar and café, a swimming pool and several meeting rooms. $$

Bed & Breakfasts / Inns

Emmanuel Hutzler House, 2036 Monument Avenue, ☎ 804-353-6900, offers four guest rooms, all with private bath, in a large 1914 home featuring stunning architectural details, leaded glass windows, mahogany paneling, and antiques and oriental rugs throughout. $$$

Patrick Henry Inn, 2300 East Broad Street, ☎ 804-644-1322, is an 1850s converted row house. There are three suites, all with private bath. Continental breakfast included. Restaurant offers lunch and dinner. Patio in rear. $$$

Richmond

The Virginia Cliffe Inn, 2900 Mountain Road, ☎ 804-266-7344, www.vacliffeinn.com, has three rooms, a suite and a cottage available, all with private bath. Reproduction of a famous historic home sits on six acres with gardens, a pond and waterfall. $$

William Catlin House, 2304 E. Broad Street, Church Hill, ☎ 804-780-3746, is a 1845 Greek Revival home with five guest rooms, three with private bath. Full breakfast served. $$

West-Bocock House, 1107 Grove Avenue in the Fan district, ☎ 804-358-6174, has three guest rooms, all with private bath. This 1871 historic home offers French linens, fresh flowers and a full breakfast at reasonable rates. $

Transportation

Richmond International Airport has daily flights with service by most major US carriers, and by several regional airlines. The airport is easily accessed via Intestates 95, 64 and 295. % 804-226-3000, www.fly-richmond.com.

The **Greyhound Lines** depot is minutes away from downtown at 2910 North Boulevard. ☎ 800-231-2222 for schedules and information.

Amtrak, located in the restored historic Main Street Station, provides eight trains daily that link with Washington DC and the northeast corridor. ☎ 804-646-MAIN, www.mainstreetstation.info.

Local bus service is provided by the **Greater Richmond Transit Company**, www.ridegrtc.com. Additional local transportation is provided by a number of taxi companies. Cab stands are at most major hotels, the airport, **Amtrak** and **Greyhound** terminals.

Information

For a free visitor's guide or assistance with hotel reservations, contact **The Richmond Convention and Visitors Bureau**, ☎ 804-782-2777, 888-RICHMOND, www.richmond.com, 401 N. Third Street, Richmond, VA 23219.

Richmond Region Visitor Center 405 N. Third Street, ☎ 804-784-7450, is open daily from 9 a.m. to 5 p.m. Another Visitor Center is located at Richmond International Airport, Exit 197 off Interstate 64, ☎ 804-236-3260. There is a **Welcome Center** on the Virginia State Capitol grounds, 101 N. Ninth Street, ☎ 804-786-4484.

Shenandoah Valley

Shenandoah – the name stirs the blood and conjures romantic images of a long-lost age of magnificence, grand country homes, horse-drawn carriages, elegant men with impeccable manners and beautiful ladies dressed in crinolines. And there's much more. It's an area of extraordinary natural beauty, of rushing rivers, broad meadows, and sweeping mountain vistas. Shenandoah, truly, is Virginia's crowning glory.

Front Royal & Warren County

Originally named Hell Town for all the wild and uproarious goings-on in the area, Front Royal, set in the magnificent Shenandoah Valley, attracts thousands of visitors every year. The area's beauty, combined with local lore and legend, continue to delight those who choose to visit. In addition to the scenic mountains, the valley and the fabled Shenandoah River, there are many local attractions, historic sites, golf courses and outdoor recreational opportunities. These include boating and fishing, hiking the Appalachian Trail and exploring Shenandoah National Park. Front Royal maintains 10 parks, playgrounds and a youth center as part of its own city park system.

Renowned for its hospitality since Colonial days, Front Royal offers a wide variety of accommodations and restaurants.

Those who enjoy shopping will find the town much to their liking. There are a large number of antique shops and the renovated downtown district is an attraction in its own right. Gift shops and crafts stores offer a variety of collectibles, area crafts and local produce, such as Virginia hams and apple products.

Sights

The **Warren Rifles Confederate Museum**, 95 Chester Street, houses a fine collection of relics and records of the Civil War. Exhibits include arms, battle flags, uniforms and accouterments, cavalry equipment, rare documents and pictures, personal and domestic items and memorabilia of Belle Boyd, Mosby's Rangers, Generals Jackson, Lee, Early, Longstreet, Turner Ashby and many more. The museum is open daily, April 15 through October 31, and by appointment from November through April 14. ☎ 540-636-6982.

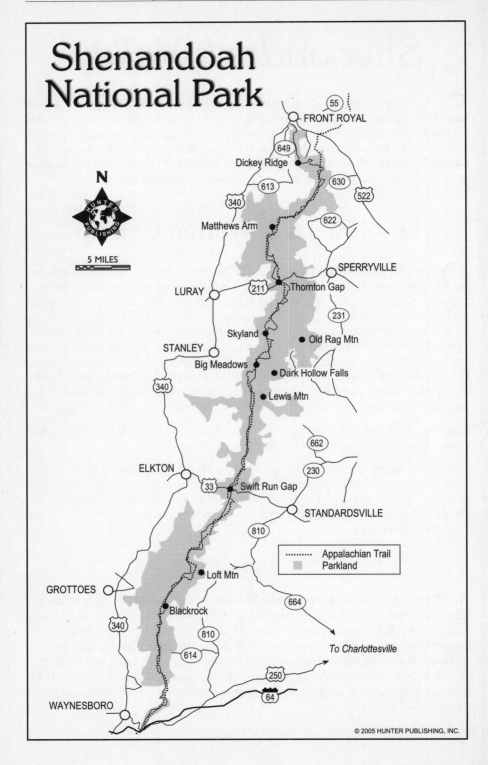

Shenandoah National Park

N

5 MILES

FRONT ROYAL
55
649
Dickey Ridge
613
630
340
522
Matthews Arm
622
SPERRYVILLE
LURAY
211
Thornton Gap
231
Skyland
Old Rag Mtn
STANLEY
Big Meadows
Dark Hollow Falls
340
Lewis Mtn
662
ELKTON
230
33
Swift Run Gap
STANDARDSVILLE
810
.... Appalachian Trail
Parkland
GROTTOES
664
Loft Mtn
To Charlottesville
340
Blackrock
810
614
250
64
WAYNESBORO

The **Belle Boyd Cottage**, 101 Chester Street, behind Ivy Lodge and next door to the Warren Rifles Confederate Museum, has served as a tavern, a private residence, military headquarters and a storeroom. During the Civil War the cottage was the home of Belle Boyd's aunt and uncle. Belle stayed in the cottage and used the opportunity to spy on Federal troops occupying the town. The old cottage has been restored as a living history museum depicting Warren County at the time of the Civil War. The cottage is open Monday, Tuesday, Thursday and Friday. ☎ 540-636-1446.

Prospect Hill Cemetery, on Prospect Street in Front Royal, is steeped in Civil War history. At the cemetery entrance stands a monument to Mosby's Rangers, commemorating the lives of seven men led by the daring confederate raider, John S. Mosby. The men were executed at the behest of Union General Ulysses S. Grant. At the top of Prospect Hill the remains of 276 soldiers are buried, representing each of the 13 Confederate states. Stonewall Jackson directed his troops from this spot during the Battle of Front Royal in May 1862.

Skyline Caverns, one mile south of the city on US 340, features rare rock formations, a 37-foot waterfall with light and sound presentations and a miniature train that provides trips through the surrounding wooded area. Cave tours start every few minutes and the caverns are open daily, year-round. ☎ 800-296-4545, www.skylinecaverns.com.

The **Raymond R. Guest Shenandoah River State Park**, on US 340 eight miles south of Front Royal, preserves six miles of river frontage on the Shenandoah River. There are 1,600 acres of camping, picnicking, hiking and boating here, as well as hiking trails. Admission charged. ☎ 540-622-6840.

Shenandoah National Park. Front Royal is where this magnificent national park system really begins. The great park boasts the unique combination of a protected mountain area plus inviting lodging and recreational amenities.

The 195,000-acre park is a hiker's paradise with many trails intersecting Skyline Drive. These trails vary in length from short hikes to trips that require 12 hours or more to complete. Skyline Drive, dedicated by President Franklin Roosevelt in 1939, takes in more than 100 miles of breathtaking mountain-top scenery from Afton in the south to Front Royal in the north along the crest of the Blue Ridge. The speed limit on Skyline Drive is 35 mph. ☎ 540-999-3500, www.nps.gov/shen.

Oasis Winery, 14141 Hume Road in the nearby town of Hume, boasts world-renowned champagne and sparkling wines, set amid breathtaking views of the Blue Ridge Mountains. Oasis offers wine tastings and food in its café, picnic areas, and outdoor heated patio. ☎ 540-635-7627, www.oasiswinery.com.

Front Royal & Warren County

Recreation

Water Activities

Front Royal Canoe Co., on Route 340, three miles past Skyline Drive, ☎ 540-635-5440 or 800-270-8808, runs float trips down the meanders of the Shenandoah River in kayaks, rafts or tubes. Bring the pet and fishing pole for a memorable ride. Open April through October. www.front-royalcanoe.com.

Shenandoah River Trips, on Indian Hollow Road (Route 613) in Bentonville, ☎ 800 RAPIDS-1, is 10 minutes from downtown Front Royal on a remote section of the South Fork of the Shenandoah River. This outfitter will put you on the renowned river to float, fish or run beginner rapids. Open April through October. www.shenandoah.cc.

Downriver Canoe Company, Indian Hollow Road (Route 613) in Bentonville, ☎ 800-338-1963, runs kayak and canoe trips on the Shenandoah River. A 10-minute drive from downtown Front Royal, Downriver offers both day trips or overnight river packages. www.downriver.com.

Golf

Blue Ridge Shadows, 7632 Winchester Road, Front Royal, ☎ 540-631-9661, www.blueridgeshadows.com.

Shenandoah Valley Golf Club, on Route 658, six miles north of I-66 at Exit 6, has 27 holes of championship golf set amid panoramic mountain views. The **Fairview House** on site offers bed-and-breakfast and golf packages. ☎ 540-636-GOLF, www.svgcgolf.com.

Bowling Green Country Club, on Bowling Green Road (Route 683) north of Front Royal, ☎ 540-635-2095, features two 18-hole courses open to the public.

Other Activities

Blue Ridge Hot Air Balloons, 552 Milldale Hollow Road, ☎ 540-622-6325, www.rideair.com, takes you high above the Blue Ridge Mountains and Shenandoah Valley for a bird's-eye view of the farms, apple orchards and small hamlets that hold so much of this region's charm. The trip ends with a toast of champagne or sparkling cider.

Town of Front Royal-Happy Creek Trail is for hikers and bicyclists. It begins on Main Street at the Happy Creek Bridge and runs a quarter-mile along Happy Creek.

Shopping

Main Street, Front Royal is lined with interesting shops selling gifts, antiques and curios.

Annual Events

The **Virginia Mushroom & Wine Festival** takes place the third Saturday of May. This is Front Royal's signature event, with crafters, wineries, art and mushroom vendors cramming the downtown historic district for a lively weekend. ☎ 800-338-2576.

The **Warren County Fair** runs the first week of August. ☎ 540-635-5827, www.warrencountyfair.com.

Riverfest makes education fun by mixing ecology and festival. The focus is the Shenandoah River, a massive, winding tributary of the Potomac River. There is food, regional art and wine. Held the third Saturday in June. ☎ 540-622-6840.

Dining

Flint Hill Public House, on Route 522 in the town of **Flint Hill**, ☎ 540-675-1700, is open for lunch and dinner, serving classic Virginia fare from a former public school house that dates back to the 1900s.

Jalisco Mexican Restaurant serves authentic Mexican fare. 510 S. Royal Avenue, ☎ 540-635-7348.

Main Grill and Sandwich Shoppe is right downtown and a good place for lunch. 117 E. Main Street, ☎ 540-636-3403.

Royal Oak Tavern serves seafood, pasta and steaks. 101 W. 14th Street, ☎ 540-551-9953.

Villa Giuseppe Italian Restaurant, 865 John Marshall Highway, ☎ 540-636-8999, serves good Italian food for lunch and dinner.

Accommodations

Accommodations in the Shenandoah National Park include the **Skyland Lodge**, ☎ 800-999-4714; **Big Meadows Lodge**, ☎ 800-999-4714; and **Lewis Mountain**, ☎ 800-999-4714.

Hotels & Motels

 Bluemont Inn, on Route 340, 522 and 55, ☎ 540-635-9447, has 28 guest rooms. Pets are welcome and free coffee is served each morning. $

Pioneer Motel, 541 S. Royal Street, near the north entrance to Skyline Drive, ☎ 540-635-4784, has 28 rooms. Next door are a swimming pool, picnic area and restaurants. $

The Quality Inn-Skyline Drive, at the end of Main Street, ☎ 540-635-3161, www.qualityinnfrontroyal.com, has more than 100 rooms, a full-service restaurant, café, bar, several meeting rooms and a pool. $

 Relax Inn – Front Royal, 1801 Shenandoah Avenue, ☎ 540-635-4101, has 20 guest rooms, a swimming pool, a picnic area, a playground and a café nearby. Children stay for free and pets are welcome. $

 Super 8 Motel, 11 South Street, ☎ 540-636-4888, has 63 rooms. Complimentary coffee and donuts are offered in the morning. $

Bed & Breakfasts / Inns

Killahevlin sits atop a hill at 1401 N. Royal Avenue, ☎ 540-636-7335, www.vairish.com, and will pamper you with Irish-style warmth and hospitality in a historic Edwardian mansion. Guest rooms come with whirlpool baths, fireplaces and mountain views. Round out your evening at a private Irish Pub on premises. $$$

Lackawanna Bed & Breakfast has three guest rooms in a farmhouse nestled on two acres between the North and South forks of the Shenandoah River. 236 Riverside Drive, ☎ 540-636-7945, www.lackawannabb.com. $$

At the **Woodward House**, 413 S. Royal Avenue, ☎ 540-635-7010, www.acountryhome.com, innkeepers Joan and Bob Kaye continue a hostelry tradition dating back to the 1930s in a historic Colonial-era home. There are three guest rooms and five guest suites, each with a private bath. Children are welcome with advance notice. A full breakfast is included with the room rate. Visit www.acountryhome.com for more information. $$

Camping

Front Royal RV Campground, adjacent to Skyline Drive and Shenandoah National Park, ☎ 540-635-2741, has 20 Kamping Kabins in resort-style setting. Kids can enjoy the waterslide.

Gooney Creek Campground, on Route 340, five miles south of Front Royal, ☎ 540-635-4066, has 45 campsites in a wooded setting for tents and RVs. There are full hook-ups for RVs, canoes for recreation and hot showers. It is open March through November.

Transportation

Washington Dulles International Airport and **Ronald Reagan Washington National Airport** outside of Washington DC provide long-range continental and international flights (www.metawashairports.com). The **Front Royal-Warren County Airport** houses companies offering airplane rides and sightseeing-by-air (☎ 540-635-3570).

Information

For more information about Front Royal and the Shenandoah Valley, including directions, points of interest, brochures, maps and lodging assistance, contact the **Front Royal Visitor Center**, in the historic train station at 414 East Main Street, Front Royal, VA 22630, ☎ 540-635-3185, www.frontroyalchamber.com.

Harrisonburg & Rockingham County

*B*ecause of their location in the heart of the Shenandoah Valley, Harrisonburg and Rockingham County are an ideal home base for quick trips to the unique stores, historical sites and museums in the area.

The busy city of Harrisonburg serves as the major financial and retail center for eight counties. In downtown Harrisonburg there are a number of unique specialty shops.

One of the downtown landmarks of Harrisonburg is the city's stately old limestone courthouse, built on land donated in 1779 by prominent area farmer Thomas Harrison. James Madison University is in the heart of Harrisonburg, where the bluestone buildings give the campus a distinctive, traditional look. Also in Harrisonburg is the Eastern Mennonite University and Seminary, an important partner in the spiritual foundation of the city.

The small towns that make up Rockingham County also offer some delightful shopping opportunities and experiences off the beaten path. The county is further known as one of the few remaining sources for primitive antiques.

Sights

The **Daniel Harrison House**, 335 Main Street in the town of Dayton, south of Harrisonburg, is also referred to as Fort Harrison. Built in 1749 by the brother of Thomas Harrison, the home features belonging of Harrison family descendants and is listed on the National Register of Historic

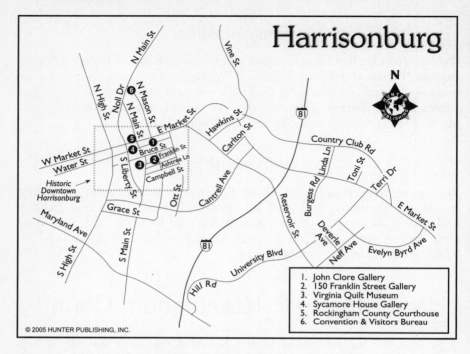

Harrisonburg

1. John Clore Gallery
2. 150 Franklin Street Gallery
3. Virginia Quilt Museum
4. Sycamore House Gallery
5. Rockingham County Courthouse
6. Convention & Visitors Bureau

© 2005 HUNTER PUBLISHING, INC.

Places. A newly renovated summer kitchen is available for tours. Seasonal festivals are also held here and tours are conducted on Saturdays and Sundays, May through October. Group tours are available by appointment throughout the year. ☎ 540-879-2280, www.heritagecenter.com.

Harrisonburg Children's Museum is a hands-on learning center for kids of all ages, 30 N. Main Street, Harrisonburg, ☎ 540-442-8900, www.hcmuseum.org.

The **Harrisonburg-Rockingham County Historical Society** at 382 High Street in Dayton houses the **Shenandoah Valley Folk Art & Heritage Center.** The center collects and preserves artifacts significant to the art and cultural life of the Valley. A huge, one-of-a-kind electronic map of Stonewall Jackson's Valley Campaign, in which more than 300 lights follow the movements of the Campaign, depicts this defining event in the region's history. There's also a genealogical library and a bookstore. It's open Monday, Thursday, Friday and on weekends. ☎ 540-879-2616, www.heritagecenter.com.

Virginia Quilt Museum, 301 S. Main Street, is a showcase for antique and contemporary quilts. Housed in the historic Warren Sipe house, the museum also houses research material for studying quilts and their role in culture and society. It is open on Monday, Thursday and Friday and on the weekend. ☎ 540-433-3818, www.vaquiltmuseum.org.

Court Square Theater in the Marketplace on Harrisonburg's Court Square is a year-round performing arts center featuring music, movies and live theater. ☎ 540-433-9189, www.courtsquaretheater.com.

The **Town of Bridgewater** was the setting for the flatboats loaded with pig iron from Miller's Iron Works on Mossy Creek. The boats were also laden with hides, skins and grain produced in the area. Everything was then floated downstream from Bridgewater to Port Republic, eventually ending up in Alexandria. Today, Mossy Creek is known for its fly-fishing. Bridgewater is also home to **Bridgewater College**, established in the 1880s and Virginia's first co-educational college.

The **Turner Ashby House**, also known as the Kemper House, is the home of the **Port Republic Museum**. This small town was a Civil War battleground, and the battlefield itself is in good condition. The museum preserves artifacts from the war, as well as exhibits and information relating to the bustling river history. It is open on Sunday afternoons, or by appointment. ☎ 540-249-5668.

Grand Caverns in Grottoes, a few miles south of Port Republic, opened in 1806, making it one of the oldest cave attractions in Virginia. Thomas Jefferson visited the system. When Stonewall Jackson and his troops came, they left their signatures on the cave walls. Visitors will see the caverns' rare "shield formations." Their formation is a mystery even today. Tours lasting an hour operate daily between April and October, on weekends the rest of the year. ☎ 888-430-2283, www.uvrpa.org.

Equal in awe-inspiring beauty to Grand Caverns are the rock formations at **Natural Chimneys Regional Park** in Mt. Solon, west of Harrisonburg near the town of Bridgewater. Today, it's difficult to imagine that the Shenandoah Valley was once the floor of a great inland sea. Millennia ago, when the sea receded, the awesome forces of nature carved out an incredible formation from the solid rock. The Natural Chimneys tower some 120 feet above the valley floor, a magnificent natural spectacle. Viewed from one angle, the mighty formations resemble enormous chimneys, standing in bleak contrast to the forests of the valley. From another angle, they resemble a medieval castle. Natural Chimneys Regional Park offers more than just the spectacle of mighty rock formations. Campers will also find plenty of activities. Open year-round. ☎ 888-430-2267, www.uvrpa.org.

Shopping

The Harrisonburg Farmers Market, in the Water Street parking deck, brings together a fine selection of the produce, baked goods and crafts produced in the county. It operates Tuesday and Saturday mornings. ☎ 540-433-1676.

Harrisonburg & Rockingham County

The Shoppes at Mauzy, off I-81 at Exit 257 near Mauzy, is a converted 1800s stagecoach inn now filled with shops and boutiques. There are antiques, furniture makers, dried flowers, candles, handcrafted items, local artwork and more. ☎ 540-896-9867.

Shenandoah Heritage Farmers Market, several miles south of Harrisonburg on Route 11, packs antiques, arts and crafts, furniture and Civil War memorabilia under an acre-sized building. Model train enthusiasts will find accessories here. If you're headed outdoors, there are also hunting, fishing and camping supplies. ☎ 540-433-3929.

Nearby, the **Dayton Farmers Market**, is another year-round source of antiques, folk art, home-baked goods and delicious country cooking. Open Thursday-Saturday. ☎ 540-879-3801, www.daytonfarmersmarket.com.

Suters Handcrafted Furniture, 2610 S. Main Street in Harrisonburg, features chairs, tables, hutches and other pieces of fine furniture. ☎ 540-434-2131, www.suters.com.

Recreation

More than 139,000 acres of the **George Washington National Forest** are found in western Rockingham County, and the county is bordered on the east by the **Shenandoah National Park**. The Forest and the Park are perfect for hiking, fishing, horseback riding and exploring nature's beauty and serenity. In addition, the Shenandoah National Park is home to **Skyline Drive**. The Swift Run Gap entrance to the Skyline Drive is in eastern Rockingham County, near Elkton.

Annual Events

Tour of Shenandoah Bicycle Race is a five-day race in late April drawing professional and top amateur cyclists from across the nation. ☎ 434-977-7146, www.tourofshenandoah.com.

The **Rockingham County Fair** runs for one week in August in Harrisonburg, 4808 South Valley Pike. Country elements such as livestock, horse shows, poultry exhibits and woodworking mix with a colorful midway and nightly country, bluegrass or gospel music headliners. For information on fair dates, admission and shows, ☎ 540-434-0005, www.rockinghamcountyfair.com.

The **Apple Butter Festival** in early September features all kinds of fresh homemade apple products at Skyland Resort. ☎ 800-999-4714.

Elkton Autumn Days Arts & Crafts Festival is in mid-October in front of the Elkton Elementary School, ☎ 540-298-9257.

Green Valley Bookfair, in the town of Mount Crawford south of Harrisonburg, features three floors of showroom space and a half-million new books filling two buildings. Open on select dates throughout the year. ☎ 800-385-0099, www.gvbookfair.com.

Dining

Boston Beanery Restaurant and Tavern, 1617 E. Market Street, Harrisonburg, ☎ 540-432-1870, www.bostonbeanery.com, offers casual lunch and dinner daily, serving big sandwiches and healthy portions of steak, seafood, and pasta.

Calhoun's Restaurant & Brewing Co., 41 Court Square, Harrisonburg, ☎ 540-434-8777, www.calhounsbrewery.com, serves lunch and dinner daily, and brunch on Sunday. Beer is brewed on the premises and the menu is an eclectic variety of American dishes.

Dave's Downtown Taverna serves Greek, Italian and American fare daily for lunch and dinner. 121 South Main Street, Harrisonburg, ☎ 540-564-1487, www.davestaverna.com.

L'Italia Restaurant serves traditional Italian fare with imaginative twists. Open daily for lunch and dinner. 815 East Market Street, Harrisonburg, ☎ 540-433-0961, http://litalia-restaurant.com.

Woodstone Deli & Pizzeria, at Massanutten Resort in McGaheysville, ☎ 540-289-4958, serves up some nice variations on the pizza-sub theme, with gourmet toppings and in-house specials on sandwiches. Also at the resort is Fareways, serving dinner ovelooking the golf course, ☎ 540-289-9431, ext. 5084.

Accommodations

Hotels & Motels

Comfort Inn, 1440 East Market Street, Harrisonburg, ☎ 540-433-6066, has 60 guest rooms, a heated pool and pets are allowed in the guest rooms. There is a complimentary continental breakfast and a senior citizen discount. $$

Courtyard by Marriott at 1890 Evelyn Byrd Avenue, Harrisonburg, ☎ 540-432-3031, has 125 guest rooms, a restaurant, lounge and meeting rooms, a fitness center and an indoor pool. $$

Econo Lodge, at Exit 247A on Interstate 81, Harrisonburg, ☎ 540-433-2576, has 89 guest rooms, a swimming pool and an exercise room. There is a complimentary continental breakfast. $

Hampton Inn, 85 University Boulevard, Harrisonburg, ☎ 540-432-1111, has 164 guest rooms, a swimming pool, and complimentary continental breakfast. $$

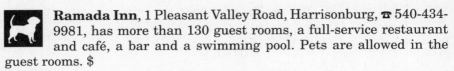

Ramada Inn, 1 Pleasant Valley Road, Harrisonburg, ☎ 540-434-9981, has more than 130 guest rooms, a full-service restaurant and café, a bar and a swimming pool. Pets are allowed in the guest rooms. $

Sheraton Four Points Hotel, 1400 East Market Street, Harrisonburg, ☎ 540-433-2521, is a well-appointed hotel with 138 guest rooms and suites, a full-service restaurant and café, a bar and two swimming pools with poolside service. Pets are allowed in the guest rooms. $$

Bed & Breakfasts / Inns

Apple Orchard Farm Bed & Breakfast, 4478 Donnelley Drive in Bridgewater, ☎ 540-828-2126, has five guest rooms, including a family suite. You get an impressive view overlooking the city and river from the front porch. Apple trees provide fruit for the breakfast pastries, hens lay eggs for breakfast and the innkeepers are always making breads and baked goods. $

Five minutes from Courthouse Circle, **By the Side of the Road Bed & Breakfast**, 491 Garbers Church Road, Harrisonburg, ☎ 540-801-0430, occupies the former home of Virginia's first Mennonite Bishop. There are five suites, each one with a private bath, television and VCR, a gas log fireplace and feather beds. Visit www.by-the-side-of-the-road-bb.com for more information. $$

Hearth N' Holly Inn, 46 Songbird Lane in Penn Laird, ☎ 540-434-6766, www.hearthnholly.com, has three guest rooms in a Colonial-style home built around the time of the Civil War. Although set amid rural surroundings, the inn is just 10 minutes from Harrisonburg. A full breakfast is served. $$

Joshua Wilton House Inn & Restaurant, 412 S. Main Street in Harrisonburg, ☎ 540-434-4464, www.joshuawilton.com, has five guest rooms, each with private bath. One of the few remaining Queen Anne Victorian-style homes left in the city, the inn is beautifully restored and decorated. It has two restaurants, one featuring fine dining, the other a café. It is conveniently located four blocks from both downtown and the college, JMU. $$

JoAnne's Bed & Breakfast, 4629 Bloomer Spring Road in Elkton, ☎ 540-298-9723, www.frederickfarm.com, is a private Shenandoah Valley farmhouse with comfortable rooms near Massanutten Resort (see below). $

The **Stonewall Jackson Inn Bed & Breakfast** near Old Town Harrisonburg is a restored mansion (circa 1885) reminiscent of stone and shingled New England cottages. There are ten guest rooms and a full breakfast is served. 547 East Market Street, Harrisonburg, ☎ 540-433-8233, 800-445-5330, www.stonewalljacksoninn.com. $$

Resort

Rockingham County is also the home of the **Massanutten Resort**, the perfect place for visitors to relax or find adventure. The resort, open year-round, is best known for its magnificent ski slopes, golf courses and its indoor sports complex. Visitors can also fish, swim, hike and ride horses. The resort is also known as a center for mountain biking. Lodging options range from hotel rooms to rental condos. ☎ 540-289-9441, www.massresort.com. $$$

Camping

Harrisonburg/New Market KOA, on Route 603 in Broadway, ☎ 540-896-8929, is a family-owned and operated campground set in the quiet, scenic woodland of the Shenandoah Valley. There are fullservices for RVs, including dump stations and LP gas, as well as cabins, a swimming pool, playground and tenting area.

Transportation

The **Shenandoah Valley Regional Airport** is in Rockingham County, ☎ 540-234-8304, www.flyshd.com; **Dulles International** and **Reagan Washington National Airports** provide continental and international service, www.metawashairports.com.

Information

For more information about Harrisonburg, Rockingham County and the Shenandoah Valley including directions, points of interest, brochures, maps and lodging assistance, contact the **Harrisonburg-Rockingham Convention and Visitors Bureau**, 10 E. Gay Street, Harrisonburg, VA 22801, ☎ 540-434-2319, www.hrcvb.org. Open 9 a.m. to 5 p.m. daily.

Lexington & Rockbridge County

*H*istoric Lexington, set deep in the rolling countryside of the Shenandoah Valley between the Blue Ridge and Allegheny Mountains, is the county seat of Rockbridge County. Lexington is known for its fine old mansions, two of the finest institutes of learning in the commonwealth and two of Virginia's greatest Confederate heroes. Robert E. Lee and Thomas J. "Stonewall" Jackson lived and are buried in the city.

Statesman Sam Houston was also born near Lexington. To the north of the city, Cyrus McCormick invented the mechanized reaper that revolutionized American agricultural production. General George C. Marshall was a graduate of the Virginia Military Institute in 1901. George Washington endowed the school now known as Washington and Lee University. Matthew Fontaine Maury, known as the Pathfinder of the Seas, was a professor at VMI. In 1774 Thomas Jefferson purchased the nearby Natural Bridge, one of the seven natural wonders of the world, and the landmark from which Rockbridge County takes its name.

Today, visitors to Historic Lexington receive a warm welcome to the old college town. The visitor center is the starting point for a self-guided walking tour. Exhibits at the center provide an introduction to the community and its heritage. Counselors can assist with information about area attractions, shopping, special events, recreation, accommodations and travel directions.

In Rockbridge County are the Theater at Lime Kiln, the Virginia Horse Center, Natural Bridge of Virginia, Goshen Pass, and Cyrus McCormick's Farm and Workshop. Buena Vista, just seven miles east of Lexington, is the home of Southern Virginia College, with its main building an 1890s hotel. Area recreational opportunities include hunting, fishing, hiking, white water canoeing, horseback riding, swimming, biking and camping.

Sights

Downtown Lexington. The downtown area of Lexington is a Virginia Historic District. The architecture at the center of the city is fascinating. Two buildings were designed by Thomas U. Walter, who designed the dome on the US Capitol Building. The downtown area offers a multitude of shopping opportunities from clothing to baked goods, and from local crafts to books. There are also several country inns and a number of fine restaurants. ☎ 540-463-3777, www.downtownlexington.com

The **Cyrus McCormick Farm and Workshop**, at Steeles Tavern just off Route 606, is where Cyrus McCormick invented the first mechanical reaper and revolutionized the world of agriculture. Visitors can view the blacksmith's shop, grist mill, museum and scenic site at the McCormick Farm, Walnut Grove. The Farm is open daily year-round. Admission is free. ☎ 540-377-2255.

The **George C. Marshall Museum**, at the Virginia Military Institute, is where you can see exhibits that trace the career of General Marshall, architect of the Marshall Plan, which provided aid to rebuild European countries devastated by World War II. A 25-minute presentation and map tell the significant events of the war. Visitors can also see General Mar-

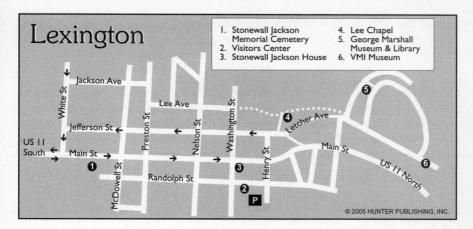

shall's Nobel Peace Prize and the Oscar won by General Frank McCarthy as producer of the movie *Patton*. Open daily except for Thanksgiving, Christmas and New Year's. ☎ 540-463-7103, www.marshallfoundation-.org.

Natural Bridge and Caverns, located on US 11 South, is one of the Seven Natural Wonders of the World. The bridge, once surveyed by George Washington and owned by Thomas Jefferson, is a rare site to behold. The Cedar Creek Trail takes visitors 215 feet below the bridge arch. After dark, you can enjoy the Drama of Creation sound and light show. The Natural Bridge site also includes a cavern with fabulous rock formations 34 stories beneath the earth, a zoo with more than 400 species and a petting area, and a wax museum with some 125 life replicas in scenes that incorporate sound, light and animation. There are lodging, conference and banquet facilities, and the Colonial Dining Room for a bite to eat. The Natural Bridge site is open daily. ☎ 540-291-2121, www.na-turalbridgeva.com.

The **Rockbridge Historical Society**, 101 E. Washington Street, offers a room-by-room tour through Campbell House, tracing the history of Lexington and Rockbridge County. Exhibits on Native Americans, early settlers, the Civil War-era and early 20th-century life fill the museum. Closed on Sundays and Mondays. Admission is free. Public gardens at the museum are open from dawn to dusk. ☎ 540-464-1058, www.rock-history.org.

The **Stonewall Jackson House** is at 8 E. Washington Street. Guided tours of the only home General Jackson ever owned interpret the man as a citizen of Lexington, a professor at the Virginia Military Institute, a church leader and family man. A five-minute slide show gives an idea of Jackson's life in Lexington. There's also a museum shop where you can purchase gifts. The house is open daily except Thanksgiving, Christmas, New Year's Day and Easter Sunday. ☎ 540-463-2552, www.stonewall-jackson.org.

The **Stonewall Jackson Memorial Cemetery**, on South Main Street, features the grave and a statue of the great Confederate general. The cemetery is also the resting place of more than a hundred Confederate veterans. It is open daily from dawn until dusk.

The Virginia Horse Center, on Route 39, is the site for various horse-related functions, including shows, auctions, educational clinics, workshops and a horse festival. A 4,000 seat coliseum hosts year-round events. Stables on site can house as many as 700 horses. ☎ 540-464-2950, www.horsecenter.org, for schedules and information.

The **Virginia Military Institute**. Founded in 1839, VMI is the oldest state-supported military college in the nation. The 12-acre parade ground is dominated by the barracks. A 15-point walking tour will take you past these imposing stone buildings and monuments. The entire complex is a designated National Historic District. Full dress parades are held most Friday afternoons during the school year. ☎ 540-464-7207, www.vmi.edu.

The VMI Cadet Museum, in the Jackson Memorial Hall at the Virginia Military Institute, features exhibits about the history and traditions of the Institute and includes Stonewall Jackson's war horse Little Sorrell, a replica of a cadet room, cadet rings and much more. The museum is open daily, except Thanksgiving, Christmas week and New Year's Day. Admission is free. ☎ 540-464-7232, www.vmi.edu/museum.

Washington and Lee University is a distinguished private non-denominational college with an enrollment of more than 1,800 students from all over the nation and many foreign countries. Named for George Washington and Confederate General Robert E. Lee, the college is a National Historic Landmark. Lee served as president of the school after the Civil War, from 1865 until 1870. He is buried in Lee Chapel on the college campus, which displays some of his personal and business effects, as well as the famous Charles Wilson Peale portrait of George Washington. Open daily throughout the year. ☎ 540-463-8768, www.leechapel.wlu.edu.

Military Memorabilia Museum, 122 S. Main Street, ☎ 540-464-3041, displays uniforms of the militaries of the United States, Great Britain, France and Germany. Open April through October, and year-round by appointment. Closed Sunday through Tuesday.

Tours

Art in Lexington Gallery Tours offers a walking tour of eight galleries in the downtown district. They begin at the Visitor Center, 106 E. Washington Street.

Carriage Tours of Lexington gives a 45-minute ride narrated by the carriage driver and tour guide. Tours run between April and October, except in bad weather, and begin across the street from the Visitors Center. Group tours are available. ☎ 540-463-5647.

Ghost Tour of Lexington is a 1½-hour twilight walk through the back streets and alleys of town, ending at the Stonewall Jackson Cemetery. For a real scare, try a Victorian-style séance re-creation (groups of 10 to 13 people only). Tours begin at the Lexington Visitor Center, Memorial Day weekend through October. ☎ 540-464-2250.

Military Tour of Historic Lexington is a suggested guide for visiting the buildings, monuments and museums that preserve this small town's military history. The 11-point tour begins at the Lexington Visitor Center. ☎ 540-463-3777.

Rockbridge Vineyard, 35 Hillview Lane in Raphine, ☎ 540-377-6204 or 888-511-WINE, www.rockbridgevineyard.com, produces award-winning vintages by winemaker Shepherd Rouse. Wines include Chardonnay, Tuscarora White and Red, Riesling and St. Mary's Blanc. Tours and tastings run May through October.

Entertainment

The **Theater at Lime Kiln**, located on Borden Road, is where master stonemasons once plied their trade and the kilns burned red-hot making lime. Today, actors and musicians delight audiences on pleasant summer evenings. The 12-acre site has three performance spaces; from May through October, stone ruins form the stage, the star-studded sky the roof; performances are presented indoors from November through April. ☎ 540-463-3074 or www.theateratlimekiln.com.

Annual Events

The **Annual Birthday Convocation** honoring Robert E. Lee is a birthday celebration for the former president of Washington and Lee University. Ceremonies are held at the University on his birthday, January 19th.

Stonewall Jackson's Birthday is celebrated at the Stonewall Jackson House where visitors are welcomed with birthday cake on January 21st.

Maury River Annual Fiddlers' Convention is held in June at the Glen Maury Park, featuring Old Time and bluegrass music, food and dancing. ☎ 540-261-2880.

Fourth of July Hot Air Balloon Rally is held Independence Day weekend at Virginia Military Institute. Food, fireworks, hot air balloon rides. 540-463-3777, www.lexingtonvirginia.com.

The **Rockbridge Community Festival**, held on the streets of Lexington the last Saturday in August, is an old-fashioned arts and crafts festival with music and events for children.

The **Rockbridge Regional Fair**, held at the Virginia Horse Center in late July, is a traditional country fair with livestock and farming exhibits. Events include an antique tractor pull, a horseshoe pitching contest, rodeo, horse show and car racing.

Recreation

Lexington, Rockbridge County and the Shenandoah Valley offer dozens of outdoor recreational opportunities. The following is only a sample. For a full list, call the Lexington Visitor Center, ☎ 540-463-3777.

Natural Areas

Woods Creek Park and **The Chessie Nature Trail** combine to form a park and pedestrian trail stretching from Lexington to Buena Vista. It's great for hiking, birdwatching, running, fishing, cross-country skiing and picnicking. There are playgrounds at the south end of Woods Creek Park in Lexington. An old canal lock on The Chessie Trail harkens back to days when boats plied the Maury and James Rivers for trading. Vehicles, including bicycles, are not allowed on the trail. A brochure is available at the Lexington Visitors Center. ☎ 540-463-3777.

Goshen Pass, on Route 39 12 miles north of Lexington, is a mountain gorge more than three miles long where visitors can enjoy such outdoor activities as fishing, swimming, tubing, canoeing, picnicking, nature watching and hiking on a trail that runs along the north side of the river. A brochure is available at the Lexington Visitors Center. ☎ 540-463-3777.

Water Sports

Swimming Areas are located at **Goshen Pass**, 12 miles west of Lexington on Route 39, and **Cave Mountain Lake**, on Route 781 six miles from Natural Bridge.

The **James River Basin Canoe Livery**, 1870 East Midland Trail (Route 60), offers canoeing for everyone. The center provides fast water or lazy paddling, big game fishing or spectacular scenery, a day out on the river or a place to go camping. The Livery is open from May 1st through September 30th. ☎ 540-261-7334 or visit www.CanoeVirginia.com.

Shopping

For the small town that it is, Lexington offers an enormous number of shops, art galleries, specialty stores and outlets. The downtown district has all sorts of opportunities for browsing, dining and just wandering the streets for an afternoon of antiquing. In the countryside, unique shops wait to be discovered. For a complete list of places to shop in Lexington and Rockbridge County, call the Lexington-Rockbridge Chamber of Commerce, ☎ 540-463-5375, www.lexingtonvirginia.com.

Dining

As befits a town with a colorful history, Lexington offers an array of fine dining choices. In downtown, more than 28 restaurants, cafés, bistros and lounges do business. Throughout Rockingham County visitors will find country-themed restaurants, many specializing in Southern cooking. For a complete list, ☎ 540-463-3777, www.lexingtonvirginia.com.

Blue Heron Café, 4 E. Washington Street, Lexington, ☎ 540-463-2800, is open for lunch during the week, and lunch and dinner on Friday and Saturday. The menu is diverse and ethnic. There's also a good selection of wines and micro-brewed beers. Closed on Sunday. Credit cards are not accepted. The restaurant is non-smoking.

The **Colonial Dining Room** at Natural Bridge serves buffets and prime rib, ☎ 540-291-2121, www.naturalbridgeva.com. Open daily for breakfast and dinner.

Country Cookin', 439 E. Nelson Street, Lexington, ☎ 540-463-3044, is open for lunch and dinner daily. This family restaurant serves hearty portions.

Maple Hall Dining is located in an 1850 home at 3111 N. Lee Hwy, Lexington, ☎ 540-463-4666, www.lexingtonhistoricinns.com. Open for dinner Monday-Saturday.

Sheridan Livery Inn Restaurant, 35 N. Main Street, Lexington, ☎ 540-464-1887, www.sheridanliveryinn.com, offers fine dining for lunch and dinner. There's a lounge and an outside patio for casual dining.

The **Southern Inn Restaurant**, 37 S. Main Street, Lexington, ☎ 540-463-3612, is open for lunch and dinner. The restaurant, in an 1828 storefront, offers Southern cuisine and a diverse wine list. Live music on Thursday and Friday.

The Willson-Walker House, 30 N. Main Street, Lexington, is in a fine old Greek-revival house, ☎ 540-463-3020, www.wilsonwalker.com. Open for lunch and dinner. Specialties of the house include medallions of veal and fresh seafood. Outdoor dining from May through October; closed on Monday.

Lexington & Rockbridge County

Accommodations

Hotels & Motels

Best Western Inn at Hunt Ridge, 25 Willow Springs Road, Lexington, ☎ 540-464-1500, has 100 guest rooms, a full-service restaurant, plus a lounge and an outdoor pool. Guest laundry service is available. $

 The **Comfort Inn**, at the junction of US 11 and Interstate 64, Lexington, ☎ 540-463-7311, has 80 rooms, an indoor swimming pool and a view of the mountains. Pets are allowed in the guest rooms. Complimentary continental breakfast is offered. There is a restaurant next door. $$

 Days Inn, one mile west of Lexington on US 60, Lexington, ☎ 540-463-2143, has 53 rooms, a restaurant and café, bar, meeting room, and picnic tables with a view of the mountains. Pets are allowed in the guest rooms. $

Hampton Inn Col Alto, 401 East Nelson Street, Lexington, ☎ 540-463-2223, www.hamptoninnlexington.com, has 76 rooms in a 19th-century manor home, set in seven-acres of parklike grounds, within walking distance of downtown. Continental breakfast is served daily. There is an outdoor pool and Jacuzzi. The staff will arrange carriage rides through town for guests. $$

 Holiday Inn Express, one mile north of Lexington on US 11, Lexington, ☎ 540-463-7351, has 72 rooms. Continental breakfast; pets allowed in the rooms. $$

Howard Johnson, six miles north of Lexington on US 11, Lexington, ☎ 540-463-9181, has 100 rooms. It offers a restaurant, café, swimming pool, meeting and banquet facilities. The hotel is located on a hillside and offers magnificent views of the mountains. Handicapped-accessible and non-smoking rooms available; pets allowed in the guest rooms. Senior citizen discount. $-$$

Natural Bridge Hotel is an historic Colonial-style brick hotel, with additional lodging in more casual cottages, at Natural Bridge. ☎ 800-533-1410, www.naturalbridgeva.com. $

 Ramada Inn, 2814 North Lee Highway, Lexington, ☎ 540-463-6400, has 80 rooms, a full-service restaurant and café, a bar, a heated indoor swimming pool and several meeting rooms. Pets permitted. $

Sheridan Livery Inn is in an 1887 building with nine rooms and three suites in downtown Lexington. 35 N. Main Street, ☎ 540-464-1887, www.sheridanliveryinn.com. $

Bed & Breakfasts / Inns

Lexington makes a serious bid for the designation "Bed and Breakfast Capital of Virginia." More than 40 inns cater to the whims of those visiting Lexington and surrounding towns. Listed below is a sampling of fine inns. For a complete list, contact the **Lexington-Rockbridge County Chamber of Commerce**, ☎ 540-463-5375.

A B&B At Llewellyn Lodge, 603 South Main Street, Lexington, ☎ 540-463-3235 or 800-882-1145, www.llodge.com, is a convenient in-town bed and breakfast within walking distance of the historic district and colleges. There are six guest rooms, each with a private bath, and a full breakfast served. Innkeepers Ellen and John Roberts offer golf, fishing and horseback riding packages. Visit www.llodge.com. $$

The **Applewood Inn & Llama Trekking**, Buffalo Bend Road, Lexington, ☎ 540-463-1962 or 800-463-1902, www.applewoodbb.com, is a short drive up scenic Buffalo Creek to a solar-powered home set amid 35 acres of private, hilly acres. Hiking, llama treks, a pool and hot tub await guests staying in the inn's four rooms, each with private bath. Innkeepers Linda and Christian Best will provide a picnic lunch or dinner with notice. $$

Brierley Hill B&B Inn, 985 Borden Road, Lexington, ☎ 540-464-8421 or 800-422-4925; sits five minutes from downtown Lexington on a sweeping eight acres with views of the Blue Ridge Mountains. There are five rooms, each with a private bath, and children over 14 are welcome. Visit www.brierleyhill.com for more information. $$

Historic Country Inns of Lexington, 11 North Main Street, Lexington, ☎ 540-463-2044, www.lexingtonhistoricinns.com, consists of three inns, each furnished with period antiques. The rate includes a continental breakfast, and the guests have pool and tennis privileges. $

Nestled between Lexington and Warm Springs is the small town of Goshen, on scenic Route 39 and 42 in northwest Rockbridge County. There you'll find the **Hummingbird Inn** at 30 Wood Lane, ☎ 540-997-9065 or 800-397-3214. The inn offers five guest accommodations, each with a private bath, in a Victorian setting. Candlelight dinner by reservation. Visit www.hummingbirdinn.com for more information. $$

Lavender Hill Farm B&B, 1374 Big Spring Drive, Lexington, ☎ 540-464-5877 or 800-446-4240, offers guests the choice of two rooms or a suite, all with private bath, in a restored 1790 working sheep farm. This outdoor get-away offers guests a chance to hike or fish, ride horses or just relax. Visit www.lavhill.com for more information. $$

Stoneridge Bed & Breakfast, Stoneridge Lane, Lexington, ☎ 540-463-4090 or 800-491-2930, www.webfeat-inc.com/stoneridge, is an 1829 Federal plantation home with five guest rooms, each with private bath.

Tucked in a wooded setting, the inn is just minutes from downtown Lexington. $$

Sugar Tree Inn is a log lodge on 28 acres at 2,800 feet. Rustic elegance with woodburning fireplaces and fine dining. Highway 56, Steeles Tavern, ☎ 800-377- 2197, www.innkeeper@sugartreeinn.com. $$$

Camping

Lake A. Willis Robertson, on Route 770 in nearby Collierstown, is a 31-acre lake and recreational area where you can camp, fish and swim. Facilities and amenities include sites with water and electric hookups, a swimming pool, a bathhouse, a comfort station with flush toilets and showers, mountain hiking trails, tennis courts, picnic areas, a group shelter and a playing area. The campground is open from March through October. ☎ 540-463-4164.

The Glen Maury Park and Campground, 2039 Sycamore Avenue in Buena Vista, is set on 315 acres of rolling land with more than a mile of river frontage. Facilities at the park include camping sites, an Olympic-size swimming pool, hiking and nature trails, ball fields, tennis courts, picnic areas and covered picnic shelters. Volunteers are restoring a 19th-century farmhouse, The Paxton House, which is listed in the Virginia Landmarks Register and the National Register of Historic Places. Open mid-March through mid-November. ☎ 540-261-7321, www.glenmaury.com.

Cave Mountain Lake Recreation Area, on Route 781 in Natural Bridge Station, 20 miles southeast of Lexington, ☎ 540-291-2188, has 42 campsites. There are no hookups for RVs, and trailers over 22 feet are not allowed. Operated by the Jefferson National Forest. Open May to October.

Long's Campground, 82 Campground Lane, five miles west of Lexington, ☎ 540-463-7672, has 45 sites with full hookups for RVs. The camp store has a pool, game room, laundry and playground. There is an 18-hole miniature golf course on site. Open March to December.

Natural Bridge/Lexington KOA Campground, 11 miles south of Lexington off Exit 180 (north) of I-81, ☎ 540-291-2770, www.naturebridgekoa.com, has Kamping Kabins and large pull-through sites for RVs, a store, laundry, recreation room, pool, bike rentals and playground. Meals are served every night to campsites.

Tye River Gap Campground, 1932 Tye River Turnpike in Vesuvius, ☎ 540-377-6168, www.tyerivergap.com, is a mile west of the Blue Ridge Parkway at Milepost 27. Campsites are wooded and there is a separate area for tents. There is a camp store, hot showers, laundry, game room, playground and swimming pool. Open March through November.

Transportation

Lexington and Rockbridge County are served by the **Roanoke Regional Airport** (www.roanokeregionalairport.com), with service offered by most major and regional carriers direct or with connections to all major domestic and international destinations.

Information

For information, brochures and a full list of area restaurants and hotels, contact the **Lexington Visitor Center** at 106 East Washington Street. Lexington, VA 24450, ☎ 540-463-3777, www.lexingtonvirginia.com. Open daily, 9 a.m. to 5 p.m.

Hot Springs & The Homestead

That Virginia's top-ranked golf course and resort exists very much off the beaten track is due to a geologic phenomenon – mineral hot springs bubbling up from the Allegheny Mountains.

Native Americans first discovered the rejuvenating properties of the 104° waters. Today the Homestead is a world-class golf, spa and ski resort.

The first lodging known as Homestead was built at Hot Springs in 1766 by Thomas Bullett, a friend of George Washington. Since then 14 presidents have visited the various incarnations of the resort. Their portraits hang in the President's Lounge, from Washington to Bill Clinton. Order a cocktail or glass of fine wine, and simply soak in the ambience.

An infusion of restoration funds from current owner, the Pinehurst Company, brought the Homestead back to its status as a world-class resort in the 1990s. The pool, built in 1903, is recently renovated with new locker rooms and a new spa reception area where guests can get a mineral bath, Swedish massage, herbal wrap or salt scrub. There's a fitness center, a salon, and a full-sized bowling alley.

Recreation

Even as the age-old traditions of formal dining and dancing every night are maintained in the main dining room, the Homestead is catering to a new breed of travelers who may not want to wear a coat and tie to dinner, or even play golf. The resort has teamed up with Orvis to offer fly-fishing instruction and guides (April through mid-August) through the Homestead's Allegheny Outfitters. Daily-guided hikes on Homestead-owned trails, mountain bike tours, caving excursions, and canoe and kayak trips on the Jackson River or Lake Moomaw depart from the outfitter, located in Cottage Row at the foot of the Homestead. They'll even organize paintball games, extreme golf, or a day on the challenge course, and rent mountain bikes for the whole family. ☎ 540-839-7760, www.thehome-stead.com.

The Homestead's 15,000 acres and 100 miles of trails could keep you busy hiking for quite some time. The Cascades Trail is a two-mile easy hike passing 13 waterfalls, across bridges and ending at the Cascades Club-house for lunch and a shuttle back to the hotel. Access is by a Homestead guide only and a fee is charged. The local guide unloads a wealth of infor-mation about the flora and fauna along the trail, from beaver activity, to why the hemlock trees are dying, to what plants are edible (the wild wa-tercress is delicious, and the Homestead uses it abundantly in its menus). Spring brings a profusion of wildflowers - trout lily, trillium, and pink and yellow Lady's Slippers. There are also three self-guided, well-groomed trails, ranging in difficulty from moderate to strenuous.

Families are catered to in every way. KidsClub provides programs for ages 3-12. There's a movie theater, four tennis courts, horseback riding and evening hayrides to a bonfire to cook s'mores. There are nine down-hill ski runs, day and night skiing, a ski school, and an Olympic sized skating rink.

Shopping

Inside the Homestead are the Tower Corridor Shops, a row of upscale boutiques with unique gifts and books. Cottage Row is a half dozen for-mer summer rental cottages, nestled at the base of the Homestead. Here are several clothing boutiques, a garden shop and Allegheny Outfitters where you get all the gear you need for your fly-fishing, hiking or moun-tain biking trip.

Just across the road, the village of Hot Springs has several gift shops and eateries, a market and a pharmacy.

Dining

Choices in dining at the Homestead include the **Dining Room** with fin-ger bowls and live music, the **Casino Club Restaurant** with patio din-ing, the **1766 Grille**, the **Players Pub**, and **Sam Snead's Pub** in town. Named for the famed golfing native of Hot Springs who passed away in 2002 in his 90s, the pub has a rustic golfing motif, fireplaces, exposed wooden beams and cozy booths in a renovated bank building (the bank vault now holds wine instead of cash). There are also restaurants at the Cascades and Lower Cascades golf courses, and the Mountain Lodge at the ski mountain. Even if you balk at the evening coat-and-tie require-ment in the Dining Room, the breakfast buffet is to-die-for and requires only "resort attire." They serve the biggest raspberries and blackberries ever seen. For all Homestead restaurants, call ahead for reservations and dress codes. ☎ 540-839-7989.

Lodging

The Homestead has 518 rooms, including 81 suites, all with terrycloth robes, mini-bars, two-line speakerphones with voice mail and data port, TV and VCR with movies on demand. Amenities include golf, fitness center, indoor pool, spa, skiing, hiking, bowling, valet parking, shuttle service, and nightly movies in the turn-of-the-century theater. Lodging ranges from cozy standard rooms to luxurious and spacious suites with fireplaces and balconies. Rates are per person, with some plans that include dinner, breakfast and afternoon tea. Off-season and weekday rates are available, ☎ 800-838-1766, 540-839-1766, www.thehomestead-.com.

Event

A Taste of Bath features a dozen area restaurants, live bluegrass music, fine arts and heritage crafts in downtown Hot Springs in early September. Bath County Chamber of Commerce, ☎ 800-628-8092, www.bath-countyva.org.

Shenandoah & Page Counties

As the Shenandoah Valley rolls through western Virginia, it bumps up against Massanutten Mountain. In the shadows of this imposing, needle-shaped ridgeline sit Shenandoah and Page counties, with histories stretching back to before the Revolutionary War. Here, more than any other part of the Shenandoah Valley, visitors may sense the life of farmers, artisans and townsfolk who work and live off the land.

Shenandoah County, anchored at its southern end by New Market, covers the western slope of Massanutten and is known for battlefields, small town museums and century-old buildings, as well as for producing high quality folk art and pottery, fine furniture and wines. Page County, on the eastern slope, is centered around the town of Luray, a major travel center for the region with hotels convenient to area attractions.

Settled primarily by German immigrants who poured south out of Pennsylvania looking for farmland and a new place to live, these two counties burst with natural beauty. Deep caverns burrow into the limestone foundations of the surrounding mountains. Massanutten rises to heights of 3,000 feet and more. Here, and in nearby Basye, four-season resorts offer golf, biking, skiing and water activities. The North Fork of the Shenandoah River passes within a mile of Woodstock, allowing for paddling, fishing and other water activities. The George Washington National Forest protects land for timber and natural gas resources, as well as recreation. Across the valley, Luray is a gateway to Shenandoah National Park.

For generations, the region's rich soil produced wheat by the bushel. Shenandoah County was the "breadbasket of the Confederacy," supplying hungry Southern soldiers with food. Today, agriculture maintains a strong presence in the form of poultry farms and apple orchards.

The Old Valley Pike, now called Route 11, wends its way through the western valley created by Massanutten and the Alleghenies. This north-to-south route dates back to the Civil War, when troops passed over its macadam surface en route to their destiny at Antietam, Gettysburg and other bloody battles. Towns along this road witnessed fighting first-hand. Their old buildings, antique shops and museums, hold rich stores of history, folk art and crafts, and music. There are several artist-owned galleries where visitors can see artisans at work. And you're never far from a quality bed and breakfast inn.

Strasburg heralds itself as the "antique capital of Virginia." Georgian and Victorian-style homes line the neighborhood streets of Woodstock, the county seat for Shenandoah County. Woodstock's 1795 stone courthouse is the oldest still in use west of the Blue Ridge Mountains. President Andrew Jackson made Mount Jackson a frequent stop en route to Washington DC from his home in Tennessee, prompting townsfolk to name it in his honor. The Meems Bottom Covered Bridge straddles the Shenandoah River at 191 feet high at Mount Jackson. Edinburg was once a regional trading center and Orkney Springs, just West of Bryce, hosts a popular annual music festival. Toms Brook and Maurertown were the sites of two battles during the Civil War, now preserved as parks.

In an area where natural beauty and history are almost commonplace, the countryside of Shenandoah and Page counties offer visitors an unspoiled link to the past.

Sights

Civil War battlefields and roadside historic markers scattered throughout the northern Shenandoah Valley preserve the legacy of near-continuous fighting that occurred here. Confederate generals used the valley twice to penetrate the northern states – advances that were twice repelled, at Antietam Creek and at Gettysburg. In between, the North and South fought skirmishes and pitched battles resulting in thousands of lost lives.

❖ *Between Strasburg and New Market stand memorials to several battles and encampments. There is a study center for Civil War history at Hupp's Hill, a rail depot and museum in Strasburg, a Confederate generals' headquarters at Belle Grove Plantation and an interpretive center at Cedar Creek. The* **Civil War Trails** *program highlights significant sites in the region.* ☎ *888-CIVIL WAR for more information.*

Crystal Caverns at Hupp's Hill is located north of Strasburg on Route 11. This is the oldest cavern in the region. It is operated as a museum, rather than a tourist destination. Like other large caves in this region, it displays impressive rock formations. A lantern-led tour adds an element of underground mystery. There is a quarter-mile trail and an interpretive museum. ☎ 540-465-5884.

Edinburg Madison District Museum & Visitor Center, 214 Main Street in the restored Edinburg Mill, preserves a collection of tools, products and information relating to the Shenandoah Telephone Company, as well as an old printing press and other memorabilia. It is open daily. ☎ 540-984-8521, www.town.edinburg.va.us.

The **Endless Caverns**, off I-81 at Exit 257 in New Market, ☎ 540-896-CAVE, www.endlesscaverns.com, are hard to miss. The Hollywood-style sign sits high on the mountain and is visible for miles. This cave system is well known for its complex rock formations and has never been fully mapped; no one has ever reached the cavern's end.

Hall of Valor Civil War Museum, at the New Market Battlefield State Historical Park on Route 305, recounts the Battle of New Market. Soldiers for the North and South, including a unit of college-aged cadets from the Virginia Military Institute, fought for several days among the apple trees and fields of the Bushong Farm. A diagram in the museum illustrates the strategies and sacrifices of both sides. The museum is closed Thanksgiving, Christmas and New Year's Day. ☎ 540-740-3101.

Luray Caverns, off I-81 at Exit 264, was formed over the course of 400 million years. Today, visitors pass by massive stone columns and pools in cathedral-sized rooms with 10-story high ceilings. An organ with pipes made of stalactites fills the cave with haunting sounds. Above ground there is a historic car and carriage museum, the Luray Singing Tower, a café and a gift shop. Guided tours are available. Open year-round. ☎ 540-743-6551 , or visit www.luraycaverns.com.

Luray Zoo, I-81 Exit 264. US 211 East, ☎ 540-743-4113 www.luray-zoo.com. Luray is a rescue zoo, home to birds of prey, exotic cats, mammals and reptiles from around the world. Boasts one of the largest venomous snake collections. Open April-October, 10 a.m.-5 p.m. daily. Open November through March, weekends and holidays. Live animal shows daily in summer. Jungle Gift Shop and petting zoo. *Crocodile Hunter* came to Luray Zoo to film for their TV show!

Mount Jackson Museum, a short walk from the Union Church behind Town Hall, chronicles the efforts of Mount Jackson townsfolk, who dedicated themselves to identifying 400 Confederate soldiers buried in nearby Old Soldiers Cemetery. It is the only cemetery in Virginia where only Confederate dead are buried. Many of the soldiers died at a hospital that opened here during the Civil War. The museum is open Thursday-Sunday, year-round. ☎ 540-477-3951.

Museum of American Presidents, 139 N. Massanutten Street in Strasburg, houses the impressive collection of one man, Leo Bernstein, who has spent a half-century collecting items relating to the presidency. Autographs from half the signers of the Declaration of Independence and most of America's 42 presidents are displayed, as well as election minutia and White House novelties, like the doors removed from the White House during Harry S. Truman's administration. Children can dress up in period costumes and play in a Colonial-era classroom. ☎ 540-465-5999.

New Market Battlefield State Historical Park, Collins Drive, New Market, ☎ 540-740-3101, www.vmi.edu/newmarket is a 280-acre battlefield, museum and historic farm with a blacksmith shop, loom house and summer kitchen. Open daily 9 a.m. to 5 p.m.

Shenandoah Caverns, two minutes from I-81 off Exit 269, four miles north of New Market, is another of the region's commercialized caves – albeit the only one with an elevator. Descending into the limestone depths of the Blue Ridge Mountains, visitors emerge into wide, expansive rooms with vaulted ceilings and impressive displays of flow rock, bacon and dome rock formations that earned this cave national recognition. For children, the cavern produces a parade featuring circus acts and Cinderella's pumpkin carriage. Open year-round. ☎ 540-477-3115, www.shenandoahcaverns.com.

At the **Stonewall Jackson Museum** at Hupp's Hill on Route 11 just north of Strasburg, the legacy of the Confederate general's Valley Campaign during the Civil War is on display. Considered a master tactician, Jackson directed the defense of the Valley in 1862 from invading Northern forces. It is said that American generals studied his work intensely in the days leading to World War II. Weapons, documents and Civil War regalia are on display. ☎ 540-465-5884.

The Strasburg Museum, on West King Street, exhibits the art and craft history of Pot Town, as Strasburg is nicknamed, and houses collections relating to blacksmiths and barrel makers. The museum building itself is an old steam potters factory listed on state and national historic registers. It is open daily May through October. Admission is free. ☎ 540-465-3175.

Woodstock Museum, 137 W. Court Street, inside the historic 18th-century Wickham House, preserves artifacts and documents important to the community's history. It is open May through September on Thursday, Friday and Saturday, and by appointment. Admission is free. ☎ 540-459-5518.

Annual Events

Mount Jackson Heritage Day is the first Saturday in May on Main Street, Mount Jackson. ☎ 540-477-3275 or www.mountjacksonva.org.

Wildflower Weekend in Shenandoah National Park is the fist weekend in May, near Luray. ☎ 540-999-3500, www.nps.gov/shen.

Strasburg Mayfest is the third weekend in May and features baseball, crafts, food, a carnival, parade and car show. ☎ 540-465-3187, www.strasburgva.com.

The **Battle of New Market** re-enactment is in May, ☎ 540-740-3101, vmi.edu/museum.nm.

The **Shenandoah Valley Music Festival** is held in Orkney Springs, bringing artists and different styles of music to the mountains over five weekends in the summer. The lineup has featured symphonic music, bluegrass and Latin music, as well as a juried arts and crafts show. ☎ 800-459-3396 or visit www.musicfest.org.

Annual Butterfly Count in Shenandoah National park takes places in early July, near Luray. ☎ 540-999-3282, www.nps.gov/shen.

The **Shenandoah County Fair** is held in late August featuring harness racing, tractor pulls, livestock exhibits, rides and live music. ☎ 540-459-3867, www.shencofair.com.

Bluegrass in the Blueridge Music Festival brings well-known artists as well as jammers to the Luray Shrine Club the first weekend in August. ☎ 615-337-8166.

Edinburg Olde Time Festival in downtown Edinburg brings crafters and special events to town during September. ☎ 540-984-8521.

The **Page County Heritage Festival** is held during October in Luray. ☎ 540-743-3915, www.luray.com.

Shenandoah Jubilee Christmas Show in early December features holiday songs and a parade at Shenandoah Caverns. ☎ 540-778-1933, www.shenandoahjubilee.com.

Christmas in Edinburg is a town-wide celebration every Saturday in December. ☎ 540-984-8318. www.edinburgchamber.com.

Recreation

Golf

Shenvalee Golf Resort, on Fairway Drive off US 11 in New Market, ☎ 540-740-3181, www.shenvalee.com, features 27 holes of golf within view of the Blue Ridge Mountains. First opened in 1927, this is a full-service resort with lodging and fine dining available, as well as a pool and lounge.

Bryce Resort, west of Mount Jackson on Route 263 in the town of Basye, ☎ 540-856-2121, www.bryceresort.com, is a four-season resort with an

18-hole championship golf course, as well as snow and grass skiing, tennis, horseback riding and a lake for water sports.

Caverns Country Club Resort, in Luray, ☎ 540-743-7111, www.luraycaverns.com, is a 27-hole golf course set in the shadows of the Blue Ridge Mountains, in the vicinity of Luray Caverns.

Water Sports

Page Valley Fly Fishing Service, 44 Carillon Drive., Luray, 540-743-7952, http://pagevalleyflyfishing.com

Lake Arrowhead is a 34-acre mountain lake for swimming, fishing and walking. Open year round, sunrise to sunset.

Shenandoah River's south fork flows through the entire length of Page County, offering canoeing, tubing, fishing and swimming.

Shenandoah River Outfitters, north of Luray on Route 684, ☎ 540-734-4159 or 800 6CANOE2, takes visitors on some of the Shenandoah River's most scenic stretches. You can canoe, kayak or tube the legendary river. Spend the night in cabins or river cottages and end your day with a steak dinner. Visit www.shenandoahriver.com for more information.

Horseback Riding

Fort Valley Stable, ☎ 888-574-5771, www.fortvalleystable.com.

Skyland Stables at Milepost 41 on Skyline Drive in Luray, ☎ 540-999-2210, www.visitshenandoah.com, will take you on one- or two-hour tours of Shenandoah National Park.

Natural Areas

Shenandoah National Park straddles the Blue Ridge Mountains, which form the eastern edge of the Appalachian chain. Skyline Drive runs 105 miles through the length of the park. The park holds more than 500 miles of trails along crests, down to waterfalls and into deep canyons. The famed Appalachian Trail also runs through the park for 101 miles. Apple trees, stone foundations, and cemeteries are reminders of the families who once called this place home. ☎ 540-999-3740, www.nps.gov/shen.

Wolf Gap Recreation Area is in the George Washington National Forest, west of Edinburg on Route 675. There are 10 primitive campsites; site #9 is the trailhead for a popular hike called Big Schloss, which takes you to impressive rock outcrops atop Massanutten Mountain. Call the Lee Ranger District at ☎ 540-984-4101, www.fs.fed.us/r8/gwi.

Shopping

Antiques, hand-crafted furniture, crafts, and locally-made foodstuffs can all be found in the Shenandoah Valley.

The Great Strasburg Emporium, 160 N. Massanutten Street, ☎ 540-465-3711, houses numerous antique dealers in a 65,000-square-foot building. Among the notable exhibitors is the Shenandoah Potters Guild.

La Dama Maya Herb and Flower Farm, on Route 340 Business in Luray, ☎ 540-743-4665, features herb plants, dried herb and flower products grown on the farm. Special events and workshops are also held here.

Murray's Fly Shop, in Edinburg, ☎ 540-984-4212, www.murraysflyshop.com, sells fly-fishing rods, flies and lures and other fishing supplies. It provides guide services for fishing in the area as well as fishing schools.

Galleries

Art – whether painting, photography or fine crafts – is a spectator event in the Shenandoah Valley, especially in the galleries and workshops of Shenandoah and Page County artisans. Chances are good you'll find an artist at work in their shop, producing work that captures the natural beauty of the region. **River Farm**, 9408 Congress Street in New Market, ☎ 540-740-3314, carries on the tradition of fiber arts in the valley by offering workshops and exhibits of local weavers. The shop supplies area weavers, spinners, knitters and felters.

Wineries

Shenandoah Vineyards, on South Ox Road in Edinburg, cultivates grapes for award-winning wines on 40 lush acres set against Massanutten Mountain. Featured wines include Cabernet Sauvignon, Merlot, Chardonnay, Riesling and Chambourcin. This is the Shenandoah Valley's oldest winery, established in 1976. There are picnic tables, a gift shop and guided tours hourly. It is closed on Thanksgiving, Christmas and New Year's Day. ☎ 540-984-8699, or visit www.shentel.net/shenvine.

North Mountain Vineyard & Winery, 4374 Swartz Road in Maurentown, north of the town of Woodstock, is within view of North Mountain. Modeled after the wineries of Europe, North Mountain Vineyards produces Chardonnay, Vidal-Riesling, Chambourcin, Claret and spiced apple wines. ☎ 540-436-9463, www.northmountainvineyard.com.

Dining

A good meal in Shenandoah and Page Counties often means dining in an unconventional setting. Whether it is a restored home or an old mill, a former stagecoach inn or a farmhouses-turned public house, restaurants serve up a bit of character with their dishes. You'll find all the major chain restaurants clustered around exits for I-81. Over the mountain to Edinburg, Strasburg and Woodstock, one-of-a-kind destinations await discovery. We've listed a sampling. For a complete list of restaurants, call the **Shenandoah Valley Travel Association** at ☎ 540-740-3132.

Farmhouse Restaurant at Jordan Hollow Farm Inn serves gourmet cuisine in a 1700s farmhouse inn. 326 Hawksbill Park Road, Stanley. ☎ 540-778-2285, www.jordanhollow.com.

Hi-Neighbor Country Restaurant is a casual country eatery in a Civil War ear dining room featuring items like scrapple, puddinmeat and turkey dinners. 192 W. King Street, Strasburg, ☎ 540-465-9987.

The **Hotel Strasburg**, 213 S. Holiday Street, ☎ 540-465-9191, occupies an 1895 restored Victorian mansion. The chef prepares daily specials for lunch and dinner, and meals are served with the charm and romanticism of turn-of-the-century Virginia.

Jackson Crossing Family Restaurant overlooks the Shenandoah Valley from atop Massanutten Mountain, seven miles west of Luray. Route 211, ☎ 540-743-7483, www.jacksoncrossing.com.

The **Lee Jackson** offers fine dining in the Congress Street Public House in New Market. ☎ 866-740-2525, www.theleejackson.com.

Parkhurst Restaurant at Rainbow Hill has food, ice cream shop, Christmas shop and gifts. Route 211, Luray, ☎ 540-743-6009, www.shen-tel.net/rainbowhill.

Post Cards Steak & Seafood Restaurant, at the Ramada Inn-Woodstock, ☎ 540-459-5000, is open for breakfast, lunch and dinner and serves a great prime rib.

The Restaurant at Victorian Inn features afternoon teas and four-course gourmet dinners, 138 E. Main Street, Luray, ☎ 540-743-1494, www.woodruffinns.com.

Southern Kitchen serves Virginia ham, seafood and fried chicken. Route 11, New Market, ☎ 540-740-3514.

The Spring House, 325 S. Main Street in Woodstock, ☎ 540-459-4755, serves lunch and dinner daily. There are five dining rooms with antique decorations and collectibles. Expect a warm atmosphere and a unique menu, including the restaurants famous homemade walnut rolls. Virginia wines served.

Accommodations

Despite its rural character, there are plenty of national chain hotels and motels in Shenandoah and Page Counties. Most are clustered in the New Market and Luray areas – 24 inns, hotels and motels in Luray alone – near exits for I-81, the major north-south route. Below is a list of some major hotels. For a complete list, contact the **Shenandoah Valley Travel Association** at ☎ 540-740-3132

Hotels & Motels

The **Best Value Cardinal Inn** has 25 rooms, mountain views and serves continental breakfast. 1005 East Main Street, Luray, ☎ 540-743-5010, www.cardinalinn.com $

Best Western Shenandoah Valley, on Route 11 at Exit 273 off I-81, ☎ 540-477-2911, has 98 guest rooms. There's a restaurant next door, and the hotel is convenient to caverns, golfing, battlefields and shopping. Ski and golf packages are available. $

Blue Ridge Inn has 18 rooms with mountain views, playground and picnic area. I-81 Exit 264, New Market. ☎ 540-740-4136, www.blueridge-inn.com $

 Budget Host Inn, on Route 11 south of Woodstock, ☎ 540-459-4086, has 43 guest rooms, a full-service restaurant and swimming pool. Pets are allowed. $

Budget Inn New Market is close to all the attractions, on US 1, I-81 at Exit 264. ☎ 800-296-6825 or 540-740-3105. $

Hotel Strasburg, 213 Holiday Street in Strasburg, ☎ 540-465-9191, www.hotelstrasburg.com, has 29 guest rooms housed in a turn-of-the-century Victorian restoration. Rooms are decked with antiques. There are three dining rooms and a Victorian pub. $$

Quality Inn-Shenandoah Valley, at Exit 264 off I-81, ☎ 540-740-3141, www.qualityinn-shenandoahvalley.com, has 101 guest rooms, a pool and a restaurant. Picnic tables, a miniature golf course, and a playground are available for guest use. $

Ramada Inn, at Exit 283 off I-81, ☎ 540-459-5000, www.ramada-woodstock.com, has 124 guest rooms, an outdoor pool and a full-service restaurant, called **Postcards**, with specialties that include prime rib and seafood. $

Bed & Breakfasts / Inns

Azalea House, 551 S. Main Street in Woodstock, ☎ 540-459-3500, www.azaleahouse.com, is a 100-year-old Victorian mansion made even more striking by the countless azaleas blooming every spring and summer. A full breakfast is served. Children over age 14 only. $$

Bluemont Bed & Breakfast has three guest rooms and serves a full country breakfast. Country setting. No children or pets allowed. 1852 US Hwy Business 340, Luray, ☎ 540-743-1268, www.bluemontbb.com. $$

Cross Roads Inn, 9222 John Sevier Road in New Market, ☎ 540-740-4157, is a white clapboard Victorian home that serves up Austrian hospitality with imported coffee and homemade strudel. There are five guest rooms, each with a private bath. Visit www.crossroadsinnva.com for more information. $$

Edinburg Inn Bed & Breakfast is an 1850 Victorian home next to Historic Edinburg Mill and Visitor Center. Main Street, Edinburg, ☎ 540-984-8286. $

Goshen House Bed & Breakfast is in a restored 1805 former tavern. Located on Hawksbill Creek in the center of town. 120 N. Hawksbill Street, Luray. ☎ 540-843-0700, www.goshenhouse.com. $$

The **Inn at Narrow Passage**, on Chapman Landing Road off Route 11 in Woodstock, ☎ 800-459-8002, is a restored Colonial inn that has been welcoming guests for 250 years. There are 12 guest rooms, each with a private bath. Rooms in the older, 1740-era section of the inn retain the feel of the Colonial past with pine floors and stenciling. Newer rooms open onto porches overlooking the Shenandoah River. Most rooms have air conditioning, queen-size bed and a fireplace. www.innatnarrowpassage.com. $$

 Mayne View B&B has five luxurious rooms, panoramic views and spa services. Children and pets welcome. 439 Mechanic Street, Luray, ☎ 540-743-7921, www.mayneview.com. $$

The **Mimslyn Inn** is a grand old country inn with 49 rooms, a dining room serving dinner, daily lunch buffet and Sunday brunch. 401 West Main Street, Luray, ☎ 540-743-5105, http://mimslyninn.com. $$

The **Ruffner House** has been in the family for eight generations. Now an elegant B&B on 21 acres. 440 Ruffner House Road, Luray, ☎ 540-743-7855, www.ruffnerhouse.com. $$

South Court Inn is an 1870s restored mansion. Rooms have fireplaces and the inn is filled with antiques. 160 South Court Street, Luray. ☎ 540-843-0980, www.southcourtinn.com. $$

Woodruff Inns are fairytale Victorian homes and riverside cabins with Jacuzzi rooms and suites. Afternoon teas, four-course dinners and full breakfasts. Restaurant is open to the public. 138 E. Main Street, Luray, ☎ 540-743-1494, www.woodruffinns.com. $$$

 The Widow Kip's, 355 Orchard Drive in Mount Jackson, ☎ 540-477-2400 or 800-478-8714, www.widowkips.com, is an 1830 home set on seven acres, chock full of antiques in six guest bedrooms and two cottages, one of which has a kitchen. Rooms have a private bath. There is a swimming pool, and the inn rents bicycles for guests. Children and pets are permitted in the guest cottages, and there's a five-acre fenced field for horses. $$

Resorts

Shenvalee Golf Resort sits on the grounds of a 1749 plantation. Today there's a golf course, pool, lodge with 42 rooms and a restaurant. ☎ 540-740-3181, www.shenvalee.com. $

Bryce Resort, west of Mount Jackson on Route 263 in the town of Basye, ☎ 540-856-2121, is a four-season resort with skiing, golf, tennis, horseback riding and a lake. There is a lodge with guest rooms, as well as condo and townhouse rentals. www.bryceresort-.com. $

Campgrounds

Creekside Campground, on the banks of Stoney Creek in Edinburg, two miles off I-81, ☎ 540-984-8516, has 30 campsites for RVs, tents and trailers. There are hot showers, full hookups for RVs, and a dump station. Pets are welcome.

Country Waye RV Resort, 3402 Kimball Road, Luray, ☎ 540-743-7222, www.countrywaye.com.

Orkney Springs Campground, on Route 610 in Orkney, ☎ 540-856-2585, www.campingva.com, has tent and trailer sites, a laundry, recreation hall, playground and is close to area golf and skiing attractions.

Rancho Compground, Valley Pike, New Market, ☎ 540-740-8313.

Yogi Bear's Jellystone Park has camping, cabins, a waterslide, mini-golf, fishing pond, paddle-boats and a swimming pool, in Luray, ☎ 540-743-4002, www.campluray.com.

Information

Learn more about attractions in Luray and Page Counties by contacting the **Luray-Page County Chamber of Commerce**, 46 E. Main Street, Luray, VA, 22835, ☎ 888-743-3915, www.luraypage.com, open daily.

Information on the sights, restaurants and lodging in Shenandoah County can be found at the **Shenandoah County Travel Council**, PO Box 802, Woodstock, VA, 22664, ☎ 540-459-2332.

For the **Town of Newmarket**, ☎ 540-740-3432, www.newmarketvirginia.com.

For region-wide travel information, contact the **Shenandoah Valley Travel Association**, PO Box 1040, New Market, VA, 22844, ☎ 540-740-3132, www.visitshenandoah.org. Their visitor center is located at Exit 264 off I-81.

The **Massanutten Visitors Center** stands atop Massanutten Mountain, halfway between Luray and New Market on Route 211, and is a good resource for people interested in exploring the George Washington National Forest. Open daily, mid-April through October. The visitor center is the starting point for several hikes. ☎ 540-740-8310.

Roanoke & Salem

*R*oanoke, capital of the Blue Ridge since the days when settlers came westward, has become the focal point of Western Virginia. The city, which began as a salt marsh named "Big Lick" and later became a booming railroad town, is now a major vacation destination.

Nestled in the midst of a rich Appalachian heritage in the heart of the mountainous west, the Roanoke Valley is a great place to discover Virginia. Just a short drive from the city, you will find a number of interesting and historical attractions, including Civil War battlefields, pioneer living at Virginia's Explore Park, and the majestic views off the Blue Ridge Parkway.

Roanoke was incorporated in 1882 when it became a junction of the Norfolk and Western Railway and the Shenandoah Valley Railroad. Nicknamed the Star City, it remains the cultural, convention and industrial center for western Virginia. The 88-foot tall, neon-lit star that overlooks the city from a perch atop Mill Mountain remains a landmark for the entire region.

A visit to the Roanoke Valley with its nearby areas of natural scenic beauty can provide a natural high. There are a number of invigorating recreational options that include bicycling along the Blue Ridge Parkway, hiking the great Appalachian Trail and a variety of smaller but no less rewarding local trails.

For the shopper, Roanoke is a haven of antique stores, tiny gift shops, arts and craft outlets and a couple of hundred specialty stores that offer everything from fresh vegetables to fashion.

Sights

The **Art Museum of Western Virginia**, in the Center in the Square complex, Roanoke, hosts major national touring exhibits and work by local artists. The Rosalie K. and Sydney Shaftman Gallery is dedicated to traditional and contemporary decorative arts; Art Venture is interactive art for families. Open Tuesday through Sunday. Admission is free. ☎ 540-342-5760, www.artmuseumroanoke.org.

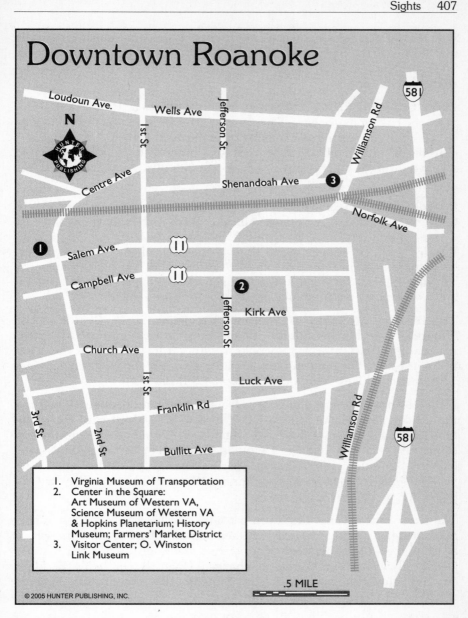

Downtown Roanoke

1. Virginia Museum of Transportation
2. Center in the Square:
   Art Museum of Western VA,
   Science Museum of Western VA
   & Hopkins Planetarium; History
   Museum; Farmers' Market District
3. Visitor Center; O. Winston
   Link Museum

.5 MILE

© 2005 HUNTER PUBLISHING, INC.

Blue Ridge Institute & Museum, at Ferrum College in Ferrum, is the official State Center for Blue Ridge Folklore, housing a vast collection of mountain crafts, music and other items relating to Blue Ridge culture. Also on site is a re-created 18th-century farmhouse highlighting the German-American roots of Blue Ridge culture. Gallery admission is free. ☎ 540-365-4416, or visit www.blueridgeinstitute.org.

The **Blue Ridge Parkway** links the Shenandoah National Park ānd the Great Smokies National Park in Tennessee via 469 miles of pristine highway. En route, it passes Roanoke at Milepost 120. Numerous hiking trails intersect with the parkway, including the renowned **Appalachian Trail**, and there are countless scenic viewing areas. ☎ 540-767-2492, www.blue-ridgeparkway.org.

Dixie Caverns, 5753 Main Street in Salem, offers a twist on the tried-and-true caving experience. This cavern goes *up* into a mountain, opens onto a large cathedral room and leads further still to interesting rock formations. There's a pottery shop, rock and mineral shop, basket shop and a souvenir shop. Open year-round. ☎ 540-380-2085, www.dixiecaverns-.com.

Roanoke's **Historic Farmer's City Market**, on First Street next door to Center in the Square, is a crowded market flush with fresh fruits and vegetables operating Monday through Saturday from 8 a.m. to 5 p.m. Besides produce, shoppers can browse specialty shops, antique stores, bookstores and gardening displays. Running since 1882, this market is Virginia's oldest farmer's market in continuous operation. ☎ 540-342-2028, www.downtownroanoke.org.

The **History Museum of Western Virginia**, in the Center in the Square at One Market Square, Roanoke, contains a number of permanent exhibits that interpret Roanoke's history from the earliest times until the present. The museum is open daily except Monday, Thanksgiving, Christmas and New Year's Day. ☎ 540-342-5770.

Mill Mountain Zoo, a short drive from downtown Roanoke and off the Blue Ridge Parkway at Milepost 120, next to **Mill Mountain Park**, exhibits 50 plus exotic and native animals on 3½ acres of mountaintop country. A Siberian tiger, red pandas, golden-lion tamarins and snow leopards are among the zoo's prize species. Special events throughout the year celebrate conservation and animals. Closed Christmas Day. ☎ 540-343-3241, or visit www.mmzoo.org.

The **O. Winston Link Museum** contains the largest collection of this photographer's prints, railway artifacts, and interactive exhibits, which all combine to tell the story of America's steam era inside the historic N&W railway station. Admission charged. Open 10 a.m. to 5 p.m., Monday-Saturday, and noon to 5 p.m. Sunday. 101 Shenandoah Avenue, ☎ 540-982-LINK, www.linkmuseum.org.

The **Salem Museum**, 801 E. Main Street in Salem, preserves relics of this small city's past. Housed in the historic Williams-Brown House, its exhibits include Civil War memorabilia, Native American artifacts, as well as photography and art. Open Tuesday through Saturday. Admission is free. Guided tours are available. ☎ 540-389-6760, or visit www.sa-lemmuseum.org.

The **Science Museum of Western Virginia**, located at the Center in the Square at One Market Square in downtown Roanoke, provides a number of hands-on exhibits that interpret the natural and physical sciences. These exhibits include animals of the land and oceans, computers and a television weather station. The museum offers a number of workshops and programs for children and adults, as well as special exhibits, shows and films. The **Hopkins Planetarium** shows films interpreting the night sky in their mega-dome. The museum is open Monday-Saturday. ☎ 540-342-5710, www.smwv.org.

To The Rescue Museum, on the upper level of Tanglewood Mall on Electric Road (US 220), commemorates the work of Julian Stanley Wise, who formed America's first rescue and first-aid crew in the Roanoke region in the 1920s. Visitors can participate in a life-saving scenario and view equipment used by today's emergency workers. Open Tuesday through Sunday and closed on major holidays. ☎ 540-776-0364.

Virginia's Explore Park, ☎ 800-842-9163, www.explorepark.org, is 1½ miles off the Blue Ridge Parkway at Milepost 115. The park exhibits life in Virginia from the 1671 to 1850, with interpreters performing skills such as flint knapping, log hewing and blacksmithing. Nearby, Brugh Tavern serves an authentic 19th-century meal. The mountain setting and 1,100 acres of park are ideal for a hike or bike ride. Guided canoe and kayak trips are offered on the Roanoke River. Pets are not allowed in the historic areas but kennels are available.

The **Virginia Museum of Transportation**, 303 Norfolk Avenue in downtown Roanoke, displays rolling stock from the past, including large steam, diesel and electric locomotives. Other exhibits include vintage cars and carriages, aviation and a large model train exhibit with 600 feet of track and seven model trains. The museum, located in a restored railway freight station next to the Norfolk Southern main track line, is open daily most of the year (closed Monday in January and February). ☎ 540-342-5670, www.vmt.org.

Recreation

Water Sports

Smith Mountain Lake, west of Roanoke on VA 24, covers 22,000 acres and 500 miles of shoreline. This 40-mile long lake is ideal for fishing and boating, water-skiing and windsurfing. Onshore, you can sunbathe, picnic or camp. ☎ 540-721-1203, www.visitsmithmountainlake.com.

Golf

Six of Roanoke Valley's golf courses have joined with area hotels to offer enticing golf/vacation packages. From tee times to car rentals to room reservations, a single telephone call can net you a great golf trip. Special rates for golf and lodging are available only by calling ☎ 877-GOLF-MTN. Participating golf courses include **Ashley Plantation**, the Valley's newest residential golf community; **Draper Valley**, regarded as one of the best conditioned courses in the Valley, **Hanging Rock**, ranked one of the top three courses in Virginia by *The Golfer's Guide*; **London Downs**, located in historic Bedford County; The **River Course** at Virginia Tech; and **Westlake**, on the shores of Smith Mountain Lake.

When the golf game is over, you can look forward to a good meal, some entertainment and quality rest at one of seven area hotels. Participating hotels include **Best Western Inn at Valley View** near the Roanoke Regional Airport, **Clarion Hotel Roanoke Airport**, **Comfort Suites: The Inn at Ridgewood Farms**, located in nearby Salem, **The Hotel Roanoke & Conference Center**, a Tudor-style hotel in the heart of downtown, and **The Patrick Henry Hotel**, in downtown Roanoke, **Sleep-Inn Tanglewood**, near Tanglewood Mall.

Spectator Sports

The Salem Avalanche, an A-level minor league team affiliated with the Houston Astros of Major League Baseball, plays home games at Salem Memorial Baseball Stadium. For schedule and ticket information, ☎ 540-389-3333, www.salemavalanche.com.

Entertainment

Center in the Square, at One Market Square in downtown Roanoke, is a unique facility housing seven independent cultural organizations under one roof, including **Mill Mountain Theatre**, with a year-round professional playbill offering a variety of dramas, musicals and comedies, as well as lectures, dance, and monthly readings of new one-act plays. **Waldron Stage**, located on Level 1 in the Center in the Square, provides a second venue for the performing arts; ☎ 540-342-5740, www.center-inthesquare.org.

Also at the Center in the Square are **The Arts Council of the Blue Ridge** and the **Art Museum of Western Virginia**. Admission to both is free. For information, ☎ 540-342-5700, www.centerinthesquare.org.

Henry Street Players presents a historical revue of downtown Roanoke in the jazz age. Duke Ellington, Count Basie and Ella Fitzgerald were once regulars at Henry Street night clubs. The players perform at various locations around Roanoke. ☎ 540-981-9110 for a listing of performances and locations.

Showtimers Community Theatre, off Route 419 across from Allstate, ☎ 540-774-2660, www.showtimers.org, is the oldest continuously performing community theater in Virginia.

Shopping

Large department stores and flagship units of leading regional retailers have been joined by a number of fascinating shops that provide exciting opportunities for antique shopping and browsing. More than 130 retailers, specialty shops, boutiques and stores call downtown Roanoke home. Travel farther afield, to Salem, Vinton and Rocky Mount, and discover a wealth of antique boutiques and specialty shops. Listed below are a sampling of Roanoke's larger shopping centers.

Valley View Mall, on Valley View Boulevard off I-581 at Hershberger Road, is the largest mall in southwest Virginia, with 130 stores, restaurants and a 10-screen cinema. Department stores include Belk, Sears, Hecht's and JC Penney. ☎ 540-563-4400 or visit www.valleyview.com for more information.

Crossroads Mall, at the corner of Hershberger and Williamson Roads, and **Towne Square**, located behind Crossroads, mix specialty shops and big box retailers such as Sam's Wholesale Discount Club and Office Max Crossroads recently opened **Cinema Grill**, a two-screen cinema and sit-down restaurant.

Tanglewood Mall, at Route 220 and 419 on Electric Road, was Roanoke's first regional mall. Today, 105 stores and eight restaurants do business in the two-story shopping center. Inside the mall's center court, antique vendors and mountain crafters display themed exhibits. ☎ 540-989-4394 or visit www.shoptanglewood.com for more information.

Towers Shopping Center, at the corner of Colonial and Brandon Avenues, is a full-service shopping center with more than 50 stores, restaurants, services and specialty shops. ☎ 540-982-6791.

Annual Events

The **Roanoke Festival in the Park** occurs over 11 days during May and June, when Roanoke celebrates arts and crafts, sports, food and live entertainment; www.roanokefestival.org. Other area activities include **Midnight on the Market** in December, www.event-zone.org; **ShrimpFest** in April and an **International Wine Tasting & Tour** in February. ☎ 540-342-2640.

The **Annual Vinton Dogwood Festival** in downtown Vinton has been a springtime tradition for 45 years in the Roanoke Valley. ☎ 540-983-0613.

The **Virginia State Championship Chili Cookoff**, held in Roanoke on the first Saturday in May, is a statewide event culminating in the award to the champion. ☎ 540-344-0876.

Roanoke & Salem

The Salem Fair and Exposition at the Salem Civic Center Complex, 1001 Roanoke Boulevard, is Virginia's largest free-admission fair. It is held in July. ☎ 540-375-4013, or visit www.salemfair.com.

Roanoke's annual **Henry Street Heritage Festival** kicks off every September in conjunction with the Harrison Museum of African-American Culture. ☎ 540-348-4818.

Taste of the Blue Ridge Blues & Jazz Festival, at Elmwood Park in Roanoke, welcomes regional artists and national performing acts for a foot-tappin' good time. Held in September. ☎ 540-342-2640, www.tobr.org.

The **Annual Lighting of the Christmas Tree** takes place in Roanoke during early December. Call the City of Roanoke at ☎ 540-342-2028.

The **Annual Christmas Parade** through downtown Roanoke is held the first week in December. ☎ 540-342-2028.

A **Dickens of a Christmas** takes place in downtown Roanoke on the first, second and third Friday evenings of December. ☎ 540-342-2028.

Dining

Roanoke has more than 60 restaurants, many of them offering live entertainment. Those listed below offer especially good value and service.

Alexander's, 105 S. Jefferson Avenue, ☎ 540-342-3937, offers visitors a fine dining experience from its gourmet menu. Open Wednesday for lunch; dinner served Tuesday through Saturday.

Billy's Ritz, on the first floor at 102 Salem Avenue, ☎ 540-342-3937, is open for dinner, with a casual but elegant atmosphere in five dining rooms, including an open-air courtyard. Specialties of the house include steaks, chops, chicken and grilled fish.

Carlos Brazilian International, 4167 Electric Road SW, ☎ 540-776-1117, is open for lunch and dinner, serving Brazilian and international cuisine. Dress is casual. Closed on Sundays and major holidays.

Corned Beef & Co., Inc., 107 South Jefferson Street, ☎ 540-342-3354, is one of Roanoke's hottest night spots for live entertainment, featuring jazz, rhythm & blues and reggae. The restaurant is famous for its overstuffed sandwiches, aged hand-cut steaks, soups, salads and fresh grilled seafood. There is outdoor patio seating, pool tables and shuffleboard.

The **Library**, 3117 Franklin Road in the Piccadilly Square shopping center, ☎ 540-985-0811, is a fine restaurant for a candlelight meal. The menu is American- and European-influenced, and the dress code is casual. Closed on Sunday, Monday, and major holidays.

Mill Mountain Coffee & Tea, 112 Campbell Avenue, ☎ 540-342-9404, specializes in dessert delicacies and a variety of coffees.

Montano's International Gourmet, 3733 Franklin Road in the Townside Festival Mall, ☎ 540-344-8960, serves an eclectic mix of food, and features great wine and tiramisu, the rich Italian dessert. In the evening, the smooth sounds of live jazz entertain diners. In the afternoons, this restaurant-delicatessen is popular with the business crowd. Children's menus and carryout are available. Closed Sunday and on Christmas, New Year's and the day before Thanksgiving.

Norberto's, 1908 Memorial Avenue, ☎ 540-342-1611, features traditional Italian fare.

The Roanoke Market Building, 32 Market Square in downtown Roanoke, was built in 1922 and once served as the place to meet and greet in Roanoke. Today, it houses a diverse sampling of lunch counters and ethnic restaurants. Great for a quick bite to eat.

Accommodations

Hotels & Motels

There is no shortage of places to say in and around Roanoke – the region's 30-plus hotels and motels have more than 5,500 rooms. Whether you need a convenient, no-nonsense evening's rest or the comfort and pampering of a luxury hotel, area hostelries offer something for all travelers. Listed below are a sampling. For more complete list, call the **Roanoke Valley Visitor Information Center** at ☎ 800-635-5535, www.visitroanoke.com.

Baymont Inn, 140 Sheraton Drive in Salem, ☎ 540-562-2717, has 68 guest rooms. There are Jacuzzis in the rooms, as well as coffee makers. A continental breakfast is delivered to the room. $

 Best Western Inn at Valley View, 5050 Valley View Boulevard, ☎ 540-362-2400, has 85 guest rooms, all equipped with in-room coffee makers and hair dryers. There is an indoor pool. $

 The Clarion Hotel Roanoke Airport, 2727 Ferndale Drive, ☎ 540-362-4500, www.roanokeclarion.com, has 154 guest rooms. Amenities include a full-service restaurant and café, bar, meeting rooms and swimming pool. Free airport transportation. $$

 Comfort Suites: The Inn at Ridgewood Farms, 2898 Keagy Road in Salem, ☎ 540-375-4800, has 78 guest rooms, and offers an outdoor pool and a fitness center. Continental breakfast is served. $$

The Colony House Motor Lodge, 3560 Franklin Road, ☎ 540-345-0411, has 69 guest rooms. There is a meeting room and a swimming pool. Free continental breakfast. $

Country Inn & Suites By Carlson, 7860 Plantation Road, ☎ 540-366-5678, has 77 guest rooms and suites, an indoor pool and serves a complimentary continental breakfast. $

 Days Inn Civic Center, 535 Orange Avenue, ☎ 540-342-4551, www.daysinnroanoke.com, has 165 guest rooms. Continental breakfast is served and pets are allowed. $$

Hampton Inn Airport, 6621 Thirlane Road, ☎ 540-265-2600, has 79 guest rooms. Each room is equipped with a small refrigerator and a VCR. $$

Hampton Inn Salem, 1886 Electric Road in Salem, ☎ 540-776-6500, www.hamptoninnsalem.com, is a large hotel with 114 guest rooms. Each room is equipped with a small refrigerator, VCR, coffee maker, hair dryer and ironing board. $$

 Holiday Inn-Tanglewood, 4468 Starkey Road, ☎ 540-774-4400, has 196 guest rooms. There is a restaurant and café, a bar, a swimming pool with poolside service, and free airport transportation. $

The Hotel Roanoke & Conference Center, 110 Shenandoah Avenue, ☎ 540-985-5900, www.hotelroanoke.com, has 332 guest rooms and occupies a sprawling 19th-century building listed on the National Register of Historic Places. The Regency dining room features a gourmet menu and daily specials. There is also a conference center. $$$

The Jefferson Lodge, 616 S. Jefferson Street, ☎ 540-342-2951, is a medium-sized hotel with 98 guest rooms. Facilities and services provided by the hotel include a swimming pool with poolside service and a café nearby. The hotel provides free airport transportation and complimentary continental breakfast. $

Motel 6, 3695 Thirlane Road, ☎ 540-563-0229, has 100 guest rooms. There is an outdoor pool, fitness facilities and the hotel offers shuttle service to nearby restaurants and shopping. $

The Patrick Henry Hotel, 617 S. Jefferson Street, ☎ 540-345-8811, www.patrickhenryroanoke.com, is a historic downtown hotel with 117 large rooms. The hotel has a full-service restaurant and café, a bar, several meeting rooms and a beauty shop. It also offers free airport transportation, health club privileges, and a senior citizen discount. $$

 Ramada Inn River's Edge, 1927 Franklin Road, ☎ 540-343-0121, has 126 guest rooms. There are fitness facilities, an outdoor pool, and a restaurant and lounge. Continental breakfast is served. $

Wyndham Roanoke Airport, 2801 Hershberger Road, ☎ 540-563-9300, is a large luxury hotel with 320 guest rooms. Facilities include a full-service restaurant and café, a bar, a swimming pool with poolside service, a free continental breakfast and free airport transportation. $-$$$

Bed & Breakfasts / Inns

Warm country inns, stately turn-of-the century mansions and old farms-turned-secluded country retreats await visitors to the Roanoke region. There are inns, lodges, and cottages sprinkled throughout the Valley, some a short drive to downtown Roanoke, others more remote, tucked in the vales and hollows of the Blue Ridge Mountains. Listed below is a sampling. For a more complete list, call the **Roanoke Valley Visitor Information Center**, ☎ 800-635-5535.

In Salem, the **Inn at Burwell Place**, 601 W. Main Street, ☎ 540-387-0250, serves up elegant fare and home-baked goods, and pampers guests with complimentary robes and slippers, custom European bedspreads and down comforters. It has two guest rooms and two guest suites, each with a private bath. The inn's 77-foot veranda overlooks the Blue Ridge Mountains. Visit www.burwellplace.com for more information. $$

Meadowood Bed & Breakfast, 6235 Buffalo Mountain Road, Milepost 174.5 (an hour south of Roanoke on the Blue Ridge Parkway), ☎ 540-593-2600, www.blueridgebedandbreakfast.net, has three spacious guest rooms, each with a private bath. The mountain estate's great room has a stone fireplace and serves a full country breakfast, and dinner on request. Outdoors, 20 acres of mountain meadows unfold from the inn's 60-foot front porch. $$

The Olde Manse, 530 E. Main Street in Salem, ☎ 540-389-3921, offers two guest rooms in an 1847 home that is listed on the National Historic Register and chock full of antiques. Innkeepers serve a full Southern breakfast. $$

Camping

Bordered by the Blue Ridge Mountain to the east and the Allegheny Mountains to the west, the Roanoke Valley offers many camping opportunities. The **George Washington and Jefferson National Forests**, ☎ 540-265-5100, have several developed recreation and tent camping areas, as well as a multitude of backcountry camping sites. **Dixie Caverns** in Salem, ☎ 540-380-2085, has 75 tent sites and 56 trailer sites with hook-ups for RVs and guest showers. The **Peaks of Otter Campground**, on the Blue Ridge Parkway at Milepost 86, ☎ 540-586-4357, is open May to November, with 86 tent sites and 59 trailer sites. Handicapped-accessible campsites are available. At **Roanoke Mountain Campground**, off the Blue Ridge Parkway at Milepost 120.5, ☎ 540-982-9242, there are 74 tent sites and 30 trailer sites, including some that are

Roanoke & Salem

handicapped-accessible. The **Rocky Knob Campground**, on the Blue Ridge Parkway at Milepost 167.1, ☎ 540-745-9664, has 81 tent sites and 28 trailer sites. **Smith Mountain Lake Campground**, on Route 1 in Huddleston, ☎ 540-297-6066, has 26 tent sites and 24 trailer sites.

Transportation

Roanoke Regional Airport (☎ 540-362-1999, www.roanokeregional-airport.com) provides service by most major and regional carriers with direct flights to many cities and connecting flights to all major domestic and international destinations. **Greyhound** serves Roanoke as well (☎ 800-231-2222).

Information

For more information about the Roanoke Valley, including directions, points of interest, brochures, maps and lodging assistance, contact the **Roanoke Valley Convention and Visitors Bureau**, 101 Shenandoah Avenue, Roanoke, VA 24016, ☎ 800-635-5535, www.visitroanokeva.com.

The **Salem Visitor's Center**, 1001 Roanoke Boulevard, contains brochures, trip planners and information on the sights in this quaint city southwest of Roanoke. ☎ 540-375-4044, 888-VA-SALEM, www.visitsalemva.com.

Information on businesses, lodging and recreation around Smith Mountain Lake is available at the **Smith Mountain Lake Chamber of Commerce**, in the Bridgewater Plaza on Route 122 in Moneta; ☎ 540-721-1203, 800-676-8203, www.visitsmithmountainlake.com.

Staunton & Augusta County

Smack dab in the heart of the Shenandoah Valley, stand **Staunton** and **Waynesboro**, two industrial cities whose close proximity belie very different histories.

Waynesboro, in the eastern portion of the county, was named for the Revolutionary War hero, "Mad Anthony" Wayne. It stands at the foot of Afton Mountain, on the west flank of the Blue Ridge. During the Civil War, Confederate troops made a final stand here, but succumbed to the superior numbers of the Northern army of General Philip Sheridan.

Since then, Waynesboro has welcomed industry and worked to preserve the links with its past. Today, the town's motto, "Hospitality in the Valley," is something shop owners in the downtown district and innkeepers at surrounding bed and breakfasts take seriously.

Staunton, about 20 miles west of Waynesboro, is one of the oldest cities in the Valley, founded in 1747. It was named for Lady Staunton, wife of the Colonial governor. Significantly, it was spared the destruction visited upon Waynesboro during the Civil War.

Because of this, Staunton's five registered historic districts contain fine examples of period architecture. The **Wharf Area** has cobblestone sidewalks, old warehouses and a train station. In **Beverly**, classic turn-of-the-century homes have been painstakingly restored.

The First Augusta Parish Church was Staunton's only church for years, and for 17 days in the summer of 1781, it became the makeshift capital of Virginia. Then-Governor Thomas Jefferson and the General Assembly had come over the mountains from Richmond, fleeing advancing British troops.

Thanks to its strategic locale, Staunton became a major link between western communities and eastern markets. In Colonial times, the westbound Parkersburg Pike and the north-south Valley Pike intersected here, and the town welcomed the commerce they brought. Railroads replaced wagon roads with the arrival of the C&O Railroad.

Staunton and Waynesboro are conveniently located at the intersection of the region's two major interstates, 81 and 64. The ease in getting here is only heightened by both town's best efforts at preserving links to frontier culture, architecture and the arts.

Sights

The hilly city of **Staunton** earned the nickname "Queen City" during the heyday of the Great Wagon Road, a trade route between the Blue Ridge and Allegheny Mountains. Wealthy merchants built three- and four-story Victorian mansions, complete with turrets and spires. Today, these buildings in the Gospel Hill historic district remain in remarkably good shape, thanks in no small part to the efforts of private citizens who've recognized their value. Antique dealers and entrepreneurs have reclaimed the city's Wharf historic district, with its old warehouses and cobblestone streets. These and three other National Historic Districts make for some interesting touring that can easily fill an afternoon.

Museum of Bank History adjoins the 1930 Beaux-Arts style hall of SunTrust Bank and is a display of objects used by the former Valley National Bank. West Beverley Street, Staunton. Open Monday-Thursday 9 a.m. to 2 p.m. and Friday 9 a.m. to 6 p.m.

The **Blackfriars Playhouse** is a recreation of Shakespeare's original 1613 theater, 13 W. Beverley Street, Staunton, 540-851-1733, 877-MUCH-ADO, www.ishakespeare.com.

The **Staunton Fire Department** on Augusta Street, ☎ 540-332-3886, has on public display its first-ever motorized fire truck, nicknamed **Jumbo**, which the city bought in 1911. The engine is restored and in pristine condition.

The **Frontier Culture Museum**, on Route 250 West in Staunton, presents the four threads that form the fabric of Shenandoah Valley life: German, English, Scotch-Irish and American. Three farms, imported from Europe and reconstructed, are staffed by interpreters in period costume living as the original settlers – both in Europe and after they arrived in America. Seasonal events are held throughout the year. ☎ 540-332-7850 for information and a schedule of events, or visit www.frontiermuseum.org.

Woodrow Wilson Birthplace and Museum, 18-24 N. Coalter Street in the Gospel Hill section of Staunton, presents the life of the 28th President of the United States. He was born in this city, and the museum records his life achievements, from Princeton to the White House, where he ably guided the country through World War I. The gardens here are well-kept and Wilson's Pierce-Arrow limousine is as classic as antique cars come. Open daily, ☎ 540-885-0897, www.woodrowwilson.org.

The **P. Buckley Moss Museum**, 150 P. Buckley Moss Drive Waynesboro, ☎ 540-949-6473, www.pbuckleymoss.com, exhibits the work of Ms. Moss, a popular Virginia folk artist who draws inspiration for her work from Valley life, especially the Amish and Mennonite people. Open daily.

McDowell Battlefield, in the town of McDowell, on Route 250 between Staunton and Monterey, preserves the site of Stonewall Jackson's first victory during the Valley Campaign of 1862, during the Civil War. The site is open daily and there is no admission. For a tour brochure, ☎ 540-468-2550.

Recreation

Natural Areas

Gypsy Hill Park is a 214-acre multi-use recreational facility with a golf course, football and baseball stadiums, playing fields, mini-train, duck pond, pool and bandstand. Intersection of Churchville Avenue (Route 250) and Thornrose Avenue, Staunton. Open daily 4 a.m. to 11 p.m. ☎ 540-332-3945.

Highland Adventures in the town of Monterey, 45 miles west of Staunton, ☎ 540-468-2722, specializes in mountain bike trips through the Allegheny Mountains and George Washington National Forest. Individuals and groups are both served. You can rent a bike, or bring your own and use the company's shuttle, mapping or guide services.

Mountain View Trails, 2607 Mt. Torrey Road in Lyndhurst, eight miles south of Exit 96 off I-81, ☎ 540-949-5346, gives horseback riding lessons for beginners and advanced riders. Trail rides through the foothills of the Blue Ridge Mountains are guided. Horse lease programs are also available.

Shenandoah National Park and **Skyline Drive** begin atop Afton Mountain, a short drive east of Waynesboro on I-64. At Rockfish Gap, Skyline Drive begins its northward trek to Front Royal. The Blue Ridge Parkway heads south from this point to Tennessee. This southern section of Shenandoah National Park is considered more remote and less congested than the central and northern regions. The **Appalachian Trail**, which winds its way through the park for 101 miles, is a great way to access the views, wildlife, plants and waterfalls that make the park so famous. The **Shenandoah Natural History Association**, ☎ 540-999-3582, is a reliable source of information on trails and history of the park. The **Waynesboro-East Augusta County Visitors Center**, located at Rockfish Gap on the southern entrance to Skyline Drive, holds a wealth of brochures and maps on the entire region.

Golf

Ingleside Resort & Country Club, on US 11 west of I-81 at Exit 225, is an 18-hole, semi-private resort with championship, regular and women's tees. You must rent and ride a cart to play. ☎ 540-248-1201

Gypsy Hill Golf Course, on Route 250 west of Staunton, ☎ 540-332-3949, is an 18-hole public course in the rolling farmland of western Virginia. There are championship, regular and women's tees. You can walk or ride the 18 holes.

The **Country Club of Staunton**, on Belle's Lane west of I-81 at Exit 275, ☎ 540-248-7273, has 18 holes of championship golf in a private resort setting. Golf packages are available only to guests staying in the adjacent Holiday Inn.

Annual Events

Wintergreen Summer Music Festival is held in July at the Wintergreen Resort (see page 340). Full symphony orchestra and chamber music are featured; ☎ 800-266-2444, www.wintergreenresort.com.

The Fall Foliage Celebration in Waynesboro fills the first two weekends of October with craft shows and other special events, including a 10K run, theater productions and a gem and mineral show. ☎ 540-949-8203.

The **Fall Foliage Bike Festival** is mid-October in Staunton, ☎ 540-885-2668, www.shenandoahbike.org.

October Festival is a family festival held in Staunton's Gypsy Hill Park each fall featuring arts, crafts, food, music and special events. Visit www.OctoberFestivalPark.net for more information, or ☎ 540-213-2027.

Dining

Belle Grae Inn, 515 W. Frederick Street, Staunton. Fine dining in a Victorian mansion in Staunton's Newtown district, four blocks from downtown. Beef, pork, seafood and quail are some of the featured menu options. Dinner served Wednesday through Sunday, 6 to 9 p.m. ☎ 540-886-5151 for reservations.

Buckhorn Inn, Route 250 in Churchville. Set in a sprawling country farmhouse, the inn welcomes fine diners and casual hikers alike. Hand-carved meats, country vegetables and wonderful homemade sauces are among the specialties. It is 12 miles west of Staunton on Route 250. Lodging available. ☎ 540-337-8660, www.thebuckhorninn.com.

Byers Street Bistro, 18 Byers Street, Staunton. Located in the historic Warehouse Row section. Gourmet pizza, pasta, chicken, steaks and sandwiches. ☎ 540-887-6100, www.byersstreetbistro.com.

Depot Grille, 12 Middlebrook Avenue, Staunton. Casual dining, with steak and seafood specialties. The restaurant is in Staunton's downtown train station, recognizable by two cabooses, yellow and red, out front. Open daily for lunch and dinner. ☎ 540-885-7332, www.depotgrille.com.

Kathy's Restaurant, 705 Greenville Avenue, Staunton. A local restaurant boasting the best breakfast in Augusta County, served all day. 705 Greenville Avenue at Statler Boulevard, downtown. ☎ 540-885-4331.

Pullman Restaurant, 36 Middlebrook Avenue, Staunton. Fine dining in a casual atmosphere, set in Staunton's downtown train station. It is locally known for its fresh fried oysters, farm-raised rainbow trout encrusted in Georgia pecans, and hand-carved meats. It is at the very end of Augusta Street, at the opposite end from the Depot Grille. Open daily for lunch and dinner. ☎ 540-885-6612, www.thepullman.com.

The Pampered Palate Café, 28 E. Beverly Street, Staunton. Casual breakfast and European-style lunch, serving up sandwiches, soups, baked potatoes and dessert. The café also features a good selection of coffee, cappuccino and fresh-baked snacks. It is at the corner of Beverly and New Street. ☎ 540-886-9463.

Purple Foot, 1035 W. Broad Street in Waynesboro, serves lunch every day from 11 a.m. to 2 p.m. Besides a wide variety of sandwiches, this local eatery features crèpes and mixed vegetable pitas. Located next to the Willow Oak Shopping Center in downtown. ☎ 540-942-9463.

South River Grille, Rt. 340, Waynesboro. Meals at this large family-style restaurant come with a huge salad bar and healthy portions. It is off

I-64, convenient to the P. Buckley Moss Museum. Lunch and dinner are served daily from 11:30 a.m. to 10 p.m. ☎ 540-942-5567.

Accommodations

There are more than 35 hotels in the vicinity of Staunton and Waynesboro, from brand-name chains to roadside hotels. Many are only a few yards from Interstates 81 and 64, and convenient to the region's attractions. Others occupy old homes and buildings in the cities themselves. Below is a sampling of hotels. For a complete list, ☎ 540-332-3972.

Hotels & Motels

 Comfort Inn, adjacent to the Frontier Culture Museum on Route 250, ☎ 540-886-5000, www.comfortinnstaunton.com, has 98 guest rooms. There are several restaurants nearby, as well as a swimming pool at the hotel. $

 Guesthouse Inn, off Route 250 in Staunton, ☎ 540-885-3117, has 91 guest rooms. Guests have the use of an indoor heated pool, a spa, exercise equipment, sauna and complimentary morning coffee. $

Holiday Inn Staunton Golf & Conference Center, on the Woodrow Wilson Parkway off I-81 at Exit 225 in Staunton, ☎ 800-648-3340, www.histaunton.com, has 115 guest rooms, including handicapped-accessible and non-smoking rooms. The management will arrange golf and ski packages for guests. There is a restaurant and a pub on premise, and rooms have coffee makers. $

Bed & Breakfasts

The Frederick House, 28 N. New Street in downtown Staunton, ☎ 540-885-4220, www.frederickhouse.com, is a complex of five restored townhouses across from Mary Baldwin College, each with private bath and entrance. Shakespeare Theater packages are available. Rooms are furnished with period pieces. Terry-cloth robes are provided. A full breakfast is served. $$

Belle Grae Inn is an historic country inn with 14 rooms and suites and a full-service restaurant. 515 West Frederick Street, ☎ 540-886-5151, 888-541-5151, www.bellegrae.com $$

Sampson Eagon Inn is a restored antebellum mansion with five guestrooms. 238 East Beverley Street, ☎ 540-886-8200, 800-597-9722, www.eagoninn.com. $$

Staunton Choral Gardens Bed and Breakfast offers rooms in the historic main house and a carriage house. 216 W. Frederick Street, ☎ 540-885-6556, www.stauntonbedandbreakfast.com $$

Resorts

Wintergreen Resort, on Route 664 off I-64 at Exit 99, ☎ 800-266-2444, www.wintergreenresort.com, is a four-season resort in the Blue Ridge Mountains east of Waynesboro. There's golfing, skiing, hiking and horseback riding for guests. $$

Camping

Shenandoah Valley KOA on Bald Rock Road in Staunton (Exit 227 off I-81), ☎ 540-248-2746, www.svkoa.net, is a full-service campsite for tents and trailers, featuring Kamping Kabins for families and activities like tubing, swimming, fishing, sports and picnicking. And yes, you *can* pet the bunnies!

Shenandoah Acres Resort, PO Box 300VR, Stuarts Draft, VA 24477. Camping cabins for that rustic experience, plus comfortable cottages, condos, and motel rooms with kitchens and fireplaces. ☎ 540-337-1911 or 800-654-1714, www.shenacres.com.

Walnut Hills Campground, on US 115, 1½ miles off Route 665, ☎ 540-337-3920, www.walnuthillscampground.com, has full-service hookups for trailers and separate tent sites. There's a playground, cabin rentals, game room and laundry. Hayrides and live music are two special events held at the campground.

Day-trip to Highland County

Highland County, west of Staunton, encompasses a mountainous landscape of high ridges and deep valleys where, as locals are fond of noting, sheep seem to outnumber people. Located 45 miles west of I-81, it exists in a world all its own when it comes to scenery and recreation.

Nicknamed "Little Switzerland," Highland County's mean average elevation is higher than any municipality east of the Mississippi. It's population is the third smallest. The major east-west highway, Route 250, takes you from soaring views atop numerous ridgelines, down corkscrew-like routes, into sweeping valleys and through tows like Hightown, a wide spot in the road comprised of a few white buildings.

The town of **Monterey** (pop. 222) is the county seat and cultural center, with several craft and antique shops, and bed and breakfasts nearby. The **Highland Maple Festival** is held the second and third weekend in March. South of town are four-season resorts in Warm Springs and Hot Springs. The South Branch of the Potomac River flows through the region. Near the town of Blue Grass, some of the state's best trout fishing awaits anglers.

And what would a Virginia destination be without some kind of tie-in with the Civil War? Confederate General Thomas "Stonewall" Jackson won the first victory of his Valley Campaign in 1862 at McDowell. The site is marked by an iron roadside marker.

The **Highland Inn** is a 1904 Victorian hotel on Main Street with 18 rooms and a restaurant. ☎ 540-468-2143, www.highland-inn.com. $

For more information about the area contact the **Highland County Chamber of Commerce**, PO Box 223, Monterey, VA, 24465, ☎ 540-468-2550, www.highlandcounty.org.

Transportation

Greyhound provides bus transportation for the region. The station is on 1143 Richmond Road (☎ 540-886-2424, 800-231-2222). **Amtrak**, at 1 Middlebrook Avenue, links the city with Washington DC, New York and Chicago (☎ 800-872-7245).

The **Shenandoah Valley Regional Airport**, located in Weyers Cave, 10 miles from Staunton, provides daily flights to Washington Dulles (www.flyshd.com).

Information

Information on attractions, dining and lodging around Staunton, as well as a brochure for a self-guided walking tour, is available at the **Staunton/Augusta County Travel Information Center**, 1303 Richmond Road, off I-81 at Exit 222, ☎ 540-332-3972, www.staunton.va.us.

You can receive information on Waynesboro from the **Rockfish Gap Tourist Information Center** at the junction of Skyline Drive and the Blue Ridge Parkway, off I-64 at Exit 99, ☎ 800-471-3109.

For information on the town of Monterey and Highland County, contact the **Highland County Chamber of Commerce**, PO Box 223, Monterey, VA 24465, ☎ 540-468-2550.

Winchester & Frederick County

Strategically situated at the northern gateway to the legendary Shenandoah Valley, Winchester has played a significant role in both Virginia and American history.

Founded in 1744 by Colonel James Wood, the town was settled predominantly by industrious, independent, Scotch-Irish, German and Quaker immigrants from Pennsylvania.

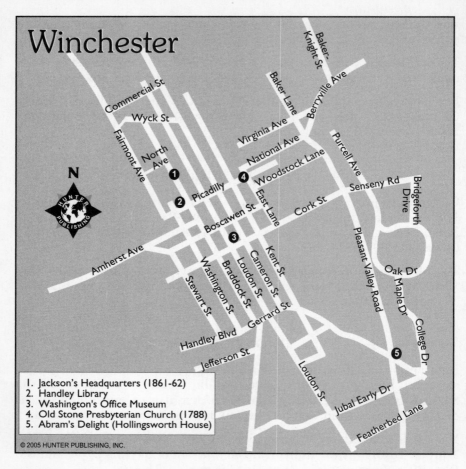

Winchester

1. Jackson's Headquarters (1861-62)
2. Handley Library
3. Washington's Office Museum
4. Old Stone Presbyterian Church (1788)
5. Abram's Delight (Hollingsworth House)

© 2005 HUNTER PUBLISHING, INC.

In 1748, 16-year-old George Washington arrived on the frontier at Winchester. Among his early endeavors, Washington surveyed Lord Fairfax's vast holdings, built a chain of forts to protect the settlers, led Virginia's forces against the French and hostile Indians and represented Frederick County in the House of Burgesses.

The Civil War devastated Winchester and Frederick County, but with the end of the hostilities the area gradually recovered. The charred acreage grew crops again, the burned barns were rebuilt, wheat and apples were marketed nationwide, new industries blossomed and the state's first public education system was established. Today, Winchester boasts a thriving economy and an inspiring historic setting bounded by one of the nation's most beautiful natural areas.

Sights

Abram's Delight and Log Cabin, 1340 South Pleasant Valley Road, are Winchester's oldest buildings. Built in 1754 by the son of the first white settler to the region, these buildings have been restored and furnished in Colonial style. The site features a log cabin, boxwood gardens and a basement kitchen. Abram's Delight is open daily, April through October. ☎ 540-662-6519.

Belle Grove Plantation, on Route 11 in Middletown, was headquarters for Northern generals during the various military campaigns in the area during the Civil War. One section of the home is devoted to quilting and fabrics. There is a gift shop and the plantation hosts a number of festivals throughout the year, including a micro-brew festival, an antique car show and a major Civil War re-enactment. Open daily, April-October. ☎ 540-869-2028 for tour and event schedules.

Blandy Experimental Farm & State Arboretum is 10 miles east of Winchester on US 50; hundreds of varieties of trees are grown here. A walk on the trails winding throughout the groves and gardens in this 170-acre preserve is both peaceful and educational. It is open dawn to dusk, year-round. ☎ 540-837-1758, www.virginia.edu/blandy.

Burwell-Morgan Mill is a stone and clapboard 200-year-old mill. Open May through October, Wednesday through Sunday. ☎ 540-837-1799.

Cedar Creek Battlefield Visitors Center, on Route 11 in Middletown, is the site of Northern General Philip Sheridan's victory over Southern forces. Maps, models and audio tools help explain this see-saw battle that saw the South advance, then suffer tremendous losses as the North regained the upper hand. Open daily, April-October. ☎ 540-869-2064.

Deer Meadow Vineyard is 12 miles southwest of Winchester. Open March through December, Wednesday through Sunday. 199 Vintage Lane, ☎ 540-877-1919, www.dmeadow.com.

Dinosaur Land, at the intersection of Rtes. 522, 340 and 277 in White Post, boasts an array of life-size dinosaur replicas, including an amazing 20-foot tyrannosaurus rex. Models of cave men and women round out this prehistoric experience. ☎ 540-869-2222, www.dinosaurland.com.

Glen Burnie Historic House, Gardens and Julian Wood Glass, Jr. Collection, 801 Amherst Street, is the home of Winchester's founder. Inside, fine examples of Colonial-era woodworking, stone cutting and decorating are preserved or re-created. Outside, gardens, fountains and a cemetery spread over 25 acres create a lush setting for this red brick, Georgian-style home. Open April through October; closed Mondays. ☎ 540-662-1473.

The Handley Library and Archives, at Bradock and Piccadilly Streets, were completed in 1913. The building, crowned by a copper-covered dome, features stained glass windows, a wrought iron staircase and glass floors. The historical archives are housed on the lower level. The Handley is open daily. ☎ 540-662-9041.

Old Court House Civil War Museum is located in the 1840 courthouse which served as a prison and hospital to both Northern and Southern troops during the Civil War. It's located on the downtown walking mall and features 3,000 relics. Open Friday through Sunday. ☎ 540-542-1145, www.civilwarmuseum.org.

Shenandoah Valley Discovery Museum, 54 S. Loudoun Street on the Old Town Mall, is a great place to bring the kids for hands-on exhibits of simple machinery, arts and crafts and nature. It's open year-round, Tuesday through Sunday. ☎ 540-722-2020, www.discoverymuseum.net.

Stonewall Jackson's Headquarters Museum, 415 North Bradock Street, was the great general's headquarters from November of 1861 until March, 1862. The museum contains many exhibits, Civil War artifacts and Jackson memorabilia. The Headquarters are open daily. ☎ 540-667-3242 for information.

Washington's Office and Museum is at the corner of Cork and Bradock Streets in Winchester. The building, used by Washington in 1755-56 during the erection of Fort Loudoun, houses many French and Indian, Revolutionary and Civil War relics, artifacts and memorabilia. The museum is open daily, April through October. ☎ 540-662-4412.

Wilson's Pet Farm is a five-acre petting zoo five miles east of Winchester off Route 50. Open daily May through Labor Day, ☎ 540-662-5715.

Recreation

Appleland Sports Center has a golf course and mini-golf on Route 11 in Stephens City. ☎ 540-869-8600.

The **Family Drive-In Theatre** shows current feature films, Route 11, Stephens City, ☎ 540-869-2175.

Jim Barnett Park has playing fields and courts, mini-golf, indoor and outdoor pools. Entrances located on Cork Street and Pleasant Valley Road, Staunton. ☎ 540-662-4946.

Sky Meadows State Park is scenic high-meadow park with an 1850s farmhouse, bridle trail and access to the Appalachian Trail. Located two miles south of Paris on Route 710 West, off Route 17 North, ☎ 540-592-3556.

Winchester Skating Rink offers roller skating on a maplewood floor. Located on Route 7, east of I-81. ☎ 540-667-6464.

Tours

The **Apple Trail Driving Tour** takes in attractions and farm markets in Virginia's Apple Capital. The 45-mile route is accompanied by an audio tape, available from the visitors center, ☎ 800-662-1360, www.apple-trail.org or www.visitwinchesterva.com.

The **Patsy Cline Nostalgia Driving Tour** is a driving tour through the hometown of the great country singer, who was born in Winchester. The Winchester-Frederick County Visitor Center and the Old Town Welcome Center have brochures available to guide visitors; ☎ 800-662-1360.

Tours of **Civil War** sites or significant **architecture** are popular activities in Winchester, lasting a few hours or an entire day. These tours are self-guided, although groups of 10 or more may make reservations for a guide to accompany them. The Old Town Welcome Center in the historic district provides brochures for both.

A guide to sites associated with **George Washington** in and around Winchester is available from the George Washington Office Museum, or call the Winchester-Frederick County Visitor Center, ☎ 800-662-1360, www.visitwinchesterva.com.

Shopping

Apple Valley Mall, 1850 Apple Blossom Drive, is the regional shopping hub for the northern Shenandoah Valley, with 90 stores. ☎ 540-665-0201.

Historic Old Town Winchester is a 45-block National Historic District full of small boutiques, cafés, craft shops and galleries. The architecture is something to behold, a mix of Colonial and turn-of-the-century designs. There are a number of restaurants offering indoor dining or sidewalk cafés. All told, there are 200 businesses in the district. This is also the site of many of Winchester's festivals, exhibits and walking tours. ☎ 540-667-1815, ext. 435.

Millwood Crossing is a renovated apple-packing warehouse and stone tenant house (boarding house) containing several specialty shops and galleries. Closed Monday. ☎ 540-662-5157.

Route 11 Potato Chips, 2325 First Street in Middletown, ☎ 540-869-0104, www.rt11.com, makes specialty chips and a delectable variety of cooked sweet potatoes and other vegetables; you can sample before you buy.

Theater

Shenandoah University Theatre at Shenandoah University in Winchester presents musicals, dramas and comedies. ☎ 540-665-4569.

Wayside Theatre is home to a professional theater company with a 32 year history of producing a wide range of contemporary and classic comedies, dramas and musicals. The Shenandoah Sampler includes a show, lunch and a tour of nearby Belle Grove. Season runs June through April. Route 11, Middletown, ☎ 540-869-1776, www.waysidetheatre.org.

Winchester Little Theater, 315 W. Boscawen Street, ☎ 540-662-3331, produces comedies and dramas year-round.

Annual Events

The Shenandoah Apple Blossom Festival, held at the end of April, features the crowning of the Apple Blossom Queen, parades, arts and crafts, band contests, music and entertainment and a number of exciting and interesting attractions. ☎ 800-230-2139 or 540-662-3863.

Shenandoah Performs Music Festival takes place over two weeks in July at Shenandoah Conservatory. ☎ 540-535-3599, www.shenandoah-performs.su.edu.

The Apple Harvest Arts & Crafts Festival, held over the third weekend in September in the Jim Barnett Park, features a number of contests, music and entertainment and arts and crafts. ☎ 540-662-3996.

Cedar Creek Living History and Re-enactment Weekend, held in October at Belle Grove Plantation and Cedar Creek Battlefield, features a major re-enactment of the 1864 battle at this site. Volunteers in period costume demonstrate weaponry, military maneuvers and camp life. ☎ 540-869-2064.

Dining

Winchester and Frederick County offer a multitude of dining options from fast food to the very best in French cuisine. For more listings see www.visitwinchester.com.

1763 Restaurant serves German-American food in a family atmosphere, open daily. Route 1, Upperville, ☎ 540-592-3848

The Ashby Inn, 692 Federal Street in Paris, 18 miles east of Winchester, ☎ 540-592-3900, is open for dinner Wednesday through Saturday and for brunch on Sunday. The inn has a pleasant Virginia hunt-country atmosphere in a beautiful setting of rolling hills. It features period antiques and plank floors that date back to the inn's origins in 1829. Specialties of the house include roast lamb, smoked seafood and crab cakes.

Café Sofia, 2900 Valley Avenue, ☎ 540-667-2950, serves homemade Bulgarian food in a small, warm atmosphere, daily except for Sunday.

Cork Street Tavern, at 8 W. Cork Street in the historic district, ☎ 540-667-3777, offers casual dining and is open for lunch and dinner seven days a week. Specialties are ribs, chicken, steaks and burgers.

La Carreta, 928 Berryville Avenue, ☎ 540-662-5759, serves Mexican food daily for lunch and dinner.

L'Auberge Provencale Inn, ☎ 540-837-1375, in White Post, nine miles east of Winchester on US 50, is open for dinner Wednesday through Sunday. The old country inn features an extensive collection of art and offers outdoor dining when weather permits.

Panda Express, 1850 Apple Blossom Drive, ☎ 540-667-6042, is open daily for lunch and dinner, specializing in fresh, healthy gourmet Chinese food.

Violino Ristorante Italiano serves northern Italian cuisine, 181 N. Loudoun Street, Winchester. Closed Sunday. ☎ 540-667-8006.

Wayside Inn serves traditional regional cuisine daily in a 1797 historic inn. 7783 Main Street, Middletown, ☎ 540-869-1797, www.wayside.org

Accommodations

Hotels & Motels

Best Western Lee-Jackson Motor Inn, 711 Millwood Avenue, Winchester, ☎ 540-662-4154, has 140 guest rooms. Amenities include a full-service restaurant and café, and a swimming pool. $

Comfort Inn, 1601 Martinsburg Pike, ☎ 540-667-8894, has 82 guest rooms, an outdoor pool and exercise equipment. $

Econo Lodge North, 1593 Martinsburg Pike, ☎ 540-662-4700, has 50 guest rooms. There is a free continental breakfast, and rooms specially equipped for senior citizens. $

The historic 1924 **George Washington Hotel** is reopening after 30 years; it's been completely renovated, with 92 guest rooms, a lobby bar and restaurant, grand ballroom, meeting space, indoor pool and a small spa. 103 E. Piccadilly Street, Winchester, ☎ 540-678-4700. $$$

Hampton Inn, 1655 Apple Blossom Drive, ☎ 540-667-8011, has 103 guest rooms, with hair dryers, irons, and sleeper sofas. $

Holiday Inn, 1017 Millwood Pike, ☎ 540-667-3300, has 175 guest rooms, a full-service restaurant and café, a bar, a swimming pool and several meeting rooms. $

Travelodge of Winchester, 160 Front Royal Pike, ☎ 540-665-0685, has 149 guest rooms and eight efficiencies. The hotel has a heated swimming pool and fitness equipment. $

Bed & Breakfasts / Inns

L'Auberge Provençale Inn in White Post, nine miles east of Winchester on US 50, ☎ 540-837-1375, www.laubergeprovencale.com, is a French country inn. It was once a sheep farm owned by Lord Fairfax. A full breakfast is served each morning. Complimentary airport transportation. $$

Inn At Vaucluse Spring is an elegant county retreat offering 15 guest rooms in six different buildings. 140 Vaucluse Spring Lane, Stephens City, ☎ 540-869-0200, www.vauclusespring.com $$$

Long Hill Bed and Breakfast is a large, 10,000 square-foot home built in the 1970s using materials from 200-year-old log homes, chimneys and barns. 547 Apple Pie Ridge Road, Winchester, ☎ 540-450-0341, 866-450-0341, www.longhillbb.com $$

Old Waterstreet Inn is an historic inn in Old Town Winchester, 217 W. Boscawen Street, Winchester. ☎ 540-665-6777, 866-665-6770, www.old-waterstreetinn.com $$

The Herds Inn at Hedgebrook is an elegant log house on a 50-acre dairy farm with two guest rooms. 688 Shady Elm Road, Winchester, ☎ 866-783-2681, www.TheHerdsInn.com $$

Wayside Inn is a 200-year-old inn at 7783 Main Street, Middletown. ☎ 540-869-1797, www.wayside.org. $$

Camping

Battle of Cedar Creek Campground, 8950 Valley Pike Road in Middletown, ☎ 540-869-1888, is open year-round. There is a swimming pool, water, electric and sewage hookups for trailers and RVs, a camp store, hot showers and fishing facilities on Cedar Creek.

Cove Campground, 980 Cove Road in Gore (Route 704) is a full-service campground with tent and trailer sites, hook-ups for RVs, a lake, bike rentals and boat rentals. ☎ 540-858-2882.

Transportation

Air transportation is provided by the **Winchester Regional Airport**. **Greyhound** also serves Winchester (☎ 800-231-2222).

Information

The **Winchester-Frederick County Visitor Center** is located at 1360 Pleasant Valley Road in the 1833 Hollingworth Mill House. There is an 18-minute video on the area, a Patsy Cline display (her music plays on the jukebox), souvenirs, maps and brochures on attractions, dining and lodging. Open daily, 9 a.m. to 5 p.m. ☎ 800-662-1360, www.visitwinchesterva.com.

Old Town Welcome Center at 2 N. Cameron Street, has tour brochures, lodging, dining and shopping information for Winchester's historic district. Open daily, ☎ 540-722-6367.

Southwest Virginia

Abingdon

Abingdon is a town rich in tradition and beauty. The oldest town west of the Blue Ridge Mountains, Abingdon has served as the Washington County seat since 1778. Lovingly restored old homes framed in a setting of mountain laurel and rhododendrons accent the vibrant rolling hills. In Abingdon, music, art, drama and unique shopping opportunities abound. The old city is a tapestry of performing artists and festivals.

Visitors to Abingdon can browse the craft shops, galleries and specialty stores, and "shop the world" at Dixie Pottery. They can stroll down shaded, brick sidewalks or take a saunter along the scenic Virginia Creeper Trail, and they can sample the culinary arts at one of a dozen or so fine restaurants.

Whether you're visiting overnight or for a vacation, Abingdon offers a world rich in hospitality, history and charm; a chance to spend a little time in a healthy atmosphere of outdoor tranquility.

Sights

Abingdon's **Historic District** covers a 20-block area. The architecture is Federal and Victorian, the gardens are impeccable. If you have an afternoon free, stroll down the tree-lined neighborhood streets, examining old homes once owned by the town's most prominent judges and business owners. Many are attractions in their own right, such as the Barter Theatre, the Martha Washington Inn, and The Tavern. The Washington County Courthouse on Court Street is of particular interest, featuring Tiffany windows installed after World War I.

The Fields/Penn 1860 House Museum, 208 West Main Street, depicts the life of a prosperous family just prior to the Civil War through period room settings and interpretive displays.

The Martha Washington Inn, 150 West Main Street, ☎ 276-628-3161, www.marthawashingtoninn.com, was the home of General Francis Preston. Built in 1832, the old house served as the Martha Washington College in 1860 and as a hospital during the Civil War. Actors at The Barter Theater across the street used it as a boarding house for a time. Today, it is a four-diamond rated lodging and stands tall as one of western Virginia's most notable inns.

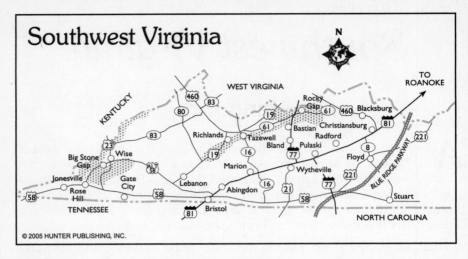

Southwest Virginia

The Barter Theatre, built around 1832 as a church for the Sinking Spring Presbyterian congregation, is now the state theater of Virginia. Across the street from the Martha Washington Inn at 133 West Main Street, it claims to be one of the oldest professional residence theaters in the United States. The theater takes its name from the long-ago practice of accepting goods in exchange for admission ("ham for Hamlet," as locals say). On the playbill you'll find Shakespeare, musical reviews and premieres. ☎ 276-628-3991, www.bartertheatre.com.

Barter Stage II, set in a historical Methodist Church across the street from the Barter Theater, offers a more intimate setting, with seating for 167 patrons. **The Café**, located in the lobby of Barter Stage II, serves lunch and dinner, specialty coffees and deserts.

The William King Regional Arts Center, a partner of the Virginia Museum of Fine Arts, features four museum-grade galleries, working studios for artists, classes, and a museum store. It is located at 415 Academy Drive. ☎ 276-628-5005, www.wkrac.org.

The Art Depot is both a gallery and a workshop, located at 314 Depot Square, and is home to the Depot Artists Association. Work by regional and state-wide artists is displayed throughout the year. Space is available for working artists. A number of media are on display – painting, weaving, pottery, sculptures – as well as performance art. ☎ 276-628-9091, www.abingdonartsdepot.org.

White's Mill, 12291 Whites Mill Road, ☎ 276-628-2960, is a National Historic Landmark and Virginia Historical Landmark. It preserves a 1797 grist and flour mill that stands as one of only a few water-powered mills in existence in Southwest Virginia. Interpreters make cornmeal in the manner of Southwest Virginia's earliest settlers. Also features a blacksmith shop and broom shop. Open Wednesday-Sunday, 10 a.m. to 6 p.m.

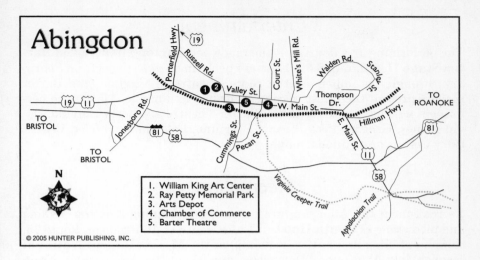

1. William King Art Center
2. Ray Petty Memorial Park
3. Arts Depot
4. Chamber of Commerce
5. Barter Theatre

© 2005 HUNTER PUBLISHING, INC.

Events

The Virginia Highlands Festival, held in Abingdon the first two weeks in August, features a large number of exhibits, demonstrations of local handicrafts, hot air ballooning, historical reenactments, musical entertainment and an antiques market. The festival has been named among the top 100 events in North America. ☎ 800-435-3440, www.va-highlandsfestival.org.

In mid-September, Abingdon hosts **The Washington County Fair**, which features a variety of exhibits that include farm equipment, livestock and crops. There's also live musical entertainment, talent shows, a beauty contest and a parade. ☎ 276-628-3789, www.washfair.com.

For additional events, call the **Abingdon Convention and Visitors Bureau**, ☎ 800-435-3440, www.abingdon.com.

Shopping

When it comes to shopping, Abingdon is everything you would imagine a hip little town should be. Shops specialize in cute country collectibles and chic décors, Christmas ornaments and locally made fine arts and crafts, the latest fashions and hard-to-find books. Elsewhere they may be called junk shops, but in Abingdon, the antique farm implements, old signs, rickety furniture and old barrels that cover the walls and hallways of several shops make for exciting exploring. After lunch, you can duck into a gallery, watch an artist at work in his or her studio, or sit under the shade of a broad-leaf tree and sip coffee as a slice of the world passes by. What you shouldn't do is rush.

Abingdon

Entertainment

The performing arts flourish at the renowned **Barter Theatre** and **Barter Stage II**, ☎ 276-628-3991. Actors perform on two stages from February through December. As the State Theatre of Virginia, the Barter players present the finest in comedy, drama and music. Among the performers who have acted with the Barter Theatre are Larry Linville, David Birney, Gregory Peck, Ernest Borgnine, Patricia Neal, Ned Beatty, Gary Collins and Hume Cronyn.

Recreation

Recreation in the Abingdon area includes swimming, boating, fishing and picnicking at **South Holston Lake**, south of Abingdon on Route 75; camping, hiking and nature watching at the **Mount Rogers National Recreation Area**, near Damascus, and along the Appalachian Trail; and hiking, bicycling, horseback riding, nature watching and cross-country skiing on the magnificent **Virginia Creeper Trail**.

Highlands Ski & Outdoor Center in Abingdon is both an outfitter and a tour provider. You'll find your kayaking, hiking, rock climbing and mountain biking supplies here. In addition, the center runs mountain bike shuttles to the Mount Rogers region and the Virginia Creeper Trail. ☎ 800-736-4174 for rates and information. Abingdon's tourism Web page lists a number of other local and regional outfitters.

The Virginia Creeper Trail is southwest Virginia's premiere multi-use trail. Mountain bikes and hikers use this 34.3-mile recreation trail, which begins at the Virginia-North Carolina border and ends in Abingdon. From one end to the other, the terrain varies from rugged to pastoral. You'll cross at least 100 train bridges and trestles. The trail name comes from the "creepers," slow-moving trains that carried coal from West Virginia mines to the port cities on the East Coast. The Virginia Creeper Trail Club (www.vacreepertrail.org) is an organization dedicated to keeping this one of the country's best rail trails.

Virginia Creeper Trail Bike Shop, ☎ 888-BIKEN4U, and Highland Bike Rental, ☎ 800-337-3629, are two Abingdon-based outfitters that specialize in Creeper Trail bike rentals and shuttles. Outfitters in nearby Damascus offer similar services.

Hot air balloons are a popular activity and a great way to see the splendor of southwest Virginia's mountain region without breaking a sweat. **Balloon Virginia**, ☎ 276-628-6353, and **Flyaway Hot Air Balloons**, ☎ 276-676-4464, run flights all year long.

Blue Blaze Bike & Shuttle Service in Damascus serves the Mt. Rogers area, including Iron Mountain, the Virginia Creeper Trail and other Appalachian Mountain areas. The shop, its guides and other employees are all-around great boosters for the Damascus area. If you need a place to stay, a bite to eat or a recommendation on where to ride, and they have a ready answer. ☎ 800-475-5095.

Dining

Abingdon offers a variety of dining opportunities. The restaurants listed below are especially good values.

Alison's, 1220 West Main Street, ☎ 276-628-8002, is casual family dining in a converted drive-in restaurant. Ribs are what it's known for, and the fresh bread, herb butter, baked potato soup, fresh salads and homemade desserts make for an eclecttic and satisfying meal.

Withers Hardware Restaurant, 260 West Main Street, ☎ 276-628-1111, is a fine restaurant with a unique dining atmosphere and the space to accommodate tour groups. Specialties of the house include fresh seafood and Western beef, as well as Asian-inspired dishes.

The Starving Artist Café, 134 Wall Street, ☎ 276-628-8445, is a local favorite featuring gourmet sandwiches. The restaurant is open for lunch and dinner and doubles as an art gallery.

The Dining Room, located in the Martha Washington Inn, ☎ 276-628-3161, is a Victorian-style restaurant that offers traditional and continental fare in an atmosphere of elegance. The restaurant is open for breakfast and dinner, with lunch on weekends or for matinee performances at the Barter Theatre.

The Tavern, 222 East Main Street, ☎ 276-628-1118, is Abingdon's oldest building, dating from 1779. It's open for dinner.

Caroline's, 301 East Main Street, ☎ 276-739-0042, is the former Abingdon General Store & Gallery. Fare is traditional American at reasonable prices.

Accommodations

Hotels & Motels

The Alpine, 882 East Main Street, ☎ 276-628-3178, has 19 guest rooms, a playground and a fine view of the mountains. Several restaurants are close by. $

The Camberley's Martha Washington Inn, 150 West Main Street, ☎ 276-628-3161, www.marthawashingtoninn.com, is an exclusive hotel with 61 rooms and suites, a full-service restaurant, meeting rooms, pool privileges, bar, tennis and golf privileges, lawn games and antique furnishings. Afternoon tea is served between 4 and 5 p.m. $$$

Abingdon

Comfort Inn, at the junction of Interstate 81 at Exit 14 and Virginia Route 140, ☎ 276-676-2222, offers 80 guest rooms. Complimentary continental breakfast. $

Days Inn, 887 Empire Drive, ☎ 276-628-7131, is located convenient to Exit 19 off Interstate 81. It's 105 rooms were renovated in 2003. A Cracker Barrel Restaurant is next door. $$

Hampton Inn, 340 Commerce Drive, Exit 17 off I-81, ☎ 276-619-4600, has 68 guest rooms, some with hot tubs, and an outdoor pool. $$

Holiday Inn Express, 940 E. Main Street, ☎ 276-676-2829, has 80 guest rooms, meeting facilities and an outdoor pool. A free continental breakfast is served daily. $$

Bed & Breakfasts / Inns

Abingdon Boarding House, 116 East Main Street, ☎ 276-628-9344 www.abingdonboardinghouse.com, has three bedrooms with either king or queen size beds. When combined with the affiliated **Wolf Hills Inn**, 112 East Main Street, there is room for a family or group of up to 18 people. $$

Cottages on the Creeper, 334 Gibson Street, ☎ 276-628-6331 www.cottagesonthecreeper.com, is a two-bedroom cottage with Jacuzzi and Internet access, convenient to the Virginia Creeper Trail and historic Abingdon. $$

The Crooked Cabin, 303 E. Main Street in Abingdon, ☎ 276-628-9582, is an interesting lodging experience. You rent the entire cabin, which can sleep up to six people in three bedrooms. There's a living room, meeting space and back yard. Food is delivered each evening and fruit, tea and coffee are always stocked. In-town attractions are a short walk away. $$

Inn On Town Creek, 445 E. Valley Street in Abingdon, ☎ 276-628-4560, www.innontowncreek.com, is set on four acres along Town Creek. There are three rooms and two suites filled with antiques. Beds are king-size; three of the rooms have private bath. The gardens here are nicely landscaped, with terraced patios The inn is non-smoking, and pets are not allowed, but children over 10 are welcome. $$

Love House, 210 East Valley Street, ☎ 276-623-1281 www.abingdon-virginia.com/loverooms, features two suites and two guest rooms in a restored post-Colonial home. Cooking classes are offered on weekends during the winter months. Breakfast is served in the affiliated Victoria & Albert Inn, a block away. $$

Maxwell Manor Bed & Breakfast, 19215 Old Jonesboro Road, ☎ 276-628-3912, is a rambling Georgian-style home with two guest rooms and one suite, each with private bath. There is an indoor pool, and a two-tier porch has swings for just plain relaxing. The living room and dining room each have a fireplace. Meeting rooms are available. A full breakfast is served. $$-$$$

Old Abingdon B&B, 200 Pecan Street NE, ☎ 276-623-1887 www.old-abingdon.com, is an inn decorated in the Italianate Victorian style located in the heat of the historic district. Two rooms feature king size beds, another a four-poster double bed with trundle. A fourth room, Cassandra's hideaway, has a king size bed and secluded back-of-the-house locale that makes it a favorite for lovebirds. $$$

Shepherd's Joy, 254 White's Mill Road in Abingdon, ☎ 276-628-3273, is a Queen Anne-style Victorian home located on a working sheep farm. There are four guest rooms tastefully decorated with antiques and a series of P. Buckley Moss paintings. This is a quiet inn, yet convenient to in-town attractions. $$-$$$

Silversmith Inn Bed & Breakfast, 102 E. Main Street in Abingdon, ☎ 276-676-3924, has four guest rooms and two suites, each with private baths set in a three-story brick home near The Barter Theater. Large front windows look out onto Main Street. Inside, there are queen-sized beds in each room, with air conditioning. $$-$$$

Summerfield Inn, 101 West Valley Street, ☎ 276-628-5905, www.summerfieldinn.com, prides itself in offering guests refined, hospitable service in the heart of historic Abingdon. There are seven guest rooms; each room features a private bath and independent heating and air conditioning controls. The large home, circa 1920, features gardens and a wrap-around porch for relaxation throughout the day. Children under 12 are welcome. No pets are allowed. $$-$$$

The Swiss Inn, at Exit 29 off I-81 in Glade Spring, ☎ 276-429-2233, offers dining and lodging with a touch of Switzerland. There are 32 rooms in the modern inn, and a gourmet restaurant in a historic 1835 home. It's located just seven miles north of Abingdon.

Victoria & Albert Inn, 224 Oak Hill Street, ☎ 276-676-2797, www-.abingdon-virginia.com/varooms, is a restored 1892 home with five guest rooms, including a second floor mini-suite. Breakfast is a four-course affair. $$-$$$

White Birches Inn, 268 White's Mill Road, ☎ 276-676-2140, www-.whitebirchesinn.com. An early-20th-century home with an eclectic décor of American and English antiques. Each room and the featured suite in this highly-decorated B&B has a mix of antique and modern furnishings, private baths, in-room fireplaces and whirlpool tubs, as well as high-speed Internet, cable and CD players. $$-$$$

Abingdon

Day-trip to Damascus

Picture this scene: You're hiking the Appalachian Trail. Have been for weeks. North Carolina's rugged mountains are behind you. Virginia lies ahead as you forge northward to Maine. Last night, in a shelter, two southbound hikers raved on about the Virginia hike, about the Grayson Highlands, Three Ridges and Skyline Drive. You wake up early, eager to make time. Crossing into Virginia, the trees fairly burst with autumn color. You come to a bend in the trail – and stop in your tracks.

In the valley sits a small town with white clapboard houses, church spires and neatly arranged streets. Kids ride bikes. A homeowner rakes the leaves into a big pile in her front yard.

Welcome to Damascus, a.k.a. Trail Town.

Such is the power of Damascus that there are actual documented cases of AT through-hikers entering town and never leaving. That may say more about the person than the town, but the fact remains: Damascus is a great place, for visitors and residents alike.

Seasons here are marked by the bloomings. Wildflowers coat the Appalachian slopes in spring, vibrant trilliums, wild iris and lady slippers; rare Catawba rhododendron bloom blue and purple in June; and Queen Anne's Lace pushes forth its white crown in August.

The proximity to the AT and Virginia Creeper Trail make Damascus a nexus for hikers. The Iron Mountain Trail heads out of town from a road dead-end, leading into the Mt. Rogers National Recreation Area.

It all comes together for Damascus during Trail Days in May, an annual celebration of the Appalachian Trail and the through-hikers who are so much a part of the town's life.

For information on visiting Damascus, call the **Town Hall** at ☎ 276-475-5131, www.damascus.org. Local retailers, like **Blue Blaze Bike & Shuttle Service**, ☎ 800-475-5095, are also a wealth of information. You can also contact the **Mount Rogers NRA office**, ☎ 276-475-5131.

Access Damascus from I-81 at Exit 19, taking Route 58 south into town. Another option is Route 91 south from I-81 at Exit 29. For a great scenic drive, head south from Marion on Route 16, then go west on Route 58.

However you get there – by trail, bike or car – be careful. Damascus just might cast that ol' mountain charm over you.

Transportation

The Tri-Cities Regional Airport is 13 miles southwest of Bristol just off Interstate 81, in Blountville, TN. Most major and regional carriers offer direct or connecting flights to all major domestic and international destinations; ☎ 423-325-6000, www.triflight.com.

By road, Abingdon is served principally by **Interstate 81** and **US Highways 11**, **19** and **58. Greyhound bus service** is also available.

Information

For information, brochures and a full list of area restaurants and hotels, contact the **Abingdon Convention & Visitors Bureau**, 335 Cummings Street, Abingdon, VA 24210, ☎ 276-676-2282 or toll-free at 800-435-3440. You can also visit their Web site at www.abingdon.com/tourism. The visitors bureau is located in the historic Hassinger House and is open daily, 9 a.m. to 5 p.m.

Big Stone Gap & Heart of Appalachia

The history of Big Stone Gap is one of boom and bust, of grand plans of outsiders to capitalize on natural resources like coal, iron ore, and timber, only to have those plans dissolve as the minerals and trees were depleted. It is the story, too, of tenacious individuals who weathered the vagaries of mountain life and carved out a lifestyle based on cherished values of independence and self-sufficiency.

In the 1850s, John Olinger bought 42,000 acres in Wise County for a total of $4.92. He called it "Mineral City" due to the huge reserves of coal and iron ore. In 1888, it returned to the name the earliest settlers had given it: Big Stone Gap.

A 40-year timber boom began in 1887. Railroads were needed to transport both lumber and coal, and the first track was laid in 1890. The streets of Big Stone Gap were laid out according to a plan, unlike most mountain towns. Lots were sold, large houses built, and property values skyrocketed. Plans were even drawn up for a 300-room hotel.

The year 1892 brought a major bank failure. The grand hotel never materialized. By 1915 most of the valuable trees had disappeared from the Appalachian slopes. They were not replanted. Production of iron ore began in Wise County in 1892, but it yielded little, and by 1920 most of the iron furnaces had closed.

Coal was the only major industry to survive around Big Stone Gap. Production peaked in 1926, and today it remains an important source of employment in Wise County.

Despite the town's "boom and bust," life changed little for those hardy inviduals who carved out homesteads in the the rugged mountains. They lived in mountain gaps and hollows much as they had for generations, hunting, farming and moonshining. Many of the place names retain the names of original setters.

Today, as tobacco – and even coal – decline, leaders hope tourism and outdoor recreation is the next boon for the area. The area, collectively marketed as the Heart of Appalachia, includes Dickenson, Lee, Russell, Scott, Tazewell and Wise counties, and the cities of St. Paul, Coeburn, Norton and Big Stone Gap. This region is again capitalizing on homegrown resources. Bluegrass music draws audiences from throughout the region, and *The Trail of the Lonesome Pine* outdoor drama, based on the novel of that name by local author John Fox, Jr., draws thousands to Big Stone Gap each year. The surrounding countryside covers thousands of acres, with miles of trails and dozens of fishing streams in the Jefferson National Forest. It's one of the few places left where you can spend days without seeing a soul and, if you're lucky, happen upon one of those early homesteader's cabins.

Sights

The **Ralph Stanley Museum & Traditional Mountain Music Center**, ☎ 276-926-5591, www.ralphstanleymuseum.com, is located in Clintwood, Dickenson County. Dr. Ralph Stanley, a native of Southwest Virginia, is a living legend of mountain music and bluegrass. This museum, opened in October 2004 inside a four-story home, celebrates his storied career and promotes appreciation of his musical genre. Besides traditional museum exhibits, there are interactive displays, listening stations, and space for conventions, seminars and workshops. Admission is $12 for adults, $10 for seniors and students. The museum is closed on Mondays.

The **Harry W. Meador Jr. Coal Museum**, at East Third Street and Shawnee Avenue, Big Stone Gap, ☎ 276-523-9209, traces the history of coal-mining in southwest Virgina, from the pick-and-shovel days to the present. Open Wednesday through Sunday; closed major holidays; free.

Historic June Tolliver House, at Jerome and Clinton Streets, Big Stone Gap, ☎ 276-523-4707. Here you can see where June Tolliver lived. She was a central character in the book *The Trail of the Lonesome Pine*. The house is decorated in period furnishings of the 1890s and has a gift and book shop. Call for opening hours.

The **Southwest Virginia Museum**, West First Street and Wood Avenue, Big Stone Gap, ☎ 276-523-1322, www.dcr.state.va.us/parks/swva-mus, is worth the visit. The mansion, built in the 1890s by Rufus Ayers, a Virginia attorney general, is made of locally-quarried limestone, sandstone and red oak; it took seven years to complete. The exhibits tell the fascinating stories of the boom and bust of Big Stone Gap and the tenacious people who settled and stayed here. It houses artifacts from mining and town life through the last 100 years. It is open daily in summer, closed during the months of January and February and Mondays the rest of the year.

John Fox, Jr. Museum, Shawnee Avenue East, Big Stone Gap, ☎ 276-523-2747, was the home of the author of *The Trail of the Lonesome Pine*, a novel based partly on reality that has been made into a film three times. A theatrical version is designated as Virginia's official Outdoor Drama, and is performed each summer in Big Stone Gap. The 1888 house contains furnishings and memorabilia of the family.

Events

Coal/Railroad Days is a festival held the first weekend of August on Main Street, Appalachia, Wise County. This old coal-mining town came into existance in 1890 when two railroad companies formed a junction. It was named for the surrounding Appalachian Mountains. This traditional village festival highlights the historical role coal and railroad played in the town's development, including the Bee Rock Tunnel, which measures all of 47 feet, 7 inches in length. ☎ 276-565-0055 for more information.

The **Dock Boggs Festival** is held the second Saturday of September in Josephine, a small burg west of Norton. Dock Boggs grew up in Southwest Virginia and his style of banjo playing, incluenced by folk and blues, is an acknowledged influence on a diverse mix of musicians, from Bob Dylan to punk bands to electronica. This annual festival is strictly mountain and bluegrass however. Admission is $8. Call ☎ 276-328-0130 or visit www.heartofappalachia.com.

The **Hills of Home Bluegrass Festival** is held annually on Memorial Day Weekend, at the Hills of Home Park (Old Home Place) near Coeburn, Virginia. This pre-eminent music festival packs three days with a who's-who in traditional and contemporary bluegrass; Gillian Welch, Jim Lauderdale, Patti Loveless and the Kentucky Mountain Boys have performed in the past. Hometown hero Ralph Stanley and His Clinch Mountain Boys are hosts and headliners. Call ☎ 606-784-9936 or visit www.dr-ralphstanley.com/events/festival.

Home Craft Days is an annual happening every third Saturday in October. Started in 1972, the festival fills Mountain Empire Community College, near Big Stone Gap, with exhibitors from throughout the Central Appalachian region. Appalachia's traditional culture is celebrated with mountain music, dancing, storytelling and food. Visit www.homecraft-days.com for information.

Pound Heritage Days take place over the Memorial Day weekend. Up and down Main Street, businesses, townfolk and visitors celebrate the heritage of Pound, in Wise County, a town which derived its name from a pounding mill once located here during the settlement era. Activities include the traditional festival line-up of crafts, music, carnival rides, street dancing and a car show. Call ☎ 276-679-0961 for information.

Gospel singing has deep roots in Appalachia. Two annual events draw especially big crowds: the **Tri-State Gospel Singing Convention**, held on the second Sunday of June in **Bullitt Park, Big Stone Gap**; and an identically-named festival held the first weekend of August at **Breaks Interstate Park**, attract large crowds. The Big Stone Gap event marks its 85th year in 2005, making it one of the regions longest-running events. The Breaks concert is the largest-attended event at the park each year. Visit www.heartofappalachia.com for information on both events.

Wise County Famous Fall Fling packs a boatload of activity into a crisp fall weekend in October. Downtown Wise bustles with activities; there is a car show, art and photo contests, chili-cook-off, quilt contest, cake competitions, talent shows and activities for kids. Music for dancing, toe-tapping or simply enjoying in a lawn chair is peformed throughout the weekend. Call ☎ 276-679-4043, www.wisefallfling.com, for information.

Beautiful natural scenery serves as backdrop for the **Guest River Rally**, held the weekend before Labor Day in Coeburn, Wise County. The two-day festival offers a traditional line-up of arts and crafts, music and food; ☎ 276-679-0961.

Entertainment

Country Cabin, Old US 23, Norton, ☎ 276-679-2632, features live bluegrass by local and regional performers every Saturday night. Family-oriented activities include clogging and mountain two-step.

At **Purely Appalachian Crafts Empowerment**, 409 Front Street, Coeburn, Virginia, country, gospel and bluegrass music ring out every Friday night, 7-9 p.m. P.A.C.E. is an Appalachian crafters outlet situated in Coeburn's historic hardware store, and an official stop on Virginia's "The Crooked Road: Virginia's Heritage Music Trail." Admission to the Friday concerts is free, although donations are accepted. Call ☎ 276-395-5160 for more information.

***Trail of the Lonesome Pine* State Outdoor Drama** is shown next door to the June Tolliver house in an outdoor amphitheater in Big Stone Gap. Each summer, from late June through early September, John Fox's romantic story of the early settlers of the area comes to life. For tickets and show times, ☎ 276-523-1235 or 800-362-0149.

Virginia-Kentucky Opry, Park Avenue, Norton, ☎ 276-679-1901, is a 250-seat theater featuring live entertainment.

Recreation

Flag Rock Recreation Area, 618 Virginia Avenue, Norton, ☎ 276-679-0754, is a city park located on the hillside, 1,000 feet above Norton. There are rental shelters, and facilities for camping and lake fishing.

George Washington & Jefferson National Forest is part of the Clinch Ranger District (headquartered in Wise, ☎ 276-328-2931; forest holdings are spread throughout the region). Among the natural highlights are the **Guest River Gorge**, a passageway cut through Stone Mountain; the trails, picnic facilities and camping around **Bark Camp Lake**, an 80-acre lake that is stocked with northern pike, blue gill, rainbow trout and catfish; **Little Stony National Recreation Trail**, an easy 2.8 mile path that begins at Hanging Rock Picnic Area and follows the Little Stony Creek to a 24-foot waterfall cascading down a natural rock ampitheater; **Cave Spring National Recreation Area**, a camping and hiking area at the foot of Stone Mountain featuring a grotto-like cave and spring; and the **Stone Mountain Trail**, which follows the top of Stone Mountain from Cave Spring NRA to Big Stone Gap.

Heart of Appalachia Bike Route, ☎ 800-SWVA-FUN or 276-523-2005, is a 128-mile route from Burkes Garden in Tazewell County to the Guest River Gorge in Wise County.

High Knob Recreation Area, in the Clinch Ranger District of the Jefferson National Forest, ☎ 276-328-2931, offers views of four states from a stone observation tower. There is also camping, lake swimming and hiking on the Chief Bengee Scout Trail.

Lake Keokee, near the community of Keokee, ☎ 276-328-2931, has a 92-acre fishing lake and a hiking trail.

Pinnacle Area Natural Reserve, 2854 Park Boulevard, in Marion, ☎ 276-781-7400, is dominated by its namesake rock formation, "The Pinnacle," but offers nature lovers a trove of sinkholes, caves, sinking streams and lush cove forest ecosystems.

In quiet St. Paul, the **Sugar Hill** and **Scenic Clinch River Trails** offer visitors a low-impact outdoor experience. Interpretive signs will familiarize you with the local flora and fauna as the trail traces first the Clinch River, than climbs into the hills through old fields and young forests. Visit www.sugarhillclinch.com for more information.

Dining

China Garden, Wise County Plaza, between Wise and Norton, ☎ 276-679-5201. Open for lunch and dinner seven days a week.

Fish Tales, VA/KY Regional Shopping Center, Norton, ☎ 276-679-1651, is a family restaurant featuring large seafood platters and fresh barbecue.

Monterey Mexican Restaurant, 154 Ridgeview Circle, Wise, ☎ 276-679-5850. Open seven days a week for breakfast, lunch and dinner.

Ms. Fritzi's Tearoom at The Victorian House, 606 Wood Avenue East, Big Stone Gap, ☎ 276-523-6245, is a Victorian home just a few steps from *The Trail of the Lonesome Pine* outdoor drama. The tearoom serves gourmet soups, salads, sandwiches and desserts. There is also a gift shop. Open for lunch and dinner.

Robert's House Restaurant, 146 Roberts Street, Wise, ☎ 276-328-2277.

Roma's Pizzeria, Wise Shopping Center, ☎ 276-328-3714.

Shannon's Restaurant, 197 Ridgeview Drive, Wise County Plaza, Norton, ☎ 276-679-5617, serves up hamburgers, seafood, and all kinds of American food. Closed on Sundays.

Stringer's Restaurant, 412 East 5th Street, Big Stone Gap, ☎ 276-523-5388, is open daily and has a bounteous, all-you-can-eat buffet, served cafeteria-style.

Accommodations

Country Hearth Inn, 375 Wharton Lane, Norton, ☎ 276-679-5340, has 58 rooms and offers a free breakfast, whirlpool suites, with shopping and restaurants nearby. $$

 Country Inn Motel & Campground, 627 Gilley Avenue, Big Stone Gap, ☎ 276-523-0374, has 42 rooms, most with a view of the mountains. Rooms have refrigerators and pets are allowed. The campground accommodates trailers and RVs and has full hookups. $

 Holiday Inn Norton, 551 Highway 58 East, Norton, ☎ 276-679-7000, has 120 rooms, an indoor pool, restaurant, and pets are allowed. $$

Day-trip to Cumberland Gap & Breaks Interstate Park

The Virginia-Kentucky border more or less follows natural ridgelines where the so-called "Virginia plates" push up and over the "Kentucky plates." This geologic phenomenon causes some of Virginia's most fascinating natural features. Among these are **Cumberland Gap** in the far southwest point of the state, and **"the Breaks"** to the northeast, the deepest gorge east of the Mississippi. As settlers forged westward, the mountains and canyons proved incredible barriers – thus the fame of Daniel Boone's Wilderness Road through the Cumberland Gap. Today, visitors can enjoy the historical and recreational opportunities they provide, from following the path of the Wilderness Road to whitewater rafting.

Breaks Interstate Park, ☎ 800-982-5122, www.breakspark.com, is a joint venture between Virginia and Kentucky. The 4,500-acre park, located on KY-VA 80, eight miles north of Haysi, VA, offers breaktaking views of the canyon and river below, camping, hiking, and live bluegrass in the outdoor amphitheater. There is a lodge and a restaurant with some of the best views in Virginia. Whitewater rafting on the Russell Fork River draws enthusiasts from all over the country to these Class VI rapids each October. The park's **Rhododendron Restaurant**, ☎ 800-982-5122, offers a panoramic view from the canyon rim and has dining outdoors on the deck.

Cumberland Gap National Historical Park, ☎ 606-248-2817, www.nps.gov/cuga, in Middlesboro, KY, commemorates America's first doorway to the West, through which thousands passed en route to settling America.

Wilderness Road State Park in Ewing, VA, ☎ 276-445-3065, www.dcr.state.va.us/parks/wildroad, offers the 10-mile Wilderness Road Trail for hiking, biking and horses. There is also a historic mansion within this day-use park.

Transportation

The nearest commercial airport is the **Tri-Cities Regional Airport** in Blountville, TN, just over the border from Bristol (www.triflight.com, ☎ 423-325-6000).

Information

Lonesome Pine Tourist & Information Center, is located in a historic train car at 627 Gilley Avenue in Big Stone Gap, ☎ 276-523-2060. The "101 Car" was built in 1870 and was once the private car of the president of the Interstate Railroad. It even has its own bathroom. During its long career, the car was used as an office and even a hunting cabin. Today, its turn-of-the-century plush interior has been restored.

Heart of Appalachia Tourism Authority, 311 Wood Avenue, Big Stone Gap, ☎ 888-SWVA-FUN or 276-523-2005, promotes tourism in far southwest Virginia.

Big Stone Gap & Heart of Appalachia

Wise County Chamber of Commerce, 765 Park Avenue, Norton, VA 24273, ☎ 276-679-0961, provides visitor information, brochures and a calendar of events.

Bristol & Washington County

*B*ristol straddles the Virginia-Tennessee state line in an elevated region where the wildflowers and scenic vistas are a delight to behold. It seems that every day is a holiday with tempting aromas of culinary delights, the lively steps of cloggers and the roar of race cars at Bristol Motor Speedway.

History

Bristol is rich in history. Around 1765 Evan Shelby, a noted "Indian fighter," settled here on a tract called Sapling Grove. His home became the neighborhood fort, where settlers sought refuge under Indian attacks. Bristol grew around the "fort," and eventually became an important railroad center. The town was incorporated in 1856, the same year the last piece of track was laid to complete the Tennessee and Virginia Railroad.

Although it's essentially a city in two states (Tennessee and Virginia), Bristol is in fact two cities – with two different area codes! In 1881, both sides of the town agreed to accept the center of the city's main street, known today as State Street, as the state line. Brass markers down the center of the street clearly indicate the state line (with even and odd addresses in different states) and acknowledge the uniqueness of the city. The Bristol Sign spans the state line, and is listed on the National Historic Register. Built in 1910 and declaring Bristol "a good place to live," it welcomed the thousands of rail passengers entering the city.

Bristol is widely recognized as the "Birthplace of Country Music." There is a museum, a mural, and a monument paying tribute to this heritage. In 1927, Ralph Peer of the Victor Talking Machine Company established a recording studio in Bristol (TN). That studio launched the careers of Jimmie Rodgers, the Stonemans and the Carter family, and what was then known as Appalachian folk music was transformed into the national sensation we know today as country music.

Sights

Birthplace of Country Music Alliance Museum, is located in the Bristol Mall at 500 Gate City Highway, ☎ 276-645-0035. Housed here are artifacts from those seminal 1927 recordings, referred to as the Bristol

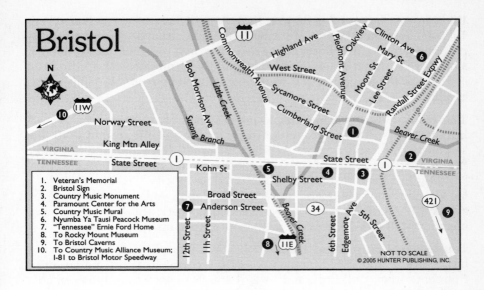

Bristol

N

1. Veteran's Memorial
2. Bristol Sign
3. Country Music Monument
4. Paramount Center for the Arts
5. Country Music Mural
6. Nyumba Ya Tausi Peacock Museum
7. "Tennessee" Ernie Ford Home
8. To Rocky Mount Museum
9. To Bristol Caverns
10. To Country Music Alliance Museum;
    I-81 to Bristol Motor Speedway

Commonwealth Avenue
Highland Ave
West Street
Sycamore Street
Cumberland Street
Bob Morrison Ave
Little Creek
Susong Branch
Norway Street
King Mtn Alley
State Street
Kohn St
Shelby Street
Broad Street
Anderson Street
12th Street
11h Street
Beaver Creek
Piedmont Avenue
Oakview
Clinton Ave
Mary St
Moore St
Lee Street
Randall Street Expwy
Beaver Creek
State Street
VIRGINIA
TENNESSEE
6th Street
Edgemont Ave
5th Street

VIRGINIA
TENNESSEE

NOT TO SCALE
© 2005 HUNTER PUBLISHING, INC.

sessions. The museum traces country music from its Appalachian roots with the Carter Family, through the radio days of Earl Scruggs, the career of Tennesee Ernie Ford, to present country stars like Dolly Parton and Patti Loveless. Admission is by donation. Every Thursday the museum presents its Pickin' Porch from 7-9 p.m. There is also a gift shop.

Bristol Caverns, located five miles southeast of Bristol off US 421, are the largest caverns in the Smoky Mountain region and are more than 200 million years old. The caverns feature many unusual rock formations that can be seen from lighted pathways winding through the caverns and along an underground river. Guided tours are conducted every 20 minutes. ☎ 423-878-2011.

The **Bristol Motor Speedway**, 2801 Highway 11E, is the world's fastest half-mile track, and hosts seven NASCAR events each year. ☎ 423-764-1161 for tickets.

Carter Family Memorial Music Center, Route 614, Hiltons, ☎ 276-386-6054, is the former home of the famous Carter Family. The family recorded for the Victor Talking Machine Company in Bristol, laying the foundation for country music. The museum is located in the old A.P. Carter Store and houses the musical artifacts of the family. Every Saturday night the tradition is carried on with live acoustic music shows in the rustic 1,000-seat theater next door. Call ahead for the museum's opening hours, show times and directions.

The **Nyumba Ya Tausi Peacock Museum**, 412 Clinton Avenue, ☎ 276-669-4596, showcases African and African-American art, artifacts, black memorabilia, and slavery and family heirlooms. Open on Saturday, 1-5 p.m., and during the week by appointment.

Bristol & Washington County

Paramount Center for the Arts, on State Street, Bristol, is housed in a 1931 art deco theater that first opened as a movie house. Today, after a $4 million restoration, it hosts Broadway tours and regional talent. There is a mighty Wurlitzer organ inside. The building is on the National Register of Historic Places. Tours can be arranged at the box office, or by calling ☎ 423-274-8920.

The Rocky Mount Museum, 11 miles southwest of Bristol on US 11E, in Piney Flats, TN, features a two-story log house built around 1770 that served as the capitol under William Blount – Governor of the United States Territory South of the Ohio River – from 1790 until 1792. The old building has been restored to its original simplicity. The site features a log kitchen, slave quarters, a blacksmith's shop and a smokehouse. Admission is charged; hours vary seasonally, check the Web site or call ahead. ☎ 423-538-7396, www.rockymountmuseum.com.

Tennessee Ernie Ford Home, 1223 Anderson Street, Bristol, is the birthplace of the world-famous entertainer, and features memorabilia from his career. Call Brenda at ☎ 276-466-9116 for a tour appointment.

The **Veteran's Memorial** at Cumberland Square, Cumberland and Lee Streets, Bristol, features five life-sized bronze sculptures by Maria Kirby-Smith. ☎ 276-645-7376.

Entertainment

Bristol's commitment to the arts is evident throughout the city. Organizations such as the **Theatre Bristol**, ☎ 423-968-4977, www.theatrebristol.com, The **Paramount Center for the Arts**, ☎ 423-274-8920, www.theparamountcenter.com, and the **Bristol Ballet Company**, ☎ 276-669-6051, form the nucleus of the city's cultural offerings.

The **Viking Hall Civic Center**, ☎ 423-764-0188, www.vikinghall.com, a popular entertainment facility, plays host to a diversity of concerts, trade shows, conventions and other activities. The **Cameo Theater**, ☎ 423-878-6279, www.cameotheater.org, built in 1925, and renovated and reopened in 1996, shows family, animation and classic films. Local colleges, theaters and civic centers also provide frequent programs.

In addition to NASCAR action at **Bristol Motor Speedway**, ☎ 423-764-1161, there is drag racing at **Bristol International Dragway**, ☎ 423-764-1161.

Shopping

Visitors will discover a new dimension in shopping with an excursion through the revived downtown district of Bristol. Quaint little restaurants and cafés cluster the streets, offering a wide variety of traditional and ethnic cuisines from seafood to bagels to homemade pastries. The downtown shops are unique, bountiful and easily accessible. A variety of shops and stores offer antiques, fine jewelry, clothing and handmade home accessories within walking distance of one another.

If you're after antiques, **Antiques Unlimited**, 620-24 State Street, ☎ 423-764-4211, **Heritage House Antiques**, 625 State Street, ☎ 276-669-9774, and more than 20 others.

Several major department stores, fine restaurants, more than 60 specialty shops and stores, along with a six-screen movie theater, are housed in the **Bristol Mall**.

Recreation

In the winter months visitors can ski at any one of a number magnificent slopes located within an hour's drive of the city. They can step back in time to journey through the geological wonders of **Bristol Caverns** and **Appalachian Caverns**, where guided tours are conducted by trained staff members.

The area offers a variety of hunting, fishing and boating opportunities.

Natural Areas

Observation Knob Park, on South Holston Lake, eight miles southeast of Bristol on US 421, is one of five TVA (Tennessee Valley Authority) lakes in the Bristol area. The lake, on the south fork of the Holston River, offers a variety of outdoor activities, including fishing, boating, swimming, camping, hiking and nature watching. ☎ 423-878-5561.

Steele Creek Park and Nature Center, 3½ miles southwest of Bristol via the Volunteer Parkway, is a 2,200-acre park with an 80-acre lake where visitors can hike, fish, swim and play golf. There is a large nature center which interprets the park's plant and animal life through exhibits and programs. ☎ 423-989-5616 for information on the nature center; ☎ 423-764-4023 for information on the park.

Sugar Hollow Park, Lee Highway, ☎ 276-645-7275, offers picnic shelters, camping and an athletic complex.

Golf

The scenic beauty of the Blue Ridge Mountains provides a relaxing atmosphere for golfing, while the mountainous terrain offers even the most experienced golfer a serious challenge. There are three private courses, **The Virginian Golf Club**, ☎ 276-645-6951; **The Country Club of Bristol**, ☎ 423-652-1700; and **The Farm**, ☎ 276-669-1042. There are five public golf courses, presenting a variety of course designs: **Cedars Golf Course**, ☎ 423-989-0064; **Clear Creek Golf Club**, ☎ 276-466-4833; **Holston Valley Golf Course**, ☎ 423-878-2021; **Steele Creek**

Golf Course, ☎ 423-764-6411; **Tri-Cities Golf Club,** ☎ 423-323-4178; and **Crockett Ridge Golf Course,** ☎ 423-279-1799.

Annual Events

Bristol Blast 4th of July Celebration is held each year at Bristol Motor Speedway. ☎ 423-764-1161.

Carter Family Traditional Music Festival, held the first weekend in August, celebrates the roots of country music at the Carter Family Fold in Hiltons. ☎ 276-386-6054.

RaceFest is a new two-week-long festival in August geared for the racing fan, coinciding with the Food City Family Race Night and the NASCAR race at Bristol Motor Speedway. For more information, call Bristol Motor Speedway at ☎ 423-764-1161.

Bristol's annual music festival is called the **Bristol Rhythm & Roots Reunion**. The three-day event in September features a variety of musical bands, from bluegrass to celtic, hosted by downtown businesses and venues. Call ☎ 423-656-6547, www.bristolrhythm.com.

Fantasy in Lights is held at Bristol Motor Speedway during November and December. ☎ 423-764-1161.

❖ *For more events in the Bristol area, call the Events Line at*
  ☎ *276-645-4238 or visit www.bristolchamber.org.*

Dining

Bristol offers an array of cafés, bakeries, gourmet shops and fine restaurants – more than 100 in all.

The Feed Room, 620 State Street, ☎ 423-764-0545, inside Antiques Unlimited, offers daily lunch specials, such as croissant sandwiches, veggie wraps and salads. Closed Sunday.

Java J's, 501 State Street, ☎ 276-466-8882, www.javajsdowntown.com, serves up hearty sandwiches with names like The Virginian, The Tennessean and The Carolinian, and a healthy offering of homemade soups, salads and deserts. The coffee bar is also a wi-fi hotspot for high-speed Internet access.

K.P. Duty Gourmet Café, 520 State Street, ☎ 423-764-3889, is located next door to the Paramount Center for the Arts. The lunch menu features dips, small pizzas and creative dishes like the portabello mushroom sandwich. Dinner fare ranges from surf-and-turf to Italian, chicken and steak entrées.

Tokyo Japanese Restaurant, 28 Commonwealth Avenue, ☎ 276-645-0399, serves lunch and dinner daily and sushi on weekends.

The Troutdale Dining Room, 412 Sixth Street, ☎ 423- 968-9099, provides ambiance with fireplaces and candlelight in an antebellum home. The award-winning restaurant serves international and American fare. Everything's made on the premises, and there's even a 750-gallon trout tank, so you know it's fresh! Their motto is "we make everything but the butter."

Vinyard Restaurant, 603 Gate City Highway, ☎ 276-466-4244, serves chicken, steak, seafood, veal and Italian dishes.

Accommodations

Hotels & Motels

All are in Bristol, VA, unless otherwise noted (the state line runs through the city, so some are in Tennessee.

Bristol Lodging, 111 Holiday Drive, Bristol, TN, ☎ 423-968-1101, has 179 rooms, a restaurant, and offers a free continental breakfast. $

Budget Host Inn, 1209 W. State Street, ☎ 276-669-5187, has 23 rooms, with non-smoking rooms available. $

Courtyard by Marriott, 3169 Linden Drive, ☎ 276-591-4400, has 170 rooms and five suites, an indoor swimming pool, a restaurant and airport shuttles.

Comfort Inn, 2368 Lee Highway, ☎ 276-466-3881, has 60 rooms and an outside pool. Free continental breakfast; senior citizen discount. $

Days Inn, 536 Volunteer Parkway, Bristol, TN, ☎ 423-968-2171, has 65 rooms, an outdoor pool and serves a free continental breakfast. It is within walking distance of the shops and restaurants along State Street. $

Econo Lodge, 912 Commonwealth Avenue, ☎ 276-466-2112, has 48 rooms, including non-smoking rooms. Pets are allowed, and there is a restaurant nearby. $

Hampton Inn, 3299 West State Street, Bristol, TN, ☎ 423-764-3600, has 91 rooms, serves a free breakfast, and has an outdoor pool. $

Holiday Inn Hotel & Suites 3005 Linden Drive, ☎ 276-466-4100, has 226 rooms. Chops is a full-service restaurant; there are meeting rooms, a pool and a bar, as well as a senior citizen discount. $

La Quinta Inn, 1014 Old Airport Road, ☎ 276-669-9353, has 123 rooms, an outdoor pool and offers a free continental breakfast. $

 Ramada Inn, 2221 Euclid Avenue, ☎ 276-669-7171, has 121 rooms, and provides a free continental breakfast. $

Bed & Breakfasts / Inns

New Hope Bed & Breakfast, 822 Georgia Avenue, ☎ 423-989-3343, has four rooms, all with private bath. All your needs are catered to, including bathrobes, hair dryers and a delicious breakfast. The late Victorian home has a wrap-around porch and swing, and a game room with a pool table. The owners host Murder Mystery Weekends with a catered gourmet dinner. $$-$$$

Robin's Nest Bed & Breakfast, 201 Robin Road, ☎ 423-274-0429, is near downtown Bristol. It has a front porch and a private back deck for enjoying early morning coffee or a quiet afternoon of reading. $$

Camping

The following are all in Bristol, TN: **Cochran's Lakeview Campground**, 821 Painter Creek Road, ☎ 423-878-8045; as well as at **Lake Front Family Campground**, 350 Jones Road, ☎ 423-878-6730, and **Observation Knob Park**, 553 Knob Park Road, ☎ 423-878-1881.

Transportation

The **Tri-Cities Regional Airport** is 13 miles southwest of Bristol just off Interstate 81 in Blountville, TN. The airport is served by most major and regional carriers with direct or connecting flights to all major domestic and international destinations. ☎ 423-325-6000, www.triflight.com.

If you are arriving by car, Bristol is accessed principally by **Interstate 81** and **US 11**, which connects to I-77 and I-40.

Information

For information, brochures and a full list of area restaurants, hotels and shops, contact the **Bristol Convention & Visitors Bureau**, 20 Volunteer Parkway, Bristol, VA/TN 24203-0519, ☎ 423-989-4850. Ask for the detailed brochure on the self-guided walking tour of the city. Visit their Web site at www.bristolchamber.org.

Montgomery County

Nestled in the heart of the Blue Ridge Mountains, Montgomery County offers the best of two worlds. The county is a combination of urban re-development, small historic communities and the outdoor world of the mountains and forests.

Established in 1776 and named for General Richard Montgomery, who served in the first Virginia regiment commanded by George Washington during the French and Indian War, Montgomery County once covered an area of more than 12,000 square miles.

History

Montgomery County is rich in history and tradition. The first settlers were predominantly Scotch-Irish from Northern Ireland. The majority of those early settlers were Protestant, fiercely independent and idealistic, with strong religious convictions. Many were indentured servants who sold themselves into service for a period of time, usually seven years, to pay for their passage to the New World.

Today, Montgomery County combines a spirit of history with modern technology. A small town atmosphere and the rolling hills and deep green valleys highlight a county community of a half-dozen or so towns and villages.

Christiansburg

The Montgomery County seat is located in Christiansburg, a town established in 1792 on land donated by James and Ann Craig. Named for General William Christian, a noted figure in the Revolutionary War and brother-in-law of Patrick Henry, the town flourished as an outpost along the Wilderness Trail and served as a source of supply for the settlers traveling west.

Many famous people passed through the town during those early days, among them Davey Crockett, Daniel Boone, Booker T. Washington and John Buchanan Floyd, a future governor of Virginia.

Christiansburg was home to the Montgomery Male Academy and the Montgomery Female Academy before a public school system of education was implemented in Virginia.

Blacksburg

Founded on land granted to Colonel James Patton in 1748, the Draper's Meadow Settlement was a forerunner to present day Blacksburg. In July of 1775, a group of Shawnee Indians killed, injured, or captured all but four from this early settlement in a raid that became known as the Draper's Meadow Massacre.

In 1772 Colonel William Preston came to the area, settled on Draper's Farm, and built what is now known as the Smithfield Plantation. On August 4, 1778, a town was established on land donated by William and Jane Black consisting of 16 square blocks. Since then, Blacksburg has grown and expanded, but the central downtown area continues to thrive to this day.

Blacksburg is also the home of **Virginia Tech**, formerly known as the Preston Olin Institute and the Virginia Agricultural and Mechanical College. Established as a land-grant college on October 1, 1872, the university covers approximately 2,300 acres, including an airport, farms and orchards, and has an enrollment of more than 25,000 students.

The bond between Virginia Tech and its host community is best summed up in the **Blacksburg Electronic Village**, or **BEV**, an effort that went online in 1993 with the goal of offering Internet access to every resident in town. Over the next decade, the community-wide network transitioned from a public effort to the private sector, spurring new high-tech ventures like ISP providers, and software and hardware developers. The BEV is noted for bringing 87 percent of Blacksburg's population online – the highest per capita use of the Internet in the world – and for being the first community in America to have all its school classrooms linked to the Internet. The BEV is accessed online at www.bev.net.

Radford

More than 200 years ago the stagecoach route followed a path through the Blue Ridge and Allegheny Mountains near the New River. It was around that time that an enterprising settler built a tavern on the route and called it Lovely Mount. In 1840, a local landowner, John McTaylor, gave 1,000 acres of land to his daughter, who married John B. Radford, from whom the town of Radford gets its name. Radford is home to Radford University, which offers undergraduate and graduate programs.

Shawsville

Shawsville is located outside of Christiansburg on Route 460. It stands on the former site of Fort Faux, a palisade constructed on the plantation that once belonged to Captain Ephraim Vaux, and built to hold the frontier for England and the colonies during the French and Indian War.

Riner

A little farther along Route 460, just beyond Shawsville, lies the tiny community of Riner. Riner was founded sometime between 1827 and 1853. Known at first as Five Points because of its location at the confluence of five rural roads, it was a spontaneous crossroads community that grew up near a local sawmill.

The little village later became known as Auburn, but didn't really grow until after the Civil War.

Recreation

The **Huckleberry Trail** is a six mile paved trail linking Christiansburg and Blacksburg. Bicyclists, walkers, runners and skaters use the trail, which is also wheelchair and stroller accessible.

Cascades National Recreation Trail, in the Jefferson National Forest, north of Blacksburg, ascends a gorge for two miles to a scenic 68-foot waterfall.

Sights

The Fine Arts Center for the New River Valley, 21 West Main Street in Pulaski. The main location features exhibits and sales of local artists, artisans and crafters. A satellite location, at 44 West Main Street, occupies a large hall where performances and classes are held. There is an "Art Mart," where artists display and sell their work. Open Monday through Saturday. ☎ 540-980-7363.

Mountain Lake, located 20 miles northwest of Blacksburg on US 460, is a resort lake, notable as one of only two naturally-formed lakes in all of Virginia. The area is most inviting in late June and early July when the azaleas and rhododendrons are in full bloom.

Smithfield Plantation, a quarter-mile west of Blacksburg on US 460 at the Virginia Tech exit, is a restored Colonial house, the former home of the Preston family, a well-connected and historically significant family. The patriarch, William Preston, a surveyor, fought in the American Revolution and helped open Kentucky lands for settlement. His son, James Patton Preston, served a term as Virginia's governor, and his grandson, William Ballard Preston, served as Secretary of the Navy under President Zachery Taylor. The old home features original woodwork, antique furniture and landscaped grounds. There is a museum and a store. The plantation is open from April through early December; admission charged. ☎ 540-231-3947, http://civic.bev.net/smithfield/.

Virginia Tech Geosciences Museum is located in Derrin Hall on the Virginia Tech campus, and exhibits gemstones, fossils, a working seismograph, and the largest display of Virginia minerals in the state. It is open Monday through Saturday; admission is free. There is a gift shop. ☎ 540-231-3001.

Montgomery County

Entertainment

Lyric Theatre, 135 College Avenue, Blacksburg, ☎ 540-951-4771, www-.thelyric.com, is a focal point for the arts of the New River Valley region. Here, patrons can see a movie, enjoy a live performance of theater, music and dance, or attend a lecture.

The **New River Valley Speedway**, 6749 Lee Highway, Radford, ☎ 540-639-1700, www.nrvsspeedway.com, hosts NASCAR-sanctioned auto races April through October.

Château Morrisette Winery, in neighboring Floyd County, has been making wine for a quarter century. Easy to find, between Mileposts 171 and 172 of the Blue Ridge Parkway, the winery features a gift shop, restaurant and wine tastings. Outdoor concerts are held each summer against a backdrop of misty Blue Ridge hills. ☎ 540-593-2865, www.chateaumorrisette.com.

Annual Events

From April through October, the farmer's markets bring the fruits (and vegetables) of the New River Valley's farms into town. The **Radford Farmer's Market** fills up Norwood Square parking lot on East Main Street from 8 a.m. to 1 p.m. ☎ 540-731-3656, www.mainstreetradford.org.

In Blacksburg, the **Downtown Farmer's Market** opens for business every Wednesday and Saturday between May and November. ☎ 540-951-0454, www.downtownblacksburg.com for information.

The Blacksburg/Virginia Tech Summer Art Festival Concerts, held on Friday evenings during June and July, host local artists in live musical concerts showcasing a variety of musical forms. ☎ 540-231-5921, www.sota.vt.edu/SAF, for schedules and information.

Independence Day Parade & Festival features a parade down Main Street, Blacksburg, bands and fireworks. Call the Blacksburg Parks and Recreation Department, ☎ 540-961-1191.

Radford After Five is a weekly concert series held on the third Friday during the warm-weather months of June, July and August. ☎ 540-731-3656, www.mainstreetradford.org, for information on local musicians, times and locations.

Radford's **Bridge Day Celebration and Chili Cookoff** happens in mid-July at Bisset Park, on the New River. A day of food, music and fun is capped with a fireworks display. ☎ 540-639-2202, www.radfordchamber.com for more information.

Steppin' Out, held in Blacksburg over the first Friday and Saturday of August, features an extensive variety of arts and crafts, clothing, jewelry, food and novelty items. It draws more than 60,000 people. Call the Downtown Merchants of Blacksburg, ☎ 540-951-0454.

The Wilderness Trail Festival, held in September in Christiansburg, is a celebration of the town's heritage and traditions. Everything happens on Main and Hickock Streets. Call the Montgomery County Chamber of Commerce for more information, ☎ 540-382-4041, www.wildernesstrail-festival.com.

The **Highlander Festival** takes place the second Saturday of October. The Celtic-themed weekend, co-sponsored by the city and Radford University, features traditional music and games, with more than 20 Scottish clans represented. The event, held at Moffett and Heth Fields, has expanded to include a day of activities in downtown Radford. ☎ 540-831-5324, www.radford.edu/festival for a schedule of events.

Oktoberfest at Mountain Lake features German food, beer, wine, and live traditional music. Takes place every Friday and Saturday night throughout the month of October. ☎ 540-626-7121.

Blacksburg's Christmas Parade occurs the first Saturday afternoon in December on Main Street. ☎ 540-961-1135 for information.

Dining

More than 50 restaurants, cafés and fast food eateries offer a wide variety of dining opportunities in the Greater Blacksburg area. Atmosphere ranges from the college coffee shop where students study at the tables to a cozy log cabin.

Anchy's Restaurant, 1600 N. Main Street, Blacksburg, ☎ 540-951-2828, serves a variety of seafood, with the catch of the day depending on what comes off the truck. Open for lunch and dinner; closed Mondays.

Bogen's Steakhouse and Bar, 622 North Main Street, Blacksburg, ☎ 540-953-2233, www.bogens.com, occupies an old house a few blocks from the Virginia Tech campus. Opened by former Hokie and professional football player Bill Ellenbogen, this restaurant features deck and balcony dining, banquet rooms and an upstairs photographic exhibit of Blacksburg.

Easy Chair Coffee, 801 University City Boulevard, Blacksburg, ☎ 540-951-1628, is located in a mall and the atmosphere is eclectic. Mornings bring bagel sandwiches and the commuting crowd grabbing cups of coffee. Afternoons and evenings – until midnight – bring in the college crowd for homemade soups, salads and a variety of 12 different sandwiches. The shop is brightly painted and features rotating works by area artists.

The Farmhouse, off Cambria Street in Christiansburg, ☎ 540-382-3965, is open dinner for dinner and special events in a renovated 1800s farmhouse, specializing in steaks and American food.

The Huckleberry Restaurant, 2790 Roanoke Street, Christiansburg, ☎ 540-381-2382, is located in a log cabin. You can get everything from prime rib to a children's meal.

Kabuki Japanese Steak House & Sushi Bar, 120 Arbor Drive, Christiansburg, ☎ 540-381-3600, is one of two locations; the other is in Roanoke. Open for dnner only.

Latitudes, in the Holiday Inn, 900 Prices Fork Road, Blacksburg, ☎ 540-552-7001, is open for breakfast, lunch and dinner and serves a full menu of American-style fare.

Portabellas, 915 Heathwood Boulevard, Blacksburg, ☎ 540-552-7111, is open for fine Italian dining, Tuesday through Friday for lunch, and Tuesday through Sunday for dinner.

Accommodations

Hotel & Motels

Best Western Radford, 1501 Tyler Avenue, Radford, ☎ 540-639-3000, has 72 rooms, including handicapped-accessible and non-smoking rooms. The hotel has a full-service restaurant, meeting rooms and a pool. There is a senior citizen discount. $$

Comfort Inn Radford, 2231 Tyler Avenue, Radford, ☎ 540-639-3333, has 32 rooms, including handicapped-accessible and non-smoking rooms. There are meeting rooms and a pool. A senior citizen discount is offered. $

 Comfort Inn Blacksburg, 3705 South Main Street, Blacksburg, ☎ 540-951-1500, has 80 rooms. Handicapped-accessible and non-smoking rooms are available. Free continental breakfast; senior citizen discount. $

 The Dogwood Lodge at Radford, 7073 Lee Highway, Radford, ☎ 540-639-9338, is a small, quiet motel with 15 rooms. Enjoy badminton, croquet and horseshoes. $

The **Donaldson Brown Hotel & Conference Center**, on Prices Ford Road, ☎ 540-231-8000, www.dbhcc.vt.edu, is a 193,000-square-foot inn and conference center on the Virginia Tech campus.

 Econo Lodge, 2430 Roanoke Street, Christiansburg, ☎ 540-382-6161, has 72 rooms, some non-smoking. There is a pool and a coffee shop nearby. Pets are allowed. $

 Quality Inn, 50 Hampton Boulevard in Christiansburg, ☎ 540-382-2055, has 125 rooms, including handicapped-accessible and non-smoking rooms. The hotel has meeting rooms, a pool and a bar. Senior citizen discount. $

Holiday Inn, 900 Prices Ford Road, ☎ 540-552-7001, is located across from Virginia Tech and a public golf course. There are 149 rooms, a restaurant, fitness center, heated indoor pool, and a tennis court. $$

Resort

Mountain Lake Hotel, State Route 700, Mountain Lake, ☎ 540-626-7121 or 800-346-3334, is about 20 miles north of Blacksburg, off US 460. This magnificent century-old retreat on 2,600 acres by Mountain Lake was used as a setting for the movie *Dirty Dancing*. There is a lodge, restaurant, cottages, hiking trails, boating, tennis, a beach and children's programs. There are 90 rooms, from a rustic cottage to a suite with fireplace and whirlpool bath. It's open May through October. $$

Bed & Breakfasts / Inns

Clay Corner Inn Bed & Breakfast, 401 Clay Street, Blacksburg, ☎ 540-953-2604, has 12 rooms in several houses with a variety of styles, some with shared kitchens. There is a pool, and non-smoking rooms available. $$$

Evergreen-The Bell Capozzi House, 201 E. Main Street, Christiansburg, ☎ 540-382-7372, www.evergreen-bnb.com, has five rooms in a three-story Victorian, all with private bath. Guests can enjoy the heated pool. $$-$$$

The Inn at Hans Meadow, 1040 Roanoke Street, Christiansburg, ☎ 888-643-2103, www.theinnathansmeadow.com, occupies a 154-year-old mansion set amid an English garden set on three acres. Four king suites are furnished with microwaves, refrigerators, private baths, thermostats and high speed wireless Internet. $$

The Oaks Victorian Inn, 311 East Main Street, Christiansburg, ☎ 540-381-1500, www.bbhost.com/theoaksinn, has seven rooms in an 1893 Queen Anne Victorian. Some rooms have whirlpool baths and all are non-smoking. $$$

River's Edge, 6208 Little Camp Road, Riner, ☎ 540-381-4147 or 888-786-9413, www.river-edge.com, has four rooms, all with private bath. The inn is located in a private valley. Sit and rock on the porch, or cozy up to a fireplace. A full breakfast served. $$$

Camping

Claytor Lake State Park, located on Virginia Route 660, six miles southwest of Radford, is set among the wooded hills of the Blue Ridge. The 4,500-acre lake and its surrounding countryside provide a variety of sporting and recreational opportunities that include boating, fishing, swimming, horseback riding, camping, hiking and birdwatching. Facilities at the park include a marina, campsites with water and electric hookups, 12 housekeeping cabins, a dumping station, flush toilets and hot showers, a snack bar and rental horses. ☎ 540-674-5492 for reservations and information.

Transportation

Montgomery County is served by the **Roanoke Regional Airport** (☎ 540-362-1999, www.roanokeregionalairport.com) and the **Virginia Tech Montgomery Executive Airport** (☎ 540-231-4444, www.vtbcb.com) with direct or connecting flights to all major domestic and international destinations.

Information & Transportation

For information, brochures and a full list of area restaurants and hotels, contact the **Montgomery County Chamber of Commerce**, 612 New River Road, New River Valley Mall, Christiansburg, VA, 24073, ☎ 540-382-4010, www.montgomerycc.org. Additional information is available online at the **Blacksburg Electronic Village**, www.bev.net/visitors.

Information may also be obtained from the **New River Valley Visitors Bureau**, 6580 Valley Center Drive, Box 21, Radford, VA 24141, ☎ 540-633-0116.

Smyth County

Smyth County may appear just a dot on the map, but don't let appearances fool you. Its mountainous terrain holds surprises waiting to be discovered by the adventurous traveler.

Marion, the county seat, has a Main Street full of shops and historic buildings. North of Marion, a winding road leads to Saltville, a town whose mineral deposits have attracted man and beast for millions of years. In the southwest portion of the county stands Mount Rogers, Virginia's highest point and a playground for thrill seekers.

History

Smyth County is rich with tales of woolly mammoths and mastodons, Indian habitation and Civil War battles. On a lighter note, it is also where a local entrepreneur bottled the first Mountain Dew soft drink.

More than 300 million years ago, a shallow, saltwater sea covered this and surrounding counties. This sea would evaporate every few million years, leaving behind rich deposits of salt and gypsum. These great stores of minerals attracted prehistoric people and animals. As a result,

Saltville today is an important site for archeological studies of woolly mammoth, musk ox, and mastodon bones. Locals say you can't drill a well in Saltville without finding some type of prehistoric bones.

Visitors can tour the archeological sites and see artifacts dating to 12,000 B.C. at the Museum of the Middle Appalachians. Today the well fields and ponds attract a variety of migrating waterfowl.

The white men's first experience with the area is shrouded in mystery. When explorers came, they found Indian villages recently abandoned. A large permanent native settlement existed near present-day Saltville, from around 1000 to 1500. But, apparently, around 1600 to 1650, Native Americans began to leave southwest Virginia. Even today, archaeologists aren't sure why.

In the early to mid-1700s, frontiersmen like Daniel Boone began exploring southwest Virginia, using the famous Wilderness Road. Today, Route 11 in Smyth County follows its path.

In 1745, James Patton obtained a land grant which included much of present-day Smyth County. He, along with John Buchanan and Charles Campbell and their descendents, played major roles in the area's settlement.

Smyth County was created in 1835 and named in honor of General Alexander Smyth, who had represented the area in Congress. In 1849, Marion was established as the county seat, named for General Francis Marion, the "Swamp Fox" of the Revolutionary War.

During the Civil War, Saltville was the "Salt Capital of the Confederacy," an important status. Salt was vital in preserving meat in the days before refrigeration. North and South fought several times for the town's saltworks, as well as the lead mines at Austinville. Today, historians are using satellite technology to unearth a dark chapter in this region's history, to learn if historical accounts of a massacre of black Union soldiers is actually true.

In 1927, one of Smyth County's most famous residents came to town. Noted short story writer Sherwood Anderson purchased Marion's two weekly newspapers, and served as editor and publisher until 1932. The Marion City Drug Store was a popular place for Sherwood his friends. In his columns, he created a fictional reporter, Buck Fever, who made observations about the happenings in the county.

In the early 1950s, Bill Jones, president of Tip Corp. in Marion, formulated the soft drink Mountain Dew. In the 1960s, the Olin Company in Saltville manufactured hydrazine, which powered the first manned moon landing in 1969. In the 1970s, Saltville's last mine closed, in part due to new environmental regulations, but the well fields and archeaological digs can still be viewed today.

Rather than fade into history as simply another of southwest Virginia's mining towns, Saltville has instead battled back and remains a viable community with a fascinating history, well worth visit.

Sights

The Museum of the Middle Appalachians, 123 Palmer Avenue in Saltville, ☎ 276-496-3633, www.museum-mid-app.org, is worth the trip up Route 107 from Exit 35 off I-81. The museum is one of southwest Virginia's newest, exhibiting Saltville's fascinating history through artifacts, photographs and exhibits. Witness how Olin Corp. brought sulphur up from the ground, how archeologists recovered mammoth bones, and how the town rebounded from the closing of the mine. The museum's rock gallery explains different types of rock strata characteristics found in southwest Virginia. It is open daily and offers tours of a nearby archeological site.

Smyth County Historical Museum and Society is a double attraction, featuring the Staley Collins house at 109 West Strother Street and a 1908 school building at 203 North Church Street, both in downtown Marion. The house belonged to former Virginia Lieutenant Governor Lewis Preston Collins II. Inside, the intricate woodworking is well preserved, as is a striking mural in the dining room. Of unknown origin, this oil-on-canvas is symbolic of the region's founding influences: castles and windmills of Europe, and rustic cabins of the settlers. In the town's first public high school across the street, the historical society displays exhibits on Southwestern State Hospital and rural life of the 19th and early 20th centuries. ☎ 276-783-7067, 276-783-7286.

Main Street Marion took on a fresh look after a landscaping project and new sidewalks were built. A self-guided pedestrian "HistoryWalk" takes in the exhibits at the Smyth County Historical Museum, the Historic Lincoln Theatre, the Lincoln Inn, and other historic buildings. ☎ 276-783-4190.

Frank Sanders Memorial Salt Park, on West Main Street, Saltville, ☎ 276-496-5342, has a furance and salt kettle dating to the Civil War.

Civil War Fortifications. On Buck Eye Hollow Road and on Walnut Street, Marion, you can see the remains of the extensive battleworks built to protect the Confederacy's salt mines during the Civil War.

The **Settlers Museum of Southwest Virginia** in Atkins, ☎ 276-686-4401, tells the story of the Scotch-Irish and Germans who came and settled in the mid-1700s. There is a restored 1790s farm, school and many outbuildings. It is open March through November.

Glade Mountain Museum, 6711 Lee Highway in Atkins, ☎ 276-783-5678, houses antique tools and equipment.

Recreation

Clinch Mountain Wildlife Area is a fisherman's dream. Big Tumbling Creek gushes and falls through this 25,000-acre wildlife area, set aside just for fishing, hunting and primitive camping. Permits and fees apply, so ☎ 276-783-4860, www.dgif.virginia.gov.

Hungry Mother State Park covers 2,000 acres of rugged mountain and pristine lakefront. There is camping, hiking, horseback riding, boating, fishing and swimming on the 108-acre lake. It is located five miles north of Marion off I-81. ☎ 276-781-7400 for activity information. For camping reservations, ☎ 800-933-7275, www.dcr.state.va.us/hungrymo.

Mount Rogers National Recreation Area encompasses Virginia's three highest mountains among its 115,000 acres of park. Mount Rogers, at 5,729 feet, is the highest. There are extensive backcountry hiking trails, a number of drive-in campsites with short day hike loops, plus fishing, horseback riding and mountain biking. Headquarters for the recreation area are located in Marion, ☎ 276-783-5196, where a visitor can pick up a number of helpful brochures. Access the recreation area by taking Highway 16 south from I-81 at Exit 45; www.fs.fed.us/r8/gwj/mr.

Annual Events

Hungry Mother Arts and Crafts Festival in July draws artisans from southwest Virginia to the state park, just north of Marion on Route 16, making for a great weekend of browsing, food and music. ☎ 276-781-7400.

Marion's Independence Day Celebration features all the fun of an old-fashioned Fourth of July, including a fireworks display. ☎ 276-783-3161 for a schedule of events.

The **Rich Valley Fair and Horse Show**, held at Rich Valley Fairgrounds on Route 630 in Smyth County in August, celebrates the area's agricultural heritage. ☎ 276-624-3263.

The **War Between the States Battle Re-Enactment** takes place in late August in Saltville, with encampments and demonstrations. ☎ 276-496-5342.

The **Saltville Labor Day Celebration** last four days, with plenty of music, and includes demonstrations of salt-making. ☎ 276-496-4212.

The **Chilhowie Apple Festival** in September in Chilhowie pays homage to the importance of apple-growing in the area. ☎ 276-646-3232.

Dining

Appletree Restaurant, Highway 16 South, Marion, ☎ 276-782-9977, serves steak, ribs, chicken and seafood, and is open daily.

Ciro's Pizza, 784 N. Main Street, Marion, ☎ 276-782-1707, serves New York-style pizza and has a full Italian menu. Open seven days a week for lunch and dinner.

Great Wall Chinese Restaurant, 1133 North Main Street in Marion, ☎ 276-783-8818, serves a full Chinese buffet daily.

Happy's Restaurant, 437 N. Main Street, Marion, ☎ 276-783-5515, serves steaks, seafood, barbechued spare ribs and cocktails. Open for lunch and dinner; closed Sundays.

Hungry Mother Restaurant at Hungry Mother State Park, ☎ 276-781-7420, has a very good restaurant that is worth the six mile drive up from Marion.

Mountain Side Restaurant, at 108 River Side Road in Chilhowie, ☎ 276-646-3086, serves seafood and country cooking. Seating comes with a great view of the moutains.

Accommodations

 Best Western-Marion, 1424 North Main Street in Marion, ☎ 276-783-3193, has 79 guest rooms, the Marion Village Café and Lounge, a pool and free breakfast. $$

Comfort Inn, 5558 Lee Highway in Atkins, ☎ 276-783-2144, has 50 guest rooms and a free continental breakfast. $

 Econo Lodge, 1424 North Main Street in Marion, ☎ 276-783-6031, has 40 guest room. Pets are welcome. $$

Fox Hill Inn B&B, 8568 Troutdale Highway in Troutdale, ☎ 800-874-3313 or 276-677-3313, has six guest rooms and a suite, all with private bath. This new house sits on 70 acres with fantastic panoramic views of the mountains. There are patios, a full breakfast and guests can use the kitchen for lunch and dinner. $$

Saltville Inn, 525 East Main Street in Saltville, ☎ 276-496-4445, has 20 guest rooms. $

 Virginia House Inn, 1419 North Main Street in Marion, ☎ 276-783-5112 or 800-505-5151, has 38 guest rooms, a pool and free breakfast. Pets are allowed. $-$$

Transportation

The nearest commercial airports are **Tri-Cities Regional Airport** in Blountville, TN, 75 miles southwest of Marion (☎ 423-325-6000, www.tri-flight.com), and **Roanoke Regional Airport**, 100 miles to the northeast (☎ 540-362-1999, www.roanokeregionalairport.com). **Greyhound** serves Marion at Dabney Road, ☎ 800-231-2222 or 276-783-7114.

Information

Chamber of Commerce of Smyth County, 214 West Main Street, ☎ 276-783-3161, has a tourism office with brochures and information available. Visit www.smythchamber.org.

Wytheville & Wythe County

History

Wytheville actually began as the incorporated town of Evansham in 1792, named in honor of Jesse Evans, a prominent citizen. Just 47 years later, the town trustees thought better of it, and the name of the county seat was changed to Wytheville.

The town became a popular stopping point for settlers heading west, and later, its mineral spas and mountain air brought vacationers from the heat of the South. Wytheville's lead mines made it an important Civil War target for Union forces operating in southwestern Virginia, and there were four major skirmishes here.

Today, Wytheville is a popular outdoor vacation destination nestled between the Blue Ridge and Allegheny Mountains.

Sights

Beagle Ridge Herb Farm is an organic farm and education center offering classes, nature trails, herbal product and crafts. Open weekends May through October. Matney Flats Road, Wytheville, ☎ 276-621-4511, www.beagleridgeherbfarm.com.

Big Walker Lookout, 12 miles north of Wytheville on Big Walker Mountain Scenic Byway, is a 120-foot observation tower at an elevation of more than 3,400 feet. The Lookout offers magnificent views of the surrounding countryside; be sure to take a camera. There's also a swinging bridge, a gift shop, a snack bar and a picnic area. Open April-October, ☎ 276-228-4401.

Haller-Gibboney Rock House, corner of Tazewell and Monroe, has been an important part of Wytheville's history since it was built in 1823 by the city's first physician, Dr. John Haller. The home was used as an in-

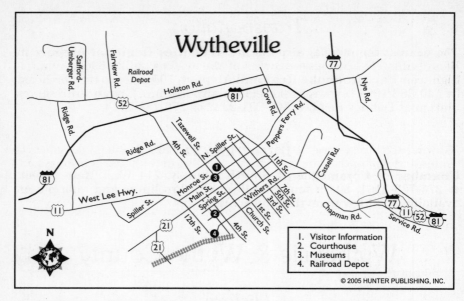

firmary and school during the Civil War, and as a boarding house when Wytheville became a popular resort. Today it is a museum, with hundreds of artifacts and furnishings that preserve family life of the 19th and early 20th century. The original part of the home is made of native limestone, and there are five gardens, including medicinal plants and herbs, on the grounds. Thirty-minute guided tours are available Tuesday through Saturday, April through October, and in December for the Christmas Tour. ☎ 276-223-3330, www.museums.wytheville.org.

The Thomas J. Boyd Museum, located adjacent to the Rock House on Tazewell Street, is named for Colonel Thomas Jefferson Boyd, "The Father of Wytheville." The building was actually Wytheville's first agricultural classroom, built in 1926. Col. Boyd came to Wythe County in 1830 and served in public office for 53 years, during which time he surveyed and laid out the town's streets. The museum preserves artifacts relating to the lives of the people of Wythe County. Exhibits include Wytheville's fire wagons, the lead mining industry, and Wytheville's famous residents. There is also a genealogical resource library. Open Tuesday-Saturday; ☎ 276-223-3331, www.museums.wytheville.org.

The Shot Tower State Park, at Jackson's Ferry, six miles east of Wytheville on Interstate 81, stands on a bluff overlooking the New River. One of only three still standing in the United States, this is a fortress-like stone shaft with walls 2½ feet thick that rises 75 feet above ground and extends below ground another 75 feet to a water tank. Molten lead was poured through sheet-iron colanders from the top of the tower. During a fall of 150 feet the molten lead formed itself into round globules that hardened when they hit the water, thus forming round shot. The park features a visitor center and interpretive programs and a number of hiking trails and picnic areas; open daily from Memorial Day to Labor Day. ☎ 276-699-6778.

At **Virginia City Pioneer Town & Gem Mine** you can pan for gemstones daily, Route 52, ☎ 276-223-1873, www.vacity.com.

Wolf Creek Indian Village & Museum in Bastian offers trained guides and historic demonstrations, open daily, ☎ 276-688-3468, www.indianvillage.org.

Entertainment

Galewinds Amusement Park, Route 2, ☎ 276-228-3020, has go-carts, miniature golf and an arcade. There is a new par 3 lighted golf course and driving range. Open all year.

Historic Millwald Theatre, Main Street, ☎ 276-228-5031, is the oldest continuously-operating theater in Virginia, and has been showing first-run films since it was built in 1928.

Wohlfahrt Haus, 170 Malin Drive, ☎ 276-223-0891, is a 200-seat dinner theater featuring a different production each month, and offering a German and American menu. There is a gift shop with German collectibles, and a lounge with a beer garden.

Annual Events

The Chautauqua Festival, held over nine days in June, includes a parade, educational events, performing arts productions, art shows, children's activities and a variety of music and entertainment, ☎ 276-228-6855.

Wythe County Heritage Days Festival is the third Saturday in September at New River Tail State Park. ☎ 276-223-6022.

Wytheville Christmas Parade is in early December in Downtown Wytheville, ☎ 276-223-3365.

Shopping

There are many specialty shops in the downtown area of Wytheville or close by. You can find outlet stores, specialized bookstores, Christmas shops, antique malls, Appalachian crafts and a wide variety of other shops.

❖ *Don't miss **Kincer-Miller Hardware** at 140 W. Main Street, ☎ 276-228-3146. It's one of the last of the old-time hardware stores. Their claim: "If we don't have it, you don't need it."*

Recreation

You can enjoy the fresh mountain air, pay a visit to the Elizabeth Brown Memorial Park in the center of downtown and take a pleasant stroll or

Wytheville & Wythe County

have a picnic. You can also visit Wither's Park, or take a swim at the McWane Pool. For a day out in the open air, however, there are several possibilities. These include:

New River Trail State Park, a 57-mile linear park or greenway that follows an abandoned railroad right-of-way and parallels the scenic and historic New River for more than 29 miles. ☎ 276-699-6778.

Fishermen and hikers can really get away from civilization in the nearby **Jefferson National Forest.** The Appalachian Trail passes through the forest.

Big Bend Picnic Area within Jefferson National Forest is open year-round, and features large boulders, oak trees, and scenic overlooks of the valley and ridge terrain. It is a prime location for birdwatching. From Wytheville, take Route 52 North for 13 miles, turn right on FS 206.

Big Walker Mountain Scenic Byway consits of 16 miles through the Jefferson National Forest. It begins at the intersection of Route 717 and Interstate 77, about five miles north of Wytheville. There are roadside markers telling the history of the area and beautiful views of the southwest Virginia mountains.

Stoney Fork Campground, on Route 717 in the forest, provides 53 sites at the foot of Big Walker Mountain. There are warm showers, flush toilets, pay phone, and disposal station. There is fishing on Stony Fork Creek and a one-mile nature trail. There is also a new, fully-equipped cabin for rent. ☎ 276-228-5551.

Rural Retreat Lake and Campground, at Exit 60 off I-81, ☎ 276-686-4331, has a 90-acre fishing lake stocked with largemouth bass, bream and catfish. The campground has 72 wooded sites with hookups, a swimming pool, boat docks and rentals.

Dining

The Wytheville area offers more than 50 restaurants offering everything from hot dogs and Southern home cooking to ethnic fare.

El Puerto, 713 Chapman Road, ☎ 276-228-3159, serves authentic Mexican food in a fun atmosphere.

Fireside Restaurant & Lounge, ☎ 276-228-5483, at the Holiday Inn on US 11, serves breakfast, lunch and dinner with a great mountain view.

Log House Restaurant, 520 East Main Street, ☎ 276-228-4139, is located in an old log cabin, the original part of it dating to 1776. The restaurant serves sandwiches for lunch, and the dinner menu features seafood, steak and regional fare such as Virginia ham and Confederate stew.

Peking Restaurant, 105 Malin Drive, ☎ 276-228-5515, is open for lunch and dinner daily, with brunch on Sunday. Good Chinese food served in a Far East atmosphere. Reservations are suggested on the weekends.

Scrooge's Restaurant, 255 Holston Road, ☎ 276-228-6622, offers casual dining, specializing in steaks, seafood and sandwiches. Open daily for dinner.

Accommodations

 Best Western, 355 Nye Road, ☎ 276-228-7300, has 100 rooms, including Jacuzzi and non-smoking rooms. There is an outdoor pool, and free continental breakfast is offered. $

Comfort Inn, at Holston Road on Interstate 81 at Exit 70, ☎ 800-228-5150, has 80 rooms, a pool and free continental breakfast. $

 Days Inn, 150 Malin Drive, ☎ 800-329-7466, has 118 rooms. Free continental breakfast. $

Hampton Inn, 1090 Pepper's Ferry Road, ☎ 800-426-7866, has 68 rooms, some of them suites, a pool and complimentary breakfast. $

 Holiday Inn, 1800 East Main Street, ☎ 800-842-7652, has 199 rooms. There is a restaurant and café, a pool and several meeting rooms. $

 Econo Lodge, 1190 East Main Street, ☎ 800-424-4777, has 72 rooms. Free coffee is available in the lobby. $

Quality Inn & Suites, 2015 East Main Street, ☎ 276-228-4241, has 61 rooms, an indoor pool, a spa, Jacuzzi, family suites, and a continental breakfast. $

 Ramada Inn, 955 Pepper's Ferry Road, ☎ 800-272-6232, has 154 rooms, a restaurant and café, a bar, a pool and several meeting rooms. $

Day-trip to Tazewell County

Tazewell County is about as close as you can get to experiencing what pioneer life was like in southwest Virginia. The county is still rural, with much of it engaged in farming. The county's five incorporated towns – Bluefield, Cedar Bluff, Richlands, Pocahontas and Tazewell – offer quaint streets, historic churches, old-fashioned festivals, and comfortable B&Bs.

At the **Crab Orchard Museum and Pioneer Park**, west of Tazewell on US 19/460, ☎ 276-988-6755, www.craborchardmuseum.com, a reconstructed village shows how settlers actually lived. The museum tells the story of the Appalachian frontier, while 13 historic log and stone buildings re-create life in the 1830s.

Across from the Crab Orchard Museum is the **Higginbotham House Museum** on Pisgah Road, ☎ 276-988-3800, www.legacyadvocacy.org. The 1811 home houses artifacts of the Colonial era and Native American collections, and there is an 18th-century garden.

In the southeast part of the county is **Burke's Garden**, a unique agricultural and geological area that is Virginia's largest rural Historic District and a National Landmark. Accessed via Route 623, this fertile area is within a bowl-shaped indentation on top of a mountain and is home to several hundred people. The Appalachian Trail passes nearby. Visit Burke's Garden General Store and Shady Pine Store.

Wytheville & Wythe County

Near Pocahontas on Route 659 is the **Pocahontas Exhibition Mine and Museum**, ☎ 276-945-2134, open daily from April through October. Here visitors can see the history of coal-mining and get a tour of a real mine that first opened in 1882. Bring your jacket: the temperature is a constant 52°.

For more information on the attractions, dining and lodging in the area, contact **Tazewell County Visitor Center**, located in a former tenant house (boarding house) behind the historic Sanders House, 200 Sanders Lane, Bluefield. Open daily, 9 a.m. to 5 p.m., ☎ 276-322-1343, www.tazewellcounty.org.

Burke's Garden Fall Festival is held on the last Saturday in September. ☎ 800-588-9401.

Tazewell County Fair, one of Virginia's largest old-fashioned fairs, is held the second week in August. ☎ 800-588-9401.

Day-trip to Galax

The new **Blue Ridge Music Center** in Galax is a 1,000-acre complex on the Blue Ridge Parkway devoted to the tradition of old-time music. The first phase includes an outdoor amphitheater hosting national and regional artists like Doc Watson, Ricky Skaggs, Del McCoury and others. An interpretive facility will tell the rich history of mountain music. ☎ 276-236-5309, www.blueridgemusiccenter.net.

Galax is also home to the **Old Time Fiddlers' Convention**, the oldest and largest event of its kind, taking place for one glorious week in August. ☎ 276-236-8541, www.oldfiddlersconvention.com.

Transportation

The nearest commercial airport is **Roanoke Regional Airport**, 75 miles east of Wytheville (☎ 540-362-1999, www.roanokeregionalairport.com). **Greyhound** serves Wytheville on Route 2, ☎ 800-231-2222 or 276-637-6373.

Information

For information, brochures and up-to-date visitor information, contact the **Wytheville Convention and Visitors Bureau**, 150 East Monroe Street, ☎ 276-223-3355, 877-347-8307, http://visit.wytheville.com; a self-guided African-American dining tour and an Historic Walking Tour are available.

Index